Health, Safety,
AND
Nutrition
FOR THE
Young Child

SIXTH EDITION

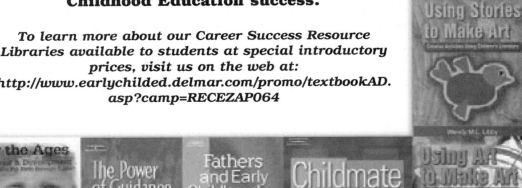

Health, Safety, AND Nutrition FOR THE Young Child

SIXTH EDITION

Lynn R. Marotz
Marie Z. Cross
Jeanettia M. Rush

THOMSON
™
DELMAR LEARNING

Australia Canada Mexico Singapore Spain United Kingdom United States

THOMSON

DELMAR LEARNING

**Health, Safety, and Nutrition
for the Young Child, Sixth Edition**
Lynn R. Marotz, Marie Z. Cross, Jeanettia M. Rush

Vice President, Career Education SBU:
Dawn Gerrain

Director of Editorial:
Sherry Gomoll

Acquisitions Editor:
Erin O'Connor

Developmental Editor:
Alexis Ferraro

Editorial Assistant:
Ivy Ip

Director of Production:
Wendy A. Troeger

Production Editor:
J.P. Henkel

Technology Project Manager:
Joseph Saba

Director of Marketing:
Wendy E. Mapstone

Channel Manager:
Donna J. Lewis

Cover Design:
Graphic World Publishing Services

Library of Congress
Cataloging-in-Publication Data

Marotz, Lynn R.
    Health, safety, and nutrition for the young child / Lynn R. Marotz, Marie Z. Cross, Jeanettia M. Rush.—6th ed.
        p. cm.
    Includes bibliographical references and index.
    ISBN 1-4018-3700-X (alk. paper)
    1. Children—Health and hygiene.
2. Children—Nutrition. 3. Children's accidents—Prevention. I. Cross, Marie Z. II. Rush, Jeanettia M. III. Title.

RJ101.M347 2004
649'.1—dc22   2004047973

NOTICE TO THE READER

Brief Contents

v

UNIT 5 Nutrition and the Young Child   393

Appendices 515

Glossary 539

Index 549

Contents

UNIT 3
Safety for the Young Child / 181

THE ORIGINAL IN A SIXTH EDITION

We are pleased to present the sixth edition of *Health, Safety, and Nutrition for the Young Child*. This best-selling, full-color early care and education text was the first to address the three most critical areas of child development in one book:

- children's health status and health education
- creating and maintaining safe, yet challenging learning environments
- proper nutrition

THE INTENDED AUDIENCE

First and foremost, *Health, Safety, and Nutrition for the Young Child* is written on behalf of young children everywhere. Ultimately, it is the children who benefit from having parents and teachers who understand and know how to protect and promote their safety and well-being. In the sixth edition, the term *teachers* is used inclusively to refer to adults who care for and work with young children in many different capacities, whether in an early care and education center, home-based program, or community activity, or as a therapist, coach, camp leader, or simply a concerned citizen. *Teachers* is also used to acknowledge the important teaching role parents play in children's daily lives. Its use also reflects and supports efforts to achieve professional recognition and status for those working in the field of early care and education.

Health, Safety, and Nutrition for the Young Child is intended for students, new and experienced early education teachers, parents, and colleagues in any role that touches children's lives. The material is based on current research and reflects the latest developments in health, safety, and nutrition as well as their application in early education settings. It is the authors' hope that after reading and studying the material addressed in this text, parents, teachers, and professional colleagues will understand and value the important role they play in fostering preventive health concepts and helping young children begin to establish good habits, attitudes, and life-long responsibility for optimizing personal well-being.

ORGANIZATION AND CONTENT

Three major topical areas are addressed in this new edition: children's health; safety concerns and management; and nutrition (basic and applied). The authors believe this arrangement gives individual instructors maximum flexibility in designing their courses and personalizing content. However, the interrelatedness of these three areas cannot be overlooked despite their artificial separation. The sixth edition of *Health, Safety, and Nutrition for the Young Child* continues to emphasize the important role parents and teachers play in promoting children's health and fostering their development of healthy attitudes, values, and practices. Information on topics included in previous editions, such as asthma, allergies, SIDS, ADD/ADHD, otitis media, childhood obesity, Fetal Alcohol Syndrome, the Food Guide Pyramid, food safety, and menu planning has been updated and expanded. Several new topics of recent concern have also been introduced, including West Nile virus, sun safety, building resiliency in children, and helping children to cope with trauma.

This new edition is written in a clear, concise, and thought-provoking manner. As always, emphasis is placed on establishing quality learning environments and practices that respect the diversity of settings, families, and teachers who care for young children. Opportunities for expanding children's understanding of health, safety, and nutrition are stressed throughout the book. This comprehensive book is a resource that no early childhood professional should be without!

NEW FEATURES

Several new features have been introduced in the sixth edition to help expand your understanding of fundamental concepts and their application in contemporary early care and education settings:

- **Focus on Families**—This new feature is designed to reinforce the collaborative efforts of parents and teachers in promoting children's health, safety, and nutrition. Teachers play a key role in ongoing parent education, helping to bridge the gap between knowledge and application in everyday situations. Ideas provided in this feature can be shared with parents in a variety of ways, such as including them in newsletters, discussing them in parent meetings, or posting the information on bulletin boards. Although topics showcased in this feature have been chosen to address select issues and problems, teachers are encouraged to identify others that are unique to the children, families, and communities they serve. The authors also hope this feature will serve as a model and that teachers will continue their efforts to support parents.
- **Information on Fast Foods**—Concerns about the increasing incidence of adult and childhood obesity and Type II diabetes are raising many questions about the relationship between these health problems and fast food consumption. Web addresses for many of the largest fast food chains are included in Appendix A to provide the reader with easy access and up-to-date nutrient information.
- **Web addresses** have also been provided for the many professional and commercial organizations listed in Appendix C so parents and teachers can take advantage of modern technology to obtain valuable educational resource information and materials. Mailing addresses and URL's have all been updated and were current at the time of printing.
- **New BMI and Growth Charts** for boys and girls are provided in Appendix B to help parents and teachers monitor children's height and weight. Explanations for their use are included.
- **A Children's Book List**—Reading to children not only enhances their literacy skills but can also be an effective method for teaching about health, safety, and nutrition. A list of suggested book titles is included in Appendix F on a variety of related topics, such as dental health, mental health, self-care, safety, and nutrition to reinforce learning in these areas and encourage parents and teachers to read often to children.

Features that have been retained from the fifth edition include:

- **Reflective Thoughts**—This feature is intended to encourage students and teachers to examine personal attitudes and practices based on the concepts presented in each chapter. Thought-provoking questions are included to stimulate individual reflection and/or class discussion.
- **Issues to Consider**—This feature showcases current events and is designed to help you relate basic principles of health, safety, and nutrition discussed in the text to everyday situa-

tions and settings. A series of questions is provided to stimulate individual thought and/or group discussion.

- Case Studies—Case studies have been provided in each chapter to encourage the application of basic concepts to everyday practice. Questions are designed to guide individual thought and/or group discussion.
- Helpful Web sites—This feature acknowledges the important role that technology plays in today's world. Web addresses are provided at the end of each chapter for readers who wish to further explore topics presented in the text.

ONLINE COMPANION

The Online Companion to accompany the sixth edition of *Health, Safety, and Nutrition for the Young Child* is your link to early childhood education on the Internet. The Online Companion contains many features to help enhance your understanding of health, safety, and nutrition issues as they relate to the young child:

- Critical Thinking Forum—In this section you have the opportunity to respond to "Reflective Thoughts" and "Issues to Consider" concepts. Various health, safety, and nutrition scenarios and thought-provoking questions test your understanding of the content provided in the text. You can share your ideas with classmates and interact informally with your instructor online.
- Web Activities—These activities direct you to a Web site(s) and allow you to conduct further research and apply content related to health, safety, and nutrition, for the young child.
- Web Links—For each chapter, a summarized list of Web links is provided for your reference.
- Sample Quizzes—Questions are provided on-line to test your knowledge of the material presented.
- Printable Forms and Charts—Many of the forms and charts that appear in this book are available online for download in PDF format.
- Online Early Education Survey—This survey gives you the opportunity to respond to what features you like and what features you want to see improved on the Online Companion.

 The Online Companion icon appears at the end of each chapter to prompt you to go online and take advantage of the many features provided.

You can find the Online Companion at *http://www.EarlyChildEd.delmar.com.*

PEDAGOGY

Pedagogy is designed to facilitate mastery of fundamental information:

1. *Terms to Know* are listed in order of appearance at the beginning of each chapter, in color where they appear within the chapter, in a running glossary at the bottom of the page on which they appear, and again in the glossary at the back of the book. Reinforcement and cross-referencing enhance comprehension.
2. *Objectives* appear at the beginning of each chapter to help you focus on key areas of learning.
3. Bulleted lists alert you to specific examples.
4. Real life, colorful photographs taken on location at centers and schools show children as they work and play in appropriate settings.

5. Full-color illustrations and tables reinforce important chapter concepts.
6. *Reflective Thoughts* encourage you to examine personal attitudes and practices based on the concepts presented in each chapter. Thought-provoking questions are included.
7. *Issues to Consider* is a feature that showcases current events and is designed to help you apply basic principles of health, safety, and nutrition to real-life situations. Questions are included to stimulate individual thought or group discussion.
8. The summary, presented in a bulleted list, concludes the chapter and is followed by:
   - Suggested Activities
   - Chapter Review Questions
   - References
   - Additional Reading (suggestions for further reading)
   - Helpful Web Sites
9. Appendices, designed to be used in conjunction with all 21 chapters, include:
   - Appendix A   Nutrient Information: Fast Food Vendor Websites
   - Appendix B   Growth and BMI Charts for Boys and Girls
   - Appendix C   Educational Resources: Health, Safety, and Nutrition
   - Appendix D   Federal Food Programs
   - Appendix E   One-Week Sample Menu
   - Appendix F   Children's Book List

A comprehensive glossary and index conclude the text with reader-friendly cross-references.

DESIGN

We were proud to present the first full-color, early childhood textbook and we continue that tradition with a beautiful contemporary design in this edition.

All new colors and attractive new unit and chapter openers invite the reader into the book. Multicultural photographs, all taken on location at child care centers and schools, plus accompanying art contribute to the visual appeal of the text.

ANCILLARIES

Instructor's Manual

The Instructor's Manual that accompanies the sixth edition includes answers to chapter review questions and case studies. Additional questions are provided to help guide class discussions or to be used for testing purposes. A list of multimedia resources is also included.

Computerized Test Bank

An updated computerized test bank that includes multiple-choice, true-false, short answer, and completion questions for each chapter is available on CD-ROM. Instructors have immediate access to approximately 900 questions that can be used to create customized printed tests, on-line tests, or computer-based tests. Additional features allow the instructor to:

- scramble choices in multiple-choice questions
- edit or add test questions
- develop multiple versions of a given test
- establish a test schedule
- provide immediate feedback to students.

Refer to the CTB User's Guide for more information on how to create and post quizzes to your school's Internet or Intranet server.

WEB TUTOR

The Web Tutor to accompany the sixth edition of *Health, Safety, and Nutrition for the Young Child* allows you to take learning beyond the classroom. This Online Courseware is designed to complement the text and benefits students in that it enables them to better manage their time, prepare for exams, organize their notes, and more. Special features include Chapter Learning Objectives, Online Course Preparation, Study Sheets, Glossary, Discussion Topics, Frequently Asked Questions, Online Class Notes, Online Chapter Quizzes, and Web Links related to chapter content. Printing features allow students to print their own customized study guides.

A benefit for instructors as well as students, the Web Tutor allows for on-line discussion with the instructor and other class members, real-time chat to enable virtual office hours and encourage collaborative learning environments, a calendar of syllabus information for easy reference, e-mail connections to facilitate communication among classmates and between students and instructors, and customization tools that help educators tailor their course to fit their needs by adding or changing content.

Web Tutor allows you to extend your reach beyond the classroom and is available on either the WebCT or Blackboard platform. Your students may also access sample quizzes created by Delmar from their Web site for Online Companion for Students at *http://www.EarlyChildEd.delmar.com.*

THE ULTIMATE GOAL

A child's health status, a safe but challenging learning environment, and proper nutrition affect the care, nurturance, and optimal physical and cognitive development of the young child. Over a decade ago, each of these subject areas was viewed as a separate entity, but research has shown the correlation among them is so intertwined that they cannot be completely separated. Philosophies concerning health care have also undergone notable change. Today, attention is being focused on the concept of health promotion and preventive health care—approaches that recognize the direct relationships which exist between health status, safety, nutrition, and numerous social and environmental factors including poverty; inequality of medical care and access to good nutrition; and informed individuals who accept responsibility for their own well-being and who work to improve social conditions affecting health.

ABOUT THE AUTHORS

Lynn R. Marotz received her Ph.D. from the University of Kansas, M.Ed. from the University of Illinois, and a B.S. in Nursing from the University of Wisconsin. She has served as the Health and Safety Coordinator and Associate Director of the Edna A. Hill Child Development Center for 27 years. In addition, she also teaches undergraduate and graduate courses in the Department of Human Development and Family Life, University of Kansas, including health/safety/nutrition, foundations of early childhood education, parenting, and administration, and provides comprehensive training related to these topics for students in the Early Childhood Teacher Education programs. Her current research interests center on children's diet and obesity. Her professional contributions include numerous conference presentations, writings, committee appointments, and involvement in state initiatives and community organizations that advocate for children and families. However, it is her daily interactions with children and families, in addition to raising two successful daughters and relishing the endearing qualities of her grandchildren, that bring real insight, meaning, and balance to the material in this book.

Jeanettia M. Rush, R.D., L.D., received her M.A. in Human Development from the University of Kansas. A graduate of the Dietetics and Institutional Management program at Kansas State University and the Dietetics Internship program of the University of California, she has worked as a hospital dietitian for 21 years and as a nutrition consultant for Meals On Wheels and Educare Laboratory Child Care Center. Other experience includes work as a nutritionist with Johnson County, Kansas Health Department Prenatal/WIC Programs. She is currently employed as a clinical dietitian serving rehabilitation, critical care, and neurology units. Other duties include serving as adjunct faculty for the AP-4 dietetics internship program.

Marie Cross received her B.S., M.S., and Ph.D. degrees from the University of Wisconsin and is currently an emeritus associate professor in the Department of Human Development, University of Kansas. Her teaching experience included undergraduate courses in basic and applied nutrition and graduate courses related to nutrition and child development. A major focus of her research involved the development of appropriate materials for nutrition education programs at levels ranging from preschool to college.

ACKNOWLEDGMENTS

The authors wish to extend a special note of appreciation to the instructors, students, and colleagues who continue to encourage our efforts and use *Health, Safety, and Nutrition for the Young Child* in their classes. We would also like to recognize the dedication and contributions of early care and education teachers to improving the lives of children everywhere.

The authors also wish to express their appreciation to a number of special people whose encouragement and technical assistance helped to make this book a valuable resource for early childhood professionals. They also wish to thank the photographers for their unique abilities to capture the delight of young children and the editorial and production staff at Delmar for their insight, encouragement, and guidance in making this an even better edition.

Special thanks to Lynne Reeves, MBA, RD, LD, for her many hours of labor on this revision of Chapters 13–21. Lynne brings a very unique perspective as a food service director, former WIC nutritionist, and child care consumer (in other words, a mom!) to this project. We appreciate her insights into the science of nutrition and the art of feeding children.

The authors would like to extend a special thank you to the following reviewers for their comments and recommendations:

Linda S. Estes, Ed.D.
St. Charles Community College
St. Peters, MO

Teresa Frazier
Thomas Nelson Community College
Hampton, VA

Jennifer Gutowsky, M.Ed.
San Jacinto College North
Houston, TX

Judith Ann Schust
Professor Emeritus
Harold Washington College
Chicago, IL

Cynthia Waters
Upper Iowa University
Fayette, IA 52142

Becky Wyatt
Murray State College
Tishomingo, OK 73460

HEALTH, SAFETY, AND NUTRITION: AN INTRODUCTION

CHAPTER 1

Interrelationship of Health, Safety, and Nutrition

● OBJECTIVES

After studying this chapter, you should be able to:

- Describe how health, safety, and nutrition are interrelated.
- List five environmental factors that have a negative effect on health.
- List five environmental factors that have a positive effect on health.
- State how nutrition affects children.
- Define the term *health promotion.*
- Identify three factors that affect children's safety.
- Discuss three measures teachers can take to promote children's health, safety, and nutrition.

● TERMS TO KNOW

health	heredity	resistance
preventive	predisposition	malnutrition
health promotion	sedentary	obesity
habits	nutrients	

In recent years, many positive changes have taken place in attitudes and practices relative to personal **health**. The concept of **preventive** health care has emerged in response to costly medical care and the realization that the medical profession is incapable of curing every health problem. On a national scale, examples of preventive initiatives include immunization programs, inspection of food supplies, fluoridation of water, monitoring of air pollutants, and regulation of chemical dumping. On a personal level, preventive practices include eating a healthy diet low in animal fats, exercising regularly, practicing effective dental hygiene and handwashing techniques, and avoiding smoking and substance abuse.

---

health – *a state of wellness. Complete physical, mental, social, and emotional well-being; the quality of one element affects the state of the others.*
preventive – *measures taken to avoid an event such as an accident or illness from occurring; implies the ability to anticipate circumstances and behaviors.*

HEALTH PROMOTION

Preventive health care is based on the principle of **health promotion** and recognizes that individuals can control many factors that affect personal health. Research data have provided conclusive evidence that changes in individual lifestyles and behaviors can lead to improved health status (Bhargava, 2002; U.S. Department of Health and Human Services, 2002; Kavanagh, 2001). Children and adults can learn to assume greater responsibility for developing and maintaining attitudes, **habits**, practices, and choices that will promote good health (Earls, 1998). This includes establishing good dietary habits, such as eating balanced meals, practicing safety behaviors such as wearing seat belts, exercising regularly, and seeking early treatment for occasional illness and injury.

The early years are an ideal time to help children begin to establish basic behaviors that will promote a healthy lifestyle. Teachers and parents can capitalize on children's endless curiosity and use opportunities throughout the day—planned as well as spontaneous—to teach about health, safety, and nutrition.

The concept of health promotion also assumes that individuals will take responsibility for social and environmental issues that affect the short- and long-term quality of everyone's health, safety, and nutritional status, such as the following:

- poverty and homelessness
- inequitable access to medical and dental care
- adverse effects of media advertising
- substance abuse
- pesticides and chemical additives in food
- child abuse and neglect
- air and water pollution
- discrimination based on diversity

Parents and teachers can begin to enhance children's awareness of complex social and environmental issues and the potential effect they may have on everyone's well-being. In addition, adults can demonstrate their initiative by supporting actions and policies that contribute to healthier environments and lifestyles for society as a whole.

National Health Initiatives

Increasingly, the benefits of preventive health care are attracting public attention. This change has been particularly notable with respect to young children. Poor standards of health, safety, and nutrition are seen as significant barriers to children's ability to learn and become healthy, productive adults. Several new, large-scale programs have been undertaken recently to improve access and preventive services for young children. Descriptions of several of these initiatives follow; information about federal food programs for children can be found in Appendix D.

Healthy People 2010. In the early 1980s, a series of general guidelines and objectives were developed to improve the nation's standard of health and to increase public awareness about the need for assuming some personal responsibility in this effort. Basic objectives targeted specific preventable health problems, including, the dissemination of health information and encouraged community and professional collaboration to aid individuals in achieving these goals.

In 1990, the U.S. Department of Health and Human Services issued an agenda titled *Healthy People 2000: National Health Promotion and Disease Prevention Objectives*, which outlined 22 national

---

health promotion – *engaging in behaviors that help maintain and enhance one's health status; includes concern for certain social issues affecting the diet and environment.*
habits – *the unconscious repetitions of a particular behavior.*

health priorities, many of which addressed the needs of children. Again, the purpose of this document was to encourage an improved standard of health through interagency collaboration and community participation. Most states have adopted these objectives and modified approaches to meet the unique needs of their local populations. Many government agencies use these objectives to monitor the health status of the U.S. population and to report measurable improvements in their well-being.

Healthy People 2010 is an updated version of the original document that continues to reinforce the philosophy of health promotion for achieving improved well-being. Goals and objectives are inclusive, targeting individuals of all ages and backgrounds, and continue to emphasize personal responsibility and the coordinated efforts of public and private organizations and agencies (Table 1–1). States are expected to maintain a critical role in this process through expansion of current programs and implementation of new initiatives. Many of the 2010 goals and objectives have direct application for early care and education programs and can easily be incorporated into existing efforts to protect and enhance children's health. For example, teaching children positive ways of expressing anger or frustration and maintaining environments respective of individual differences helps to promote good mental health. Serving nutritious foods, making physical activity a daily priority, and creating safe classroom conditions are also practices teachers can implement to foster children's growth and development.

National Children's Agenda. A similar Canadian initiative aimed at health promotion for children is outlined in a report titled *A National Children's Agenda: Developing a Shared Vision.* This document presents a comprehensive agenda of goals and objectives for addressing children's critical health care and safety needs. It also embraces the importance of the early years and supports the vision of a unified approach to helping children achieve their full potential.

State Children's Health Insurance Program (SCHIP). Legislation included in the Balanced Budget Act of 1997, also know as Title XXI, established a national health insurance program for uninsured income-eligible children. This program is administered by individual states through annual appropriations. To qualify for funding, states must submit a Child Health Plan that describes how the program will be administered, how eligibility will be determined, and how eligible children will be located.

Although many eligible children still do not participate in this program, approximately 2.3 million children were enrolled during 2001 (Centers for Medicare & Medicaid Services, 2001). Services covered by this plan include free or low-cost medical care, prescriptions, and hospitalization. Improved access to preventive health care not only ensures children a better quality of life but also has immediate benefits for improved learning.

Healthy Child Care America. The primary objective of the Healthy Child Care America (HCCA) Initiative is the improvement of quality in early care and education programs. HCCA, supported by the U.S. Department of Health and Human Services, the Child Care Bureau, and the Maternal and Child Health Bureau, was established in 1995 to coordinate the mutual interests of health professions, early education professionals, and families in addressing children's health and

TABLE 1–1 Healthy People 2010 Objectives

Areas targeted for improving children's health include the following:

• physical activity and fitness	• unintentional injury
• nutrition—overweight and obesity	• immunizations
• substance abuse	• oral health
• mental health	• maternal and infant health
• violent and abusive behavior	• access to health care

TABLE 1-2   National Health and Safety Performance Standards

Comprehensive guidelines address the following areas of child care:

- staffing
- activities for healthy development
- health promotion and protection
- nutrition and food services
- facilities, supplies, equipment, and transportation
- infectious diseases
- children with special needs
- administration
- recommendations for licensing and community action

safety needs in out-of-home programs. They have also been instrumental in launching several large-scale educational campaigns, including Child Care Passenger Safety, Back to Sleep (for parents), and Back to Sleep in Child Care Settings (2003). Grant-supported offices, located in every state, have been set up to evaluate and strengthen existing community infrastructure and to assist with new initiatives for improving children's access to health care.

National Health and Safety Performance Standards for Child Care. National concern for children's welfare also resulted in a collaborative project between the American Academy of Pediatrics (AAP) and the American Public Health Association (APHA) to develop health, safety, and nutrition guidelines for out-of-home child care programs. The resulting document, *National Health and Safety Performance Standards: Guidelines for Out-of-Home Child Care Programs*, provides detailed quality standards and procedures for ensuring children's health and safety while they are in organized care (Table 1–2) (American Public Health Association & American Academy of Pediatrics, 2002). Because the current system of child care regulation allows states to establish individual licensing standards, there is notable variation in quality. This project was an attempt to develop and recommend standards that would improve uniformity and consistency. Similar guidelines have also been proposed by the National Association for the Education of Young Children (NAEYC), the professional organization of early childhood educators and advocates.

No Child Left Behind.   The importance of children's health and learning during their earliest years received one of its strongest acknowledgments with the recent passage of the No Child Left Behind Act of 2001. This bill authorized significant reforms of the K–12 educational system and strengthens partnerships with Head Start, Even Start, and early education programs in center- and home-based settings. It recognizes parents as children's first and most important teachers, the valued contribution of early childhood care and education programs, and the need to foster early literacy skills (understanding and using language) to ensure children's success in school. In addi-

REFLECTIVE THOUGHTS

The word *diversity* appears frequently in the media and conversation. What does the term *diversity* mean to you? What biases do you have that would influence your attitudes toward people of diverse backgrounds? Why do you think these developed? Consider how you might go about changing any biases. How can you help children develop positive attitudes toward all people?

tion, this bill authorized additional funding to cover child care costs for low-income families and to expand prenatal services for pregnant women and children's health services for improved well-being. Parent education program and subsidized research are also important components of this initiative to improve the quality of care and education for children.

HEALTH

Definitions of *health* are as numerous as the factors that affect it. In the past, the term referred only to an individual's physical status, and emphasis was placed on the medical treatment of disorders. Today, the concept of health is much broader and encompasses more than the absence of illness and disease. International professional groups such as the World Health Organization recognize health as a state or quality of complete physical, mental, and social well-being. Each element is assumed to make an equally important contribution to health. Furthermore, factors affecting the quality of one element are known to have an effect on the others. For example, a stressful home environment may contribute to a child's frequent illnesses, stomachaches, or headaches. Also, a child's chronic illness or disability may have a profound effect on the parents' mental, social, and physical well-being.

This broader concept of health also recognizes that children and adults do not live in isolation. Rather, they are important members of multiple groups, including family, peer, neighborhood, ethnic, cultural, recreational, and community. Social interaction and participation in these groups often affects, and is affected by, the state of an individual's health. Consider, for example, the recent severe acute respiratory syndrome (SARS) epidemic and how quickly a communicable illness can spread given the ease of modern-day travel. Thus, environment also becomes an important and influential factor.

Factors Influencing Children's Health

Health is a complex state determined by ongoing interactions between biological material inherited at conception and environmental factors (Figure 1–1). For example, a baby's immediate and long-term health is affected by the mother's health practices and personal state of health; diet; avoidance of substances such as alcohol, tobacco, and certain medications; regular medical supervision; and exposure to communicable illnesses during pregnancy. A baby who is born prematurely and has a low birth weight faces a greater risk of health problems and early death. In contrast, a child growing up in a loving family in which a healthy diet, safe environment, and opportunities for learning and recreation are provided is more likely to experience good health.

Heredity. Characteristics transmitted from parents to their children at the time of conception determine all of the genetic traits of a new, unique individual. **Heredity** sets the limits for growth, development, and health potential (Figure 1–2). It explains, in part, why children in one family are short while those from another family are tall or why some individuals have allergies or need glasses while others do not.

Understanding how heredity influences health can also be useful for predicting an inherited tendency, or **predisposition**, to certain health problems, such as heart disease, deafness, cancer, diabetes, allergies, or mental health disorders. However, it should be noted that having a family history of heart disease, for example, does not necessarily mean that a child will develop this condition. Many lifestyle factors, including exercise, diet, and stress levels, interact with genetic material (genes) to ultimately determine whether a child will develop heart disease or any other health disorders.

---

heredity – *the transmission of certain genetic material and characteristics from parents to child at the time of conception.*
predisposition – *having an increased chance or susceptibility.*

FIGURE 1–1

The interactive components of health.

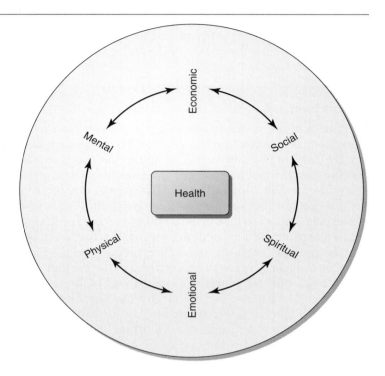

Environment.   Although heredity provides the basic building materials that determine one's health, environment plays an equally important role. In a simplified way, environment is made up of physical, social, economic, and cultural factors. These factors influence the way individuals perceive and respond to their surroundings (Figure 1–3). In turn, these responses affect one's physical, social, emotional, and economic choices and behaviors (Charlesworth, 2004). For example, two drivers both see the light turning red as they approach an intersection; one races through, and the and other stops. The driver who chose to run the red light is hit by an oncoming car and seri-

FIGURE 1–2

Heredity sets the limits for growth, development, and health potential.

FIGURE 1–3

Physical, social, and cultural factors affect the nature of our responses.

ously injured. That driver's unfortunate decision will have obvious health, economic, social, and psychological consequences.

Some environmental factors are positive and promote good health:

- good dietary habits
- recreation, regular exercise, and adequate rest
- access to medical and dental care
- stress reduction
- homes, child care facilities, schools, and workplaces that are clean and safe
- opportunities to form stable and respectful relationships

On the other hand, exposure to chemicals and pollution, abuse, illness, obesity, **sedentary** lifestyles, poverty, stress, violence, poor diet, and inadequate medical and dental care are negative influences and interfere with the achievement of optimal growth and development.

SAFETY

Safety refers to the behaviors and practices that protect children and adults from risk or injury. Safety is of special concern with young children because their well-being is directly affected by the condition of their environment. Unintentional injury is the single leading cause of death among children birth to 14 years in the United States. As greater numbers of children with diverse needs and abilities are included in early education programs, the need for high standards of safety management becomes increasingly important. Consequently, efforts to prevent unintentional injury and death must be a major responsibility of every adult (Aronson, 2002; Marotz, 2000).

Accidents resulting in even minor injuries have an immediate effect on a child's health. Serious injury can cause an extended absence and temporarily interrupt a child's learning and partici-

sedentary – *unusually slow or sluggish; a lifestyle that implies a general lack of physical activity.*

FIGURE 1–4

Children can be encouraged to explore in safe environments.

pation in daily activities. It may also result in added medical expense and increased stress for the child's family.

Factors Affecting Children's Safety

Providing for children's safety requires a keen awareness of the skills and abilities typical of each developmental stage (Allen & Marotz, 2003; Berk, 2003). Teachers can use this information to identify and correct sources of potential harm in children's environments. For example, knowing that an infant enjoys hand-to-mouth activities should alert teachers to continuously monitor the environment for small objects or poisonous substances that could be ingested. Recognizing the toddler's curiosity and desire to explore should make adults concerned about such things as children wandering away, pedestrian safety, unsupervised sources of water, and availability of unsafe play materials.

Limits or rules offer another important form of protection (Figure 1–4). Rules stated in simple terms are easy for children to understand and provide the type of positive guidance that encourages mastery of personal safety skills. Frequent reminders and consistent enforcement also make rules more meaningful for young children. However, teachers must never become overly trusting of a child who has supposedly "learned the rules." Children's spontaneity often takes precedence over their learned behaviors. Consequently, awareness and efforts to protect children's safety are a continuous adult responsibility. It also requires parents and teachers to be aware of personal limitations and circumstances that could interfere with their ability to effectively protect children from injury.

NUTRITION

Nutrition can be defined as "all processes used by an adult or child to take in food and to digest, absorb, transport, utilize, and excrete food substances" (Endres, 1994). Components or substances found in foods are called **nutrients**.

---

nutrients – *the components or substances that are found in food.*

Food is essential for life; what children and adults eat affects their nutritional status and their health. Food supplies essential nutrients that the body requires for the following:

- energy
- growth and development
- normal behavior
- resistance to illness and infection
- tissue repair

A daily intake of essential nutrients depends on eating a variety of foods in adequate amounts. However, the quality of one's diet is often influenced by a number of environmental factors, such as financial resources and availability, transportation, geographical location, cultural preferences, convenience, and knowledge of good nutrition. Most children in the United States live in a time and place where food is reasonably abundant. Yet, there is increasing concern about the number of children who may not be getting enough to eat or whose diets do not include the right types of foods (Forum on Child and Family Statistics, 1999). Also, because many young children spend the majority of their waking hours in out-of-home child care arrangements, special efforts must be made to provide essential nutrients needed for growth and good health.

Effects of Nutrition on Children

Nutritional status affects children's behavior. Well-nourished children are more alert, attentive, and better able to benefit from physical activity and learning experiences. Poorly nourished children may be quiet and withdrawn, or hyperactive and disruptive, during class activities (Brown & Pollitt, 1996). Children who are overweight also face many social, emotional, and physical problems. They are often slow and less able to participate in physical activity. They may also suffer ridicule, have emotional stress, and be excluded from their peer groups (Belfield, 2003; Latner & Stunkard, 2003: Davidson & Birch, 2001).

Children's **resistance** to infection and illness is also directly influenced by their nutritional status (Trahms & Pipes, 2000). Children who are well nourished are less likely to become ill; they also recover more quickly when they are sick. Poorly nourished children are more susceptible to infections and illness, while illness increases the need for some nutrients. Thus, poor nutrition creates a cycle of illness, poorer nutritional status, and lowered resistance to illness.

Malnutrition.   **Malnutrition** is always a serious problem, but it is especially harmful for infants and young children. A lack of essential nutrients and adequate calories can severely interfere with a child's early growth and brain development. Feeding these children a healthy diet later in their lives does not entirely reverse the harmful effects caused by earlier malnutrition (Gordon, 1997; Super, Herrera, & Mora, 1990). Although malnutrition is commonly thought to be associated with poverty and a deprived environment, this is not always true. Children of middle- and upper-income families may also be malnourished simply because of unwise food selections. Frequent fast food meals, snacking habits, unrealistic concern regarding weight control, and skipped meals can significantly limit the variety of food types and nutrients ingested (Satter, 2000). However, some children do experience malnutrition as a result of chronic health conditions and diseases.

Obesity.   Another significant nutritional concern is the recent and dramatic increase in childhood **obesity**. Studies indicate that approximately 25 percent of school-aged children are either

---

resistance – *the ability to avoid infection or illness.*
malnutrition – *prolonged inadequate or excessive intake of nutrients and/or calories required by the body.*
obesity – *a condition characterized by an excessive accumulation of fat.*

overweight or obese (Ball & McCargar, 2003; Kimm & Obarzanek, 2002). Excessive intake of calories, sugars, and dietary fat, coupled with a significant decrease in physical activity, has spelled trouble for many young children (Denehy, 2003; Orlet Fisher, Rolls, & Birch, 2003). Not only do overweight children experience immediate health and psychological consequences, but many are also developing serious long-term health problems, such as type 2 diabetes and heart disease, conditions not previously seen at this age (Gale, 2002; Moran, 1999).

HEALTH, SAFETY, AND NUTRITION: AN INTERDEPENDENT RELATIONSHIP

Health, safety, and nutrition are closely related and dependent on one another. The status of each has a direct effect on the quality of the others. For example, a child whose diet contains inadequate iron or who has medical problems that interfere with iron absorption may develop anemia. Children who are anemic typically experience loss of appetite, fatigue, and a diminished alertness that may affect their safety. At a time when it becomes even more important for children to increase their intake of iron, they may not find food appealing. In other words, nutritional status affects the quality of children's health, while the condition of their health influences nutritional requirements needed to restore and maintain good health, and also challenges their safety.

Good nutrition also plays an important role in accident prevention. The child or adult who arrives at school having eaten little or no breakfast may experience low blood sugar. This results in decreased alertness and slowed reaction time, which causes the individual to be more accident-prone and less able to avoid serious injury. Children and adults who are overweight are also more likely to experience accidental injury. Excess weight can restrict their physical activity, slow reaction times, and cause them to tire more quickly.

IMPLICATIONS FOR TEACHERS

The mothers of more than 64 percent of all children younger than age six currently work outside of the home (U.S. Bureau of the Census, 2000). As a result, early care and education programs serve more children now than at any other time in history. Because these children spend many hours away from their families, it is important that teachers be alert to children's health, safety, and nutritional needs. Activities, environments, meal planning, and supervision should reflect a strong commitment to promoting each child's optimal growth and development. Programs can fulfill this commitment to children by providing the following:

- protection
- services
- education

Protection

Early care and education programs and professionals have a moral and legal obligation to protect the children in their care. The physical arrangement of all spaces occupied by children should receive utmost attention. Planning of indoor and outdoor areas must be carried out carefully to provide environments that are safe and designed to meet children's developmental needs. Daily inspections, prompt removal of hazardous materials, and careful selection of developmentally appropriate equipment and activities help prevent accidents. Appropriate supervision and the establishment of rules also reduce the chances for unintentional injury.

Early education programs must also establish policies and procedures that address and safeguard children's health, safety, and nutritional needs. These policies should also reflect the goals and philosophy of an individual program, and address important issues such as the following:

- Who is responsible for providing first aid?
- What types of emergency information should be obtained from parents?
- When and how are emergency procedures, for example, fire drills and earthquake preparedness, practiced with children and staff?

Licensing requirements often require early care and education programs to adopt specific health policies, such as the following:

- How are sanitary conditions in the classrooms and food preparation areas to be monitored?
- Which staff members will be permitted to administer medications? Will a physician's prescription be required before over-the-counter medications can be given?
- How will children's medical procedures, such as nebulizer treatments, catheter irrigations, or dressing changes, be handled? Who will perform these routines?

For legal protection, programs may also to establish policies such as those that follow:

- What types of activities require special parental permission?
- When can information concerning a child be released? To whom?
- What pick-up procedures must be followed before releasing a child? Special identification? Permission forms?

To be most useful, policies must be written in clear, concise terms that teachers and parents can easily understand. Policies should describe the expectations, actions, and any penalty for noncompliance. New policies should be explained fully and copies provided to parents and staff members who may be directly affected.

Measures taken to protect infants and young children from unnecessary illness and disease are also an important responsibility of teachers. Adherence to good sanitary standards and personal health practices such as disinfecting tables after each diaper change and careful handwashing help control the spread of infectious disease in group settings. Ongoing educational programs for children and adults also help ensure success.

Services

Changes in social and family structure have led to increased collaboration between teachers and parents in order to address children's health needs. However, primary responsibility for a child's health care always belongs to the parents. Parental consent always must be obtained before arrangements are made for any special testing, screening procedures, or treatment. To function effectively in this new role, teachers must have up-to-date information; a sound understanding of health, safety, and nutrition issues that affect young children; and a cooperative partnership with parents.

Early identification of health impairments is critical to optimal realization of a child's growth and development (Allen & Marotz, 2003). Teachers occupy an ideal position for observing children's health and identifying children who require professional evaluation. Programs should make arrangements to provide basic screening tests, such as vision, hearing, and speech evaluations, for the early detection of any problems. Teachers should also be prepared to make referrals and assist families in locating appropriate community services.

Education

Early childhood is a prime time to promote good health, safety, and nutrition education. It is also a time when teachers can help young children begin to develop an awareness of social and

ISSUES TO CONSIDER • Teacher's Role in Children's Health Care

Legislation has opened classrooms to children with a diverse range of abilities and disabilities. Recently, the family of a student who requires continuous monitoring for his complex physical needs challenged school officials in the Supreme Court for refusing to cover the cost of these services. School officials believed the boy's medical needs were beyond their expertise, financial capabilities, and time limitations. However, the courts upheld the student's right to attend school and to have all necessary services provided by the school district. As increasing numbers of children who require some form of medical assistance are being served in inclusive child care programs, teachers are beginning to ask serious questions about their role in, and responsibility for, administering these procedures:

- What laws address children with disabilities and protect their right to an education?
- Should teachers be required to administer medications and medical treatments?
- What rights does a teacher have in these situations? How would a teacher research his or her rights?
- What steps can teachers take in these situations to protect themselves from legal problems?

environmental issues that affect their well-being. Teachers have an obligation to provide children with accurate information and help them learn good habits and attitudes. Often these behaviors become well established during the early years and are carried over into adulthood (Hendricks et al., 1988; Green & Bird, 1986). For these reasons, it is important that parents and teachers capitalize on children's developmental readiness to learn. Learning positive behaviors from the very beginning is much easier than having to reverse poor habits later in life (Figure 1–5).

Health, safety, and nutrition educational experiences should be interesting to children and should encourage them to use the lessons learned in their daily lives. Learning becomes more meaningful when it is woven into children's daily experiences (Figure 1–6). For example, exercise can be incorporated into musical activities, good nutrition can be stressed during snack time or science activities, and the importance of handwashing can be combined with cooking or art activities.

FIGURE 1–5

Good health habits, such as handwashing, are learned through early and repeated experiences.

FIGURE 1–6

Daily experiences provide ideal opportunities for learning about health, safety, and nutrition.

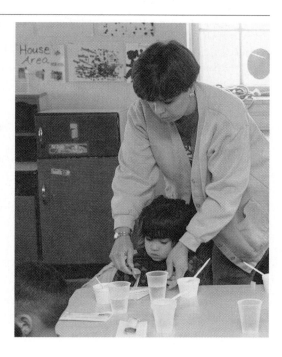

By integrating health, safety, and nutrition concepts into daily learning activities, teachers help children gain a better understanding of their personal value and relevance (Figure 1–7).

Educational experiences, however, must gradually go beyond teaching children basic facts and rules. Teachers must also help children develop problem-solving skills and learn to apply practices in a variety of settings and situations.

FIGURE 1–7

Good health allows children to function effectively with their peers.

The fact that children often learn more from what they see than what they are told cannot be overlooked. Setting good examples of positive health, safety, and nutrition practices is one of the most important responsibilities that teachers and families share. Some of these positive practices include buckling safety belts, eating a variety of foods, engaging in frequent handwashing, and getting adequate daily exercise. Such role modeling helps create environments where young children begin to learn, understand, and assume responsibility for their own well-being.

FOCUS ON FAMILIES • Healthy Living

A healthy body often leads to positive effects on attitude, self-confidence, interest, and energy levels. A nutritious diet and participation in regular physical activity are necessary to maintain a healthy body and to keep it performing at its best. Parents play a key role in this process and help shape children's early attitudes and habits about the value of good nutrition and exercise.

- Be a good role model! Eat a variety of foods and engage in daily physical activity with your children.

- Start the day with breakfast and encourage children to eat. Studies show they will be more alert, better able to learn, and have more energy for play.

- Serve healthy meals that are low in fat and refined sugars. Include five or more daily servings of fruits and vegetables and choose low-fat dairy products.

- Encourage children of all ages to help with meal preparation. Involvement often improves children's interest in eating. Very young children can help by putting napkins and utensils on the table; older children can assist with washing fruits and vegetables or stirring.

- Involve children in 60 minutes of physical activity each day. Plan family activities that everyone can do together, such as walking the dog, swimming, riding bicycles, skating, playing golf or baseball, or playing badminton in the backyard.

- Tell children they are loved. Acknowledge the positive things they do and minimize criticism.

- Assign children age-appropriate responsibility around the house, such as feeding the dog, bringing in the newspaper, or folding clothes. Encourage their efforts, even if the results aren't perfect.

CASE STUDY

Jose, seven years old, and his mother live alone in a one-bedroom apartment close to his school. Most afternoons Jose walks home from school, lets himself into their apartment, and watches television until his mother arrives home from work. Because his mother is usually tired after working all day, she often brings home dinner from one of the local fast food restaurants.

1. How would you rate Jose's short- and long-term health potential?
2. How would you rate his safety?
3. What potential health problems might Jose develop if he does not change his current behavior?
4. What environmental risk factors may be contributing to these problems?
5. If you were working with this family, what suggestions would you have for improving their health?

SUMMARY

- Preventive health care is a relatively new concept.
  - It recognizes that health attitudes and practices are learned behaviors.
  - It encourages individuals to assume an active role in developing and maintaining practices that promote good health.
  - It suggests a need to begin teaching children about good health in the early years.
- Health is determined by one's genetic makeup and environment.
  - It is a dynamic state of physical, mental, and social well-being that is continuously changing as a result of lifestyle decisions.
- Children's growth and development potentials are influenced by the interactions of health, safety, and nutrition.

SUGGESTED ACTIVITIES

1. Contact local law enforcement, fire, and public school authorities. Find out what types of safety programs are available for young children. Invite several representatives to present their information to your class. Discuss how appropriate and effective their programs are for children.

2. Observe a child eating lunch or dinner. What foods does the child eat? What foods are refused? Based on your observation, do you think the child is developing healthy eating habits? If there is an adult present, observe the adult's eating practices. Do you think the adult exhibits healthy eating habits? Do the adult's food likes and dislikes have any influence on what the children eat?

3. Review a menu from an early education center. Are a variety of foods served to the children? Are meals and snacks offered at times when children are likely to be hungry? Are foods nutritious and appealing to children? Are the children likely to eat the food?

4. Contact your local public health department. Make arrangements to observe a routine well-child visit. What preventive health information was given to the parents?

5. Compile a list of early care and education programs available in your community. Note the variety of schedules and services offered. Select five programs at random; check to see if they have waiting lists. If there is a waiting list, how long can parents expect to wait for placement of their child? How many of these programs accept children with special needs, such as physical disabilities, behavior problems, giftedness, or learning disabilities? What adaptations are made for these children in their programs?

CHAPTER REVIEW

A. **Define the following terms:**

1. preventive health care

2. nutrient

3. heredity

4. malnutrition

B. **Briefly answer each of the following:**

1. List five environmental factors that have a negative effect on health.

2. List five environmental factors that have a positive effect on health.

3. Explain how heredity contributes to health.

4. Explain why an abundant food supply does not ensure good nutrition for everyone.

5. List three bodily processes that are sustained through the consumption of food.

6. Explain how illness affects a child's nutritional needs.

7. Name three ways an early care and education program can promote and protect the health, safety, and nutrition of young children enrolled.

REFERENCES

Allen, K. E., & Marotz, L. R. (2003). *Developmental profiles: Pre-birth through twelve* (4th ed.). Clifton Park, NY: Delmar Learning.

American Public Health Association & American Academy of Pediatrics. (2002). *Caring for our children. National health and safety performance standards: Guidelines for out-of-home care.* Washington, DC: Authors.

Aronson, S. (2002). *Health young children: A manual for programs.* (4th ed.). Washington, DC: NAEYC.

Ball, G. D., & McCargar, L. J. (2003). Childhood obesity in Canada: A review of prevalence estimates and risk factors for cardiovascular diseases and type 2 diabetes. *Canadian Journal of Applied Physiology, 28*(1), 117–140.

Belfield, J. (2003). Childhood obesity—a public health problem. *School Nurse News, 20*(1), 20, 22, 24.

Bhargava, A. (2003). A longitudinal analysis of the risk factors for diabetes and coronary heart disease in the Framingham Offspring Study. *Population Health Metrics, 1*(1), 3.

Braet, C., Mervielde, I., & Vandereycken, W. (2003). Psychological aspects of childhood obesity: A controlled study in a clinical and nonclinical sample. *Journal of Pediatric Psychology, 22*(1), 59–71.

Brown, L. J., & Pollitt, E. (1996). Malnutrition, poverty, and intellectual development. *Scientific American, 274*(2), 38–43.

Centers for Medicare & Medicaid Services (CMS). (2001). *CMS: State children's health insurance program annual enrollment report—2001.* Washington, DC: U.S. Department of Health and Human Services.

Charlesworth, R. (2004). *Understanding child development* (6th ed.). Clifton Park, NY: Delmar Learning.

Davison, K., & Birch, L. (2001). Weight status, parent reaction, and self-concept in five-year-old girls. *Pediatrics, 107*(1), 46–53.

Denehy, J. (2003). The health effects of soft drinks. *Journal of School Nursing, 19*(2), 63–67.

Earls, F. (1998). The era of health promotion for children and adolescents—a cross-sectional survey of strategies and new knowledge. *American Journal of Public Health, 88*(6):869–871.

Endres, J. B., & Rockwell, R. E. (1994). *Food, nutrition, and the young child* (4th ed.). Columbus, OH: Merrill.

Forum on Child and Family Statistics. (1999). *America's children: Key national indicators of well-being, 1999.* Washington, DC: National Center for Health Statistics. [http://www.cdc.gov/nchswww/default.htm.]

Gale, E. A. (2002). The rise of childhood type 1 diabetes in the 20th century. *Diabetes, 51*(12), 3353–3361.

Gordon, N. (1997). Nutrition and cognitive function. *Brain Development, 19*(3), 165–170.

Hendricks, C., Peterson, F., Windsor, R., Poehler, D., & Young, M. (1988). Reliability of health knowledge measurement in very young children. *Young Children, 58*(1), 21–25.

Kavanagh, T. (2001). Exercise in the primary prevention of coronary artery disease. *Canadian Journal of Cardiology, 17*(2), 155–161.

Kimm, S. Y., & Obarzanek, E. (2002). Childhood obesity: A new pandemic of the new millennium. *Pediatrics, 110*(5), 1003–1007.

Latner, J. D., & Stunkard, A. J. (2003). Getting worse: The stigmatization of obese children. *Obesity Research, 11*(3), 452–456.

Marotz, L. R. (2000). Childhood and classroom injuries. In J. L. Frost (Ed.), *Children and injuries.* Tucson, AZ: Lawyers & Judges Publishing Co., Inc.

Moran, R. (1999). Evaluation and treatment of childhood obesity. *American Family Physician, 59*, 861.

Office of Disease Prevention and Health Promotion. (2000). *Healthy People 2010.* Washington, DC: Office of Disease Prevention and Health Promotion. U.S. Department of Health and Human Services. Accessed June 9, 2003, from [http://www.healthypeople.gov].

Orlet, L., Fisher, J., Rolls, B. J., & Birch L. L. (2003). Children's bite size and intake of an entree are greater with large portions than with age-appropriate or self-selected portions. *American Journal of Clinical Nutrition,77*(5), 1164–1170.

Super, C., Herrera, M., & Mora, J. (1990). Long-term effects of food supplementation and psychological intervention on the physical growth of Columbian infants at risk of malnutrition. *Child Development, 61*, 21–49.

Trahms, C. M., & Pipes, P. L. (2000). *Nutrition in infancy and childhood.* Columbus, OH: McGraw-Hill.

U.S. Bureau of the Census. (2001). Washington, DC: Author.

U.S. Department of Health and Human Services. (2002). *Health, United States, 2002 With Chartbook on Trends in the Health of Americans.* 430 pp. (PHS) 2002-1232. Washington, DC: Author.

ADDITIONAL READING

ADA Reports. (1999). Position of the American Dietetic Association: Dietary guidelines for healthy children aged 2 to 11 years. *Journal of the American Dietetic Association, 99*, 93.

Centers for Disease control and Prevention. (1997). *CDC's guidelines for school and community programs to promote lifelong physical activity among young people.* Washington, DC: U.S. Department of Health and Human Services, National Center for Chronic Disease Prevention and Health Promotion.

Guthrie, J. F., Lin, B. H., & Frazao, E. (2002). Role of food prepared away from home in the American diet, 1977–78 versus 1994–96: Changes and consequences. *Journal of Nutrition Education & Behavior, 34*(3), 140–150.

Kanarek, N., & Bialek, R. (2003). Community readiness to meet *Healthy People 2010* targets. *Journal of Public Health Management & Practice, 9*(3), 349–354.

Kennedy, E. & Goldberg, J. (1995). What are American children eating? Implications for public policy. *Nutrition Reviews, 53*(5), 111–125.

Mei, Z., Scanlon, K. S., & Grummer-Strawn, L. M. (1998). Increasing prevalence of overweight among U.S. low-income preschool children: The Centers for Disease Control and Prevention Nutrition Surveillance, 1983–1995. *Pediatrics, 101*, 12.

Poest, C. A., Williams, J. R., Witt, D. D., & Atwood, M. E. (1990). Challenge me to move: Large muscle development in young children. *Young Children, 45*(5), 4–10.

Salmeron, J., Hu, F. B., Manson, J. E., Stampfer, M. J., Colditz, G. A., Rimm, E. B., & Willett, W. C. (2001). Dietary fat intake and risk of type 2 diabetes in women. *American Journal of Clinical Nutrition, 73*(6), 1019–1026.

Tuchfarber, B. S., Zins, J. E., & Jason, L. A. (1997). Prevention and control of injuries. In R. Weissberg, T. P. Gullotta, R. L. Hampton, B. A. Ryan, & G. R. Adams (Eds.), *Enhancing children's wellness* (pp. 250–277). Thousand Oaks, CA: Sage Publications.

HELPFUL WEB SITES

Canadian Institute of Child Health (CICH)	http://www.cich.ca
Canadian Pediatric Society	http://www.cps.ca/
Children's Defense Fund	http://www.childrensdefense.org
Healthy People 2010	http://www.health.gov/healthypeople
National Center for Health Statistics	http://www.cdc.gov/nchswww/default.htm
National Resource Center for Health and Safety in Child Care	http://nrc.uchsc.edu/national
No Child Left Behind	http://www.nochildleftbehind.gov
No Child Left Behind (for parents)	http://www.nclb.gov/parents
Office of Disease Prevention and Health Promotion (Dept. of Health and Human Services)	http://odphp.osophs.dhhs.gov/pubs
Centers for Medicare & Medicaid Services	http://cms.hhs.gov/schip/
U.S. Department of Education	http://www.ed.gov/offices/OESE/esea

For additional health, safety, and nutrition resources, go to
http://www.EarlyChildEd.delmar.com

Health of the Young Child: Maximizing the Child's Potential

CHAPTER 2

Promoting Good Health

After studying this chapter, you should be able to:

- Identify growth and developmental characteristics of the infant, toddler, and preschool child.
- List three areas of special concern regarding children's health.
- Describe how teachers can provide for the safety of infants, toddlers, and preschool children.
- Explain how teachers influence children's mental health.
- Describe at least four practices that contribute to a child's improved dental health.

● **TERMS TO KNOW**

autonomy	head circumference	development
norms	bonding	well child
normal	deciduous teeth	characteristics
growth		

The period of infancy is truly a marvel when one considers the dramatic changes in growth and development that occur in a relatively short span of time. The infant progresses from a stage of dependency and relative passiveness to one that enables the child to explore the environment and communicate with others. The spectacular changes in growth and development that occur during this first year will never again be repeated throughout the entire life span.

The toddler years are characterized by an explosive combination of improved locomotion, seemingly unending energy, delightful curiosity, and an eagerness to become independent. Driven by the desire for **autonomy**, or personal identity, toddlers display an intense determination to do things for themselves. As a result, special attention to safety and accident prevention must be a prime concern for teachers and parents.

The preschool years are a time of great excitement and tremendous accomplishments. As children pass through this stage of life, they continue to explore the world around them, but with an

---

autonomy – *a state of personal or self-identity.*

added dimension of understanding. The preschool child's efforts and skills become increasingly sophisticated, while concentration on basic needs such as eating, sleeping, mobility, and communicating grows less intense. Moving toward a sense of independence becomes a major task. Unlimited energy is united with a spirit of curiosity, imagination, and adventurous instincts. This creates a dynamic child who continues to need careful adult supervision and guidance.

GROWTH AND DEVELOPMENT

Early care and education programs serve children of all ages, abilities, and backgrounds. Because the needs and expectations of this population are often quite diverse, it is imperative that teachers be familiar with the normal changes in growth and development associated with each age. Teachers who understand normal growth and development are able to appreciate and work more effectively with young children (Charlesworth, 2004). They are better prepared to help children master critical skills and behaviors at each developmental level. They can create learning experiences and set goals for children that are developmentally appropriate and help foster positive self-esteem. They are able to design quality environments that are safe based on this information. Teachers also find their knowledge of growth and development effective for promoting children's well-being, as well as identifying health problems and abnormal behaviors.

Discussions of growth and development often refer to the "average" or "normal" child; such a child probably does not exist. Every child is a unique individual—a product of different experiences, environments, interactions, and heredity (Figure 2–1). These factors lead to considerable variation in the rate at which children grow and acquire various skills and behaviors (Allen & Marotz, 2003). As a result, each child differs in many ways from every other child.

FIGURE 2–1

Each child is a unique individual—a product of different experiences, environments, interactions, and heredity.

Norms have been established for children's growth and development to serve as useful frames of reference. These norms represent the average or approximate age when the majority of children demonstrate a given behavior or skill. Therefore, the term **normal** implies that while many children can perform a particular skill, some will be more advanced and others may be somewhat slower, yet they are still considered within the normal range.

Growth

The term **growth** refers to the many physical changes that occur as a child matures. Although the process of growth takes place without much conscious control, there are many factors that affect both the quality and rate of growth:

- genetic potential
- cultural influences
- adequate nutrition
- health status
- level of emotional stimulation
- socioeconomic factors
- parent responsiveness

Infants (0–12 months). The average newborn weighs approximately 7 to 8 pounds (3.2–3.6 kg) at birth and is approximately 20 inches (50 cm) in length. Growth is rapid during the first year; an infant's birth weight nearly doubles by the fifth month and triples by the end of the first year (Berk, 2003). An infant who weighs 8 pounds (3.6 kg) at birth should weigh 16 pounds (7.3 kg) at 5 months and approximately 24 pounds (10.9 kg) at 12 months.

Increases in length during the first year represent approximately 50 percent of the infant's original birth length. An infant measuring 21 inches (52.5 cm) at birth should reach a length of approximately 31.5 inches (78.7 cm) at 12 months of age. A larger percentage of this gain takes place during the first six months when an infant may grow as much as 1 inch (2.5 cm) per month.

Rapid growth of the brain causes the infant's head to appear large in proportion to the rest of the body. Thus, measurements of **head circumference** are important indicators of normal growth. Measurements should increase steadily and equal the chest circumference by the end of the first year.

Additional physical changes that occur during the first year include the growth of hair and eruption of teeth (four upper and four lower). The eyes begin to focus and move together as a unit by the third month, and vision becomes more acute. Special health concerns for infants include the following:

- nutritional requirements
- adequate provisions for sleep
- **bonding** or maternal attachment
- early brain development
- safety and injury prevention
- identification of birth defects and health impairments

---

norms – *an expression (e.g., weeks, months, years) of when a child is likely to demonstrate certain developmental skills.*

normal – *average; a characteristic or quality that is common to most individuals in a defined group.*

growth – *increase in size of any body part or of the entire body.*

head circumference – *the distance around the head obtained by measuring over the forehead and bony protuberance on the back of the head; it is an indication of normal or abnormal growth and development of the brain and central nervous system.*

bonding – *the process of establishing a positive and strong emotional relationship between an infant and his or her parent; sometimes referred to as attachment.*

During the weeks and months following birth, a baby's brain undergoes rapid change as the result of maturation and experience. Genetic makeup and maternal practices during pregnancy (such as diet, smoking, ingestion of alcohol or drugs, infections) can have a significant effect on this process. The quality of attachment infants establish with their primary caregivers also plays an important role. Early learning experiences provide critical stimulation within the brain that forces it to begin establishing, organizing, and maintaining complex electrical connections (Rushton, 2001). Gradually, through new and repetitive learning experiences, the baby's brain is transformed from an otherwise disorganized system to one capable of profound thought, emotions, and learning. Most of this transformation occurs during the first three years, when the brain appears to be more receptive to shaping and change. Researchers have also discovered what they believe to be certain "critical periods," or windows of opportunity, when some forms of learning and sensory development are more likely to occur (Bailey, Symons, & Lichtman , 2001). Parents and teachers can use this information to provide infants and young children with environments and experiences that are enriching and will foster healthy brain development (Vaught, 2001; Eisenberg, 1999).

Toddlers (12–30 months). The toddler continues to make steady gains in height and weight, but at a much slower rate than during infancy. A weight increase of 6 to 7 pounds (2.7–3.2 kg) per year is considered normal and reflects a total gain of nearly four times the child's birth weight by the age of two. The toddler grows approximately 3 to 5 inches (7.5–12.5 cm) in height per year. Body proportions change and result in a more erect and adultlike appearance.

Eruption of "baby teeth," or **deciduous teeth**, is completed by the end of the toddler period. (Deciduous teeth consist of a set of 20 temporary teeth.) Toddlers can learn to brush their new teeth as an important aspect of preventive health care, although considerable adult supervision is still needed. Special attention should also be paid to providing foods that promote good dental health; are colorful, appealing, and easily chewed; and include all of the essential nutrients since toddlers typically have smaller appetites. Foods from all food groups—fruits, vegetables, dairy, protein, whole-grains—should be part of the toddler's daily meal pattern.

High activity levels require that the toddler get at least 10 to 12 hours of uninterrupted nighttime sleep. In addition, most toddlers continue to nap one to two hours each day. Safety awareness and injury prevention continue to be major concerns that demand careful adult attention (Figure 2–2).

Preschoolers/Early School-age (2½–8 years). During the preschool years a child's appearance becomes more streamlined and adultlike in form. Head size remains approximately the same, while the child's trunk (body) and extremities (arms and legs) continue to grow. Gradually, the head appears to separate from the trunk as the neck lengthens. Legs grow longer and at a faster rate than the arms, adding extra inches to the child's height. The characteristic chubby shape of the toddler is gradually lost as muscle tone and strength increase. These changes are also responsible for the flattening of the abdomen, or stomach, and straighter posture.

Gains in weight and height are relatively slow but steady throughout this period. By three years of age, children weigh approximately five times their weight at birth. An ideal weight gain for a preschool child is approximately 4 to 5 pounds (1.8–2.3 kg) per year. However, a greater proportion of the preschool child's growth is the result of increases in height rather than weight. The typical preschool child grows an average of 2 to 2.5 inches (5.0–6.3 cm) per year. By the time children reach six years of age, they have nearly doubled their original birth length (from approximately 20 inches

deciduous teeth – *a child's initial set of teeth; this set is temporary and gradually begins to fall out around 5 years of age.*

FIGURE 2–2

Safety is a major concern in any early childhood setting.

to 40 inches [50–100 cm]). This combination of growth and muscle development causes children to take on a longer, thinner appearance.

Adequate nutrition continues to be a prime consideration (Satter, 2000). High activity levels replace the rapid growth of earlier years as the primary demand for calories. A general rule for estimating a child's daily caloric needs is to begin with a base of 1,000 calories and add an additional 100 calories per birthday. (For example, a seven-year-old would need approximately 1,700 calories.) However, this period is often marked by decreased appetite and poor eating habits. Consequently, parents and teachers must be aware of children's actual food intake and work to encourage healthy eating habits.

Sleep is also required for optimal growth and development. When days are long and tiring or unusually stressful, children's need for sleep may be even greater. Most preschool and early school-aged children require 8 to 12 hours of uninterrupted sleep at night in addition to daytime periods of rest. However, bedtime and afternoon naps often become a source of conflict between children and adults. Preschool children have a tendency to become so intensely busy and involved in play activities that they are reluctant to take time out for sleep. Nevertheless, young children benefit from short periods of rest during their normal daytime routine. Planned quiet times, with books, puzzles, quiet music, or a small toy, may be sufficient for helping children relax.

By the time children reach school-age, they begin to enjoy one of the healthiest periods of their lives. They generally experience fewer colds and upper respiratory infections due to improved resistance and physical maturation. Their visual acuity also continues to improve, resulting in a gradual decrease of farsightedness. Once again, children will undergo fairly rapid growth as height and muscle mass increase to give them a more adultlike appearance.

REFLECTIVE THOUGHTS

Adequate sleep is important for children during their early years. What strategies could you use to encourage children to rest quietly during naptime? What suggestions would you have for parents to improve children's compliance with bedtimes?

Development

In the span of one year, remarkable changes take place in the infant's **development**. The child progresses from a stage of complete dependency on adults to one marked by the acquisition of language and the formation of rather complex thought patterns. Infants also become more social and outgoing near the end of the first year and seemingly enjoy and imitate the adults around them (Allen & Marotz, 2003).

The toddler and preschool periods reflect a continued refinement of language, perceptual, motor, cognitive, and social achievements. Improved motor and verbal skills enable the toddler to explore, test, and interact with the environment for the purpose of determining personal identity, or autonomy.

Developmental gains enable the preschool-aged child to perform self-care and fine motor tasks with improved strength, speed, accuracy, control, and ease. The beginning of a conscience slowly emerges. This is an important step in the process of socialization because it allows children to exercise control over some of their emotions. Friendships with peers become increasingly important as preschool children begin to extend their sphere of acquaintances beyond the limit of family members.

Six-, seven-, and eight-year-olds are motivated by a strong desire to achieve. Participation in sports and other vigorous activities help children improve their motor skills. Rewards and adult approval continue to be important and help children build self-esteem. During this stage, children also begin to sort out gender identity through increased social contacts.

A summary of major developmental achievements is presented in Table 2–1. It should be remembered that such a list represents accomplishments that a majority of children can perform at a given age. It should also be noted that not every child achieves all of these tasks. Many factors, including nutritional adequacy, opportunities for learning, access to appropriate medical and dental care, a nurturing environment, and parental support, exert a strong influence on children's skill acquisition.

PROMOTION OF GOOD HEALTH

Today, concern for children's health and welfare is a shared vision. Changes in current lifestyles, trends, and expectations have shifted some responsibilities for children's health to the collaborative efforts of parents, teachers, and service providers. Communities are also valued members of this partnership and must be proactive in creating environments that are safe, enriching, and healthy places for children to live.

How can parents and teachers determine whether children are healthy? What qualities or indicators are commonly associated with being a healthy or **well child**? **Characteristics** of normal growth and development can be helpful in evaluating children's overall health status and developmental progress. However, there is much variation within the so-called normal range, so they must be used cautiously. Table 2–2 identifies a sampling of physical and developmental expectations for the healthy preschool child based on these norms. Similar lists can be generated for infants and toddlers based on characteristics of growth and development (Allen & Marotz, 2003).

---

development – *commonly refers to the process of intellectual growth and change.*
well child – *a child in a good physical, mental, social, and emotional state.*
characteristics – *qualities or traits that distinguish one person from another.*

TABLE 2–1 Major Developmental Achievements

AGE	ACHIEVEMENTS
2 months	lifts head up when placed on stomach follows moving person or object with eyes imitates or responds to smiling person with occasional smiles turns toward source of sound begins to make simple sounds and noises grasps objects with entire hand; not strong enough to hold on enjoys being held and cuddled
4 months	has good control of head reaches for and grasps objects with both hands laughs out loud; vocalizes with coos and giggles waves arms about holds head erect when supported in a sitting position rolls over from side to back to stomach recognizes familiar objects (e.g., bottle, toy)
6 months	grasps objects with entire hand; transfers objects from one hand to the other and from hand to mouth sits alone with minimal support deliberately reaches for, grasps and holds objects plays games and imitates (e.g., peek-a-boo) shows signs of teeth beginning to erupt prefers primary caregiver to strangers babbles using different sounds raises up and supports weight of upper body on arms
9 months	sits alone; able to maintain balance while changing positions picks up objects with pincer grasp (first finger and thumb) begins to crawl attempts to say words such as "mama" and "dada" is hesitant toward strangers explores new objects by chewing or placing them in mouth
12 months	pulls up to a standing position may "walk" by holding on to objects stacks several objects one on top of the other responds to simple commands and own name babbles using jargon in sentence-like form uses hands, eyes, and mouth to investigate new objects can hold own eating utensils
18 months	crawls up and down stairs one at a time walks unassisted; has difficulty avoiding obstacles in pathway is less fearful of strangers enjoys being read to; likes toys for pushing and pulling has a vocabulary consisting of approximately 5–50 words, can name familiar objects helps feed self; manages spoon and cup

(Continued)

TABLE 2-1 Major Developmental Achievements (Continued)

AGE	ACHIEVEMENTS
2 years	runs, walks with ease; can kick and throw a ball; jumps in place speaks in two- to three-word sentences; asks simple questions; knows about 200 words displays parallel play achieves daytime toilet training voices displeasure
3 years	climbs stairs using alternating feet can hop and balance on one foot feeds self can help dress and undress; washes own hands and brushes teeth with help is usually toilet trained is curious; asks and answers questions enjoys drawing, cutting with scissors, painting, clay, and make-believe can throw and bounce a ball states name; recognizes self in pictures
4 years	dresses and undresses self; helps with bathing; manages own toothbrushing enjoys creative activities: paints, draws with detail, models with clay, builds imaginative structures with blocks rides a bike with confidence, turns corners, maintains balance climbs, runs, and hops with skill and vigor enjoys friendships and playing with small groups of children enjoys and seeks adult approval understands simple concepts (e.g., shortest, longest, same)
5 years	expresses ideas and questions clearly and with fluency has vocabulary consisting of approximately 2,500–3,000 words substitutes verbal for physical expressions of displeasure dresses without supervision seeks reassurance and recognition for achievements engages in active and energetic play, especially outdoors throws and catches a ball with relative accuracy cuts with scissors along a straight line; draws in detail
6 years	plays with enthusiasm and vigor develops increasing interest in books and reading displays greater independence from adults; makes fewer requests for help forms close friendships with several peers exhibits improved motor skills; can jump rope, hop and skip, ride a bicycle enjoys conversation sorts objects by color and shape
7 and 8 years	enjoys friends; seeks their approval shows increased curiosity and interest in exploration develops greater clarity of gender identity is motivated by a sense of achievement begins to reveal a moral consciousness

Adapted from Allen K. E., & Marotz, L. R. (2003). *Developmental profiles* (4th ed.). Clifton Park, NY: Delmar Learning.

TABLE 2-2 Characteristics of the Healthy Preschool Child

	YES	NO
A. Physical Characteristics		
1. alert and enthusiastic	X	
2. enjoys vigorous, active play		X
3. appears rested		
4. firm musculature		
5. growth—slow, steady increases in height and weight		
6. not easily fatigued		
7. inoffensive breath		
8. legs and back straight		
9. teeth well formed—even, clean, free from cavities		
10. lips and gums pink and firm		
11. skin clear (color is important) and eyes bright		
12. assumes straight posture		
13. large motor control well developed		
14. beginning to develop fine motor control		
15. good hand-eye coordination		
B. Social Behaviors		
1. enthusiastic		
2. curious—interested in surroundings		
3. enters willingly into a wide range of activities		
4. happy and friendly; cheerful most of the time		
5. developing self-confidence; anticipates success, copes with failure		
6. shares in group responsibilities		
7. works and plays cooperatively with peers		
8. respects other's property		
9. appreciates and understands other's feelings		
10. adapts to new situations		
11. enjoys friends and friendships		
12. participates in cooperative play		
13. understands language; can express thoughts and feelings to adults and peers		
14. demonstrates courage in meeting difficulties; recovers quickly from upsets		
15. begins to exercise self-control		
C. Characteristic Work Behaviors		
1. attentive		
2. begins to carry tasks through to completion		
3. increasing attention span		
4. is persistent in activities; is not easily frustrated		
5. can work independently at times		
6. demonstrates an interest in learning; curiosity		
7. shows originality, creativity, imagination		
8. accepts responsibility		
9. responds quickly and appropriately to directions and instructions		
10. works and shares responsibilities with others		
11. accepts new challenges		
12. adaptable		

Download this form online at http:// www.Early ChildEd.del mar.com

SPECIAL AREAS OF CONSIDERATION

Teachers, in cooperation with families, have considerable influence on children's well-being. In addition to providing safe environments, nutritious meals, health supervision, stimulating learning experiences, and valuable guidance, teachers have many opportunities throughout the day to promote children's health and development of healthy behaviors (Marcon, 2003). Again, knowledge of children's growth and development serves as an important guide for understanding the special needs associated with each stage. Four areas of special concern will be addressed here: injury prevention, posture, dental health, and mental health.

Injury Prevention

Unintentional injuries, especially those involving motor vehicles, pose the greatest threat to the lives of young children (Schieber & Vegaga, 2002; Simpson, Moll, Kassam, Miller, & Winston, 2002). They are responsible for more than one-half of all deaths among children under five years of age in the United States. Each year an additional one million children sustain injuries that require medical attention, and many are left with permanent disabilities (Dellinger, 2002; U.S. Department of Health and Human Services, 2001).

An understanding of normal growth and development is particularly useful when planning for children's safety. Many of the characteristics that make children exciting and a joy to work with are the same characteristics that make them likely to sustain injury. Children's skills are seldom as well developed as their determination, and in their zealous approach to life, they often fail to recognize inherent dangers. Their inability to judge time, distance, and speed accurately contributes to many injuries, including those resulting from falls, as a pedestrian, or riding toys out into the street (Crowley-Coha, 2002; Marotz, 2000). Limited experience also makes it difficult for children to always anticipate the consequences of their actions. The inclusion of infants and children with disabilities raises additional safety concerns. For these reasons, safety awareness and injury prevention must be given prime consideration in group care settings and in a child's home (Figure 2–3). Approaches to safety management will be discussed in Chapter 9.

Posture and Physical Activity

Good posture, balance, and correct body *alignment* are necessary for many of the physical activities children engage in, such as walking, jumping, running, skipping, standing and sitting. Encouraging children's development of good postural habits can help avoid some types of chronic problems related to poor posture later in life. Early recognition and treatment of ear infections is also important because a child's balance can be affected.

Orthopedic problems (those relating to skeletal and muscular systems) are not common among young children. However, there are several conditions that warrant early diagnosis and treatment:

- birth injuries, such as hip dislocation, fractured collarbone
- abnormal or unusual walking patterns, such as limping, walking pigeon-toed
- bowed legs
- knock-knees
- flat feet
- unusual curvature of the spine
- difference in length of the extremities (arms and legs)

Some irregularities of posture disappear spontaneously as young children mature. For example, it is not uncommon for infants and toddlers to have bowed legs or to walk slightly pigeon-toed. By age three or four, these problems should correct themselves. However, if these conditions

FIGURE 2–3

Adults must be continuously aware of hazards in children's environments.

persist beyond the age of four, they should be evaluated by a health professional. Early detection and treatment can prevent many long-term or permanent deformities.

Good posture is an excellent topic for classroom discussion, demonstrations, rhythm and movement activities, games, and art projects (Bronson, 2003; Arnsdorff, 2001) (Figure 2–4). Concepts and techniques that children learn can be shared with parents so that they can reinforce them at home (Kalata, 1998). Parent newsletters can include suggestions for good posture, children can illustrate basic posture concepts in pictures, and parents can be invited to attend a class demonstration of good body alignment.

Although the acts of sitting and standing seem quite natural, it is important that children learn the following good body mechanics:

- Sit squarely in a chair, resting the back firmly against the chair back with both feet flat on the floor.
- Sit on the floor with legs crossed in front or with both legs extended out in front. Children should be discouraged from sitting in a "W" position because this position strains developing joints (Figure 2–5).
- Stand with the shoulders square, the chin up, and the chest out. Distribute body weight evenly over both feet to avoid placing added stress on one or the other hip joints.
- Lift and carry heavy objects using the stronger muscles of the arms and legs rather than the weaker muscles of the back. Get close to the object to be lifted. Stand with the feet slightly apart to give a wider base of support, and stoop down to lift rather than just bend over.

Good posture and body mechanics are also important for parents and teachers to practice (Table 2–3). Because they perform many activities each day that involve lifting and bending,

FIGURE 2-4

Good posture is an excellent topic for rhythm and movement activities.

following proper technique can help reduce chronic fatigue and work-related injury (Cantu, 2002). Exercising regularly also helps improve muscle strength and makes demanding physical tasks easier to manage while avoiding injury.

Vigorous physical activity should also be an essential part of every child's daily routine. Evidence continues to establish a strong correlation between declining rates of physical activity, especially among children, and increasing obesity (Belfield, 2003; Berg, Buechner, & Parham, 2003; Kimm & Obarzanek , 2002). Because lifelong habits are being established throughout childhood, this is an ideal time to help children develop ones that will promote good health. Frequent opportunities for vigorous indoor and outdoor play should be planned throughout the day. Current guidelines recommend that children get a minimum of 30 to 60 minutes of moderate physical activity daily (Wehling, Weepie, & McCarthy, 2002; Troiano, Macera, & Ballard-Barbash, 2001). Not only are these periods important for children's physical well-being, but they are also effective for relieving excess energy, stress, and boredom. Parents and teachers must also serve as good role models for children and engage in daily physical activity (Hodges, 2003).

Dental Health

Dental problems can have an obvious effect on children's overall health, as well as their appearance and self-esteem. Advancements in dentistry and ongoing educational efforts have improved children's dental health. The value of good nutrition during pregnancy, dental visits for children before age two, the addition of fluoride to water supplies, and application of sealants have contributed significantly to a decrease in dental caries and gum disease (Horowitz, 2003). Yet, there

TABLE 2-3 **Good Body Mechanics for Parents and Teachers**
• Use proper technique when lifting children; flex the knees and lift using leg muscles; avoid lifting with back muscles, which are weaker.
• Adjust the height of children's cribs and changing tables to avoid bending over.
• Provide children with step stools so that they can reach water fountains and faucets without having to be lifted.
• Bend down by flexing the knees rather than bending over at the waist; this reduces strain on weaker back muscles and decreases the risk of possible injury.
• Sit in adult-sized furniture with feet resting comfortably on the floor to lessen strain on the back and knees.
• Transport children in strollers or wagons rather than carrying them.
• Exercise regularly to improve muscle strength, especially back muscles, and to relieve stress.
• Lift objects by keeping arms close to the body versus extended; this also reduces potential for back strain.

are still many children who have never been treated by a dentist because their families cannot afford dental insurance or costly preventive dental care (Edelstein, 2002; Yu, Bellamy, Kogan, Dunbar, Schwalberg, & Schuster, 2002). Also, many parents erroneously believe that "baby teeth," or deciduous teeth, are relatively unimportant because they will eventually fall out (Riedy, 2001). This belief is incorrect because temporary teeth are necessary for the following:

- chewing
- the spacing of permanent teeth
- shaping of the jaw bone
- development of speech

The condition of children's teeth can also have a direct effect on their behavior and ability to learn. Neglected dental care can result in painful cavities and infected teeth, making it difficult for children to concentrate and maintain interest in tasks and activities. Proper dental care must be practiced from birth, with special attention given to the following:

- diet
- hygienic practices—e.g., toothbrushing, flossing
- regular dental examinations
- prompt treatment of dental problems

FIGURE 2–5

Children should be discouraged from sitting in the "W" position.

A child's first visit to the dentist should be scheduled when the child is between two and two-and-one-half years of age. Initial visits should be a pleasant experience and allow the child to become acquainted with the dentist, routine examinations, and cleanings without the discomfort of painful dental work. Hopefully, such positive experiences will foster a healthy attitude toward dental care and discourage children from anticipating future dental examinations with fear and anxiety. Routine checkups at 6- to 12-month intervals are generally recommended as part of a preventive dentistry program.

Diet has an unquestionable effect on children's dental health (Satter, 2000). Proper tooth formation depends on an adequate intake of protein and minerals, particularly calcium and fluoride. One of the most devastating influences on diet, however, is the consumption of large amounts of highly refined and sticky carbohydrates. This includes those found in cakes, cookies, candies, gum, soft drinks, sweetened cereals, and dried fruits (for example, raisins, dates, and prunes). Parents and teachers can help young children begin to adopt good dietary habits by limiting the frequency and amounts of sweets they are served and by substituting foods that are nutritious. Because many children's medications and chewable vitamins are sweetened with sugars, toothbrushing should always be encouraged following their ingestion.

A daily routine of good oral hygiene is also essential for the promotion of good dental health (Price, 1999). An infant's teeth should be wiped with a small, wet washcloth to remove pieces of food. Around 15 months of age, children can begin learning how to brush their teeth. Several steps teachers and parents can take to increase children's interest in learning to brush their own teeth follow:

- purchasing a small, soft toothbrush in the child's favorite color
- storing the toothbrush where the child can reach it
- providing a footstool or chair so that the child can reach the sink

Caution: Supervise the child closely to prevent slipping or falling.

- demonstrating the toothbrushing procedure so that the child knows what to expect
- encouraging the child to brush teeth at least twice daily—once in the morning and again before going to bed
- constructing a simple chart where children can place a check each time they brush their teeth; this provides a good method for reinforcing regular toothbrushing habits

Toddlers can be taught to brush their teeth with an adult's help. At this age, toothbrushing can be accomplished by using a soft brush and water to clean the teeth. Most toddlers do not like the taste or foaming action of toothpastes and are unable to spit them out after brushing. When a child is first learning toothbrushing skills, it is a good idea for an adult to brush over the teeth at least after one of the brushings each day to be sure all areas are clean. Children can also be taught alternative methods for cleaning teeth between brushings. These methods include rinsing out the mouth with water after eating, and eating raw foods such as apples, pears, and celery that provide a natural cleansing action on the teeth. Some cheeses, such as cheddar, swiss, and Monterey Jack, have also been found beneficial for reducing dental decay.

Preschool children are usually able to brush with minimal adult supervision. Although their technique may not always be perfect, children are establishing a lifelong habit of good toothbrushing. In addition to proper technique, the use of a toothpaste containing fluoride has proved to be very beneficial in reducing dental cavities. However, caution children not to swallow the toothpaste: too much fluoride can be harmful.

The question of whether young children should learn to floss their teeth is best answered by the individual child's dentist. Although the practice is regarded as beneficial, much depends on the child's maturity and fine motor skills. Flossing is often not stressed until after permanent teeth begin erupting and the spaces between teeth disappear. If children are too young to floss their own teeth, parents can provide assistance.

Regular dental supervision also contributes to good dental health. However, it cannot replace daily attention to good nutrition and hygiene. During routine examinations, dentists look for signs of any dental problems and also review the child's toothbrushing technique, diet, and personal habits that may have an effect on the teeth (such as thumbsucking or grinding the teeth). Cleaning and an application of fluoride are generally included with routine examinations. Fluoride added to city water supplies has also been proved to significantly reduce tooth decay (Horowitz, 2003). New

REFLECTIVE THOUGHTS

Bottle mouth syndrome or baby bottle tooth decay (BBTD) is a preventable condition that results in extensive decay when a baby's teeth are exposed to sugary substances, including juices, formula, and breast milk, for prolonged periods. Practices such as putting a baby to bed with a bottle, nursing a baby frequently or for extended periods at night, and giving a toddler a bottle with juice to carry around are harmful to children's teeth (Barnes, et al., 1992; King, 1998). Because saliva flow is decreased during sleep, it is less effective in rinsing off the teeth.

- What cautions would you offer to new parents who want to prevent their infants from developing bottle mouth syndrome?
- What practices can a mother who wants to feed her infant on demand use to avoid BBTD?
- What practices can parents use with older children to encourage good dental health?

preventive treatments, such as sealants (a plasticlike material applied over the grooves of permanent molars to protect them from decay), also help reduce children's dental problems (Feigal, 2002).

Mental Health

Children's mental health has received increasing attention as problems of juvenile delinquency, school dropout rates, substance abuse, violence, gang membership, and child suicide escalate. Approximately 15 to 22 percent of children in the United States experience mental health problems that seriously interfere with learning and the ability to become productive adults (Chow, Jaffee, & Snowden, 2003; Kataoka, Zhang, & Wells, 2002). This statistic reinforces the necessity of helping young children develop and strengthen skills that will enable them to cope with fast-paced lifestyles and the tough problems many are likely to face (Parlakian, 2002; Elias & Weissberg, 2000).

Early education teachers play a major role in this process (Collins, Mascia, Kendall, Golden, & Schock, 2003). They can use a variety of strategies to promote children's healthy mental development, including the following:

- practicing good mental health principles, such as encouraging children's efforts, respecting their differences, teaching positive social skills
- preventing emotional problems through child and parent education, including how to manage conflict, behavior guidance, problem-solving techniques, and communication skills
- identifying and referring children with potentially serious emotional problems, such as excessive fear or anger, aggressive behavior, difficulty making and keeping friends
- assisting parents in locating appropriate community resources and arranging for treatment services

Basic Needs. The preventive health care model recognizes that a close relationship exists between children's mental and physical well-being (Dawson, Ashman & Carver, 2000). To achieve sound emotional health, children must first have their basic needs for food, water, shelter, sleep, love, security, and achievement satisfied. Only then are children able to develop a sense of autonomy, form meaningful relationships with others, and function effectively in group settings (Maslow, 1970). How children feel about themselves and how readily they adapt to environmental change are important qualities that influence lifelong emotional well-being.

Teachers must recognize the value of helping young children develop positive attitudes and socially acceptable behaviors. They can provide opportunities where children can learn to communicate effectively, control their impulsive and aggressive behaviors, express their emotions, develop independence, handle success and failure, respond with ease to new situations, solve problems, and feel good about themselves (Gartrell, 2002; Parlakian, 2002). In other words, they should understand children's developmental needs and promote personal and social mental health skills.

REFLECTIVE THOUGHTS

Making friends is an important part of growing up. Gaining acceptance and respect from peers helps shape one's sense of self-esteem. However, friendships are not always easy for children to establish. What social skills are required for making friends? What behaviors are likely to alienate friends? Should parents get involved in their children's friendships? As a parent, what would you do if your child became friends with someone you didn't care for?

Role Models. Teachers must carefully examine their own emotional state if they are to be successful in helping young children achieve good mental health. They, too, must have a strong sense of self-worth and confidence in what they are doing. They should be aware of personal prejudices, be able to accept constructive criticism, and recognize their strengths and limitations. They must have effective communication skills and be able to work collaboratively with families, community service providers, health care professionals, and other members of the child's educational team.

If teachers are to serve as positive role models, they must be able to exercise the same control over their emotions that they expect of children. Personal problems and stressors must be left at home so that full attention can be focused on the children. Teachers must respect children as individuals—for who they are, and not what they can or cannot do—because every child has qualities that are endearing and worthy of recognition. Teachers must also be impartial in their treatment of children; favoritism cannot be tolerated.

Working with young children can be a rewarding career, but it can also be stressful and demanding in terms of the patience, energy, and stamina required. Noise, children's continuous requests, long hours, staff shortages, low wages, and occasional conflicts with parents or co-workers are everyday challenges. Physical demands and unresolved stress can gradually take their toll on teachers' health, commitment, and everyday performance. Eventually, this can lead to job burnout and an intense desire to leave their current position or, in some case, the profession (Gruenberg, 1998; Manning, Rubin, Perdigao, Gonzalez, & Schindler, 1996). For this reason, it is important to identify the sources of stress in one's job and take the necessary steps to address, reduce, or eliminate them to the extent possible (Kunitz, 2000) (Table 2–4).

Emotional Climate. The emotional climate of a classroom or child care setting has a significant impact on children's mental health. Consider the following situations and decide which classroom is most inviting:

> Kate enters the classroom excited and eager to tell her teacher about the tooth she lost last night and the quarter she found under her pillow from the "tooth fairy." Without any greeting, the teacher hurries to check Kate in and informs her that she is too busy to talk right now, "but maybe later." When they are finished, the teacher instructs Kate to find something to do without getting into trouble. Kate quietly walks away to her locker.

TABLE 2–4 Strategies for Managing Teacher Stress

- Seek out training opportunities where you can learn new skills and improve your work effectiveness.
- Learn and practice time management techniques.
- Develop program policies and procedures that will increase efficiency and reduce sources of tension and conflict.
- Join professional organizations; expand your contacts with other child care professionals, acquire new ideas, advocate for young children.
- Take care of your personal health—get plenty of sleep, eat a nutritious diet, and participate in some form of physical exercise several times each week.
- Develop new interests, hobbies, and other outlets for releasing tension.
- Practice progressive relaxation techniques. Periodically, concentrate on making yourself relax.
- Plan time for yourself each day—read a good book, watch a movie or favorite TV program, go for a long walk, paint, go shopping, play golf, or participate in some activity that you enjoy.

Ted arrives at the child care center and is reluctant to leave his mother. The care provider greets Ted and his mother. "Ted, I am so glad that you came to school today. We are going to build with the wooden blocks, and I know that is one of your favorite activities. Perhaps you would like to build something for your mother before it is time for her to go home." Ted eagerly builds a barn with several "animals" in the yard around it and proudly looks to his mother for approval. When Ted's mother is ready to leave, he waves good-bye.

Clearly, the classroom atmosphere or mood is influenced by the teacher's actions and responses, which in turn have a direct effect on children's behavior (Figure 2–6). Young children are more receptive and likely to respond enthusiastically to teachers who are warm, nurturing, and sensitive to their special needs. The use of ridicule, sarcasm, threats, or discipline that is harsh or inconsistent is never appropriate and can harm children's short- and long-term emotional development. When children are exposed to this type of adult response, they tend to learn behaviors that are inappropriate and socially undesirable. However, an emotional climate that encourages and supports mutual cooperation, respect, trust, acceptance, and independence encourages children to develop a strong foundation of positive mental health skills and attitudes.

Curriculum planning can also be used effectively to promote children's mental health. Learning activities that are developmentally appropriate and adapted to meet children's special needs and abilities improve their chances for achieving success. In addition to building self-esteem, positive learning outcomes translate into continued motivation and interest in learning (Fallin, Wallinga, & Coleman, 2001). Curriculum planning that takes into account children's need for periods of active play and quiet time, indoor and outdoor experiences, and group versus individual activities also contributes to their overall emotional health.

Stress. Prolonged or intense stress in children's lives will sooner or later affect their mental and physical well-being. Stressful situations, such as abusive treatment, poverty, unrealistic parental demands, chronic illness, unsafe neighborhoods, being left alone for long periods, or natural disasters (floods, tornadoes), can have a serious impact on children's emotional states (Jewett & Peterson, 2002). Even many everyday experiences that adults take in stride can provoke feelings of undue anxiety, tension, and stress in young children:

- separation from parents
- new experiences—for example, moving, placement in a childcare center, mother going to work, birth of a sibling, getting a new teacher, being left with a sitter

FIGURE 2–6

Teachers influence the classroom atmosphere, which, in turn, affects children's behavior.

- chronic illness and hospitalization
- divorce of parents
- death of a pet, family member, or close friend
- conflict of ideas; confrontations with parents, friends, or teachers
- overstimulation due to hectic schedules, participation in numerous extracurricular activities
- learning problems

Inexperience and immature development of defense mechanisms challenge children's ability to handle stressful events in a healthy manner (Berk, 2003). Sudden changes in behavior may be an early indication that a child is experiencing undue stress, anxiety, or inner turmoil (Parlakian, 2002; Honig, 1986). Signs of behavior disturbances can range from those that are less serious—nail biting, hair twisting, body rocking, or shyness—to more serious problems—repeated aggressiveness, destructiveness, withdrawal, depression, nightmares, psychosomatic illnesses, or poor performance in school.

Childhood Depression. Some children are unsuccessful or unable to cope with chronic stress and turmoil. They may develop a sense of extreme and persistent sadness and hopelessness that begins to affect the way they think, feel, and act. Some early signs of childhood depression follow:

- apathy or disinterest in activities or friends
- loss of appetite
- difficulty sleeping
- complaints of physical discomforts, such as headaches, stomachaches, vomiting, diarrhea, ulcers, repetitive tics (twitches), or difficulty breathing (Cullinan, Evans, Epstein, & Ryser, 2003; Luby, Heffelfinger, Mrakotsky, Brown, Hessler, Wallis, & Spitznagel, 2003)
- lack of energy or enthusiasm
- indecision
- poor self-esteem

Children who have learning and behavior disorders are known to experience an increased risk of also developing depression (National Institutes of Mental Health, 2000). Having a family history of mental health problems also places some children at higher risk. Even children as young as three may show early signs of depression particularly when their mothers are also suffering from this condition (Lyons, Wolfe, Lyubchik, & Steingard, 2002).

The onset of childhood depression may occur abruptly following a traumatic event, such as parental divorce, death of a close family member or friend, abusive treatment, or chronic illness (Hopkins, 2002). However, it can also develop slowly over time, making the early signs more difficult to notice. In either case, teachers must be knowledgeable about the behaviors commonly associated with childhood depression so that they can refer children for evaluation and diagnosis. Childhood depression requires early recognition and treatment to avoid serious and debilitating effects on children's social, emotional, and cognitive development and long-term mental health disorders (Emslie, Mayes, Laptook, & Batt, 2003).

Childhood Fears. Most childhood fears and nightmares are a normal part of the developmental process and are eventually outgrown as children mature. Basic fears are relatively consistent across generations, although they vary from one developmental stage to the next (Yamamoto, et al., 1996). For example, a three-month-old infant is seldom fearful, whereas a three-year-old may awake during the night because of "monsters under the bed." Five- and six-year-olds tend to experience fears that reflect real-life events, such as fire, kidnaping, thunderstorms, or homelessness, whereas ten- and eleven-year-olds express fears related to appearance and social rejection (Allen & Marotz, 2003). Some fears are unique to an individual child and stem from personal experiences, such as an earthquake, tornado, witness to a shooting, car accident, abuse, or abandonment. (Cjte, Tremblay, Nagin, Zoccolillo, & Vitaro, 2002).

Fears and nightmares are often accentuated during the preschool years, a time when children have a heightened imagination and are trying to make sense of their world. Also, children's literal interpretation of the things they see and hear can easily lead to misunderstanding and fear. For example, children may believe an adult who says, "I'm going to give you away if you misbehave one more time." Some childhood fears also develop from adult reactions that have been witnessed or from previous bad experiences, such as being frightened by a large dog.

It is important that adults acknowledge children's fears and understand they are real to the child. Although it may be difficult to remain patient and caring when a child wakes up repeatedly at 2 AM, children need consistent adult reassurance and trust to overcome their fears. Children may also find comfort in talking about the things that frighten them or rehearsing what they might do, for example, if they got lost at the supermarket or if it began to thunder.

Poverty and Homelessness. Nearly 23 percent of children younger than age six currently live at or below the poverty level (Centers for Disease Control and Prevention, National Center for Health Statistics, & National Vital Statistics System, 2001). Most of these children live in families that have recently immigrated to the United States, are categorized as minorities (especially Hispanic, Native American, and African American), or are headed by a single parent—usually a mother. Living in a single versus two-parent family places children at the highest economic risk for poverty. Children living in rural areas also comprise an often overlooked group who are increasingly being affected by poverty. Difficult economic times and lack of employment opportunities have placed many rural families in jeopardy. Consequently, families with young children

 ISSUES TO CONSIDER • Children and Television

In a policy statement titled "Children, Adolescents, and Television," the American Academy of Pediatrics (AAP, 2001) recommends that children younger than two years be discouraged from watching television and that viewing time for older children be limited to no more than two hours of "quality programming" per day. Increasing concerns regarding television's negative impact on children's emotional, social, and physical well-being, including its effect on aggressive behavior and obesity, have prompted the AAP and other professional groups to issue guidelines and recommendations for children's television viewing. Although they recognize that parents are unlikely to discontinue children's access to television and other media forms (for example, movies, videos, and computer games), they encourage families to engage in more activities, such as reading together, conversing with one another, and playing together to foster children's early brain development and promote learning. In addition, parents are encouraged to watch television programs with their children and to monitor their exposure to media violence.

- What are your thoughts about the role of television for very young children? Is it inappropriate for children younger than two years?
- Should parents prevent children from watching violence on television or playing games that involve violence?
- What other factors might contribute to children's violent behavior?
- How can parents help children to view television and other media in a healthy context?

represent the fastest-growing segment of the homeless population today (Children's Defense Fund, 1998).

Poverty places additional burdens on the already challenging demands of parenting. Struggles simply to provide basic food, clothing, shelter, health care, and adult attention for children are often compromised by increased stress, fear, conflict, and even violence. Economic hardship also forces many families into undesirable housing and living arrangements. There is often increased parental tension, domestic violence and abusive treatment of children, and inability to provide the nurturing and support children require.

Unfortunately, the impact of poverty has both immediate and long-term consequences for children's growth and development. Children born into poverty have a higher rate of birth defects, early death, and chronic illnesses, such as anemia and lead poisoning (Allen & Marotz, 2003). Often the quality of their diets, access to health and dental care, and mental health status are compromised (Weinreb, Wehler, Perloff, Scott, Hosmer, Sagor, & Gundersen, 2002). Consequently, children are more likely to experience child abuse, learning and behavior problems in school, and teen pregnancy and to have lowered earning potential as adults (Krieger, Chen, Waterman, Soobader, Subramanian, & Carson, 2003; Margai & Henry, 2003; Duncan & Brooks-Gunn, 1997). Ultimately, poverty threatens their chances of growing up to become healthy, educated, and productive adults (Brooks-Gunn & Duncan, 1997; Duncan, Brooks-Gunn, & Klebanov, 1994; Elkind, 1994).

Violence.   Children today live in a world where daily exposure to violence is not uncommon. Neighborhood crime, substance abuse, the presence of gangs, and access to guns have created environments that place many young children's lives at risk. Violence and death are frequently portrayed in movies, video games, and cartoons and on television (Bushman & Cantor, 2003; Levin, 2003; Muscari, 2002). Many children have personally witnessed family violence or are themselves victims of child abuse (Baliff-Spanvill, Clayton, & Hendrix, 2003). Although studies conclude that children do not necessarily become aggressive from observing violence in the media, the dynamics are considerably different for children who grow up in environments where violence is part their daily lives (McCloskey, Figueredo, & Koss, 1995; Wright, Huston, Reitz, & Piemyat, 1994). Because young children have limited ability to understand the dysfunctional nature of these events, they often have lasting and damaging psychological effects. Many of these children are at risk for becoming violent adults or developing serious mental health (McCloskey, et al., 1995; McCord, 1991). Teachers who understand this potential can reach out to children and their families and refer them to appropriate mental health resources in the community.

Resilient Children

Children face many challenges while growing up in this complex world. Stress, violence, uncertainty, and negative encounters are everywhere. What makes some children more vulnerable to the negative effects of stress and aversive treatment or more likely to develop inappropriate behaviors? Many factors have been suggested, including genetic predisposition, malnutrition, prenatal exposure to drugs or alcohol, poor attachment (bonding) to primary caregivers, physical or learning disabilities, and an irritable personality. Children's home environments can also contribute to this problem. Chaos, inconsistent responsiveness, and unsupportive relationships make it difficult for children to achieve normal developmental tasks and positive self-esteem (Blum, 1998).

Why are some children better able to survive the negative effects of an impoverished, traumatic, violent, or stressful life? Researchers continue to study this question in an effort to learn what qualities make some children more **resilient** in the face of such adversity. Although much

---

resilient – *the ability to withstand or resist difficulty.*

remains to be understood, several important protective factors have been identified. These include having certain personal characteristics (such as above-average intelligence, positive self-esteem, and good social and problem-solving skills), having a strong and dependable relationship with a parent or parent substitute, and having a social support network outside of one's immediate family (such as a church group, local recreation center, organized sports, Boys and Girls clubs, or youth groups).

Competent parenting is, beyond a doubt, the most important and critical factor in helping children manage adversity and avoid its potentially damaging consequences (Table 2–5). Children who grow up in an environment where families are caring and emotionally responsive, provide meaningful supervision and discipline that is consistent and developmentally appropriate, offer encouragement and praise, and help their children learn to solve problems in a peaceful way are more likely to demonstrate resilient behavior (Brooks & Goldstein, 2002; Henry, 2001). Teachers, likewise, can facilitate children's development of resiliency skills through nurturing environments and relationships that are consistent and supportive (Wyman, Crow, Work, Hoyt-Meyers, Magnus, & Fagen, 1999).

Management Strategies. Understandably, all children undergo occasional periods of emotional instability or undesirable behavior. Short-term or one-time occurrences are usually not cause for concern. However, when a child consistently demonstrates abnormal or antisocial behaviors, an intervention program or counseling therapy may be necessary.

At times, it may be difficult for parents to recognize abnormal behaviors in their own children. Some emotional problems develop slowly over time and therefore may be difficult to distinguish from normal behaviors. Some parents may find it difficult to talk about or admit that their child has an emotional disturbance. Others, unknowingly, may be contributing to their children's problems.

For whatever reasons, it may be teachers who first identify children's abnormal social and emotional behaviors. Teachers occupy an ideal position for observing children's mental health status and documenting inappropriate conduct. They can also use their expertise to help families become aware of these problems, counsel them in appropriate behavior management techniques, or help them arrange for professional counseling.

Teachers can also be instrumental in promoting children's mental health and resiliency by recognizing early changes in behavior, providing stable and supportive environments, and fostering

---

TABLE 2–5 Strategies for Increasing Children's Resilient Behaviors

- Be a good role model for children; demonstrate how you expect them to behave.
- Accept children unconditionally; avoid being judgmental.
- Help children develop and use effective communication skills.
- Listen carefully to children to show that you value their thoughts and ideas.
- Use discipline that is developmentally appropriate and consistently enforced.
- Help children understand and express their feelings; encourage them to have empathy for others.
- Avoid harsh physical punishment and angry outbursts.
- Help children establish realistic goals, set high expectations for themselves, and have a positive outlook.
- Promote good problem-solving skills; help children make informed decisions.
- Reinforce children's efforts with praise and encouragement.
- Give children responsibility; assign household tasks.
- Involve children in activities outside of their home.
- Encourage children to believe in themselves, to feel confident rather than seeing themselves as failures or victims.

children's communication and problem-solving skills (Honig, 1986). They can also teach children methods for coping with stressful events (Wittmer & Honig, 1994):

- the use of music for relaxation
- progressive relaxation techniques—the process of contracting and relaxing various body parts, beginning at one end of the body and moving toward the other
- relaxation activities—the use of imagery and visualization, make-believe, let's pretend, books and stories, movement activities
- short periods of vigorous physical activity followed by rest
- art activities—water play, clay and play dough, painting
- dramatic play—using dolls and puppets to act out feelings of fear, anger or frustration

There are also many books available to read and discuss with children (see Appendix F).

Thus, teachers have many opportunities to promote children's development of positive mental health skills. Children who learn conflict resolution, problem-solving, and effective communication skills will have powerful resources available to help them cope with daily problems in an effective manner. Parent–child relationships can also be strengthened by sharing information and providing training to families. Although most parents welcome an opportunity to improve their parenting skills, the benefit to high-risk or dysfunctional families may be even greater.

FOCUS ON FAMILIES • Helping Children Cope with Trauma

Children are exposed to violence on may levels—from viewing events on television and hearing others talk about it to witnessing traumatic acts in their own neighborhoods or even being personally involved. Their reactions to these experiences can range from a heightened concern or expressed fear to serious and prolonged behaviors, such as withdrawl, nightmares, aggression, sadness, complaints of physical ailments (such as headache, stomachache, sleep disturbances, and loss of appetite), excessive fear, and depression. When children have a supportive environment and caring adults in their lives, they are often able to gradually recover form negative experiences.

- Examine your own personal reactions and responses. Children often imitate adult behaviors. If adults appear to lack self-control, children are likely to exhibit similar characteristics.

- Provide added comfort and reassurance that the child will be safe.

- Foster open communication without judgment. Encourage children to talk about the experiencce and acknowledge their feelings. Let them know these are normal. Do not call children "sissys" or tell them to "grow up" because of the way they are reacting.

- Maintain regular schedules, routines, and rules to help children feel more secure.

- Restrict children's media exposure. Monitor what they listen to and see.

- Aviod temporary separations. Children may be afraid to sleep alone at night; allowing them to stay in the same room may be helpful in overcoming their fear.

- Involve children in outside activities to minimize focusing on a traumatic event.

- Obtain the help of a mental health counselor if children continue to experience problems.

- Build children's resilience through positive self-esteem.

CASE STUDY

Azumi's family recently moved when her father was transferred to another company location. Her mother, a librarian, was successful in getting a job at the local library soon after they arrived. Azumi's mother called the local resource and referral agency to determine the availability of early-morning child care openings. After visiting several programs, her mother chose one that was only a few blocks from her workplace. Azumi's mother knew that her three-year-old daughter would probably have difficulty adjusting to new teachers and children.

1. What are some of the feelings a "new" child is likely to experience?
2. What strategies can teachers use to help integrate a "new" child into an existing group?
3. What personal qualities make this transition easier for some children than others?
4. How can the other children help to make the "new" child feel welcomed?
5. How can teachers help parents with this transition?

SUMMARY

- Growth is rapid during infancy; the rate slows considerably during the preschool years.
- Preschoolers can manage most of their own personal care, but they may still need some adult assistance.
  - Good dental hygiene is important for all children once they have teeth.
  - A baby's gums and teeth can be wiped with a damp cloth to remove food particles.
  - Parents should brush a toddler's teeth at least once each day.
- Changes in socialization are dramatic from infancy to early school years.
  - Friendships and group interaction become important to older children.
  - Some children continue to experience difficulty separating from parents.
- Children's mental health requires special adult attention and consideration to promote healthy development and prevent emotional problems.
  - Positive self-esteem is a key component of good mental health.
  - Sudden changes in children's behavior may be an indication of stress.
  - Childhood fears are common during the preschool years.
  - Poverty, homelessness, violence, and other social ills contribute to increasing concerns about the quality of children's mental health.

SUGGESTED ACTIVITIES

1. Observe a small group of preschool-aged children during free-play or outdoor times for two 15-minute intervals. For each observation, select a different child and record the number of times that child engages in cooperative play. Repeat this observation procedure with a group of toddlers. Note any differences.
2. Select and read 10 children's books from the Mental Health section in Appendix F. Prepare a brief annotation of the theme and content for each book. Describe how you might use each book to promote children's positive mental health skills or as part of a classroom learning activity.

3. Write to the American/Canadian Dental Association or contact a local dentist and request information on children's dental care. Decide how you could implement this knowledge in a child care program.

4. Invite a child mental health specialist to speak to your class. Find out what types of problems are treated most often and how caregivers can help prevent these problems in young children.

5. Develop a checklist, similar to the one in Table 2–2, identifying appropriate characteristics for infants and for toddlers.

6. Visit your Public Health Department. What services/programs would be available to you if you were a single, unemployed parent of two children, ages six months and two-and-one-half years?

CHAPTER REVIEW

A. **Answer the following questions by filling in the blanks. Then, take the first letter of each answer and place it in the appropriate square that follows Question 6 to form an important word.**

1. Major gains in the preschool child's growth are due to increases in _____.

2. A comprehensive health program should include services, _____, and provisions for a healthy environment.

3. _____ are the leading cause of death among children younger than age 14.

4. Teachers can promote children's mental health by planning activities that are appropriate for their _____ of skill.

5. _____ have a professional and ethical responsibility to protect the safety of young children in their programs.

6. Good dental care depends on a nutritious diet, good oral _____, and routine dental examinations.

B. **Briefly answer each of the following questions.**

1. How many hours of sleep are recommended for the toddler each day?

2. What methods might a parent or teacher use to encourage a child, who refuses to sleep, to relax and rest quietly?

3. How much can an infant be expected to grow in length during the first year?

4. What is another term used to describe "baby teeth"?

5. How does environment affect children's mental health?

6. Explain the relationship between good dental health and learning.

7. Would it be realistic to expect an 11-month-old infant to be toilet trained? Explain. Should parents be concerned if their nine-month-old infant cannot sit up without support?

8. Describe at least five ways that parents and teachers can help children become more resilient when faced with stressful or adverse situations.

REFERENCES

Allen, K. E., & Marotz, L. R. (2003). *Developmental profiles: Pre-birth through twelve* (4th ed.). Clifton Park, NY: Delmar Learning.

Arnsdorff, M. (2001). *Pete the posture parrot.* Annapolis, MD: Body Mechanics, Inc.

Bailey, D., Bruer, J. R., Symons, F., & Lichtma, J. (Eds.). (2001). *Critical thinking about critical periods.* Baltimore: Paul H. Brookes.

Ballif-Spanvill, B., Clayton, C. J., & Hendrix, S. B. (2003). Gender, types of conflict, and individual differences in the use of violent and peaceful strategies among children who have and have not witnessed interparental violence. *American Journal of Orthopsychiatry, 73*(2), 141–153.

Barnes, G., Parker, W., Lyon, T., Drum, M., & Coleman, G. (1992). Ethnicity, location, age, and fluoridation factors in baby bottle tooth decay and caries prevalence of Head Start children. *Public Health Reports, 107,* 167–173.

Belfield, J. (2003). Childhood obesity—a public health problem. *School Nurse News, 20*(1), 20, 22, 24.

Berg, F., Buechner, J., Parham, E., Weight Realities Division of the Society for Nutrition Education (2003, January–February). Guidelines for childhood obesity prevention programs: Promoting healthy weight in children. *Journal of Nutrition Education and Behavior, 35*(1), 1–4.

Berk, L. (2003). *Child development* (6th ed.). Boston: Allyn & Bacon.

Blum, R. W. (1998). Healthy youth development as a model for youth health promotion. *Journal of Adolescent Health, 22,* 368–375.

Bronson, M. B. (2003). Choosing play materials for primary school children (ages 6–8). *Young Children, 58* (3), 24– 25.

Brooks, R., & Goldstein, S. (2002). *Nurturing resilience in our children: Answers to the most important parenting questions.* New York: McGraw-Hill/Contemporary Books.

Brooks-Gunn, J., & Duncan, G. (1997, Summer–Fall). The effects of poverty on children. *The Future of Children, 7,* 55–71.

Bushman, B. J., & Cantor, J. (2003). Media ratings for violence and sex. Implications for policymakers and parents. *American Psychologist, 58*(2), 130–141.

Cantu, C. (2002). Protect your back: Guidelines for safer lifting. *Texas Child Care, 26*(1), 24–27.

Centers for Disease Control and Prevention, National Center for Health Statistics, & National Vital Statistics System. (2001). *America's children 2001.* Accessed June 6, 2003, from [http://www.childstats.gov].

Charlesworth, R. (2004). *Understanding child development.* (6th ed.). Clifton Park, NY: Delmar Learning.

Children's Defense Fund. (1998). *The state of America's children: Yearbook 1998.* Washington, DC: Author.

Chow, J. C., Jaffee, K., & Snowden, L. (2003). Racial/ethnic disparities in the use of mental health services in poverty areas. *American Journal of Public Health, 93*(5), 792–797.

Cjte, S., Tremblay, R. E., Nagin, D., Zoccolillo, M., & Vitaro, F. (2002). The development of impulsivity, fearfulness, and helpfulness during childhood: Patterns of consistency and change in the trajectories of boys and girls. *Journal of Child Psychology & Psychiatry, 43*(5), 609–701.

Collins, R., Mascia, J., Kendall, R., Golden, O., & Schock, L. (2003, March). Promoting mental health in child care settings: Caring for the whole child. *Zero to Three, 23*(4), 39–45.

Crawley-Coha, T. (2002). Childhood injury: A status report, part 2. *Journal of Pediatric Nursing, 17*(2), 133–136.

Cullinan, D., Evans, C., Epstein, M., & Ryser, G. (2003). Characteristics of emotional disturbance of elementary school students. *Behavioral Disorders, 28*(2), 94–110.

Dawson, G., Ashman, S. B., & Carver, L. J. (2000). The role of early experience in shaping behavioral and brain development and its implications for social policy. *Developmenal Psychopathology, 12*(4), 695–712.

Dellinger, A. M., Groff, P. C., Mickalide, A. D., & Nolan, P. A. (2002). Kids in cars: Closing gaps in child occupant restraint laws. *Journal of Law & Medical Ethics, 30*(3 Suppl), 150–156.

Duncan, G., & Brooks-Gunn, J. (Eds.). (1997). *Consequences of growing up poor.* New York: Russell Sage Press.

Duncan, G., & Brooks-Gunn, J., & Klebanov, P. (1994). Economic deprivation and early childhood development. *Child Development, 65*(2), 296–318.

Edelstein, B. L. (2002). Disparities in oral health and access to care: Findings of national surveys. *Ambulatory Pediatrics, 2*(2 Suppl), 141–147.

Eisenberg, L. (1999). Experience, brain, and behavior: The importance of a head start. *Pediatrics, 103,* 1031–1035.

Elias, M. J., & Weissberg, R. P. (2000). Primary prevention: educational approaches to enhance social and emotional learning. *Journal of School Health, 70*(5), 186–190.

Elkind, D. (1994). *Ties that stress: The new family imbalance.* Cambridge, MA: Harvard University Press.

Emslie, G. J., Mayes, T. L., Laptook, R. S., & Batt, M. (2003). Predictors of response to treatment in children and adolescents with mood disorders. *Psychiatric Clinics of North America, 26*(2), 435–456.

Fallin, K., Wallinga, C., & Coleman, M. (2001). Helping children cope with stress in the classroom setting. *Childhood Education, 78*(1), 17–24.

Feigal, R. J. (2002). The use of pit and fissure sealants. *Pediatric Dentistry, 24*(5), 415–422.

Furman, R. A. (1995). Helping children cope with stress and deal with feelings. *Young Children, 50*(2), 33–41.

Gartrell, D. (2002). Replacing time-out. Part two—using guidance to maintain an encouraging classroom. *Young Children, 57*(2), 36–43.

Gruenberg, A. (1998). Creative stress management: "Put your own oxygen mask on first." *Young Children, 53*(1), 38–42.

Henry, D. L. (2001). Resilient children: what they tell us about coping with maltreatment. *Social Work Health Care, 34*(3–4), 283–298.

Hodges, E. A. (2003). A primer on early childhood obesity and parental influence. *Pediatric Nursing, 29*(1), 13–16.

Honig, A. (1986). Stress and coping in children (part I). *Young Children, 41*(4), 50–63.

Honig, A. (1986). Stress and coping in children (part II). *Young Children, 41*(5), 47–59.

Hopkins, A. R. (2002). Children and grief: The role of the early childhood educator. *Young Children, 57*(1), 40–47.

Horowitz , H. S. (2003). The 2001 CDC recommendations for using fluoride to prevent and control dental caries in the United States. *Journal of Public Health Dentistry, 63*(1), 3–8.

Jewett, J., & Peterson, K. (2002, December). Stress and young children. *ERIC Digests, #EDO-PS-02-20.* Accessed June 6, 2003, from [http://ericeece.org/pubs/digests/2002/jewett02.html].

Kataoka, S. H., Zhang, L., & Wells, K. B. (2002). Unmet need for mental health care among U.S. children: Variation by ethnicity and insurance status. *American Journal of Psychiatry, 159*(9), 1548–1555.

Kalata, D. E. (1998). Parents! Let's play! *Young Children, 53*(5), 40–41.

Kimm, S. Y., & Obarzanek, E. (2002). Childhood obesity: A new pandemic of the new millennium. *Pediatrics, 10*(5), 1003–1007.

King, K. (1998). Healthy smiles: Multidisciplinary baby bottle tooth decay prevention program. *Journal of Health Education, 29*(1), 4–7.

Krieger, N., Chen, J. T., Waterman, P. D., Soobader, M. J., Subramanian, S. V., & Carson, R. (2003). Choosing area based socioeconomic measures to monitor social inequalities in low birth weight and childhood lead poisoning: The Public Health Disparities Geocoding Project (US). *Journal of Epidemiology & Community Health, 57*(3), 186–199.

Kunitz, J. (2000). Avoiding provider burnout. *Child Care Health Connections, 13*(6), 9.

Levin, D. E. (2003). Beyond banning war and superhero play: Meeting children's needs in violent times. *Young Children, 58*(3), 60–64.

Luby, J., Heffelfinger, A., Mrakotsky, C., Brown, K., Hessler, M., Wallis, J., & Spitznagel, E. L. (2003). The clinical picture of depression in preschool children. *Journal of the American Academy of Child and Adolescent Psychiatry, 42*(3), 340–348.

Lyons, R., Wolfe, R., Lyubchik, A., & Steingard, R. (2002). Depressive symptoms in parents of children under age 3: Sociodemographic predictors, current correlates, and associated parenting behaviors. In N. Halfon & K. McLearn (Eds.), *Child rearing in America: Challenges facing parents with young children* (pp. 217–259). New York: Cambridge University Press.

Manning, D., Rubin, S., Perdigao, H., Gonzalez, R., & Schindler, P. (1996). A "worry doctor" for preschool directors and teachers: A collaborative model. *Young Children, 51*(5), 68–73.

Marcon, R. A. (2003). Growing children: The physical side of development. *Young Children, 58*(1), 80–87.

Margai, F., & Henry, N. (2003). A community-based assessment of learning disabilities using environmental and contextual risk factors. *Social Science Medicine, 56*(5), 1073–1085.

Marotz, L. R. (2000). Childhood and classroom injuries. (2000). In J. L. Frost (Ed.), *Children and injuries.* Tucson: Lawyers & Judges Publishing Co.

Maslow, A. H. (1970). *Motivation and personality* (2nd ed.). New York: Harper & Row.

McCloskey, L., Figueredo, A., & Koss, M. (1995). The effects of systemic family violence on children's mental health. *Child Development, 66,* 1239–1261.

McCord, J. (1991). Family relationships, juvenile delinquency, and adult criminality. *Criminology, 29,* 397–414.

Muscari, M. (2002). Media violence: Advice for parents. *Pediatric Nursing, 28*(6), 585–591.

National Center for Injury Prevention and Control. (2001). *Unintentional injury prevention.* Washington, DC: Office of Statistics and Programming, Centers for Disease Control and Prevention, U.S. Department of Health & Human Services.

National Institutes of Mental Health (NIMH). (2000). *Depression in children and adolescents.* Bethesda, MD: Author.

Parlakian, R. (2002). *Building strong foundations: Practical guidance for promoting the social/emotional development of infants and toddlers.* Herndon, VA: Zero to Three.

Pica, R. (1997). Beyond physical development: Why young children need to move. *Young Children, 52*(6), 4–11.

Price, S., & Vaughan, D. A. (1999). Dental health issues in child-care centers. *Journal of Dental Hygiene, 73*(3), 135–140.

Riedy, C. A., Weinstein, P., Milgrom, P., & Bruss, M. (2001). An ethnographic study for understanding children's oral health in a multicultural community. *International Dental Journal, 51*(4), 305–312.

Rushton, S. P. (2001). Applying brain research to create developmentally appropriate learning environments. *Young Children, 56*(5), 76–82.

Satter, E. (2000). *Child of mine: Feeding with love and good sense.* Palo Alto, CA: Bull Publishing Co.

Schieber, R. A., & Vegega, M. E. (2002). Reducing childhood pedestrian injuries. *Injury Prevention, 8*(Suppl 1), i1–10.

Simpson, E. M., Moll, E. K., Kassam-Adams, N., Miller, G. J., & Winston, F. K. (2002). Barriers to booster seat use and strategies to increase their use. *Pediatrics, 110*(4), 729–736.

Troiano, R. P., Macera, C. A., & Ballard-Barbash, R. (2001). Be physically active each day. How can we know? *Journal of Nutrition, 131*(2S-1), 451S–460S.

U.S. Department of Health and Human Services. (2001). *Health United States 2000–2001 and injury chartbook.* Washington, DC: Author.

Vaught, M. (2001). Another look at brain research. *Young Children, 56*(4), 33.

Wehling Weepie, A. K., & McCarthy, A. M. (2002). A healthy lifestyle program: Promoting child health in schools. *Journal of School Nursing, 18*(6), 322–328.

Weinreb, L. L., Wehler, C., Perloff, J., Scott, R., Hosmer, D., Sagor, L., & Gundersen, C. (2002). Hunger: Its impact on children's health and mental health. *Pediatrics, 110*(4), e41.

Wittmer, D., & Honig, A. (1994). Encouraging positive social development in young children. *Young Children, 49*(5), 4–12.

Wright, J. C., Huston, A. C., Reitz, A. L., & Piemyat, S. (1994). Young children's perceptions of television reality: Determinants and developmental differences. *Developmental Psychology, 30*(2), 229–239.

Wyman, R. A., Cowe, E. I., Work, W. C., Hoyt-Meyers, L., Magnus, K. B., & Fagen, D. B. (1999). Care-giving and developmental factors differentiating young at-risk urban children showing resilient versus stress-affected outcomes: A replication and extension. *Child Development, 70,* 645–659.

Yamatoto, K., Davis, O. L., Dylak, S., & Whittaker, J. (1996). Across six nations: Stressful events in the lives of children. *Child Psychiatry & Human Development, 26*(3), 139–150.

Yu, S. M., Bellamy, H. A., Kogan, M. D., Dunbar, J. L., Schwalberg, R. H., & Schuster, M. A. (2002). Factors that influence receipt of recommended preventive pediatric health and dental care. *Pediatrics, 110*(6), e73.

ADDITIONAL READING

Adelman, H., Taylor, L., Bradley, B., & Lewis, K. (1997). Mental health in schools. *Journal of School Nursing, 13*(3), 6–12.

Anderson, M. P. (2001). ACT against violence. *Young Children, 56*(4), 60–61.

Beardslee, W., Versage, E., Velde, P., Swatling, S., & Hoke, L. (2002). Preventing depression in children through resiliency promotion: The Preventive Intervention Project. In R. McMahon & R. Peters (Eds.), *The effects of parental dysfunction on children* (pp. 71–86). New York: Kluwer Academic/Plenum Publishers.

Bullock, J. (1993). Lonely children. *Young Children, 48*(6), 53–57.

Carlsson-Paige, N., & Levine, D. (1992). Making peace in violent times: A constructivist approach to conflict resolution. *Young Children, 48*(1), 4–13.

Doris, B., & Coscia , J. (2001). *Brain research and childhood education: Implications for educators.* Olney, MD: Association for Childhood Education International.

Dinwiddie, S. (1994). The saga of Sally, Sammy and the red pen: Facilitating children's social problem solving. *Young Children, 49*(5), 13–17.

Duarte, G., & Rafanello, D. (2001). The migrant child: A special place in the field. *Young Children 56*(2), 26–34.

Eaton, M. (1997). Positive discipline: Fostering the self-esteem of young children. *Young children, 52*(6), 43–46.

Flores, G., Fuentes-Afflick, E., Barbot, O., Carter-Pokras, O., Claudio, L., Lara, M., McLaurin, J. A., Pachter, L., Gomez, F. R., Mendoza, F., Valdez, R. B., Villarruel, A. M., Zambrana, R. E., Greenberg, R., Weitzman, M. (2002). The health of latino children: Urgent priorities, unanswered questions, and a research agenda.. *JAMA, 288*(1), 82–90.

Gross, T. & Clemens, S. G. (2002). Painting a tragedy. Young Children, *Young Children, 57*(3), 44–51.

Kantrowitz, D., & Kalb, C. (1998, May 11). Boys will be boys. *Newsweek,* 54–60.

Levin, D. E. (1998). Play with violence: Understanding and responding effectively. In D. Fromberg and D Bergen (Eds.), *Play from birth to twelve and beyond: Contexts, perspectives, and meanings.* New York: Garland.

Marion, M. (1997). Guiding young childen's understanding and management of anger. *Young Children, 52*(7), 62–67.

Marshall, T. A. (2003). Diet and nutrition in pediatric dentistry. *Dental Clinics of North America, 47*(2), 279–303.

Nelson, D. W. (2000). Connections count: An alternative framework for understanding and strengthening America's vulnerable families. *Young Children, 55*(6), 39–42.

Nixon, P. D. (1999). Negotiating with toddlers. *Young Children, 54*(3), 60–61.

Novick, R. (2002). Nurturing emotional literacy. *Young Children, 57*(3), 84–89.

Phelan, K. J., Khoury, J., Grossman, D. C., Hu, D., Wallace, L. J., Bill, N., & Kalkwarf, H. (2002). Pediatric motor vehicle related injuries in the Navajo Nation: The impact of the 1988 child occupant restraint laws. *Injury Prevention, 8*(3), 216–220.

Pica, R. (2004). *Experiences in movement with music, activities, and theory* (3rd ed.). Clifton Park, NY: Delmar Learning.

Shore, R. (2003). *Rethinking the brain: New insights into early development.* New York: Families and Work Institute.

Thornburg, K. R. (2002). Exporting TV violence—what do we owe the world's children? *Young Children, 57*(2), 6, 74.

Wardle, F. (2001). Viewpoint. Supporting multiracial and multiethnic children and their families. *Young Children, 56*(6), 38–39.

HELPFUL WEB SITES

American Academy of Pediatric Dentistry	http://www.aapd.org
American Institute of Stress, The	http://www.stress.org
Children's Television Workshop Online	http://www.ctw.org
Council for Exceptional Children	http://www.cec.sped.org
Indian Health Service	http://www.ihs.gov
Kids Health	http://www.kidshealth.org
Mental Health Net	http://www. cmhc.com

National Academy for Child Development   http://www.nacd.org.
National Center for Children in Poverty   http://cpmcnet.columbia.edu/dept
National SAFE KIDS Campaign   http://www.safekids.org

For additional health, safety, and nutrition resources, go to
http://www.EarlyChildEd.delmar.com

CHAPTER 3

Health Appraisals

OBJECTIVES

After studying this chapter, you should be able to:

- State why it is important for teachers to observe children's health.
- Explain the relationship between health and learning.
- List four sources where information about a child's health can be obtained.
- Identify five health specialists who may be called upon to evaluate children's health.
- Describe how to conduct a health check.
- Discuss how good parent-teacher communications can enhance children's health.

TERMS TO KNOW

impairment	atypical	anecdotal
chronic	observations	diagnosis
health assessment	symptoms	

The *Healthy People 2010* national initiative reinforces the important relationship between a child's health and ability to learn (U.S. Department of Health & Human Services, 2000). It also recognizes that not all children have equal access to medical and dental care or to environments that promote well-being. It underscores the collaborative effort necessary for assuring children's health and educational success, and challenges communities to address these problems. Teachers and other professionals play a critical role in this process through their early identification of children's health problems, assisting parents to obtain appropriate medical treatment and working with families to encourage a healthy lifestyle.

When children enjoy good health, they are more likely to benefit from participation in learning experiences. However, an acute or chronic illness, undetected health **impairment**, or emotional problem can interfere with a child's interest, degree of involvement, and effectiveness in school. For example, even a mild hearing loss may distort a child's perception of

---

impairment – *a condition or malfunction of a body part that interferes with optimal functioning.*

letter sounds, pronunciations, and responsiveness. If left undetected, such problems can have a profound and long-term effect on children's learning abilities. Health problems do not have to be obvious or complex to have a negative effect. Even a simple cold, toothache, allergic re-action, or chronic tonsillitis will disrupt a child's energy level, cooperation, attention span, interest, and enjoyment of learning. Thus, it is imperative that teachers be continuously aware of children's health status. Recognizing the early signs of health conditions and arrang-ing for early intervention often limits their negative impact on children's development and learning.

PROMOTING CHILDREN'S HEALTH

Early care and education programs make a significant contribution to children's well-being through their provision of health services, educational programs, safe and healthy learning envi-ronments, and good nutrition. Quality programs employ a variety of techniques, including teacher observations and daily health checks, to continually monitor children's health status and identify potential health needs. This process must be ongoing because children's health status changes continuously, as illustrated in the following example:

> Joshua bounded into the classroom and greeted his classmates with the usual "Hi guys." However, by 10:00 A.M. his teacher noticed that Joshua had retrieved his blanket and was lying quietly in the book area. Despite several minutes of coaxing, Joshua ve-hemently refused to budge. His teacher continued to observe Joshua for the next few minutes and noted that he was holding his hand over his left ear and whimpering. When the teacher took Joshua's temperature, it was 103°F and he complained of an earache.

Thus, it is important for teachers to always be alert to changes in children's appearance and be-havior (Figure 3–1). These signs may be the first indication of an impending acute illness or **chronic** health problem.

Gathering Information

Information about children's health can be gathered from a variety of sources, including:

- dietary assessment
- health histories
- results of medical examinations
- teacher observations and health checks
- dental examinations
- parent interviews
- vision and hearing screenings
- speech evaluations
- psychological testing
- developmental evaluations

chronic – *frequent or repeated incidences of illness; can also be a lengthy or permanent status, as in chronic disease or dysfunction.*

FIGURE 3–1

Teachers should be alert to changes in children's appearance and behavior.

Several of these assessment tools can be administered by teachers or volunteers, while others require the skills of specially trained health professionals. Often, the process of identifying a specific health impairment requires the cooperative efforts of specialists from several different fields:

- pediatric medicine
- nursing
- speech
- dietetics
- dentistry

- psychology
- education
- ophthalmology
- social work
- audiology

Health information should always be collected from a variety of sources before any final conclusions about the child's condition are reached. Relying on the results of a single **health assessment** can present a biased and often unrealistic picture of the child's problem (Allen & Cowdery, 2005). Children sometimes behave or respond in ways that are **atypical** when confronted with new surroundings or an unfamiliar adult examiner, thereby making it difficult to obtain reliable results. By gathering information from multiple sources, a more accurate assessment of the illness or impairment and its effect on the child can be formed. For example, combining teacher and parent observations with the results of a hearing evaluation may confirm the need to refer a child to a hearing specialist.

OBSERVATION AS A SCREENING TOOL

Teachers are valuable members of a child's comprehensive health team. Their knowledge of children's developmental patterns and involvement with children in a classroom setting places them

---

health assessment – *the process of gathering and evaluating information about an individual's state of health.*
atypical – *unusual; different from what might commonly be expected.*

FIGURE 3-2

Teachers see children functioning in various settings. This
gives them an excellent opportunity to observe the children
for potential health problems.

in an excellent position for observing potential health problems (Figure 3–2). Information obtained from daily **observations** provides a useful baseline for determining what is typical behavior and appearance for each child. When combined with an understanding of normal growth and
development, this information allows teachers to quickly note any changes or deviations
(Bentzen, 2001).

Health observations are a simple and effective screening tool readily available to teachers.
Many of the skills necessary for making objective health observations are already at their disposal. Sight, for example, is one of the most important senses; much can be learned about children's health by merely watching them in action. A simple touch can detect a fever or enlarged
lymph glands. Odors may indicate lack of cleanliness or an infection. Careful listening may reveal breathing difficulties or changes in voice quality. Problems with peer relationships, eating
habits, self-esteem, or abuse in the child's home may be detected during a conversation. Utilizing one's senses to the fullest—seeing children as they really are, hearing what they really have
to say, and responding to their true needs—is a skill that requires time, patience, and practice to
perfect.

As with any form of evaluation, conclusions drawn from teacher observations should be made
with caution. It must always be remembered that a wide range of normal behavior and skill at-
tainment exists at each developmental stage. Norms merely represent the average age at which
most children are able to perform a given skill. For example, many three-year-olds can reproduce
the shape of a circle, name and match primary colors, and walk across a balance beam. There will
also be some three-year-olds, however, who will not be able to perform these tasks. This does not
imply that they are not "normal." Some children simply take longer than others to master certain
skills. However, developmental norms can be useful for identifying children who may be experiencing health problems, as well as those who may simply require additional help in acquiring
these skills.

---

observations – *to inspect and take note of the appearance and behavior of other individuals.*

DAILY HEALTH CHECKS

Evaluating children's health status on a daily basis provides valuable information about their well-being and readiness to learn. Health checks require only a minute or two to complete. They enable teachers to detect early signs and symptoms of many illnesses and health impairments and should, therefore, be conducted in addition to ongoing observations. Daily health checks also help teachers become familiar with each child's typical appearance and behavior so they can quickly recognize when changes develop.

Parents should be encouraged to remain with their child until the health check has been completed. Children may find comfort in having their parent nearby. Often, parents can provide valuable information about conditions or behaviors the teacher may observe. Parents may also be less apprehensive if they have an opportunity to witness health checks firsthand and to ask their own questions. However, if a parent is unavailable, it may be advisable to have a second teacher witness the procedure so as to avoid any allegations of misconduct.

Method

A quiet area set aside in the classroom is ideal for conducting health checks. A teacher may choose simply to sit on the floor with the children or provide a more structured setting with a table and chairs. Health checks should be conducted in the same area each day, so children become familiar with the routine.

A systematic approach is often the most efficient method for conducting health checks. With an established routine, health checks will be consistent and thorough each time. Table 3–1 illustrates a simple observation checklist. It is arranged so observations are conducted from head to foot, first looking at the child's front- and then back-side. However, this procedure can easily be modified to meet a program's unique needs in terms of setting and children being served.

A teacher should begin the daily health checks by observing children as they first enter the classroom. Many clues about their well-being, such as personal cleanliness, weight changes, signs of illness, facial expressions, posture, skin color, balance and coordination, can be quickly noted. The nature of parent–child interactions and their relationship with one another can also be noted. Information gathered from observations may help to explain why some children exhibit certain behaviors. For example, does the parent have a tendency to do everything for the child—take off boots, hang up coats, pick up items the child has dropped—or does the parent encourage the child to be independent? Is the child allowed to answer questions or does the parent provide all of the answers?

Following these initial observations, a flashlight is used to inspect the mouth and throat (Figure 3–3). A quick look inside alerts the teacher to any child with an unusually red throat, swollen or infected tonsils, dental cavities, sores, or unusual breath odors. Observations of the hair

REFLECTIVE THOUGHTS

Daily health checks serve many important functions. They help teachers monitor children's health, and can also be a valuable teaching tool. How can teachers involve children in the process? What can children learn from this experience? What are some health and safety topics that teachers might discuss with children during health checks? What strategies can a teacher use to improve a child's cooperation? How might parents be involved?

TABLE 3–1 Health Observation Checklist

1. *General appearance*—note changes in weight (gain or loss), signs of fatigue or unusual excitability, skin tone (pallor or flushed), and size for age group.

2. *Scalp*—observe for signs of itching, head lice, sores, hair loss, and cleanliness.

3. *Face*—notice general expression (e.g., fear, anger, happy, anxious), skin tone, and any scratches, bruises, or rashes.

4. *Eyes*—look for redness, tearing, puffiness, sensitivity to light, frequent rubbing, styes, sores, drainage, or uncoordinated eye movements.

5. *Ears*—check for drainage, redness, and appropriate responses to sounds or verbal requests.

6. *Nose*—note any deformity, frequent rubbing, congestion, sneezing, or drainage.

7. *Mouth*—look inside at the teeth; note cavities, malformations, sores, or mouth-breathing.

8. *Throat*—observe for enlarged or red tonsils, red throat, white patches on throat or tonsils, drainage, or unusual breath odors.

9. *Neck*—feel for enlarged glands.

10. *Chest*—watch the child's breathing and note any wheezing, rattles, shortness of breath, coughing (with or without other symptoms).

11. *Skin*—lift up clothing and observe the chest and back for color (pallor or redness), rashes, scratches, bumps, bruises, scars, unusual warmth, and perspiration.

12. *Speech*—listen for clarity, stuttering, nasality, mispronunciations, monotone voice, and appropriateness for age.

13. *Extremities*—observe posture, coordination; note conditions such as bowed legs, toeing-in, or arms and legs of unequal length.

14. *Behavior and temperament*—note any changes in activity level, alertness, cooperation, appetite, sleep patterns, toileting habits, irritability or uncharacteristic restlessness.

FIGURE 3–3

Through careful observation, a teacher can identify clues about the child's well-being.

FIGURE 3–4

Checklists are useful for systematically observing and recording children's health status.

and face, including the eyes, ears, and nose, can provide clues about the child's general hygiene as well as any communicable illness.

Next, the child's clothing can be lifted. Rashes, unusual scratches, bumps or bruises, and skin color on the chest, abdomen, and arms should be noted. Patches of blue discoloration, called Mongolian spots, are sometimes visible on the lower backs of children of Asian, Native American, and Middle Eastern origin. These spots appear similar to bruises, but do not undergo the changes typical of an injury. Mongolian patches tend to disappear gradually as children reach eight or nine years of age. Because many of the rashes associated with communicable disease begin on the warmer areas of the body, for example, chest, back, neck, and forearms, these parts should be inspected carefully (Figure 3–4). Finally, the child is asked to turn around and similar checks are made of the head, hair, and back.

Teachers should continue their observations after the health check has been completed. For example, balance, coordination, and posture can easily be noted as an infant crawls away or an older child walks over to join friends in the art center. Information gathered from health checks and teacher observations contributes to a well-rounded picture of a child's health status—physical, mental, emotional, and social well-being.

With time and practice, teachers become skilled in conducting daily health checks and making invaluable observations. They gain confidence in their ability to recognize signs and **symptoms** that indicate illness or problems requiring further evaluation. Gradually, teachers also become skilled in picking up on subtle changes in children's behavior or appearance that may be cause for concern.

Recording Health Observations

Teachers are indispensable as observers and recorders of information concerning children's health. Through their skilled questioning, careful listening, keen observation, understanding of children's development, and precise recording skills, they contribute information valued by health care professionals. Therefore, observations should be recorded immediately following health checks and placed in each child's permanent health file or maintained in a notebook designated for this purpose. Programs may develop a form similar to the one illustrated in Figure 3–5, or use daily attendance records to record **anecdotal** health information. Checklists can also be useful for conducting and recording observations in a systematic manner. Throughout the day, any changes in a child's condition, such as a seizure or episode of diarrhea, should also be recorded carefully and reported to parents.

---

symptoms – *changes in the body or its functions that are experienced by the affected individual.*
anecdotal – *a brief note or description that contains useful and important information.*

FIGURE 3–5

Form to record anecdotal information.

Sunny Days Child Care Center

Daily Health Check Recording Form

Week of: ____________________

Observations and Comments

Child's Name	Monday	Tuesday	Wednesday	Thursday	Friday

ONLINE COMPANION

Download this form online at http://www.EarlyChildEd.delmar.com

Recorded observations must be accurate and precise in order to be meaningful to others. To say that a child "looks sick" is vague and open to interpretation by anyone reading this description. However, stating that a child is flushed, has a fever of 101 °F. (38.3 °C), and is covered with a fine red rash on his torso is definitive and less likely to be confusing. A meaningful description is also helpful to parents who may need to convey this information to the child's physician (Dailey, 1999).

Confidentiality of Health Information

Information obtained from daily health checks and teacher observations should be treated with utmost confidentiality and not left out where it may be accessible to other parents or staff members. Anecdotal records and health checklists should be kept in a notebook or folder to protect children's identity until the information can be transferred to their personal files. Additionally, this information must never be released to another individual or organization without first obtaining written parental permission. However, federal law guarantees parents the right to access information in their child's health file at any time and to request correction of errors or mistakes.

Benefits of Health Observations

Monitoring children's health status on a regular basis offers several distinct advantages. First, teachers are obligated, professionally and morally, to protect the health of other children in a group setting (Aronson, 2002). Observations and daily health checks provide an effective way to achieve this goal. For example, a teacher may note changes in a child's appearance or behavior that signal the onset of a communicable illness. This information can be used to determine if a child is too ill to remain in group care based on the program's exclusion policies. Sending a sick child home reduces unnecessary exposure to other children.

Daily health checks and teacher observations provide several additional benefits. Teachers' descriptive records can be helpful to health care professionals when they are evaluating a child's condition. A teacher's perspective adds a unique dimension in the identification and understanding of how a health problem may be affecting a child's development. The earlier health impairments, such as a hearing loss, allergy, or diabetes, are recognized and treatment is begun, the less negative the impact will be on a child's ability to learn.

Caution: Responsibility for interpreting signs and symptoms of an illness or health condition and arriving at a final **diagnosis** *always belongs to trained health care professionals.*

REFLECTIVE THOUGHTS

Parent involvement in children's education has been shown to have a positive effect on their development. Finding ways to increase parent participation is, therefore, important. How do children benefit from parent involvement? What are some of the ways parents can become more involved in children's programs? What strategies can teachers use to successfully increase parent participation? What approaches can be used with parents who feel uncomfortable in a school setting?

---

diagnosis – *the process of identifying a disease, illness, or injury from its symptoms.*

Children also benefit from the individualized attention given to their well-being and to the informal health education that can take place during health checks. This daily routine also enhances children's awareness of their personal health and may help them become more comfortable with visits to their health care provider.

Patterns of illness or significant behavioral changes can also be traced from daily health records. For example, knowing that children have been exposed to chicken pox or that there has been a reported outbreak of head lice in the community should alert teachers to be even more vigilant in the coming weeks.

INVOLVING PARENTS

Daily health checks provide an excellent opportunity for involving parents in children's preventive health care. Frequent contact with parents helps build a relationship of understanding and trust with staff (Wright & Stegelin, 2003; File, 2001; Turbiville, Umbarger & Guthrie, 2000) (Figure 3–6). Some parents may be hesitant, at first, to initiate contacts with the teacher regarding their child's health needs. However, through repeated encouragement, interest, and assistance, effective lines of communication can gradually be established (Lundgren & Morrison, 2003).

During the health check procedure, parents should be encouraged to ask questions and voice concerns about their child's behavior, physical condition, habits, or adjustment to care. In addition, parents may be able to provide simple explanations for problems the teacher observes. For example, a child's fatigue or aggressiveness may be the result of a new puppy, a grandmother's visit, a new baby in the home, or a seizure the night before. Allergies or a red vitamin taken at breakfast may be the cause of a questionable red throat. Without this direct sharing of information, such symptoms might otherwise be cause for concern.

Contacts with parents during health checks are also a good time to alert them to outbreaks of communicable illnesses. They can be informed of specific signs and symptoms to watch for and are thus more likely to keep sick children at home.

FIGURE 3–6

A partnership of trust and understanding is built on effective communication between parents and teachers.

ISSUES TO CONSIDER • The Impact of Health on Learning

High drop-out rates among school-age children continue to attract national attention. According to several recent studies, many of these children have undiagnosed health problems, such as vision and hearing impairments, allergies, asthma, and anemia, that interfere with their ability to learn and perform adequately in school. After years of struggle and failure, some children simply choose to abandon the source of their frustration.

The visionary founders of Head Start clearly understood the importance of early identification of children's health problems to assure that they were ready and able to learn upon entering school. This fundamental principle was again recognized in the *Goals 2000* and reiterated in the *Healthy People 2010* initiatives. Together, these programs continue to reinforce the essential role teachers play in assessing children's health.

- Should teacher education programs include more training about children's health needs? Explain.
- Do state child care licensing regulations support this important role?
- What rights does a teacher have in terms of making sure that children receive treatment for their health problems?
- What health care options exist for children whose families cannot afford needed treatments?

Parents' Responsibility

Primary responsibility for a child's health care always belongs to the parents. Parents are ultimately responsible for maintaining their child's health, following through with recommendations, and obtaining any necessary evaluations and treatments.

Often parents are the first to sense that something is wrong with their child (Allen & Marotz, 2003). However, they may delay seeking professional advice, either denying that a problem exists or hoping the child will eventually outgrow it. Some parents may not realize the serious consequences that health problems can have on their child's development and learning potential. Others may not be able to determine the exact nature of a child's problem or know where to go to obtain appropriate diagnosis and treatment.

Occasionally, parents fail to take the initiative to provide for any type of routine health care. Some parents find it difficult to understand the need for medical care when a child does not appear to be sick, while others simply cannot afford preventive health care. With today's rising medical care costs, it is easy to understand why this might occur. Cost, however, must not discourage parents from obtaining necessary medical attention. Health insurance is now available for income-eligible children through the national State Children's Health Insurance Program (SCHIP) to help improve their access to health care. In addition, most communities offer a variety of free or low-cost health services for young children, including:

- Head Start
- Child Find Screening Programs
- Medicaid Assistance

- Well Child Clinics
- University-Affiliated Training Centers and Clinics
- Public Health Immunization Centers
- Community Centers
- Interagency Coordinating Councils

These agencies and services can generally be located in the telephone directory or by contacting the local Public Health Department.

Teachers can be supportive and instrumental in helping parents understand the importance of scheduling routine health care for children. They can also become familiar with community resources and assist families in securing appropriate health care services (Allen & Cowdery, 2005).

HEALTH EDUCATION

Daily health checks also provide many opportunities for teaching children about good health. Teachers can begin to encourage children's interest in practices that promote a healthy lifestyle.

Simple questions about topics, such as hygiene, nutrition, exercise, and sleep, can be discussed with even very young children. For example:

- "Sandy, did you brush your teeth this morning? Brushing helps to keep teeth healthy and prevents cavities."
- "Alexander, what did you eat for breakfast this morning before coming to school? Food gives us energy to work and play."
- "Marion, have you had a drink of water yet today? Our bodies need water in order to grow and stay healthy."

Brief and spontaneous conversations such as these can capture children's immediate interest and help them begin to understand the importance of taking good care of themselves.

Parent Education

Daily health checks also provide an effective opportunity for educating parents. Many issues related to children's health care and education lend themselves to informal discussions with parents during the daily health check assessment.

- toy safety
- the importance of eating breakfast
- nutritious snack ideas
- the benefits of exercise
- cleanliness
- children dressing appropriately for the weather
- dental hygiene

Including parents in health education programs brings about an improved understanding of the health principles and goals that a program shares with the children. It also assures greater consistency in terms of information and practices between school and the child's home.

FOCUS ON FAMILIES • Children's Oral Health

Good oral health and a bright smile are important components of children's well-being. Teeth are necessary for chewing, speech, maintaining proper space for permanent teeth, and appearance. Decay and infection can make it difficult for children to fully participate and learn in school. Unfortunately, tooth decay continues to affect many young children today despite increased public education and improved dental treatments. However, parents can do many things at home to promote children's dental health.

- Keep baby's gums clean by wiping them with a damp washcloth after each feeding.

- Dampen a soft toothbrush and use twice daily to clean baby's first teeth.

- Don't put babies to bed with a bottle containing juice, formula, or breast milk. These solutions can pool around gums and teeth and lead to early decay. Offer water if your baby takes a bottle to bed. Also, stop breast-feeding once baby falls asleep.

- Apply a pea-sized dab of toothpaste to a soft brush and encourage toddlers to begin brushing thir own teeth. Be sure to follow their efforts by "going around the block" once again.

- Purchase fluoride toothpaste to help reduce dental decay. Fluoride is also added to the water supply in many cities. Your doctor or dentist may prescribe fluoride drops or tablets if your local water supply does not contain adequate fluoride.

- Continue to supervise preschool children's twice-daily tooth brushing. Discourage children from swallowing too much fluoride toothpaste; this can cause spots to develop on children's permanent teeth.

- Schedule your child's first routine dental check between one and two years of age. If you can't afford dental care, contact local public health personnel for information about free or low-cost options in your community. Reduced-cost dental insurance is also available to low income families in some states.

- Serve nutritious meals and snacks. Include fresh fruits and vegetables, whole-grain breads, crackers and cereals, and dairy products.

- Offer children water when they are thirsty. Limit their consumption of carbonated beverages, fruit drinks, and sport drinks, which tend to be high in sugars.

 ## CASE STUDY

Lynette's teacher recently became concerned about her ability to see. He has noticed that when stories are read to the children, Lynette often loses interest, frequently leaves her place in the circle, and crawls closer to him in order to see the pictures he holds up. The teacher also observed that Lynette looks very closely at puzzles and pictures she is coloring. Lynette's parents have expressed some concern about her clumsiness at home. An initial vision screening test, administered by the school nurse, reveals that Lynette's vision is not within normal limits. She was referred to an eye specialist for further evaluation.

1. What behaviors did Lynette exhibit that made her teacher suspect some type of vision disorder?

2. Identify the sources from which information concerning Lynette's vision problem was obtained before she was referred to an eye specialist.

3. If the teacher suspected a vision problem, why didn't he just go ahead and recommend that Lynette get glasses?

4. What responsibilities do teachers have when they believe that a child has a health impairment?

SUMMARY

- Good health is essential for effective learning.
  - Health problems can interfere with children's ability to learn.

- Teachers play a valuable role in promoting children's health.
  - Their observations provide information about children's physical, mental, social, and emotional well-being.
  - Their daily health checks yield additional information that is useful for identifying changes in children's health status, including communicable illness.
  - They must never attempt to diagnose children's health problems; this is the health professional's responsibility.
  - They can help parents understand the need for professional health care, and assist them in locating appropriate and affordable community services.

- Information gathered from daily health checks and teacher observations can be useful to health professionals for diagnosing and/or ruling out children's health problems.

- Parents must always be involved in children's health care and health education.

SUGGESTED ACTIVITIES

1. With another student, role-play the daily health check procedure. Record your findings.

2. Invite a public health nurse from a well-child clinic or a local pediatrician to speak to the class about routine health care for children birth to six years.

3. Visit several early education programs in your community. Note whether health checks are conducted as children arrive. Describe the method you observed at each center. Also, briefly discuss how this information was recorded.

4. Develop a list of resources available in your community and state for children with vision impairments, speech impairments, deafness, cerebral palsy, autism, and learning disabilities. Be creative in your search; consider child care options, special equipment needs, availability of special therapists, family financial assistance, etc.

CHAPTER REVIEW

A. **Match the term in column II with the correct definition in column I.**

<table>
<tr><td colspan="2" align="center">**Column I**</td><td align="center">**Column II**</td></tr>
<tr><td>1.</td><td>the process of writing down health data</td><td>a. health</td></tr>
<tr><td>2.</td><td>a problem that interferes with a child's ability to function</td><td>b. impairment</td></tr>
<tr><td>3.</td><td>evaluation or assessment of an individual's health</td><td>c. observations</td></tr>
<tr><td></td><td></td><td>d. symptom</td></tr>
<tr><td>4.</td><td>to gather information by looking and listening</td><td>e. appraisal</td></tr>
<tr><td>5.</td><td>physical maturation</td><td>f. recording</td></tr>
<tr><td>6.</td><td>a bodily change noticed by the affected individual</td><td>g. diagnosis</td></tr>
<tr><td>7.</td><td>to examine or look at carefully</td><td>h. parent contacts</td></tr>
<tr><td>8.</td><td>formal or informal meetings</td><td>i. development</td></tr>
<tr><td>9.</td><td>a state of complete physical, mental, and social well-being</td><td>j. inspection</td></tr>
<tr><td>10.</td><td>development toward maturity</td><td>k. growth</td></tr>
<tr><td>11.</td><td>the act of determining an illness or disorder from signs and symptoms</td><td></td></tr>
</table>

B. **Questions for small group discussion.**

1. What sources are available to teachers for gathering information about a child's health?
2. Describe the relationship between health and learning.
3. How do daily health checks benefit the child?
4. How can teachers involve parents in their child's preventive health care?
5. Describe the health check routine. What are some of the health problems/conditions that teachers should be looking for?
6. Why is it important that teachers conduct daily health checks?

REFERENCES

Allen, K. E. & Cowdery, G. (2005). *The exceptional child: Inclusion in early childhood education.* (5th ed.). Clifton Park, NY: Delmar Learning.

Allen, K. E. & Marotz, L. R. (2003). *Developmental profiles: Pre-birth through twelve.* (4th ed.). Clifton Park, NY: Delmar Learning.

Aronson, S. (2002). *Health young children: A manual for programs.* (4th ed.). Washington, DC: NAEYC.

Bentzen, W. R. (2001). *Seeing young children: A guide to observing and recording behavior.* (4th ed.). Clifton Park, NY: Delmar Learning.

Dailey, L. (1999). Communicating health, safety, and developmental concerns to parents. *Child Care Health Connections, 12*(5), 4.

File, N. (2001). Family-professional partnerships: Practice that matches philosophy. *Young Children, 56*(4), 70–74.

Lundgren, D. & Morrison, J. W. (2003) Involving Spanish-speaking families in early education programs. *Young Children, 58*(3), 88–95.

Turbiville, V. P., Umbarger, G. T., & Guthrie, A.C. (2000). Father's involvement in programs for young children. *Young Children, 55*(4), 74–79.

U.S. Department of Health & Human Services (HHS). (2000). *Healthy people 2010.* Office of Disease Prevention and Health Promotion. Washington, DC: U.S. Department of HHS.

U.S. Department of Health & Human Services (HHS). (2003). Fact sheet: Protecting the privacy of patients' health information. Accessed May 25, 2003 from http://www.hhs.gov/news/facts/privacy.html.

Wright, K. & Stegelin, D.A. (2003). *Building school and community partnerships through parent involvement.* Upper Saddle River, NJ: Merrill/Prentice Hall.

ADDITIONAL READING

Aronson, S. (2002). *Model child care health policies.* (4th ed.) Washington, DC: NAEYC.

Beaty, J. (2001). *Observing the development of young children.* New York: Prentice-Hall.

Diffily, D., & Morrison, K. (Eds.). (1997). *Family-friendly communication for early childhood programs.* Washington, DC: NAEYC.

Dodd, A. W. (1996). Involving parents, avoiding gridlock. *Educational Leadership, 53*(7), 44–49.

Hemmeter, M., Maxwell, K. L., Ault, M. J., & Schuster, J. W. (2001). *Assessment of Practices in Early Elementary Classrooms.* New York: Teachers College Press.

Hills, T. (1993). Assessment in context—teachers and children at work. *Young Children, 48*(5), 20–28.

Leavitt, R. L. & Eheart, B. K. (1991). Assessment in early childhood programs. *Young Children, 46*(5), 4–9.

Mindes, G., Ireton, H., & Mardell-Czudnowski, C. (1996). *Assessing young children.* Clifton Park, NY: Delmar Learning.

Schweinhart, L. (1993). Observing young children in action: The key to early childhood assessment. *Young Children, 48*(7), 29–33.

Shepard, L. A., Kagan, S. L., & Wurtz, E. (1998). Goal/Early childhood assessments resources group recommendations. *Young Children, 53*(3), 52–55.

HELPFUL WEB SITES

Canada's Schoolnet staff room	http://www.schoolnet.ca/home/e/
Canadian Institute of Child Health (CICH)	http://www.cich.ca/html
Early Head Start National Resource Center	http://www.ehsnrc.org
Head Start Bureau	http://www2.acf.dhhs.gov/program
Parents information	http://www.parentsoup.com
Zero to Three; National Center for Infants, Toddlers, and Families	http://www.zerotothree.org

 *For additional health, safety, and nutrition resources, go to http://www.EarlyChildEd.delmar.com*

CHAPTER 4

Health Assessment Tools

It is essential for teachers to familiarize themselves with the variety of methods and screening tools available for evaluating children's health. Several of the ost common procedures are described in this unit. Used appropriately, each is designed protect and improve children's health. Information collected in an objective manner and from a comvination of screening procedures yields: (1) reliable data for health promotion, (2) the early detection of potentially disabling conditions that can affect children's growth and development, and (3) an opportunity to adjust programs and environments to meet a child's unique needs.

HEALTH RECORDS

Information in children's permanent health files can be useful for promoting well-being if it is current and sufficiently detailed (Table 4–1). Unfortunately, good recordkeeping is not a priority in many early education programs. The types of records centers and home-based programs are re-

TABLE 4–1 Children's Health Records
Children's permanent health records should include:
• child/family health history
• copy of a recent medical assessment (physical examination)
• immunization records
• emergency contact information
• record of dental examinations
• attendance data
• school-related accidents or injuries
• parent conferences related to the child's health
• screening results, e.g., vision, hearing, speech, development
• medications administered while the child is at school

quired to maintain are usually specified in state child care licensing regulations. However, because these regulations typically reflect only minimal standards, programs may want to consider keeping additional forms of documentation. Selection of appropriate health-related records and forms should be consistent with a program's goals and philosophy. Records should include comprehensive information about individual children and provide adequate legal protection for the children, staff, and center. Information in children's permanent health records can be used for many purposes, including:

- determining health status
- identifying possible problem areas
- developing **intervention** programs
- evaluating the outcome of special services, e.g. speech therapy, occupational therapy.
- coordinating services
- making **referrals**
- following a child's progress
- research

Health records often include private information about children and their families. Only information that teachers require to work effectively with a child should be shared. Personal details about a child or family should remain confidential and must never serve as topics of conversation outside of the classroom. No portion of a child's health record should ever be released to another agency, school, health professional, or clinician until written permission has been obtained from the child's parent or guardian. A special release form, such as the one shown in Figure 4–1, can be used for this purpose. The form should clearly designate the nature of information that is to be released and the agency or person to whom it is to be sent. It must also be dated and signed by the parent or guardian, and a copy retained in the child's folder.

Recordkeeping is most efficient when one person is responsible for maintaining all health-related records. However, input from all members of a child's teaching team is important for determining the overall effect of health problems and for monitoring progress. Because health records are viewed as legal documentation, they should be kept on file for at least five years.

---

intervention – *practices or procedures implemented to modify or change a specific behavior or condition.*
referrals – *directing an individual to other sources, usually for additional evaluation or treatment.*

FIGURE 4–1

A sample information release form.

Download this form online at http://www.Early ChildEd.del mar.com

INFORMATION RELEASE FORM

I understand the confidentiality of any personally identifiable information concerning my child shall be maintained in accordance with the Family Education Rights and Privacy Act (P.L.93-380), federal and state regulations, and used only for the educational benefit of my child. Personally identifiable information about my child will be released only with my written consent. With this information, I hereby grant the

_____
(Name of program, agency, or person)

permission to release the following types of information:

Medical information   _____
Assessment reports   _____
Child histories   _____
Progress reports   _____
Clinical reports   _____
(Other)   _____

to:_____
(Name of agency or person to whom information is to be sent)

regarding _____ _____ _____
                    Child's Name   Birthdate   Gender

_____
Signature of Parent or Guardian

_____
Relationship of Representative

_____
Date

Child Health Histories

Health histories include valuable information about children's backgrounds, past medical condition, as well as current developmental status and health problems. Questions about family history are generally included to gain a more comprehensive picture of the child. Parents should complete a health history form when children are initially enrolled in an early care and education program and review the information annually to update any changes in the child's condition.

The nature of the information programs request on a child's health history form varies considerably. Unless a standard form is required by a licensing agency, programs may wish to develop a format that best suits their own needs. Sample forms can often be obtained from other programs or state agencies and reviewed to determine the types of questions a program wants to include. However, a child health history form should request basic information, including:

- facts related to the child's birth
- family structure, e.g., siblings and their ages, family members, predominant language spoken, legal custody issues
- major developmental milestones
- previous injuries, illnesses, surgery, or hospitalizations
- daily habits, e.g., toileting, food problems, napping
- parent concerns, e.g., behavior problems, social development, language, eating habits
- special health conditions, e.g., allergies, asthma, epilepsy, diabetes, blindness, hearing loss

Information included in health histories also contributes to a better understanding of each child's uniqueness, including past health events and potential risks for future health problems. This knowledge can be extremely useful for assessing a child's general state of health and enables teachers to set reasonable goals and expectations for individual children. Programs can be modified to accommodate children's special needs, such as a hearing loss, the use of a wheelchair for locomotion, or a mild heart condition. However, caution must be exercised not to set expectation levels unnecessarily low for children based on this information alone. A child's potential for learning must never be discounted unless an impairment is definitely known to restrict the educational process or performance. Lowering goals and expectations may limit what a child is willing to try, for often children will achieve only what is expected and may not be encouraged to progress or achieve their true potential.

Child health histories also provide teachers with insight into the type of routine medical supervision a child has received in the past. This knowledge may be useful when making referrals, because it often reflects the value parents place on preventive health care.

Medical and Dental Examinations

In most states, child care licensing regulations require children to have a complete health examination and current immunizations before they enroll in child care. Some states require this examination to be updated annually, while others request it only at the time of admission. It is generally recommended that well children who are less than one year of age have a routine medical checkup every two to three months. Children two to three years of age should be examined every six months and children four and older should be seen by their doctor annually. More frequent medical supervision may be necessary when health problems exist.

Current information is obtained from the parent and child during the course of the health examination. Questions related to physical, mental, and social development are asked to help the examiner assess the child's total state of health. The child's immunization record is reviewed and additional immunizations are administered as indicated. Body parts and systems, such as the heart, lungs, eyes, ears, **skeletal** and **neurological** development, and gastrointestinal function (stomach and intestines) are carefully examined. Head circumference is routinely measured on all infants and children until thirty-six months of age to be certain that head size continues to increase at an acceptable rate. Height, weight, and blood pressure readings (after age three) are also taken and compared to past records to determine if a child's growth is progressing satisfactorily. Lack of growth may be an indication of other health problems. Specialized tests, such as blood tests for anemia, sickle cell disease, or lead poisoning, may be ordered to identify or rule out any

skeletal – *pertaining to the bony framework that supports the body.*
neurological – *pertaining to the nervous system, which consists of the nerves, brain, and spinal column.*

of these conditions. Urinalysis, tuberculin testing, vision screening, and hearing evaluation may also be requested to provide more complete information about a child's health.

Although dental examinations are seldom required for enrollment in early education programs, their benefits are unquestionable. Preventive checkups for young children are generally recommended at 6 to 12-month intervals and include a visual inspection of the teeth, cleaning, and an application of fluoride.

SCREENING PROCEDURES

Screening tests are also an essential component of the comprehensive health assessment process. They support the philosophy of preventive care by ensuring that health problems and physical impairments do not interfere with a child's ability to learn. They can also help children become accustomed to screening as an integral part of routine health care.

A number of screening tools are available for assessing children's health. Most are relatively quick, inexpensive, and efficient to administer to groups of young children. Some of these tests can be conducted by teachers, while others require the services of professional clinicians. Screening tests are used to identify children who may have an impairment that requires professional evaluation, *never* to diagnose specific conditions. Test results simply provide additional information about a child to be used in combination with parent and teacher observations, assessments of growth and development, and the results of daily health checks.

Measurements of Height and Weight

The first five years of life are an important period of growth. Changes in height and weight are dramatic during infancy, while growth continues steadily, but at a much slower rate in the preschool years (Allen & Marotz, 2003). Measurements of height are particularly important because they provide a reliable means for evaluating a child's long-term health and nutritional status (see Appendix B for growth curves that show norms by children's age and gender). Fluctuations in weight, on the other hand, tend to reflect short-term variables, such as a recent illness, infection, emotional stress or overeating. However, it must be remembered that a child's growth potential is ultimately governed by genetics. This is especially important to remember when working with children from different cultures and ethnic backgrounds.

The practice of measuring height and weight is one method teachers can readily use to assess children's health (Figure 4–2). It does not require special skills or training and can be completed in a relatively short period of time. Children are usually fascinated to see how much they have grown or how "big" they are in comparison to friends. Teachers can also use this opportunity as a valuable learning experience to encourage children's interest in their own growth and health. Simple individual or group growth charts can be constructed with crayon and paper. By plotting measurements of height and weight each time, children can visualize their growth from one measurement to the next.

Ideally, height and weight should be measured at four- to six-month intervals and recorded in the child's permanent health file. However, a child's growth cannot be accurately evaluated from one measurement. A single measurement is unlikely to identify the child who is experiencing a growth disturbance related to physical illness, emotional problems, or eating disorders. Rather, what is more important is the pattern of changes that occur over a period of time. More important is the pattern of change that occurs over time. Measurements can be recorded on standardized growth charts and comparisons made with previous data to determine if growth is progressing satisfactorily. Recently revised (2000) growth charts are available from the National Centers for Health Statistics, Department of Health and Human Services, or on their Web site: http://www.cdc.gov/growthcharts/ (see Appendix B).

FIGURE 4–2

Measurements of height and weight provide a good index of children's health.

The Body Mass Index (BMI) is a new measure of children's growth currently replacing the standard weight-for-height (growth) assessment (see Appendix B). The BMI is recommended for the use with children two years and older to determine their risk for being underweight, overweight, or becoming overweight based on a weight-for-age relationship. Special gender-specific charts are available for plotting children's BMI-for-age and can also be obtained on the National Centers for Health Statistics' Web site. Examples of growth charts are also included in Appendix B.

REFLECTIVE THOUGHTS

Children enjoy being weighed and measured. Monitoring their growth is important for assuring good health. Teachers can use this activity for periodic assessment of children's well-being and to reinforce their learning of good health practices. However, ethnic differences must be taken into consideration when using standardized tables (such as Appendix B) to evaluate children's measurements of height and weight. Data in these tables are based on middle-class, Caucasian children and do not account for ethnic variations in body structure. How could you determine if an Asian or Hispanic child's growth was appropriate? How does nutrition influence a child's growth? What classroom activities (science, art, language, motor) could you incorporate to help children understand the concept of good health? How can teachers include parents in children's health education? What Internet sites provide reliable health and nutrition information for young children?

SENSORY DEVELOPMENT

The sensory system affects all parameters of a child's growth and development. Five special senses comprise the sensory system: vision, hearing, smell, touch, and taste. The young child depends on these senses to receive, interpret, process, and respond to information in the environment. Optimal functioning of the sensory system is, therefore, of critical importance, especially during the early stages of growth and development. Of the five senses, perhaps vision and hearing are two of the most critical to young children, since much of early learning is dependent on what the child hears and sees (Allen & Cowdery, 2004).

VISION SCREENING

It is often falsely assumed that because children are young and healthy they naturally have good vision. The Eye Care Council (1999) estimates that 20 percent of children entering kindergarten have undetected vision problems that interfere with learning. Approximately one in five children entering kindergarten has a vision impairment (Eyecare Council, 1999). Some impairments, such as cataracts or blindness, may be present at birth, or they can develop as the result of an injury or infectious illness, such as meningitis. Vision problems also are more prevalent in children who have other types of disabilities, such as cerebral palsy, Down syndrome, or fetal alcohol syndrome (FAS) (Erin, 2000; Topor, 1999; Lewis & Russo, 1998). For this reason, an infant's eyes should be examined for abnormalities and muscle imbalance at 3, 6, and 12 months of age and yearly, thereafter, to avoid the risk of permanent vision loss (Teplin, 1995). It is also recommended that all children have a professional eye evaluation by an **ophthalmologist** or **optometrist** before starting kindergarten. Early detection of vision impairments generally improves a child's chances for rapid and successful treatment.

Often, it is the teacher who first notices clues in a young child's behavior that suggest a vision disorder (Figure 4–3). As greater demands are placed on a child to perform tasks accurately, vision problems become more apparent. Also, it is unlikely that young children will recognize when their vision is not normal, especially if they have never experienced good vision. A careful comparison of screening results and adult observations can provide reliable information about a child's vision and the need for professional referral.

Special attention should be paid to children who have other known physical disabilities or are repeatedly unsuccessful in achieving tasks that depend on visual cues (Allen & Cowdery, 2004; Orel-Bixler, 1999). Delays in identifying vision problems can seriously affect the learning process and reduce the chance for successful treatment. Undiagnosed vision problems can also cause the inappropriate labeling of children as cognitively delayed or mentally retarded when, in fact, they simply cannot see well enough to learn (Allen & Marotz, 2003). The following case study illustrates the point:

> The teachers were concerned about Tina. She was easily frustrated and unable to complete many preacademic tasks, such as puzzles, color identification, and simple object labeling. She appeared clumsy and often avoided participation in large motor activities during outdoor time. These problems were not typical of most children Tina's age (three years, eight months). Her teachers considered placing Tina in a special classroom for children with learning disabilities. However, during routine vision screening, Tina's vision was discovered to be 20/200. With corrective glasses and slight modifications in teaching techniques, immediate improvement was observed in Tina's performance.

---

ophthalmologist – *a physician who specializes in diseases and abnormalities of the eye.*
optometrist – *a specialist (nonphysician) trained to examine eyes and prescribe glasses and eye exercises.*

FIGURE 4–3

Often it is the teacher who first notices signs of a child's vision problem.

Methods of Assessment

Early detection of visual defects requires observing children carefully for specific behavioral indicators (Tables 4–2 and 4–3). Talking with parents may also confirm a teacher's suspicions about a child's possible vision problems.

Vision problems are not outgrown, nor do they improve. Some vision problems have no outwardly visible signs or symptoms. Therefore, routine screenings are important for monitoring children's vision to be sure it is developing properly, and also to identify children with impaired vision (Figure 4–4) (Greenwald, 2003).

An infant's vision can be tested by holding an object, such as a rattle, 10 to 12 inches away and observing the infant's ability to focus on (fixation) and track (follow), the object as it is moved in a 180° arc around the child's head. The infant's eyes should also be observed carefully for any uncoordinated movements as the object is brought closer (convergence) and farther away from the face. In addition, the blink reflex (sweep hand quickly in front of the eyes; observe for blinking), and pupil response (shine a penlight, held four to six inches away, into the eye; pupil should become smaller) should also be checked. A child showing abnormal responses should be referred for professional evaluation.

TABLE 4–2   Early Signs of Visual Abnormalities in Infants and Toddlers

Observe the infant closely for:

- roving eye movements that are suggestive of blindness
- jerky or fluttering eye movements
- eyes that wander in opposite directions or are crossed (after three months)
- inability to focus or follow a moving object (after three months)
- pupil of one eye larger than the other
- absence of a blink reflex
- drooping of one or both lids
- cloudiness on the eyeball
- chronic tearing

TABLE 4–3 Signs of Visual Acuity Problems in Older Children

- rubs eyes frequently
- attempts to brush away blurs
- is irritable with close work
- is inattentive to distant tasks, e.g., a movie, catching a ball
- strains to see distant objects, squints, or screws up face
- blinks often when reading; holds books too close or far away
- is inattentive with close work; quits after a short time
- closes or covers one eye to see better
- tilts head to one side
- appears cross-eyed at times
- reverses letters, words
- stumbles over objects; runs into things
- complains of repeated headaches or double vision
- poor eye–hand coordination
- experiences repeated styes, redness, or watery eyes

Teachers and parent volunteers can be trained by health professionals to administer many of the standardized visual acuity tests (Table 4–4). Printable versions of the Eye Tests for Children (near and distance vision) are also available on the Prevent Blindness America Web site (www. preventblindness.org) or by contacting the organization's headquarters (500 E. Remington Road, Schaumburg, IL, 60173). In addition, children's eyes should be checked for:

- convergence
- depth perception (Titmus Fly test)
- binocular fusion (Worth 4-Dot test; Random Dot E)
- deviations in pupil position (test by holding a penlight 12 inches from the child's face, direct light at the bridge of the nose; the light reflection should appear in the same position on both pupils; any discrepancy requires professional evaluation.)

FIGURE 4–4

Early detection and treatment of vision problems improves children's learning success.

TABLE 4–4 Examples of Acuity Tests for Preschool Children
• Denver Eye Screening Test (DEST) • HOTV Symbols Visual Acuity Test • Screening Test for Young Children and Retardates (STYCAR); (this test can be used with children who have developmental delays) • Snellen Illiterate E • Allen Card Test • Cover-Uncover Test • Lea Symbols Visual Acuity Test • Random Dot E Stereoacuity Test

Photoscreening is a relatively new screening option that is gaining attention for use with young children, especially those who are preverbal or nonverbal or have developmental delays or disabilities that would make it difficult for them to complete conventional screening procedures (American Academy of Pediatrics, 2002; Enzenauer, Freeman, Larson, & Williams, 2000). A special camera records light reflected on the eye and is thus especially useful for the early detection of amblyopia and strabismus. Although it is an efficient and effective screening technology, the equipment is expensive and the test requires special training to administer.

Whenever screening tests are administered to children, it is important that they understand the instructions and expected method of response, or the results may be invalid. Children who fail an initial screening should be retested within two weeks. If a second screening is failed, testing results should be shared with parents and the child referred to a professional eye specialist for a comprehensive assessment.

The early detection and successful treatment of vision impairments in children has been targeted as a major goal in the *Healthy People 2010* initiative. Efforts to increase public awareness and to reach children in medically underserved areas are aimed at combating unnecessary and irreversible vision loss. Valuable information concerning symptoms of visual impairments, testing procedures, and treatments is also available on the Web sites of many professional organizations, including Prevent Blindness America (http://www.preventblindness.org), American Academy of Ophthalmology (http://www.aao.org), American Academy of Pediatrics (http://www.aap.org), and the American Association of Pediatric Ophthalmology and Strabismus (http://www.aapos.org).

Common Disorders

Vision screening programs are designed to detect three common disorders in young children, including:

- amblyopia
- strabismus
- myopia

Amblyopia, or "lazy eye," is a distortion of vision that forces one eye to assume primary responsibility for seeing. It is one of the most common vision problems affecting young children (Mittelman, 2003; Blackman, 1997). Amblyopia is thought to be caused by some form of dysfunction in the visual pathway of the brain, although other factors have also been suggested. Chil-

---

amblyopia – *a condition of the eye commonly referred to as "lazy eye"; vision gradually becomes blurred or distorted due to unequal balance of the eye muscles. The eyes do not present any physical clues when a child has amblyopia.*

dren with amblyopia typically experience double (blurred) vision because images received from one eye are weaker and, therefore, not seen as clearly. The brain begins ignoring (suppressing) images from the weaker (affected) eye, which leads to a gradual deterioration of vision and eventual blindness in the eye.

Early identification and treatment of amblyopia is critical for preventing a permanent loss of vision. If the condition is diagnosed before the age of five or six, a significant portion of the child's eyesight can often be restored. Treatment is even more successful when this condition is diagnosed between six months and two years of age (Mittelman, 2003). Early diagnosis requires a comprehensive eye examination by a professional eye specialist. Unfortunately, there are no physical signs or indicators in the child's appearance or behavior that would suggest this condition. Children themselves are often not aware of problems with their vision and, therefore, unable to tell an adult. Consequently, amblyopia too often goes undetected.

Amblyopia is commonly treated by having the child wear a patch over the stronger (unaffected eye) to gradually build up the strength of the visual pathway (Figure 4–5). Other methods for treating amblyopia include corrective glasses, eye drops, and special eye exercises (Repka, et al., 2003; Healthlink, 2002).

Strabismus, also sometimes referred to as crossed eyes, is another vision impairment occasionally seen in young children. The eyes of children with strabismus do not work together as a unit. Children with strabismus have an observable misalignment of their eyes (e.g., both eyes turn in, one eye turns in or out) that occurs intermittently or consistently. As a result, both eyes do not appear to be focused on an object at the same time. As in amblyopia, double vision occurs because the eyes are unable to focus together. Images from the weaker eye are ignored in the brain and vision gradually deteriorates.

Early recognition and treatment of strabismus is also essential for restoring normal vision. Today, even infants are being treated aggressively for this condition. Although uncoordinated eye movements are common in very young infants, by four months of age an infant's eyes should move together as a unit. Several methods are used to treat strabismus, including surgical correction, patching of the unaffected eye, and eye exercises.

FIGURE 4–5

Common vision defects affecting young children can include amblyopia, strabismus, and myopia.

strabismus – *a condition of the eyes in which one or both eyes appear to be turned inward (crossed) or outward (walleye).*

Myopia, or nearsightedness, affects young children, but is more common in school-aged children. A child who is nearsighted can see near objects, but has poor distant vision. Children with myopia may appear clumsy and stumble or run into objects. Squinting is also typical behavior, as children attempt to bring distant objects into focus.

Farsightedness, or **hyperopia**, is thought to be a natural occurrence in children under the age of five, and is caused by a shortness of the eyeball. As children grow older, this condition often corrects itself. Children who are farsighted can see objects clearly at a distance but have difficulty focusing on near objects. They may complain of headaches, tired eyes, and blurred vision following periods of close work. Hyperopia cannot be detected with most routinely administered screening procedures. For this reason, teacher and parent observations may provide the best clues to this disorder. A child who exhibits signs of hyperopia should be referred to a professional eye specialist for evaluation.

Color blindness affects a small percentage of children and is generally limited to males. Females are usually the carriers of this hereditary defect but are rarely affected themselves. The most common form of color blindness involves the inability to discriminate between red and green. Testing very young children for color blindness is difficult and often omitted, since learning is not seriously affected and there is no treatment available.

Management

When a child is suspected of having vision problems, parents should be counselled to arrange for professional screening. Vision testing is available through a number of sources, including pediatricians, "well-child" clinics, public health departments, professional eye doctors, and public schools. Some local service organizations, such as the Lions Clubs, offer assistance with the cost of professional eye examinations and glasses to individuals in need.

Children who do not pass an initial vision screening should be retested. Failure to pass a second screening necessitates referral to a professional eye specialist for more extensive evaluation and diagnosis. However, results obtained from routine vision testing should be viewed with some caution because they do not guarantee that a child does or does not have a problem. Most routine

REFLECTIVE THOUGHTS

Children who experience vision problems may require extra care and direction in the classroom (Koenig & Holbrook, 2000; Desrochers, 1999). They may not be able to complete tasks as quickly or precisely as other children.

Some children have difficulty tolerating treatments, such as patching for amblyopia, because their visual field is temporarily distorted. Daily application and removal of adhesive patches can cause skin irritation and also attract peer attention and curiosity. How can teachers turn this opportunity into a learning experience for young children? What strategies can teachers use in the classroom to help a child with vision problems? How might vision problems affect children in outdoor settings? What observable behaviors would suggest to a parent or teacher that a child may have vision problems?

---

myopia – *nearsightedness; an individual has good near vision but poor distant vision.*
hyperopia – *farsightedness; a condition of the eyes in which an individual can see objects clearly in the distance but has poor close vision.*

screening procedures are not designed to test for all types of vision impairments. Consequently, there will always be some overreferral of children who do not have any problems, while other children with vision defects will be missed. It is for this reason that the observations of teachers and parents are extremely important. Visual acuity also changes over time, so it is important for teachers and parents to be continuously vigilant of children's visual performance.

HEARING SCREENING

A child's ability to hear is essential for the development of speech patterns, **language**, and many other facets of learning. Undetected hearing impairments may also affect a child's social interactions, emotional development, and performance in school (Kaderavek & Pakulski, 2002). The early diagnosis of any hearing loss is extremely critical. Unfortunately, children with hearing losses are sometimes inappropriately labeled as slow learners, retarded, or "behavior problems." Failure to hear properly can cause children to respond and behave in seemingly inappropriate ways.

Methods of Assessment

Inappropriate responses and behaviors may be the first indication that a child is not hearing properly (Guralnick, 2000; Chen, 1998). Signs of hearing loss range from very obvious problems to those that are subtle and more difficult to identify. An observant parent or teacher may notice behaviors that could indicate a hearing loss, such as:

- frequent mouth breathing
- failure to turn toward the direction of a sound
- delays in acquiring language; development of poor speech patterns
- difficulty understanding and following directions
- asking to have statements repeated
- rubbing or pulling at ears
- mumbling, shouting, or talking loudly
- quiet, withdrawn; reluctant to interact with others
- using gestures rather than words
- excelling in activities that do not depend on hearing
- imitating others at play
- responding to questions inappropriately
- mispronouncing many word sounds
- having an unusual voice quality—one that is extremely high, low, hoarse, or monotone
- failing to respond to normal sounds and voices

Hearing tests are usually conducted by trained paraprofessionals, nurses, and audiologists (Figure 4–6). An audiologist is a specially prepared clinician who uses nonmedical techniques to diagnose hearing impairments. Routine hearing screening procedures test for the normal range of tones used in everyday conversation.

Today, hospitals in many states are complying with Universal Infant Hearing Screening recommendations (see Reflective Thoughts). Trained hospital staff test infants' hearing shortly after birth to detect hearing loss. An infant's hearing can also be evaluated informally by checking for responses such as eye blinking and turning of the head or interruption of sucking in an attempt to

---

language – *form of communication that allows individuals to share feelings, ideas, and experiences with one another.*

FIGURE 4–6

Hearing tests are conducted by audiologists or trained professionals.

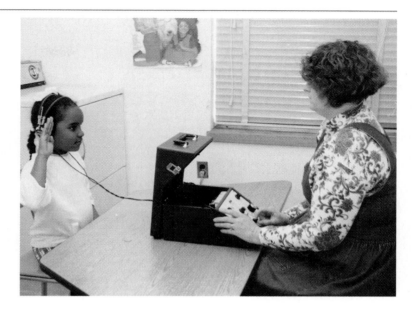

locate sounds (Table 4–5). Older infants and toddlers can be tested by observing as they turn to locate sounds (often emitted through speakers in formal testing procedures), as well as by the appropriateness of their responses and language development (Figure 4–7).

Children's hearing should be tested at least once during the preschool years and more often if a hearing problem is suspected. Most preschool children are able to complete routine hearing screening with little trouble. However, an unfamiliar situation involving new people, instruments and equipment, a novel task, a lack of understanding, or failure to cooperate may occasionally interfere with the child's performance and cause unreliable test results. These problems must be taken into consideration whenever children fail an initial screening. Children should always be retested to be sure screening results are valid. Parents and teachers should also be aware of the child who passes a hearing test yet continues to exhibit behaviors suggestive of a hearing loss.

Teachers and parents can be extremely helpful by preparing and training young children in advance for a hearing screening (Brown & Collar, 1982). In the classroom and at home, children can practice concentrated listening for short periods of time. Also, play activities that involve the use of headphones—telephone operators, airplane pilots, radio announcers, or musicians—will help children feel more comfortable when they are asked to wear headphones for screening purposes.

TABLE 4–5 Early Signs of Hearing Abnormalities in the Infant and Toddler

Observe an infant or toddler carefully for:

- absence of a startle response to a loud noise
- failure to stop crying briefly when adult speaks to baby (3 months)
- failure to turn head in the direction of sound, such as a doorbell or a dog barking (4 months)
- absence of babbling or interest in imitating simple speech sounds (6–8 months)
- no response to adult commands, such as "no"

FIGURE 4-7

An infant's response to sound can be used to test hearing.

Teachers should try to find out what response method, for example, raising one hand, pressing a button, pointing to pictures, or dropping a wooden block into an empty can, the children will be expected to use. This activity can also be practiced in the classroom. If a special room will be used for testing purposes, teachers should arrange for children to visit the facilities and look at the equipment beforehand. These special preparations will make hearing screening less frightening for young children and increase the reliability of test results.

REFLECTIVE THOUGHTS

Universal Newborn Hearing Screening and Intervention programs are currently available in 42 states and the District of Columbia (ASHA., 1999). Many other countries around the world are making efforts to adapt and implement similar screening initiatives. These programs are designed to evaluate newborn infants for significant hearing loss before they leave the hospital nursery or maternity center and to arrange for further testing and intervention as needed. Trained staff administer the test in a matter of minutes. A small earpiece, through which soft sounds are emitted, is placed in the ear canal and the baby's response (brain waves) is measured. Babies experience no discomfort during this test, and parents can learn the results within minutes. The average cost for this testing is around $30 to $40 and often covered by insurance plans. Numerous studies have demonstrated the significant advantage of identifying children with hearing loss and initiating appropriate intervention before six months of age (Thompson, et al. 2001; Mitka, 2000). Yet not every hospital offers this type of screening; some reserve it only for babies considered to be at high risk for having a hearing impairment (e.g., low birth weight, prematurity, family history, maternal infection during pregnancy, presence of other disabilities). Why is the early identification of hearing loss so important to children's development? Why are hearing impairments often not diagnosed before the age of two to three years? What areas of development are most likely to be affected by hearing loss? What community resources are usually available to parents if they are concerned about their child's hearing? Should all insurance companies be required to pay for newborn hearing screening? Explain.

Common Disorders

Children born with any physical disability are at greater risk of also having hearing problems (Allen & Marotz, 2003; Chen, 1998). Temporary and permanent hearing losses are more commonly associated with:

- a family history of hearing problems
- prenatal exposure to maternal infections, e.g., herpes, German measles, cytomegalovirus
- prematurity, low birthweight
- bacterial meningitis, measles, mumps
- allergies
- frequent colds and ear infections (otitis media)
- birth defects, such as Down syndrome, Fetal Alcohol syndrome (FAS), cleft lip/cleft palate, cerebral palsy
- head injuries

Any parent who expresses concern about their child's hearing should always be listened to carefully and encouraged to seek professional advice.

The most common forms of hearing loss are classified as conductive, receptive, and sensorineural.

- **Conductive loss** affects the volume of word tones. (For example, a child usually hears loud, but not soft sounds. This type of hearing loss occurs because sound waves are transmitted improperly from the external ear to structures of the inner ear, as when fluid accumulates in the child's middle ear.)
- **Receptive loss** affects the range of tones heard. (For example, a child may hear high, but not low tones. This type of hearing loss occurs when the sensory structures of the inner ear have been damaged.)
- **Sensorineural loss**, a less common form of hearing loss, results when sound impulses cannot reach the brain because of damage to the auditory nerve or brain itself. (These children can actually hear sounds, but are not able to understand what they hear.) These children are considered to have a learning disability that requires special educational management.

Management

Many hearing impairments can be successfully treated if they are identified in the early stages. Treatment depends on the underlying cause, and ranges from antibiotic therapy to surgery (Child Health Alert, 1999). Some children benefit from hearing aids, while others eventually learn sign language.

A child who experiences a sudden or gradual hearing loss should be referred to a family physician for medical diagnosis or to an audiologist for a complete hearing evaluation. Parents can arrange for this testing through the child's doctor, a speech and hearing clinic, public health department, public schools, or an audiologist.

---

conductive loss – *affects the volume of word tones heard, so that loud sounds are more likely to be heard than soft sounds.*

receptive loss – *affects the range of tones heard, so that high tones are more likely to be heard than low tones.*

sensorineural loss – *a type of loss that occurs when sound impulses cannot reach the brain due to damage of the auditory nerve, or cannot be interpreted because of prior brain damage.*

A teacher who understands how different impairments affect children's ability to hear, can take appropriate steps to improve learning conditions. Such measures might include:

- giving individualized instructions
- facing or standing near the child when speaking
- bending down to the child's level to make it easier for the child to hear and understand what is being said
- speaking slowly and clearly
- using gestures to illustrate what is being said, e.g., pointing to the door when it is time to go outside
- demonstrating what the child is expected to do, e.g., picking up a bead and threading it on a shoestring

Additional information about hearing impairments and testing procedures can be obtained from:

American Association of Speech-Language-Hearing
10801 Rockville Pike
Rockville, MD 20852

SPEECH AND LANGUAGE EVALUATION

Throughout the early years, children make impressive gains in both the number of words they understand (receptive vocabulary) and use to express themselves (expressive vocabulary) (Table 4–6). Children's receptive vocabulary is usually more extensive than their expressive vocabulary. For example, most toddlers can follow instructions and understand simple directions long before they can clearly express themselves with words. Children's language becomes increasingly fluent and complex with time and experience.

Many factors influence children's **speech** and language development. Most important is their ability to hear. Hearing is especially critical during the early years, when children are beginning to learn and imitate sounds, words, and word patterns. Hearing disorders can jeopardize the normal acquisition of speech and language development and lead to long-term speech impairments. Whenever there is concern about a child's progress, a comprehensive hearing evaluation should always be considered.

It is also important to take a child's home environment into consideration. Parents who engage children in frequent verbal interactions, read stories to their children, and support children's efforts to express themselves encourage early literacy and language development. Homes where these opportunities are lacking can place severe limits on children's ability to experience and practice important verbal and learning skills.

Young children also acquire early speech and language skills by imitating speech heard in their homes (Jaffe, 1997). For example, children whose parents are bilingual, have an unusual voice inflection, or speech impairment are often likely to exhibit similar qualities. Cultural values and variations also exert a strong influence on children's language usage and speech patterns. Thus, it is important for teachers to consider all of these factors and work collaboratively with parents when evaluating a child's speech and language development.

speech – *the process of using words to express one's thoughts and ideas.*

TABLE 4-6   Speech and Language Developmental Milestones

Infants

birth–4 months	turns to locate the source of sound
	begins to coo and make babbling sounds, *(baa, aah, ooh)*
	imitates own voice and sounds
4–8 months	repeats syllables in a series: *ba, ba, ba*
	"talks" to self
	responds to simple commands: "no" and "come"
8–12 months	recognizes labels for common objects: shoe, blanket, cup.
	"talks" in one word sentences to convey ideas or requests: "cookie" (meaning "I want a cookie")

Toddlers

12–24 months	follows simple directions
	knows and uses 10–30 words.
	points to pictures and body parts on request
	asks frequently "What's that," "Why?"
	enjoys being read to
	understands 200–300 words
	speaks in two–three word sentences
	65–70% of speech is intelligible
24–36 months	refers to self as "me": "Me do it myself."
	uses language to get desired attention or object
	understands simple concepts when asked: "Find the small ball."
	follows simple directions: "It's time to get dressed."
	understands and uses 50–300 new words
	70–80% of speech is intelligible
3–6 years	answers simple questions appropriately.
	describes objects, events, and experiences in fairly detailed terms
	sings simple songs and recites nursery rhymes
	carries on detailed telephone conversations
	enjoys making up and telling stories
	acquires a vocabulary of approximately 10,000–14,000 words by age six
	uses verb tenses and word order correctly
6–8 years	enjoys talking and conversing with adults
	uses language, in place of physical aggression, to express feelings
	loves to tell jokes and riddles
	understands complex statements and performs multistep requests
	finds pleasure in writing stories, letters, and e-mail messages
	expresses self fluently and in elaborate detail

Adapted from: Developmental profiles: Pre-birth through twelve, by K. Eileen Allen & L. Marotz, 2003, Clifton Park, NY: Delmar Learning.

Methods of Assessment

Parents are often aware that their child has a speech problem but may not know what to do about it. Many adults believe erroneously that children eventually outgrow such impairments. Indeed, some children have developmentally appropriate **misarticulations** that will improve as they grow older. For example, a three-year-old may pronounce "r" as "w" as in "wabbit" (rabbit) or "s" as "th" as in "thong" (song). Nevertheless, children who demonstrate speech or speech patterns that are not developmentally appropriate should be referred to a speech therapist for a thorough evaluation. A hearing test should be included in this evaluation to rule out the possibility of a hearing loss that could be affecting the child's speech. Speech and hearing clinics are often affiliated with colleges and universities, medical centers, child development centers, public health departments, public schools, and Head Start programs. A listing of certified speech and hearing specialists can be obtained by writing to the American Speech, Language, and Hearing Association (see Appendix C).

Common Disorders

The term *speech impairment* has many different meanings to persons working with children. For some, the term refers only to more obvious problems, such as stuttering, lisping, or unintelligent speech patterns. For others, a wide range of conditions are cause for concern, for example, a monotone voice, nasality, improper pitch of the voice, a voice tone that is too high or too low, omissions of certain letter sounds, or misarticulations of word sounds.

The range of speech and language disorders is as great as the variations in normal speech and language development (Hamaguchi, 2001; Venn, 2000). Some abnormal speech patterns include:

- no speech by two years of age
- stuttering
- substitution of word sounds
- rate of speech that is too fast or unusually slow
- monotone voice
- no improvement in speech development
- unintelligent speech by three years of age
- inattentive behavior or ignoring others

Management

Parents and teachers are important role models in a child's speech and language development. Early language experiences and stimulation encourage the child's effective use of language. However, teachers should never hesitate to refer children for professional evaluation if their speech and language patterns interfere with effective communication. Early recognition and treatment is critical for helping young children successfully overcome many speech impairments.

NUTRITIONAL ASSESSMENT

There is no question that the quality of children's diets has a direct effect on their behavior and state of health. Problems related to over- and underconsumption of food and nutrients are of increasing concern. Rising food costs and difficult economic conditions are forcing many families to

---

misarticulations – *improper pronunciations of words and word sounds.*

sacrifice the quality and quantity of food they purchase and serve (Casey, Szeto, Lensing, Bogle, & Weber, 2001). Furthermore, television advertising, increased consumption of fast foods, and availability of prepackaged and convenience foods have all contributed to a further decline in the quality of children's diets (Belfield, 2003; Freeman-Fobbs, 2003).

A preliminary assessment of children's state of nutrition and general health can be obtained through direct observation of their behavior and physical appearance. Many significant indicators can be noted during daily health checks. For example, facial **pallor**, dry skin, or **lethargy** may be indications of poor eating habits. Healthy, well-nourished children usually exhibit the following physical signs:

- height appropriate for age
- weight appropriate for height
- bright, clear eyes—no puffiness, crusting, or paleness of inner lids
- clear skin—good color; no pallor or scaliness
- teeth—appropriate number for age; no caries or **mottling**
- gums—pink and firm; not puffy, dark red, or bleeding
- lips—soft, moist; no cracking at corner of mouth
- tongue—pink; no cracking, smooth spots, or deep red color

Assessment Methods

Selecting an appropriate method for assessing children's nutritional status depends upon the child's age, reason for evaluation, type of information desired, and available resources. The methods most commonly used include:

- dietary assessment—is used to determine adequacy of nutrient intake and other nutritional deficiencies. The child's eating patterns are monitored for various lengths of time (24 hours, one to seven days) and actual food intake is recorded (Figure 4–8). Dietary information is then analyzed for nutritional content according to one of several methods, e.g., Food Guide Pyramid, nutrient analysis, RDAs (see Chapter 13) to determine if **nutrient intake** is adequate.
- anthropometric assessment—is based on simple measurements of height, weight, and head circumference. Comparisons are made with standardized norms (see Appendix B). Additional measurements of **skinfold** thickness and mid-arm circumference are sometimes also taken (Trahms & Pipes, 2000). These measurements yield specific information about a child's growth.
- clinical assessment—involves observing a child for signs of nutritional deficiency (Table 4–7). It is not a reliable method because of its subjective nature and the fact that physical symptoms often do not appear until a deficiency is severe.
- biochemical assessment—involves laboratory testing of various body tissues and fluids, such as urinalysis or hemoglobin (testing for iron level) to validate concerns related to over- or under-consumption of nutrients. These tests are usually ordered by a health care provider and performed by trained laboratory technicians.

---

pallor – *paleness.*
lethargy – *a state of inaction or indifference.*
mottling – *marked with spots of dense white or brown coloring.*
nutrient intake – *consumption of foods containing chemical substances (nutrients) essential to the human body.*
skinfold – *a measurement of the amount of fat under the skin; also referred to as fat-fold measurements.*

FIGURE 4–8

Sample questionnaire for obtaining information about a child's eating habits.

NUTRITIONAL ASSESSMENT

Dear Parent:

Nutrition is a very important part of our program. In order for us to plan appropriate nutrition-education activities and menus to meet your child's needs, we need to know your child's eating patterns. This information will also help us obtain an overview of the eating habits of young children as a group. Please take the time to fill out the questionnaire carefully.

NAME _____ AGE _____ DATE _____

1. How many days a week does your child eat the following meals or snacks?
   a morning meal _____ a midafternoon snack _____
   a lunch or midday meal _____ an evening snack _____
   an evening meal _____ snack during the night _____
   a midmorning snack _____

2. When is your child most hungry?
   morning _____
   noon _____
   evening _____

3. What are some of your child's favorite foods? _____

4. What foods does your child dislike?
   _____

5. Is your child on a special diet? Yes _____ No _____
   If yes, why? _____
   Describe diet _____
   Diet prescribed by whom? _____

6. Does your child eat things not usually considered food e.g., paste, dirt, paper? _____
   If yes, how often? _____
   What is eaten? _____

7. Is your child taking a vitamin or mineral supplement?
   Yes _____ No _____ If yes, what kind? _____

8. Does your child have any dental problems that might create a problem when eating certain foods? _____

9. Has your child ever been treated by a dentist? _____

10. Does your child have any diet-related health problems?
    Diabetes _____ Allergies _____ Other _____

11. Is your child taking any medication for a diet-related health problem?
    _____

12. How much water does your child normally drink throughout the day?
    _____

13. Please list as accurately as possible what your child eats and drinks on a typical day. If yesterday was a typical day, you may use those foods and drinks.

TIME	PLACE	FOOD	AMOUNT

TABLE 4–7 Physical Signs of Malnutrition

Tissue	Sign	Cause
Face	Pallor	Niacin, iron deficiency
	Scaling of skin around nostrils	Riboflavin, B$_6$ deficiency
Eyes	Hardening of cornea and lining: pale lining	Iron deficiency
	Foamy spots in cornea	Vitamin A deficiency
Lips	Redness: swelling of mouth and lips; cracking at corners of mouth	Riboflavin deficiency
Teeth	Decayed or missing	Excess sugar (or poor dental hygiene)
	Mottled enamel	Excess fluoride
Tongue	Red, raw, cracked, swollen	Niacin deficiency
	Magenta color	Riboflavin deficiency
	Pale	Iron deficiency
Gums	Spongy, red, bleeding	Vitamin C deficiency
Skin	Dry, flaking	Vitamin A deficiency
	Small underskin hemorrhages	Vitamin C deficiency
Nails	Brittle, ridged	Iron deficiency

Common Disorders

Teachers and parents need to be alert to several nutritional problems that may affect children's health. Poor dietary habits, resulting in inadequate intake of essential nutrients, can lead to malnutrition over a period of time. Vitamins A and C, iron, and calcium are the nutrients most commonly missing from children's diets today. Long-term use of certain medications, such as steroids, aspirin, antibiotics, and laxatives, can also interfere with the absorption of some nutrients. Many children are undernourished simply because they do not get enough to eat. These children are often below average in height and weight, irritable, anemic, and listless (see Appendix B). Their poor state of nutrition can severely limit their ability to learn.

Not all malnourished children are thin and emaciated. Children who are overweight can also be malnourished. Because the bulk of their diet often consists of sugars and starches, these children may appear to be well fed, yet lack many of the nutrients essential for good health. Inactivity also contributes significantly to their weight problems.

Another serious nutritional health problem is that of obesity (Belfield, 2003; Berg, 2003). Approximately 20 to 25 percent of all children in the United States are considered overweight for their age. Inactivity and poor eating habits are the primary causes of this current national childhood epidemic (Freeman-Fobbs, 2003).

Children who are overweight or obese often face additional health problems. Excess weight limits their participation in much needed physical activity. Children who are obese tend to have poor coordination and shortness of breath with exertion, and they tire more quickly. Teasing, ridicule, and rejection by peers can also lead to serious maladjustment problems. Children who are overweight also have a tendency to remain overweight as adults and, therefore, face an increased risk of short- and long-term health problems, including heart disease, stroke, asthma, and diabetes.

Management

Obesity in young children cannot be ignored. Ideally, prevention is always the most effective method. However, promising results can also be obtained by taking action while a child is young and still in the process of establishing lifelong eating habits (Hodges, 2003; Dyson, 2000). For maximum success, a treatment program for weight control must include the cooperation of the child, parents, teachers, and health personnel.

The goal of any weight control program is to help young children and their parents develop a new awareness about:

- meal planning and nutritious eating habits.
- methods for increasing children's daily activity level (Figure 4–9). (For example, children can be asked to run errands, walk a pet, help with daily household chores or ride their bike to school.)
- acquainting children with new outside interests, hobbies, or activities, such as swimming, dance, neighborhood baseball, or learning to ride a bike (Involvement in fun activities can divert children's attention away from food.)
- finding ways to help children experience success and develop a positive self-image. (For example, praise received for simple achievements can make children feel good about themselves—"Lonnie, you did a nice job of sweeping all the sand off the sidewalk." For many children, praise replaces food as an important source of satisfaction.)

Long-term weight control is enhanced by attending to all aspects of a child's well-being, physical, emotional, and social. Children should not be placed on weight reduction programs unless they are under a doctor's supervision. Weight reduction programs must be designed to meet all the nutritional needs of children to ensure normal growth and development. Education and positive role modeling are also important factors in the management of good nutrition and promotion of healthier lifestyles.

FIGURE 4–9

Increasing children's activity levels can help control their weight.

REFERRALS

The initial step in making successful referrals involves gaining the parent's trust and cooperation. Referrals are of little use unless parents are willing and able to follow through with recommendations. Knowing something about the beliefs, customs, habits, and people of the community can influence the way in which referrals are handled. For example, mistrust of the medical profession, poverty, job conflicts, religious beliefs, a lack of transportation, or limited education will undoubtedly affect a parent's response.

ISSUES TO CONSIDER • Children's Health

The U.S. Census Bureau redefined the term *poverty* so it more accurately reflects today's economic standards. Current guidelines exclude many families whose income is often not adequate to meet even minimal requirements for food, clothing, shelter, and health care. Data show that the adults in a majority of these families are employed, but often in jobs paying minimum wages. Health care and insurance are luxuries that many cannot afford. Eligibility changes in various government assistance programs (food, cash, and housing) have further reduced access to resources that affect children's health. An increase in poverty has also contributed to an increase in homelessness, especially for families with children—currently the fastest growing segment of the homeless population (CDC, 2001).

- Why is it important for teachers to be aware of changes in national fiscal policy and federal programs?
- How does increasing poverty and homelessness affect a teacher's role in monitoring children's health?
- How can teachers become stronger advocates for children?
- What types of partnerships with parents can help improve children's health status?

Meeting with the child's parents, or calling them on the telephone, is often the most effective method for making referrals:

Teacher: "I am concerned about Ryan's vision. On several occasions, I have noticed that his right eye turns inward more than the left eye and that he holds his head close to materials when he is working. Have you observed any of these behaviors at home?"

Parent: "Yes, but we didn't know if it was anything to worry about. We thought it would go away when he was older."

Teacher: "I cannot be sure if Ryan has anything wrong with his eyes, but the behaviors I have observed can sometimes be an indication of vision problems and should be checked carefully by an eye specialist. If you need help locating a doctor or making an appointment, I will be glad to help you. I will also give you a written copy of my observations to take with you. Please let me know the date of Ryan's appointment after you have made it."

Although a face-to-face meeting with parents is preferable, a well-written letter may be the only way to reach some families today. Parents should be given copies of screening test results, which they can forward to the specialist who will be evaluating their child. This step also improves the efficiency of the referral process. Familiarity with various community services, such as hospitals, clinics, health departments, medical specialists, public and private service agencies, volunteer organizations, and funding sources, also improves teachers' ability to assist families in securing appropriate help for the child and alleviate some of their frustration in the process.

Follow-up contact should be made after several days to determine if parents have been successful in arranging for professional evaluation, or to learn the outcome of diagnostic testing. Teachers can use these findings to make adjustments in the child's instructional program or learning environment. Follow-up contacts can also be beneficial for reinforcing parents' efforts to obtain necessary services for the child and to convey the teacher's genuine interest in the child's well-being.

FOCUS ON FAMILIES • Children's Eye Safety

Each year, thousands of children sustain eye injuries as the result of hazardous conditions at home or school. The majority of these eye injuries are preventable through appropriate supervision, selection of toys and equipment, and instruction. Parents can play a major role in identifying potentially dangerous situations and taking measures to eliminate children's exposure to unnecessary risk. They should also take similar precautions to protect their own eye safety and serve as a positive role model for children.

- Never shake a baby! Vigorous shaking can cause serious eye damage and blindness.

- Insist that children wear sunglasses whenever they play outdoors to limit exposure to ultraviolet (UV) light. Over time, UV exposure increases the risk of developing a number of serious eye conditions, including macular degeneration and cataracts. Purchase sunglasses that fit closely, cover the entire eye area, and provide UV protection.

- Keep children indoors whenever mowing or edging the lawn. Stones, sticks, and small debris can easily become dangerous projectiles.

- Select toys and play equipment based on your child's age and abilities. Avoid toys with projectile parts, such as darts, slingshots, pellet guns, and missile-launching devices. Stones, rubber bands, balls, wire coat hangers, and fish hooks also pose a serious eye danger.

- Supervise children closely whenever they are using a sharp item, such as a fork, pencil, toothpicks, wire paperclips, scissors, or small wooden dowels.

- Keep children away from fireworks. Do not allow them to light fireworks or to be near anyone who is doing so.

- Lock up household cleaners, sprays, paints, paint thinners, and chemicals such as garden fertilizers, and pesticides that could injure children's eyes.

- Make sure children wear appropriate protective eyewear, such as goggles or a helmet with a face guard, when participating in sports.

- Don't allow children to shine a laser pointer or aim a squirt gun or spray nozzle toward someone's eyes.

- Remind children to avoid touching their eyes with unwashed hands.

CASE STUDY

A friend encouraged Mrs. Howard to take her son to the developmental screening clinic being held at the community recreation center. Parker was nearly two years old and spoke only a few words that were understandable. He usually stayed with his grandmother during the day while his mother worked, so he didn't have many opportunities to play with other children his age. The developmental screening team checked his height, weight, vision, hearing speech, cognitive abilities, and motor skills. The team leader noted that Mrs. Howard indicated on the history intake form that Parker had several food allergies and frequent upper respiratory and ear infections. His hearing tests revealed a significant loss in one ear and a moderate loss in the other.

1. Is Parker's speech development appropriate for his age?

2. What significance do Parker's ear infections have to his hearing loss?

3. Should the screening team's recommendation for Parker include a referral to his physician? Why?

4. What strategies can Parker's mother and others use to improve their communication with him?

5. What things can Parker's mother do to encourage his speech development?

SUMMARY

- Teachers play an important role in the health assessment of young children.
  - They can use a variety of information to evaluate children's health status, including observations, health records, screening procedures, daily health checks, and interactions with parents.
- Results of screening procedures are not always accurate and can be affected by children's ability to respond.
- Teachers can initiate the referral process after gathering and evaluating data from multiple sources.
  - Referrals should be followed-up to make certain that recommendations have been carried out and to learn how teachers can implement suggestions in the classroom.

SUGGESTED ACTIVITIES

1. Locate and read instructions for administering the Snellen E and one additional acuity screening test. With another student, practice testing one another. What were the advantages of each test? Disadvantages?

2. Devise a monitoring system whereby daily food intakes are recorded for each child in a group setting. This information is primarily intended to provide information about daily food consumption to parents. Factors to consider are:

   a. What nutritional information is needed? In what form?

   b. Who is responsible for collecting this data?

   c. How can this information be obtained efficiently?

   d. How can food intake records increase opportunities for communication with parents?

   e. What other uses can food intake records serve for the teacher?

3. Collect samples of child history forms from several child care programs in your area. Review the type of information that is requested most often. Design your own form.

4. Attend a signing class. Learn to say "hello" and "good-bye" and 10 additional words in sign language.

5. Make arrangements with a local child care program to conduct a comparison study of children's growth. Measure and record the heights and weights of 15 children, ages three to six years, on the standard Growth Charts (Appendix B). Then, determine their BMI and plot this information on the BMI-for-age charts. Which method provides the most accurate in-

formation about children's growth? What about their potential risk for becoming over-weight? Locate and read further about the BMI measure.

6. Obtain an audiometer. Have a nurse or audiologist demonstrate the technique for testing hearing. Locate a partner and practice administering the test with one another.

7. Research the Internet or contact the American Heart Association for educational programs designed to improve cardiovascular health. Are the materials/programs developmentally appropriate? How is improvement determined?

CHAPTER REVIEW

A. **Define the following terms:**

1. audiologist
2. conductive hearing loss
3. sensorineural hearing loss
4. receptive vocabulary
5. expressive vocabulary
6. anthropometric assessment
7. nutrient deficiency

B. **Select the screening test that would be recommended for children with the following behaviors, signs, or symptoms. Place the appropriate code letter in each space for questions 1–15.**

H	Hearing screening	Dt	Dental screening
V	Vision screening	S	Speech evaluation
D	Developmental screening	N	Nutrition evaluation
HW	Height and weight		

_____ 1. frequent blinking; often closes one eye to see

_____ 2. stutters whenever tense and in a hurry to speak

_____ 3. usually listless; appears very small for her chronological age

_____ 4. stumbles over objects in the classroom; frequently walks into play equipment in the play yard

_____ 5. very crooked teeth that make his speech difficult to understand

_____ 6. seems to ignore the teacher's requests; shouts at the other children to get their attention

_____ 7. awkward; has great difficulty running and climbing; tires easily because of obesity

_____ 8. a five-year-old who has trouble catching a ball, pedaling a bicycle and cutting with scissors

_____ 9. appears to focus on objects with one eye while the other eye looks off in another direction

_____ 10. multiple cavities; in recent weeks has not been able to concentrate on any task

_____ 11. is extremely shy and withdrawn; spends the majority of her time playing alone, imitating the actions of other children

_____ 12. seems extremely hungry at snack time; always asks for extra servings and takes food left on other children's plates when the teacher isn't looking

_____ 13. becomes hoarse after shouting and yelling during outdoor time

_____ 14. arrives at school each morning with potato chips, candy, or a cupcake

_____ 15. a four-and-a-half-year-old who whines and has tantrums to get his own way

C. **Questions for small group discussion.**

1. What vision disorders are most common among young children? How is each typically treated?

2. How can children's health records be used to assess children's health?

3. What strategies can a teacher use to evaluate the adequacy of a child's diet?

4. What recommendations could a teacher offer the parent of an obese child for managing this condition?

5. What resources are available in your community for a parent who is interested in having her twenty-month-old infant's hearing tested?

REFERENCES

American Speech-Language-Hearing Association. (1999). Universal newborn hearing screening. Accessed May 17, 2003, from http://www.asha.org/hearing/testing.

Allen, K. E. & Cowdery, G. (2004). _The exceptional child: Inclusion in early childhood education._ (5th ed.). Clifton Park, NY: Delmar Learning.

Allen, K. E., & Marotz, L. R. (2003). _Developmental profiles: Pre-birth through twelve._ (4th ed.). Clifton Park, NY: Delmar Learning

American Academy of Pediatrics (2002). Use of photoscreening for children's vision screening. _Pediatrics, 109_(3), 524–525.

Belfield J. (2003). Childhood obesity—a public health problem. _School Nurse News, 20_(1), 20–24.

Berg F., Buechner, J., & Parham, E. (2003). Guidelines for childhood obesity prevention programs: promoting healthy weight in children. _Journal of Nutrition Education & Behavior, 35_(1), 1–4

Blackman, J. A. (1997). _Medical aspects of developmental disabilities in children birth through three._ Rockville, MD: Aspen Publishers.

Casey, P. H., Szeto, K., Lensing, S., Bogle, M., & Weber, J. (2001). Children in food-insufficient, low-income families: Prevalence, health, and nutritional status. _Archives of Pediatrics & Adolescent Medicine, 155_(4), 508–514.

CDC. (2001). _Health, United States, 2001 with socioeconomic status and health chartbook._ National Center for Health Statistics. Washington, DC: U.S. Department of Health and Human Services (DHHS).

Chen, D. (1998). Early identification of infants who are deaf-blind: A systematic approach for early interventionists. _Deaf-Blind Perspectives, 5_(3), 1–5.

Child Health Alert. (1999). Are doctors changing the way they treat ear infections? _Child Health Alert, 17,_ 1–2.

Desrochers, J. (1999). Vision problems—How teachers can help. _Young Children, 54_(2), 36–38.

Dyson, L. (2000). American cuisine in the 20th century. _Food Review, 23_(1), 2–7.

Enzenauer, R., Freeman, H., Larson, M., & Williams, T. (2000). Photoscreening for amblyogenic factors by public health personnel: The Eyecor Camera System. _Ophthalmic Epidemiology, 7,_ 1–12.

Erin, J. N. (2000). Students with visual impairments and additional disabilities. In A. J. Koenig & M. C. Holbrook (Eds.), _Foundations of education: Instructional strategies for teaching children and youths with visual impairments_ (Vol. 2, pp. 720–752). New York: American Foundation for the Blind.

Eyecare Council, Inc. (1999). See to learn program. Accessed on May 24, 2003, from http://www.see-tolearn.com.

Freeman-Fobbs, P. (2003). Feeding our children to death: The tragedy of childhood obesity in America. *Journal of National Medical Association, 95*(2), 119.

Greenwald, M. J. (2003). Refractive abnormalities in childhood. *Pediatric Clinics of North America, 50*(1), 197–212.

Guralnick, M. J. (Ed.) (2000). *Interdisciplinary clinical assessment of young children with developmental disabilities.* Baltimore, MD: Paul H. Brookes.

Hamaguchi, P. (2001). *Childhood speech, language & listening problems.* (2nd ed.). Indianapolis, IN: John Wiley & Sons.

Healthlink. (2002). Amblyopia: Eye drops could be as effective as patching. Accessed May 24, 2003, from http://healthlink.mcw.edu/article/1030635385.html.

Hodges, E. A. (2003). A primer on early childhood obesity and parental influence. *Pediatric Nursing, 29*(1), 13–60.

Jaffe, M. (1997). *Understanding parenting.* Dubuque, IA: William C. Brown.

Kaderavek, J. N., & Pakulski, L. A. (2002). Minimal hearing loss is not minimal. *Teaching Exceptional Children, 34*(6), 14–18.

Lewis, S., & Russo, R. (1998). Educational assessment for students who have visual impairments and other disabilities. In S. Sacks & R. Silberman (Eds.), *Education of students who have visual impairments and other disabilities* (pp. 39–71). Baltimore, MD: Paul H. Brookes.

Mahon, L.K. & Escott-Stump, S. (Eds.). (2000). *Krause's food, nutrition, & diet therapy.* (10th ed.). Darien, IL: W. B. Saunders.

Mitka, M. (2000). Neonatal screening varies by state of birth. *JAMA, 284,* 2044–2046.

Mittelman, D. (2003). Amblyopia. *Pediatric clinics of North America, 50*(1), 189–196.

Repka, M. X., Beck, R. W., Holmes, J. M., Birch, E. E., Chandler, D. L., Cotter, S. A., Hertle, R. W., Kraker, R. T., Moke, P. S., Quinn, G. E., & Scheiman, M. M. (2003). A randomized trial of patching regimens for treatment of moderate amblyopia in children. *Archives of Ophthalmology, 121*(5), 603–611.

Satter, E. (2000). *Child of mine: Feeding with love and good sense.* Palo Alto, CA: Bull Publishing Co.

Teplin, S. W. (1995). Visual impairment in infants and young children. *Infants and Young Children, 8*(1), 18–51.

Thompson, D., McPhillips, H., Davis, R., Lieu, T., Homer, C.J., & Helfand, M. (2001). Universal newborn hearing screening: Summary of evidence. *JAMA, 286,* 2000–2010.

Topor, I. (1999). Functional vision assessments and early interventions. In D. Chen (Ed.), *Essential elements in early intervention: Visual impairment and multiple disabilities* (pp.157–206). New York: American Foundation for the Blind.

Trahms, C. M., & Pipes, P. L. (2000). *Nutrition in infancy and childhood.* Columbus, OH: McGraw-Hill.

Venn, J. (2000). *Assessing students with special needs.* Upper Saddle River, NJ: Merrill.

ADDITIONAL READING

American Academy of Pediatrics, Task Force on Newborn and Infant Screening. Newborn and infant hearing loss: detection and intervention. (1999). *Pediatrics, 103,* 527–530.

Besing, J., Koehnke, J., Abouchacra, K., & Letowski, T. (1998). Contemporary approaches to audiological assessment in young children. *Topics in Language Disorders, 18*(3), 52–70.

Blasi, M. J., & Priestley, L. (1998). A child with severe hearing loss joins our learning community. *Young Children, 53*(20), 44–49.

Bowe, F. G. (2004). *Birth to five: Early childhood special education* (3rd ed.). Clifton Park, NY: Delmar Learning.

Cunningham, M., & Cox, E. O. (2003). Hearing assessment in infants and children: recommendations beyond neonatal screening. *Pediatrics, 111*(2), 436–44.

D'Andrea, F. M., & Farrenkopf, C. (2000). *Looking to learn: Promoting literacy for students with low vision.* New York: American Foundation for the Blind.

Discolo, C. M., & Hirose, K. (2002). Pediatric cochlear implants. *American Journal of Audiology, 11* (20), 114–118.

Dobson, V., Miller, J. M., Harvey, E. M., & Mohan, K. M. (2003). Amblyopia in astigmatic preschool children. *Vision Research, 43* (9), 1081–1090.

Holbrook, M.C. (Ed.). (1996). *Children with visual impairments: A parents' guide.* Bethesda, MD: Woodbine House.

Joint Committee on Infant Hearing. (2000). Year 2000 position statement: principles and guidelines for early hearing detection and intervention. *Pediatrics, 106,* 798–817.

Kennedy, E., & Goldberg, J. (1995). What are American children eating? *Nutrition Reviews, 53*(5), 111–126.

Koenig, A. J. & Holbrook, M. C. (2000). *Foundations of education: instructional strategies for teaching children and youths with visual impairments.* New York: American Foundation for the Blind.

Madell, J. R. (1998). *Behavioral evaluation of hearing in infants and young children.* New York: Thieme Medical Publishers.

Maples, W. C. (2003) Visual factors that significantly impact academic performance. *Optometry, 1,* 35–49.

Mei, Z., Scanlon, K. S., & Grummer-Strawn, L. M. (1998). Increasing prevalence of overweight among US low-income preschool children: The Centers for Disease Control and Prevention Nutrition Surveillance, 1983–1995, *Pediatrics, 101,* 12.

Overton, T. (2000). *Assessment in special education.* Upper Saddle River, NJ: Merrill/Prentice Hall.

Satter, E. (1999). *Secrets of feeding a healthy family.* Madison, WI: Kelay Press.

Telzrow, C. F., & Bonar, A. M. (2002). Responding to students with nonverbal learning disabilities. *Teaching Exceptional Children, 34*(6), 8–13.

Tripathi A., O'Donnell N. P., Holden R., Kaye L., & Kaye S. B. (2002). Occlusion therapy for the treatment of amblyopia: letting the parents decide. *Ophthalmologica, 216*(6), 426–429.

Wasserman, R., Croft, C., & Brotherton, S. (1992, May). Preschool vision screening in pediatric practice: A study from the Pediatric Research in Office Settings (PROS) Network. *Pediatrics, 101,* 834–838.

Watt, M., Roberts, J., & Zeisel, S. (1993). Ear infections in young children: The role of the early childhood educator. *Young Children, 49*(1), 65–72.

Yoshinaga-Itano, C., Sedey A. L., Coulter, D. K., & Mehl, A. L. (1998). Language of early and later-identified children with hearing loss. *Pediatrics, 102,* 1161–1171.

HELPFUL WEB SITES

American Speech, Language, and Hearing Association (ASHA)	http://www.asha.org
Children with Special Needs	http://www.children-special-needs.org/parent.html
National Eye Institute	http://www.nei.nih.gov
Parent's guide to middle ear fluid in children	http://www.kidsource.com
Prevent Blindness America	http://www.preventblindness.org

For additional health, safety, and nutrition resources, go to http://www.EarlyChildEd.delmar.com

CHAPTER 5

Conditions Affecting Children's Health

Today, many more children with disabilities, medical problems, and chronic illnesses are enrolling in community early childhood programs. Legislative enactments, increased public awareness, and improved intervention strategies have opened educational doors to all children regardless of their special needs. Consequently, teachers must be prepared to address children's learning as well as their medical and safety needs. Efforts to define the teacher's role in managing various medical procedures are beginning to receive increasing attention.

Children who develop symptoms of a chronic illness that has not yet been diagnosed present another classroom challenge. These conditions may be difficult to recognize because their signs and symptoms are often less obvious than those of an acute illness. Some chronic diseases, such as sickle cell anemia and diabetes, may be present from birth. Other conditions, such as allergies and lead poisoning, may develop slowly so that their appearance is less noticeable; even the child may not be aware that anything is wrong. Also, because parents see their child every day, it may be difficult for them to be objective and to recognize the early symptoms of a chronic illness.

Undiagnosed and untreated chronic illnesses can interfere with a child's overall growth and development. Teachers must work closely with parents to identify these early symptoms and assist families in obtaining appropriate medical evaluation and treatment. The earlier a chronic illness is diagnosed and treatment initiated, the less serious its impact will be on a child's developmental progress. When evaluating children for signs of chronic illness, environmental factors should also be taken into consideration. For many children, daily circumstances may contribute to their health conditions and/or serve as barriers to needed treatment:

- where they live—urban neighborhoods, rural areas, or without a home (homeless)
- family's financial situation, which in turn affects access to medical care, quality of nutrition, living arrangement
- exposure to environmental pollution, including air, water, noise, and chemicals
- presence of stress, trauma, violence
- disruption of the traditional family unit
- exposure to persuasive advertising

ALLERGIES

Allergies are the single most common cause of chronic health problems among young children and may affect as many as one in every 10 children. Although many allergies can be successfully treated, it is estimated that more than 50 percent of children with symptoms are undiagnosed (American Academy of Allergy, Asthma, and Immunology, 2003). Allergic reactions range in severity from symptoms that are mildly annoying to those that are disabling and severely restrict a child's activity and even to unexpected death.

Signs and Symptoms

A substance capable of triggering an allergic reaction is called an *allergen*. An error in the body's immune system causes it to overreact to an otherwise harmless substance in the environment, such as dust, pollen, foods, or medicines (Beers & Berkow, 1999).

Allergic reactions are generally classified according to the body site where symptoms most commonly occur:

- ingestants—cause digestive upsets and respiratory problems. Common examples include foods such as milk, citrus fruits, eggs, wheat, chocolate, nuts, and oral medications.
- inhalants—affect the respiratory system causing a runny nose, cough, wheezing, and itchy, watery eyes. Examples include pollens, molds, dust, animal dander, and chemicals, such as perfumes and cleaning fluids.
- contactants—cause skin irritations, rashes, hives, and eczema. Common contactants include soaps, cosmetics, dyes, fibers, latex, medications placed directly on the skin, and some plants, e.g., poison ivy, poison oak, and grass.
- injectables—trigger respiratory, digestive, and/or skin disturbances. Examples of injectables include insect bites, especially those of bees, wasps, hornets, spiders, and medications that are injected directly into the body.

REFLECTIVE THOUGHTS

Examine your feelings regarding children with chronic health disorders. Are you more apprehensive about working with these children? Do you consider them to be different in some way from children without long-term health problems? Do you respond to them differently in the classroom? Do you expect less of these children or are you more likely to be protective? What do you see as your role in helping children adjust to chronic health problems? Why is good communication with parents even more important in these situations?

Children who have chronic allergies often experience long-term irritability and malaise in addition to the discomfort that accompanies an acute reaction. To understand how allergies affect children on a day-to-day basis, a simple comparison can be made to the generalized fatigue and uneasiness that one feels during the onset of a cold. Certainly, children cannot benefit fully from learning when they are not feeling well. For these reasons, children's allergies may be an important contributing factor in many behavior and learning problems, including disruptive behaviors, hyperactivity, chronic fatigue, disinterest, irritability, and poor concentration.

Teachers can be instrumental in recognizing the early signs of allergic conditions in young children. Daily observations and anecdotal records can help detect patterns of repetitious symptoms that may otherwise be blamed on everyday childhood illnesses (Table 5–1) (Marks, 1983). Common signs and symptoms of allergic disorders include:

- frequent colds and ear infections
- chronic congestion, e.g., runny nose, cough, or throat clearing; mouth-breathing
- headaches
- frequent nosebleeds
- unexplained stomachaches
- hives, eczema, or other skin rashes
- wheezing or shortness of breath
- intermittent or permanent hearing losses
- reactions to foods or medications
- dark circles beneath the eyes
- mottled tongue
- frequent rubbing, twitching, or picking of the nose
- chronic redness of the throat
- red, itchy eyes; swollen eyelids
- irritability; restlessness; lack of energy or interest

Management

At present, there are no known cures for allergic conditions. Sensitivities are thought to be inherited and are seldom outgrown. However, the types and numbers of substances that a child is allergic to can change periodically. This may give the impression that an allergy has disappeared, only to resurface and become troublesome again at some later time.

TABLE 5–1 Cold or Allergy . . . . How to Tell?

	Cold	Allergy
time of year	more likely in fall and winter	depends on what child is allergic to could be year round or seasonal (fall, spring)
nasal drainage	begins clear; may turn color after 2–3 days.	remains clear
fever	common with infection	no fever
cough	may become loose and productive	usually not productive; nasal drainage irritates throat causing frequent throat clearing and shallow cough
itchy eyes	no	typical
muscle aches	may be present during first 1–2 days	none
length of illness	7–10 days	may last an entire season or year round

Symptoms and complications of allergies are generally less severe and easier to control if they are identified early. Treatment is aimed primarily at limiting a child's exposure to annoying allergens. In some instances, steps can be taken to completely remove these substances from the child's environment. For example, if a child is allergic to milk, all dairy products can be eliminated from the child's diet. If the pet dog is the cause of a child's allergies, the dog can be kept outside or at least out of the child's bedroom. In other cases, only the amount of exposure can be controlled, as in allergies to dust or pollens. Smoking should always be avoided around children with respiratory allergies because it can aggravate and intensify their problems (*American Lung Association*, 2003). Left untreated, allergies can lead to more serious chronic health problems, including chronic bronchitis, permanent hearing loss, sinusitis, asthma, and emphysema.

Antihistamines, decongestants, bronchodilators, and anti-inflammatory nasal sprays are commonly used to treat the symptoms of respiratory allergies. Many children also receive medication through aerosol breathing treatments (Delgado, Chou, Silver, & Crain, 2003; Frieri, 1998; Goldberg, 1994). Although effective, most of these medications simply provide temporary relief from symptoms. Children taking antihistamines and decongestants often experience drowsiness, difficulty concentrating, and excessive thirst. They need to be supervised closely, especially during outdoor times and activities that involve risk. Some children experience restlessness or agitation from their medications. These side effects make it particularly difficult for children to pay attention and learn, especially if they are prescribed for extended periods of time. Teachers must observe children who are taking these medications carefully and discuss any concerns about their effectiveness or side effects with the child's parents. A different medication with fewer side effects can sometimes be prescribed.

Caution: Teachers should always obtain approval from the child's physician and receive proper training before administering breathing treatments or any other form of medication.

In some cases, allergy shots (desensitization therapy) are given when other forms of treatment have been unsuccessful in controlling the child's symptoms. Many children experience improvement, but the full effect may take from 12 to 18 months.

Most allergic conditions are not life threatening. However, bee stings, medications, and certain foods can lead to a condition known as **anaphylaxis** in children who have a severe allergic reaction to these substances (Neugut, Ghatak, & Miller, 2001). This life-threatening response can cause shock, extreme difficulty in breathing, and requires urgent medical attention.

Caution: An ambulance should be called at once if anaphylaxis occurs.

Symptoms of anaphylaxis develop suddenly and may include:

- wheezing or difficulty breathing
- swelling of the lips, tongue, throat, and/or eyelids
- itching and hives
- nausea, vomiting, and/or diarrhea
- anxiety and restlessness
- blue discoloration around the mouth and nailbeds

Children who have a history of severe allergic reactions may keep an EpiPen at school. EpiPens are an autoinjecting device that administers a single dose of epinephrine when quickly pressed against the skin (usually on the leg) (Figure 5–1) (Child Health Alert, 2003; Sicherer, Foreman, & Noone, 2000). However, this medication provides only temporary relief, so it is essential to call for emergency medical assistance.

---

anaphylaxis – *a severe allergic reaction that may cause difficulty breathing, itching, unconsciousness, and possible death.*

FIGURE 5–1

An EpiPen auto-injector.

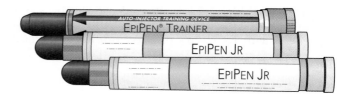

The emotional effects of allergies on the quality of children's lives cannot be overlooked. Frequently, these children are overly protected from many everyday experiences in order to avoid the risk of unpleasant reactions. They are continually reminded to be cautious so that exposure to offending allergens is limited. Children may also be sensitive about their appearance—frequent sneezing, runny nose, red and swollen eyes—along with feeling moody, irritable, or even depressed. In some cases, severe allergies may actually place limits on a child's level of physical activity. Eventually, these feelings can lead to excessive fear, withdrawn behaviors, and other maladjustment problems.

It is also important that children not be allowed to use their allergies as a means of gaining attention or special privileges. Instead, they can learn to become independent and self-confident in coping with their problems. Teachers can often help children make simple adjustments in their daily lifestyles so they can lead normal, healthy lives. Also, parenting classes and individual counseling can teach parents the skills they need to help children achieve these goals. Some clinics and hospitals offer special classes for parents and children to help them cope with allergies. A wealth of information can also be found on many professional Web sites.

ASTHMA

Asthma has become a significant health problem affecting millions of children (American Lung Association, 2003). For many young children, asthma is both a chronic and acute respiratory disorder affecting boys twice as often as girls (Mailick, Holden, & Walther, 1994). It is a form of allergic response and often seen in children who also have other allergies. Like allergies, asthma tends to be an inherited tendency that can become progressively worse without treatment (Burke, Fesinmeyer, Reed, Hampson, & Carlsten, 2003). Children who are obese also experience increased rates of asthma, raising additional alarms about their long-term health (Rodriguez, Winkleby, Ahn, Sundquist, & Kraemer, 2002; Belamarich et al., 2000).

A number of theories are currently under investigation in an attempt to determine why the incidence of asthma is increasing at such an alarming rate. Researchers are looking at multiple factors, including the quality of indoor environments, early infant feeding practices, sanitation standards, and increased air pollution. Mothers are being encouraged to breast-feed and to withhold solid foods until infants reach six months of age to decrease the potential risk of childhood allergies (Wong, 2001; Trahms, & Pipes, 2000). Women are also being urged to not smoke during pregnancy; babies born to mothers who smoke are more likely to develop asthma later in life (Gilliland, Berhane, Li, Rappaport, & Peters, 2002). Recent studies have also found the rate of asthma to be significantly higher among minority children and those living in poverty (Akerman, et al., 2003; Akinbami, LaFleur, & Schoendorf, 2002). Asthma attacks are thought to be triggered by a number of factors, including:

- airborne allergens, e.g., pollen, animal dander, dust, molds, perfumes, cleaning chemicals, paint, ozone, cockroaches (Lierl & Hornung, 2003; Ross, et al., 2002)
- foods, e.g., nuts, wheat, milk, eggs
- second-hand cigarette smoke (AAP, 1997)
- respiratory infections, e.g., colds, bronchitis
- stress (especially anger) and fatigue
- changes in temperature, e.g., cold, rain, wind
- vigorous exercise

Signs and Symptoms

Symptoms of acute attacks include wheezing, coughing, and difficulty breathing, especially exhalation. These symptoms are caused by swelling and spasms of the respiratory tract (bronchial tubes) (Figure 5–2). As mucous collects in the airways, breathing becomes labored, and it becomes more difficult to expel air. Many children will outgrow asthma attacks as the size of passageways increases with age.

Management

Treatment of asthma consists of identifying substances that cause flare-ups and removing them from the child's environment whenever possible (Table 5–2). For children with airborne allergies, frequent dusting and vacuuming of the environment may be necessary. Furnace filters should be replaced on a regular basis. Furnaces can also be equipped with electrostatic air purifiers to help remove offending particles from the air. Some families find that smaller child care programs are more desirable for children with asthma because the environment can be monitored more closely

REFLECTIVE THOUGHTS

Some medications used to treat the symptoms of allergies and asthma can cause undesirable side effects, including restlessness, nervousness, trembling, thirst, difficulty sleeping, drowsiness, nausea, headache, dilated pupils, difficult urination, and decreased appetite. What should you do if you observe any of these effects? What actions would you take if a child began developing difficulty breathing? How might these medications affect children's classroom behaviors and social interactions? What can teachers do to help children adjust to chronic health problems, such as asthma and allergies?

FIGURE 5-2

Swelling and excess mucus in the airways make breathing difficult during an asthma attack.

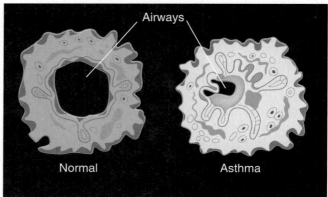

An artist's representation of bronchial tubes, or airways in the lung, in cross section. The normal airway, left, is open. The airway affected by asthma, right, is almost completely closed off. The allergic reaction characteristic of asthma causes swelling, excess mucus production, and muscle constriction in the airways, leading to coughing, wheezing, and difficult breathing.

From: http://www.niaid.nih.gov

and there is less exposure to respiratory infections. Medications, such as anti-inflammatory drugs and bronchodilators may also be prescribed to decrease swelling and open air passages. These are usually administered in the form of an inhaler or aerosol breathing treatment.

Teachers should always arrange a parent meeting when children with asthma are first enrolled so they are familiar with the child's condition—what symptoms does the child show, what substances are likely to trigger an attack, what, when, and how should medications be administered—and to develop an emergency plan of action. This information should be reviewed frequently with the child's parents so teachers are aware of any changes.

If weather triggers an attack, children may need to be kept indoors on days when there are abrupt temperature changes. However, children should be encouraged to participate in regular activities as much as their condition permits. If asthma attacks are caused by strenuous play, teachers

TABLE 5-2 Strategies for Managing Children's Asthma Attacks

- If you know that certain substances trigger a child's attack, remove the child from the environment (cold air, fumes).
- Encourage the child to remain quiet. Do not leave the child alone.
- Allow the child to assume a position that makes breathing easier; sitting upright is usually preferred.
- Administer any medications prescribed for the child.
- Offer small sips of room-temperature liquids (not cold).
- Contact the child's parents if there is no relief from medications or if parents request to be notified in the event of an attack.
- Do not delay calling for emergency medical assistance if the child shows any signs of struggling to breathe, fatigue, anxiety, restlessness, blue discoloration of the nail beds or lips, or loss of consciousness.
- Record your observations—child's condition prior to, during, and following an attack, factors that appeared to trigger the attack, medications that were administered, parents contacted.
- Stay calm; this helps put the child at ease and makes breathing easier.

ISSUES TO CONSIDER • Childhood Asthma

It is 10 A.M. and six children are lined up on small plastic chairs in the director's office at the Wee Care 4 Kids Child Care Center. Steam hisses from clear plastic masks being held by older children over their noses and mouths while a teacher assists those who are still too young to manage the procedure alone. All of these children have one thing in common—asthma. Twice each day, teachers must administer breathing treatments to increasing numbers of young children who suffer from frequent bouts of wheezing. Unfortunately, this scene is not uncommon in many schools today as the reported incidence of childhood asthma continues to soar.

- What is asthma?
- Why are more children than ever experiencing this chronic condition?
- Why does the incidence of asthma appear to be higher among minorities and children living in poverty?
- Should teachers be responsible for administering medical procedures?
- What steps should you take to prevent administering the procedure incorrectly and, thus, protect yourself from liability?

should monitor children's activity level and have them rest until the symptoms subside. In any event, teachers should always be prepared to respond quickly if a child develops difficulty breathing (see Chapter 10).

ATTENTION DEFICIT DISORDERS (WITH OR WITHOUT HYPERACTIVITY)

The term **hyperactivity** is often used inappropriately to label children who may actually be behaving within normal limits (Bussing, Zima, Gary, & Garvan, 2003). Many young children are, by nature, exceedingly energetic, curious, impatient, and restless. Using this term indiscriminately and without professional validation can lead to inappropriate treatment and altered expectations of children.

Attention deficit disorder (ADD) is a developmental disorder that includes a wide range of behavior and learning problems, including reading, expressive, and receptive disabilities. Some children have an attention deficit disorder accompanied by hyperactivity (ADHD). The American Psychiatric Association (2000) defines the disorder as "a **syndrome** of attention and behavior disturbances that may improve when stimulant-type drugs are administered."

Signs and Symptoms

Despite attempts to describe the condition more precisely, much controversy still remains about its causes, diagnosis, and effective management. A number of causes are currently being studied,

---

hyperactivity – *a condition characterized by attention and behavior disturbances, including restlessness, impulsive and disruptive behaviors. True cases of hyperactivity respond to the administration of stimulant-type medication.*

syndrome – *a grouping of symptoms and signs that commonly occur together and are characteristic of a specific disease or illness.*

including the role of genetics, prenatal exposure to smoke, alcohol, viral infections, sugar and food additives, environmental toxins, and biochemical disorders of the brain. However, ADD/ADHD is known to affect boys four to five times more often than girls and that it often runs in families (APA, 2000; Gaub & Carlson, 1997).

Some terms commonly used to describe children's behaviors include:

- explosive
- inattentive
- fidgety
- aggressive

- defiant
- forgetful
- easily frustrated
- clumsy

Unfortunately, there are no clear symptoms or simple medical tests available for accurately diagnosing this disorder. Often the decision is based on a combination of personal beliefs and observations. The American Psychiatric Association has established a series of diagnostic guidelines for identifying children with ADD/ADHD, including:

- excessive levels of motor activity based on the child's age
- limited attention span; is easily distracted and forgetful
- repeated incidences of impulsive behavior; aggressive and easily frustrated
- poor motor coordination
- disturbances of sleep
- engages in dangerous behavior (e.g., running out into the street) and is unaware of the consequences

In addition, the guidelines suggest that the behaviors must have been present before a child reaches seven years of age, be observed for at least six months and be inconsistent with the child's expected level of development (APA, 2000).

Management

No one simple method is available to treat this cluster of disorders (Selekman 2002; O'Connor, 2001). Each child requires an individualized approach. Often a combination of methods is used, although some are still considered to be controversial. Children's vision and hearing should also be tested to eliminate them as a cause of behaviors that could mimic ADD/ADHD.

Medications, such as Ritalin, Cylert, and Dexedrine, are commonly prescribed for children diagnosed with ADD/ADHD (Parr, Ward, & Inman, 2003; AAP, 1998). These stimulant and antidepressant-type drugs tend to have an opposite effect in children with ADD/ADHD. Rather than increasing children's activity level, these drugs often have a calming effect.

The medical profession has been criticized for its over diagnosis and overuse of medication to treat children with hyperactivity (O'Connor, 2001). Drugs are sometimes viewed as an easy way out for parents, doctors, and teachers and are often prescribed before other forms of intervention are tried. Many of these medications cause undesirable side effects in children, including a depression of appetite, slowing of growth, sleeplessness, listlessness, and stupor-like state. Furthermore, medication alone is not a cure (Schachar, et al., 2002; Child Health Alert, 1998). The child's problem behaviors generally reappear once the medication wears off or drug therapy is discontinued. However, medication can be beneficial for some children when it is used under medical supervision, over a short period of time, and in combination with behavior management therapy (Bussing, et al., 2003; Selekman, 2002).

Behavior management and special intervention strategies have been used successfully to treat children with ADD/ADHD. Their effectiveness can be attributed to the fact that these methods deal directly with the child's problem behaviors (Webster-Stratton, Reid, & Hammond, 2001). Through carefully planned and controlled experiences, children can learn behaviors that are socially acceptable and appropriate. Some basic principles include:

- Creating a structured environment. The degree of structure depends on the type and severity of the child's problems. For example, structure for one child may involve restricting the number of furnishings in a classroom to a single table and chair. For another child, structure may be achieved by limiting the number of choices, e.g., choosing between only two toys or activities.
- Establishing a daily routine that is consistent and predictable. Children with ADD/ADDH function best when things are familiar, including a routine that is the same from day to day.
- Giving directions that are clear and easy for the child to follow. Let the child know exactly what is expected. "Andy, I want you to put the toys in this basket." The use of repetition is also important.
- Offering praise and positive reinforcement. This is an effective means for gaining children's cooperation. It also encourages them to attempt and complete even simple tasks. "Good work, Nel. You put on your shoe."
- Providing experiences that are challenging, yet within the child's skill and tolerance level. Thus, a child can begin to experience frequent success and avoid repeated frustration and failure.
- Providing opportunities for developing new interests, especially physical activities where children can channel excess energy and learn to relax.

Implementing these strategies can provide children with opportunities to learn positive behaviors and, thus, lessen the emotional problems that often accompany attention deficit disorders. Gradually, children's self-confidence will improve as they become more successful and no longer see themselves as "always bad" or "failures" at whatever they do. Dietary management has also been suggested as a treatment (*Child Health Alert*, 1995). The controversial Feingold diet, introduced during the 1970s, linked sugar, artificial colors and flavorings, and foods containing an aspirin-related compound to the uncontrollable behaviors associated with hyperactivity. Feingold (1975) reported that when sugar and foods with these additives were omitted from the child's diet, behavior improved dramatically.

Many authorities continue to question Feingold's theories and results. However, like many other forms of therapy, what works for one child does not necessarily work for another. If parents understand this fact beforehand, they are less likely to be frustrated if dietary changes do not produce the results they hoped for. However, there is certainly no harm in feeding children foods that are nutritious, lower in sugar, and additive-free.

DIABETES

Although the incidence of diabetes among young children is still relatively low, it is rapidly becoming a major public health concern. At present, approximately 25 percent of all persons diagnosed with diabetes, particularly Type II, are children (CDC, 2002a). However, there is growing fear that it could soon reach epidemic proportions in children due to the strong correlation between obesity and diabetes (Ilardi, 2003; Mokdad, et al., 2003).

Teachers should be familiar with the signs, symptoms, and treatment of diabetes as many of these children will be enrolled in early care and education programs (Shipley, 2002). Treatment of childhood diabetes requires careful regulation and control. Growth, unpredictable changes in activity levels, irregular eating habits, and frequent exposure to respiratory infections often challenge successful management in children (Wong, 2001).

Signs and Symptoms

Diabetes is a chronic, incurable, and often hereditary condition that occurs when the pancreas does not produce an adequate amount of the **hormone** insulin. Type I diabetes typically develops during childhood and is caused by a failure of the pancreas to produce insulin (Gale, 2002). Type II diabetes is caused by an insufficient amount of insulin being produced or the cell's inability to use insulin properly (Knehans, 2002). Insulin is necessary for the metabolism of carbohydrates (sugars and starches) and the storage and release of glucose (blood sugar/energy). If insulin is absent or the amount is insufficient, glucose continues to circulate freely in the bloodstream rather than being stored. This condition is known as **hyperglycemia**. Serious complications, including death, can occur if it is left untreated. The onset of diabetes in children is usually rather abrupt, and includes early symptoms such as:

- rapid weight loss
- fatigue and/or weakness
- nausea or vomiting
- frequent urination

- **dehydration**
- excessive thirst and/or hunger
- dry, itchy skin

Management

Teachers must become familiar with each child's unique situation and treatment regime—whether the child has Type I or Type II diabetes, what dietary restrictions the child requires, what medical treatments (urine testing, insulin injections, medications) must be administered. Children who have Type I diabetes must be given insulin injections several times each day, have their glucose levels checked, and closely regulate their diet and activity. Some children with Type II diabetes may also require insulin injections, while others are able to regulate this condition through careful dietary management or medications to help their bodies utilize glucose. Teachers must also be knowledgeable about the complications that are associated with diabetes. For example, an insulin dose that is too large or too small requires different emergency care (see Chapter 10).

Arrangements should be made to meet with parents before their diabetic child begins to attend an out-of-home program (Shipley, 2002; Grabeel, 1997). Parents can alert teachers to changes in their child's behavior and appearance that may signal impending complications. Teachers also need to learn about dietary restrictions and medical procedures so they can be followed carefully while the child is in care (Figure 5–3). Plans for handling medical emergencies should also be worked out with parents at this time. Telephone numbers and names of additional contact persons should be reviewed with parents frequently.

hormone – *special chemical substance produced by endocrine glands that influences and regulates certain body functions.*

hyperglycemia – *a condition characterized by an abnormally high level of sugar in the blood.*

dehydration – *a state in which there is an excessive loss of body fluids or extremely limited fluid intake. Symptoms may include loss of skin tone, sunken eyes, and mental confusion.*

FIGURE 5–3

It is important to follow all special dietary restricitons.

Equipped with this knowledge, a teacher is better prepared to respond to emergencies. This can be reassuring to parents who may be reluctant to leave their diabetic child in the care of others. Teachers are also in a unique position to help diabetic children learn to accept and manage their condition and lead well-adjusted lives (Table 5–3).

ECZEMA

Eczema is a chronic inflammatory skin condition. Initial symptoms commonly appear in infants and children younger than five, and affect between 10 and 12 percent of all children (Wong, 2001). Eczema often disappears or significantly improves between the ages of 5 and 15 years in approximately 50 percent of these children. Consequently, approximately 15 percent of all adults in the United States will continue to experience some form of this chronic condition (National Institutes of Health, 2003).

Signs and Symptoms

Eczema is caused by an abnormal immune system response. It is commonly associated with allergies, especially to certain foods (e.g., eggs, wheat, milk) and substances that come in contact with

TABLE 5-3   Strategies for Helping Children Who Have Diabetes

- Begin to understand diabetes in simple terms (not to be ashamed of, afraid of, or embarrassed by).
- Understand that good eating habits are important.
- Recognize the relationship between good eating habits and feeling well.
- Learn to enjoy physical activity.
- Assist with their own medical management, e.g., practice good hand washing before glucose tests (finger sticks), cleansing the injection site.
- Participate in opportunities that help build good self esteem.

the skin (e.g., wool, soaps, perfumes, disinfectants, animal dander). Often there is strong family history of allergy and similar skin problems.

Reddened patches of irritated skin may first appear on an infant's or toddler's cheeks, forehead, scalp, or neck. Older children typically develop dry, itchy, scaly areas on the knees, elbows, wrists, and/or back of hands. Repeated scratching can lead to open, weeping skin that can easily become infected. Changes in weather can trigger an eczema flare-up or cause it to get worse, especially during summer heat or in winter cold when full-length clothing is likely to be worn. Older children may be reluctant to put on short-sleeved shirts and shorts when warmer weather arrives because of eczema's appearance.

Management

Eczema is not curable, but can be controlled through a number of preventive measures. Eliminating environmental allergens is always the preferred and first line of defense. However, in some cases these substance may not yet be known or are difficult to eliminate, such as dust or pollen, but steps can be taken to reduce the child's exposure. Reminding children not to scratch irritated skin and keeping their skin moisturized, especially after bathing or washing is also helpful.

Limiting exposure to extreme temperature changes can also be effective for controling symptoms. Keeping children cool in warm weather prevents sweating, which can lead to skin irritation. Reducing room temperatures, dressing infants and children in light clothing, and wiping warm areas of their body (creases in neck, elbow, knees, and face) with cool water can improve the child's comfort. Teachers may also be asked to administer antihistamines or topical cortisone ointments that the child's doctor has prescribed. Reducing stress in children's lives and helping them to develop a healthy self-image are also important strategies for reducing flare-ups.

FATIGUE

Most children enjoy a refreshing sense of energy, enthusiasm, and curiosity for life. Their stamina and intensity of play is often amazing (Figure 5–4). However, children may also experience periods of fatigue and listlessness from time to time. In most instances, both the cause and symptoms are temporary. Growth spurts, late bedtimes, moving to a new home, recovery from a recent cold, the birth of a sibling, or participation in too many activities may temporarily disrupt a child's normal sleeping pattern or increase the need for additional sleep.

Signs and Symptoms

Repeated or prolonged fatigue is not considered a normal condition for young children and should be investigated because of its potentially negative effect on growth and development. Chronic fatigue may be an indication of other health problems, including:

- poor nutrition
- chronic infection, such as otitis media
- **anemia**
- allergies

---

anemia – *a disorder of the blood commonly caused by a lack of iron in the diet, resulting in the formation of fewer red blood cells and lessened ability of the cells to carry oxygen. Symptoms include fatigue, shortness of breath, and pallor.*

FIGURE 5–4

Children are naturally energetic and curious.

- lead poisoning
- hepatitis
- **endocrine** (hormonal) disorders, such as diabetes, thyroidism
- heart disorders

Management

Careful evaluation of the child's personal habits and lifestyle may reveal a reason for chronic fatigue. A complete medical examination may be necessary to detect any existing health problems. If
no specific cause can be identified, there are several steps parents and teachers can take to improve
the child's general well-being (Table 5–4). Many of these measures can be built into daily classroom routines and are beneficial for all children.

TABLE 5–4 Strategies for Improving Chronic Fatigue in Children

- Help children develop good dietary habits.
- Encourage children to participate in moderate exercise, such as walking, swimming, riding bikes.
- Provide opportunities for improved sleep, e.g., earlier bedtimes, short naps during the day, a
  quiet sleeping area away from activity.
- Alternate periods of activity with quiet times, e.g., reading a book, playing quietly with a favorite
  toy, listening to music.
- Reduce environmental stress.
- Help children build effective coping skills.

endocrine – *refers to glands within the body that produce and secrete substances called hormones directly into the
bloodstream.*

FETAL ALCOHOL SYNDROME (FAS)/FETAL ALCOHOL EFFECT (FAE)

A mother's consumption of alcohol during pregnancy has been linked directly to the preventable conditions known as Fetal Alcohol Syndrome (FAS) and Fetal Alcohol Effect (FAE) in the unborn child (Project CHOICES Intervention Research Group, 2003). It is estimated that between 2,000 and 9,000 babies are born each year with Fetal Alcohol Syndrome, although it is difficult to obtain an exact number since the signs may not be identified until after the child's first birthday (CDC, 2003; Eustace, Kang, & Coombs, 2003). How severely a child will be affected is difficult to predict, but often depends on the amount and point in the pregnancy when alcohol was ingested (Streissguth, Bookstein, & Barr, 1996). Babies born to mothers who drank heavily during pregnancy are more likely to suffer from FAS; babies exposed to less alcohol typically experienced fewer and more mild abnormalities, such as difficulty with problem-solving, memory, and judgement (FAE). While alcohol can affect fetal development throughout the pregnancy, the most serious consequences tend to occur during the first three months when all major fetal organs (e.g., brain, heart, lungs, sensory and immune systems) are forming.

Signs and Symptoms

Unfortunately, the baby's brain development is most significantly affected by this syndrome—the way it develops and the way it works. Children with mild symptoms may not be diagnosed immediately, especially if their involvement is relatively mild. Fetal alcohol syndrome typically causes three major categories of disability—delayed growth, abnormalities of the brain and central nervous system, and distinct facial malformations (Johnson & Lapadat, 2000). Characteristics commonly associated with FAS include:

- low birth weight
- mental retardation
- poor muscle strength and coordination
- small head circumference (microcephaly)
- heart defects
- behavior problems
- learning disabilities
- irritability; restlessness; difficulty sleeping
- droopy or short eyelids
- thin upper lip
- eyes set far apart
- ears set lower on the head
- hearing and/or vision problems
- difficulty remembering; poor attention span

Slow growth, limited cognitive development, and numerous health problems continue to plague these children for life.

Management

FAS and FAE are entirely preventable conditions. No child would experience the physical and developmental disabilities associated with this syndrome if their mothers had avoided consumption of *all* alcohol prior to and during pregnancy. Studies have not been able to determine if any amount of alcohol is safe, so complete abstinence is recommended (Committee on Substance Abuse & Committee on Children with Disabilities, 2000). The incidence of FAS and FAE is considerably higher among minority populations who may not have ready access to preventive information. Public service efforts to spread this critical message are being stepped up as a result (Project CHOICES Intervention Research Group, 2003).

Early identification and early educational and behavioral interventions for children with these syndromes are important for their long-term success (Harwood & Kleinfeld, 2002; Duckworth, & Norton, 2000; Johnson & Lapadat, 2000). Some children are able to participate in traditional learning activities, while others require considerable adaptation. A predictable routine and limited environmental distractions improve children's ability to stay focused. Educational goals should be aimed at helping children develop effective social and communication skills (oral, written, signing) and to become as independent as their disability permits (Green, Diaz-Gonzalez de Ferris, Vasquez, Lau, & Yusim, 2002). Because these children are prone to health problems, teachers should monitor them closely so their progress is not disrupted. Teachers must also be extremely vigilant about children's safety. Their inability to remember, inability to understand cause and effect, and poor coordination place them at high risk for injury.

LEAD POISONING

Lead poisoning continues to be a major public health concern despite a significant decline in the numbers of children affected (Figure 5–5) (CDC, 2003b). Aggressive educational campaigns, legislation, and abatement programs have been successful in eliminating many common sources of lead contamination. Despite these efforts, the CDC estimates that approximately 434,000 U.S. children between one and five years of age have blood levels in excess of safety recommendations (CDC, 2003b).

While lead poisoning is not a problem exclusively associated with poverty and inner city populations, the incidence is typically higher among children living in these areas because of the lead-based paints (prior to 1978) used on houses and furniture (Table 5–5). Legislation passed in 1978 banned the production of these paints, although many existing sources still remain (Stephenson, 2002; Su, Barrueto, & Hoffman, 2002). Renovation of old houses can produce considerable contamination in the form of loose paint chips and paint dust that children may inhale (Lanphear, Succop, Roda & Henningsen, 2003). Inexpensive test kits are available at hardware stores for detecting lead-based paint on surfaces.

Caution: Use care when purchasing used toys and furniture at garage sales or from second-hand stores, as some of these items may contain lead-based paints.

Signs and Symptoms

Young children are especially vulnerable to lead poisoning. They frequently put toys and hands in their mouths, their bodies absorb lead more readily, and their brain and nervous systems are especially sensitive to lead's harmful effects (Canfield, et al., 2003; Lanphear, Dietrich, & Berger, 2003). Lead gradually accumulates in the child's bones, brain, central nervous system, tissues, and kidneys (Piomelli, 2002).

These children can present a range of symptoms, including:

- irritability
- loss of appetite and nausea
- headaches
- unexplained abdominal pain, muscle aches
- constipation
- listlessness

FIGURE 5–5

Lead poisoning continues to affect many young children.

TABLE 5-5   Common Sources of Environmental Lead
• old lead-based house paint (prior to 1978), including dust from remodeling projects
• soil contaminated by leaded gasoline emissions and old paint chips
• plastic mini blinds (manufactured before 1996, not made in the U.S.A.)
• contaminated drinking water (from lead solder in old water pipes)
• imported dishware and crystal
• lead shot and fishing weights
• used toys and furniture manufactured before 1978
• areas around lead smelters and mining operations
• working with, or around, motor vehicle batteries

- learning problems; short attention span; easily distracted
- behavior problems; aggression; impulsivity

Children younger than six years of age, living in low-income residential areas, and who consume a poor-quality diet, especially one low in vitamin C and iron, are at greatest risk for developing lead poisoning.

Management

Research has demonstrated that elevated levels of lead can lower a child's IQ by as much as 4 to 5 percent (Stephensen, 2002). Consequently, the Center for Disease Control (CDC) now recommends that all children, especially those at risk, be screened for lead poisoning between 6 and 72 months of age (AAP, 1998). However, a teacher who has concerns about an older child's physical complaints, behavior, or learning problems and thinks there may be a risk of lead poisoning should encourage parents to have their child tested.

Prevention of lead poisoning requires that environmental sources be located and removed. Early identification of children already affected by this condition is also important so that additional exposure to lead contamination can be stopped. Children should be encouraged to practice good hand washing habits, and to keep their hands and objects out of their mouths. Children who have elevated blood levels of lead may be treated with special medications and increased dietary intake of iron and vitamin C (Wright, Tsaih, Schwartz, Wright, & Hu, 2003; MMWR, 2002; Simon & Hudes, 1999). Unfortunately, there is little evidence to date suggesting that educational interventions can reverse or offer any improvement in children's behavior and/or learning problems if lead has already had detrimental effects (CDC, 2002b). Thus, public awareness and community education continue to be the most effective measures for combating this preventable condition.

SEIZURE DISORDERS

It is not uncommon to have children who experience **seizures** in an early childhood setting. Unlike many other chronic health problems, the mention of terms such as seizures, convulsions, or epilepsy arouses feelings of fear and anxiety in many adults. However, prior knowledge and plan-

---

seizures – *a temporary interruption of consciousness sometimes accompanied by convulsive movements.*

TABLE 5-6 Strategies for Helping Children Who Experience Seizure Disorders

1. Be aware of any children with a seizure disorder in the classroom. Find out what the child's seizures are like, if medication is taken to control the seizures, and whether the child is limited in any way by the disorder.

2. Know emergency first aid measures. Develop guidelines for staff members to follow whenever a child has a seizure; review the guidelines periodically.

3. Use the presence of a child with a seizure disorder as a learning opportunity for other children. Provide simple explanations about what seizures are; encourage children to ask questions and express their feelings. Help children learn to accept those who have special problems.

4. Gain a better understanding of epilepsy and seizure disorders. Read books and articles, view films, and talk with health professionals and parents.

5. Obtain and read the following books and pamphlets that are written for children. Share them with children in the classroom.

   - Gosselin, K. (1998). *Taking seizure disorders to school: A story about epilepsy.* St. Louis, MO: JayJo Books.

   - Moss, D. (1989). *Lee, the rabbit with epilepsy.* Bethesda, MD: Woodbine House.

   - Silverstein, A. (1980). *Epilepsy.* Philadelphia: J. B. Lippincott Co.

   - Young, M. (1980). *What difference does it make, Danny?* London: Andre Deutsch Limited.

ning will enable teachers to respond with skill and confidence when caring for children who experience these types of disorders (Table 5–6).

The term seizure disorder describes a cluster of symptoms rather than a particular disease (Figure 5–6). Seizures are caused by a rush of abnormal electrical impulses in the brain. This abnormal activity leads to involuntary or uncontrollable movements in various parts of the body. Their intensity and location vary, depending on the type of seizure. Some seizures involve only

FIGURE 5-6

Teachers must know what to do in the event of a seizure.

a momentary lapse of attention or interruption of thought while others may last several minutes and cause vigorous, spasmodic contractions of the entire body. Temporary loss of consciousness, frothing, and loss of bowel and bladder control may also accompany some types of seizures.

The specific cause of a seizure disorder is often difficult to determine (Cowan, 2002). Heredity is a contributing factor in some families. Children who have certain disabilities and syndromes are also at higher risk of experiencing a seizure disorder. However, an exact cause may never be identified. Several conditions are known to initiate seizure activity in young children:

- fevers that are high or rise rapidly (especially in infants)
- brain damage
- infections that affect the central nervous system, such as meningitis or encephalitis
- tumors
- head injuries
- lead, mercury, and carbon monoxide poisoning
- hypoglycemia (low blood sugar)
- drug reactions

Signs and Symptoms

Seizures are generally classified according to the pattern of symptoms a child presents (Wong, 2001; McBrien & Bonthius, 2000). The most common types of seizures include:

- febrile
- petit mal
- grand mal
- focal
- temporal lobe

Approximately 5 to 10 percent of infants and children under three years of age experience *febrile seizures* (Baumann, 2001). A higher percentage occurs in infants between 6 and 12 months. Febrile seizures are triggered by high fever and may cause a child to lose consciousness and have involuntary jerking movements involving the entire body. They usually stop when the fever subsides, and are, therefore, not thought to be serious or to result in any permanent damage.

Teachers may be the first to notice the subtle, abnormal behaviors exhibited by children with *petit mal seizures.* This type of seizure is characterized by momentary losses of attention, including:

- repeated incidences of daydreaming
- staring off into space
- a blank appearance
- brief fluttering of the eyes
- temporary interruption of speech or activity
- twitching or dropping of objects

Petit mal seizures generally occur in children 4 to 10 years of age and are characterized by a brief loss of consciousness, usually lasting 10 to 30 seconds. Children may suddenly stop an activity and resume it almost as quickly once the seizure subsides. Parents should be informed of the teacher's observations and encouraged to consult the child's physician.

Grand mal seizures are the most common form of seizure disorder. Convulsive movements usually involve the entire body, often making them frightening to the observer. Some children experience an aura or warning immediately before a seizure begins. This warning may be in the form of a certain sound, smell, taste, sensation, or visual cue. Sudden rigidity or stiffness (tonic phase) is followed by a loss of consciousness and uncontrollable muscular contractions (clonic phase).

TABLE 5–7   Information to Include in a Child's Seizure Report

- child's name
- date and time the seizure occurred
- events preceding the seizure
- how long seizure lasted
- nature and location of convulsive movements (what parts of the body were involved?)
- child's condition during the seizure, e.g., difficulty breathing, loss of bladder or bowel control, change in skin color (pallor, blue discoloration)
- child's condition following the seizure, e.g., any injuries, complaints of headache, difficulty with speech or memory, desire to sleep
- name of person who observed and prepared the report

When the seizure ends, children may awaken briefly and complain of a headache or dizziness before falling asleep.

Focal seizures are characterized by involuntary convulsive movements that begin at the tip of an extremity and spread toward the body trunk. The child does not always lose consciousness with this type of seizure.

Temporal lobe seizures are distinguished by spontaneous episodes of unusual behavior; the behavior is considered unusual because it is inappropriate for the circumstances. For example, a child may burst out in sudden hysterical laughter, utter unintelligible sounds, run around in circles, or cry out without apparent reason. It is also common to experience an aura before this type of seizure begins. Although there is usually not a total loss of consciousness during the seizure, children may appear drowsy or momentarily confused following the episode and should be encouraged to rest for a short time.

Management

Most seizures can be controlled with medication. It is vital that children take their medications every day, even after seizures are under control. Initially, children may experience undesirable side effects to these drugs, such as drowsiness, nausea, and dizziness. However, these problems usually disappear after a short time. Children should be monitored closely by their physician to ensure that prescribed medications and dosages continue to be effective in controlling seizure activity and do not interfere with learning.

Whenever a child experiences a seizure, parents should be notified. Also, any time seizures change in character or begin to recur after having once been under control, parents should be informed and encouraged to consult with the child's physician. Informing parents enables them to keep accurate records of seizure activity and to monitor medical treatment. Teachers should also complete a brief, written report documenting their observations following any seizure (Table 5–7). Completed reports should be filed in the child's permanent health record. The child's physician may also find this information useful for diagnosing a seizure disorder and evaluating medical treatments.

Teachers play an important role in the inclusion of children with seizure disorders in early education programs. By arranging environments that are safe and mastering emergency response techniques (See Chapter 10), teachers can fully involve all children in activities. Teachers can help young children learn to accept and cope with their seizure disorder. They can also encourage children to develop positive attitudes toward persons who experience seizures. A teacher's own reactions and displays of genuine acceptance can go a long way in teaching understanding and respect for persons with special health problems.

SICKLE CELL ANEMIA

Sickle cell anemia is an inherited disorder that interferes with the red blood cells' ability to carry oxygen (Wong, 2001). It primarily affects the African-American population, as well as individuals of Mediterranean, Middle Eastern, and Latin American descent. Approximately 10 percent of African Americans carry the trait for sickle cell anemia but do not necessarily experience symptoms of the disease themselves; these people are called carriers. When both parents have the sickle cell trait, some of their children may be born with the actual disease, while others may be carriers.

Signs and Symptoms

The abnormal formation of red blood cells in sickle cell anemia causes chronic health problems for the child (Palermo, Schwartz, Drotar, & McGowan, 2002). Red blood cells form in the shape of a comma or sickle, rather than their typical round shape. As a result, blood flow throughout the body is slowed and occasionally blocked. Symptoms of the disease do not usually appear until sometime after the child's first birthday.

Clumping of deformed blood cells results in periods of acute illness called *crisis*. A crises can be triggered by infection, injury, strenuous exercise, dehydration or, in some cases, for no known reason. Symptoms of a sickle cell crisis include fever, swelling of the hands or feet severe abdominal and leg pain, vomiting, and ulcers (sores) on the arms and legs. Children are usually hospitalized during a crisis. Between flare-ups, they may be free from acute symptoms. However, because of chronic infection and anemia, these children often are small for their age, irritable, easily tired, and possibly at risk for cognitive delays (Barden, Kawchak, Ohene-Frempong, Stallings, & Zemel, 2002; Thompson, Gustafson, Bonner, & Ware, 2002). They are also more susceptible to infections, a fact that parents should consider when placing children in group care.

Management

At present there is no known cure for sickle cell anemia. A new drug has recently been approved to treat persons who have multiple crises per year (Steinberg, et al., 2003). Currently, hospitals in many states test newborns to determine if they have sickle cell disease or are a carrier before they are sent home. This measure allows early medical intervention and reduces mortality. Genetic counseling offers prospective parents who are carriers the chance to decide whether or not they want to risk having children. Also, screening programs are now available to help parents obtain early diagnosis and medical care for infants and young children with sickle cell disease. Antibiotics, such as penicillin, may be given on a routine basis to prevent infections which are the leading cause of death for this group. New studies have also found that frequent blood transfusions can be helpful in preventing acute crises (Miller, et al., 2001).

FOCUS ON FAMILIES • Protecting Children from West Nile Virus

The West Nile virus is transmitted to humans through the bite of an infected mosquito. Although the number of identified cases remains relatively low, the infection continues to spread. Few people who are bitten will actually develop symptoms of the disease, which include fever, headache, body aches, skin rash, and swollen lymph glands. Simple, preventive steps can be taken to protect children against this newly emerging infectious illness.

- Eliminate sources of standing water in bird baths, plants, fountains, tire swings, buckets, and wading pools.

- Keep children indoors during early-morning hours, or at dusk when mosquitoes are more active.

- Dress children in light-colored, protective clothing, such as a long-sleeve shirt, long pants, and hat.

- Apply insect repellant containing no more than 10 percent DEET sparingly to exposed skin. Do not apply around the eyes, nose, or mouth, and wash hands carefully when you are finished. Be sure to wash the repellant off when children come indoors. Do not use DEET repellants on children younger than two years or if you are pregnant.

- Install or repair screens on doors and windows.

- Keep grass cut short and eliminate areas of overgrown vegetation.

- Contact a physician if your child develops any early signs of the West Nile virus.

CASE STUDY

Read the case study and fill in the blanks with a word (or words) selected from the following list.

breathing	headache
sleep	anticonvulsants
seizure	consciousness
informed	written report
aura	time length
grand mal	
permanent health file	

While climbing up the playhouse ladder, Jamie let out a sudden shriek, released her grip and fell to the ground. Her teacher quickly ran to see what had happened. Jamie lay on the ground unconscious, her arms and legs jerking. The teacher realized that Jamie was having a _____, and that it was probably a _____ type. A warning or _____ precedes this kind of seizure.

Jamie's teacher stood back and watched until the muscular contractions ended. In addition to the loss of consciousness, the teacher also carefully noted the exact _____ of the seizure, the parts of the body _____, and whether Jamie had any difficulty _____. Later, this information would be included in a _____, which would be placed in the child's _____.

When Jamie regained _____ she complained of a _____. The teacher encouraged her to _____ for a short while. Meanwhile, Jamie's parents were _____ of her seizure. Her mother explained that the doctor had recently prescribed a new medication and was trying to regulate the dosage. The most common group of medications used to treat seizure disorders are _____.

SUMMARY

- Many children in group care settings are affected by chronic illness.
  - Some conditions, such as diabetes, allergies, and lead poisoning, may develop slowly and, therefore, be difficult to recognize.
  - Parents may find it difficult to acknowledge children's health problems or not be certain where to go for help.
  - Teachers play an important role in helping young children cope with health conditions.

- Allergies are another common chronic condition experienced by many young children.
  - Symptoms are caused by an abnormal response to substances called allergens and can include nasal congestion, headaches, eczema, rashes, asthma, stomachaches, and behavioral changes.
  - Treatment is often symptomatic and based on identification of offending allergens.

- ADD/ADHD causes a variety of behavioral and learning problems.
  - Causes, diagnosis, and treatments are not clear-cut and are sometimes controversial.
  - Combinations of medication and behavior management strategies are often used to treat the disorder.

- Diabetes in children is caused by an inadequate amount or lack of the hormone insulin.
  - Early symptoms include weight loss, frequent urination, fatigue, and excessive thirst.
  - Treatment includes daily insulin injections and careful dietary regulation.

- The incidence of asthma, a form of allergic response, is increasing.
  - Many potential causes are being investigated, including exposure to chemicals and air pollution, infant feeding practices, obesity, and smoking during pregnancy.
  - Treatment is aimed at alleviating symptoms and acute attacks.

- Fetal Alcohol Syndrome (FAS) and Fetal Alcohol Effect (FAE) have been linked directly to maternal alcohol consumption during pregnancy; no amount is considered safe.
  - Abnormal facial features, vision and hearing impairments, learning disabilities, and behavior problems are common.

- Lead poisoning affects thousands of children in the United States.
  - Environmental sources of lead contamination can be found in paint on older houses (prior to 1978), lead shot and fishing weights, contaminated soil, and car batteries.
  - Children with elevated blood levels of lead show signs of impaired cognitive abilities, headaches, loss of appetite, fatigue, and behavior problems.

SUGGESTED ACTIVITIES

1. Locate and read at least eight children's books written about the various chronic diseases discussed in this chapter.

2. Interview teachers in three different settings. Find out what types of allergies they encounter most often and how they manage children's problems in the classroom. Develop a simple, five-day snack menu for a toddler who is allergic to milk and milk products, chocolate, and eggs.

3. Invite a speaker from the nearest chapter of the Feingold Association. Read at least one of the following articles beforehand and be prepared to ask questions:

Feingold, B. F. (1975). Hyperkinesis and learning disabilities linked to artificial food flavors and colors. *American Journal of Nursing, 75,* 797.

Herbert W. (1982, January 23). Hyperactivity—diet link questions. *Science News, 121,* 53.

Kaplan, B., McNicol, J., Conte, R., & Moghadam, H. (1989). Overall nutrient intake of preschool hyperactive and normal boys. *Journal of Abnormal Child Psychology, 17*(2), 127–132.

Lipton, M. A., & Mayo, J. P. (1983). Diet and hyperkinesis—an update. *Journal of the American Dietetics Association, 83*(2), 132–134.

Robinson, L. A. (1980). Food allergies, food additives and the Feingold Diet. *Pediatric Nurse, 6,* 38.

Wolraich, M., Milich, R., Stumbo, P., & Schultz, F. (1985). The effects of sucrose ingestion on the behavior of hyperactive boys. *Pediatrics, 106,* 675–682.

4. Design an educational poster on fetal alcohol syndrome prevention and display it in a prominent public area where potential mothers are likely to see it.

CHAPTER REVIEW

A. **Define the following terms:**

1. chronic
2. orthopedic problem
3. allergen
4. insulin
5. hyperglycemia
6. allergic reaction

B. **Discuss the following questions:**

1. What factors may be contributing to the increased incidence of childhood allergies and asthma?
2. Why has the use of medication to treat hyperactive children stirred so much controversy?
3. What are some of the early signs of diabetes? What resources are available in your community to help teachers improve their understanding of the condition and learn how to administer injections?
4. Distinguish between petit mal and grand mal seizures.
5. Why are many chronic health problems difficult to identify in the young child?

REFERENCES

Akerman, M., Valentine-Maher, S., Rao, M., Taningco, G., Khan, R., Tuysugoglu, G., & Joks, R. (2003). Allergen sensitivity and asthma severity at an inner city asthma center. *Journal of Asthma, 40*(1), 55–62.

Akinbami, L. J., LaFleur, B. J., & Schoendorf, K. C. (2002). Racial and income disparities in childhood asthma in the United States. *Ambulatory Pediatrics, 2*(5), 382–387.

American Academy of Allergy, Asthma, and Immunology. (2003). *Prevention of allergies and asthma in children.* http://www.aaai.org/public/publicedmat/tips.stm.

American Academy of Pediatrics (AAP). (1997). Environmental tobacco smoke: A hazard to children. *Pediatrics, 99,* 639–642.

AAP. (1998). *Caring for your baby and young child.* Steven Shelov (Ed.). New York: Bantam Books.

American Lung Association. (2003). Asthma in children factsheet. Accessed on June 14, 2003, from http://www.lungusa.org/asthma/.

American Psychiatric Association (APA). (2000). *Diagnostic and statistical manual of mental disorders DSM-IV-TR.* (4th ed.). Washington, DC: American Psychiatric Press.

Barden, E. M., Kawchak, D. A., Ohene-Frempong, K., Stallings, V. A., & Zemel, B. S. (2002). Body composition in children with sickle cell disease. *American Journal of Clinical Nutrition, 76*(1), 218–225.

Baumann, R. J. (2001). Prevention and management of febrile seizures. *Paediatric Drugs, 3*(8), 585–592.

Beers, M. H., & Berkow, R. (Eds.). (1999). *Merck Manual Diagnosis & Therapy.* Los Angeles, CA: Merck & Co.

Belamarich, P. F., Luder, E., Kattan, M., Mitchell, H., Islam, S., Lynn, H., & Crain, E. F. (2000). Do obese inner-city children with asthma have more symptoms than nonobese children with asthma? *Pediatrics, 106*(6), 1436–1441.

Burke, W., Fesinmeyer, M., Reed, K., Hampson, L., & Carlsten, C. (2003). Family history as a predictor of asthma risk. *American Journal of Preventive Medicine, 24*(2), 160–169.

Bussing, R., Gary, F. A., Mason, D. M., Leon, C. E., Sinha, K., & Garvan, C. W. (2003). Child temperament, ADHD, and caregiver strain: exploring relationships in an epidemiological sample. *Journal of the American Academy of Child & Adolescent Psychiatry, 42*(2), 184–192.

Bussing, R., Zima, B. T., Gary, F. A., & Garvan, C. W. (2003). Barriers to detection, help-seeking, and service use for children with ADHD symptoms. *Journal of Behavioral Health Service & Research, 30*(2), 176–189.

Canfield, R. L., Henderson, C. R., Cory-Slechta, D. A., Cox, C., Jusko, T. A., & Lanphear, B. P. (2003). Intellectual impairment in children with blood lead concentrations below 10 microg per deciliter. *New England Journal of Medicine, 348*(16), 1517–1526.

CDC. (2003). *Childhood lead poisoning: What is the problem?* National Center on Environmental Health. Centers for Disease Control and Prevention. Accessed on June 14, 2003 from http://www.cdc.gov/nceh/lead/factsheets/childhoodlead.htm.

CDC. (2002a). *New state data show obesity and diabetes still on the rise.* Washington, DC: National Center for Chronic Disease Prevention & Health Promotion.

CDC. (2002b). *Managing elevated blood lead levels among young children: Recommendations from the Advisory Committee on Childhood Lead Poisoning Prevention.* Washington, DC: Author.

Child Health Alert. (2003, March). Making sure an EpiPen works when it's needed. *Child Health Alert, 21,* 2.

Child Health Alert. (1998). Hyperactivity: Symptoms vs. medication side effects. *Child Health Alert, 16,* 2.

Child Health Alert. (1995). Synthetic food colorings: Do they affect children's behavior? *Child Health Alert, 13,* 1.

Committee of Substance Abuse and Committee on Children with Disabilities. (2000). Fetal Alcohol Syndrome and alcohol-related neurodevelopmental disorders. *Pediatrics, 106,* 358–361.

Cowan, L. D. (2002). The epidemiology of the epilepsies in children. *Mental Retardation and Developmental Disabilities Research Reviews, 8*(3), 171–181.

Delgado, A., Chou, K. J., Silver, E. J., & Crain, E. F. (2003). Nebulizers vs metered-dose inhalers with spacers for bronchodilator therapy to treat wheezing in children aged 2 to 24 months in a pediatric emergency department. *Archives of Pediatric & Adolescent Medicine,157*(1), 76–80.

Duckworth, S. V., & Norton, T. L. (2000). Fetal Alcohol Syndrome and Fetal Alcohol Effects—Support for teachers and families. *Dimensions of Early Childhood, 28*(3), 19–23.

Eustace, L. W., Kang, D. H., & Coombs, D. (2003). Fetal alcohol syndrome: a growing concern for health care professionals. *Journal of Obstetrical, Gynecological & Neonatal Nursing, 32*(2), 215–221.

Feingold, B. F. (1975). *Why your child is hyperactive.* New York: Random House.

Frieri, M. (1998, September/October). Managing asthma in infants. *Asthma,* 15–17.

Gale, E. A. (2002). The rise of childhood type 1 diabetes in the 20th century. *Diabetes, 51*(12), 3353–3361

Gaub, M., & Carlson, C. (1997). Gender differences in ADHS: A meta-analysis and critical review. *Journal of the American Academy of Child & Adolescent Psychiatry, 36,* 1036–1045.

Gilliland, F. D., Berhane, K., Li, Y. F., Rappaport, E. B., & Peters, J. M. (2002). Effects of early onset asthma and in utero exposure to maternal smoking on childhood lung function. *American Journal of Respiratory Critical Care Medicine, 167*(6), 917–924.

Goldberg, E. (1994). Including chidren with chronic health conditions: Nebulizers in the classroom. *Young Children, 49*(2), 34–37.

Grabeel, J. (1997). A health care plan for the student with diabetes. *Journal of School Nursing, 13*(2), 30–34.

Green, H. L., Diaz-Gonzalez de Ferris, M. E., Vasquez, E., Lau, E. M., & Yusim, J. (2002). Caring for the child with fetal alcohol syndrome. *Journal of Alcohol Abuse and Prevention Association, 15*(6), 37–40.

Harwood, M., & Kleinfeld, J. S. (2002). Up front, in hope: The value of early intervention for children with fetal alcohol syndrome. *Young Children, 57*(4), 86–90.

Ilardi, D. (2003). Obesity: the widening issue we can't ignore. *School Nurse News, 20*(1), 21, 23, 25.

Johnson, C. L., & Lapadat, J. C. (2000). Parallels between learning disabilities and fetal alcohol syndrome/effect: No need to reinvent the wheel. *Exceptionality Education Canada, 10*(3), 65–81.

Knehans, A. W. (2002). Childhood obesity: why is this happening to our children? *Journal of the Oklahoma State Medical Association, 95*(8), 539–544.

Lanphear, B. P., Dietrich, K. N., & Berger, O. (2003). Prevention of lead toxicity in US children. *Ambulatory Pediatrics, 3*(1), 27–33.

Lanphear, B. P., Succop, P., Roda, S., & Henningsen, G. (2003). The effect of soil abatement on blood lead levels in children living near a former smelting and milling operation. *Public Health Report, 118*(2), 83–91.

Lierl, M. B., & Hornung, R. W. (2003). Relationship of outdoor air quality to pediatric asthma exacerbations. *Annual Allergy & Asthma Immunology, 90*(1), 28–33.

Mailick, M., Holden, G., & Walther, V. (1994). Coping with childhood asthma: Caretaker's view. *Health & Social Work, 19*(2), 103–108.

Marks, M. (1983). Recognition of the allergic child at school: Visual and auditory signs. *Journal of School Health, 44*(5), 227–235.

McBrien, D. M., & Bonthius, D. J. (2000). Seizures in infants and young children. *Infants and Young Children, 13*(2), 21–31.

Miller, S. T., Wright, E., Abboud, M., Berman, B., Files, B., Scher, C. D., Styles, L., & Adams, R. J. (2001). Impact of chronic transfusion on incidence of pain and acute chest syndrome during the Stroke Prevention Trial (STOP) in sickle-cell anemia. *Journal of Pediatrics, 139*(6), 785–789.

Mokdad, A. H., Ford, E. S., Bowman, B. A., Dietz, W. H., Vinicor, F., Bales, V. S., & Marks, J. S. (2003). Prevalence of obesity, diabetes, and obesity-related health risk factors, 2001. *JAMA, 289*(1), 76–79.

National Institutes of Health. (2003). Eczema. Accessed on June 10, 2003, from http://www.niams.nih.gov/hi/topics/dermatitis

Neugut, A. I., Ghatak, A. T., & Miller, R. L. (2001). Anaphylaxis in the United States: an investigation into its epidemiology. *Archives of Internal Medicine, 161*(1), 15–21.

O'Connor, E. M. (2001, December). Medicating ADHD: Too much? Too soon? *APA Monitor, 32*(11), 11–15.

Palermo, T. M., Schwartz, L., Drotar, D., & McGowan, K. (2002). Parental report of health-related quality of life in children with sickle cell disease. *Journal of Behavior Medicine, 25*(3), 269–283.

Parr, J. R., Ward, A., & Inman, S. (2003). Current practice in the management of Attention Deficit Disorder with Hyperactivity (ADHD). *Child Care Health & Development, 29*(3), 215–218.

Piomelli, S. (2002). Childhood lead poisoning. *Pediatric Clinics of North America, 49*(6), 1285–1304.

Project CHOICES Intervention Research Group. (2003). Reducing the risk of alcohol-exposed pregnancies: a study of a motivational intervention in community settings. *Pediatrics, 111*, 1131–1135.

Ramey, C., & Ramey, S. (1998). Early intervention and early experience. *American Psychologist, 53*, 109–120.

Rodriguez, M. A., Winkleby, M. A., Ahn, D., Sundquist, J., & Kraemer, H. C. (2002). Identification of population subgroups of children and adolescents with high asthma prevalence: findings from the Third National Health and Nutrition Examination Survey. *Archives of Pediatric & Adolescent Medicine, 156*(3), 269–275.

Ross, M. A., Persky, V. W., Scheff, P. A., Chung, J., Curtis, L., Ramakrishnan, V., Wadden, R. A.., & Hryhorczuk, D. O. (2002). Effect of ozone and aeroallergens on the respiratory health of asthmatics. *Archives of Environmental Health, 57*(6), 568–578.

Schachar, R., Jadad, A. R., Gauld, M., Boyle, M., Booker, L., Snider, A., Kim, M., & Cunningham, C. (2002). Attention-deficit hyperactivity disorder: Critical appraisal of extended treatment studies. *Canadian Journal of Psychiatry, 47*(4), 337–348.

Selekman, J. (2002). Attention-deficit/hyperactivity disorder. *Journal of School Nursing, 18*(5), 270–276.

Shipley, T. E. (2002). Child care centers and children with special needs: Rights under the Americans with Disabilities Act and Section 504 of the Rehabilitation Act. *Journal of Law & Education, 31*(3), 327–349.

Sicherer, S. H., Forman, J. A., & Noone, S. A. (2000). Use assessment of self-administered epinephrine among food-allergic children and pediatricians. *Pediatrics, 105*(2), 359–362.

Simon, J. A., & Hudes, E. S. (1999). Relationship of ascorbic acid to blood levels. *JAMA, 272*, 277–283.

Steinberg, M. H., Barton, F., Castro, O., Pegelow, C. H., Ballas, S. K., Kutlar, A., Orringer, E., Bellevue, R., Olivieri, N., Eckman, J., Varma, M., Ramirez, G., Adler, B., Smith, W., Carlos, T., Ataga, K., DeCastro, L., Bigelow, C., Saunthararajah, Y., Telfer, M., Vichinsky, E., Claster, S., Shurin, S., Bridges, K., Waclawiw, M., Bonds, D., & Terrin, M. (2003). Effect of hydroxyurea on mortality and morbidity in adult sickle cell anemia: risks and benefits up to 9 years of treatment. *JAMA, 289*(13), 1645–1651.

Stephenson, J. (2002). CDC report on environmental toxins: some progress, some concerns. *JAMA, 289*(10), 1230, 1233.

Streissbuth, A. P., Bookstein, F. L., & Barr, H. M. (1996). A dose-response study of the enduring effects of prenatal alcohol exposure: Birth to 14 years. In J. L. Spohr & H. C. Steinhausen (Eds.). *Alcohol, prenancy and the developing child* (pp. 144–168). New York: Cambridge University Press.

Su, M., Barrueto , F., & Hoffman, R. S. (2002). Childhood lead poisoning from paint chips: a continuing problem. *Journal of Urban Health, 79*(4), 491–501.

Thompson, R. J., Gustafson, K. E., Bonner, M. J., & Ware, R. E. (2002). Neurocognitive development of young children with sickle cell disease through three years of age. *Journal of Pediatric Psychology, 27*(3), 235–244.

Trahms, C. M. & Pipes, P. L. (2000). *Nutrition in infancy and childhood.* Columbus, OH: McGraw-Hill.

Webster-Stratton, C., Reid, J., & Hammond, M. (2001). Social skills and problem-solving training for children with early-onset conduct problems: who benefits? *Journal of Child Psychology & Psychiatry, 42*(7), 943–952.

Wong, D. (2001). *Wong's Essentials of Pediatric Nursing.* (6th ed.). St. Louis: Mosby.

Wright, R. O., Tsaih, S. W., Schwartz, J., Wright, R. J., & Hu, H. (2003, January). Association between iron deficiency and blood lead level in a longitudinal analysis of children followed in an urban primay care clinic. *Journal of Pediatrics, 142*(1), 9–14.

ADDITIONAL READING

Amr, S., Bollinger, M. E., Myers, M., Hamilton, R. G., Weiss, S. R., Rossman, M., Osborne, L., Timmins, S., Kimes, D. S., Levine, E. R., & Blaisdell, C. J. (2003). Environmental allergens and asthma in urban elementary schools. *Annuals of Allergy & Asthma Immunology, 90*(1), 34–44.

Arbes, S. J., Cohn, R. D., Yin, M., Muilenberg, M. L., Burge, H. A., Friedman, W., Zeldin, D. C. (2003). House dust mite allergen in U.S. beds: results from the First National Survey of Lead and Allergens in Housing. *Journal of Allergy & Clinical Immunology, 111*(2), 408–414.

Cowley, G. (2003, February 17). Getting the lead out. *Newsweek, 141*(7), 54–56.

Cunningham, C. E., & Boyle, M. H. (2002). Preschoolers at risk for attention-deficit hyperactivity disorder and oppositional defiant disorder: family, parenting, and behavioral correlates. *Journal of Abnormal Child Psychology, 30*(6), 555–569.

Gaudreau, J. M. (2000). The challenge of making the school environment safe for children with food allergies. *Journal of School Nursing, 16*(2), 5–10.

Glass, J. (1999, April). Breathing easy. *Parents,* 140–148.

Haslam, R., & Valletutti, P. (2004). *Medical problems in the classroom* (4th ed.). Austin, TX: ProEd Press.

Liu, A. H. (2002). Early intervention for asthma prevention in children. *Allergy & Asthma Proceedings, 23*(5), 289–293.

Liu, A. H., & Szefler, S. J. (2003). Advances in childhood asthma: hygiene hypothesis, natural history, and management. *Journal of Allergy & Clinical Immunology, 111*(3 Suppl), S785–792.

Mazur, L. J. (2003). Pediatric environmental health. *Current Problems in Pediatric & Adolescent Health Care, 33*(1), 6–25.

McCall, B. P., Horwitz, I. B., Kammeyer-Mueller, J. D. (2003). Have health conditions associated with latex increased since the issuance of universal precautions? *American Journal of Public Health, 93*(4), 599–604.

NAEYC. (1997). *Model child care health policies.* Washington, DC: Pennsylvania Chapter of American Academy of Pediatrics.

National Institutes of Health. (1993). Early identification of hearing impairment in infants and young children. *NIH Consensus Statement, 11*(1), 1–25.

Presler, B., & Routt, M. L. (1997). Inclusion of children with special health care needs in early childhood programs. *Dimensions of Early Childhood, 23*(3), 26–31.

Striph, K. (1995). Prevalence of lead poisoning in a suburban practice. *Journal of Family Practice, 41*(1): 65–70.

Video Resource: *Type I Diabetes in Children: A Passport to Knowledge.* [CD-ROM]. Available from EDRS.; Savvy Knowledge Systems Corp., #701, 550-11 Avenue, Calgary Alberta T2R 1M7, Canada. Tel: 403-264-7224; Tel: 800-230-5593 (Toll-Free); Fax: 403-264-7224; Web site: http;//www.savvyknowledge.com.

Waldron, K. A. (1996). *Introduction to special education: The inclusive classroom.* Albany, NY: Delmar.

Yoshinaga-Itano, C. (1995). Universal hearing screening for infants: Simple, risk-free, beneficial, and justified. *Audiology Today, 7*(1), 13.

Zametkin, A. (1999). Current concepts: Problems in the management of attention-deficit hyperactivity disorder. *New England Journal of Medicine, 340,* 40–46.

HELPFUL WEB SITES

American Diabetes Association	http://www.diabetes.org
American Lung Association	http://www.lungusa.org
Canadian Pediatric Society	http://www.cps.ca/
Centers for Disease Control and Prevention	http://www.cdc.gov/nccdphp/ddt/tcoyd
Children with Diabetes	http://www.kwd.org
Indian Health Service	http://www.ihs.gov
Kids Health–Nemours Center for Children's Health Media	http://www.kidshealth.org
National Diabetes Information Clearinghouse	http://www.niddk.nih.gov/brochures

For additional health, safety, and nutrition resources, go to
http://www.EarlyChildEd.delmar.com

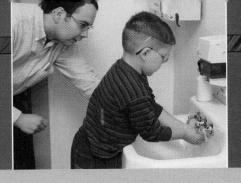

CHAPTER 6

The Infectious Process and Effective Control

Young children, especially those under three years of age, are highly susceptible to communicable illness (Slack-Smith, Reed & Stanley, 2002). Frequent upper respiratory infections are common, especially during a child's first experiences in group care (Bradley, 2003). Several factors may contribute to this increased risk. First, children with limited exposure to groups of children have had fewer opportunities to encounter illness and, thus, to build up **antibodies** for protection. This lowered immunity makes young children more vulnerable to germs that cause communicable and acute illnesses. Chronic illness and physical disabilities also increase children's susceptibility to infections.

Second, immature development of body structures contributes to a higher rate of illness. For example, shorter distances between an infant's or toddler's ears, nose, and throat encourage frequent respiratory infections.

Third, group-care settings, such as preschools, early education centers and homes, and elementary schools are conducive to the transfer of illness. However, children are also exposed to

---

antibodies – *special substances produced by the body that help protect against disease.*

FIGURE 6–1

Mouthing of toys contributes to the spread of communicable illness.

communicable illnesses in many other places, including grocery stores, shopping centers, churches, libraries, and restaurants. Many of children's habits, such as sucking on fingers, mouthing toys, carelessness with bodily secretions (runny noses, drool, urine, stool), and lots of physical contact encourage the rapid spread of communicable illness (Figure 6–1). For this reason, every attempt must be made to establish and implement policies, practices, and educational programs that will protect young children from unnecessary exposure.

COMMUNICABLE ILLNESS

A **communicable** illness is an illness that can be transmitted or spread from one person or animal to another. Three factors, all of which must be present at approximately the same time, are required for this process to occur (Figure 6–2).

- a pathogen
- a susceptible host
- a method of transmission

First, a **pathogen** or disease-causing agent, such as a bacteria, virus, or parasite, must be present and available for transmission. These invisible germs are specific for each illness and are most commonly located in discharges from the respiratory (nose, throat, lungs) and intestinal tract of infected persons. They can also be found in the blood, urine, and discharges from the eyes and

---

communicable – *a condition that can be spread or transmitted from one individual to another.*
pathogen – *a microorganism capable of producing illness or infection.*

FIGURE 6–2

Key components required for the spread of a communicable illness.

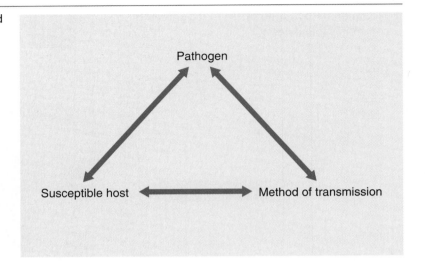

skin. Most pathogens require a living host for their survival. One exception, however, is the organism that causes tetanus; it can survive in soil and dust for several years.

Second, there must be a **susceptible host** or person who can become infected with the pathogen. The types of communicable illnesses experienced most often by young children generally enter their new host through either a break in the skin, the **respiratory tract**, or digestive tract. The route of entry depends on the specific illness or disease involved.

Not every child who is exposed to a particular virus or bacteria will become infected. Conditions must be favorable to allow an infectious organism to successfully avoid the body's defense systems, multiply, and establish itself. Children who are well rested, adequately nourished, **immunized**, and in a good state of health are generally less susceptible to communicable illnesses. Also, a previous case of the same illness may provide protection against additional infection. However, the length of this protection varies with the illness and can range from several days to a lifetime. Children who experience a very mild or subclinical case of an illness or who are carriers of an infection are often resistant to the illness without realizing that they have actually experienced it.

Third, a method for transmitting the infectious agent from the original source to a new host is necessary to complete the communicable process (Figure 6–2). One of the most common modes of transmitting infectious agents in early education settings involves **airborne transmission**. Disease-causing pathogens are carried on tiny droplets of moisture that are expelled during coughs, sneezes, or while talking (Figure 6–3). Influenza, colds, meningitis, tuberculosis, and chickenpox are examples of infectious illnesses spread in this manner.

Fecal-oral transmission is the second most common route by which infectious illnesses are spread in early education settings, particularly when there are infants and toddlers in diapers. Teachers who fail to wash their hands properly after changing diapers or helping children with

---

susceptible host – *an individual who is capable of being infected by a pathogen.*
respiratory tract – *pertains to, and includes, the nose, throat, trachea, and lungs.*
immunized – *a state of becoming resistant to a specific disease through the introduction of living or dead microorganisms into the body, which then stimulates the production of antibodies.*
airborne transmission – *when germs are expelled into the air through coughs/sneezes, and transmitted to another individual via tiny moisture drops.*
fecal-oral transmission – *when germs are transferred to the mouth via hands contaminated with fecal material.*

FIGURE 6–3

Common methods for the spread of communicable illness.

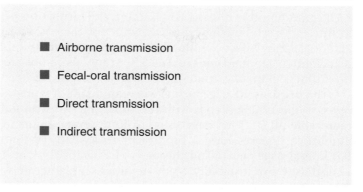

- ■ Airborne transmission
- ■ Fecal-oral transmission
- ■ Direct transmission
- ■ Indirect transmission

toileting needs are often responsible for spreading disease-causing germs, especially if they also handle food. For this reason, it is advisable to assign diaper changing and food preparation responsibilities to different teachers. It is also critical to wash children's hands after diaper changes or using the bathroom because their hands often end up in their mouths. Pinworms, hepatitis A, salmonella, and giardiasis are examples of illnesses transmitted by fecal-oral contamination.

A third common method of transmission involves direct contact with body fluids, such as blood or mucous, or an area of infection on another individual. The infectious organisms are transferred directly from the original source of infection to a new host. Ringworm, athlete's foot, impetigo, Hepatitis B, and conjunctivitis are some of the conditions spread in this manner.

Communicable illnesses can also be transmitted through indirect contact. This method involves the transfer of infectious organisms from an infected individual to an intermediate object, such as water, milk, dust, food, toys, towels, eating utensils, animals, or insects, and finally to the new susceptible host. Recent studies suggest that it may be possible to infect oneself with certain viruses, such as those causing colds and influenza, by touching the moist linings of the eyes and nose with contaminated hands.

The absence of any one of these factors (pathogen, host, or method of transmission) will prevent the spread of communicable illness. This is an important concept for teachers to remember when trying to control outbreaks of communicable illness in group settings. It also lessens the risk of teachers carrying illnesses home to their families.

STAGES OF ILLNESS

Communicable illnesses generally develop in predictable stages:

- incubation
- prodromal
- acute
- convalescence

Since many of these stages overlap, it can be difficult to identify when each begins and ends.

The **incubation** stage includes the time between exposure to a pathogen and the appearance of the first signs or symptoms of illness. During this period, the infectious organisms enter the

---

incubation – *the interval of time between exposure to infection and the appearance of the first signs or symptoms of illness.*

body and multiply rapidly in an attempt to overpower the body's defense systems and establish themselves. The length of the incubation stage is described in terms of hours or days and varies for each communicable disease. For example, the incubation period for chickenpox ranges from two to three weeks following exposure, while for the common cold it is thought to be only 12 to 72 hours. Many infectious illnesses are already communicable near the end of this stage. The fact that children are often **contagious** before any symptoms are apparent makes the control of infectious illness in the classroom more difficult, despite teachers' careful observations.

The **prodromal** stage begins when an infant or young child experiences the first nonspecific signs of infection and ends with the appearance of symptoms characteristic of a particular communicable illness. This stage may last from several hours to several days. However, not all communicable diseases have a prodromal stage. Early symptoms commonly associated with the prodromal stage may include headache, low-grade fever, a slight sore throat, and a general feeling of restlessness or irritability. Many of these complaints are so vague that they often go unnoticed. However, because children are highly contagious during this stage, teachers and parents must learn to recognize that these subtle changes may signal impending illness.

During the **acute** stage an infant or child is definitely sick. This stage is marked by the onset of symptoms that are typical of the specific communicable illness. Some of these symptoms such as fever, sore throat, cough, runny nose, rash, or enlarged lymph glands are common to many infectious diseases. However, there are also characteristic patterns and variations of these symptoms that can be used to identify a specific communicable illness. An infant or child continues to be highly contagious throughout this stage.

The **convalescent** or recovery stage generally follows automatically unless complications develop. During this stage, symptoms gradually disappear, the child begins to feel better, and usually he or she is no longer contagious.

CONTROL MEASURES

Teachers have an obligation and responsibility to help protect young children from communicable illnesses. Classrooms, early education centers, and homes are ideal settings for the rapid spread of many infectious conditions. However, many practical control measures can be implemented in these settings to reduce the incidence of illness.

Observations

Teachers' daily health observations can be effective for identifying children in the early stages of a communicable illness. By removing sick children from group settings, a direct source of infection can be eliminated. However, because many illnesses are communicable before actual symptoms appear, not all spread can be avoided. Early recognition of sick children requires that adults develop a sensitivity to changes in children's normal appearance and behavior patterns (Aronson, 2002). This process is facilitated by the fact that young children generally look and behave

---

contagious – *capable of being transmitted or passed from one person to another.*
prodromal – *the appearance of the first nonspecific signs of infection; this stage ends when the symptoms characteristic of a particular communicable illness begin to appear.*
acute – *the stage of an illness or disease during which an individual is definitely sick and exhibits symptoms characteristic of the particular illness or disease involved.*
convalescent – *the stage of recovery from an illness or disease.*

○ **REFLECTIVE THOUGHTS**

Outbreaks of communicable illnesses such as colds, flu, and head lice are common in settings where there are groups of young children. Explain why this occurs. Why is it important for teachers to understand the infectious process? What resources are available to teachers and parents for improving their understanding of various childhood illnesses?

differently when they are not feeling well. Their actions, facial expressions, skin color, sleep habits, appetite, and comments provide valuable warnings of impending illness and may include:

- unusually pale or flushed skin
- red or sore throat
- enlarged **lymph glands**
- nausea, vomiting, or diarrhea
- rash, spots, or open lesions
- watery or red eyes
- headache or dizziness
- chills, fever, or achiness
- fatigue or loss of appetite

It is also important to be alert to signs of illness during certain seasons of the year when some illnesses are more prevalent, or whenever there is known outbreak in the community.

However, these same signs and symptoms may not always warrant concern in all children. For example, a teacher who knows that Tony's allergies often cause a red throat and cough in the fall, or that Shadra's recent irritability is probably related to her mother's hospitalization, would not be alarmed by these observations. Teachers must be able to distinguish between children with potentially infectious illnesses and those with health problems that are explainable and not necessarily contagious.

Policies

Written policies offer another important method for controlling infectious illnesses (Richardson, Elliman, Macguire, Simpson, & Nicoll, 2001). Policies should be consistent with state regulations, and in place before a program begins to enroll children. Frequent review of policies with staff members assures their familiarity with the information, and that enforcement will be more consistent.

General health and exclusion policies should also be included in parent handbooks and given to parents when children are accepted into a program. This lets parents know in advance what to expect if their child becomes ill and helps build strong partnerships with parents. Exclusion and inclusion policies provide parents and teachers with clear guidelines to follow when deciding if children should be kept home because of illness, and when they are well enough to return (Figure 6–4).

Opinions differ on how restrictive exclusion policies should be (Lucarelli, 2002). Some experts believe that children with mild illnesses can remain in group care, while others feel that children exhibiting symptoms should not attend. Because many early signs of communicable illnesses are similar, it is often difficult for teachers to distinguish between conditions that warrant exclusion and medical attention and those that involve only mild infections. Consequently, early

---

lymph glands – *specialized groupings of tissue that produce and store white blood cells for protection against infection and illness.*

FIGURE 6–4

Sample exclusion policy.

> ## EXCLUSION POLICY
>
> Control of communicable illness among the children is a prime concern. Policies and guidelines related to outbreaks of communicable illness in this center have been developed with the help of the health department and local pediatricians. In order to protect the entire group of children, as well as your own child, we ask that parents assist us by keeping sick children at home if the have experienced any of the following symptoms *within the past 24 hours:*
>
> - a fever over 100°F (37.8°C) orally or 99°F (37.2°C) axillary (under the arm)
> - signs of a newly developing cold or uncontrollable coughing
> - diarrhea, vomiting, or an upset stomach
> - unusual or unexplained loss of appetite, fatigue, irritability, or headache
> - any discharge or drainage from eyes, nose, ears, or open sores
>
> Children who become ill with any of these symptoms will be returned home. We appreciate your cooperation with this policy. If you have any questions about whether or not your child is well enough to attend school or group care that day, please call the center *before* bringing your child.

education programs may decide to set exclusion policies that are fairly restrictive unless they are set up to care for sick children.

It is also important for programs to adopt policies for notifying parents when children are exposed to communicable illnesses. This measure enables parents to watch for early symptoms and to keep sick children home (Figure 6–5). Immunization requirements should also be addressed in program policies, as well as actions the program will take if children are not in compliance. Local

FIGURE 6–5

Sample letter to parents indicating their child has possibly been exposed to a communicable disease.

> Date_____
>
> Dear Parent:
>
> There is a possibility that your child has been exposed to chickenpox. If your child has not had chickenpox, observe carefully from _____ to _____ (more likely the first part of this period), for signs of a slight cold, runny nose, loss of appetitie, fever, listlessness, and/or irritability. Within a day or two, watch for a spot (or spots) resembling mosquito bites on which a small blister soon forms. Chickenpox is contagious 24–48 hours before the rash appears. Children who develop chickenpox may return when all pox are covered by a dry scab (about 5 or 6 days).
>
> If you have any questions, please call the Center before bringing your child. We appreciate your cooperation in helping us keep incidences of illness to a minimum.

public health authorities can offer much useful information and assistance to programs when they are formulating new policies or are confronted with a communicable health problem about which they are unsure.

Guidelines for Teacher Illness. Teachers are exposed to many infectious illnesses through their daily contact with young children. Often, they experience an increased incidence of illness, especially during the initial months of employment, that is similar to when young children begin group care. This resistance tends to improve over time. Completing a pre-employment health assessment, having a tuberculin test, and updating immunizations are some of the precautionary measures teachers can take to minimize their risk of illness. However, practicing good handwashing always offers the most effective protection. Teachers who are pregnant may want to reconsider their position since some communicable illnesses, such as Cytomegalovirus (CMV) and German measles can affect the fetus, especially during the early months.

When teachers do become ill, it is important for them to follow the same exclusion guidelines established by the center with regard to sick children when deciding whether or not to come to work. Adults who do not feel well will find it difficult to meet the rigorous demands of caring for children and will run an increased risk of sustaining injury. Programs should maintain a list of available substitute teachers so that staff members do not feel pressured to work when they are ill.

Administration of Medication. The administration of medicine to young children is a responsibility that should always be taken seriously (Table 6–1). Policies and procedures for the administration of prescription and nonprescription medications, including ointments and creams, eye, ear, and nose drops, cough syrups, baby aspirin, inhalers, and nebulizer breathing treatments should be developed carefully in accordance with state licensing regulations to safeguard children, as well as teaching staff. These policies and procedures should be in writing, familiar to all staff members, filed in an accessible location, and distributed to every parent (Figure 6–6).

When children are enrolled in part times programs, parents may be able to alter medication schedules and administer prescribed medications at times when childeren are home. However, this option is not feasible for the majority of children enrolled in full-day programs. In these instances parents will need to make prior arrangements to have the child's teachers administer prescribed medication.

Medication should never be administered by a teacher without the written consent of the child's parent and written direction of a licensed physician. The label on a prescription drug is considered an acceptable directive from the physician. In the case of nonprescription medicines, parents should obtain written instructions from the physician stating the child's name, the medication to be given, the dose, frequency it is to be administered, and any special precautions that may be necessary. There are risks associated with giving children over-the-counter medications that have not been authorized by a physician. Thus, to protect themselves from possible liability, teachers should not assume these risks. It is the physician's professional and legal responsibility to determine the type and exact dosage of a medication that is appropriate for an individual child.

Immunization

Immunization offers permanent protection against all preventable childhood diseases, including diphtheria, tetanus, whooping cough, polio, measles, mumps, rubella, Haemophilus influenza, and chickenpox (Luman, McCauley, Stokley, Chu & Pickering, 2002). Yet, despite several large-scale national, state, and local campaigns, many children still are not fully immunized. At present, it is estimated that only 77 percent of children have received all of the recommended age-appropriate immunizations (National Center for Health Statistics, 2002). Thus, a major goal of the *Healthy People 2010* initiative is to increase this rate to 90 percent by the year 2010 (U.S. Department of Health & Human Services, 2000).

Why are some parents so seemingly unconcerned about obtaining immunizations for their children? Perhaps they do not realize how life threatening some communicable illnesses still are.

TABLE 6–1 Guidelines for Administering Medications to Children

1. Be honest when giving young children medication! Do not use force or attempt to trick children into believing that medicines are candy. Instead, use the opportunity to help children understand the relationship between taking a medication and recovering from an illness or infection. Also, acknowledge the fact that the taste of medicine may be disagreeable or a treatment may be somewhat unpleasant; offer a small sip of juice or cracker to eliminate an unpleasant taste or read a favorite story as a reward for cooperating.
2. Designate one individual to accept medication from parents and administer it to children; this could be the director or the head teacher. This step will help minimize the opportunity for errors, such as omitting a dose or giving a dose twice.
3. When medication is accepted from a parent, it should be in the original container, labeled with the child's name, name of the drug, and include directions for the exact amount and frequency the medication is to be given.

   Caution: NEVER give medicine from a container that has been prescribed for another individual.

4. Store all medicines in a locked cabinet. If it is necessary to refrigerate a medication, place it in a locked box and store on a top shelf in the refrigerator.
5. Be sure to wash your hands before and after administering medication.
6. Concentrate on what you are doing and do not talk with anyone until you are finished.
   a. Read the label on the bottle or container three times:
      * when removing it from the locked cabinet
      * before pouring it from the container
      * after pouring it from the container
   b. Administer medication on time, and give *only* the amount prescribed.
   c. Be sure you have the correct child! If the child is old enough to talk, ask "What is your name?" and let the child state his/her name.
7. Record and maintain a permanent record of each dose of medicine that is administered (Figure 6–6). Include the:
   * date and time the medicine was given
   * name of the teacher administering the medication
   * dose of medication given
   * any unusual physical changes or behaviors observed after the medicine was administered.
8. Inform parents of the dosage(s) and time medication was given, as well as any unusual reactions that may have occurred.
9. NOTE: Adults should never take any medication in front of children.

Others may believe these diseases have been eliminated and are, therefore, no longer anything to worry about. Some parents have also expressed concern about the number of recommended immunizations and possible side effects associated with some vaccines (Hobson, 2003; Kimmel, 2002; Halsey, 2001). Also, the convenience of modern medicines has created a general complacency about serious infections and disease in general.

Most states require children's immunizations to be current when they enter early care and education programs. In states where no immunization laws exist, teachers must insist on complete immunization of every child unless parents are opposed on religious or medical grounds (Salmon, Harber, & Cangarosa, 1999). At the same time, teachers must continue to support legislation establishing minimal immunization requirements at the state level.

The human body produces protective substances, called antibodies, whenever organisms are introduced by an infectious illness or vaccine. Babies are born with limited immunity, acquired from their mothers, to some communicable illnesses. However, this maternal protection is only temporary and, therefore, the immunization process must be started early in a baby's life. Table 6–2 shows

FIGURE 6–6

Sample medication record.

Download this form online at http://www.Early ChildEd.del mar.com

ADMINISTRATION OF MEDICATION FORM

Child's name _____

Prescription number _____

Date of prescription _____

Doctor prescribing medicine _____

Medication being given for _____

Time medication is to be given by staff _____

Time medication last given by parent _____

Amount to be given at each time (dosage) _____

....

I, _____ give my permission for the staff to administer the above prescription medication (according to the above guidelines) to _____
_____ . I understand that the staff cannot be held
　　　　　　(child's name)

responsible for allergic reactions or other complications resulting from administration of the above medication given according to the directions.

Signed _____
　　　　　　　　(parent or guardian)

Date _____

....

Staff Record

Name of staff accepting medication and form _____

Is medication in its original container? _____

Is original label intact? _____

Is there written permission from the doctor attached (or the original prescription)? _____

Signature of accepting staff _____

....

Administration Record

DATE	TIME	AMOUNT GIVEN	STAFF ADMINISTERING	INITIALS

TABLE 6-2 Recommended Childhood and Adolescent Immunization Schedule—United States, 2003

Legend: range of recommended ages | catch-up vaccination | preadolescent assessment

Vaccine ▼ / Age ▶	Birth	1 mo	2 mos	4 mos	6 mos	12 mos	15 mos	18 mos	24 mos	4-6 yrs	11-12 yrs	13-18 yrs
Hepatitis B[1]	HepB #1 only if mother HBsAg (-)		HepB #2		HepB #3						HepB series	
Diphtheria, Tetanus, Pertussis[2]			DTaP	DTaP	DTaP			DTaP		DTaP	Td	Td
Haemophilus influenzae Type b[3]			Hib	Hib	Hib	Hib						
Inactivated Polio			IPV	IPV	IPV					IPV		
Measles, Mumps, Rubella[4]						MMR #1				MMR #2	MMR #2	
Varicella[5]						Varicella					Varicella	
Pneumococcal[6]			PCV	PCV	PCV	PCV				PCV	PPV	
Hepatitis A[7]										Hepatitis A series		
Influenzae[8]					Influenza (yearly)							

Vaccines below this line are for selected populations

This schedule indicates the recommended ages for routine administration of currently licensed childhood vaccines, as of December 1, 2002, for children through age 18 years. Any dose not given at the recommended age should be given at any subsequent visit when indicated and feasible. ■ Indicates age groups that warrant special effort to administer those vaccines not previously given. Additional vaccines may be licensed and recommended during the year. Licensed combination vaccines may be used whenever any components of the combination are indicated and the vaccine's other components are not contraindicated. Providers should consult the manufacturers' package inserts for detailed recommendations.

1. Hepatitis B vaccine (HepB). All infants should receive the first dose of hepatitis B vaccine soon after birth and before hospital discharge; the first dose may also be given by age 2 months if the infant's mother is HBsAg-negative. Only monovalent HepB can be used for the birth dose. Monovalent or combination vaccine containing HepB may be used to complete the series. Four doses of vaccine may be administered when a birth dose is given. The second dose should be given at least 4 weeks after the first dose, except for combination vaccines which cannot be administered before age 6 weeks. The third dose should be given at least 16 weeks after the first dose and at least 8 weeks after the second dose. The last dose in the vaccination series (third or fourth dose) should not be administered before age 6 months.

Infants born to HBsAg-positive mothers should receive HepB and 0.5 mL Hepatitis B Immune Globulin (HBIG) within 12 hours of birth at separate sites. The second dose is recommended at age 1–2 months. The last dose in the vaccination series should not be administered before age 6 months. These infants should be tested for HBsAg and anti-HBs at 9–15 months of age.

Infants born to mothers whose HBsAg status is unknown should receive the first dose of the HepB series within 12 hours of birth. Maternal blood should be drawn as soon as possible to determine the mother's HBsAg status; if the HBsAg test is positive, the infant should receive HBIG as soon as possible (no later than age 1 week). The second dose is recommended at age 1–2 months. The last dose in the vaccination series should not be administered before age 6 months.

2. Diphtheria and tetanus toxoids and acellular pertussis vaccine (DTaP). The fourth dose of DTaP may be administered as early as age 12 months, provided 6 months have elapsed since the third dose and the child is unlikely to return at age 15–18 months. **Tetanus and diphtheria toxoids (Td)** is recommended at age 11–12 years if at least 5 years have elapsed since the last dose of tetanus and diphtheria toxoid-containing vaccine. Subsequent routine Td boosters are recommended every 10 years.

3. *Haemophilus influenzae* type b (Hib) conjugate vaccine. Three Hib conjugate vaccines are licensed for infant use. If PRP-OMP (PedvaxHIB® or ComVax® [Merck]) is administered at ages 2 and 4 months, a dose at age 6 months is not required. DTaP/Hib combination products should not be used for primary immunization in infants at ages 2, 4 or 6 months, but can be used as boosters following any Hib vaccine.

4. Measles, mumps, and rubella vaccine (MMR). The second dose of MMR is recommended routinely at age 4–6 years but may be administered during any visit, provided at least 4 weeks have elapsed since the first dose and that both doses are administered beginning at or after age 12 months. Those who have not previously received the second dose should complete the schedule by the 11–12 year old visit.

5. Varicella vaccine. Varicella vaccine is recommended at any visit at or after age 12 months for susceptible children, i.e. those who lack a reliable history of chickenpox. Susceptible persons aged ≥13 years should receive two doses, given at least 4 weeks apart.

6. Pneumococcal vaccine. The heptavalent **pneumococcal conjugate vaccine (PCV)** is recommended for all children age 2–23 months. It is also recommended for certain children age 24–59 months. **Pneumococcal polysaccharide vaccine (PPV)** is recommended in addition to PCV for certain high-risk groups. See *MMWR* 2000;49(RR-9);1–38.

7. Hepatitis A vaccine. Hepatitis A vaccine is recommended for children and adolescents in selected states and regions, and for certain high-risk groups; consult your local public health authority. Children and adolescents in these states, regions, and high risk groups who have not been immunized against hepatitis A can begin the hepatitis A vaccination series during any visit. The two doses in the series should be administered at least 6 months apart. See *MMWR* 1999;48(RR-12);1–37.

8. Influenza vaccine. Influenza vaccine is recommended annually for children age ≥6 months with certain risk factors (including but not limited to asthma, cardiac disease, sickle cell disease, HIV, diabetes, and household members of persons in groups at high risk; see *MMWR* 2002;51(RR-3);1–31), and can be administered to all others wishing to obtain immunity. In addition, healthy children age 6–23 months are encouraged to receive influenza vaccine if feasible because children in this age group are at substantially increased risk for influenza-related hospitalizations. Children aged ≤12 years should receive vaccine in a dosage appropriate for their age (0.25 mL if age 6–35 months or 0.5 mL if aged ≥3 years). Children aged ≤8 years who are receiving influenza vaccine for the first time should receive two doses separated by at least 4 weeks.

Approved by the Advisory Committee on Immunization Practices (www.cdc.gov/nip/acip), the American Academy of Pediatrics (www.aap.org), and the American Academy of Family Physicians (www.aafp.org).

For additional information about vaccines, including precautions and contraindications for immunization and vaccine shortages, please visit the National Immunization Program Website at www.cdc.gov/nip or call the National Immunization Information Hotline at 800-232-2522 (English) or 800-232-0233 (Spanish).

ISSUES TO CONSIDER • Childhood Immunizations

The number of young children who are not fully immunized against preventable communicable diseases continues to remain high. Poverty, lack of education, and poor accessibility to medical care are often cited as reasons for noncompliance. In addition, some parents have expressed concern that vaccines can make children sick. Television programs, magazine articles, and word-of-mouth have attempted to link everything from SIDS, HIV/AIDS, arthritis, multiple sclerosis, and autism to childhood vaccines. However, to date, there has been no substantiated evidence that vaccines cause any of these problems (Kimmell, 2002; Rapin, 1997). While minor discomforts, including mild fever, achiness, and pain at the injection site, may occur, vaccines are considered safe. To further improve the safety of immunizing children, the American Academy of Pediatrics has urged physicians to administer the injectable form of polio vaccine (IPV), rather than the oral version (OPV), thus eliminating exposure to the live, but weakened, virus.

- As a teacher, how would you respond to parents who were opposed to immunization because they felt they were unsafe?
- Where could you locate accurate information about the safety of immunizations?
- How would you handle situations where there is conflict between parental beliefs and state regulation?
- On what basis does your state grant exceptions to immunization requirements for children?

the immunization schedule currently recommended by the Center for Disease Control and Protection, the American Academy of Pediatrics (AAP), and the American Academy of Family Physicians (AAFP). Similar recommendations are available for Canadians and children in other countries (Pan American Health Organization, 2003).

Infants and young children, especially those who are in group care, are encouraged to be immunized against Haemophilus influenza Type b (Hib), an upper respiratory infection and common cause of meningitis (see Table 6–2). Newer vaccines for chickenpox (Varicella) and hepatitis B, a viral infection spread through contact with body secretions and feces, are also recommended for children in early childhood settings (Zimmerman, 2003). Immunizations can be obtained from most health care providers, neighborhood clinics, or local health departments where the cost is reduced or often free.

Programs that employ more than one teacher (including aides and substitutes) are required to offer free hepatitis B immunizations to employees during the first 10 days of employment or within 24 hours following exposure to blood or body fluids containing blood (Child Care Law Center, 1994).

Environmental Control

A variety of practices and environmental changes can be used effectively to reduce the spread of communicable illness (Rubino, 2002). Working with young children requires teachers to also take added precautions to protect themselves from unnecessary exposure.

Universal Infection Control Precautions. The U.S. Department of Labor's Occupational Safety and Health Administration (OSHA) is responsible for protecting workers' safety and assuring that environments and practices meet federal standards. Regulations passed by

TABLE 6–3 Universal Precautions for Handling Body Fluids

Whenever handling body fluids or items contaminated with body fluids be sure to:

- Wear disposable latex gloves when you are likely to have contact with blood or other body fluids, e.g., vomitus, urine, feces, or saliva.
- Remove glove by grasping the cuff and pulling it off inside out.
- Wash hands thoroughly (lather for approximately 30 seconds).
- Dispose of contaminated materials properly. Seal soiled clothing in plastic bags to be laundered at home. Dispose of diapers by tying them securely in garbage bags. Place broken glass in a designated container.
- Clean all surfaces with a disinfectant, such as a bleach solution (one tablespoon bleach/one cup water mixed fresh daily).
- Subsidize the cost of hepatitis B immunizations for all employees.

OSHA (1992) were recently amended (2001) and require child care programs (except those without paid employees) to develop and practice **universal infection control precautions** for handling contaminated body fluids (Table 6–3).

In addition, programs must also have a written plan for handling potentially infectious material, provide annual training for employees and maintain records of any exposure (OSHA, 2001; Child Care Law Center, 1994).

The purpose of universal precautions is to protect teachers from accidental exposure to blood borne pathogens, including hepatitis B and HIV/AIDS. All body fluids are considered potentially infectious and, therefore, should be treated in the same manner. Any material that has been contaminated with blood or body fluids that might contain blood, such as urine, feces, saliva, and vomitus, must be handled with caution, regardless of whether or not a child is known to be ill.

Disposable latex gloves should always be accessible to teachers. They must always be worn whenever handling soiled objects or caring for injuries. Gloves should be removed by pulling them off inside out and carefully discarding them after use with an individual child. Good handwashing must follow so as to prevent any spread of infection; wearing gloves does not eliminate the need for washing one's hands. Children's hands and skin should also be washed with soap and running water to remove any blood. Washable objects, such as rugs, pillows or stuffed toys belonging to the center, should be laundered separately from other items. Children's clothing can be rinsed out, sealed in a plastic bag, and sent home to be washed. Bloodstains on surfaces must be wiped up and disinfected with a commercial germicide or mixture of bleach and water (one tablespoon bleach to one cup water).

Handwashing. Handwashing is perhaps the single most effective control measure against the spread of communicable and infectious illness in child care environments (Table 6–4 and Table 6–5) (Aronson, 2002).

Particular attention should also be given to infants and toddlers who are crawling and eating with their hands. Individual washcloths moistened with soap and water or washing children's hands under running water are the methods of choice (Figure 6–7).

---

universal infection control precautions – *special measures taken when handling bodily fluids, including careful hand-washing, wearing latex gloves, disinfecting surfaces, and proper disposal of contaminated objects.*

TABLE 6-4 Times When Handwashing Is Essential

Good handwashing technique should be used:

- upon arrival or return to the care setting
- before handling food or food utensils
- before and after feeding children
- before and after administering medication
- after handling items contaminated with mucus, urine, feces, vomitus or blood
- after personally using the restroom
- after cleaning up from snack, play activities, or handling art materials such as clay and paint

Cleaning. Frequent cleaning of furniture, toys, and surfaces is also effective for limiting the spread of communicable illness (Harkavy, 2002; Aronson, 2001). A solution of one-quarter cup bleach to one gallon of water (or one tablespoon/one quart) can be used to wipe off large play equipment, cribs, sleeping mats, and strollers. Tables, tops of gates, car seats, and crib rails should be scrubbed daily with soap and water and then disinfected. **Note:** *A new bleach solution must be prepared daily to maintain its disinfecting strength.* Changing tables, mats, and potty chairs should be constructed of nonporous materials and free of any tears or cracks for ease of cleaning. They should be disinfected thoroughly after each use with a bleach solution that can be sprayed on and wiped off with paper towels. A stronger bleach solution (one part chlorine bleach to 10 parts water) should be used to disinfect surfaces contaminated with blood or large amounts of urine, stool, or vomitus.

Toys that infants place in their mouths should be removed for cleaning before they are used by another child. Items should be washed with soap and water, rinsed in a bleach solution, and allowed to air-dry. Some toys can be sanitized in the dishwasher. Washable cloth and stuffed objects should be laundered between use by children. Other surfaces, such as tables, gate tops, car seats, and crib rails that children mouth or drool on, should be scrubbed daily with soap and water and disinfected.

TABLE 6-5 Correct Handwashing Technique

Following proper hand washing technique is critical for controlling the spread of infectious illnesses:

- Pull down paper towel.
- Wet hands and lower arms under warm, running water.
- Apply soap and lather hands to loosen dirt and bacteria.
- Rub hands and lower arms vigorously for 20 to 30 seconds. Friction helps to remove microorganisms and dirt. (Encourage children to complete singing the ABC's while rubbing their hands with soap.)
- Pay special attention to rubbing soap on the backs of hands, between fingers, and under nails.
- Rinse hands thoroughly under running water to remove dirt and soap. Keep hands lower than wrists to prevent recontamination. Leave the water running.
- Dry hand and arms carefully with paper towel.
- Use the paper towel to turn off water faucets. (This prevents hands from becoming contaminated again.)
- Open bathroom door with paper towel and discard it in an appropriate receptacle.

FIGURE 6–7

Infants and toddlers should have their hands washed under running water.

Room Arrangements.   Modifications in child care environments can also have a positive effect on the control of communicable illnesses. For example, room temperatures set between 68°–70°F are less favorable for the spread of infectious illnesses and are often more comfortable for children. Their smaller body surfaces make them less sensitive than adults to cooler temperatures.

Rooms should also be well ventilated. Circulating fresh air helps to reduce the concentration of infectious organisms within a given area. Large child care facilities should be equipped with an efficient mechanical ventilating system that is in good operating condition. Doors and windows can be opened for brief periods, even on cold days, to introduce fresh air. Screens should be used to prevent disease-carrying flies and insects from entering. Encouraging children to play outdoors, even in winter, can also improve their resistance to illness.

The humidity level in rooms should also be checked periodically, especially in winter when rooms are heated and there are fewer opportunities to let in fresh air. Extremely warm, dry air increases the chances of respiratory infection by causing the mucous lining of the mouth and nose to become dry and cracked. Moisture can be added to rooms by installing a humidifier in the central heating system. A cool-mist vaporizer can also be used to increase the humidity in individual rooms. (Cool-mist units eliminate the possibility of burns.) These units should be emptied, washed out with soap and water, disinfected, and refilled with fresh distilled water each day to prevent bacterial growth. Plants or small dishes of water placed around a room will also provide increased humidity. However, they will also encourage the growth of mold spores which can aggravate children's allergies and asthma.

The physical arrangement of a classroom can also be an effective method for controlling communicable and infectious illness. Keeping infants and toddlers in an area separate from older children who are toilet-trained can reduce the spread of intestinal illnesses. Surfaces, e.g., floors, walls, counter tops, and furniture should be smooth and easy to clean. Laundry and food preparation areas should be separated from each other as well as from the classrooms. Pedal-operated sinks or infrared-triggered faucets are ideal for encouraging frequent handwashing and avoiding recontamination.

Measures taken to group children and limit the amount of close contact are also desirable. Crowding at tables or in play areas can be avoided by dividing children into smaller groups.

During naptimes, children's rugs, cots, or cribs can be arranged in alternating directions, head to foot, to decrease talking, coughing, and breathing in each other's faces. Provisions should also be made for children to have individual lockers or storage space for personal items, such as blankets, coats, hats, toys, toothbrushes, and combs to reduce the transfer of communicable illnesses.

Several additional areas in children's environments deserve special attention. Sandboxes should be covered to prevent contamination from animal feces. Water tables and wading pools need to be emptied and washed out daily to prevent the spread of communicable illness; a water pH of 7.2–8.2 and chlorine level of 0.4–3.0 parts per million should be maintained in swimming pools at all times (as specified in commercial test kits). Items that children put on their heads, such as hats, wigs, and beauty parlor items can spread head lice and, therefore, may not be appropriate to use in group settings. Play clothes should be washable and laundered often.

Education

Teachers also make a valuable contribution to the control of communicable illness through education. Ongoing classroom instruction on topics such as personal health habits, exercise, and nutrition can be a key factor in improving children's resistance to infectious organisms and shortening the length of convalescence (Ackerman, Duff, Dennehy, Mafilis, & Krilov, 2001). Topics of special value for young children include:

- appropriate technique and times for handwashing
- proper method for covering coughs and blowing noses
- sanitary use of drinking fountains
- not sharing personal items, e.g., drinking cups, toothbrushes, shoes, hats, towels, eating utensils
- dressing appropriately for the weather
- good nutrition
- the need for rest and exercise

Outbreaks of communicable illness provide excellent opportunities for teachers to review important preventive health concepts and practices with children. Learning is more meaningful for young children when it is associated with real-life experiences, such as having a classmate with chickenpox or pink eye. Teachers can also reinforce learning by modeling good health practices; children frequently imitate adult behaviors.

Parents must be included in any educational program that is aimed at reducing the incidence of communicable illness. Families should be informed of special health practices and information being taught to the children. Teachers can also reinforce the importance of (1) serving nutritious meals and snacks, (2) making sure that children get sufficient rest and exercise, (3) obtaining immunizations for infants, toddlers and older children, and (4) routine medical and dental supervision. Teachers and parents must work together to control the spread of communicable illness and promote children's health.

REFLECTIVE THOUGHTS

Teachers who work with young children are often exposed to communicable illness in the classroom. Sometimes parents unknowingly bring sick children to school or child care. How do you feel about being exposed to contagious illness? Could you care for a child who was acutely ill knowing that you too might become sick? What precautions can you take to protect yourself from such illnesses? How could you help parents address the problem of bringing sick children to child care?

FOCUS ON FAMILIES • Giving Children Medication

Special precautions should be taken whenever administering medication to young children. Their bodies tend to be more sensitive to many medications, and they may respond differently than an adult. It is also easy to give children too much of a medication because their dosages are typically quite small. Medications left unattended may attract a curious child's attention and lead to an unintentional poisoning, so they should always be stored in a locked cabinet. Additional precautions for the safe administration of medication to children include:

- Always check with your child's physician before giving over-the-counter medications, especially to children under two years.

- Read the label carefully. Be sure you are giving the correct medication to the right child at the appropriate time interval. Also, double-check the dose that has been prescribed, and give only that amount. Make sure the medication is approved for children; many drugs are not advised for children under 12 years.

- Ask your pharmacist about potential drug interactions—with other medications or food—that should be avoided. Also, learn about possible reactions that should be noted before giving your child any new medication.

- Always follow the instructions for administering a medication, and finish giving the full course that has been prescribed.

- Throw away any outdated medication. Old medications may lose their effectiveness or cause unexpected reactions. Always check with a pharmacist if in doubt.

- Store medications in their original container and according to instructions.

- Never tell children medicines are "candy," and avoid taking medication in front of children.

CASE STUDY

Laura arrived at the day-care center with a runny nose and cough. Her mother informed the teachers that it was probably just allergies and left before Laura could be checked in. In addition to having a part-time job, Laura's mother is a single parent and student at the local community college. Shortly after Laura's mother left, the teachers discovered that Laura had a fever, red throat, and swollen glands.

1. How should the teachers handle Laura's immediate situation? Should she be allowed to stay or should an attempt be made to contact Laura's mother?

2. If Laura is allowed to stay at the center, what measures can be taken to limit the risk of spreading illness to other children?

3. If this is a repeated occurrence, what steps can be taken to make sure Laura's mother complies with the center's policies?

4. How can the center help Laura's mother avoid similar situations in the future?

SUMMARY

- Frequent incidences of communicable illness are common in child care settings for a number of reasons, including children playing in close proximity, immature development of children's respiratory system, children's habits like mouthing of objects, and careless practices and handwashing by adults.

- Communicable illness is passed from one person to another via airborne, fecal-oral, direct, or indirect methods.

- To be communicable, an illness requires a pathogen, susceptible host, and a method for successful transmission.

- Teachers can implement practices to effectively control and manage communicable illness in group settings, including observations, health policies and sanitation procedures, enforcing immunization requirements, modifying the environment, working with parents, and educating children.

SUGGESTED ACTIVITIES

1. Obtain several agar growth medium plates. With sterile cotton applicators, culture one toy and the top of one table in a preschool classroom or child care center. Observe the "growth" after 24 hours and again after 48 hours. Wash the same item with a mild chlorine solution and repeat the experiment. Compare the results.

2. Write to the Office of Public Health in your state (province/territory). Request information on the immunization requirements for children attending early childhood programs. If possible, obtain data on the percentage of children under six years of age who are immunized in your state.

3. Obtain a copy of the OSHA pamphlet on regulations and instructions for implementing a bloodborne pathogen policy (CFR 1910.1030) from your nearest regional office. Prepare a written compliance plan for an early education center.

4. Discuss how you would handle the following situations:
   a. The father of a toddler in your center is upset because his child has frequent colds.
   b. You observe your teacher covering a cough and then continuing to prepare snacks for the children.
   c. Your toddler group has experienced frequent outbreaks of strep throat in the past six months.
   d. While reviewing immunization records, you discover that one child has received only one dose of DTaP, IPV, and Hib.
   e. During health checks, Gabriel announces that he threw up all night. You notice that his eyes appear watery and his cheeks are flushed.
   f. You find that one of your aides has stored all of the children's toothbrushes together in a sealed, plastic container.

5. Review and compare health care policies from a child care center, home day care, Head Start program and elementary school. How are they similar? How do they differ?

CHAPTER REVIEW

A. **Define the following terms:**

1. pathogen
2. contagious
3. universal precautions
4. incubation period

5. immunity
6. convalescence
7. antibodies
8. communicable illness

B. **Briefly answer the following questions:**

1. Describe how an illness can be spread by:
   a. airborne transmission
   b. indirect contact

2. What immunizations, and how many of each, should a thirty-month-old child have?

3. Where can parents obtain immunizations for their children?

4. Children are contagious during what stage(s) of most communicable diseases?

5. What three factors must be present for an infection to be communicable?

6. Name three early signs of communicable illness that can be observed in young children.

7. Describe specific practices that teachers can use to limit the spread of illnesses transmitted via:
   a. the respiratory tract
   b. the fecal-oral route
   c. skin conditions
   d. contaminated objects, e.g., toys, towels, changing mats

REFERENCES

Ackerman, S. J., Duff, S. B., Dennehy, P. H., Mafilis, M. S., & Krilov, L. R. (2001). Economic impact of an infection control education program in a specialized preschool setting. *Pediatrics, 108*(6), E102.

American Public Health Association (APHA) & American Academy of Pediatrics (AAP). (2002). *Caring for our children: National health and safety performance standards: Guidelines for out-of-home care.* Washington, DC: Author.

Aronson, S. (2002). *Healthy young children: A manual for programs.* (4th ed.). Washington, DC: NAEYC.

Bradley, R.H. (2003). Child care and common communicable illnesses in children aged 37 to 54 months. *Archives of Pediatric & Adolescent Medicine, 157*(2),196–200.

CDC. (1999, June). Vaccine-preventable diseases: Improving vaccination coverage in children, adolescents, and adults. *MMWR, 48,* 1–10.

Child Care Law Center. (1994, October). *Revised description of OSHA regulations on bloodborne pathogens.* San Francisco, CA: Author.

Children's Defense Fund (CDF). (2001). *The state of America's children: Yearbook 2001.* Washington, DC: Author.

DHHS. (2000). *Healthy People 2010.* Washington, DC: Author.

Halsey, N. A. (2001). Safety of combination vaccines: perception versus reality. *Pediatric Infectious Disease Journal, 20*(11 Suppl), S40–44.

Harkavy, L. M. (2002). Role of surface disinfection and hand hygiene in reducing illness. *Journal of School Health,* Oct. Suppl, 27–30.

Hobson, K. (2003). The vaccine conundrum. Should parents be concerned about the number of childhood inoculations? *U.S. News World Report, 134*(8), 44–45.

Kimmel, S. R. (2002). Vaccine adverse events: separating myth from reality. *American Family Physician, 66*(11), 2113–2120.

Lucarelli, P. (2002). Raising the bar for health and safety in child care. *Pediatric Nursing, 28*(3), 239–241.

Luman, E. T., McCauley, M. M., Stokley, S., Chu, S. Y., & Pickering, L. K. (2002). Timeliness of childhood immunizations. *Pediatrics, 110*(5), 935–939.

National Center for Health Statistics. (2002). *Health United States, 2002 with chartbook on trends in the health of Americans.* Washington, DC: Author.

Pan American Health Organization (PAHO). (2003). Health workers mobilize to vaccinate children in the Americas. *News release,* May 22, 2003.

Occupational Safety and Health Administration (OSHA). (1992; 2001). *Bloodborne pathogens.* Washington, DC: U. S. Department of Labor, Occupational Safety and Health Administration. (As amended).

Rapin, I. (1997, July). Autism. *New England Journal of Medicine, 337*(2), 97–104.

Richardson, M., Elliman, D., Macguire, H. Simpson, J., & Nicoll, A. (2001). Evidence base of incubation periods, periods of infectiousness and exclusion policies for the control of communicable diseases in schools and preschools. *Pediatric Infectious Disease Journal, 20*(2), 380–391.

Rubino, J. R. (2002). Economic impact of a healthy school environment. *Journal of School Health,* Oct. Suppl., 27–30.

Slack-Smith, L., Read, A., & Stanley, F. J. (2002). A prospective study of absence for illness and injury in childcare children. *Child Care Health & Development, 28*(6), 487–494.

U.S. Department of Health & Human Services (HHS). (2000). *Healthy people 2010.* Office of Disease Prevention and Health Promotion. Washington, DC: U.S. Department of HHS.

Zimmerman, R. K. (2003). Recommended childhood and adolescent immunization schedule, United States, 2003 and update on childhood immunizations. *American Family Physician, 67*(1), 188, 190, 195–196.

ADDITIONAL READING

Aronson, S. (2001). Maintaining a sanitary chid care environment—Six tips for germ control. *Child Care Information Exchange* (137), 94–97.

Building Quality Child Care: Health and Safety. Washington, DC: NAEYC. (This video addresses handwashing, diapering, and food service practices for teachers.)

CDC. *Six common misconceptions about vaccinations.* National Immunization Program. Washington, DC: U.S. Department of Health and Human Services.

CDC. (2003). Vaccination coverage among children enrolled in Head Start programs, licensed child care facilities, and entering school—United States, 2000–2001 school year. *JAMA, 289*(13),1629–1630.

CDC. (2003). Recommended childhood and adolescent immunization schedule, United States, 2003. *Morbidity and Mortality Weekly Report (MMWR), 52*(4), Q1–4.

Child Health Alert. (2001, April). Fever and pain medication: Getting the dose right. *Child Health Alert,* 19, 1.

Child Health Alert. (1995, May). Bacterial contamination in child care centers and diaper types. *Child Health Alert,* 1.

Child Health Alert. (1995, July/August). Child care issues: More on fecal contamination, diapers, and child care. *Child Health Alert,* 2.

Child Health Alert. (1997, December). Chicken pox vaccine—more reasons to use it. *Child Health Alert,* 15, 1–2.

Cohen, N. J., Lauderdale, D. S., Shete, P. B., & Daum, R. S. (2003). Physician knowledge of catch-up regimens and contraindications for childhood immunizations. *Pediatrics, 111*(5 Pt 1), 925–932.

Moukaddem, V. (1990). Preventing infectious diseases in your child care setting. *Young Children, 45*(2), 28–29.

NAEYC. (1999). *Preparing for illness: A joint responsibility for parents and caregivers.* Washington, DC: Author.

Rivest, P. (1995). Risk factors for measles and vaccine efficacy during an epidemic in Montreal. *Canadian Journal of Public Health, 86*(2), 86–88.

Tamblyn, S. E. (1995). Measles elimination—Time to move forward. *Canadian Journal of Public Health, 86*(2), 83–85

U. S. Department of Health and Human Services. (1990). *Healthy people 2000: National health promotion and disease prevention objectives.* Public Health Service. Washington, DC: DHHS Publication No. PHS91–50212.

HELPFUL WEB SITES

American Public Health Association	http://www.apha.org
Canadian Pediatric Society	http://www.cps.ca/
Centers for Disease Control and Prevention (CDC)	http://www.cdc.gov
Children's Defense Fund	http://www.childrensdefense.org
Maternal and Child Health	http://www.os.dhhs.gov/hrsa/mchb
National Center for Health Statistics	http://www.cdc.gov/nchswww
National Foundation for Infectious Diseases	http://www.medscape.com/nfid
National Institutes of Health	http://www.nih.gov

For additional health, safety, and nutrition resources, go to
http://www.EarlyChildEd.delmar.com

CHAPTER 7

Communicable and Acute Illness: Identification and Management

TERMS TO KNOW

symptoms	abdomen	Lyme disease
asymptomatic	hyperventilation	Reye's syndrome
apnea	temperature	intestinal
infection	fever	urination
dehydration	tympanic	salmonellosis
listlessness	disorientation	

Children, especially those under three years of age, have an increased susceptibility to illness and infection. Group settings such as schools, early childhood centers, and home child-care programs encourage the rapid transfer of illness among children and adults. Therefore, every effort must be made to establish policies and practices that will protect young children from unnecessary exposure.

IDENTIFYING SICK CHILDREN

Every teacher should know how to identify sick children (Figure 7–1). By learning to recognize the early signs and **symptoms** of common illnesses, teachers can exclude children from group settings when they are sick. Teachers can also use children's illnesses to promote wellness education and strengthen principles of good health.

---

symptoms – *changes in the body or its functions that are experienced by the affected individual.*

FIGURE 7–1

Every teacher should know how to identify sick children.

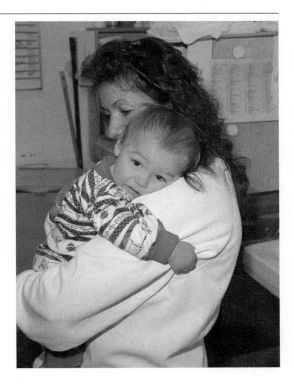

COMMON COMMUNICABLE ILLNESSES

Effective control and protection of other children in group-care settings require teachers to have a sound understanding of communicable illnesses. Their ability to recognize early symptoms and practice good sanitary procedures, including handwashing, is important for limiting the spread of illness. Table 7–1 provides brief descriptions of communicable illnesses common among young children.

Teachers should also be familiar with local public health policies regarding which communicable illnesses must be reported. Notifying health officials of existing cases enables them to monitor communities for potential outbreaks.

SPECIAL CONCERNS

Acquired Immunodeficiency Syndrome (AIDS)

One of the most controversial and emotionally-laden communicable illnesses of recent years is HIV/AIDS (acquired immunodeficiency syndrome). AIDS has become a major public health concern. The Centers for Disease Control and Prevention (CDC) report that approximately 9,000 U.S. children under age 13 are currently infected with the AIDS virus (CDC, 2001).

Cause. Many children have acquired the virus from their HIV positive mothers during pregnancy, delivery, or through breast-feeding (Nakashima & Fleming, 2003). Only a small number of children have been infected through contaminated blood transfusions. Recent and dramatic

TABLE 7-1 Common Communicable Illnesses

AIRBORNE TRANSMITTED ILLNESS

Communicable Illness	Signs and Symptoms	Infectious Agent	Methods of Transmission	Incubation Period	Length of Communicability	Control Measures
Chickenpox	Slight fever, irritability, cold-like symptoms. Red rash that develops blister-like head, scabs later. Most abundant on covered parts of body, e.g., chest, back, neck, forearm.	Virus	Airborne through contact with secretions from the respiratory tract. Transmission from contact with blisters less common.	2–3 weeks after exposure	2–3 days prior to the onset of symptoms until 5–6 days after first eruptions. Scabs are not contagious.	Specific control measures: (1) Exclusion of sick children, (2) Practice good personal hygiene, especially careful handwashing. Children can return to group care when all blisters have formed a dry scab (approximately 1 week). Immunization is now available
Common Cold	Highly contagious infection of the upper respiratory tract accompanied by slight fever, chills, runny nose, fatigue, muscle and headaches. Onset may be sudden.	Virus	Airborne through contact with secretions from the respiratory tract, e.g., coughs, sneezes, eating utensils, etc.	12–72 hours	About 1 day before onset of symptoms to 2–3 days after acute illness.	Prevention through education and good personal hygiene. Avoid exposure. Exclude first day or two. Antibiotics not effective against viruses. Avoid aspirin products (possible link to Reye's syndrome). Watch for complications, e.g., earaches, bronchitis, croup, pneumonia.
Fifth's disease	Appearance of bright red rash on face, especially cheeks.	Virus	Airborne contact with secretions from the nose/mouth of infected person.	4–14 days	Prior to appearance of rash; probably not after rash develops.	Don't need to exclude children once rash appears. Frequent handwashing; frequent washing/disinfecting of toys/surfaces. Use care when handling tissues/nasal secretions.

(Continued)

TABLE 7-1 Common Communicable Illnesses (Continued)

Communicable Illness	Signs and Symptoms	Infectious Agent	Methods of Transmission	Incubation Period	Length of Communicability	Control Measures
Haemophilus influenza Type b	An acute respiratory infection; frequently causes meningitis. Other complications include pneumonia, epiglottitis, arthritis, infections of the bloodstream and conjunctivitis	Bacteria	Airborne via secretions of the respiratory tract (nose, throat). Persons can also be carriers with or without symptoms.	2–4 days	Throughout acute phase; as long as organism is present. Noncommunicable 36–48 hours after treatment with antibiotics	Identify and exclude sick children. Treatment with antibiotics 3–4 days before returning to group care. Notify parents of exposed children to contact their physician. Immunize children. Practice good handwashing techniques; sanitize contaminated objects.
Measles (Rubeola)	Fever, cough, runny nose, eyes sensitive to light. Dark red blotchy rash that often begins on the face and neck, then spreads over the entire body. Highly communicable.	Virus	Airborne through coughs, sneezes and contact with contaminated articles.	8–13 days; rash develops approximately 14 days after exposure	From beginning of symptoms until 4 days after rash appears.	Most effective control method is immunization. Good personal hygiene, especially handwashing and covering coughs. Exclude child for at least 4 days after rash appears.
Meningitis	Sudden onset of fever, stiff neck, headache, irritability, and vomiting; gradual loss of consciousness, seizures, and death.	Bacteria	Airborne through coughs, nasal secretions; direct contact with saliva/nasal discharges.	Varies with the infecting organism; 2–4 days average	Throughout acute phase; noncommunicable after antibiotic treatment.	Encourage immunization for Exclude child from care until medical treatment is completed. Use Universal Precautions when handling saliva/nasal secretions, frequent handwashing, and disinfecting of toys/surfaces.
Mononucleosis	Characteristic symptoms include sore throat, intermittent fever, fatigue, and enlarged lymph glands in the neck. May also be accompanied by headache and enlarged liver or spleen.	Virus	Airborne; also direct contact with saliva of an infected person.	2–4 weeks for children; 4–6 weeks for adults	Unknown. Organisms may be present in oral secretions for as long as one year following illness.	None known. Child should be kept home until over the acute phase (6–10 days). Use frequent handwashing and careful disposal of tissues after coughing or blowing nose.

(Continued)

TABLE 7-1 Common Communicable Illnesses (Continued)

Communicable Illness	Signs and Symptoms	Infectious Agent	Methods of Transmission	Incubation Period	Length of Communicability	Control Measures
Mumps	Sudden onset of fever with swelling of the salivary glands.	Virus	Airborne through coughs and sneezes; direct contact with oral secretions of infected persons.	12–26 days	6–7 days prior to the onset of symptoms until swelling in the salivary glands is gone (7–9 days).	Immunization provides permanent protection. Peak incidence is in winter and spring. Exclude children from school or group settings until all symptoms have disappeared.
Roseola Infantum (6–24 mo.)	Most common in the spring and fall. Fever rises abruptly (102°–105°F) and lasts 3–4 days; loss of appetite, listlessness, runny nose, rash on trunk, arms, and neck lasting 1–2 days.	Virus	Person to person; method unknown.	10–15 days	1–2 days before onset to several days following fading of the rash.	Exclude from school or group care until rash and fever are gone.
Rubella (German Measles)	Mild fever; rash begins on face and neck and rarely lasts more than 3 days. May have arthritis-like discomfort and swelling in joints.	Virus	Airborne through contact with respiratory secretions, e.g., coughs, sneezes.	4–21 days	From one week prior to 5 days following onset of the rash.	Immunization offers permanent protection. Children must be excluded from school for at least 7 days after appearance of rash.
Streptococcal Infections (strep throat, scarlatina, rheumatic fever)	Sudden, onset. High fever accompanied by sore, red throat; may also have nausea, vomiting, headache, white patches on tonsils, and enlarged glands. Development of a rash depends on the infectious organism.	Bacteria	Airborne via droplets from coughs or sneezes. May also be transmitted by food and raw milk.	1–4 days	Throughout the illness and for approximately 10 days afterward, unless treated with antibiotics. Medical treatment eliminates communicability within 36 hours. Can develop rheumatic fever or become a carrier if not treated.	Exclude child with symptoms. Antibiotic treatment is essential. Avoid crowding in classrooms. Practice frequent handwashing, educating children, and careful supervision of food handlers.

(Continued)

TABLE 7-1   Common Communicable Illnesses (Continued)

Communicable Illness	Signs and Symptoms	Infectious Agent	Methods of Transmission	Incubation Period	Length of Communicability	Control Measures
Tuberculosis	Many people have no symptoms. Active disease causes productive cough, weight loss, fatigue, loss of appetite, chills, night sweats.	Bacteria	Airborne via coughs or sneezes.	2–3 months	As long as disease is untreated; usually noncontagious after 2–3 weeks on medication.	TB skin testing, especially babies and young children, if there has been contact with an infected person. Seek prompt diagnosis and treatment if experiencing symptoms; complete drug therapy. Cover coughs/sneezes. Practice good handwashing.
BLOOD BORNE TRANSMITTED ILLNESSES						
Acquired Immuno-deficiency Syndrome (AIDS)	Flu-like symptoms, including fatigue, weight loss, enlarged lymph glands, persistent cough, fever, and diarrhea.	Virus	Children acquire virus when born to infected mothers from contaminated blood transfusions and possibly from breast milk of in-fected mothers. Adults acquire the virus via sexual transmission, con-taminated drug needles, and blood transfusions.	6 weeks to 8 years	Lifetime	Exclude children 0–5 yrs. if they have open lesions, uncontrollable nosebleeds, bloody diarrhea, or are at high risk for exposing others to blood-contaminated body fluids. Use Universal Precautions when handling body fluids, including good handwashing techniques. Seal contaminated items, e.g., diapers, paper towels in plastic bags. Disinfect surfaces with bleach/water solution (1:10) or other disinfectant.
Hepatitis B	Slow onset; loss of appetite, nausea, vomiting, abdominal pain, and jaundice. May also be asymptomatic.	Virus	Through contact with blood/body fluids containing blood.	45–180 days; average 60–80 days	Varies; some persons are lifetime carriers.	Immunization is preferable. Use Universal Precautions when handling any blood/body fluids; use frequent handwashing. *(Continued)*

asymptomatic – *having no symptoms.*

TABLE 7-1 Common Communicable Illnesses (Continued)

Communicable Illness	Signs and Symptoms	Infectious Agent	Methods of Transmission	Incubation Period	Length of Communicability	Control Measures
CONTACT (direct and indirect) TRANSMITTED ILLNESSES						
Conjunctivitis (Pinkeye)	Redness of the white portion (conjunctiva) of the eye and inner eyelid, swelling of the lids, yellow discharge from eyes and itching.	Bacteria or virus	Direct contact with discharge from eyes or upper respiratory tract of an infected person; through contaminated fingers and objects, e.g., tissues, washcloths, towels.	1–3 days	Throughout active infection; several days up to 2–3 weeks.	Antibiotic treatment. Exclude child for 24 hours after medication is started. Frequent handwashing and disinfection of toys/surfaces is necessary.
Cytomegalovirus (CMV)	Often no symptoms in children under 2 yrs.; sore throat, fever, fatigue in older children. High risk of fetal damage if mother is infected during pregnancy.	Virus	Person to person contact with body fluids, e.g., saliva, blood, urine, breast milk, in utero.	Unknown; may be 4–8 weeks	Virus present (in saliva, urine) for months following infection.	No need to exclude children. Always wash hands after changing diapers or contact with saliva. Avoid kissing children's mouths or sharing eating utensils. Practice careful handwashing with children; wash/disinfect toys and surfaces frequently.
Hand, Foot, and Mouth Disease	Affects children under 10 yrs. Onset of fever, followed by blistered sores in the mouth/cheeks; 1–2 days later raised rash appears on palms of hands and soles of feet.	Virus	Person to person through direct contact with saliva, nasal discharge, or feces.	3–6 days	7–10 days	Exclude sick children for several days. Practice frequent handwashing, especially after changing diapers. Clean/disinfect surfaces.
Herpes simplex (Cold sores)	Clear blisters develop on face, lips, and other body parts that crust and heal within a few days	Virus	Direct contact with saliva, on hands, or sexual contact.	Up to 2 weeks	Virus remains in saliva for as long as 7 weeks following recovery.	No specific control. Frequent handwashing. Child does not have to be excluded from school. *(Continued)*

TABLE 7-1 Common Communicable Illnesses (Continued)

Communicable Illness	Signs and Symptoms	Infectious Agent	Methods of Transmission	Incubation Period	Length of Communicability	Control Measures
Impetigo	Infection of the skin forming crusty, moist lesions usually on the face, ears, and around the nose. Highly contagious. Common among children.	Bacteria	Direct contact with discharge from sores; indirect contact with contaminated articles of clothing, tissues, etc.	2–5 days; may be as long as 10 days	Until lesions are healed.	Exclude from group settings until lesions have been treated with antibiotics for 24–48 hours. Cover areas with bandage until treated.
Lice (head)	Lice are seldom visible to the naked eye. White nits (eggs) are visible on hair shafts. The most obvious symptom is itching of the scalp, especially behind the ears and at the base of the neck.	Head louse	Direct contact with infected persons or with their personal articles, e.g., hats, hair brushes, combs, or clothing. Lice can survive for 2–3 weeks on bedding, carpet, furniture, car seats, clothing, etc.	Nits hatch in 1 week and reach maturity within 8–10 days	While lice remain alive on infested persons or clothing; until nits have been destroyed	Infested children should be excluded from group settings until treated. Hair should be washed with a special medicated shampoo and rinsed with a vinegar/water solution (any concentration will work) to ease removal of all nits (using a fine-toothed comb). Heat from a hair dryer also helps destroy eggs. All friends and family should be carefully checked. Thoroughly clean child's environment; vacuum carpets/upholstery, wash/dry or dry clean bedding, clothing, hair-brushes. Seal nonwashable items in plastic bag for 2 weeks.
Ringworm	An infection of the scalp, skin, or nails. Causes flat, spreading, oval-shaped lesions that may become dry and scaly or moist and crusted. When it is present on the feet it is commonly called athlete's foot. Infected nails may become discolored, brittle, or chalky or they may disintegrate.	Fungus	Direct or indirect contact with infected persons, their personal items, swimming pools, theater seats, etc. Dogs and cats may also be infected and transmit it to children or adults.	4–10 days, (unknown for athlete's foot)	As long as lesions are present.	Exclude children from gyms, pools, or activities where they are likely to expose others. May return to group care following medical treatment with a fungicidal ointment. All shared areas, such as pools and showers should be thoroughly cleansed with a fungicide.

(Continued)

TABLE 7–1 Common Communicable Illnesses (Continued)

Communicable Illness	Signs and Symptoms	Infectious Agent	Methods of Transmission	Incubation Period	Length of Communicability	Control Measures
Rocky Mountain Spotted Fever	Onset usually abrupt; fever (101°–104°F); joint and muscle pain, severe nausea and vomiting, and white coating on tongue. Rash appears on 2nd to 5th day over forehead, wrist, and ankles; later covers entire body. Can be fatal if untreated.	Bacteria	Indirect transmission: tick bite.	2–14 days; average 7 days	Not contagious from person to person.	Prompt removal of ticks; not all ticks cause illness. Administration of antibiotics. Use insect repellent on clothes when outdoors.
Scabies	Characteristic burrows or linear tunnels under the skin, especially between the fingers and around the wrists, elbows, waist, thighs, and buttocks. Causes intense itching.	Parasite	Direct contact with an infected person.	Several days to 2–4 weeks	Until all mites and eggs are destroyed.	Children should be excluded from school or group care until treated. Affected persons should bathe with prescribed soap and carefully launder all bedding and clothing. All contacts of the infected person should be notified.
Tetanus	Muscular spasms and stiffness, especially in the muscles around the neck and mouth. Can lead to convulsions, inability to breathe, and death.	Bacteria	Indirect: organisms live in soil and dust; enter body through wounds, especially puncture-type injuries, burns and unnoticed cuts.	4 days to 2 weeks	Not contagious.	Immunization every 8–10 years affords complete protection.

(Continued)

TABLE 7-1 Common Communicable Illnesses (Continued)

Communicable Illness	Signs and Symptoms	Infectious Agent	Methods of Transmission	Incubation Period	Length of Communicability	Control Measures
FECAL/ORAL TRANSMITTED ILLNESSES						
Dysentery (Shigellosis)	Sudden onset of vomiting; diarrhea; may be accompanied by high fever, headache, abdominal pain. Stools may contain blood, pus or mucus. Can be fatal in young children.	Bacteria	Fecal-oral transmission via contaminated objects or indirectly through ingestion of contaminated food or water and via flies.	1–7 days	Variable; may last up to 4 weeks or longer in the carrier state.	Exclude child during acute illness. Careful handwashing after bowel movements. Proper disposal of human feces; control of flies. Strict adherence to sanitary procedures for food preparation
E. coli	Diarrhea, often bloody	Bacteria	Spread through contaminated food, dirty hands.	3–4 days; can be as long as 10 days	For duration of diarrhea; usually several days.	Exclude infected children until no diarrhea; practice frequent handwashing, especially after toileting and before preparing food.
Encephalitis	Sudden onset of headache, high fever, convulsions, vomiting, confusion, neck and back stiffness, tremors, and coma.	Virus	Indirect spread by bites from disease-carrying mosquitoes; in some areas transmitted by tick bites.	5–15 days	Man is not contagious	Spraying of mosquito breeding areas and use of insect repellents; public education.
Giardiasis	Many persons are asymptomatic. Typical symptoms include chronic diarrhea, abdominal cramping, bloating, pale and foul-smelling stools, weight loss, and fatigue.	Parasite (protozoa)	Fecal-oral transmission; through contact with infected stool (e.g., diaper changes, helping child with soiled underwear), poor handwashing, passed from hands to mouth (toys, food). Also transmitted through contaminated water sources.	7–10 days average; can be as long as 5–25 days	As long as parasite is present in the stool.	Exclude children until diarrhea ends. Scrupulous handwashing before eating, preparing food, and after using the bathroom. Maintain sanitary conditions in bathroom areas.

(Continued)

TABLE 7-1   Common Communicable Illnesses (Continued)

Communicable Illness	Signs and Symptoms	Infectious Agent	Methods of Transmission	Incubation Period	Length of Communicability	Control Measures
Hepatitis (Infectious; Type A)	Fever, fatigue, loss of appetite, nausea abdominal pain (in region of liver). Illness may be accompanied by yellowing of the skin and eyeballs (jaundice) in adults, but not always in children. Acute onset.	Virus	Fecal-oral route. Also spread via contaminated food, water, milk, and objects.	10–50 days (average range 25–30 days)	7–10 days prior to onset of symptoms to not more than 7 days after onset of jaundice.	Exclude from group settings a minimum of 1 week following onset. Special attention to careful handwashing after going to the bathroom and before eating is critical following an outbreak. Report disease incidents to public health authorities. Immunoglobulin (IG) recommended for protection of close contacts.
Pinworms	Irritability, and itching of the rectal area. Common among young children. Some children have no symptoms.	Parasite; not contagious from animals.	Infectious eggs are transferred from person to person by contaminated hands (oral-fecal route). Indirectly spread by contaminated bedding, food, clothing, swimming pool.	Life cycle of the worm is 3–6 weeks; persons can also reinfect themselves.	2–8 weeks or as long as a source of infection remains present.	Infected children must be excluded from school until treated with medication; may return after initial dose. All infected and noninfected family members must be treated at one time. Frequent handwashing is essential; discourage nail biting or sucking of fingers. Daily baths and change of linen are necessary. Disinfect school toilet seats and sink handles at least once a day. Vacuum carpeted areas daily. Eggs are also destroyed when exposed to temperatures over 132°F. Education and good personal hygiene are vital to control.
Salmonellosis	Abdominal pain and cramping, sudden fever, severe diarrhea (may contain blood), nausea and vomiting lasts 5–7 days.	Bacteria	Fecal-oral transmission: via dirty hands. Also contaminated food (especially improperly cooked poultry, milk, eggs) water supplies, and infected animals.	12–36 hours	Throughout acute illness; may remain a carrier for months.	Attempt to identify source. Exclude children/adults with diarrhea; may return when symptoms end. Carriers should not handle or prepare food until stool cultures are negative. Practice good handwashing and sanitizing procedures.

REFLECTIVE THOUGHTS

Teachers recognize the importance of addressing issues of diversity in their programs. However, little is often understood about how individuals from various backgrounds—cultures, recent immigrants, homeless families—view the concepts of health, illness, and traditional Western medicine. Notable differences between mainstream values, beliefs, and practices and those held by a particular group are common. Thus, teachers must make an effort to learn more about individual parents and their unique beliefs and priorities in order to best serve children's health needs.

decreases in mother-to-infant transmission are being achieved through national efforts to identify and treat mothers during their pregnancy (CDC, 2001; Bush-Parker, 2000).

Management. Infants infected with the HIV virus at, or prior to, birth typically develop symptoms of the disease within the first year and are usually quite ill. Many of these children will die before the age of five because of complications from pneumonia or a special form of cancer. However, early diagnosis and treatment with new medications appear to be helping these children to live longer. Consequently, the number of children in early education programs who are HIV positive is likely to continue increasing. This presents an emotional and ethical dilemma for some teachers (Black, 1999).

The HIV virus, which causes AIDS, is not transmitted through casual contact, such as hugging, touching, kissing, sitting next to an infected person, or even sharing his or her bathroom or eating utensils (AAP, 2003; Raper & Aldridge, 1998). It is spread primarily through sexual contact with an infected individual or from blood or blood products contaminated with the HIV virus. For these reasons, the risk of HIV transmission to teachers or other children in group care is unlikely. To date, no cases of HIV transmission are known to have occurred in child care programs. Even biting behavior does not cause the spread of HIV (Black, 1999).

Because teachers may not always know when there are HIV positive children in attendance, they must always follow Universal Precautions when handling items contaminated with blood or other body fluids, including vomit, urine, saliva, and feces (see Chapter 6, Table 6–3). Disposable gloves should always be worn when administering first aid or changing diapers, and followed by thorough handwashing *(always an effective control measure)*. Contaminated surfaces should be disinfected promptly. A 1:10 solution of household bleach to water (one tablespoon to three-quarters cup water) is inexpensive and effective against the virus when cleaning up body fluids. Disposable paper should be used under children when changing diapers; tissues and towels should also be disposable. Soiled items should be sealed in plastic bags for proper disposal. Mops should be soaked in disinfectant for 20 to 30 minutes at least once a week.

Children who have HIV/AIDS are protected under the Americans with Disabilities Act (ADA) of 1990 and, therefore, cannot be denied access to educational programs (Raper & Aldridge, 1998; Stegelin, 1997). Parents are also not required to inform school personnel about their child's condition. Some parents choose to withhold this information to protect their child from potential discrimination and stigma. For the same reasons, teachers who test positive may also prefer to remain anonymous. Again, this should pose no risk to the children or coworkers if Universal Precautions and strict sanitary practices are always followed.

The Centers for Disease Control recommends that HIV positive children be excluded from group child care settings *only* if they have open sores, uncontrollable nose bleeds, bloody diarrhea, or are at high risk for exposing others to blood-contaminated body fluids. Actually, children who are HIV positive are at greater risk of contracting illnesses and infections from the other children because their immune systems are not functioning properly (Grier & Hodges, 1998). Many of these illnesses are life-threatening.

Each day, more is understood about HIV and AIDS. Local health departments, medical centers, national agencies (e.g., Centers for Disease Control and Prevention, Canadian Public Health Association, American Academy of Pediatrics, National Pediatric HIV Resource Center) are valuable resources, and can provide information and guidance to child care programs when they are establishing policies or procedures.

Sudden Infant Death Syndrome (SIDS)

Sudden infant death syndrome (SIDS) is a leading cause of death among seemingly healthy infants under one year with most deaths occuring between the second and fourth months (National SIDS Resource Center, 2003; NICHD, 1997). Approximately 2,000–3,000 infants die each year (National Center for Health Statistics, 2002). Infants often appear to be in good health at the time of death. Several factors seem to place some babies at higher risk of dying from SIDS, including being born with a low-birth-weight, being male, being African American, having a sibling who also died of SIDS, being born into poverty, and premature birth. Deaths often occur at night, and especially during the fall and winter months.

Cause. While no one single cause has yet been identified, several things are known about babies who die of SIDS. Many of these infants experience repeated interruptions of breathing called **apnea**. Researchers continue to look for connections between this breathing disturbance and factors that put babies at high risk (Cote, Russo, & Michaud, 1999; Skadberg, Morild, & Markestad, 1998). Other possible factors that are being studied include:

- baby's sleep position
- lack of prenatal care
- mothers who smoked or used drugs (such as cocaine, heroin or methadone) during pregnancy
- premature or low birth weight babies (less than 3.5 pounds; 1.6 kg)
- second-hand smoke and air pollution
- overheating due to overdressing a baby
- brain abnormalities (the mechanisms that affect regulation of breathing and waking during sleep)
- respiratory infections (such as colds and flu)
- birth to a teenage mother

Management. To date, a baby's sleeping position has proven to be the strongest link in preventing SIDS. This discovery lead to the launching of a nationwide "Back to Sleep" campaign in 1994. Currently, multiple child and maternal government and private agencies are partnering to conduct a new initiative (2003) called "Healthy Child Care Back to Sleep Campaign" (DHHS, 2003). This effort is designed to spread information about SIDS and recommended infant sleeping positions to teachers in early education and care programs. Parents and teachers are now counseled to *always put babies down to sleep on their backs* (Figure 7–2). Initial fears that babies would be more likely to choke in this position have not proven true. It isn't clear whether back-sleeping improves babies' oxygen intake or reduces their breathing in of carbon monoxide. However, since this practice was initially recommended, the death rate from SIDS has been reduced by nearly 50 percent (National SIDS Resource Center, 2003).

---

apnea – *momentary absence of breathing.*

FIGURE 7–2

Putting babies to sleep on their backs significantly reduces the risk of Sudden Infant Death Syndrome (SIDS).

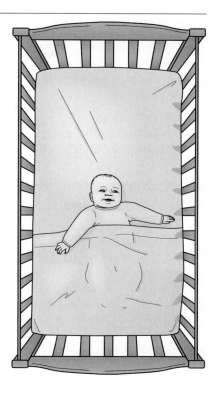

Soft or loose bedding has also been studied as a possible contributing factor. Infants can easily become buried in pillows and blankets, making it difficult for them to breathe. Crib mattresses should be firm and fluffy blankets left out of babies' beds. Babies should also *never* sleep on a waterbed, soft sofa cushions, sheepskin pad, pillows, or other soft materials. Babies can be dressed in blanket sleepers and covered with a thin blanket for warmth. Soft items, such as stuffed toys, pillows, or comforters should *never* be left in an infant's crib to prevent smothering. Other recommendations for reducing the risk of SIDS are included in Table 7–2.

TABLE 7–2 Practices to Reduce the Risk of Sudden Infant Death Syndrome (SIDS)

- Always put babies to sleep on their back or side unless a health condition prevents this.
- Use a firm mattress in crib. Never place babies on a waterbed, sheepskin, comforter, or other soft material.
- Remove pillows, fluffy blankets, and soft toys from baby's bed.
- Cover babies with a thin blanket, tucking bottom half under the mattress (Figure 7–2).
- Dress babies so they do not become overheated.
- Avoid exposing babies to second-hand smoke and persons with colds or other respiratory infections.
- Encourage mothers to obtain professional prenatal care.
- Encourage and support breast-feeding; this may give babies extra protection against SIDS.

Since there is often no identifiable cause for SIDS, parents tend to blame themselves for having been negligent or using poor judgment. They believe that somehow they could have prevented this tragedy. Consequently, parents who have experienced the unexpected death of an infant from SIDS require special emotional support and counseling. Siblings may also be affected by a baby's death and should be included in counseling therapy. Local chapters of several national SIDS organizations offer information and support groups to help families cope with their grief, including (see Appendix C):

- SIDS Alliance
- National SIDS Resource Center
- Association of SIDS and Infant Mortality Programs

COMMON ACUTE ILLNESSES

Children experience many forms of acute illness; however, not all of these are contagious (Bradley, 2003). Teachers must be able to distinguish conditions that are contagious from those that are limited to an individual child. *However, teachers must never attempt to diagnose children's health problems.* Their primary responsibilities include identifying children who are ill, making them comfortable until parents arrive, and advising the family to contact their health care provider. The remainder of this unit is devoted to several acute illnesses and health complaints commonly experienced by young children.

Colds

Colds are a common ailment of young children; they may experience as many as seven to eight colds during a year (Figure 7–3). This number typically decreases as children's respiratory passageways grow, their immune systems become more effective, and they begin to develop healthy

FIGURE 7–3

Treatment for colds, including plenty of rest, helps prevent more serious complications.

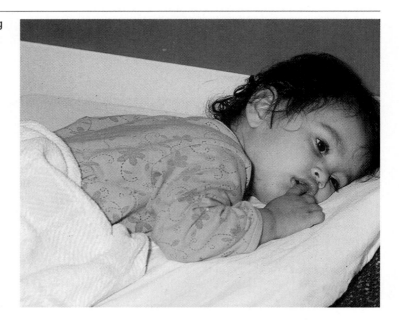

habits. Cold symptoms can range from frequent sneezing and runny nose to fever, sore throat, cough, headache, and muscle aches.

Cause. Most colds are caused by a viral **infection**, primarily rhinoviruses and coronoviruses. They spread rapidly and have a short incubation stage of one to two days.

Management. Because colds are highly contagious during the first day or two, it is best to exclude children from group-care settings. Rest, increased intake of liquids (water, fruit juices, soups), and nonaspirin, fever-reducing medication can be provided by the child's parents and are usually adequate for treating most colds. Antibiotics are not effective against most viruses and are, therefore, of limited value for treating simple colds. However, a physician may prescribe antibiotics to treat complications, or secondary infections, that may develop.

Although colds themselves are not serious, complications can sometimes develop. Toddlers and preschool-aged children are often more susceptible to these complications such as earaches, bronchitis, croup, and pneumonia. Parents should watch children closely and contact their physician if any complications develop or the child does not improve within four to five days. Parents should also be advised to seek immediate medical attention for children who develop white spots in their throats or on tonsils in order to rule out the possibility of strep throat.

Diaper Rash

Diaper rash is an irritation of the skin in and around the buttocks and genital area. Babies with sensitive skin are more likely to experience periodic outbreaks. Diaper rash also occurs more often in infants who are formula-fed versus breast-fed (Wong, 2001).

Cause. Prolonged contact with ammonia in urine and organic acids in stools can burn baby's skin, causing patches of red, raised areas or tiny pimples. Open, weeping areas may develop if the rash is severe, leaving irritated skin open to infection from yeast or bacteria. Reactions to fabric softeners, soaps, lotions, powders, and certain brands of disposable diapers may also cause diaper rash in some infants and toddlers.

Management. Prompt changing of wet and soiled diapers followed by a thorough cleansing of the skin is often sufficient prevention and treatment of diaper rash. Avoid using baby powders and talcs because babies are apt to inhale the fine powder (Child Health Alert, 1991). Also, when combined with urine, powders become good media for bacterial growth. A thin layer of petroleum jelly or zinc oxide ointment can be applied to help protect irritated areas. Allowing the infant to go without diapers (when at home) and exposing irritated skin to the air can also help speed the healing process.

Diarrhea

The term diarrhea refers to frequent watery or very soft bowel movements. They may be foul-smelling and also contain particles of blood or mucus. It is not uncommon for young children to experience several episodes of diarrhea during the course of a year.

Cause. Diarrhea can either be infectious or noninfectious. Infectious forms of diarrhea include:

- viral or bacterial infections, such as hepatitis A or salmonellosis
- parasitic, such as giardia

---

infection – *a condition that results when a pathogen invades and establishes itself within a susceptible host.*

ISSUES TO CONSIDER • Implications of SARS for Children and Adults

Recent events have drawn attention to the fact that communicable illnesses of epidemic proportions are not a thing of the past. The frequency and relative ease of modern travel and dense living arrangements make it easy for a disease to spread quickly, often before its victims are even aware of exposure. Scientists are working intensely to understand SARS (severe acute respiratory syndrome), how to contain its spread, and how to treat its victims (Lawrence, 2003; Poutanen, Low, & Henry, 2003; Soares, 2003). The appearance of SARS in many parts of the world has raised additional concerns about other new strains of viruses and bacteria that could possibly threaten world health. Practicing basic sanitation measures, such as frequent hand washing, disinfection of surfaces, and improvement of personal health, affords protection against many communicable illness. Knowledge can also be a powerful tool for understanding these illnesses and developing appropriate preventive strategies. A wealth of information about SARS is available on many Web sites. (http://www.cdc.gov/ncidod/sars/; http://www.who.int/csr/sars/en/; http://www.hsc.mb.ca/corporate/sars.htm; http://www.caringforkids.cps.ca/whensick/sarsdetailed.htm). Conduct a search before considering these questions:

- What is SARS? What are its symptoms? How does it spread?
- What factors would place the children in your program at risk for exposure to SARS?
- What community resources are available to help you learn more about this disease?
- What precautionary practices would be helpful for your program to implement?
- Is SARS a reportable disease?

Causes of noninfectious diarrhea can include:

- fruit juices containing sorbital, especially apple and pear (Child Health Alert, 2002)
- antibiotic therapy
- recent dietary changes
- food allergies
- food poisoning
- illnesses, such as earaches, colds, strep throat, or cystic fibrosis

Frequent or prolonged diarrhea can result in **dehydration**, especially in infants and toddlers. Dehydration involves a loss of body water and can occur quickly in young children because of their small body size. Excessive dehydration can be fatal (Wong, 2001). For this reason, it is critical that teachers observe infants and young children carefully for signs of dehydration:

- dryness of the mouth
- **listlessness**
- sunken eyes
- absence of tears
- decreased or no urinary output
- rapid, weak pulse
- skin loses elasticity; doughlike

---

dehydration – *a state in which there is an excessive loss of body fluids or extremely limited fluid intake. Symptoms may include loss of skin tone, sunken eyes, and mental confusion.*
listlessness – *a state characterized by a lack of energy and/or interest in one's affairs.*

Management. It is important to monitor and record the frequency (number) and amount (small, large) of bowel movements. The color, consistency, and presence of any blood, mucus, or pus should also be noted. Be sure to check the child's temperature and observe for any signs of discomfort. Prompt medical advice should be sought if diarrhea is severe or prolonged, or the child becomes lethargic or drowsy. Special care should always be taken to practice meticulous hand washing by teachers and children.

Most cases of diarrhea can be treated by temporarily replacing solid foods in the child's diet with a commercially prepared electrolyte solution. This solution replaces important fluids and salts lost through the diarrhea. Liquids and soft foods can gradually be added to the diet once diarrhea has stopped. Any complaint of pain that is continuous or located in the lower right side of the **abdomen** should be reported promptly to the child's parents and checked by a physician.

Children who have experienced diarrhea during the past 24 hours should be excluded from group-care settings. Exceptions to this policy would include children whose diarrhea resulted from noncontagious conditions such as food allergies, changes in diet, or recent treatment with antibiotics. However, even these children may not feel well enough to attend school or group care and participate in the day's activities. The problem and inconvenience of frequent accidental soiling may also be too time-consuming for teachers to manage.

Diarrhea lasting longer than a week should be cause for concern, especially if it is accompanied by bloating, change of appetite, or weight loss. The child should be excluded from group-care settings until a cause is determined, and conditions such as giardia, dysentery, or hepatitis A have been ruled out.

Dizziness

It is not unusual for children to complain of momentary dizziness or a spinning sensation after vigorous play. However, repeated complaints of dizziness should be noted and reported to the child's parents. They should be advised to contact the child's physician to investigate a possible underlying cause.

Cause. Dizziness can be a symptom of other health conditions, including:

- ear infections
- fever
- headaches
- head injuries
- anemia

REFLECTIVE THOUGHTS

Sometimes parents knowingly or unknowingly bring sick children to school or child care. Examine your feelings about being exposed to children's communicable illnesses. Do you feel differently depending on the illness? What steps can teachers take to improve their resistance to communicable illness? How would you respond to parents who repeatedly ignore a program's exclusion policies? How might cultural differences influence what parents view as illness? What could you do to help parents understand and respect a program's policies?

---

abdomen – *the portion of the body located between the diaphragm (located at the base of the lungs) and the pelvic or hip bones.*

- nasal congestion and sinus infections
- brain tumor (rare)

Management. Temporary episodes of dizziness usually respond to simple first aid measures. Have the child lie down quietly or sit with head resting on or between the knees until the sensation has passed. Quiet play can be resumed when the child no longer feels dizzy. Inform parents of this experience so they can continue to monitor the child at home.

If dizziness is accompanied by any loss of balance or coordination, parents should be encouraged to check with the child's physician at once. Dizziness that results from an underlying health problem will usually not respond to most first aid measures.

Earaches

Earaches and ear infections are frequently a problem during the first three or so years of a child's life, affecting boys more often than girls (Bradley, 2003). More than half of all infants, especially those who are formula-fed versus breast-fed, experience an ear infection before their first birthday (Warren, Levy, Kirchner, Nowak, & Bergus, 2001). However, by age five, children usually begin experiencing fewer ear infections as structures in the ear, nose, and throat mature (lengthen) and resistance to infection (antibody formation) increases. Children of Native American and Eskimo descent appear to experience a higher rate of ear infections, possibly related to structural differences in the ear (Curns, et al., 2002). Exposure to second-hand smoke has also been suggested as a possible contributing factor. Studies have also shown that children in group care tend to have a higher incidence ear infections and of otitis media than those who stay at home (Zeisel, Roberts, Burchinal, Neebe, & Henderson, 2002).

Cause. A number of conditions can cause earache in children, including:

- upper respiratory infections, such as a cold
- allergies
- dental cavities and eruption of new teeth
- excessive ear wax
- foreign objects, e.g., plastic beads, food, small toy pieces, stones
- bacterial infections, such as "swimmer's ear," otitis media
- feeding infants in a reclining position

Earaches caused by an acute bacterial infection of the middle ear are known as *otitis media*. This condition causes an inflammation of the eustachian tube (passageway connecting the ear, nose, and throat), which can lead to a backup of fluid in the middle ear and resulting pain, fever, and temporary or chronic hearing loss (Roberts, Burchinal, & Zeisel, 2002; Gravel & Wallace, 2000). Often, only one ear will be affected at a time, and the infection may or may not be accompanied by fluid accumulation behind the eardrum. New research findings suggest that placing infants on their backs to sleep is also effective in decreasing the incidence of ear infection (Hunt, Lesko, et al., 2003). Children, especially infants and toddlers with limited language, should be observed carefully for signs of a possible ear infection, including:

- nausea, vomiting, and/or diarrhea
- tugging or rubbing of the affected ear
- refusal to eat or swallow
- redness of the outer ear
- fever
- dizziness
- irritability
- discharge from the ear canal
- difficulty hearing
- crying when placed in a reclining position

Management. Children who develop otitis media do not need to be excluded from group care unless they are too ill to participate in daily activities or have other symptoms that are contagious. Teachers may be able to provide temporary relief from earache pain by having the child lie down with the affected ear on a soft blanket; the warmth helps soothe discomfort. A small, dry cotton ball placed in the outer ear may also help reduce pain by keeping air out of the ear canal. Excess wax and foreign objects should only be removed by a physician.

A child's complaints of persistent ear pain or earache should be checked by the child's health care provider if symptoms last longer than a day or two. If fluid is present, it may clear up with the infection or sometimes persist for weeks. Chronic otitis media with fluid can interfere with children's speech and language development and, therefore, requires medical treatment (Roberts, et al., 2002; Minter, Roberts, Hooper, Burchinal, & Zeisel, 2001).

Physicians are now using several approaches to treat acute bacterial ear infections (Jackson, 2001). If children are placed on oral antibiotics, it is important that all medication be taken; failure to finish medication can result in a recurrence of the infection. When all medication is finished, children should be rechecked by a physician to make certain the infection is gone. In some cases, additional medication may be needed. Surgical insertion of small plastic tubes into the eardrum is sometimes recommended for children with repeated infections and chronic fluid buildup to lessen the risk of permanent hearing loss (Paradise, et al., 2001). Teachers should be alert to any children with tubes in their ears. Special precautions must be taken to avoid getting water in the outer ear canal during activities that involve water play, such as swimming, bathing, or playing in pools or sprinklers. Ear plugs or a special plastic putty are commonly used for this purpose.

Fainting

Fainting, a momentary loss of consciousness, occurs when blood supply to the brain is temporarily reduced.

Cause. Possible causes for this condition in young children include:

- anemia
- breathholding
- **hyperventilation**
- extreme excitement or hysteria
- drug reactions
- illness or infection
- poisoning

Management. Initially, children may complain of feeling dizzy or weak. Quickly, the skin appears pale, cool, and moist, and the child may collapse. If this occurs, help the child to lie down, elevate the legs eight to ten inches on a pillow or similar object, and observe breathing and pulse frequently. A light blanket can be placed over the child for extra warmth. Breathing is made easier if clothing is loosened from around the neck and waist. No attempt should be made to give the child anything to eat or drink until consciousness is regained. Parents should be notified and encouraged to consult with the child's physician.

Fever

Activity, age, eating, sleeping, and the time of day cause normal fluctuations in children's temperatures. However, a persistent elevated **temperature** is usually an indication of illness or infection,

---

hyperventilation – *rapid breathing often with forced inhalation; can lead to sensations of dizziness, lightheadedness, and weakness.*

temperature – *a measurement of body heat; varies with the time of day, activity, and method of measurement.*

especially if the child complains of other discomforts such as headache, coughing, nausea, or sore throat (Aronson, 2000).

Cause.   Common causes of fever in children include,

- viral and bacterial illnesses, such as ear, skin, and upper respiratory infections
- urinary tract infections
- heat stroke and overheating

Parents and teachers may first notice a child's **fever** by observing them carefully for:

- flushed or reddened face
- listlessness or desire to sleep
- skin that is warm to the touch
- "glassy" eyes
- loss of appetite
- complaints of not feeling well
- increased perspiration

Management.   Children's temperatures should be checked if there is reason to believe that they may have a fever. Only digital and infrared **tympanic** thermometers are recommended for use in group care settings because of safety and liability concerns (Table 7–3). These thermometers are quick and efficient to use, especially with children who may be fussy or uncooperative, and provide readings that are reasonably accurate (Table 7–4) (Sganga, Wallace, Kiehl, Irving, & Witter, 2000; Lanham, Walker, Klocke, & Jennings, 1999). Glass mercury thermometers are considered unsafe to use with young children and also pose environmental concerns (Hoffman, Boyd, Briere, Loos, & Norton, 1999).

Children with an axillary temperature over 99.1°F (37.4°C) or a tympanic reading over 100.4°F (38°C) should be observed carefully for other symptoms of illness. Unless a program's exclusion policies require children with fevers to be sent home, they can be moved to a separate room or quiet area in the classroom and monitored. If there are no immediate indications of acute illness, children should be encouraged to rest. Lowering the room temperature, removing warm clothing, and offering extra fluids can also help make a child feel more comfortable. Fever-reducing medications should only be administered with a physician's approval. Parents should also be notified so they can decide whether to take the child home or wait to see if anything further develops.

TABLE 7–3   Preferred Methods for Checking Children's Temperature in Group Settings (in Rank Order)

infants and toddlers	axillary
2–5 year olds	tympanic axillary oral
5 years and older	oral tympanic axillary

fever – *an elevation of body temperature above normal; a temperature over 99.4°F or 37.4°C orally is usually considered a fever.*
tympanic – *referring to the ear canal.*

TABLE 7-4 A Comparison of Thermometer Options

Type	Advantages	Disadvantages	Normal Range	How to Use	How to Clean
Digital thermometer	Can be used to check oral and axillary temperatures Safe, unbreakable Numbers are easy to read Beeps when ready Easy to clean	Takes 1–2 minutes to obtain a reading Requires child to sit still Axillary readings are less accurate than oral Must purchase batteries and disposable covers	(Axillary) 94.5°–99.0° F (34.7°–37.2° C) (Oral) 94.5°–99.5° F (34.7°–37.3° C)	Turn switch on; wait for beep to signal ready Apply disposable sanitary cover (optional) Place under tongue (oral) or in crease of armpit; hold in place wait for beep to signal reading	Remove disposable cover. Wipe with alcohol or clean with soap and cool water.
Tympanic thermometer	Yields a quick reading Easy to use Can check child's temperature while asleep Requires limited child cooperation	Thermometer is expensive to buy (approximately $40–60) Accuracy of reading depends on correct positioning in child's ear canal (differs from child to child) Must purchase batteries and disposable ear piece coverings	96.4°–100.4° F (35.8°–38° C)	Apply disposable earpiece Turn on start button Insert probe carefully into ear canal opening reading appears in seconds	Wipe instrument (probe) with alcohol.

Headaches

Headaches are not a common complaint of young children. However, when they do occur, headaches are usually a symptom of some other condition. Repeated episodes of headache should be brought to parents' attention.

Cause. Children may experience headaches as the result of several conditions, including:

- bacterial or viral infections
- allergies
- head injuries
- emotional tension or stress
- reaction to medication
- lead poisoning
- hunger
- eye strain
- nasal congestion
- brain tumor (rare)
- constipation
- carbon monoxide poisoning

Management. In the absence of any fever, rash, vomiting or **disorientation**, children who experience headaches can remain in care but should continue to be observed for other indications of illness or injury. Frequently, their headaches will disappear with rest. Patterns of repeated or intense headaches should be noted and parents encouraged to discuss the problem with the child's physician.

Heat Rash

Heat rash is most commonly seen in infants and toddlers.

Cause. Heat rash is caused by a blockage in the sweat glands. It occurs primarily during the summer months, although it can occur at any other time when an infant or child is dressed too warmly. Clothing made of synthetic fabrics and overdressing can also encourage the development of heat rash, especially in young children with sensitive skin.

Management. Heat rash is not contagious. However, there are several measures that can be taken to make a child more comfortable. Affected areas can be washed with cool water, dried thoroughly, and dusted sparingly with cornstarch.

Lyme Disease

Lyme disease is a tick-borne infection most prevalent along the East Coast, although it has been identified in nearly every U.S. state and many provinces of Canada (MMWR, 2002). As a result, the incidence continues to increase, with over 17,000 cases reported in children ages five to nine in the year 2000 (Orloski, Hayes, Campbell, & Dennis 2000).

Cause. This bacterial illness is caused by the bite of a tiny, infected deer tick; however, not all deer ticks are infected, nor will everyone who is bitten develop Lyme disease. Many species of the deer tick are commonly found in grassy and wooded areas during the summer and fall months.

Management. The most effective way to prevent Lyme disease is to take preventive measures whenever children will be spending time outdoors, especially in grassy or wooded areas (Table 7–5).
Because deer ticks are exceptionally small, they are easily overlooked. Development of any unusual symptoms following a tick bite should be reported immediately to a physician. Early symptoms of Lyme disease are often vague and difficult to diagnose. Within the first few weeks of a bite, a small red, flat, or raised area may develop at the site, followed by a localized rash that gradually disappears. Flulike symptoms, including fever, chills, fatigue, headache, and joint pain may also be

---

disorientation – *lack of awareness or ability to recognize familiar persons or objects.*
Lyme disease – *bacterial illness caused by the bite of infected deer ticks found in grassy or wooded areas.*

TABLE 7-5 Measures to Prevent Tick Bites

- Encourage children to wear long pants, a long-sleeved shirt, socks, shoes, and a hat; light colored clothing makes it easier to spot small deer ticks.
- Apply insect/tick repellants containing DEET to clothing and exposed areas of the skin (Eppes, 2003; Gayle & Ringdahl, 2001). Be sure to follow manufacturer's directions and avoid aerosol sprays that children might inhale.
- Discourage children from rolling in the grass or sitting on fallen logs.
- Remove clothing as soon as children come indoors and check all areas of the body (under arms, around waist, behind knees, in the groin, neck) and hair.
- Bathe or shower to remove any ticks.
- Wash clothing in soapy water and dry in drier (heat will destroy ticks).
- Continue to check children for any sign of ticks that may have been overlooked on a previous inspection.
- Promptly remove any tick discovered on the skin and wash the area carefully.

experienced during this stage. If the bacterial infection is not diagnosed early and treated with antibiotics, complications, including arthritis, heart, and/or neurological problems can develop within two years of the initial bite. A blood test is available for early detection.

Reye's Syndrome

Reye's syndrome is an acute illness that almost exclusively affects young children. It occurs more often in the winter months, particularly during the flu season. Symptoms associated with this illness typically don't develop until three days to three weeks following a viral infection, making it somewhat difficult and puzzling to diagnose (Cooper, 2003).

Cause. Although an exact cause is unknown, Reye's syndrome is commonly linked to a prior viral infection, such as an upper respiratory infection, influenza, or chickenpox (National Reye's Syndrome Foundation, 2003). While aspirin does not cause Reye's syndrome, its use has been linked to the onset of this disease in over 90 percent of the cases (Food & Drug Administration, 2003; Casteels-Van Daele, Van Greet, Wouters, & Eggermont, 2001). Consequently, parents are now warned not to administer aspirin to children who have chickenpox or flulike symptoms. Aspirin bottles also carry this mandatory warning on the label. Many cold medications contain aspirin or aspirin-like compounds and should be used only on the advice of a physician.

Reye's syndrome affects boys and girls alike, especially those under 16 years of age. The onset of symptoms appears just as the child seems to be recovering from a viral illness. Frequent vomiting, sudden fever, mental confusion, drowsiness, irritability, body rigidity, and coma are characteristic indicators.

Management. Reye's syndrome is a medical emergency requiring intensive treatment. Fortunately, the incidence of this illness continues to decrease as parents understand the importance of not giving children aspirin or aspirin-like medications for viral infections.

Sore Throat

Sore throats are a fairly common complaint among young children, especially during the fall and winter seasons. Teachers must often rely on their observations to determine when infants and

---

Reye's syndrome – *an acute illness of young children that severely affects the central nervous system; symptoms include vomiting, coma, and seizures.*

toddlers may be experiencing a sore throat because children of this age are unlikely to verbalize their discomfort. Fussiness, lack of interest in food or refusal to eat, fever, and fatigue may be early indications that the child is not feeling well.

Cause.   Most sore throats are caused by a viral or bacterial infection. Some children may also experience a scratchy throat as the result of sinus drainage, mouth breathing, or allergies.

Management.   It is extremely important not to ignore a child's complaint of sore throat. A small percentage of sore throats are caused by a highly contagious streptococcal infection (Table 7–1). Although most children are quite ill with these infections, some may experience only mild symptoms or none at all. Unknowingly, they may become carriers of the infection and capable of spreading it to others. Strep throat must be identified and treated with antibiotics. A routine throat culture can safely determine whether or not a strep infection is present. Left untreated, strep throat can lead to serious complications, including rheumatic fever and rheumatic heart disease (Wong, 2001).

Sore throats resulting from viral infections are not usually harmful, but they can cause the child considerable discomfort. Antibiotics are not effective against most viral infections and, therefore, seldom prescribed.

Stomachaches

Most children experience an occasional stomachache from time to time. However, children may use this term to describe a range of discomforts, from hunger or a full bladder to actual nausea, cramping, or emotional upset. Teachers can use their observation and questioning skills in an effort to determine a probable cause.

Cause.   Children's stomachaches are often a symptom of some other condition. There are many possible causes, including:

- food allergies or intolerance
- appendicitis
- **intestinal** infections, e.g., giardiasis, salmonella, E. Coli
- urinary tract infections
- gas or constipation
- side effect to medication, especially antibiotics
- change in diet
- emotional stress or desire for attention
- hunger
- diarrhea and/or vomiting
- strep throat

Management.   There are several ways to determine whether or not a child's stomach pain is serious. Is the discomfort continuous or a cramping-type pain that comes and goes? Does the child have a fever? Is the child able to continue playing. If no fever is present, the stomachache is probably not serious. Encourage the child to use the bathroom and see if **urination** or having a bowel movement relieves the pain. Have the child rest quietly to see if the discomfort goes away. Check with parents to determine if the child is taking any new medication or has had a change of diet. Stomach pain or stomachaches should be considered serious if they:

---

intestinal – *pertaining to the intestinal tract or bowel.*
urination – *the act of emptying the bladder of urine.*

- disrupt a child's activity, e.g., running, playing, eating, sleeping
- cause tenderness of the abdomen
- are accompanied by diarrhea, vomiting, or severe cramping
- last longer than three to four hours
- result in stools that are bloody or contain mucus

If any of these conditions occur while the child is attending school or group care, parents should be notified and advised to seek prompt medical attention for the child.

Teething

Teething is a natural process. Infants usually begin getting their first teeth around four to seven months of age. Older children will begin the process of losing and replacing their baby teeth with a permanent set about the time they reach their fifth or sixth birthday.

Cause.   New teeth erupting through gum tissue can cause some children mild discomfort. However, most children move through this stage with relatively few problems.

Management.   An increase in drooling and chewing activity for several days or weeks may be the only indication that an infant is teething. Some babies become a bit more fussy, run a low-grade fever (under 100° F), and may not be interested in eating. However, high fevers, diarrhea, and vomiting are usually not caused by teething, but may be an indication of illness. Chilled teething rings and firm objects for children to chew often provide comfort and relief to swollen gums.

Toothache

Toothache should not be a complaint of young children. Dental-related problems cause children pain and suffering and can interfere with speech and language development, make eating difficult, and result in early tooth loss. Children should not have to forgo necessary treatment of dental problems because of limited family income (Satcher, 2001; Community Voices: HealthCare Underserved, 2001). Low-cost insurance and community resources are often available to help children and families obtain essential dental care.

Infants and toddlers may experience temporary discomfort when they are teething. Older children may feel a similar tooth discomfort when they begin losing their baby teeth and permanent teeth erupt.

Cause.   Tooth decay is the most common cause of toothache. Children may complain of a throbbing pain that sometimes radiates into the ear. Redness and swelling may be observed around the gumline of the affected tooth. Foods that are hot or very sweet may intensify pain. Similar tooth discomfort may be experienced by older children when children begin losing baby teeth and permanent teeth erupt.

Management.   Complaints of toothache should be checked promptly by the child's dentist. In the meantime, an icepack applied to the cheek on the affected side may make the child feel more comfortable. Aspirin-free products can also be administered by the child's parents for pain relief. Proper brushing after eating eliminates a significant percentage of early tooth decay (Figure 7–4).

Vomiting

Vomiting can be a frightening and unpleasant experience for children. True vomiting is different from a baby who simply spits up after eating. Vomiting is a symptom often associated with an acute illness or other health problem (Wong, 2001).

FIGURE 7–4

Brushing teeth after eating helps to reduce tooth decay.

Cause. A number of conditions can cause children to vomit, including:

- emotional upset
- viral or bacterial infection, e.g., stomach flu, strep throat
- Reye's syndrome
- ear infections
- meningitis
- **salmonellosis**
- indigestion
- severe coughing
- drug reactions
- head injury
- poisoning

Management. The frequency, amount, and composition of vomited material is important to observe and record. Dehydration and disturbances of the body's chemical balance can occur with prolonged or excessive vomiting, especially in infants and toddlers. Children should be observed carefully for:

- high fever
- abdominal pain
- signs of dehydration
- headache
- excessive drowsiness
- difficulty breathing
- sore throat
- exhaustion

Children who continue to vomit and show signs of a sore throat, fever, or stomach pains should be sent home as soon as possible. The teacher should also advise the child's parents to contact their physician for further advice.

In the absence of any other symptoms, a single episode of vomiting may simply be due to an emotional upset, dislike of a particular food, excess mucus, or reaction to medication. Usually the child feels better immediately after vomiting. These children can remain at the school and be encouraged to rest until they feel better.

In addition to not feeling well, the act of vomiting itself may be very upsetting and frightening to the young child. Extra reassurance and comforting can help make the experience less traumatic.

---

salmonellosis – *a bacterial infection that is spread through contaminated drinking water, food or milk or contact with other infected persons. Symptoms include diarrhea, fever, nausea, and vomiting.*

Infants should be positioned on their stomachs, with their hips and legs slightly raised to allow vomited material to flow out of the mouth and prevent choking. Older children should also be watched closely so they don't choke or inhale vomitus.

FOCUS ON FAMILIES • When to Call the Doctor

Frequent bouts of illness are not uncommon among young children. With time, their bodies mature, they begin to build up resistance (immunity) to many illnesses, and their immunizations will have been completed. In the meantime, parents often face the difficult task of deciding at what point their child is sick enough to warrant a call to the doctor. While each child's symptoms and needs are different, there are guidelines that may be helpful in making this decision. Call the physician if your child:

- Experiences serious injury, bleeding that cannot be stopped, or excessive or prolonged pain.

- Is less than one month old and develops a fever, or is between one and three months of age and has a rectal temperature over 100.4° F.

- Has difficult, rapid, or noisy breathing.

- Experiences any loss of consciousness, including a seizure.

- Complains of unusual pain in an arm or leg. X-rays may be necessary to rule out a fracture.

- Has repeated episodes of vomiting or diarrhea and is unable to keep down liquids. Symptoms of dehydration include urination fewer than three times per day, dry lips or tongue, headache, lack of tears, excessive drowsiness, and sunken fontanel (soft spot) in infants. Young children can become dehydrated quickly.

- Develops an unusual skin rash, especially one that spreads.

- Has blood in his/her vomit, urine, or stool.

- Suffers an eye injury or develops an eye discharge. Children who have sustained an eye injury should always be seen by a physician.

- Develops stomach pain that is prolonged or interferes with appetite or activity.

- Becomes excessively sleepy and difficult to arouse.

Finally, rely on your intuition. Don't hesitate to call the doctor if you are unsure about the symptoms your child may be experiencing. Most physicians would rather be aware of a child's condition than be called only when a crisis arises.

CASE STUDY

The teacher observes that Kati seems quite restless today and is having difficulty concentrating on any task she starts. She is continuously squirming, whether in a chair or sitting on the floor. On a number of occasions throughout the morning, the teacher has observed Kati tugging at her underwear and scratching her bottom.

1. What type of problem might the teacher suspect Kati is having?
2. What control measures should be taken? At school? At home?
3. When can she return to school?
4. For what length of time after an outbreak must the teacher watch for the development of similar problems in other children?
5. What special personal health measures should be emphasized with the other children?

SUMMARY

- Illness is common among young children in group settings.
- Teachers can help control the spread of illnesses through:
  - observation and early identification of sick children.
  - implementation of exclusion policies.
  - careful hand washing.
  - environmental sanitation.

SUGGESTED ACTIVITIES

1. With a partner, practice taking each other's axillary, oral, and tympanic temperatures. Follow steps for correct cleaning of the thermometer between each use.

2. Divide the class into groups of five to six students. Discuss how each member feels about caring for children who are ill. Could they hold or cuddle a child with a high fever or diarrhea? What are their feelings about being exposed to children's contagious illnesses? How might they react if an infant just vomited on their new sweater? If they feel uncomfortable around sick children, what steps could they take to better cope with the situation?

3. Select another student as a partner and observe that person carefully for twenty seconds. Now look away. Write down everything you can remember about this person, such as eye color, hair color, scars or moles, approximate weight, height, color of skin, shape of teeth, clothing, etc. What can you do to improve your observational skills?

CHAPTER REVIEW

A. **Match the signs/symptoms in column I with the correct communicable illness in column II.**

Column I

1. swelling and redness of white portion of the eye
2. frequent itching of the scalp
3. flat, oval-shaped lesions on the scalp, skin; infected nails become discolored, brittle, chalky, or they may disintegrate
4. high fever; red, sore throat
5. mild fever and rash that lasts approximately three days
6. irritability and itching of the rectal area
7. red rash with blisterlike heads; coldlike symptoms
8. sudden onset of fever; swelling of salivary glands
9. burrows or linear tunnels under the skin; intense itching
10. vomiting, abdominal pain, diarrhea that may be bloody

Column II

a. chickenpox
b. strep throat
c. lice
d. shigellosis
e. conjunctivitis
f. ringworm
g. German measles
h. scabies
i. pinworms
j. mumps

B. **Describe what you would do in each of the following situations:**

1. You have just finished serving lunch to the children, when Mara begins to vomit.
2. The class is involved in a game of keep-away. Ted suddenly complains of feeling dizzy.
3. During check-in, a parent mentions that his son has been experiencing stomachaches every morning before coming to school.
4. Leandra wakes up from her afternoon nap, crying because her ear hurts.
5. You have just changed a toddler's diaper for the third time in the last hour because of diarrhea.
6. Sami enters the classroom, sneezing and blowing his nose.
7. While you are helping Erin put on her coat to go outdoors, you notice that her skin feels very warm.
8. Richard refuses to eat his lunch because it makes his teeth hurt.
9. While you are cleaning up the blocks, Tommy tells you that his throat is sore and it hurts to swallow.
10. You have just taken Juanita's temperature (orally) and it is 102° F.

REFERENCES

American Academy of Pediatrics (AAP) (2003). *Red book: Report of the Committee on Infectious Disease.* (26th ed.). Elk Grove, IL: Author.

Aronson, S. (2000, November). Exclusion of children with fevers from child care. *Child Care Information Exchange,* 88–89.

Black, S. (1999). HIV-AIDS in early childhood centers. The ethical dilemma of confidentiality versus disclosure. *Young Children, 54*(2), 39–45.

Bradley, R. H. (2003). Child care and common communicable illnesses in children aged 37 to 54 months. *Archives of Pediatric & Adolescent Medicine, 157*(2), 196–200.

Bush-Parker, T. Perinatal HIV: Children with HIV grow up. *Focus,* January 2000; *15*(2), 1–6

Casteels-Van Daele, M., Van Geet, C., Wouters, C., & Eggermont, E. (2001). Reye's syndrome. *Lancet, 358*(9278), 334.

CDC. (2001). *HIV/AIDS surveillance report.* Washington, DC: Centers for Disease Control and Prevention (CDC).

Child Health Alert. (2002, June). Can fruit juices cause irritable bowel syndrome? *Child Health Alert, 20,* 1.

Child Health Alert. (1991, June). Persistent hazards to young children: Inhalation of baby powder. *Child Health Alert, 20,* 1.

Community Voices: HealthCare for the Underserved. (2001). *Poor oral health is no laughing matter.* Washington, DC: Author.

Cooper, C. (2003). Would you recognize this syndrome? *RN, 66*(4), 49–52.

Cote, A., Russo, P., & Michaud, J. (1999, October). Sudden unexpected deaths in infancy: What are the causes? *Journal of Pediatrics, 135*(4), 437–443.

Curns, A. T., Holman, R. C., Shay, D. K., Cheek, J. E., Kaufman, S. F., Singleton, R. J., & Anderson L. J. (2002). Outpatient and hospital visits associated with otitis media among American Indian and Alaska native children younger than 5 years. *Pediatrics, 109*(3), E41–1.

Eppes, S. (2003). Diagnosis, treatmen, and prevention of lyme disease in children. *Pediatric Drugs, 5*(6), 363–372.

Food & Drug Administration. (2003). Labeling for oral and rectal over-the-counter drug products containing aspirin and nonaspirin salicylates: Reye's Syndrome warning. Final rule. *Federal Registry, 68*(74), 1423–1424.

Gayle, A. & Ringdahl, E. (2001). Tick-borne diseases. *American Family Physician, 64*(3), 461–466.

Gravel, J. S. & Wallace, I. F. (2000). Effects of otitis media with effusion on hearing in the first 3 years of life. *Journal of Speech, Language, & Hearing Research, 43*(3), 631–644.

Grier, E. C. & Hodges, H. F. (1998). HIV?AIDS: A challenge in the classroom. *Public Health Nursing, 15*(4), 257–262.

Hoffman, C., Boyd, M., Briere, B., Loos, F., & Norton, P. J. (1999). Evaluation of three brands of tympanic thermometer. *Canadian Journal of Nursing Research, 31*(1), 117–130.

Hunt, C. E., Lesko, S. M., Vezina, R. M., McCoy, R., Corwin, M. J., Mandell, F., Willinger, M., Hoffman, H., Mitchell, A. A. (2003). Infant sleep position and associated health outcomes. *Archives of Pediatric & Adolescent Medicine, 157*(5), 469–474.

Jackson, P. L. (2001). Healthy People 2010 objective: Reduce number and frequency of courses of antibiotics for ear infections in young children. *Pediatric Nursing, 27*(6), 591–593.

Lanham, D. M., Walker, B., Klocke, E., & Jennings, M. (1999). Accuracy of tympanic temperature readings in children under 6 years of age. *Pediatric Nursing, 25*(1), 39–42.

Lawrence, D. (2003). Coronavirus confirmed as cause of SARS. *Lancet, 361*(9370), 1712.

Minter, K. R., Roberts, J. E., Hooper, S. R., Burchinal, M. R., & Zeisel, S. A. (2001). Early childhood otitis media in relation to children's attention-related behavior in the first six years of life. *Pediatrics, 107*(5), 1037–1042.

MMWR Weekly. (2002, January 18). Lyme disease—United States, 2000. *MMWR, 51*(2), 29–31.

Nakashima, A. K., & Fleming, P. L. (2003) HIV/AIDS surveillance in the United States, 1981-2001. *Journal of Acquired Immune Deficiency Syndrome, 32* Suppl 1, S68–85.

National Center for Health Statistics. (2002). *National Vital Statistics Reports, 50*(16), 110.

National Reye's Syndrome Foundation. (2003). Accessed on June 3, 2003, from http://www.reyessyndrome.org/default.htm.

National SIDS Resource Center. (2003). *What is SIDS? Sudden infant death syndrome: Some facts you should know, and facts about apnea and other apparent life-threatening events.* Vienna, VA: Author.

Orloski, K. A., Hayes, E. B., Campbell, G. L., & Dennis, D. T. (2000). Surveillance for Lyme disease—United States. In: CDC surveillance summaries (April 28, 2000). *MMWR, 49*(SS-3), 1–11.

Paradise, J. L., Feldman, H. M., Campbell, T. F., Dollaghan, C. A., Colborn, D. K., Bernard, B. S., Rockette, H. E., Janosky, J. E., Pitcairn, D. L., Sabo, D. L., KursLasky, M., & Smith, C. G. (2001). Effect of early or delayed insertion of tympanostomy tubes for persistent otitis media on developmental outcomes at the age of three years. *New England Journal of Medicine, 344*(16), 1179–1187.

Poutanen, S.M., Low, D. E., Henry, B. (2003). Identification of severe acute respiratory syndrome in Canada. *New England Journal of Medicine, 348*(20), 1995–2005.

Raper, J. & Aldridge, J. (1998). What every teacher should know about AIDS. *Childhood Education, 64,* 146–149.

Roberts, J. E., Burchinal, M. R., & Zeisel, S. A. (2002). Otitis media in early childhood in relation to children's school-age language and academic skills. *Pediatrics, 110*(4), 696–706.

Satcher, D. (2001). *Oral health and learning.* Washington, DC: National Center for Education in Maternal and Child Health.

Sganga, A., Wallace, R., Kiehl, E., Irving, T., & Witter, L. (2000). A comparison of four methods of normal newborn temperature measurement. *The American Journal of Maternal/Child Nursing, 25*(2), 76–79.

Skadberg, B. T., Morild, I., & Markestad, T. (1998, February). Abandoning prone sleeping: Effect on the risk of sudden infant death syndrome. *Journal of Pediatrics, 132*(2), 340–343.

Soares, C. (2003). Caught off gaurd. SARS reveals gaps in global disease defense. *Scientific American, 288*(6), 18–19.

Stegelin, D. (1997, Fall/Winter). Early childhood professionals and HIV/AIDS-impacted children and families. Strategies for professional preparation. *Journal of Early Childhood Teacher Education, 18*(3), 26–34.

U. S. Department of Health and Human Services (DHHS). (2003). *Healthy Child Care America Back to Sleep Campaign.* Child Care Bureau & Maternal & Child Health Bureau. Accessed on June 3, 2003, from http://www.aap.org/advocacy/hcca/backtosleep/.

Warren, J. J., Levy, S. M., Kirchner, H. L., Nowak, A. J., & Bergus, G. R. (2001). Pacifier use and the occurrence of otitis media in the first year of life. *Pediatric Dentistry, 23*(2), 103–107.

Wong, D. (2001). *Wong's essentials of pediatric nursing.* (6th ed.). St. Louis: Mosby, Inc.

Zeisel, S. A., Roberts, J. E., Burchinal, M., Neebe, E., & Henderson, F. W. (2002). A longitudinal study of risk factors for otitis media in African American children. *Maternal & Child Health, 6*(3), 189–193.

ADDITIONAL READING

American Academy of Pediatrics and American Public Health Association (AAP & APHA, (2002). *Caring for our children: National health and safety performance standards: Guidelines for out-of-home care.* Washington, DC: American Academy of Pediatrics.

Center for Disease Control and Prevention. (1996). *ABC's of safe and healthy child care.* Washington, DC: Author.

Child Health Alert. (1995, May). Can we predict when children have ear infections? *Child Health Alert, 13,* 1.

Child Health Alert. (1997). Information on ear tubes for children. *Child Health Alert, 15,* 4.

Child Health Alert. (1998, October). Yikes—Lice: A storybook to help children cope with head lice. *Child Health Alert, 16,* 3.

Child Health Alert. (1999). Are doctors changing the way they treat ear infections? *Child Health Alert, 17,* 1–20.

Child Health Alert. (2002, March). Chickenpox declines with vaccine use. *Child Health Alert, 20,* 2.

Child Health Alert. (2002, June). Lyme disease and prevention. *Child Health Alert, 20,* 5.

Child Health Alert. (2002, December). Protecting children from the flu: Vaccine and handwashing. *Child Health Alert, 20,* 2.

Child Health Alert. (2003, May). Resource: where to get the latest information on SARS. *Child Health Alert, 21,* 5.

Dailey, L. (2000). Is that nit dead or alive—or does it matter? *Child Care Health Connections, 13*(6), 4.

De la Cruz, A. (1998). The changing treatment paradigm for acute otitis media. *JAMA, 280*(2), 1903.

Ecklund, C. R., & Ross, M. C. (2001). Over-the-counter medication use in preschool children. *Journal of Pediatric Health Care, 15*(4), 168–172.

Gershon, N. B., & Moon, R. Y. (1997). Infant sleeping position in licensed child care centers. *Pediatrics, 100*(1), 75–78.

Groves, M. (1997). Keeping children healthy! *Early Childhood News, 9*(3), 16–21.

Ibarra, J., & Hall, D. M. B. (1996). Head lice in school children. *Archives of Disease in Childhood, 75*(6), 471–473.

Kaiser, B., & Rasminsky, J. S. (1995). *HIV/AIDS and child care: A fact book.* Ottawa, Ontario: Canadian Child Care Federation, AIDS Clearinghouse.

Larkin, M. (2003). Web serves as conduit for SARS information. *Lancet Infectious Diseases, 3*(6), 388–389.

Lieu, J. E., & Feinstein, A. R. (2002). Effect of gestational and passive smoke exposure on ear infections in children. *Archives of Pediatric & Adolescent Medicine, 156*(2), 147–154.

Merrifield, M. (1990). *Come sit by me.* Toronto, Ontario, Canada: Women's Press.

MMWR (2003, April 4). Update: Outbreak of Severe Acute Respiratory Syndrome—Worldwide, 2003. *MMWR Weekly, 52*(13), 269–272.

MMWR. (1999, October). Progress in reducing risky infant sleeping positions—13 states, 1996–97. *MMWR, 48*(39), 878–882.

National Institute of Child Health & Human Development (NICHD). (1997). *Sudden infant death syndrome: Fact sheet.* Washington, DC: Author.

Sachs, S. (2000, January 3). More screening of immigrants for TB sought. *New York Times,* 149.

Schonfeld, D. T. (1996). Talking with elementary and school-age children about AIDS and death. *Journal of School Health Nursing, 12*(1), 26–32.

Sorum, P. C., Shim, J., Chasseigne, G., Mullet, E., Sastre, M. T., Stewart, T., & Gonzalez-Vallejo, C. (2002). Do parents and physicians differ in making decisions about acute otitis media? *Journal of the American Family Practitioner, 51*(1), 51–57.

Squibb, B., & Yardley K. (1999). Playing healthy, staying healthy: A prevention program for contagious disease. *Early Childhood Education Journal, 26*(3), 143–147.

Vernon-Feagans, L. (1996). Otitis media and the social development of daycare-attending children. *Child Development, 67*(4), 1528–1539.

Williams, L., Reichert, A., Mackenzie, W., Hightower, A., & Blake, P. (2001). Lice, nits, and school policy. *Pediatrics, 107*(5), 1011–1015.

HELPFUL WEB SITES

Center for Disease Control	http://www.cdc.gov/health/diseases
Early Childhood and Parenting Collaborative	http://ecap.crc.uiuc.edu/info
Harvard Health Letter	http://www.med.Harvard.edu
Kid Source	http://www.kidsource.com
National Institutes of Health	http://www.nih.gov
Your Child's Health	http://www.yourchildshealth.echn.ca

For additional health, safety, and nutrition resources, go to http://www.EarlyChildEd.delmar.com

SAFETY FOR THE YOUNG CHILD

CHAPTER 8

Creating Quality Environments

OBJECTIVES

After studying this chapter, you should be able to:

- Discuss the relationship between environment and a child's growth and development.
- State the purpose of licensing requirements.
- List the necessary steps for securing a license to operate an early education program.
- Describe ways of making a child's environment safe.

TERMS TO KNOW

environment	regulations	developmentally appropriate practice (DAP)
cognitive	compliance	
accreditation	registration	notarized
licensing		

Children's growth and development are continually shaped and influenced by their **environment**. Growth is enhanced through nurturing and responsive caregiving, good nutrition, homes and schools that are clean and safe, access to appropriate health care, and communities that are free of drugs and violence. Opportunities for learning, experiencing new challenges, and positive social interaction are important for promoting children's intellectual and psychological development. Thus, there are many aspects of children's environments for teachers and parents to consider. Every effort must be made to create physical, **cognitive**, and psychological environments that have positive effects on children's growth and development (Figure 8–1).

---

environment – *the sum total of physical, cultural, and behavioral features that surround and affect an individual.*
cognitive – *the aspect of learning that refers to the development of skills and abilities based on knowledge and thought processes.*

FIGURE 8–1

Environments can have a positive effect on children's growth and development.

LOCATING QUALITY PROGRAMS

Demands for early childhood programs continue to increase. For many working parents, locating out-of-home care for their children is a necessity. Some parents simply want their children to benefit from enriching experiences and opportunities to socialize with others. Children with special needs may be enrolled in early intervention programs where they can receive individualized learning experiences and special services, such as speech or physical therapy (Allen & Cowdery, 2005). Regardless of the reason, finding high-quality and affordable programs can be a challenging task for parents. In the rush to meet increased demand, many new programs and centers have opened, but quality has not always been a top priority.

Research continues to demonstrate that high-quality programs make a difference in children's development and family relationships (Booth, & Jean, 2002; Clarke-Stewart, Vandell, Lowe, Burchinal, O'Brien, & McCartney, 2002; Weaver, 2002). Children enrolled in higher quality care show long-term gains in language and cognitive skills, improved readiness for school, and fewer problem behaviors (Peth-Pierce, 2002). While most parents would prefer to have their child in a quality program, the urgency and, at times, desperation of simply finding an available opening may force them to overlook this important issue. Cost and location can also be determining factors that overshadow a parent's concern about quality.

It is also true that many parents simply do not know how to begin evaluating the quality of a program. Some parents feel uncomfortable questioning teachers. Others may not be able to find a convenient high-quality program even when they are dissatisfied with poor conditions in a current arrangement.

Parent Education

Many advocacy groups and professional organizations have begun to launch national efforts to educate parents about key quality indicators and assist them in locating these programs in their communities. Similar information is also available on many Web sites, making it easy for parents to retrieve.

Researchers have identified three common features that are characteristic of high-quality early care and education programs (Bredecamp & Copple, 1997):

- small group size
- low teacher–child ratio (fewer children per teacher)
- teachers with training and education in early childhood

Parents should always take time to observe any new program they are considering and determine how the program measures up to these criteria. Additional areas that should also be noted include:

- physical facilities, e.g., clean, safe, spacious, licensed
- program philosophy, e.g., goals, objectives, developmentally appropriate
- nutritious meals and snacks
- opportunities for parent involvement
- respectful of diversity
- toys and educational activities, e.g., developmentally appropriate, variety, adequate number, organized learning experiences
- health services

Educating parents about how to recognize quality programs has obvious benefits for children. And, as demand for quality increases, some programs may be forced to improve their services or go out of business.

Resource and Referral Services

Resource and referral agencies were developed to help parents locate available child care. Many of these agencies were originally established as independent services but are now linked together to form state and national computerized networks; the National Association of Child Care Resource and Referral Agencies (NACCRRA) is one of the largest.

These agencies maintain a registry of programs and current openings for a range of child care options, from center-based to in-home care. Parents receive a list of available spaces based on their specific child care needs, such as location, cost, preferred hours, philosophy, and child's age. However, agencies do not always restrict their listings to high-quality programs. Some agencies include any program with available openings, while others screen programs carefully to ensure quality care. Resource and referral agencies also play an active role in educating parents about how to select quality child care. Many states have launched massive educational campaigns targeting this topic. These agencies are also committed to providing support and ongoing training for early childhood teachers.

REFLECTIVE THOUGHTS

Parents are often faced with difficult choices when they try to locate child care options. While efforts to improve the quality of child care continue, it is well known that not all programs reflect excellence. What does the literature suggest about how parents select child care? What features distinguish quality in early childhood programs? How can communities work together to improve the overall quality of care provided in their area? What efforts are needed to improve accessibility to quality care for all children?

Professional Accreditation

A national system of voluntary **accreditation** for early childhood programs was established in 1985 by the National Association for the Education of Young Children (NAEYC). Its primary objective is aimed at promoting excellence and improving the quality of child care through a process of self-study (NAEYC, 1999). The accreditation process identifies and recognizes outstanding early education programs and offers centers an added credential signifying their commitment to quality care. Programs are accredited for three years, at which time they must reapply. NAEYC is currently conducting an extensive review and revision of its accreditation process and standards for evaluating quality in early education programs.

Several other organizations, such as Head Start and Montessori, have initiatives to recognize outstanding programs. Some states have also begun to develop quality standards and systems for voluntary program accreditation (Kansas Stakeholders Advisory Committee for Early Childhood Education, 2001; Warman, 1998).

LICENSING

Licensing standards, established by individual states, represent an attempt to encourage and ensure that child care environments are safe and healthful for young children (Snow, Teleki, & Reguero-de-Atiles, 1996). However, these standards reflect only minimal health and safety requirements and vary considerably from one state to another. They in no way guarantee quality conditions, programs, or care. This is an issue of great concern, as programs are increasingly serving infants and children with special behavior, learning, and medical needs (Figure 8–2).

Licensing requirements serve a twofold purpose. First, they are aimed at protecting children's physical and psychological well-being by regulating the safety of environments and educational programs. Second, licensing **regulations** afford minimal protection to the program and its personnel. By complying with licensing requirements, programs are not as likely to encounter situations involving negligence.

FIGURE 8–2

Licensing standards help protect children's well-being.

---

accreditation – *the process of certifying an individual or program as having met certain specified requirements.*
licensing – *the act of granting formal permission to conduct a business or profession.*
regulations – *standards or requirements that are set to ensure uniform and safe practices.*

Early attempts to regulate child care programs dealt primarily with the sanitation and safety of facilities. However, current licensing regulations often go beyond narrow concern only for the safety of physical settings. Today, teacher qualifications and the quality of educational programs planned for young children are also recognized as important.

Each state has a designated agency that is authorized and responsible for conducting inspections and issuing or revoking licenses to operate. This agency also oversees the review and development of licensing standards and methods for enforcing **compliance**. Again, there are significant differences in licensing standards and levels of enforcement from one state to another. This fragmented approach also lacks a system for ensuring that individual states are actually carrying out their responsibilities.

In many states, home-based child programs are governed by a separate set of regulations and often include an option of either becoming licensed or registered. Those choosing to be licensed are usually inspected by a member of the licensing agency and are expected to meet certain standards. In contrast, the requirements for **registration** are often minimal. Teachers may simply be asked to place their name on a list, complete a self-administered checklist attesting to safe conditions, or attend a brief preservice informational program. An on-site inspection of these homes is seldom conducted unless a complaint is registered. Child care programs based in churches and public schools are exempt from licensing regulation in many states.

Understandably, there is always controversy around the issue of licensing for early childhood programs. Establishing licensing requirements that adequately protect young children's health and safety, yet are realistic for teachers and programs to achieve, is a challenging task. Some people believe that too much control or standards that are set too high will reduce the number of programs. The licensing process is also costly to administer and often difficult to enforce. Lowering standards may be a tempting option. On the other hand, many parents and teachers favor stricter regulations to ensure high-quality programs and improved respect for the early childhood profession.

Despite the ongoing controversy, licensing of early childhood programs is necessary. Ideally, licensing standards should adequately safeguard children, yet not be so overly restrictive that qualified individuals and programs are eliminated. The development of separate licensing requirements for in-home and center-based programs has been offered as one practical solution to this dilemma (Clarke-Stewart, Vandell, Burchinal, O'Brien & McCartney, 2002; Kendall, 1989).

Obtaining a License

A license permits a teacher to conduct a child care program on a regular basis. As mentioned earlier, the process for obtaining a license differs from one state to another. However, the steps described here are generally representative of the procedure involved. In some cases, the process may require considerable time and effort, especially if major renovations must be made to the proposed facility. For others, approval may be obtained in a reasonably short time.

Persons interested in operating an early childhood program should first contact their state or local licensing agency. Questions regarding the applicant's qualifications and specific program requirements can usually be answered at this time.

In addition to complying with state licensing regulations, child care facilities must also be in accordance with local laws and ordinances. Zoning codes must be checked carefully to determine whether or not the location of a center or in-home program is permissible in a given neighborhood. Often this requires meeting with local planning authorities and reviewing proposed floor plans.

Buildings that house child care programs must also pass a variety of inspections to be sure they meet fire, safety and sanitation codes. These inspections are usually conducted by personnel

---

compliance – *the act of obeying or cooperating with specific requests or requirements.*

registration – *the act of placing the name of a child care program on a list of active providers; usually does not require on-site inspection.*

from the local fire and public health departments. From these inspections, it is possible to determine what, if any, renovations may be necessary in order to comply with licensing regulations. In most cases, these are relatively simple; in other cases, it may not be feasible or economical to complete all of the required changes.

Once these steps have been completed, the licensing office should again be contacted. Formal applications for a permanent license can be made at this time. Copies of the program's plans and policies are then submitted to the licensing authorities for review. Final approval typically includes an on-site inspection of the facilities to see that all requirements and recommendations have been satisfied.

Federal Regulations

In addition to meeting state licensing regulations, early childhood programs receiving federal funds must also conform to special supplemental guidelines (U.S. DHEW, 1981). Governmental requirements adopted in the spring of 1981 apply to all child care centers funded through Title XX of the Social Security Act. Additional regulations also exist for all Head Start programs. All child care facilities built or remodeled after 1990 must also meet standards established by the Americans with Disabilities Act (ADA).

FEATURES OF QUALITY PROGRAMS

Researchers are continually studying children in home- and center-based programs to determine what conditions and experiences are best for promoting learning and healthy development. Through the years, they have identified several key components that distinguish high-quality programs. The National Association for the Education of Young Children (NAEYC) (the largest organization representing early care and education in the United States) and other professional organizations have embraced these findings and incorporated them into their accreditation standards and recommended guidelines (Goffin, 2002; APHA & AAP, 2002; Aronson, 2002).

Teacher Qualifications

Perhaps one of the weakest areas in many state licensing regulations pertains to staff qualifications. Emphasis is usually focused on the safety of physical settings, while staff requirements such as years of experience, educational preparation, and personal qualities are often lacking or poorly defined. Even when these issues are addressed in the licensing regulations, there is little consistency from one state to another.

Research has documented a positive correlation between teacher's educational preparation and ability to provide high-quality early childhood education (Peth-Pierce, 2002). Teachers who have a strong background in child development, value parent involvement and communication, understand and respect diversity, and know how to create developmentally appropriate experiences are more effective in facilitating positive learning outcomes for children (Essa, 2003). As more and more children with behavior problems and disabilities are enrolled in early education programs, teachers must also be prepared to meet their special needs (Booth & Jean, 2002). In addition, teachers must also be able to work and communicate effectively with children and families of diverse backgrounds.

Unfortunately, the licensing requirements in many states do not reflect what we currently know about the importance of having teachers who have obtained formal education in early childhood. Often, anyone who is 18 years of age, has a high school diploma, and passes a background check is qualified to be hired as an early childhood teacher. As a result, they are generally not prepared to handle the daily challenges involved in working with young children. This, combined with poor salaries and long hours, contributes to a high turnover rate in many programs, which is difficult for children. Initiatives to improve teacher preparation and salaries are being studied, funded, and incorporated into licensing regulations in an effort to improve the quality of care and education young children receive (Kagan, Brandon, Ripple, Maher, & Joesch, 2002; Whitebook & Eichberg, 2002). However, teachers must also take steps to continue their education and better prepare themselves to work with young children. Many scholarship programs and professional educational opportunities are currently available, including:

- on-the-job training/inservice training
- CDA (Child Development Associates credential)
- one-year vocational training; Child Care or Child Development certificate
- two-year associate degree (A.A.) (community college)
- four-year bachelor degree
- advanced graduate training (M.A. and Ph.D.)

At a minimum, all directors and head teachers should have a CDA (Child Development Associate) credential or a two-year associate arts degree with specialized training in early childhood (Kagan, Brandon, Ripple, Maher, & Joesch, 2002; Kontos, Howes, & Galinsky, 1996). However, in many areas of the country, teachers with advanced preparation are in short supply.

Some early childhood programs include paraprofessionals as part of their teaching team. These individuals may be aides who work for wages or unpaid volunteers. Regardless of their position or previous experience, it is essential that paraprofessionals receive a brief, but thorough, orientation to their job responsibilities and program procedures before working in the classrooms. This preparation allows paraprofessionals to be productive and effective when they begin working with the children. These are important considerations for employee retention and also benefit children in the long run.

Teachers who work in quality programs often have many special personal qualities and additional skills. They value communication and know how to develop meaningful relationships with children, families, and colleagues. They understand and respect diversity and make it a priority. They also possess qualities of warmth, patience, sensitivity to children's needs, respect for individual differences, and a positive attitude. They have the ability to plan, organize, make decisions, and resolve conflict. They also enjoy good personal health which allows them to cope with the physical and emotional demands of long, action-packed days. Individuals with these qualities are not only better teachers, but they are also more likely to have a positive effect on young children's lives.

Staffing Ratios

Staff/child ratios are determined by individual states and typically reflect only the minimal number of adults considered necessary to protect children's well-being (Wishard, Shivers, Howes & Ritchie, 2003). However, quality learning experiences, individualized care, and maintaining conditions that safeguard children's health and safety require more teachers than is usually recommended.

Ideally, high-quality early childhood programs provide one full-time teacher for every seven to eight children three to six years of age. Programs serving children with disabilities should have one teacher for every four to five children, depending on the age group and severity of their limitations. If children younger than two years are included, the staff/child ratio should be no more than one full-time teacher per three to four children. A list of substitutes should be available in the event of teacher illness or other absence.

Research also suggests that small group size and low teacher/child ratios improve the quality of child care programs. However, low ratios do not always guarantee that children will be safer (Burchinal, Howes, & Kontos, 2002; Munton, Blackburn, Barreau, 2002; Bredekamp & Copple, 1997). Much depends on the knowledge and supervisory skills of individual teachers.

Teachers who are part of high-quality programs practice life-long learning by attending professional meetings, inservice programs, workshops, and college classes. Exposure to new concepts, ideas, and approaches promotes continued professional growth and competence. Interaction with other teachers provides opportunities for discussing common problems, sharing ideas, and discovering unique solutions.

Group Size and Composition

When a license is issued to an early childhood program, specific conditions and restrictions under which it is allowed to operate are clearly defined. These conditions usually spell out:

- ages of children that can be enrolled
- group size per classroom
- maximum enrollment per program
- special populations of children to be served, e.g., children with behavior problems; children with developmental disabilities; infants, school age

For example, a preschool program may be licensed to provide three half-day sessions for children three to five years of age, with a maximum enrollment of 18 children per session. An in-home program might be licensed for at total of six children, ages birth to four years.

Group size is recognized as one of the most important indicators of quality child care (APHA & AAP, 2002; Bredekamp & Copple, 1997). For this reason, restrictions are usually placed on the number of children a program can enroll. This figure is determined by the amount of available space, ages and special populations of children served, as well as the number of teachers. However, it should be remembered that state regulations allow total group sizes that are often much larger than is ideal for quality care.

Admission policies should include a description of the categories of children a program is willing and able to serve. The age range, special needs, and total number of children that a program is licensed to enroll must clearly be spelled out to avoid parent misunderstanding.

Program Curriculum

The value of early learning experiences is well documented (Clarke-Stewart, Vandell, Burchinal, O'Brien, & McCartney, 2002; Kagan, Brandon, Ripple, Maher, & Joesch, 2002; Peth-Pierce, 2002). Because many children spend the majority of their waking hours in out-of-home early childhood programs, it is essential that **developmentally appropriate practices** (DAP)—learning environments and enriching opportunities—be provided (Figure 8–3). Quality early education programs plan learning experiences that address children's needs across all developmental areas, including:

- physical
- cognitive
- emotional
- social
- language
- self-care
- motor

It is important that the curriculum be stimulating and help children develop new skills. Time should be devoted to planning and organizing learning experiences and then sharing this information with parents. A schedule of daily activities and lesson plans should be posted where parents can easily read them. How activities are presented throughout the day affects children's physical stamina and mental receptiveness. Fatigue and lack of interest can often be avoided by planning activities that provide alternating periods of rest and active play. For example, a long walk outdoors might be followed by a teacher-directed flannel board story or puppet show. When teachers pay careful attention to planning, they can take advantage of times when children are most likely to learn.

---

developmentally appropriate practice (DAP) – *learning experiences and environments that take into account children's individual abilities, interests, and diverse needs. DAP also reflects differences among families and values them as essential partners in children's education.*

FIGURE 8–3

Carefully planned activities foster children's development.

Health Services

Safeguarding children's health and well-being is a fundamental part of any early childhood program (Aronson, 2002; Cryer & Phillipsen, 1997). Only when children are healthy can they fully benefit from everyday experiences and learning opportunities. Quality programs take this responsibility seriously and address children's health needs by:

- having written policies and procedures
- maintaining comprehensive health and safety records
- training personnel to administer first aid and emergency care
- developing emergency response plans
- planning for health, safety, and nutrition education

State child care licensing regulations generally establish the types of policies and records that programs are required to maintain. Although not every state's requirements are the same, quality programs often find it prudent to take a more comprehensive approach to record-keeping for improved understanding and added legal protection. Basic records that programs should maintain include:

- children's health assessments
- attendance
- emergency contact information
- developmental profiles
- adult health assessments
- fire and storm drills
- accidents and injuries
- daily health checks

Licensing authorities will carefully review the information in these records during renewal visits.

Teachers in quality child care programs are trained to handle emergencies and provide first aid and emergency care to ill or injured children. They also have completed training in cardiopulmonary resuscitation (CPR). Programs choosing to meet minimal standards should have at least one staff member who is trained in these techniques and can respond immediately to emergencies.

| **FIGURE 8–4** |

An emergency contact information form.

Download this form online at http://www.Early ChildEd.del mar.com

EMERGENCY CONTACT INFORMATION

Child's Name _____ Date of Birth _____

Address _____ Home Phone _____

Mother's Name _____ Business Phone _____

Father's Name _____ Business Phone _____

Name of other person to be contacted in case of an emergency:

1. _____ Address _____

Relationship (sitter, relative, friend, etc.) _____ Phone _____

2. _____ Address _____

Relationship (sitter, relative, friend, etc.) _____ Phone _____

Authorization is hereby given for the Child Development Center Staff to release the above named child to the following persons, provided proper identification is first established (list all names of authorized persons, including immediate family):

1. _____ Relation: _____

2. _____ Relation: _____

3. _____ Relation: _____

Physician to be called in an emergency:

1. _____ Phone _____ or _____

2. _____ Phone _____ or _____

I, the undersigned, authorize the staff of the Child Development Center to take what emergency medical measures are deemed necessary for the care and protection of my child enrolled in the Child Development Center program.

_____
(Signature of Parent or Guardian/date)

Signature witnessed by:
(Notary)

_____
(Signature of Parent or Guardian/date)

The above statement sworn before me on:

_____

_____

Notarized permission forms, similar to the one shown in Figure 8–4, listing the name, address, and telephone number of the child's physician should be completed by parents when the child is first enrolled. This measure grants teachers authority to administer emergency care or secure emergency medical treatment. Emergency numbers for fire, police, ambulance, and poison control should be posted next to the telephone for quick reference.

notarized – *official acknowledgment of the authenticity of a signature or document by a notary public.*

TABLE 8-1   Principles of Emergency Preparedness

- Remain calm—do not panic.
- Be informed. Tune in a local station on your battery-powered radio.
- Get to a safe place. Develop and practice an appropriate disaster plan.
- Keep a first-aid kit and flashlight handy.
- Take along children's health forms and emergency contact information.
- Learn basic emergency first aid.

Programs that provide care for mildly ill children should develop policies that address their special needs and care. Whether they remain in a separate area of the classroom away from other children or are moved to a different room, provisions should be made so they can rest and not expose other children to their illnesses. Medical supplies and equipment should be nearby so they are readily accessible.

Early childhood programs should also develop emergency plans and procedures so they are prepared to respond immediately and in an organized manner (Table 8-1). These plans should outline steps for protecting children's safety in the event of fire, severe storms such as tornadoes, and major disasters such as earthquakes, floods, or hurricanes. Representatives from fire and police departments, Red Cross, and local emergency preparedness groups are available to assist programs in developing their emergency plans. These plans should be shared with parents so they will know what to expect in the event of an emergency and can also use them to model similar procedures at home.

GUIDELINES FOR SAFE ENVIRONMENTS

Nowhere is health and safety more important than in group programs serving young children. When parents enroll their children in a program, they expect them to be safe. They assume the facilities, toys, and equipment will be safe for children's use, that teachers will carefully supervise their children's activities, and that the environment and food are healthy. These expectations require teachers to be well informed and knowledgeable about how to create and maintain environments that assure children's health and safety.

As previously described, there are no national child care licensing requirements. However, several organizations have developed similar recommendations for out-of-home early childhood programs. The National Association for the Education of Young Children (NAEYC) has consistently defined and supported high standards for early-childhood programs. The American Academy of Pediatrics and the American Public Health Association recently revised a document entitled *Caring for Our Children: National Health and Safety Performance Standards Guidelines for Out-of-Home Child Care Programs,* which identifies approximately 180 regulation standards and safety practices. The remainder of this chapter will address features of children's indoor and outdoor environments that require special attention.

Indoor Safety

A great deal of thought and preparation is needed to create rooms that are safe for young children. Everything from the placement of furniture and choice of floor coverings to the design of changing tables and proper storage requires careful study. Knowledge of children's abilities at each stage of development plays a key role in anticipating and eliminating potential safety hazards. (Refer to Table 9-1.) A safe environment encourages children to explore and learn through play, and is also less stressful for adults.

Building and Site Location.   In a time of increasing demand for child care and shrinking budgets, the selection of an appropriate building often requires a creative approach. It would be ideal to plan and design a facility specifically for this purpose. However, few programs have sufficient funds for new construction. More often, existing buildings, such as unused classrooms in public schools, older houses, unoccupied stores, church basements, or places of business such as factories or hospitals are modified or remodeled to make them suitable for early education programs. This type of work can be expensive and may not be practical in some instances. However, it may also be possible to use the talents of willing parents to help complete at least a small portion of the work and, thus, reduce the cost.

With the exception of church-based programs, home- and center-based programs are considered public facilities under the 1990 Americans with Disabilities Act (ADA) even if they are privately owned (Surr, 1992). Consequently, they too must comply with guidelines set forth in this historical piece of legislation requiring the removal of physical barriers that would otherwise deny access to individuals with disabilities. Early childhood-programs cannot refuse to admit children on the basis of their disabilities. They are expected to make reasonable adjustments in policies, practices, and facilities in order to accommodate all children. Admission can be denied only if these modifications are unduly difficult or costly to complete, or if there is no alternative solution to meet a child's special needs. Consequently, this law has important implications throughout the site selection, building and/or remodeling stages as more children with disabilities enroll in early childhood programs.

Location is always important to consider when selecting an appropriate site. Buildings chosen to house child care programs must meet local zoning requirements. These ordinances often make it difficult to locate programs in residential neighborhoods where they may be most needed. Buildings should be located away from heavy traffic, excessive noise, air pollution, animals, exposure to chemicals, bodies of water, large equipment, and other similar hazards to protect children's safety. However, these conditions may be unavoidable for programs in inner city and rural areas. It then becomes even more essential to devote time and extra effort to safety awareness, policy development, and educational programs for children, teachers, and parents.

Local fire codes also affect building selection. Older buildings and those not originally designed for infants and young children may require extensive changes before they pass inspection. Rooms that children occupy must have a minimum of two exits, one leading directly outdoors. All doors should be hinged so they swing out of the room; this will prevent doors from slowing the evacuation process. Programs located on upper levels should also have an enclosed stairwell for safe escape in the event of a fire.

How much space is needed depends to some extent on the type of program and services that will be offered. Thirty-five square feet of usable floor space per child is considered an absolute minimum for adequate child care. Teachers often find even this amount of space crowded and difficult to work in. Quality programs may provide 45 to 50 square feet of space per child. This amount seems to be more workable for both children and teachers. Additional space may be needed to accommodate large indoor play structures, special equipment for children with physical disabilities, or cribs for infants. However, it should also be kept in mind that spaces that are too large may be difficult to supervise. Ground floor levels are always preferable for infants and preschool-aged children, although basement areas can be used for several hours at a time provided there are at least two exits.

Space.   The arrangement of space, or basic floor plan, should be examined carefully to determine the ease of conducting specific activities. For example, the traffic flow should allow ample room for children to arrive and depart without disturbing others who are playing. Small rooms that lack storage space, good lighting, accessible bathrooms or adequate outdoor play areas are inconvenient and frustrating for both the staff and children.

⊙ REFLECTIVE THOUGHTS

As adults, we often take great efforts to create environments and rules that will protect children from harm. Yet, it can be perplexing to understand why children continue to get themselves into situations that are unsafe. Why do you think this occurs? Are adult's and children's expectations and perceptions the same? (Try getting down on your hands and knees to understand how children view their environment.) How do cultural differences affect one's definition of a safe environment?

Play spaces for infants and toddlers should be separated from those of older children to avoid injuries and confrontations. Large, open space, free of obstacles, also encourages very young children to move about and explore without hesitation (Figure 8–5).

Building Security. Added precautions should be taken to protect children from unauthorized individuals while assuring legitimate visitors safe access. Buildings and outdoor play spaces should be evaluated carefully to determine if the areas are secure. Safety measures, such as locking outside doors and gates, installing key pads, or issuing card keys (used in hotels), are effective for controlling unauthorized access. Teachers and staff members should always be alert to persons entering the building and greet them as a way of acknowledging their presence. Surveillance cameras can also be installed to monitor entrances and exits. Programs should develop and review plans for handling unauthorized visitors and summoning assistance. They may also want to establish a safe area of the building where children can be moved for added protection.

Fire Safety. Smoke and carbon monoxide detectors should be present in child care settings, especially where infants and young children will be sleeping. Additional fire safety precautions can

FIGURE 8–5

Infants need open space where they can move about and explore.

TABLE 8-2 How to Conduct a Fire Drill

Develop an Evacuation Plan

- Plan at least one alternate escape route from every room.
- Post a written copy of the plan by the door of each room.
- Inform new personnel.

Assign Specific Responsibilities

- Designate someone to call the fire department, preferably from a telephone outside of the building. Be sure to give the fire department complete information: name, address, approximate location of the fire inside the building, whether or not anyone is inside. Do not hang up until the fire department hangs up first.
- Designate several adults to assemble children and lead them out of the building; assign extra adults, e.g., cooks, secretaries, to assist with evacuation of younger children.
- Designate one adult to take a flashlight and the notarized emergency cards or class list.
- Designate someone to turn off the lights and close the doors to the rooms.

Establish a Meeting Place

- Once outside, meet at a designated location so that everyone can be accounted for.
- DO NOT GO BACK INTO THE BUILDING!

Practice Fire Evacuation Drills

- Conduct drills at least once a month; have some of these be unannounced.
- Practice alternate routes of escape.
- Practice fire evacuation safety, e.g., feel closed doors before opening them, select an alternate route if hallway or stairwells are filled with smoke, stay close to the floor (crawl) to avoid heat and poisonous gases, learn the stop-drop-roll technique.
- Use a stopwatch to time each drill and record the results; work for improvement.

be taken by installing flame-retardant floor coverings and draperies and having at least one multi-purpose fire extinguisher available. Staff should be familiar with the location of building exits and emergency procedures. Teachers should be trained to conduct monthly fire drills so children will be familiar with the routine and not be frightened in the event of a real emergency (Table 8–2). Plans for evacuating children with special needs should also be given careful attention.

Extension cords should not be used. All electrical outlets should be covered with safety caps, which can be purchased in most grocery or hardware stores. However, caps are only a temporary solution; they are frequently removed and not replaced, and can become a choking hazard for young children. Conventional outlets can be replaced with childproof receptacles by an electrician.

Bathroom Facilities. Adequate bathroom facilities are also essential. They should be accessible to both indoor and outdoor play areas. Installation of child-sized fixtures, including sinks, toilets, soap dispensers, and towel racks, allow children to care for their own needs (Figure 8–6). If only adult-sized fixtures are available, foot stools, large wooden blocks, or platforms securely anchored to the floor will facilitate children's independence. One toilet and sink should be available for every 10 to 12 children. Programs serving children with disabilities should be designed to meet their special needs and be in compliance with ADA standards (Surr, 1992). A separate bathroom area should also be available for adults and staff members.

FIGURE 8–6

Child-sized fixtures encourage independence.

Handwashing facilities located near toilets and sleeping areas encourage good handwashing habits. Hot water temperatures should be maintained between 105° F (40.5° C) and 120° F (48.8° C) to protect children from accidental burns (Child Health Alert, 2003). Liquid soap dispensers placed near sinks encourage handwashing, are easy for children to use, and are less likely to end up on the floor. The use of individual paper towels and cups also improves sanitation and limits the spread of communicable illness. Smooth surfaces on walls and floors facilitate cleaning. Light colors, especially in bathrooms, make dirt visible and, therefore, able to be cleaned more promptly. Fixtures such as mirrors, light switches, and towel dispensers placed within children's reach, good lighting, and bright paint create a functional and pleasant atmosphere in which young children can develop self-care skills.

Surface and Furnishings. Furniture and equipment should be selected carefully. Children are less likely to be injured if chairs and tables are appropriately proportioned. Quality is also an important feature to consider. Furniture should be sturdy so that it can withstand hard use by groups of children and meet federal safety standards (see Chapter 9). Items with sharp corners or edges should be avoided. Bookcases, lockers, pianos and other heavy objects should be anchored securely to the wall or floor to prevent children from pulling them over. Tall bookshelves should be replaced or cut in half to make them more child sized.

Materials used for wall and floor coverings should be easy to clean. Vinyl floor covering is a popular choice for use in child care centers for this reason. However, they do become very slippery when wet. Care must be taken to wipe up spills immediately or to place rugs or newspapers in areas where floors are likely to get wet. Often a combination of carpeted and tiled areas is most satisfactory because it provides soft, warm surfaces where children can sit as well as surfaces that can easily be cleaned.

Each child should have an individual storage space, cubby, or locker where personal belongings can be kept (Figure 8–7). A child's private space is particularly important in group settings. It offers the psychological benefit of belonging to only that child, whereas most other objects in the classroom are expected to be shared. Individual cubbies help minimize the loss of prized possessions. They also are effective for controlling the spread of communicable illnesses that are transmitted through direct and indirect contact (such as head lice and pinkeye).

FIGURE 8-7

Each child should have a personal space or cubby to store belongings.

Other standards aimed at improving the quality and safety of child care facilities include having locked cabinets available for storing medicines and other potentially poisonous substances, for example, cleaning products, paints, gasoline.

For emergency use, a telephone should be located conveniently in the building. A list of emergency phone numbers, including the fire department, police, hospital, ambulance and poison control center, should be posted next to the telephone. A checklist for evaluating the safety of indoor and outdoor areas is illustrated in Table 8-3.

Lighting and Ventilation. Low windows and glass doors should be constructed of safety glass or plastic to prevent serious injuries if they are broken. Colorful pictures or decals placed at children's eye level also help to discourage children from accidentally walking into the glass. Doors and windows should be covered with screens that can also be locked. Cords from draperies or blinds should be fastened up high and out of children's reach to prevent stangulation.

Good lighting is essential in classrooms and hallways. Rooms that are sunny and bright are inviting and attractive to both teachers and children. Natural light from windows and glass doors is one of the most desirable ways to supply rooms with light. Sunlight costs nothing to use and has a positive psychological effect.

Proper arrangement of artificial lighting is equally as important as the amount of brightness it produces. Areas of a room that are used for close activities, such as reading centers or art tables, require more lighting. Fluorescent lights are ideal for this purpose because they give off more light that is less glaring than incandescent bulbs. Although fluorescent lighting is initially more costly to install, it uses less electricity to operate.

Heating and cooling systems should be in good operating condition and able to maintain room temperatures between 68° F (20° C) and 85° F (29.4° C) year round (Ferng & Lee, 2002). Rooms occupied by young children should not have hot radiators, pipes, furnaces, or fireplaces exposed where children can come in contact with them; wire screen can be wrapped around free-standing heaters and fans to prevent injury.

Indoor Air Quality. Every day, children are exposed to a variety of indoor air pollutants, including formaldehyde (in carpet and building materials), carbon monoxide, radon, asbestos, cigarette smoke, paint fumes, lead, numerous household chemicals, and pesticides. More studies are

TABLE 8-3 Safety Checklist

	Date Checked	Pass/Fail	Comments
Indoor Areas			
1. A minimum of 35 square feet of usable space is available per child			
2. Room temperature is between 68°–85° F (20°–29.4° C)			

3. Rooms have good ventilation
  a. windows and doors have screens
  b. mechanical ventilation systems in working order			

4. There are two exits in all rooms occupied by children			
5. Carpets and draperies are fire-retardant			
6. Rooms are well lighted			
7. Glass doors and low windows are constructed of safety glass			
8. Walls and floors of classrooms, bathrooms, and kitchen appear clean; floors are swept daily, bathroom fixtures are scrubbed at least every other day			
9. Tables and chairs are child sized			
10. Electrical outlets are covered with safety caps			
11. Smoke detectors are located in appropriate places and in working order			
12. Furniture, activities and equipment are set up so that doorways and pathways are kept clear			
13. Play equipment and materials are stored in designated areas; they are inspected frequently and are safe for children's use			
14. Large pieces of equipment, e.g., lockers, piano, bookshelves, are firmly anchored to the floor or wall			
15. Cleaners, chemicals and other poisonous substances are locked up			

16. If stairways are used
  a. a handrail is placed at children's height
  b. stairs are free of toys and clutter
  c. stairs are well lighted
  d. stairs are covered with a nonslip surface			

17. Bathroom areas:
  a. toilets and washbasins are in working order
  b. one toilet and washbasin available for every 10–12 children; potty chairs provided for children in toilet training
  c. water temperature is no higher than 120° F (48.8° C)
  d. powdered or liquid soap is used for handwashing
  e. individual or paper towels are used for each child
  f. diapering tables or mats are cleaned after each use			

(Continued)

TABLE 8–3 Safety Checklist (Continued)

	Date Checked	Pass/ Fail	Comments
18. At least one fire extinguisher is available and located in a convenient place; extinguisher is checked annually by fire-testing specialists			
19. Premises are free from rodents and/or undesirable insects			
20. Food preparation areas are maintained according to strict sanitary standards			
21. At least one individual on the premises is trained in emergency first aid and CPR; first aid supplies are readily available			
22. All medications are stored in a locked cabinet or box			
23. Fire and storm/disaster drills are conducted on a monthly basis			
24. Security measures (plans, vigilant staff, key pads, locked doors, video cameras) are in place to protect children from unauthorized visitors.			
Outdoor Areas			
1. Play areas are located away from heavy traffic, loud noises and sources of chemical contamination			
2. Play areas are located adjacent to premises or within safe walking distance			
3. Play areas are well drained			
4. Bathroom facilities and drinking fountain easily accessible			
5. A variety of play surfaces, e.g., grass, concrete, sand are available; there is a balance of sunny areas and shady areas			
6. Play equipment is in good condition, e.g., no broken or rusty parts, missing pieces, splinters, sharp edges, frayed rope			
7. Selection of play equipment is appropriate for children's ages			
8. Soft ground covers present in sufficient amounts under large, climbing equipment; area is free of sharp debris			
9. Large pieces of equipment are stable and anchored in the ground			
10. Equipment is placed sufficiently far apart to allow a smooth flow of traffic and adequate supervision			
11. Play areas are enclosed by a fence at least four feet high, with a gate and workable lock for children's security and safety			
12. There are no poisonous plants, shrubs, or trees in the area			
13. Chemicals, insecticides, paints and gasoline products are stored in a locked cabinet			
14. Grounds are maintained on a regular basis and are free of debris; grass is mowed; broken equipment is removed			
15. Wading or swimming pools are always supervised; water is drained when not in use			

TABLE 8–4 Some Common Air Pollutants and Their Health Effects

Sources

- organic particles (e.g., dust mites)
- molds
- pollen
- carbon monoxide
- formaldehyde
- insulation (e.g., asbestos, fiberglass)
- ozone

Common Health Effects

• chronic cough	• fatigue	• skin irritation
• headache	• eye irritation	• shortness of breath
• dizziness	• sinus congestion	• nausea

demonstrating a close relationship between these pollutants and an increased rate of respiratory illnesses, allergies, and asthma among children (Brugge, et al., 2003; Gold, 2002; Weisel, 2002). The toxic properties of these substances may pose an even greater health risk for young children because of their immature body systems and rapid growth (Table 8–4). However, little is known about the long-term effects of air pollutants on children's health.

While it is impossible to avoid exposure to all toxic chemicals in an environment, increased awareness and understanding of control measures can effectively reduce the risks to young children (Daisey, Angell, & Apte, 2003; Dishop, 2002). Aerosol sprays should always be avoided around children. Indoor air quality can be improved significantly by simply increasing ventilation (opening doors and windows daily, turning on air conditioning) and substituting alternative products for toxic chemicals. Many new building materials manufactured without toxic chemicals are now available. Toys and art materials should always be nontoxic (Figure 8–8). Also, the safety of all building materials and heating and ventilating systems should be checked regularly.

FIGURE 8–8

Children's toys should always be made from nontoxic materials.

Outdoor Safety

The outdoors presents an exciting environment for an endless array of imaginative play and learning opportunities for children (Sutterby & Frost, 2002; Barrett, 2001). It also has important implications for their health in terms of promoting physical activity and acquiring a lifelong appreciation for fitness and outdoor recreation. As studies continue to reveal an alarming increase in obesity among young children, the positive value of active outdoor physical activity on well-being cannot be overlooked. However, outdoor play areas are also a major source of unintentional injury for children and, therefore, require a heightened awareness of design, maintenance, and supervisory strategies (Frost, Wortham, & Reifel, 2001; Thompson & Hudson, 2000).

Space. Safety must be a major consideration in the design of outdoor play areas. No less than 75–100 square feet of space per child (using it at the same time) should be available to encourage active play and decrease the potential for accidents. The National Health and Safety Performance Standards recommend that play areas for infants include a minimum of 33 square feet per child; 50 square feet per child is suggested for toddlers (APHA and AAP, 2002). Ideally, play areas should be located adjacent to the child care facility so bathrooms are also readily accessible and children are not required to walk long distances. Traveling even a short distance to playgrounds with young children requires considerable time and effort, and often discourages spontaneous outdoor play.

A fence at least four feet in height should surround the play area and include two exits with latched gates to prevent children from wandering away. Railings or slats should be spaced less than three-and-one-half or more than nine inches apart to prevent children's heads or bodies from becoming entrapped. Sharp wire and picket-type fences are inappropriate and should not be used around young children.

An important design element in children's play areas involves the use of space (DeBord, Hestenes, Moore, Cosco, & McGinnis, 2002; Flynn & Kieff, 2002). Play areas should be arranged so that children are clearly visible from all directions. Large open areas encourage active play such as running and tossing balls. Hard, flat surfaces allow children to use riding toys and play out-

---

ISSUES TO CONSIDER • Security in Child Care Programs

Recent media reports of shootings in school, child mistreatment, and workplace violence have heightened concerns about security (Tang, 1999; Glassner, 1999). Many businesses have installed additional security devices in office buildings and enhanced existing security procedures, but child care programs have been slower to respond. Routine background checks of child care employees, the ability of staff to recognize a child's parent, and parental permission for releasing a child to other individuals are often the primary safety measures programs rely on. Some centers are implementing more innovative security measures, including touch key pads and Web cameras that allow parents to view children on their computer screens while at work (Morris, 1999).

- What resources are available for learning more about appropriate steps to take?
- What workplace policies and procedures are necessary to protect the safety of children and teachers?
- What are some advantages and disadvantages of increasing security in child care programs?
- What does the need for increased security in child care programs say about contemporary society?
- What newer technologies can be used in centers to improve building security?

doors during inclement weather, especially if these areas are covered. Flower beds provide children with space for gardening, while sand promotes imaginary play. Grassy areas and trees create a natural touch and offer protection from the sun. If trees are not available, large colorful awnings or tents can also be purchased from play equipment companies or home improvement stores to provide shade. Separate areas designed for quiet and active play also help to reduce the potential for accidents. Always be sure to check with a local nursery or county extension office to be sure that flowers, trees, and other plantings are not poisonous to children. See Table 8–5 for a partial list and Figure 8–9. A comprehensive listing, complete with photographs is available to http://www.ansci.cornell.edu/plants/comlist.html.

Designing outdoor playgrounds so they can also be enjoyed by children with disabilities presents another unique and challenging opportunity. Guidelines are now available for applying the Americans with Disabilities Act (ADA) standards to playgrounds. Solid, flat surfaces that are at least three-and-one-half feet wide allow children to maneuver safely in their wheelchairs. Bright colors, textures, ramps, and handrails can easily be incorporated into play environments, improving their accessibility to children. Also, a wider selection of modified outdoor play equipment serving the needs of all children is now available from many manufacturers.

FIGURE 8–9

Examples of poisonous plants.

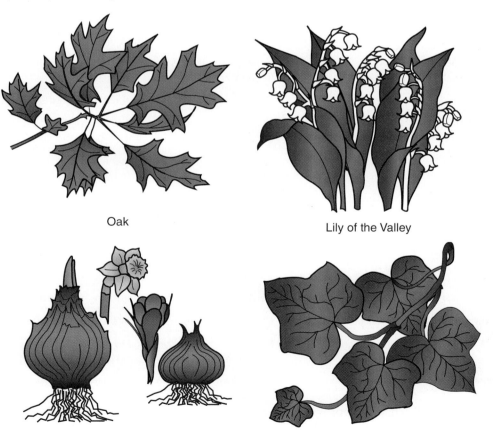

Oak

Lily of the Valley

Daffodil & Crocus Bulbs

English Ivy

TABLE 8–5 Some Common Poisonous Vegetation

Vegetation	Poisonous Part	Complications
Bittersweet	Berries	Causes a burning sensation in the mouth. Nausea, vomiting, dizziness, and convulsions.
Buttercup	All parts	Irritating to the digestive tract. Causes nausea and vomiting.
Castor Bean	Beanlike pod	Extremely toxic. May be fatal to both children and adults.
Daffodil, hyacinth, narcissus, jonquil, iris	Bulbs Underground roots	Nausea, vomiting, and diarrhea. Can be fatal.
Dieffenbachia	Leaves	Causes immediate burning and swelling around mouth.
English Ivy	Leaves and berries	Ingestion results in extreme burning sensation.
Holly	Berries	Results in cramping, nausea, vomiting, and diarrhea.
Lily-of-the-Valley	Leaves and flowers	Nausea, vomiting, dizziness, and mental confusion.
Mistletoe	Berries	Extremely toxic. Diarrhea and irregular pulse.
Oleander	Flowers and sap	Highly toxic; can be fatal. Causes nausea, vomiting, diarrhea, and heart irregularities.
Philodendron	Leaves	Ingestion causes intense irritation and swelling of the lips and mouth.
Rhubarb	Raw leaves	Can cause convulsions, coma, and rapid death.
Sweet Pea	All parts, especially the seeds	Shallow respirations, possible convulsions, paralysis, and slow pulse.
Black Locust Tree	Bark, leaves, pods and seeds	Causes nausea and weakness, especially in children.
Cherry Tree	Leaves and twigs	Can be fatal. Causes shortness of breath, general weakness, and restlessness.
Golden Chain Tree	Beanlike seed pods	Can cause convulsions and coma.
Oak Tree	Acorns and leaves	Eating large quantities may cause poisoning. Gradually causes kidney failure.
Rhododendron	All parts	Causes vomiting, convulsions, and paralysis.
Wisteria	Seed pods	Causes severe diarrhea and collapse.
Yews	Berries and foliage	Foliage is very poisonous and can be fatal. Causes nausea, diarrhea, and difficult breathing.

Equipment.   Each year approximately 200,000 children under the age of 12 are treated in emergency rooms as a result of playground injuries (CPSC, 2001). Because most injuries involve play equipment, careful attention must be given to its selection, placement, and maintenance (Table 8–6; also see Chapter 9). Choices of equipment should be based on:

TABLE 8–6 General Guidelines for Purchasing Outdoor Play Equipment

Consider:

- height of platforms and decks; these should be no higher than four–five feet for preschoolers, six feet for school-age children
- railings present on all decks and platforms, especially those higher than 30 inches above ground
- the size of all openings (including those between rungs and guard rails) should be closer than three-and-one-half inches or more than nine inches apart to prevent entrapment
- hardware such as "S" hooks, protruding nuts and bolts, or moving pieces of rope that could injure fingers or catch on clothing; rope swings that could cause strangulation
- materials used in construction. Wood/wood products require maintenance to avoid splintering and deterioration. Metal is strong, but gets hot in sunlight and becomes slippery when wet. Paints and chemicals used for wood treatment must be nontoxic
- the type of surface material that will be needed under equipment
- the amount of area required for safe installation. A clearance area of nine feet is needed for stationary equipment; fifteen feet is needed for equipment with moving parts such as swings
- ladders that are set straight up and down (vs. on an angle) encourage children to hold onto rungs when climbing

- amount of available play space
- age and developmental appropriateness
- variety of learning experiences provided
- quality and safety of construction

Large pieces of equipment and portable climbing structures should be firmly anchored in the ground; posts should be sunk 12 to 18 inches below ground surface if anchored with metal pins or at least six inches if set in concrete. Play equipment for preschoolers should be no taller than six feet and located at least nine feet from other equipment or surfaces such as concrete and asphalt to avoid injury in the event of a fall. This distance should be increased to 15 feet if the equipment has moving parts such as swings (Figure 8–10).

Because children are frequently injured on swings and teeter totters, many states no longer permit child care programs to include them on newly constructed playgrounds (Tinsworth & McDonald, 2001). When they are allowed, swing seats should be constructed of plastic or rubber to decrease the risk of impact injuries. If tires are used for swings, holes should be drilled to prevent water from collecting and allowing mosquitoes to breed. The size of any opening on equipment should also be carefully checked (less than three-and-one-half inches or greater than nine inches) to be sure children's heads will not accidentally become entrapped. While large trampolines have recently increased in popularity, they are not appropriate in child care settings (Furnival, Street, & Schunk, 1999). Due to an increasing number of deaths and serious injuries, the American Academy of Pediatrics has discouraged their use in private backyards, schools, and for athletic activities and has recommended that they be prohibited for use by children under age six (American Academy of Pediatrics, 1999).

Sand boxes require special care and attention to keep them safe for children (Table 8–7). Play sand, made specifically for children's sandboxes, can be purchased at garden centers or from building contractors or cement suppliers. (**Note:** Sands used in construction may contain hazardous materials, such as asbestos, and should not be used for children). Sandboxes should have good drainage and a tightly fitting cover to keep out animals and insects. If they cannot be covered when not in use, sand should be inspected carefully for animal feces. Sand should be raked and

FIGURE 8–10

Climbing structures should be located away from hard surfaces.

checked each day for spiders, insects, sticks, stones, or other sharp debris before children play. Frequent sweeping of adjoining surfaces reduces the potential for slipping and falling.

Wading or swimming pools can add interest to outdoor play areas. However, they require extra supervision, safety, and sanitation precautions.

Caution: Children must never be left unattended around any source of water, including sprinklers, wading pools, water tables, puddles, ditches, fountains, buckets, or toilets.

Every teacher should be familiar with water safety procedures and at least one adult on site should be CPR certified. Children's water activities are safer and easier to monitor if the number of children is limited. Safety rules should be carefully explained to the children before an activity begins and then strictly enforced.

It is essential that pool water be disinfected prior to use by each group of children to prevent the spread of disease. Inexpensive water-quality test kits are available from pool supply stores. Permanent pools and natural bodies of water must be fenced (at least five feet in height; be sure to check local codes) and have self-closing gates. Additional protection from childhood drowning can be provided by gate alarms, pool safety covers, motion alarms, and the availability of proper flotation devices.

TABLE 8–7 Sandbox Care and Maintenance

- Purchase only special play sand for children's sandboxes.
- Make sure there is adequate drainage to prevent water from pooling.
- Rake and check sand daily for spiders, stones, and sharp objects.
- Cover sand if at all possible; if not, be sure to check for animal feces before children play.
- Sweep adjoining surfaces to prevent slipping and falling.

Tricycles and other small riding toys are always children's favorites. However, they also are involved in many serious childhood injuries and a common cause of head trauma (Lalloo & Sheiham, 2003; Stanken, 2000). Children should always be required to wear bike helmets when they are riding. It is important that helmets fit properly, are worn correctly, and meet new safety standards mandated by the Consumer Product Safety Commission (Figure 8–11) (Lohse, 2003; CPSC, 1999). A designated riding area away from where other children are playing makes riding less hazardous. It is also important to discuss rules for safe riding with children to avoid collisions and subsequent injury. Encouraging all children to ride in the same direction and only one child on a bike at a time makes riding even safer.

Surface Materials. Protective materials that are soft and resilient should always be placed under play equipment to protect children from harm (Table 8–8). A minimum of 9–10 inches of

FIGURE 8–11

Helmets must fit and be worn correctly to protect children from serious injury.

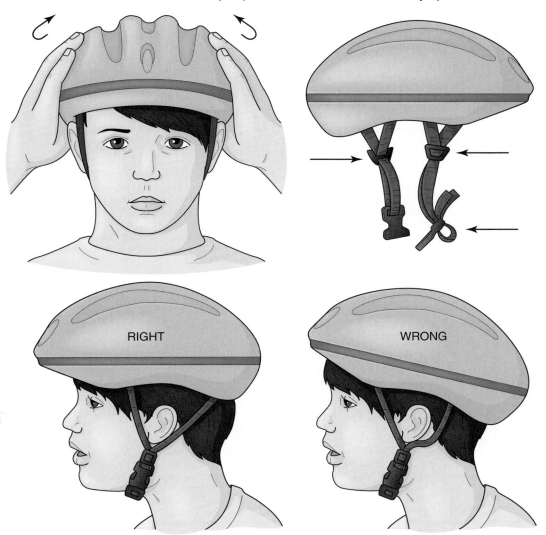

RIGHT

WRONG

TABLE 8–8 Comparison of Surfacing Materials

Material	Advantages	Disadvantages
gravel, pea (3/8 inch diameter) (6–9 inches depth)	• relatively inexpensive • readily available • long-lasting; won't decompose • drains quickly • doesn't attract animals • easy to install	• requires a barrier for containment • becomes compact if wet and freezes • must be replenished periodically; may mix with soil below • not recommended with children under 5 years; small pebbles may be thrown or stuffed into noses, ears, or mouths • not wheelchair accessible. Hazardous if gravel is scattered on hard surfaces nearby; can cause slipping and falls
gravel, medium (12 inches depth)	• qualities are similar to pea gravel	• disadvantages are similar to pea gravel • larger pieces tend to cause more superficial scrapes
bark mulch (6 inches depth)	• inexpensive • easy to install • drains quickly • readily available	• decomposes rapidly • must be contained with barriers; can wash away with heavy rains • absorbs moisture and freezes • compacts easily • difficult to find sharp objects, e.g. broken glass, sticks, nails, stones in loose mulch • prone to microbial infestations
wood chips (6 inches)	• air trapped between chips promotes cushioning effect • low in cost • accessible to wheelchairs	• washes away with heavy rains • decomposes and must be replenished to maintain cushion-effect • may be thrown about by children but not likely to cause injury
sand (coarse or masonry sand) (12 inches)	• easy to obtain • inexpensive • does not deteriorate over time • easy to install • not as prone to microbial or insect infestation • accessible by wheelchairs	• must be replenished periodically to maintain cushioning effect • may be thrown about or eaten by children • gets into shoes and clothing • hazardous when spilled onto nearby hard surfaces such as cement and tile floors; causes slipping and falls • attractive to animals, especially cats if area not covered • must be raked and sifted frequently to check for undesirable objects, e.g., sticks, broken glass, stones • requires good drainage beneath
shredded tires (10–12 inches)	• relatively low initial cost • requires good drainage system • doesn't deteriorate over time • not as likely to compact • less conducive to microbial and insect infestation • wheelchair accessible	• is flammable • may stain clothing if not treated • may contain metal particles from steel belted tires • easily thrown about by children but unlikely to cause injury
rubber tiles or mat systems (Check manufacturer's recommendations.)	• uniform cushioning effect • easy to clean and maintain • material remains in place • foreign objects are easily noticed • good accessibility to wheelchairs	• expensive to install • requires a flat surface; difficult to use on hills or uneven area • mat or tile edges may curl up and present a tripping hazard • some materials affected by frost

Note: Suggested material depths (noncompacted) are based on shock absorbancy from falls of 6 feet.
Source: *Handbook for Public Playground Safety*, U.S. Consumer Product Safety Commission, 2003.

sand, pea gravel, finely chopped rubber, or bark mulch will provide adequate shock resistance (CPSC, 1997). However, these materials must be loosened frequently to prevent them from packing and be replaced as they deteriorate. They must also be checked frequently to remove any sharp debris. Specially designed rubber mats are also an acceptable choice for fall zones and can be purchased through most outdoor equipment catalogues. Surface materials should extend approximately four feet beyond the designated fall zone to ensure children's protection.

Maintenance. Hazardous conditions can often be spotted if outdoor play areas are inspected carefully each day before children begin to play. Equipment with broken pieces, jagged or sharp edges, loose screws or bolts, or missing parts should be removed or made off-limits to children. Frequent inspections of play areas for poisonous vegetation, snakes, rodents or other small animals, sharp sticks, fallen branches, broken glass, or other harmful debris can avoid unintentional injury.

Supervision. Although individuals may go to great lengths to design attractive playgrounds and safe equipment, there is without a doubt no substitution for good supervision. Children must never be left unattended. Outdoor times provide valuable opportunities for helping children learn self-protection skills that will last a lifetime. A detailed discussion of safety management will be presented in Chapter 9.

Transportation

Some early childhood programs transport children to and from other school settings or on occasional field trips. Large passenger vans are often used for this purpose, but they are not considered safe and, in the event of an accident, may actually place occupants at increased risk for serious injury (National Transportation Safety Board, 2002). Vans have a tendency to roll over and offer poor structural protection to passengers. As a result, federal transportation officials currently recommend that early childhood programs replace existing passenger vans with small-scale school buses. These buses are designed with improved structural safety features (roof and fuel tanks) and, thus, offer greater protection.

Any vehicle used to transport children should be fitted with an appropriate safety restraint system (based on height, weight, and age) for each child:

- an infant carrier for infants weighing up to 20–22 pounds (9.1–10.0 kg) (installed facing the rear of the car) with a 3- or 5-point harness.
- a child safety seat for children weighing 20–40 pounds (9.1–18.2 kg) and able to sit up by themselves (installed facing the front of the car)
- a booster seat used in combination with a lap belt and shoulder harness for children who have outgrown child seats and are under 54 inches (135 cm) in height
- a vehicle lap belt and shoulder harness for children who are at least 55–58 inches (137.5–145 cm) in height

It is also critical that safety seats and restraints be installed according to manufacturer's specifications and used correctly whenever children are in transit:

- they must be correctly installed (facing the front or back as is appropriate) and securely anchored in the vehicle
- they must meet federal standards for manufacturing
- children must always be buckled into the seat

Children and adults must always be buckled in securely on every trip even though it may be a time-consuming process. Young children should always ride in the back seat of a vehicle to avoid accidental injury from airbags.

The driver of any vehicle must be a responsible individual and possess a current license appropriate for the number of passengers to be transported. Parents of children who are transported on a regular basis should get to know the driver so they feel comfortable with the arrangement. Written permission and special instructions should always be obtained from each parent before children are transported.

Motor vehicles used to transport children must be in good repair. Air conditioning and heating should be operational to protect children from temperature extremes. Copies of children's health forms and emergency contact information should also be kept in the vehicle. Periodic inspections of all safety and mechanical features ensure the vehicle's safe performance. An ABC-type fire extinguisher should be fastened in the front of the vehicle where it is readily available for emergencies. Liability insurance should be purchased to cover the vehicle, driver, and maximum number of passengers it will be carrying.

Whether parents or programs are responsible for transporting children, additional precautions can be taken to safeguard children. Special off-street areas can be designated for the sole purpose of loading and unloading young children. If programs do not have adequate space to provide this feature, greater emphasis will need to be placed on safety education. Parents and children should continually be reminded to use caution around traffic. Parents should be encouraged to help children enter and exit from the curb-side rather than the street-side of a car. Programs can also reduce traffic congestion around centers and improve children's safety by providing adequate parking for parents.

Some programs ask parents, on occasion, to provide transportation for off-site field trips. However, this practice is risky and has the potential for creating serious legal problems in the event of an accident. Programs have no guarantee that privately owned vehicles or individual drivers meet the standards and qualifications previously discussed. As a result, programs may be even more vulnerable to lawsuits and charges of negligence. To avoid this risk, programs may want to use public transportation, such as a city bus, or contract with a private transportation company.

When private vehicles are used for transportation, several steps can be taken to protect children's safety. Travel routes should be planned well in advance, reviewed with the director, and followed precisely by all drivers. Names of drivers, additional adults, and children riding in each vehicle, as well as anticipated departure and arrival times should also be left with a program administrator. Rules for safe traveling should be reviewed with drivers and children. Plans for responding to an unplanned emergency, such as an ill child, flat tire, car jacking, or unusual weather, should be also be discussed and reviewed regularly with drivers. At least one adult should have first aid and CPR training.

FOCUS ON FAMILIES • How to Choose Quality Child Care

All parents want to find the best early childhood education placement for their children, but knowing what features to look for is often difficult. Small group size, a small ratio of adults to children, and teachers who have educational preparation in early childhood are three indicators commonly associated with quality programs. Parents should always take time to visit a program before enrolling their children and attempt to answer some of the following questions:

- Does the environment appear to be clean, safe, and appealing to children? For example, are electrical outlets covered, are sharp items stored out of children's reach, is the carpet intact and free of snags or stains, and do children wash their hands before eating?

- Is the program accredited or licensed?

- Do the children seem happy and under control? Are children encouraged in their efforts and allowed to express their feelings? Are teachers playing and talking with the children? Do they help children solve their own problems?

- Are children treated with respect and as individuals? Is the teacher's tone of voice warm and friendly versus harsh and demanding?

- Is there adequate adult supervision? Are enough adults present to respond to an injured child or classroom emergency, and to assure the safety of other children?

- Are there a sufficient number and variety of toys and materials for all children to use, or must children wait for others to finish? Are items easily accessible to children?

- Is the food served to children nutritious, age appropriate, and adequate in amount? If your child has food allergies, would special needs be accommodated? Are weekly menus posted?

- Have the teachers been trained to work with young children? Do they appear to enjoy working with the children and take pride in their efforts? Are they knowledgeable about how to facilitate children's development and spot problems? Be sure to ask about their educational preparation and years of experience.

- Do you feel welcomed and encouraged to ask questions? Are there opportunities for you to become involved in your child's classroom?

- Are learning experiences planned for children, or are they left to wander or watch television? Is a daily schedule of the children's activities posted for you to read?

- Do you agree with the program's philosophy, and is it appropriate for your child's needs?

- Have the program's policies been explained clearly, and are they acceptable to you?

 CASE STUDY

Linh Nam cares for several neighborhood children while their parents work at the local meatpacking factory. In the beginning, she agreed to take in one or two children on days when their parents were unable to find other child care arrangements. However, now Linh has seven children, 19 months to six years, who show up on a regular basis. Their parents are grateful and pleased with the loving care Linh provides. She fears that local licensing authorities will discover her activities, but is reluctant to contact them because she has no formal training in child care and isn't sure that her house will meet safety standards. She also knows that her friends depend on her for child care and could lose their jobs if they don't have anywhere to leave their children.

1. What are Linh's options?
2. What steps can Linh take to improve her chances of becoming licensed?
3. Should licensing (or registration) be mandatory for in-home child care?
4. Should programs that don't meet state licensing standards be closed down?
5. How can increasing demands for child care be balanced against a need to improve their quality?

SUMMARY

- Environment affects all aspects of children's growth and development.

- Children's environments must be planned to be enriching and safe.

- Regulation of early childhood facilities and programs is essential for protecting children's safety.

- Adhering to licensing regulations can help protect teachers, however, not everyone agrees about how much regulation is necessary.

- Licensing procedures vary from state to state.

- The review process generally includes:
  - meeting local zoning, fire, safety, and sanitation codes.
  - review of staff qualifications and training.
  - evaluation of curriculum plans and program policies.
  - assurance that transportation, food service, and health care are adequate.

- Parents can be advocates for quality programs by supporting licensing and accreditation efforts, selecting quality care for their children, and being informed.

SUGGESTED ACTIVITIES

1. Develop a safety checklist that teachers and parents could use to inspect children's outdoor play areas for hazardous conditions. Using your list, conduct an inspection of two different play yards (for example, public vs. private), or the same play area on two separate occasions. Repeat the process for indoor areas.

2. Contact your local licensing agency. Make arrangements to accompany licensing personnel on an on-site visit of a center-based program. Be sure to review state licensing regulations beforehand. Observe how the licensing inspection is conducted. In several short paragraphs, describe your reactions to this experience.

3. Often licensing personnel are viewed as unfriendly or threatening authority figures. However, their major role is to offer guidance and help teachers create safe environments for children. Role play how you would handle the following situations during a licensing visit. Keep in mind the positive role of licensing personnel, e.g., offering explanations, providing suggestions, planning acceptable solutions and alternatives:
   - electrical outlets not covered
   - all children's toothbrushes found stored together in a large plastic bin
   - open boxes of dry cereals and crackers in kitchen cabinets
   - an adult-sized toilet and wash basin in the bathroom
   - a swing set located next to a cement patio
   - incomplete information on children's immunization records
   - a teacher who prepares snacks without first washing his or her hands

4. Obtain and read a copy of your state's licensing regulations. Organize a class debate on the topic of minimal vs. quality standards for early childhood programs.

5. Prepare a brochure or simple checklist for parents on how to select quality child care.

6. Send for information about the Child Development Associate program (available from the Council for Professional Recognition, 2460 16th St., NW, Washington, DC, 20009-3575, (800) 424–4310). After reading the materials, write a brief summary describing the program.

7. Invite a county extension agent or florist to bring in examples or cuttings of poisonous plants.

8. Go to the U.S. Consumer Product Safety Commission Web site (www.cpsc.gov). Review and summarize the recommended safety standards for at least eight playground items. Prepare a handout for parents highlighting safety conditions they should observe in public play areas.

CHAPTER REVIEW

A. **Briefly answer the following questions:**

1. How does environment affect a child's growth and development?

2. What steps are generally involved in obtaining a license to operate an early childhood program?

3. Why is it important for each child to have a personal locker or cubby?

4. Name three features that help to make an outdoor play yard safe for young children.

5. Describe eight features of a quality child care program.

B. **Match the definition in column I with the term in column II.**

Column I	Column II
1. local ordinance that indicates what type of facility shall be in an area	a. regulation
2. rule dealing with procedures	b. minimal standards
3. method of action that determines present and future decisions	c. staff qualification
4. witnessed form that indicates the signature that appears on the form is really that of the person signing the form	d. notarized permissions
5. skills possessed by the people responsible for the operation of a business	e. policy
6. meeting the least possible requirements	f. zoning code

REFERENCES

Allen, K. E., & Cowdery, G. (2005). *The exceptional child: Inclusion in early childhood education.* Clifton Park, NY: Delmar Learning.

Allred, K., Briem, R., & Black, S. (1998). Collaboratively addressing the needs of young children with disabilities. *Young Children, 53*(5), 32–36.

American Academy of Pediatrics (AAP). (1999, May). Trampolines at home, school, and recreational centers. *Pediatrics, 103*(5), 1053–1056.

American Public Health Association (APHA) and American Academy of Pediatrics (AAP). (2002). *Caring for our children: National health and safety performance standards for out-of-home care.* Washington, DC: Authors.

Aronson, S. (2002). *Healthy young children: A manual for programs.* (4th ed.). Washington, DC: NAEYC.

Barrett, B. (2001). Play now, play later: Lifetime fitness implications. *Journal of Physical Education, Recreation, & Dance, 72*(8), 35–39.

Booth, C. L., & Jean, F. (2002). Child care effects on the development of toddlers with special needs. *Early Childhood Research Quarterly; 17*(2), 171–196.

Bredekamp, S., & Copple, C. (Eds.) (1997). *Developmentally appropriate practice in early childhood programs.* Washington, DC: NAEYC.

Brugge, D., Vallarino, J., Ascolillo, L., Osgood, N., Steinbach, S., & Spengler, J. (2003). Comparison of multiple environmental factors for asthmatic children in public housing. *Indoor Air, 13*(1), 18–27.

Burchinal, M., Howes, C., & Kontos, S. (2002). Structural predictors of child care quality in child care homes. *Early Childhood Research Quarterly, 17*(1), 87–105.

Cartwright, S. (1999). What makes good early childhood teachers? *Young Children, 54*(4), 4–7.

Child Health Alert. (2003, March). Injury prevention: Accidental scald burns in skins. *Child Health Alert, 21,* 4–5.

Clarke-Stewart, K. A., Vandell, D. L., Burchinal, M., O'Brien, M., & McCartney, K. (2002). Do regulable features of child-care homes affect children's development? *Early Childhood Research Quarterly 17*(1), 52–86.

Consumer Product Safety Commission (CPSC). (2003). *Handbook of public playground safety.* Washington, DC: Author.

Consumer Product Safety Commission (CPSC). (2002). *Injuries and deaths associated with children's playground equipment.* Washington, DC: Author.

Consumer Product Safety Commission (CPSC). (2001). *National electronic injury surveillance system 1998–2000.* Washington, DC: Author.

Crowley, A. L. (1999). Training family childcare providers to work with children who have special needs. *Young Children, 54*(4), 58–61.

Cryer, D., & Phillipsen, L. (1997). Quality details: A close-up look at the child care program strengths and weaknesses. *Young Children, 52*(5), 51–61.

Daisey, J. M., Angell, W. J., &, Apte, M. G. (2003). Indoor air quality, ventilation and health symptoms in schools: An analysis of existing information. *Indoor Air, 13*(1), 53–64.

DeBord, K., Hestenes, L., Moore, R. C., Cosco, N., & McGinnis, J. R. (2002). Paying attention to the outdoor environment is as important as preparing the indoor environment. *Young Children, 57*(3), 32–34.

Dishop, M. L. (2002). Maintaining environmental cleanliness in school. *Journal of School Nursing,* Oct (Suppl), 23–26.

Essa, E. (2003). *Introduction to early childhood education.* Clifton Park, NY: Delmar Learning.

Ferng, S. F., & Lee, L. W. (2002). Indoor air quality assessment of daycare facilities with carbon dioxide, temperature, and humidity as indicators. *Journal of Environmental Health, 65*(4), 14–18, 22.

Flynn, L. L., & Kieff, J. (2002). Including everyone in outdoor play. *Young Children, 57*(3), 20–26.

Frost, J. L., Wortham, S. C., & Reifel, S. (2001). *Play and child development.* Upper Saddle River, NJ: Merrill Prentice Hall.

Furnival, R. A., Street, K. A., & Schunk, J. E. (1999, May). Too many pediatric trampoline injuries. *Pediatrics, 103*(5), e57.

Glassner, B. (1999, August 13). School violence: The focus, the facts. *New York Times.*

Goffin, S. G. (2002). Accreditation Reinvention. Recommendations for the next era of NAEYC's accreditation system from the National Commission on Accreditation Reinvention. *Young Children, 57* (3), 75– 83.

Gold, D. R. (2002). Environmental tobacco smoke, indoor allergens, and childhood asthma. *Environmental Health Perspectives, 108*(Suppl 4), 643–651.

Kagan, S. L., Brandon, R. N., Ripple, C. H., Maher, E. J., & Joesch, J. M. (2002). Supporting quality early childhood care and education: Addressing compensation and Infrastructure. *Young Children, 57*(3), 58–65.

Kansas Stakeholders Advisory Committee for Early Childhood Education. (2001). *Quality standards for early childhood education for children birth through eight.* Topeka, KS: Kansas State Department of Education (available on-line, http://www.kskits.org/html/bestpractice/qs.html). (Also available, *Quality standards in family child care homes*).

Kantos, S. C., Howes, C., & Galinsky, E. (1996). Does training make a difference in quality in family child care? *Early Childhood Research Quarterly, 11*(4), 427–445.

Lalloo, R. & Sheiham, A. (2003). Risk factors for childhood major and minor head and other injuries in a nationally representative sample. *Injury, 34*(4), 261–266.

Lohse, J. L. (2003). A bicycle safety education program for parents of young children. *Journal of School Health, 19*(2), 100–110.

Morris, B. (1999, December 2). Webcam's focus on day care. *New York Times.*

Munton, A. G., Blackburn, T., & Barreau, S. (2002). Good practice in out of school care provision. *Early Child Development and Care, 172*(3), 223–230.

National Association for the Education of Young Children (NAEYC). (1999). NAEYC position statement on developing and implementing public policies to promote early childhood and school-age care program accreditation. *Young Children, 54*(4), 36–40.

National Transportation Safety Board. (2002). *Evaluation of the rollover propensity of 15-passenger vans.* Washington, DC: Author.

Newberger, J. (1997). New brain development research—A wonderful window of opportunity to build public support for early childhood education. *Young Children, 52*(4), 4–9.

Oliver, S. J., & Klugman, E. (2002, May–June). Playing the day away: The importance of constructive play in early childhood settings. *Child Care Information Exchange 145,* 66–70.

Peth-Pierce, R. (2002). Early child care and children's development prior to school entry: Results from the NICHD study of early child care. *American Educational Research Journal, 39*(1), 133–164.

Snow, C. W., Teleki, J. K., & Reguero-de-Atiles, J. T. (1996). Public policy report: Child care center licensing standards in the United States, 1981–1995. *Young Children, 51*(6): 36–41.

Stanken, B.A. (2000). Promoting helmet use among children. *Journal of Community Health Nursing, 17*(2), 85–92.

Surr, J. (1992). Early childhood programs and the American Disabilities Act (ADA). *Young Children, 47*(5), 18–21.

Sutterby, J. A., & Frost, J. L. (2002). Making playgrounds fit for children and children fit on playgrounds. *Young Children, 57*(3), 36–42.

Tang, A. (1999, December 15). Trends: The workplace can be threatening, especially for women. *New York Times.*

Thompson, D., & Hudson, S. (2000). Children and playground injuries. In J. Frost (Ed.)., *Children and injuries.* Tucson, AZ: Lawyers & Judges Publishing Co.

Tinsworth, D. & McDonald, J. (2001). *Special study: Injuries and deaths associated with children's playground equipment.* Washington, DC: U.S. Consumer Product Safety Commission.

U.S. Consumer Product Safety Commission (CPSC). (1997). *Playground surfacing technical information guide.* Washington, DC: U.S. Government Printing Office.

U.S. Department of Health, Education, and Welfare. (1981). *Summary report of the assessment of current state practices in Title XX funded day care programs: Report to Congress.* Washington, DC: Day Care Division Administration for Children, Youth, and Families, Office of Human Development Services.

Warman, B. (1998). Trends in state accreditation policies. *Young Children, 53*(5), 52–55.

Weisel, C. P. (2002). Assessing exposure to air toxics relative to asthma. *Environmental Health Perspectives, 110*(Suppl 4), 527–537.

Whitebrook, M., & A. Eichberg. (2002). Finding a better way: Defining policies to improve child care workforce compensation. *Young Children, 57*(3): 66–72.

Whitebrook, M., Howes, C., & Phillips, D. (1998). *Worthy work, unliveable wages: The national child care staffing study, 1988–1997.* Washington, DC: Center for Child Care Workforce.

Wishard, A. G., Shivers, E. M., Howes, C., & Ritchie, S. (2003). Child care program and teacher practices: Associations with quality and children's experiences. *Early Childhood Research Quarterly, 18*(1), 65–103.

ADDITIONAL READING

Briss, P., Sacks, J., Addiss, D., Kresnow, M., & O'Neil, J. (1995, August). Injuries from falls on playgrounds: Effects of day care regulations and enforcement. *Archives of Pediatrics & Adolescent Medicine, 148*(8), 906–11.

DiNatale, L. (2002). Developing high-quality family involvement programs in early childhood settings. *Young Children, 57*(5), 90–95.

Dorrell, A. (1999, January/February). Tips for choosing and using children's toys. *Early Childhood News,* 36–37.

Galinsky, E., Howes, C., Kontos, S., & Shinn, M. (1994). The study of children in family child care and relative care—Key findings and policy recommendations. *Young Children, 50*(1), 58–61.

Goffin, S. (2002). Accreditation reinvention. Frequently asked questions about the next era of NAEYC accreditation. *Young Children, 57*(5), 52–53.

Goffin, S. (2003). Learning more about the Commission on NAEYC Early Childhood Program Standards and Accreditation Criteria. *Young Children, 58*(2), 82–83.

Harms, T., & Clifford, R. (1998.) *Early childhood environmental rating scale.* New York: Teachers College Press.

Harms, T., Cryer, D., & Clifford, R. (2003). *Infant/toddler environment rating scale (ITERS).* New York: Teachers College Press.

Harms, T., Jacobs, E., & White, D. (1996). *School-age care environment rating scale (SACERS).* New York: Teachers College Press.

Lyons, M. (1997, September). Carefree backyard playgrounds. *Home,* 72–78.

National Association for the Education of Young Children (NAEYC). (2002). Professional Development. Preparing tomorrow's teachers: NAEYC announces new standards. *Young Children 57*(2), 78–79.

National Association for the Education of Young Children (NAEYC). (1995). NAEYC position statement on quality, compensation, and affordability. *Young Children, 51*(1), 39–41.

Rothenberg, P. V. (2002). Liabilities and lullabies: On-site childcare facilities are a risky but important business. *Journal of Property Management, 67*(6), 16.

Tonyan, H. A., & Howes, A. (2003). Exploring patterns in time children spend in a variety of child care activities: Associations with environmental quality, ethnicity, and gender *Early Childhood Research Quarterly, 18*(1), 121–142.

Wardle, F. (1999, January/February). Educational toys. *Early Childhood News,* 38.

Weaver, R. (2002). Predictors of quality and commitment in family child care: Provider education, personal resources, and support. *Early Education and Development, 13*(3), 265–282.

Weaver, R. H. (2002). The roots of quality care: Strengths of master providers. *Young Children, 57*(1), 16–22.

Wiechel, J. (2003). From our President. "A new day, a new year, a new frontier." *Young Children, 58*(1), 6.

HELPFUL WEB SITES

Child and Family Canada	http://www.cfc-efc.ca
National Association for Family Child Care	http://www.assoc-mgmt.com/users.nafcc
National Association for the Education of Young Children (NAEYC)	http://www.naeyc.org
National Association of Child Care Resource and Referral Agencies (NACCRRA)	http://www.naccrra.org
National Network for Child Care	http://www.exnet.iastate.edu/pages/ families/nncc
National Program for Playground Safety	http://www.uni.edu/playground
Parent Soup	http://www.parentsoup.com
U.S. Product Safety Commission	http://www.cpsc.gov

For additional health, safety, and nutrition resources, go to http://www.EarlyChildEd.delmar.com

CHAPTER 9

Safety Management

OBJECTIVES

After studying this chapter, you should be able to:
- List the most frequent causes of unintentional death among young children.
- Explain why infants and toddlers are at greatest risk for unintentional injury.
- Describe the four basic principles of safety management.
- Identify two types of negligence.

TERMS TO KNOW

unintentional injury   supervision   liability
risk management   incidental learning   negligence

Unintentional injuries are the leading cause of death and permanent disability among children under the age of 14 (Hambridge, Davidson, Gonzales & Steiner, 2002; National Center for Injury Prevention and Control, 2000). They are also responsible for thousands of nonfatal injuries and are costly in terms of time, energy, suffering, and medical expense. Although children experience many different types of injuries, the most common causes of death due to unintentional injury include (Table 9–1):

- motor vehicles—as pedestrians, riding a bicycle or wheeled toy
- drowning—in swimming pools, spas, bathtubs, ponds, toilets, buckets
- burns—from fireplaces, appliances, grills, chemicals, electrical outlets, residential fires, fireworks
- suffocation—from plastic bags, entrapment in chests or appliances, bedding, aspiration of small objects
- falls—from stairs, furniture, play equipment, windows
- poisoning—from pain relievers, carbon monoxide, cleaning products, insecticides, cosmetics

Thus, parents and teachers must take extra precautions to provide environments and activities that are safe for children of all ages and stages of development.

217

TABLE 9–1   Common Causes of Childhood Death Due to Unintentional Injury

Cause of Death	1–4 year olds	5–9-year-olds
motor vehicle/pedestrian	36.1%	55%
drowning	27%	14.5%
fire/burns	16.3%	13.2%
suffocation	8.3%	3.2%
falls	2.0%	1.2%
poisoning	1.8%	1.2%

National Center for Injury Prevention and Control, Office of Statistics and Programming. Centers for Disease Control and Prevention, U.S. Department of Health & Human Services, 2001.

WHAT IS UNINTENTIONAL INJURY?

The term *unintentional injury* has replaced *accidents* when referring to injuries sustained by children. This is because, in most instances, factors contributing to an accident are preventable. Childhood injuries are most often attributed to environmental hazards, lack of appropriate planning and adult supervision, or a child's immature development—conditions that are all manageable with improved knowledge and awareness.

Infants and toddlers are at highest risk for sustaining life-threatening injuries and medical emergencies. Their zealous interest and curiosity in learning about their surroundings, impulsive play, and immature development can unfortunately also lead children into new and unexpected dangers. Likewise, older children continue to explore their environment with an even greater sense of interest, yet still lack an adult's maturity, experience, and understanding necessary to anticipate the consequences of their behavior. Thus, assuring children's safety requires continuous awareness of children's abilities, stage of development, potential hazards, and preventive measures (Table 9–2).

FIGURE 9–1

Parents expect child care facilities to be safe.

TABLE 9-2 Developmental Characteristics and Injury Prevention

Age	Developmental Characteristics	Hazards	Preventive Measures
Birth to 4 months	Eats, sleeps, cries Rolls off flat surfaces Wriggles	Burns	Set hot water heater to a maximum of 120°F. Always keep one hand on baby.
		Falls	Never turn back or walk away from a baby who is on a table or bed.
		Toys/Choking	Select toys that are too large to swallow, too tough to break, have no sharp points or edges, and have nontoxic finishes.
		Sharp objects	Keep pins and other sharp objects out of baby's reach.
		Suffocation	Filmy plastics, harnesses, zippered bag, and pillows can smother or strangle. A firm mattress and coverings that are tucked in are safest. Babies of this age need complete protection.
4–12 months	Grasps and moves about Puts objects in mouth	Play areas	Keep baby in a safe place near an adult. The floor, full-sized bed, and yard are unsafe without supervision.
		Bath	Check temperature of bath water with elbow. Keep baby out of reach of faucets. *Never* leave baby alone in bath.
		Toys	Large beads on strong cord and unbreakable, rounded toys or smooth wood or plastic are safe.
		Small objects	Keep buttons, beads, coins, and other small objects from baby's reach.
		Poisoning	Children of this age still need full-time protection.
		Falls	Don't turn your back or walk away when baby is on an elevated surface. Place gates in doorways and on stairways.
		Burns	Place guards around registers and floor furnaces. Keep hot liquids, hot foods, and electric cords on irons, toasters, and coffee pots out of baby's reach. Use sturdy and round-edged furniture. Avoid hot steam vaporizers.
1–2 years	Investigates, climbs, opens doors and drawers; takes things apart; likes to play	Gates, windows, doors	Securely fasten doors leading to stairways, driveways, and storage. Put gates on stairways and porches. Keep screens locked or nailed.
		Play areas	Fence the play yard. Provide sturdy toys with no small removable parts or with unbreakable materials. Keep electric cords to coffee pots, toasters, irons, and radios out of reach.
		Water	*Never* leave child alone in tub, wading pool, or around open or frozen water.
		Poisons	Store all medicines and poisons in locked cabinets. Store cosmetics and household products, especially caustics, out of child's reach. Store kerosene and gasoline in metal cans and out of children's reach.
		Burns	Provide guards for wall heaters, registers, and floor furnaces. Never leave children alone in the house. Close supervision is needed to protect child from accidents. *(Continued)*

TABLE 9–2 Developmental Characteristics and Injury Prevention (Continued)

Age	Developmental Characteristics	Hazards	Preventive Measures
2–3 years	Fascinated by fire. Moves about constantly. Tries to do things alone. Imitates and explores. Runs and is lightning fast. Is impatient with restraint.	Traffic	Keep child away from street and driveway with strong fence and firm discipline.
		Water	Even shallow wading pools are unsafe unless carefully supervised.
		Toys	Large sturdy toys without sharp edges or small removable parts are safest.
		Burns	Keep matches and cigarette lighters out of child's reach. Teach them about the danger of fire. Never leave children alone in the house.
		Dangerous objects	Lock up medicine, household and garden poisons, dangerous tools, firearms, and garden equipment. Teach safe ways of handling appropriate tools and kitchen equipment.
		Playmates	Accidents are more frequent when playmates are older—the two-year-old may be easily hurt by bats, hard balls, bicycles, rough play.
3–6 years	Explores the neighborhood, climbs, rides tricycles. Likes and plays rough games. Frequently out of sight of adults. Likes to imitate adult actions.	Tools and equipment	Store in a safe place, out of reach, and locked. Teach safe use of tools and kitchen equipment.
		Poisons and burns	Keep medicines, household cleaning products, and matches locked up. Provide nontoxic art materials.
		Falls and injuries	Check play areas for attractive hazards such as old refrigerators, deep holes, trash heaps, construction, and old buildings.
		Drowning	Teach the danger of water and begin swimming instruction.
		Traffic	Help children learn rules and dangers of traffic, insist on obedience where traffic is concerned.
6–12 years	Enjoys spending time away from home. Participates in active sports, is part of a group and will "try anything once" in traffic on foot or bicycle. Teaching must gradually replace supervision.	Traffic	Drive safely as an example. Use safety belts. Teach pedestrian and bicycle safety rules. Don't allow play in the streets or alleys.
		Firearms	Store unloaded in a locked cabinet. Teach children to stay away from guns and tell an adult if they find one.
		Sports	Provide instruction, safe area, and equipment, and supervise any competition.
		Drowning	Teach swimming and boating safety.

Teachers and administrators assume a major role and responsibility for protecting the safety of children in their care. This can be a particularly challenging task because of the ages of children typically enrolled in early education programs. However, teachers are uniquely positioned to eliminate needless tragedies and assure children's well-being with appropriate training and experience.

RISK MANAGEMENT: PRINCIPLES AND PREVENTIVE MEASURES

Prevention of **unintentional injury** requires continuous awareness and implementation of safe practices (MMWR, 2001). Teachers and parents must consider the element of safety in everything they do with young children (Table 9–2). This includes the rooms they organize, toys they purchase, and learning activities that are planned. To new teachers or busy parents, this step may seem unnecessarily slow or too time-consuming. However, these are precisely the times when it is important to focus extra attention on children's safety. Any amount of time and effort is worthwhile if it spares only one child from injury!

Knowledge of developmental skills is essential for protecting children's safety (Berk, 2003). Understanding the differences in their cognitive, motor, social, and emotional abilities at various stages helps adults anticipate children's actions, and take steps to avoid unintentional injury. For example, understanding that infants put everything into their mouths should alert teachers to be extra vigilant of small items, such as a paper clip or pen cap, that might be dropped on the floor. Knowing that toddlers enjoy climbing should caution adults to securely fasten bookshelves and large pieces of play equipment to the wall or floor. Recognizing that four-year-old's limited understanding of cause and effect makes them more vulnerable to hazardous situations in their environment is useful when designing a classroom or play yard. Or, knowing that boys are more likely to be involved in accidents than girls due to their preference for play that involves active, aggressive, and risk-taking behaviors can be used when planning large motor activities (Schwebel, Speltz, Jones, & Bardina, 2002; Eisenberg & Fabes, 1998; Matheny, 1991). Teachers and parents will also find information about children's development helpful for:

- planning children's environments
- preparing learning activities
- selecting appropriate play equipment (indoor and outdoor)
- establishing rules
- supervising children's learning and play experiences
- developing safety education programs

An awareness of circumstances and adult behaviors that can contribute to an increased risk of unintentional injury in early education settings, as well as in children's homes, is also essential (Table 9–3).

It is also known that children in group care settings are more likely to be injured while playing outdoors, especially on swings, climbing apparatus, and slides (Briss, Sacks, Addiss, Kresnow, & O'Neil, 1995). For this reason, some states no longer permit swings, teeter-totters, or large slides on new playgrounds. In homes, children typically experience a higher rate of accidents indoors, particularly in the kitchen and bathroom areas (U.S. Consumer Product Safety Commission, 1998).

Environmental design and maintenance are also important considerations in the prevention of children's accidents. Local building codes and state child care licensing regulations provide guidelines for the construction of facilities that are safe. Consulting with licensing personnel during the planning phase of any new construction or remodeling project is helpful for identifying safety features and assuring that the facilities will comply with recommended standards. The National Association for the Education of Young Children (NAEYC) and National Association of Child Care Resource and Referral Agencies (NACCRRA) have also issued recommendations that address quality standards for children's environments.

---

unintentional injury – *an unexpected or unplanned event that may result in physical harm or injury.*
risk management – *measures taken to avoid an event such as an injury or illness from occurring; implies the ability to anticipate circumstances and behaviors.*

TABLE 9-3 **Behaviors and Conditions that Contribute to Unintentional Injury**

- not feeling well; suffering from symptoms of illness or discomfort
- experiencing anger or an emotional upset; facing a difficult situation, such as an uncooperative child, an unpleasant conversation with a parent, a strained relationship with a staff member, or a personal problem
- the presence of new teachers, staff members, or visitors who are unfamiliar with the children and their routines
- conditions that are rushed
- a shortage of teachers; too few adults to provide adequate supervision
- times when children are not able to play outdoors due to inclement weather
- new children are included in a group and are unfamiliar with the environment, rules, and expectations
- when rules have not been formulated or explained carefully to children

---

National Health and Safety Performance Standards *(Guidelines for out-of home-child care programs)* have also been developed by the American Academy of Pediatrics and American Public Health Association (http://nrc.uchsc.edu/national).

Despite adults' best efforts, it is not possible to prevent every childhood injury. Regardless of how much care is exercised, some circumstances will be beyond a teacher's or parent's ability to control. For example, no amount of appropriate planning or supervision can prevent a toddler from suddenly bumping into a table edge or an older child's unexpected release of a climber railing. However, the number and seriousness of accidents can be significantly reduced when basic safety principles are followed:

- planning in advance
- establishing rules
- maintaining quality supervision
- providing for safety education

Advanced Planning

Considerable thought and careful planning should go into the selection of equipment and activities that are appropriate for young children (Lucarelli, 2002; Gestwicki, 1999). Choices must take into account children's developmental abilities and also encourage the safe acquisition of new skills. Activities should be planned, and equipment selected to stimulate children's curiosity, exploration, and sense of independence without endangering their safety (Hart, Burts, & Charlesworth, 1997). When programs invest time in planning and providing a variety of developmentally appropriate learning opportunities, they typically experience a lower incidence of unintentional injury because children find the activities interesting, engaging, and suited to their abilities.

Planning for children's safety requires that teachers consider the risks involved in each activity. Many problems can easily be avoided if time is taken to examine materials, methods, and

---

REFLECTIVE THOUGHTS

Teachers are exposed to children's communicable illnesses on a daily basis. Calling in sick often creates a staff shortage since substitutes may be difficult to locate. How can a teacher determine if he/she is too sick to come to work? What are the risks involved in coming to work when you are sick? How can teacher illness contribute to children's unintentional injury?

equipment before they are presented to children. This process also includes thinking through each step of an activity carefully before allowing children to begin. Advanced planning implies being prepared for the unexpected. This includes anticipating children's often unpredictable behaviors and developing safety rules for each activity (Figure 9–2). It also infers that adults check the safety of play equipment (indoor and outdoor) before children begin to play.

Organization is fundamental to effective advanced planning. Teachers must carefully review, from start to finish, each step of an activity before presenting it to children. Forgetting supplies or being unsure of how to proceed greatly increases the risk of unintentional injury. Thinking a project through also enables teachers to make adjustments and substitute safer alternatives for any that may be potentially hazardous.

An examination of accident records can also be useful during the planning stage. A pattern of similar injuries may suggest that teachers need to alter the way an activity is being conducted. For example, if it is noted that children are repeatedly hurt on a piece of outdoor play equipment, a cause must be investigated immediately. Plans to modify the rules, amount of supervision, or the equipment itself may be necessary to assure children's safety.

FIGURE 9–2

Teachers should anticipate children's often unpredictable behaviors.

Establishing Rules

Rules are statements about behavior that is considered acceptable as it relates to the welfare of an individual child, concern for group safety, and respect for shared property (Table 9–4). Too often, rules only inform children about what they should not do. They leave unclear what behaviors are acceptable or valued. However, when rules are based on developmentally appropriate expectations, they can promote children's cooperation and understanding of how to use play equipment safely.

Teachers can use rules to encourage children's appropriate behavior by stating them in positive terms, e.g., "Slide down the slide on your bottom, feet first, so you can see where you are going." The only time "no" should be used is when a child's immediate safety is endangered. To be most effective, rules should be stated clearly and in terms that are simple enough for even very young children to understand. Children are often more willing to accept a rule when they have been given a brief explanation of why it is necessary.

There are no universal safety rules. Individual programs must develop their own safety guidelines and rules based on the:

- population of children being served
- type of program and equipment (indoor and outdoor)
- number of adults available for supervision
- nature of the activity involved

Programs serving very young children and children whose behavior is difficult to manage may need to establish rules and limits that are more explicit and comprehensive. The type of equipment and whether it is being used in the classroom, outdoors, or in home-based settings also influences the thoroughness of rules necessary to protect children.

TABLE 9-4 Rules for Safe Use of Play Equipment

Climbing Apparatus

Rules for Children
- Always hold on with both hands.
- Keep hands to self.
- Look carefully before jumping off equipment; be sure the area below is clear of objects and other children.
- Be extra careful if equipment or shoes are wet from snow or rain.

Guidelines for Adults
- Inspect equipment before children begin to play on it. Check for broken or worn parts and sharp edges; be sure the equipment is firmly anchored in the ground.
- Be sure surface material under equipment is adequate and free of sharp stones, sticks, and toys.
- Limit the number of children on climber at any one time.
- Always have an adult in direct attendance when children are on the equipment.
- Supervise children carefully if they are wearing slippery-soled shoes, sandals, long dresses or skirts, mittens, bulky coats, or long scarves.

Swings

Rules for Children
- Wait until the swing comes to a full stop before getting on or off.
- Always sit on the swing seat.
- Only one child per swing at any time.
- Only adults should push children.
- Stay away from moving swings.
- Hold on with both hands.

Guidelines for Adults
- Check equipment for safety, e.g., condition of chain/rope and seat, security of bolts or S-rings; also check ground beneath swings for adequate cushioning material and sharp debris.
- Designate a "safe" area where children can wait their turn.
- An adult should be in attendance at all times.

When rules are established, they must also be enforced consistently or children quickly learn that they have no meaning. However, a teacher must never threaten children or make them afraid in order to gain compliance. Rather, children should be praised whenever they demonstrate appropriate safety behaviors. For example, a teacher might recognize a child's efforts by saying, "Carlos, I liked the way you rode your bike carefully around the other children who were playing," or "Tricia, you remembered to lay your scissors on the table before getting up to leave." Through repeated positive encouragement, children quickly begin to learn safety behaviors that are considered acceptable and desirable.

Occasionally, a child will misuse play equipment or not follow directions. A gentle reminder concerning rules is usually sufficient. If this approach fails and the child continues to behave inappropriately, the teacher must remove the child from the activity or area. A simple statement such as, "I cannot allow you to hit the other children," lets the child know that this is not acceptable behavior. Permitting the child to return later to the same activity conveys confidence in the child's ability to follow expectations.

FIGURE 9–3

Rules never replace adult supervision.

Rules never replace the need for careful adult **supervision** (Figure 9–3). Young children tend to quickly forget rules, especially when they are busy playing or excited about what they are doing. However, rules should also be realistic and allow children sufficient freedom to work and play within the boundaries of safety. Rules that are overly restrictive create fear and discourage children from exploring and experimenting with their environment. Gradually, as children learn to recognize danger and begin to assume responsibility for their own behavior, the need for extensive rules can be lessened.

Quality Supervision

Parents and teachers of young children are faced with many responsibilities. However, their supervisory role is, perhaps, one of the most important (Marotz, 2000). Children depend on responsible adult guidance for protection, as well as for learning appropriate safety behaviors. The younger children are, the more protective this supervision must be. As children gain additional motor coordination, cognitive skill, and experience in handling potentially dangerous situations, adult supervision can become less restrictive.

Quality supervision is also influenced by the nature of children's activities (Figure 9–4). For example, a cooking project involving the use of a hot appliance must be supervised more carefully than painting at an easel or putting together a puzzle. Certain pieces of play equipment may also be more challenging for some children and, thus, require close teacher supervision at all times. The nature of an activity also affects the number of children a teacher can safely manage. One adult may be able to oversee several children building with hollow blocks or riding their bikes around a play yard, while a field trip to the fire station would require the supervision of several adults.

Caution: Never leave children unattended. If a teacher must leave an area, it should be supervised by another adult.

Occasionally, there are children in a group setting who are known to be physically aggressive or who engage in behaviors that could possibly bring harm to themselves or other children.

---

supervision – *watching carefully over the behaviors and actions of children and others.*

FIGURE 9–4

The amount of adult supervision depends on the activity.

Teachers are obligated to supervise these children more closely and to protect other children from harm. However, their responsibility goes beyond merely issuing a verbal warning to the child to stop—they must intervene and actually stop the child from continuing the dangerous activity even if it means physically removing the child from the area. Failure to intervene could result in legal action. However, there are a number of additional approaches that teachers can use to effectively manage children's disruptive behaviors (Table 9–5).

An adequate number of adults must always be available to supervise children, especially in out-of-home programs. Minimal adult/child ratios are generally established by individual state child care licensing regulations for indoor and outdoor settings. NAEYC has also recommended that there never be fewer than two adults with any group of children. However, there are considerable differences in adults' abilities to supervise and manage children's behavior. Some teachers are less effective at controlling unruly or disruptive children. In these situations, it may be necessary to have more than the required number of adults available to safely monitor children's play.

Safety Education

One of the primary methods for avoiding unintentional injury is through safety education (McCracken, 1999). Children can begin learning safe behaviors as soon as they understand the

TABLE 9–5   Positive Strategies for Managing Children's Inappropriate Behavior

- Offer frequent praise and attention for desired behavior.
- Redirect the child's attention to some other activity.
- Provide the child with an opportunity for choices.
- Model the appropriate and desired behavior.
- Teach and encourage children to use problem-solving techniques.
- Ignore inappropriate behaviors, unless doing so is unsafe.
- Make changes in the environment to discourage inappropriate behavior.

meanings of words. The earlier children learn about safety, the more naturally they will develop the attitudes and respect that lead to lifelong patterns of safe behavior.

Much safety education takes place through **incidental learning** experiences and imitation of adult behaviors. Young children who already show many safe attitudes and practices can also serve as role models for other children. For example, several children may be jumping from the top of a platform rather than climbing down the ladder. Suddenly, one child yells, "You shouldn't be doing that. You could get hurt!" As a result, the children stop and begin using the ladder. Taking advantage of teachable moments can also prove to be an effective educational tool. For example, when children stand up on a swing or run with sharp objects in their hand, teachers should use these opportunities to explain why these actions are not appropriate. Safer alternatives can also be suggested. Often this form of learning is most meaningful to a young child.

Safety education should also prepare young children to cope with emergencies. Personal safety awareness and self-protection skills enable even young children to avoid many potentially harmful situations. Children must know what to do in an emergency and how to get help. They should learn their home address and phone number as well as how to use the telephone. Older children can also begin to learn basic first aid skills.

Teachers should not overlook their own safety in their concern for children. It is easy for adults to be careless when they are under stress or have worked long, hard hours. Sometimes, in their zealous attempts to help children, teachers take extraordinary risks; it is at these times that even greater caution must be exercised.

IMPLEMENTING SAFETY PRACTICES

Much of the responsibility for maintaining a safe environment belongs to teachers. Their knowledge of child development and daily contact with children gives them an advantageous position for identifying problem areas. However, safety must be a concern of all school personnel, including support staff such as aides, cooks, janitors, receptionists, and bus drivers. One person may spot a safety hazard that had previously gone unnoticed by others.

Safety must be a continual concern. Each time teachers rearrange the classroom, add new play equipment, plan an activity, or take children on a field trip or walk they must first stop to assess the risks involved for the children. Even differences among groups of children can affect the nature of safety problems that may occur and the types of rules necessary. Extra precautions may be needed whenever children with special needs, chronic health problems, or behavior problems are present.

Toys and Equipment

The majority of childhood deaths and injuries related to toys and play equipment are due to choking and improper use (U.S. Consumer Product Safety Commission, 2003a; Nakamura, Pollack-Nelson, & Chidekel, 2003). Many of these injuries can be prevented by carefully selecting equipment and toys that are developmentally appropriate (CDC, 1999). Children's interests, behavioral characteristics, and developmental abilities should serve as key considerations when choosing these items (Tables 9–6 and 9–7). Age warnings on product labels do not take into account children's individual differences and, therefore, are not always reliable. Some toys on the market scarcely meet required U.S. safety standards and, thus, may pose a hazard for children who are not as developmentally advanced. Injuries are also more likely to occur when

---

incidental learning – *learning that occurs in addition to the primary intent or goals of instruction.*

TABLE 9–6 Guidelines for Selecting Safe Toys and Play Equipment

1. Consider children's age, interests, and developmental abilities (including problem-solving and reasoning skills); check manufacturers' labels carefully for recommendations and warnings.
2. Choose fabric items that are washable and labeled flame-retardant or nonflammable.
3. Look for quality construction; check durability, good design, stability, absence of sharp corners or wires, and strings longer than 12 inches (30 cm).
4. Select toys that are made from nontoxic materials.
5. Avoid toys and play materials with small pieces that a child could choke on.
6. Select toys and equipment that are appropriate for the amount of available play and storage space.
7. Avoid toys with electrical parts or those that are propelled through the air.
8. Choose play materials that children can use with minimal adult supervision.

children attempt to use educational materials and play equipment intended for older children, such as:

- toys that are too heavy for young children to lift
- rungs that are too large for small hands to grip securely
- steps that are too far apart
- climbing equipment and platforms too far above the ground
- balloons and small objects that can cause choking or suffocation (Figure 9–5).

The opposite may also occur. When play equipment has a singular purpose or is designed for younger children, older children may misuse it in an effort to create interest and challenge.

The amount of available classroom or play yard space will also influence choices. Large pieces of equipment or toys that require a big area for their use will be a constant source of accidents if they are set up in spaces that are too small.

TABLE 9–7 Examples of Appropriate Toy Choices for Infants, Toddlers, and Preschoolers

Infants	Toddlers	Preschoolers
nonbreakable mirrors	peg bench	puppets
cloth books	balls	dolls and doll houses
wooden cars	records	dress-up clothes
rattles	simple puzzles	simple art materials,
mobiles	large building blocks	e.g., crayons, markers,
music boxes	wooden cars and trucks	watercolors, playdough,
plastic telephone	dress-up clothes	blunt scissors
balls	bristle blocks	books, puzzles, lacing cards
toys that squeak	large wooden beads	simple musical instruments
blocks	to string	cars, trucks, fire engines
nesting toys	cloth picture books	tricycle
teething ring	nesting cups	simple construction sets, e.g.,
washable, stuffed animals	pull and riding toys	Legos®, bristle blocks
	plastic dishes, pots and pans	play dishes, empty food
	fat crayons and paper	containers

FIGURE 9–5

There are devices available for measuring small parts to prevent choking. Notice that the domino gets caught in the tube, but the die passes through the tube, indicating a choking hazard.

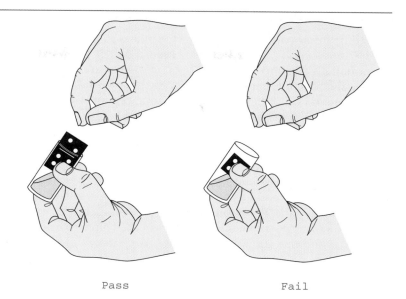

Pass   Fail

Quality is also very important to consider when purchasing toys. The materials and construction of toys and play equipment should be examined carefully and not purchased if they have:

- sharp wires, pins, or staples
- small pieces that could come loose, e.g., buttons, "eyes," screws
- moving parts that can pinch fingers
- pieces that are smaller than 1.5 inches (3.75 cm) or balls less than 1.75 inches (4.4 cm) in diameter (for children under three years)
- objects too heavy or large to be handled easily
- unstable bases or frames
- toxic paints or materials
- sharp metal edges or rough surfaces
- defective parts
- construction that will not hold up under hard use
- possibility of causing electrical shock
- brittle plastic or glass parts that could easily break
- objects that become projectiles, such as darts, arrows, air guns

The amount of noise a toy produces should also be considered. Children's hearing is more sensitive than that of an adult's and can easily be damaged through repeated exposure to loud noises. Many children's toys emit sounds that exceed the 85-decibel threshold recommendation for safe hearing levels (OSHA, 2003). Adults should use their judgment and be cautious in purchasing toys that produce loud music and sounds to protect young children from unnecessary hearing loss.

New toys and children's products that don't always meet these standards are continually being introduced; imported items can be a particular problem if they are not manufactured according to U.S. safety standards (CPSC, 2002b). Extreme care should also be taken when purchasing children's toys or equipment on the Internet. Hazard warnings and age recommendations may be absent, misrepresented, or not in compliance with statutory label requirements (Public Interest Research Group, 2002). Caution should also be exercised when purchasing used toys and children's equipment. Often, products that have been recalled because of hazardous features continue to appear on Web sites or in garage sales. Parents and teachers should take time to inspect these items carefully and be sure they meet all current safety standards.

REFLECTIVE THOUGHTS

Manufacturers are now labeling toys with age guidelines to help parents make safer choices. However, a child's chronological age does not necessarily reflect his/her developmental skills and abilities. What is meant by the term developmentally appropriate? How can a parent determine this? Why are age guidelines not always a reliable method for selecting children's toys and play equipment? Where can a parent or teacher locate information about product safety and recalls?

Toys and play equipment should be inspected on a daily basis, especially if they are used frequently by children or are located outdoors and exposed to variable weather conditions. They should always be in good repair and free of splinters, rough edges, protruding bolts or nails, and broken or missing parts. Ropes on swings or ladders should be checked routinely and replaced if they begin to fray. Large equipment should be checked often to be sure that it remains firmly anchored in the ground and that surface materials are adequate and free of debris (see Chapter 8) (Frost & Sutterby, 2002; National Center for Injury Prevention & Control, 2001; Thompson & Hudson, 2000).

Regularly scheduled maintenance ensures that toys and play equipment will remain in a safe condition. Equipment that is defective or otherwise unsafe for children to use should be removed promptly until it can be repaired. Items that cannot be repaired should be discarded.

Special precautions are necessary whenever large equipment or climbing structures are set up indoors. Placing equipment in an open area limits opportunities for children to get hurt on nearby furniture or other objects. Mats, foam pads, or large cushions placed around and under elevated structures will protect children in the event of an accidental fall. Rules for the safe use of indoor climbers are also important and should be explained carefully to children before they begin to play. The potential for injuries can be further reduced when an adult is situated near the equipment and monitors children's activity (Figure 9–6).

Safety is a prime concern whenever new equipment, toys, or educational materials are introduced into a classroom or outdoor setting. Some rules may be necessary to protect children's well-being. However, too many rules may dampen children's enthusiasm for exploring new equipment

FIGURE 9–6

An adult should always be in direct attendance when children are using playground structures.

and restrict their inventiveness. If several new item are being introduced, it is best to do this over a period of time so that children are not overwhelmed by too many instructions.

Selection of furnishings, for example, beds, cribs, playpens, strollers, carriers, and toys for infants and toddlers, must be made with great care. As a consumer, it is important to remember that product design has contributed to a significant number of child deaths. As a result, strict criteria have been established by the U.S. Consumer Safety Product Commission and Canadian Consumer Corporate Affairs for the manufacturing of children's furniture since 1977 (Table 9–8). However, toys and furniture purchased at second-hand shops, garage sales, or on the Internet may have been manufactured before these standards went into effect. They should, therefore, be examined carefully. Consequently, consumers must be knowledgeable about critical quality and safety features whenever purchasing children's toys and furniture (CPSC, 2002). Information concerning product recalls is available from the Consumer Product Safety Commission at (www.cpsc.gov) or from (www.SafeChild.net) sponsored by the Consumer Federation of America.

Classroom Activities

Safety must always be a priority when teachers select, plan, and implement learning activities for children. The potential for injury is present in nearly every activity, whether it is planned for indoor or outdoor settings. Even metal trucks or plastic golf clubs can cause harm when children use them incorrectly. Teachers should ask themselves the following questions when evaluating the safety of any activity:

- Is the activity age- and developmentally-appropriate?
- What potential risks or hazards does this activity present?
- What special precautions do I need to take to make the activity safe?
- What would I do in the event that a child is hurt while the activity is in progress?

After these questions have been given careful thought, teachers can begin to consider how basic safety principles, e.g., advanced planning, formulating rules, determining appropriate supervision, and safety education training will be applied.

Materials selected for classroom activities should always be evaluated for safety risks before they are presented to children. Added safety precautions and more precise planning may be necessary whenever the following high-risk items are used as part of an activity:

- pointed or sharp objects such as scissors, knives, and woodworking tools, e.g., hammers, nails, saws
- pipes, boards, blocks, or objects made of glass
- electrical appliances, e.g., hot plates, radio, mixers
- hot liquids, e.g., wax, syrup, oil, water
- cosmetics or cleaning supplies

For added safety, projects that include any of these items can be set up in an area separated from other activities. Boundaries created with portable room dividers or a row of chairs improve a teacher's ability to monitor children's actions more closely.

Restricting the number of children who can participate in an activity at any one time is another effective way to ensure safe conditions. Some activities may need to be limited to even one child. Limiting the number of children improves a teacher's ability to effectively supervise a given space. Color-coded necklaces, badges, or number of chairs at a table are a few methods teachers can use to control the number of children in a given area at any one time. These systems also help children determine if there is available space.

When electrical appliances are included in an activity, their condition should be checked very carefully before they are used. Be sure that the plugs are intact and cords are not frayed. Avoid the

TABLE 9-8 Infant Equipment Checklist

	YES	NO

Back Carriers (not recommended for use before 4–5 months)
1. Carrier has restraining strap to secure child.
2. Leg openings are small enough to prevent child from slipping out.
3. Leg openings are large enough to prevent chafing.
4. Frames have no pinch points in the folding mechanism.
5. Carrier has padded covering over metal frame near baby's face.

Bassinets and Cradles
1. Bassinet/cradle has a sturdy bottom and a wide base for stability.
2. Bassinet/cradle has smooth surfaces—no protruding staples or other hardware that could injure the baby.
3. Legs have strong, effective locks to prevent folding while in use.
4. Mattress is firm and fits snuggly against sides of bed.

Carrier Seats
1. Carrier seat has a wide, sturdy base for stability.
2. Carrier has nonskid feet to prevent slipping.
3. Supporting devices lock securely.
4. Carrier seat has crotch and waist strap.
5. Buckle or strap is easy to use.

Changing Tables
1. Table has safety straps to prevent falls.
2. Table has drawers or shelves that are easily accessible without leaving the baby unattended.

Cribs
1. Slats are spaced no more than 2 3/8 inches (6 cm) apart.
2. No slats are missing or cracked.
3. Mattress fits snugly—less than two fingers width between edge of mattress and crib side.
4. Mattress support is securely attached to the head and footboards.
5. Corner posts are no higher than 1/16 inch (1.0 mm) to prevent entanglement.
6. There are no cutouts in head and footboards to allow head entrapment.
7. Drop-side latches cannot be easily released by a baby.
8. Drop-side latches securely hold sides in raised position.
9. All screws or bolts which secure components of crib together are present and tight.

Crib Toys
1. Crib toys have no strings longer than 7 inches (178 cm) to prevent entanglement.
2. Crib gym or other crib toy suspended over the crib must have devices that securely fasten to the crib to prevent it from being pulled into the crib.
3. Components of toys are large enough not to be a choking hazard.

Gates and Enclosures
1. Gate or enclosure has a straight top edge.
2. Openings in gate are too small to entrap a child's head.
3. Gate has a pressure bar or other fastener so it will resist forces exerted by a child.

High Chairs
1. High chair has restraining straps that are independent of the tray.
2. Tray locks securely. *(Continued)*

TABLE 9-8 Infant Equipment Checklist (Continued)

	YES	NO
3. Buckle on waist strap is easy to fasten and unfasten.		
4. High chair has a wide base for stability.		
5. High chair has caps or plugs on tubing that are firmly attached and cannot be pulled off and choke a child.		
6. If it is a folding high chair, it has an effective locking device.		
Hook-On Chairs		
1. Hook-on chair has a restraining strap to secure the child.		
2. Hook-on chair has a clamp that locks onto the table for added security.		
3. Hook-on chair has caps or plugs on tubing that are firmly attached and cannot be pulled off and choke a child.		
4. Hook-on chair has a warning never to place chair where child can push off with feet.		
Pacifiers		
1. Pacifier has no ribbons, string, cord, or yarn attached.		
2. Shield is large enough and firm enough so it cannot fit in child's mouth.		
3. Guard or shield has ventilation holes so baby can breathe if shield does get into mouth.		
4. Pacifier nipple has no holes or tears that might cause it to break off in baby's mouth.		
Playpens		
1. Drop-side mesh playpen or mesh crib has warning label about never leaving a side in the down position.		
2. Playpen mesh has small weave (less than 1/4–inch openings).		
3. Mesh has no tears or loose threads.		
4. Mesh is securely attached to top rail and floorplate.		
5. Top rail has no tears or holes.		
6. Wooden playpen has slats spaced no more than 2 inches (60 mm) apart.		
7. If staples are used in construction, they are firmly installed—none missing, or loose.		
Rattles/Squeeze Toys/Teethers		
1. Rattles and teethers have handles too large to lodge in baby's throat.		
2. Rattles have sturdy construction that will not cause them to break apart in use.		
3. Squeeze toys do not contain a squeaker that could detach and choke a baby.		
Strollers		
1. Stroller has a wide base to prevent tipping.		
2. Seat belt and crotch strap are securely attached to frame.		
3. Seat belt buckle is easy to fasten and unfasten.		
4. Brakes securely lock the wheel(s).		
5. Shopping basket low on the back and located directly over or in front of rear wheels.		
Toy Chests		
1. Toy chest has no latch to entrap child within the chest.		
2. Toy chest has a spring-loaded lid support that will not require periodic adjustment and will support the lid in any position to prevent lid slam.		
3. Chest has ventilation holes or spaces in front or sides, or under lid.		

Adapted from *The Safe Nursery,* U.S. Consumer Product Safety Commission, Washington, DC.

FIGURE 9–7

Nontoxic art materials must be used by young children.

use of extension cords that children could trip over. Always place electrical appliances on a table nearest the outlet and against the wall for safety. Never use appliances near a source of water, including sinks, wet floors, or large pans of water.

When children will actually be operating an electrical appliance, it should be set on a low table or the floor so that it is easy to reach. Equipment that is placed higher than children's waist level is dangerous. Children must continuously be reminded to stand away from any machinery with moving parts to prevent their hair, fingers, or clothing from getting caught or burned. Special precautions such as turning the handles of pots and pans toward the back of the stove or hot plate should be taken whenever hot liquids or foods are involved. Always detach cords from the electrical outlet, never the appliance. Promptly replace safety caps in all electrical outlets when the project has been completed.

Safety must also be a concern in the selection of art media and activities. Art materials such as paints, glue, crayons, and clay must always be nontoxic when they are used by young children (Figure 9–7). Avoid using dried beans, peas, berries, or small beads, which children can stuff into their ears or nose, or swallow. Toothpicks and other sharp objects should also be avoided. Fabric pieces, dried leaves or grasses, Styrofoam, packing materials, yarn, or ribbon are safer alternatives for children's art creations. Other safe substitutions for hazardous art materials are provided in Table 9–9. Storing liquid paints and glue in plastic containers eliminates any risk of broken glass.

Special precautions should be taken in classrooms with hard-surfaced or highly polished floors. Spilled water, paint, or other liquids and dry materials such as beans, rice, sawdust, flour, or cornmeal cause these floors to be very slippery. Spills should be cleaned up promptly. Spreading newspapers or rugs out on the floor can help prevent children from slipping and falling.

Environments and activities that are safe for young children are also less stressful for adults. When classrooms and play yards are free of potential hazards, teachers can concentrate their attention on selecting safe activities and providing quality supervision. Also, being familiar with a program's safety policies and procedures and having proper emergency training, such as first aid and CPR, can increase teacher confidence and lessen stress levels.

TABLE 9-9 Safe Substitutes for Hazardous Art Materials

Avoid	Safe Substitutes
Powders—dry tempera paints, silica, pastels, chalk, dry clay, cement. Use plaster of paris only in well-ventilated area.	Use liquid tempera paints, water colors, crayons, and nontoxic markers.
Aerosol sprays—adhesives, fixatives, paints	Use brushes or spray bottles with water-based glues, paints, and inks.
Solvents and thinners—turpentine, rubber or epoxy cements, or those containing benzene, toluene, lacquers, or varnish. Avoid enamel-based paints that require Solvents for cleanup	Select water-based paints, glues, and inks.
Permanent markers, dyes, and stains	Prepare natural vegetable dyes (e.g., beets, walnuts, onions) or commercial cold water dyes.
Minerals and fibers—instant paper-mache (may contain lead and asbestos fibers); glazes, printing inks (colored newsprint, magazines), paints, especially enamels (may contain lead); builder's sand (may contain asbestos)	Use black-white newspaper and water-based glue to make paper-mache; choose water-based paints and inks; purchase special sandbox sand that has been cleaned.
Photographic chemicals	Use blueprint or colored paper set in the sun.

Additional precautions:
- Read ingredient labels carefully. Only choose materials that are labeled nontoxic. Older supplies may not comply with new federal labeling requirements and contain harmful chemicals
- Mix and prepare art materials in a well-ventilated area (only by an adult), away from children
- Make sure children wash their hands after working with art materials
- Keep food and beverages away from areas where art activities are in progress.

Field Trips

Excursions away from a center's facilities can be an exciting part of children's educational experiences. However, field trips present added risks and liability concerns for early education programs and, therefore, require special precautions to be taken.

Most importantly, programs should have written policies outlining procedures for field trips. Parents should be informed in advance of an outing and their written permission obtained for each excursion. On the day of the trip, a posted notice will remind parents and staff of the trip, where the children will be going, and when they will leave and return to the center. At least one adult accompanying the group should have first aid and CPR training. A first aid kit should also be taken along and include money for emergency telephone calls or access to a cell phone. Tags can be pinned on children with the center's name and phone number. However, *do not* include children's names: this enables strangers to call children by name, making it easier to lure them away from a group. A list with children's emergency information, for example, parents' telephone numbers, name of physician, and number of various emergency services, should also be taken along. Prior to the outing, procedures and safety rules should be carefully reviewed with the staff and children.

Special consideration should also be given to the legal issues involved in conducting a field trip. Transporting children in the private vehicles of other parents, staff, or volunteers, for example,

ISSUES TO CONSIDER • Transportation Safety

Evening newscasters described the tragic death of a toddler forgotten in a day-care van. The child had been picked up from his home early that morning, placed in a safety car seat, and transported to a local day-care center. However, personnel did not realize the child was missing until the end of the day when it was time for the children to return home. The unconscious toddler was found still strapped in his car seat. Despite emergency medical efforts, heat stroke claimed the child's life as temperatures outside the van climbed into the 90s during the day.

- What steps should have been taken to prevent this tragedy?
- What policies and procedures would keep this from happening again?
- What measures should be taken to assure children's safety during transportation? In private vehicles? In center vans?

can present serious liability issues (see Chapter 8) (Marotz, 2000; Child Care Law Center 1991). There is almost no way of assuring that a car is safe or an adult is a good driver. Also, most states have laws that require appropriate safety restraints for each passenger, and not all vans and cars are properly equipped to provide these for multiple children. Therefore, it may be in a program's best interest not to use private vehicles for transporting children on field trips. Vehicles owned and operated by a program are generally included in their liability insurance and, therefore, are preferable. Neighborhood walks and public bus rides are always safe alternatives.

Pets

Pets can be a special addition to early childhood settings, but care must be taken so it is also a safe experience for both the children and animals. Children's allergies should be considered before pets visit or become permanent residents of a classroom. Also, make sure animals are free of disease and current on immunizations (if appropriate). Some animals, such as turtles and birds, are known carriers of illnesses that are communicable to humans and are not good choices for young children (Child Health Alert, 1998). Instructions for the animal's care should be posted to serve as both a guideline and reminder to staff. Precautions must also be taken to protect pets from curious and exuberant children who may unknowingly cause harm or injury to the animal. Careful handwashing after petting or handling animals is a must for everyone.

LEGAL IMPLICATIONS

Safety generates more concern than any other aspect of early childhood education. Recent lawsuits, legal decisions, and increased public awareness have added to feelings of uneasiness and scrutiny. As demand for early childhood programs continues to grow, interest in regulating programs and facilities has also increased. Parents want, and have a right, to be assured that facilities are safe. Parents also expect schools and early education programs to protect their children's safety.

Teachers should be familiar with the legal issues and responsibilities that affect their positions. There are several reasons why this is essential. First, teachers are expected, by law, to provide for children's safety. Second, the incidence of injury and accidents is known to be especially high among young children. The combination of immaturity and the unpredictable behavior of young children always necessitates careful safety management.

The most important legal concerns for teachers center around the issue of liability (Child Care Law Center, 1992). The term **liability** refers to the legal obligations and responsibilities, especially those related to safety, that are accepted by administrators and teachers when they agree to care for children. Failure to carry out these duties in an acceptable manner is considered **negligence**.

Negligence often results from questionable safety practices and management. For legal purposes, negligent acts are generally divided into two categories according to the circumstances and resulting damages or injuries. The first category includes situations in which a teacher fails to take appropriate precautionary measures to protect children from danger. Standards for judging a teacher's actions would be set by first determining what measures a teacher with similar training and experience would be expected to take in the same situation. A teacher who failed to adhere to these standards would then be considered negligent. A lack of adequate supervision, play equipment that is defective or in need of repair, and allowing children to engage in harmful activities such as throwing rocks or standing on swings are some examples of this form of negligence.

A second category of negligent acts includes situations in which the actions or decisions of a teacher put children at risk. An example of this type of negligence might include a teacher making arrangements to have children transported in private vehicles that are not insured, or planning classroom activities that allow children to use poisonous chemicals or unsafe electrical equipment without proper supervision.

Prevention is always the best method for ensuring the safety of young children and avoiding unpleasant legal problems and lawsuits. However, there are many steps individuals and programs can take for added protection (Marotz, 2000).

Teachers are always legally responsible for their actions. Despite careful attempts at providing safe conditions for children, they may, at some time, be accused of negligence or wrongdoing. For this reason, it is wise for every administrator and teacher to obtain personal liability insurance. Policies can be purchased from most private insurance companies and through the National Association for the Education of Young Children (NAEYC). Accident insurance, purchased on individual children who are enrolled, also affords programs necessary protection.

Administrators and staff should not hesitate to seek legal assistance on issues related to their roles and responsibilities. Legal advice can be a valuable source of protection. Programs might also consider selecting a member of the legal profession to fill a position on their board of directors or advisory council.

Teachers should always examine job descriptions carefully and be familiar with employer expectations before accepting a new position. This step helps assure that they will have the appropriate qualifications and training necessary to perform all required duties. For example, if a teacher is responsible for administering first aid to injured children, she/he should have completed basic first aid and CPR training prior to beginning employment. It is also imperative for administrators to screen potential candidates for teaching positions through careful interviewing and follow-up contacts with the individual's references. Background checks also help identify persons with a history of criminal behavior. Although these steps may seem time-consuming, they will help protect a program from hiring unqualified personnel.

Accurately maintained records, particularly accident reports, also provide added legal protection (Figure 9–8). Information in these reports can be used in court as evidence to support a

---

liability – *legal responsibility or obligation for one's actions owed to another individual.*
negligence – *failure to practice or perform one's duties according to certain standards; carelessness.*

FIGURE 9–8

A sample individual injury report form.

INDIVIDUAL INJURY REPORT FORM

Child's Name _____ Date of Injury _____

Parent _____ Time _____ AM ____ PM ____

Address _____ Parent notified _____ AM ____ PM ____

Description of injuries _____

_____

First aid or emergency treatment administered:_____

_____

Was a doctor consulted? _____ Doctor's name and address _____

Doctor's diagnosis_____

_____

Number of days child was absent as a result of injury _____

Adult in charge when injury occurred _____

Description of activity, location in facility and circumstances, immediately before and at the time of the injury

_____

_____

_____

_____

_____

_____

Report prepared by (full name):_____ Date _____

teacher's or program's innocence against charges of negligence. A thorough report should be completed for each accident, regardless of how minor or unimportant it may seem at the time. This is very important because the results of some injuries are not always immediately apparent. There is also the possibility that complications may develop at a later date. A special form such as the one shown in Figure 9–9 can be used for this purpose. This form should be completed by the teacher who witnessed the accident and administered first aid treatment. The information should be clear, precise, and objective. Such forms provide a composite picture of the accident and are also useful for detecting patterns of injury. Accident records are considered legal documents and should be kept on file for a minimum of five years.

FIGURE 9-9

A sample running injury record form.

SUNNY DAYS CHILD CARE CENTER
Record of Children's Injuries

Date and Time	Child's Name	Nature of Child's Injuries	How the Injury Occurred	Observed By	Type of First Aid Treatment Administered	By Whom (Full name)

Download this form online at http://www.Early ChildEd.del mar.com

FOCUS ON FAMILIES • Sun Safety

Exposure to too much sun over a lifetime can have harmful health consequences, including skin cancer, premature aging of the skin, eye damage, and interference with the immune system's ability to function. Children's skin—even that of dark-skinned children—is especially sensitive to the sun's ultraviolet (UV) rays and tends to burn quickly and easily. Steps should always be taken to protect children's skin and minimize their sun exposure. Adults should also follow these same precautions.

- Avoid going outdoors between 10 A.M. and 4 P.M., when the sun's rays are the strongest and most damaging.

- Encourage children to play in the shade whenever possible. Rule of thumb—you shouldn't be able to see their shadow!

- Dress them in protective clothing that is cool and loose fitting. Keep as much skin surface covered as possible. Children should be discouraged from wearing tank or halter tops. A hat with a brim provides shade protection for the face and eyes.

- Apply sunscreen, with at least a 15+ Sun Protection Factor (SPF) 30 minutes before going outdoors. Reapply every two hours or more often if children are swimming, perspiring, or drying themselves with a towel. Sunburn occurs more quickly when the skin is wet.

- Wear sunglasses to protect eyes from UV radiation. Light-colored eyes (blue, gray) are particularly sensitive to sunlight.

- Become a SunWise school by registering at http://www.epa.gov/sunwise/join.html.

CASE STUDY

Teachers at the Wee Ones Child Care Center, located in an inner-city neighborhood, know that field trips can be an important part of the curriculum. They have discussed organizing a trip to the local city zoo as part of a learning unit on animals. However, the teachers also realize the challenges involved in taking a group of 20 three- and four-year-olds on this field trip, but feel the experience is especially valuable for these children. Since the zoo is located on the other side of town, the teachers have made arrangements to ride the city bus.

1. What criteria can teachers use to determine if a field trip is worthwhile?
2. What types of planning are necessary to assure a safe and successful field trip?
3. What are the advantages/disadvantages of using public transportation?
4. What safety precautions must teachers take before leaving the premises?
5. How might visiting a site ahead of time help teachers better plan for a field trip?
6. What types of problems should teachers anticipate when taking children on field trips?
7. What information should parents be given?
8. Are off-premise field trips typically covered by liability insurance policies for early care and education programs?

SUMMARY

- Unintentional injuries are the leading cause of death for young children.
  - Children's curiosity and inability to understand cause and effect contribute to a high injury rate.
  - Adults take steps to prevent injuries through advanced planning, establishing rules, providing careful supervision, and conducting safety education.

- Teachers have a professional and moral obligation to protect children's safe-being.
  - Failure to uphold this responsibility can result in charges of negligence.
  - Acts of omission involve failure to take precautionary measures.
  - Acts of commission include knowingly exposing children to elements of risk.

- Teachers can take steps to protect themselves from personal liability, including purchasing liability insurance, meeting required job qualifications, completing on-going training in CPR and first aid, and documenting all children's injuries.

SUGGESTED ACTIVITIES

1. Visit an early childhood program play yard or a public playground. Select one piece of play equipment and observe children playing on or with it for at least 15 minutes. Make a list of actual or potential dangers that could result from improper use. Develop a set of workable safety rules for children to follow.

2. Role play how a teacher might handle a child who is not riding a tricycle in a safe manner.

3. You have been asked to purchase outdoor play equipment for a new child development center. Prepare a list of safety features you would look for when making your selections. Write to several companies for equipment catalogues. Using the catalogues, select basic outdoor equipment to furnish the play yard of a small child-care center that has two classes of 20 children each and a budget of $8,000.

4. Prepare a separate room-by-room home safety checklist for parents of: infants; toddlers; and preschooler-age children.

CHAPTER REVIEW

A. **Match the item in column I with those in column II.**

Column I	Column II
1. basic element of advanced planning	a. foresight
2. legal responsibility for children's safety	b. supervision
3. the ability to anticipate	c. education
4. limits that define safe behavior	d. planning
5. failure to protect children's safety	e. rules
6. watching over children's behavior	f. safe
7. environments free of hazards	g. negligence
8. the process of learning safe behavior	h. prevention
9. a key factor in injury prevention	i. liability
10. measures taken to insure children's safety	j. organization

B. **Fill in the blanks with one of the words listed below:**

removed   unintentional injury   anticipate
legal   responsible   safety principles
supervision   safety education   safety
inspected

1. Broken play equipment must be _____ immediately from a classroom or play yard.

2. The leading cause of death for young children is _____ .

3. Adults must be able to _____ children's actions as part of advanced planning.

4. Parents expect teachers to be _____ for their child's safety.

5. Basic _____ _____ include advanced planning, establishing rules, careful supervision, and safety education.

6. Injury records are _____ records.

7. A continuous concern of teachers is _____ .

8. Rules never replace the need for adult _____ .

9. Toys and play equipment should be _____ daily.

10. A prime method for avoiding accidents is through _____ _____ .

REFERENCES

Berk, L. (2003). *Child development.* (6th ed.). Boston, MA: Allyn & Bacon.

Briss, P., Sacks, J., Addiss, D., Kresnow, M., & O'Neill, J. (1995). Injuries from falls on playgrounds: Effects of day care center regulation and enforcement. *Archives of Pediatric & Adolescent Medicine, 148*(8), 906–911.

Center for Disease Control and Prevention (CDCP). (1999). Playground safety—United States, 1998–99. *MMWR, 48*(16), 329–332.

Child Care Law Center. (1992). *Legal aspects of caring for sick and injured children.* San Francisco, CA: Author.

Child Care Law Center. (1991). *Vehicle and property insurance: Insuring your program.* San Francisco, CA: Author.

Child Health Alert. (1998). Animals in schools: What are the risks of infection? *Child Health Alert, 16,* 1.

Eisenberg, N., & Fabes, R. A. (1998). Prosocial development. In N. Eisenberg (Ed.). *Handbook of child psychology: Vol 3. Social, emotional and personality development* (5th ed.). 701–778. New York: Wiley.

Frost, J. L., & Sutterby, J. A. (2002). Making playgrounds fit for children and children fit for playgrounds. *Young Children, 57*(3), 36–41.

Gestwicki, C. (1999). *Developmentally appropriate practice: Curriculum and development in early education* (2nd ed.). Albany, NY: Delmar.

Hambridge, S. J., Davidson, A. J., Gonzales, R., & Steiner, J. F. (2002). Epidemiology of pediatric injury-related primary care office visits in the United States. *Pediatrics, 109*(4), 559–565.

Hart, C. H., Burts, D. C., & Charlesworth, R. (1997). *Integrated curriculum and developmentally appropriate practice: Birth to age 8.* SUNY Series. New York: State University of New York Press.

Hudson, S., Mack, J., & Thompson, D. (2000). *How safe are America's playgrounds? A national profile of children, school, and park playgrounds.* Cedar Falls, IA: National Program for Playground Safety.

Lucarelli, P. (2002). Raising the bar for health and safety in child care. *Pediatric Nursing, 28*(3), 239–241, 291.

Marotz, L. R. (2000). Childhood and classroom injuries. (2000). In, J. L. Frost (Ed.), *Children and injuries.* Tucson, AZ: Lawyers & Judges Publishing Co.

Matheny, A. R. (1991). Children's unintentional injuries and gender: Differentiation and psychosocial aspects. *Children's Environment Quarterly, 8,* 51–61.

McCracken, J. B. (1999). *Playgrounds: Safe and sound.* Washington, DC: NAEYC.

MMWR. (2001, December 7). School health guidelines to prevent unintentional injuries and violence. *MMWR, 50*(RR-22), 1–73.

Nakamura, S. W., Pollack-Nelson, C., & Chidekel, A. S. (2003). Suction-type suffocation incidents in infants and toddlers. *Pediatrics, 111*(1), e12–16.

National Center for Injury Prevention and Control. (2001). *Unintentional injury prevention.* Washington, DC: Office of Statistics and Programming. Centers for Disease Control and Prevention, U.S. Department of Health & Human Services.

OSHA Noise exposure standard, 39FR23502 (as amended) section 19010.95. U.S. Department of Labor (2003).

Public Interest Research Group. (2002). *Trouble in toyland, 2002: 17th annual survey of potential toy hazards.* Accessed on June 3, 2003, at http://www.toysafety.net.

Schwebel, D. C., Speltz, M. L., Jones, K., & Bardina, L. (2002). Unintentional injury in preschool boys with and without early onset of disruptive behavior. *Journal of Pediatric Psychology, 27*(8), 727–737.

Thompson, D. & Hudson, S. (2000). Cause and prevention of playground injuries. In, J. L. Frost (Ed.), *Children and injuries.* Tucson, AZ: Lawyers & Judges Publishing Co.

U.S. Consumer Product Safety Commission (CPSC). (2002a). *Age determination guidelines: Relating children's ages to toy characteristics and play behavior.* Author.

U.S. Consumer Products Safety Commission (CPSC). (2002b). *California company pleads guilty to importing and selling dangerous toys to children.* Author.

U.S. Consumer Product Safety Commission (CPSC). (1986). *The safe nursery.* Washington, DC: Author.

U.S. Consumer Product Safety Commission (CPSC). (1992). *Labeling of hazardous art materials.* Washington, DC: Author.

U.S. Consumer Product Safety Commission (CPSC). (1997). *Handbook for public playground safety.* Washington, DC: Author.

U.S. Consumer Product Safety Commission (CPSC). (1998). *For kids sake: Think toy safety.* (CPSC #281). Washington, DC: Author.

Zavitkovsky, A., & Thompson, D. (2000). Preventing injuries to children: Interventions that really work. *Child Care Information Exchange, 100*(1), 54–56.

ADDITIONAL READING AND RESOURCES

Are playgrounds safe? Canadian Safety Council. Accessed on June 3, 2003, at http://www.safety-council.org.

Bredekamp, S., & Copple, N. (1997). *Developmentally appropriate practice in early childhood programs.* Washington, DC: NAEYC.

Child Health Alert. (2003). When one sibling is injured, another one at risk—for a while. *Child Health Alert, 21,* 3.

Child Health Alert. (1999, June). Children can strangle in window covering cords. *Child Health Alert, 17,* 2–3.

Child Health Alert. (1998, May). Trampoline injuries: A soaring problem. *Child Health Alert, 16,* 2.

Dorrell, A. (1999). Tips for choosing and using children's toys. *Early Childhood News, 11*(1), 36–37.

Griffin, C., & Rinn, B. (1998). Enhancing outdoor play with an obstacle course. *Young Children, 53*(3), 18–23.

Hendricks, C., (1993). Safer playgrounds for young children. *ERIC Digests* (ED 355206).

Kendrick, A., Kaufmann, R., & Messenger, K. (Eds.). (1995). *Healthy young children.* Washington, DC: NAEYC.

National Program for Playground Safety. (1999). *America's playgrounds receive C- in safety: National study details state-by-state result.* Washington, DC: U.S. Consumer Product Safety Commission (CPSC).

Rivkin, M. (1997). *The great outdoors: Restoring children's right to play outside.* Washington, DC: NAEYC.

Scott, C. L. (1983). Injury in the classroom: Are teachers liable? *Young Children, 38*(6), 10–18.

Tamburro, R. F., Shorr, R. I., Bush, A. J., Kritchevsky, S. B., Stidham, G. L., & Helms, S. A. (2002). Association between the inception of a SAFE KIDS Coalition and changes in pediatric unintentional injury rates. *Injury Prevention, 8*(3), 242–245.

Thompson, D., Hudson, S., Mack, M. (1999). Who should supervise the children? *Child Care Information Exchange, 99*(5), 74–77.

When child's play is adult business. Canadian Institute of Child Health. (pamphlet).

VIDEOS

Can be ordered from:

- American Academy of Pediatrics (1–800–433–9016)
  - *Caring for our children: National health and safety performance standards—Guidelines for out-of-home child care.*
  - *Child safety at home*
  - *Child safety outdoors*

- National Association for the Education of Young Children (NAEYC)
  - *Safe active play: A guide to avoiding play area hazards*
  - *Tools for teaching developmentally appropriate practice (video series)*
  - *Nurturing growth: Child growth and development*
  - *Early intervention: Natural environments for children*

- National program for playground safety. School of Health, Physical Education and Leisure Services, University of Northern Iowa, Cedar Falls, IA, 50614–0618.
  - *ABC's of supervision*

HELPFUL WEB SITES

American Society for Testing and Materials   http://www.astm.org

Canadian Institute of Child Health   http://www.cich.ca

Center for Injury Research and Control   http://www.injurycontrol.com

Child Care Law Center   http://www.childcarelaw.org

National Center for Injury Prevention
and Control   http://www.cdc.gov/ncipc/ncipchm

National Program for Playground Safety   http://www.uni.edu/playground

Safety Link   http://www.safetylink.com

U.S. Consumer Product Safety Commission   http://www.cpsc.gov

*For additional health, safety, and nutrition resources, go to
http://www.EarlyChildEd.delmar.com*

CHAPTER 10

Management of Injuries and Acute Illness

OBJECTIVES

After studying this chapter, you should be able to:

- Describe the difference between emergency care and first aid.
- Identify the ABCs for assessing emergencies.
- Name eight life-threatening conditions and state the emergency treatment for each.
- Name 10 non-life-threatening conditions and describe the first aid treatment for each.
- Discuss the teacher's role and responsibilities as they relate to management of unintentional injuries and acute illness.

TERMS TO KNOW

negligent	resuscitation	hypothermia
aspiration	paralysis	heat exhaustion
recovery position	ingested	heat stroke
sterile	alkalis	reimplanted
elevate	submerge	

Prevention of unintentional childhood injuries is a major responsibility of parents and teachers (Aronson, 2002; Preboth, 2002). This goal is best achieved when programs provide safe environments, include health/ safety education, and establish proper procedures for handling emergencies (Marotz, 2000).

Unfortunately, many programs overlook the necessity for developing emergency policies and plans until something unexpected happens. This can result in unnecessary confusion and ineffective response, and it can place children and adults at risk of additional injury. Advanced preparation and training assures that staff will respond to an emergency in a prompt and knowledgeable manner (Figure 10–1). Programs serving children should establish emergency response plans that address:

- personnel trained in infant/child CPR and basic first aid techniques (Figure 10–2)
- staff member(s) assigned to coordinate and direct emergency care
- notarized parental permission forms for each child authorizing emergency medical treatment

FIGURE 10–1

Sample emergency plan for centers: management of serious illness and injury.

Serious Injury and Illness Plan

1. **Remain with the child at all times.** Keep calm and reassure the child that you are there to help. Your presence can be a comfort to the child, especially when faced with unfamiliar surroundings and discomfort. You can also provide valuable information about events preceding and following the injury/illness, symptoms the child exhibited, etc.

2. **Do not** move a child with serious injury unless there is immediate danger from additional harm, such as fire or electrical shock.

3. Begin appropriate emergency care procedures immediately. Meanwhile, send for help. Have another adult or child alert the person designated to handle such emergencies in your center.

4. **Do not** give food, fluids, or medications unless specifically ordered by the child's physician or Poison Control Center.

5. Call for emergency medical assistance if in doubt about the severity of the situation. Don't attempt to handle difficult situations by yourself. A delay in contacting emergency authorities could make the difference in saving a child's life. If you are alone, have a child dial the emergency number in your community (commonly 911).

6. If the child is transported to a medical facility before parents arrive, a teacher should accompany, and remain with, the child until parents arrive.

7. Contact the child's parents. Inform them of the nature of the illness/injury and the child's general condition. If the child's condition is not life-threatening, discuss plans for follow-up care, e.g., contacting the child's physician, transporting the child to a medical facility. If parents cannot be reached, call the child's emergency contact person or physician.

8. Record all information concerning serious injury/illness on appropriate forms within twenty-four hours; place in the child's folder and provide parents with a copy. If required, notify local licensing authorities.

FIGURE 10–2

Every teacher should know the fundamentals of emergency and first aid care.

TABLE 10–1 Basic First Aid Supplies

activated charcoal	safety pins
adhesive tape—1/2 and 1 inch widths	scissors—blunt tipped
antibacterial soap or cleanser	soap—preferably liquid
bandages—assorted sizes	spirits of ammonia
blanket	splints (small)
bulb syringe	syrup of ipecac—1 oz. bottle
cotton balls	thermometers—2
flashlight and extra batteries	tongue blades
gauze pads—sterile, 2x2s, 4x4s	towel—large and small
instant cold packs or plastic bags for ice cubes	triangular bandages for slings
needle—(sewing-type)	tweezers
roller gauze—1- and 2-inch widths; stretch	Vaseline
latex or vinyl gloves	first aid book or reference cards
pen and small notepad	emergency telephone numbers

- a list of emergency numbers should be posted near the telephone and include those of parents and additional emergency contacts, hospital, fire department, ambulance, police, and local poison control
- the availability of a telephone
- arrangements for emergency transportation
- a fully equipped first aid kit (Table 10–1)

Copies of a program's emergency response plans should be made available to parents and staff members and reviewed on a regular basis.

Whenever emergency policies and procedures are being formulated, special attention should be given to protecting children and adults from transmissible illnesses, such as hepatitis B and C, and AIDS/HIV. Universal Precautions are special infection-control guidelines that have been developed to prevent the spread of diseases transmitted via blood and other body fluids (see Chapter 6). These guidelines address several areas of precaution—barrier protection (including the use of latex/vinyl gloves and handwashing), environmental disinfection, and proper disposal of contaminated materials—and must be followed carefully whenever caring for children's injuries.

Despite careful planning and supervision, accidents, injuries, and illness are inevitable. For this reason, it is important that teachers learn the fundamentals of emergency care and first aid (Table 10–2). Appropriate training and preparation allow personnel to handle emergencies with skill and confidence (Siwula, 2003; American Academy of Pediatrics, 1999).

TABLE 10–2 The ABCs for Assessing Emergencies

A—Airway	Make sure the air passageway is open and clear. Roll the infant or child onto his/her back. Tilt the head back by placing your hand on the child's forehead and gently push downward (unless back or neck injuries are suspected). At the same time, place the fingers of your other hand under the child's chin and lift it upward.
B—Breathing	Watch for the child's chest to move up and down. Feel and listen for air to escape from the lungs with your ear.
C—Circulation	Note the child's skin color (especially around the lips and nailbeds), and if the child is coughing or moving.

Teachers are responsible for administering initial and urgent care to children who are seriously injured or acutely ill. These measures are considered to be temporary and aimed at saving lives, reducing pain and discomfort, and preventing complications and additional injury. Responsibility for obtaining additional treatment can then be transferred to the child's parents (Marotz, 2000).

EMERGENCY CARE VS. FIRST AID

Emergency care refers to immediate treatment administered for life-threatening conditions. It includes a quick assessment of the emergency ABCs (Table 10–2). The victim is also checked and treated for severe bleeding, shock, and signs of poisoning.

First aid refers to treatment administered for injuries and illnesses that are not considered life-threatening. Emergency care and first aid treatments are based on principles that should be familiar to anyone who works with young children.

1. Summon emergency medical assistance (911 in many areas) for any injury or illness that requires more than simple first aid.
2. Stay calm and in control of the situation.
3. Always remain with the child. If necessary, send another adult or child for help.
4. Don't move the child until the extent of injuries or illness can be determined. If in doubt, have the child stay in the same position and await emergency medical help.
5. Quickly evaluate the child's condition, paying special attention to an open airway, breathing, and circulation.
6. Carefully plan and administer appropriate emergency care. Improper treatment can lead to other injuries.
7. Don't give any medications unless they are prescribed for certain lifesaving conditions.
8. Don't offer diagnoses or medial advice. Refer the child's parents to health care professionals.
9. Always inform the child's parents of the injury and first aid care that has been administered.
10. Record all the facts concerning the accident and treatment administered; file in the child's permanent folder.

In most states, legal protection is granted to individuals who administer emergency care, unless their actions are judged grossly **negligent** or harmful. This protection is commonly known as the Good Samaritan Law.

LIFE-THREATENING CONDITIONS

Situations that require emergency care to prevent death or serious disability are discussed in this section. The emergency techniques and suggestions included here are not intended as substitutes for certified first aid and cardiopulmonary resuscitation (CPR) training. Rather, they are included as a review of basic instruction and to enhance the teacher's ability to respond to children's emergencies. A course involving hands-on practice is necessary to master these skills. It is also important to take a refresher course from time to time.

---

negligent – *failing to practice or perform one's duties according to certain standards; careless.*

> ## ◯ REFLECTIVE THOUGHTS
>
> When you place an emergency telephone call, it is important to remain calm and stay on the line. What information should you be prepared to give the dispatcher? Why shouldn't you hang up after making a report? What emergency numbers should be posted in child care facilities? Where should they be posted? What emergency numbers should children learn to dial?

Absence of Breathing

Breathing emergencies accompany many life-threatening conditions, for example, asthma, drowning, electrical shock, convulsions, poisoning, severe injuries, suffocating, choking, and Sudden Infant Death Syndrome (SIDS). Adults who work with young children should complete certified training in basic first aid and cardiopulmonary resuscitation (CPR). This training is available from most chapters of the American Red Cross and the American Heart Association or from a local ambulance service, rescue squad, fire department, high school, or community parks and recreation departments.

It is important to remain calm and perform emergency lifesaving procedures quickly and with confidence. Have someone call for an ambulance or emergency medical assistance while you begin mouth-to-mouth breathing. The procedure for mouth-to-mouth breathing follows and is also illustrated in Figure 10–3.

1. Gently shake the child or infant to determine if conscious or asleep. Call out the child's name in a loud voice. If there is no response, quickly assess the child's condition and immediately begin emergency breathing procedures.
2. Position the infant or child on his/her back on a hard surface. Using extreme care, roll an injured child as a unit, keeping the spine straight.
3. Remove any vomitus, excess mucus, or foreign objects (only if they can be seen) by quickly sweeping a finger around the inside of the child's mouth.
4. To open the airway, gently tilt the child's head up and back by placing one hand on the forehead and *the fingers (not thumb)* of the other hand under the chin; push downward on the forehead and lift the chin upward.

   > *Caution: Do not tip the head back too far. Tipping the head too far can cause obstruction of the airway in an infant or small child. Keep your fingers on the jawbone, not on the tissue under the chin.*

5. Listen carefully for 5–10 seconds for any spontaneous breathing by placing your ear next to the child's nose and mouth; also watch for a rise and fall of the chest and abdomen.
6. *For an infant,* place your mouth over the infant's nose and mouth to create a tight seal. Gently give two small puffs of air (1–1 1/2 seconds per breath with a short pause in between) into the infant's nose and mouth.

   > *Caution: Too much air forced into an infant's lungs may cause the stomach to fill with air (may cause vomiting and increased risk of* **aspiration**). *Always remember to use small, gentle puffs of air from your cheeks.*

7. *For the child one-to-eight years old,* gently pinch the nostrils closed, place your open mouth over the child's open mouth forming a tight seal. Give two small breaths (1–1 1/2 seconds per breath) of air in quick succession, pausing between breaths.

---

aspiration – *accidental inhalation of food, fluid, or an object into the respiratory tract.*

FIGURE 10–3

Emergency breathing techniques for the infant and child.

If vomitus or foreign objects are visible, use the tongue-jaw lift to open the mouth. Then use a finger to quickly check for the object. Remove if visible.

Position child on his/her back. Gently tilt the head up and back by placing one hand on child's forehead and fingers of the other hand under the jawbone. Lift upwards (head tilt/chin lift). **Look** for the chest to rise/fall. **Listen** for breathing. **Feel** for breath on your cheek.

For an infant, place your mouth over the infant's nose and mouth creating a tight seal. Slowly and gently, give two small puffs of air (1–1 1/2 seconds), pausing between breaths. Check (look/listen) for breathing at the rate of one breath every three seconds. If air does not go in, reposition and try to breathe again.

For a child one to eight years, place your mouth over the child's mouth forming a tight seal. Gently pinch the child's nostrils closed. Quickly give two small breaths of air (1–1 1/2 seconds per breath). Continue breathing for the child at a rate of one breath every three seconds. If air does not go in, reposition and try to breathe again.

Lift your head and turn it to the side after each breath. This allows time for air to escape from the child's lungs and also gives you time to take a breath and to observe if the child is breathing.

FIGURE 10–4

The child should be placed in a recovery position to rest.

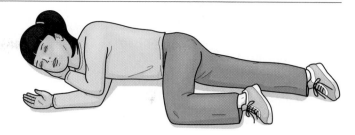

8. Observe the child's chest and abdomen for movement (rising and falling) to be sure air is entering the lungs.
9. Continue breathing at the rate of one breath every three seconds for infants and children one to eight years; or, one breath every five seconds for children eight years and older.
10. Pull your mouth away and turn it to the side after giving each breath. This allows time for air to escape from the child's lungs and also gives you time to take a breath and see if the child is breathing on his own.
11. DO NOT GIVE UP! Continue breathing procedures until the child breathes alone or emergency medical assistance arrives. Failure to continue mouth-to-mouth breathing can lead to cardiac arrest in children.

If the entry of air seems blocked or the chest does not rise while administering mouth-to-mouth breathing, check for foreign objects in the mouth and airway and remove only if they are visible (refer to Airway Obstruction). Continue mouth-to-mouth breathing until the child breathes alone or medical help arrives.

If the child resumes breathing, keep him/her lying down and roll (as a unit) onto one side; this is called the **recovery position** (Figure 10–4). Maintain body temperature by covering with a light blanket. Closely observe the child's breathing until medical help arrives.

Airway Obstruction

Children under five years of age account for nearly 90 percent of deaths due to airway obstruction (National Safekids Campaign, 2003). More than 65 percent of the deaths occur in infants (American Heart Association, 1997). Certain foods (Table 10–3) and small objects (Table 10–4) are common causes of aspiration and should not be accessible to children under age five.

TABLE 10–3 Foods Commonly Linked to Childhood Choking

raw carrots	seeds (pumpkin), peanuts and other nuts
hot dogs	chewy cookies
pieces of raw apple	cough drops
grapes (whole)	raisins
fruit seeds and pits	pretzels
gummy or hard candies	popcorn
peanut butter sandwich	chewing gum

recovery position – *placing an individual in a side-lying position.*

TABLE 10–4 **Objects Commonly Linked to Childhood Choking**

latex balloons (uninflated or pieces)
small batteries (calculator, hearing aid)
marker or pen caps
paper clips
small objects (less than 1.5 inches; 3.75 cm) in diameter
toys with small pieces
coins
marbles
small balls, blocks, beads, or vending machine toys

However, older children whose development is immature or delayed may require similar supervision for a much longer period of time. In most instances, children are successful in coughing the object out without emergency intervention. However, emergency lifesaving measures must be started immediately if:

- breathing is labored or absent
- lips and nailbeds turn blue
- cough is weak or ineffective
- the child becomes unresponsive
- there is a high-pitched sound when the child inhales

Respiratory infections in children can sometimes lead to swelling and obstruction of their airway. If this occurs, call immediately for emergency medical assistance. Time should not be wasted on attempting techniques for clearing airway obstruction (foreign body). They are not effective and may actually cause more harm to the child. Emergency techniques to relieve an airway obstruction should only be attempted if a child has been observed choking on an object or is unconscious and not breathing after attempts have been made to open the airway and to breathe for the child.

Different emergency techniques are used to treat infants, toddlers, and older children who are choking (American Heart Association, 2001). Regardless of the child's age, attempt to remove the object only if it can be clearly seen. Extreme care must be taken not to push the object further back into the airway. If the object cannot be removed easily and the infant **IS CONSCIOUS,** quickly:

- Have someone summon emergency medical assistance.
- Position the infant face down over the length of your arm, with the child's head lower than his/her chest and the head and neck supported in your hand (Figure 10–5). The infant can also be placed in your lap with its head lower than its chest.
- Use the heel of your hand to give five quick back blows between the infant's shoulder blades.

Caution: Do not use excessive force as this could injure the infant.

- Support and turn the infant over, face up, with the head held lower than the chest.
- Give five chest thrusts, using the hand not supporting the infant's head. Place two fingers over the breastbone and approximately the width of one finger below the infant's nipples (Figure 10–6). Rapidly compress the infant's chest approximately 1/2–1 inch (1.3–2.5 cm); release pressure between thrusts, allowing the chest to return to its normal position.
- Look inside the child's mouth for the foreign body. If clearly visible and reachable, remove it.
- Repeat the steps alternating five back blows, five chest thrusts until the object is dislodged or the infant loses consciousness.

FIGURE 10–5

Position the infant with the head lower than the chest.

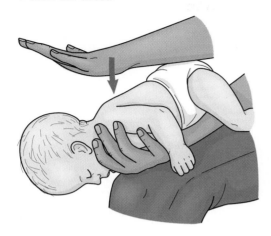

FIGURE 10–6

Location of fingers for chest thrusts on an infant.

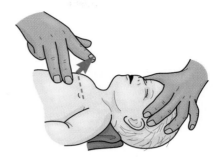

If the infant **LOSES CONSCIOUSNESS AND IS NOT BREATHING:**

- Have someone call for an ambulance or emergency medical assistance if this has not already been done.
- Place the infant on his/her back. Perform jaw lift. Look inside the child's mouth for the foreign body. If clearly visible and reachable, remove it.
- Begin lifesaving breathing procedures. Open the airway using head tilt/chin lift.
- Give the infant two small breaths of air, 1–1 1/2 seconds per breath. Watch for the chest to rise and fall.
- If the infant's lungs inflate, continue breathing assistance, giving one breath every three seconds. If the lungs cannot be inflated, give one breath of air, five back blows, five chest thrusts, check in mouth for the object, reposition the airway, and give one breath of air. Repeat these steps until help arrives or the object is dislodged: **open airway, breath, five back blows, five chest thrusts, reposition the airway, breath.**

To give emergency aid to the child one to eight years who is choking, first attempt to remove the object from the blocked airway only if it is clearly visible and reachable. Use care not to push the object further back into the throat. If the object cannot be dislodged and the child **IS CONSCIOUS,** quickly:

- Summon emergency medical assistance.
- Stand or kneel behind the child with your arms around the child's waist (Figure 10–7).
- Make a fist with one hand, thumbs tucked in.
- Place the fisted hand (thumb-side) against the child's abdomen, midway between the base of the rib cage (xiphoid process) and the navel.
- Press your fisted hand into the child's abdomen with a quick, inward and upward thrust.
- Continue repeating abdominal thrusts until the object is dislodged or the child becomes unconscious.

If the child **LOSES CONSCIOUSNESS AND IS NOT BREATHING:**

- Immediately summon emergency medical assistance.
- Assess the ABCs first unless the victim is known to be choking.
- Place the child flat on the floor (on back, face up).

FIGURE 10–7

The Heimlich maneuver.

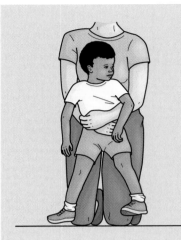

Stand or kneel behind the child with your arms around the child's waist.

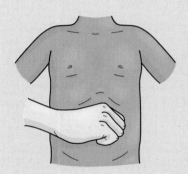

Make a fist with one hand. Place the fisted hand against the child's abdomen below the tip of the rib cage, slightly above the navel.

Grasp the fisted hand with your other hand. Press your fists into the child's abdomen with a quick upward thrust.

- Straddle the child's hips and kneel at the foot of a small child (Figure 10–8).
- Perform the jaw lift and look inside of the child's mouth; carefully remove any object that is clearly visible and reachable.
- Begin lifesaving breathing procedures. Open the airway using head tilt/jaw lift technique. Give two small breaths of air, 1–1 1/2 seconds each. Stop if the child begins breathing.
- If the child does not begin to breathe, place the heel of one hand on the child's abdomen, slightly above the navel and well below the base of the breastbone. Position the other hand on top of the first hand.
- Press hands into the child's abdomen with a quick upward thrust. Always keep hands positioned in the middle of the abdomen to avoid injuring nearby organs.
- Repeat abdominal thrusts five times. Repeat the sequence: **perform head tilt/chin lift technique, visually inspect the mouth for the object, attempt mouth-to-mouth breathing, give five abdominal thrusts and repeat the sequence. Do not give up!** Continue this sequence until the object is dislodged and you can get air in and out of the child's lungs or emergency medical help arrives.
- If the child begins to breathe on his own, stop mouth-to-mouth breathing, and continue to observe closely until medical help arrives. Roll the child (as a unit) onto his/her side (recovery position).

After the object is dislodged and breathing is restored, always be sure the child receives medical attention.

FIGURE 10–8

Heimlich maneuver with child lying down.

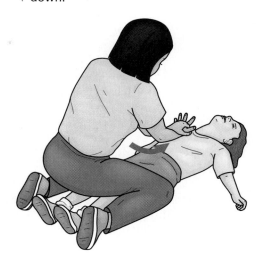

Shock

Shock frequently accompanies many types of injuries, especially those that are severe, and should be anticipated. However, shock can also result from extreme emotional upset, and less severe injuries, such as bleeding, pain, heat exhaustion, poisoning, burns, and fractures. It is a life-threatening condition and requires prompt emergency treatment. Early indicators of shock include:

- skin that is pale, cool, and clammy
- confusion, anxiety, restlessness
- increased perspiration
- weakness
- rapid, shallow breathing

Later, and more serious, signs of shock may include:

- rapid, weak pulse
- bluish discoloration around lips, nails, and ear lobes
- dilated pupils
- extreme thirst
- nausea and vomiting
- unconsciousness

To treat a child in shock:

1. Have someone call for emergency medical assistance.
2. Quickly assess the ABCs. Try to identify what may have caused the shock (e.g., bleeding, poisoning) and treat the cause first.
3. Keep the child lying down.
4. Elevate the child's feet 8 to 10 inches, if there is no indication of fractures to the legs or head, or back injuries.
5. Maintain body heat by covering the child lightly with a blanket.
6. Moisten a clean cloth and use it for wetting the lips and mouth if the child complains of thirst.
7. Stay calm and reassure the child until medical help arrives.
8. Observe the child's breathing closely; give mouth-to-mouth resuscitation if necessary.

Asthma

Asthma is a chronic disorder of the respiratory system characterized by periods of wheezing, gasping, and labored breathing. Numerous factors are known to trigger an acute asthma attack, including allergic reactions, respiratory infections, emotional stress, air pollutants, and physical exertion (Delfino, Gong, Linn, Pellizzari, & Hu, 2003; Simon, 2002). Asthma attacks make breathing intensely difficult and, therefore, must be treated as a life-threatening event (Whaley & Wong, 2003; Slack-Smith, Read, & Stanley, 2002).

Remaining calm and confident during a child's asthmatic attack is crucial. To treat a child who is having an asthma attack:

1. Summon emergency medical help immediately if the child shows signs of anxiety, wheezing, restlessness, loss of consciousness, or blue discoloration of the nailbeds or lips. Fatigue, inability to recognize teachers, or loss of consciousness are dangerous signs of impending respiratory failure and/or cardiac arrest.
2. Reassure the child.
3. Administer any medications prescribed for the child's acute asthmatic symptoms immediately.
4. Encourage the child to relax and breathe slowly and deeply (anxiety makes breathing more difficult).
5. Have the child assume a position that is most comfortable. (Breathing is usually easier when sitting or standing up.)
6. Notify the child's parents.

Bleeding

Occasionally, young children receive injuries, such as a deep gash or head laceration, that bleed profusely. Severe bleeding requires prompt emergency treatment. Again, it is extremely important that the teacher act quickly, yet remain calm. To stop bleeding:

1. Summon emergency medical assistance immediately if bleeding comes in spurts or is profuse and cannot be stopped.
2. Follow Universal Precautions, including the use of latex gloves.
3. Place a pad of **sterile** gauze or clean material over the wound.
4. Apply firm pressure directly over the site of bleeding, using the flat parts of the fingers.
5. Maintain pressure for approximately 5 to 10 minutes before letting up.

---

sterile – *free from living microorganisms.*

FIGURE 10–9

Important pressure points used to control bleeding.

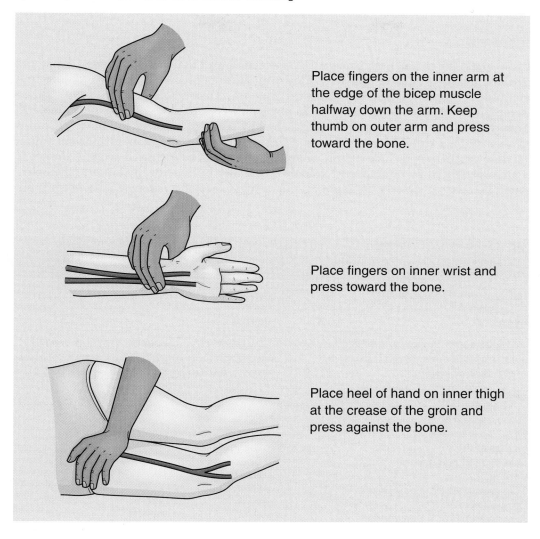

Place fingers on the inner arm at the edge of the bicep muscle halfway down the arm. Keep thumb on outer arm and press toward the bone.

Place fingers on inner wrist and press toward the bone.

Place heel of hand on inner thigh at the crease of the groin and press against the bone.

6. **Elevate** the bleeding part if there is no sign of a fracture.
7. Apply an ice pack, wrapped in a cloth or towel, to the site to help slow bleeding and decrease swelling.
8. Place additional pads over the bandage next to the skin if blood soaks through; bleeding may be restarted if the wound is disturbed.
9. Secure the bandage in place when bleeding has stopped.
10. Locate the nearest pressure point above the injury and apply firm pressure if bleeding cannot be stopped with direct pressure and elevation (Figure 10–9).

> *Caution: Tourniquets should only be used as a last resort and with the understanding that the extremity will probably have to be amputated.*

elevate – *to raise to a higher position.*

Save all blood-soaked dressings. Doctors will use them to estimate the amount of blood loss. Contact the child's parents when bleeding is under control and advise them to seek medical attention for the child.

Diabetes

Two potentially life-threatening emergencies associated with diabetes are hypoglycemia and hyperglycemia. Teachers must be able to quickly distinguish between these two conditions in order to determine appropriate emergency measures (American Diabetes Association, 1999). The causes and symptoms of these complications are, in many respects, opposites of each other (Table 10–5).

Hypoglycemia, or insulin shock, is caused by low levels of sugar in the blood. It can occur whenever a diabetic child either receives an excessive dose of insulin or an insufficient amount of food. Other causes may include illness, delayed eating times, or increased activity. Similar symptoms are experienced by nondiabetic children when they become overly hungry. Hypoglycemia can often be reversed quickly by administering a sugar substance. Orange juice is ideal for this

TABLE 10–5 Signs and Symptoms of Hyperglycemia and Hypoglycemia

Hyperglycemia (diabetic coma)	Hypoglycemia (insulin shock)
Causes	**Causes**
High blood sugar caused by too little available insulin, improper diet, illness, stress, or omitted dose of insulin.	Low blood sugar caused by too much insulin, insufficient amounts of carbohydrates, increased activity, decreased food intake, and illness.
Symptoms	**Symptoms**
• Slow, gradual onset • Slow, deep breathing • Increased thirst • Skin flushed and dry • Confusion • Staggering; appears as if drunk • Drowsiness • Sweet smelling, winelike breath odor • Nausea, vomiting • Excessive urination	• Sudden onset • Skin cool, clammy, and pale • Dizziness • Shakiness • Nausea • Headache • Hunger • Rapid, shallow breathing • Confusion • Seizures • Unconsciousness
Treatment	**Treatment**
Summon emergency medical assistance. Keep the child quiet and warm.	Summon emergency medical assistance if the child's state of consciousness is altered. If *conscious* and alert, quickly administer orange juice or a concentrated glucose source, such as Glucose™. If *unconscious*, maintain airway, summon emergency medical assistance or rush the child to the nearest hospital.

⊙ ISSUES TO CONSIDER • Water Safety

Several times each month, the Arizona five o'clock news and local newspapers carry heartbreaking stories of childhood drownings. More often than not, the victim is a toddler who momentarily escapes a parent's watchful eye, wanders through an unlocked gate, and falls into a residential swimming pool. While current regulations require new houses and pool installations to meet strict building codes, many existing homes do not have these safety features in place. However, pools and spas are not the only water hazards that contribute to childhood drowning.

- What water sources are present in most homes that could contribute to a potential childhood drowning?
- What characteristics place the toddler at greater risk for drowning?
- What safety measures should be taken to protect children from drowning in residential pools or spas?
- What Web sites provide information about prevention of childhood drowning?
- How would you care for a toddler who has just been pulled from the water and is unconscious?

---

purpose because it is absorbed rapidly by the body. Concentrated glucose gel or tablets can also be purchased and used for emergency purposes. Hard candies, such as Life Savers™ or lollipops, **should not** be given because a child could easily choke.

Hyperglycemia (which can lead to diabetic coma), results when there is too much sugar circulating in the blood stream. This condition is a potential problem for every diabetic child. Illness, infection, emotional stress, poor dietary control, fever, or a dose of insulin that is too small or forgotten can lead to hyperglycemia. Whenever a teacher observes the symptoms of hyperglycemia in a diabetic child, local emergency medical services should immediately be contacted. Emergency treatment of hyperglycemia usually requires the administration of insulin by medical personnel. The child's parents should also be notified so they can consult with their physician.

Drowning

Drowning is a leading cause of unintentional death among young children (Centers for Disease Control and Prevention, 2002). Even small amounts of water, such as toilet bowls, buckets, wading pools, and bathtubs, pose a serious danger. Poor muscle coordination and large upper body proportion make it difficult for young children to escape from water hazards.

Cardiopulmonary **resuscitation** must be started immediately upon rescuing a child from a drowning emergency. For this reason, every parent and teacher should complete basic CPR training. A child who has been rescued from drowning is likely to vomit during resuscitation attempts because large amounts of water are often swallowed. To reduce the risk of choking, the child should be placed in a recovery position (side-lying). Also, observe closely for signs of shock. Even if a child appears to have fully recovered from a near drowning incident, medical care should be obtained immediately. Complications, such as pneumonia, can develop from water, chemicals, or debris remaining in the lungs.

---

resuscitation – *to revive from unconsciousness or death; to restore breathing and heartbeat.*

Electrical Shock

Exposure to electrical shock can be a life-threatening condition in children. Although it is natural to want to immediately grab the child, this must *never* be attempted until the source of electricity has be turned off or disconnected. This can be accomplished by unplugging the cord, removing the appropriate fuse from the fuse box, or turning off the main breaker switch. If the source cannot be located quickly, a dry nonconductive object, such as a piece of wood or plastic, a folded newspaper or magazine, or rope can be used to push or pull the child away from the current. Always be sure to stand on something dry such as a board or cardboard while attempting to rescue the child.

Severe electrical shock can cause breathing to cease, surface burns, deep tissue injury, symptoms of shock, and the heart to stop beating. To treat the infant or young child who has received an electrical shock:

1. Have someone call for emergency medical assistance while you remove the child from the source of electrical current.
2. Check the child's breathing.
3. Begin cardiopulmonary resuscitation (CPR) immediately if the child is not breathing.
4. Observe for, and treat, signs of shock and burns.
5. Have the child transported to a medical facility as quickly as possible.

Head Injuries

The greatest danger of severe head injuries is internal bleeding and swelling (Wong, 2003; Lalloo & Sheiham, 2003). Signs of bleeding and internal swelling may develop within minutes or hours following the injury, or sometimes not for several days or weeks later.

Early signs of head injury may include:

- repeated or forceful vomiting
- bleeding or clear fluid coming from nose or ears
- confusion, aggressive behavior, apathy, or loss of consciousness
- drowsiness
- severe headache

Symptoms that can occur immediately with severe injury or develop later with less serious injury include:

- weakness or **paralysis**
- poor coordination or gait
- unequal size of the pupils of the eye
- speech disturbances
- double vision
- seizures
- an area of increasing swelling beneath the scalp

If any of these signs develop, summon emergency medical help, and contact the child's parents immediately.

Children who receive even a minor blow or bump to the head should not be moved until it can be determined that there are no fractures or additional injuries. If the injury does not appear to be serious, the child should be encouraged to rest or play quietly for the next few hours. Always inform parents of any blow or injury to a child's head regardless of how insignificant it may seem

---

paralysis – *temporary or permanent loss of sensation, function, or voluntary movement of a body part.*

Children who wear bicycle helmets are significantly less likely to experience head injury. The National Bike Safety Network (www.cdc.gov/ncipc/bike) and the Bicycle Helmet Safety Institute (www.bhsi.org) strongly urge children and adults to wear safety helmets to reduce serious head injuries. Children are also encouraged to wear helmets when riding scooters, skiing, or in-line skating (AAP, 2002; Adeboye & Armstrong, 2002; Child Health Alert, 1999). How much do you know about current standards that apply to bicycle helmets? What criteria should parents use to select a helmet that is safe? Should children be required to wear helmets while attending child care programs? What are the advantages? Disadvantages?

at the time. It is also important to observe these children carefully during the next 24 to 36 hours for any changes in behavior or appearance that may indicate the development of complications.

Scalp wounds have a tendency to bleed profusely, causing even minor injuries to appear more serious than they actually are. Therefore, when a child receives an injury to the scalp, it is important not to become overly alarmed at the sign of profuse bleeding. Pressure applied directly over the wound with a clean cloth or gauze dressing is usually sufficient to stop most bleeding. An ice pack can also be applied to the area to decrease swelling and pain. Parents should be advised of the injury so they can continue to monitor the child's condition.

Poisoning

Accidental poisoning results when harmful substances have either been inhaled, ingested, touched, or injected into the body. The majority of incidences occur in children under the age of six and involve substances that have been ingested (Litovitz, et. al, 2002). The possibility of a child ingesting medication from a purse, or seed pods from a plant on the way to school, must not be overlooked. Signs of poisoning may appear quickly or be delayed, and can include:

- nausea or vomiting
- abdominal cramps or diarrhea
- unusual odor to breath
- skin that feels cold and clammy
- burns or visible stains around the mouth, lips, or skin
- restlessness
- difficulty breathing
- convulsions
- confusion, disorientation, apathy, or listlessness
- loss of consciousness
- seizures

Emergency treatment of accidental poisoning is determined by the type of poison the child has **ingested** (Wong, 2003; Liebelt & DeAngelis, 1999). Poisons are classified into three basic categories: strong acids and **alkalis**, petroleum products, and all others. Examples of each type are shown in Table 10–6.

ingested – *the process of taking food or other substances into the body through the mouth.*
alkalis – *groups of bases or caustic substances that are capable of neutralizing acids to form salts.*

TABLE 10-6 Poisonous Substances

Strong Acid and Alkalis	Petroleum Products	All Others
bathroom, drain, and oven cleaners	charcoal lighter	medicines
battery acid	cigarette lighter fluid	plants
dishwasher soaps	furniture polish and wax	berries
lye	gasoline	cosmetics
wart and corn remover	kerosene	nail polish remover
ammonia	naphtha	insecticides
	turpentine	mothballs
	floor wax	weed killers
	lamp oil	

If a child is suspected of swallowing a poisonous substance:

- Quickly check for redness or burns around the child's lips, mouth, and tongue. These are indications of a chemical burn, usually caused by strong acids or alkalis. **Do not make the child vomit.**
- Smell the child's breath. If the poison is a petroleum product the odor of gasoline or kerosene will be present. **Do not make the child vomit.**

If the child is *conscious:*

- Quickly try to locate the container, which may provide clues about what the child has ingested. If you cannot find a container, do not delay in calling Poison Control.
- Call the nearest Poison Control Center or your city's emergency number (911 in many areas) and follow their instructions. *Be sure to keep the number posted by the telephone.*
- Observe the child closely for signs of shock and/or difficulty breathing.

If the child is *unconscious:*

- Summon emergency medical assistance immediately.
- Monitor and maintain the child's airway, breathing, and circulation.
- **Do not give any fluids to drink.**
- Position the child in the recovery position (side-lying) to prevent choking on vomited material.
- Observe the child closely for signs of difficulty breathing.

If the ingested poison is not an acid, alkali, or petroleum product, you may be instructed to make the child vomit; check with the Poison Control Center first. Be sure to keep the child's head lower than the stomach to prevent aspiration. Contact the child's parents as soon as possible.

NON-LIFE-THREATENING CONDITIONS

The majority of children's injuries and illnesses are not life-threatening but may require some type of basic first aid care. Teachers who have received proper training can administer this type of care, but they are not qualified or expected to provide comprehensive medical treatment. With training they can perform initial first aid to limit complications and make children more comfortable until parents arrive and assume responsibility for the child's care. The remainder of this unit describes conditions typically encountered by young children that require first aid care.

Abrasions, Cuts, and Other Minor Skin Wounds

Minor cuts, scrapes, and abrasions are among the most common types of injury young children experience. First aid care is concerned primarily with the control of bleeding and the prevention of infection. To care for the child who has received a simple skin wound, do the following:

1. Follow Universal Precautions (Chapter 6), including the use of latex or vinyl gloves.
2. Apply direct pressure to the wound using a clean cloth or sterile pad if there is bleeding.
3. Apply a cold pack, wrapped in a disposable paper towel or plastic bag, to the area; this will slow bleeding and reduce swelling.
4. Cleanse the wound carefully with soap and water after bleeding has been stopped.
5. Cover the wound with a sterile bandage.
6. Inform parents of the injury. Have them check the child's tetanus immunization to be sure it is current.
7. Watch for signs of infection, such as warmth, redness, swelling, or drainage.

Puncture-type wounds and cuts that are deep or ragged require medical attention because of the increased risk of infection. Stitches may be needed to close a gash greater than 1/2 inch (1.2 cm), especially if it is located on the child's face, chest, or back.

Bites

Human and animal bites are painful and can lead to serious infection. The possibility of rabies should be considered with any animal bite that is unprovoked, unless the animal is known to be free of the rabies virus. A suspected animal should be confined and observed by a veterinarian. In cases where the bite was provoked, the animal is not as likely to be rabid. First aid care for human and animal bites includes the following:

1. Allow the wound to bleed for a short while, if the skin is broken, to remove any saliva before applying direct pressure to stop bleeding.
2. Wearing latex gloves, cleanse the wound thoroughly with soap and water or hydrogen peroxide.
3. Cover the wound with a clean dressing.
4. Notify the child's parents and advise them to have the wound checked by the child's physician.
5. Notify local law enforcement authorities immediately if the injury is due to an animal bite; provide a description of the animal and its location (unless it is a classroom pet).

REFLECTIVE THOUGHTS

Risk of exposure to blood-borne diseases, such as hepatitis B and C, and HIV/AIDS, is ever present when attending to injuries that involve blood or other body fluids. What steps can teachers take to protect themselves from exposure? What additional precautions can be taken? Where can teachers locate current information about these diseases? What is OSHA? What role does it play in establishing safe workplace conditions?

Most insect bites cause little more than local skin irritations. However, some children are extremely sensitive to certain insects, especially bees, hornets, wasps, and spiders. Signs of severe allergic reaction include:

- sudden difficulty breathing
- joint pain (delayed reaction)
- abdominal cramps
- vomiting
- fever
- red, swollen eyes
- hives or generalized itching
- shock
- weakness or unconsciousness
- swollen tongue

Allergic reactions to insect bites can be life-threatening and should be observed for carefully. To treat a child for severe allergic reactions:

1. Call for emergency medical assistance (911), especially if the child has never experienced this type of reaction before.
2. Encourage the child to rest quietly. Let the child assume a position that is most comfortable for breathing.
3. Administer any medication the child may have at school for allergic reactions immediately.

First aid measures for insect bites provide temporary relief from discomfort and prevent infection. If a stinger remains in the skin, an attempt should be made to remove it quickly with tweezers. The area should then be washed and an ice/cold pack applied to decrease swelling and pain. A paste of baking soda and water applied to the area may provide temporary pain relief.

Blisters

A blister is a collection of fluid (white blood cells) that builds up beneath the skin's surface to protect the area against infection. Blisters most commonly develop from rubbing or friction, burns, or allergic reactions.

First aid care of blisters is aimed at protecting the affected skin from infection. If at all possible, blisters should not be broken. However, if they do break, wash the area with soap and water and cover with a bandage.

Bruises

Bruises result when small blood vessels rupture beneath the skin. They are often caused by falls, bumps, and blows. Fair-skinned children tend to bruise more easily. First aid care is aimed at controlling subsurface bleeding and swelling. Apply an ice or cold pack to the bruised area for 15 to 20 minutes and repeat three to four times during the next 24 hours. Later, warm moist packs can be applied to improve circulation and healing. Alert parents to watch for signs of infection or unusual bleeding if the bruising is extensive or severe.

Burns

Burns result when body surfaces come in contact with heat, electrical current, or chemicals. Several factors affect the severity of an accidental burn and the need to call for emergency medical assistance, including the source, temperature of the source, affected body part or area, length of exposure, and victim's age and size (Table 10–7).

Burns that involve children are always considered more serious because of their smaller body surface (Wong, 2003; Ying & Ho, 2001). Burns caused by heat are usually classified according to the degree (depth and extent) of tissue damage.

- first degree—surface skin is red
- second degree—surface skin is red and blistered

TABLE 10-7 Burns—When to Call for Emergency Medical Assistance

Always call for emergency medical assistance if:

- a child or elderly person is involved
- the victim experiences any difficulty breathing
- burned areas are located on the face, head, neck, feet, hands, or genitalia
- multiple areas of the body have been burned
- chemicals, electrical current, smoke, or an explosion has caused the burn

- third degree—burn is deep; skin and underlying tissues are brown, white and/or charred. These burns require emergency medical attention—call for help immediately.

Immediate first aid care of burns (first and second) includes the following:

1. Use caution to protect yourself from the heat source.
2. Quickly **submerge** the burned areas in cool water, hold under running water, or cover with a cool, wet towel for 10 to 15 minutes. Cool water temperatures lessen the depth of burn as well as decrease swelling and pain (Figure 10-10).
3. Elevate the burned body part to relieve discomfort.
4. Cover the burn with a sterile gauze dressing and tape in place. Do not use greasy ointments or creams. Dirt and bacteria can collect in the ointments and creams increasing the risk of infection.
5. Burns that involve feet, face, hands, or genitals, cover a large area or cause moderate blistering are critical and require immediate medical attention. Parents should be advised to contact the child's health care provider.

FIGURE 10-10

Burns can be cooled under running water.

submerge – *to place in water.*

Chemical burns should be rinsed for 10 to 15 minutes under cool, running water. Remove any clothing that might have the chemical on it. Call for emergency medical assistance or the nearest Poison Control Center for further instructions. The child's parents should also be advised to contact their physician.

Burns caused by smoke or electrical current should not be cooled with water and require immediate medical attention.

Eye Injuries

Most eye injuries are not serious and can be treated by teachers (Marin Child Care Council, 2002). However, because eyes are delicate structures, it is important to know proper care strategies for different types of injuries. Also, parents should always be informed of injuries involving their child's eye(s), so they can continue to observe and consult promptly with their physician.

A sudden blow to the eye from a snowball, wooden block, or other hard object is usually quite painful. First aid treatment includes the following:

1. Keep the child quiet.
2. Apply an ice pack to the eye for 15 minutes if there is no bleeding.
3. Use direct pressure to control any bleeding around the eye. *Do not* apply pressure to the eyeball itself. Cleanse and cover skin wounds with a sterile gauze pad.
4. Summon emergency medical assistance at once if the child complains of inability to see or is seeing spots or flashes of light.
5. Inform parents of any blow to the eye so they can continue to monitor the child's condition.

Foreign particles such as sand, cornmeal, or specks of dust frequently find their way into children's eyes. Although it is very natural for children to want to rub their eyes, this must be discouraged to prevent further injury to the eyeball. Often spontaneous tearing will be sufficient to wash the object out of the eye. If the particle is visible, it can also be removed with the corner of a clean cloth or by flushing the eye with warm water (Child Health Alert, 2002). If the particle cannot be removed easily, the eye should be covered and medical attention sought.

An object that penetrates the eyeball *must never be removed.* Place a paper cup, funnel or small cardboard box over *both* the object and the eye. Cover the uninjured eye with a gauze pad and secure both dressings (cup and gauze pad) in place by wrapping an elastic roller bandage around the head. Movement of the injured eyeball should be kept to a minimum and can be achieved by covering both eyes. Seek immediate medical treatment.

A thin cut on the eye's surface can result from a piece of paper, toy, or child's fingernail. Injuries of this type cause severe pain and tearing. The teacher should cover *both* of the child's eyes with a gauze dressing. Notify the parents and advise them to take the child for *immediate* medical care.

Chemical burns to a child's eye are very serious. Another staff member should call immediately for emergency medical assistance so the child can be transported to the nearest medical facility. Quickly tip the child's head toward the affected eye. Gently flush the eye with a large amount of warm water, using a small bulb syringe or bottle, for at least 15 minutes. Meanwhile, contact the child's parents.

Fractures

A fracture is a break or crack in a bone. A teacher can check for possible fractures by observing the child for:

- particular areas of extreme pain or tenderness
- an unusual shape or deformity of a bone
- a break in the skin with visible bone edges protruding

- swelling
- a change in skin color around the injury site

A child who complains of pain after falling should not be moved, especially if a back or neck injury is suspected. Have someone call immediately for an ambulance or emergency medical assistance. Keep the child warm and observe carefully for signs of shock. Avoid giving the child anything to eat or drink in the event that surgery is necessary. Stop any bleeding by applying direct pressure.

If no emergency medical help is available, only persons with prior first aid training should attempt to splint a fracture. Splinting should be completed before the child is moved. Splints can be purchased from medical supply stores or improvised from items such as a rolled-up magazine or blanket, a ruler, a piece of board or a tissue box. Never try to straighten a fractured bone. Cover open wounds with a sterile pad but do not attempt to clean the wound. Elevate the splinted part on a pillow and apply an ice pack to reduce swelling and pain. Watch the child closely for signs of shock. Contact the child's parents immediately and have them notify the child's physician.

Frostbite and Hypothermia

Frostbite results when body tissues freeze from exposure to extremely cold temperatures. Certain parts of the body are especially prone to frostbite, including the ears, nose, fingers, and toes. Wet clothing, such as mittens and shoes, can hasten the chances of frostbite. It can occur within minutes, causing the skin to take on a hard, waxy, gray-white appearance with or without blisters. Infants and young children should be watched carefully during extremely cold weather so they don't remove hats, boots, or mittens. Initially, the child may experience considerable pain or have no discomfort. However, when tissues begin to warm, there is often a tingling and painful sensation. First aid treatment for frostbite consists of the following:

- Rewarm the affected part by immersing it in lukewarm, then warm, water (104°F, 40°C).

  Caution: Never use hot water.

- Handle the frostbitten part with care; avoid rubbing or massaging the part as this could further damage frozen tissue.
- Cover the frostbitten area with sterile gauze.
- Elevate the affected area to decrease pain and prevent swelling.
- Wrap the child in a blanket for extra warmth.
- Contact the parents so they can take the child for medical treatment.

Exposure to cold temperatures can also cause **hypothermia**, a drop in body temperature that slows heart rate, respirations, and metabolism. This slowing of body functions reduces the amount of available oxygen and can lead to shivering, drowsiness, loss of consciousness, and cardiac arrest. Emergency medical personnel should be summoned at once.

Heat Exhaustion and Heat Stroke

First aid treatment of heat-related illness depends on distinguishing heat exhaustion from heat stroke. A child who has lost considerable fluid through sweating and is overheated may be suffering from **heat exhaustion**. The following symptoms would be observed:

- skin is pale, cool, and moist with perspiration
- weakness or fainting
- thirst

---

hypothermia – *below normal body temperature caused by overexposure to cold conditions.*
heat exhaustion – *above normal body temperature caused by exposure to too much sun.*

- nausea
- abdominal and/or muscle cramps
- headache
- normal or below normal body temperature

Heat exhaustion is not considered life-threatening. It usually occurs when a child has been playing vigorously in extreme heat or humidity. First aid treatment for heat exhaustion is similar to that for shock:

1. Have the child lie down in a cool place.
2. Elevate the child's feet 8–10 inches (20–25 cm).
3. Loosen or remove the child's clothing.
4. Sponge the child's face and body with cool water.
5. Offer frequent sips of cool water.

Heat stroke is a life-threatening condition that requires immediate treatment. The child's temperature begins to rise quickly and dangerously as perspiration stops and the body's temperature-regulating mechanism fails. Symptoms of heat stroke include:

- high body temperature (102°–106°F; 38.8°–41.1°C)
- dry, flushed skin
- headache or confusion
- seizures
- diarrhea, abdominal cramps
- loss of consciousness
- shock

Emergency treatment for heat stroke is aimed at cooling the child as quickly as possible:

1. Summon emergency medical assistance at once.
2. Move the child to a cool place and remove outer clothing.
3. Sponge the child's body with cool water. The child can also be placed in a shallow tub of cool water or gently sprayed with a garden hose. *Do not leave child unattended!*
4. Elevate the child's legs to decrease the possibility of shock.
5. Offer small sips of cool water only if the child is fully conscious.
6. Notify the child's parents.

Nosebleeds

Accidental bumps, allergies, nose picking, or sinus congestion can all cause a child's nose to bleed. Most nosebleeds are not serious and can be stopped quickly. If a nosebleed continues more than 30 minutes, get medical help. To stop a nosebleed, do the following:

1. Place the child in a sitting position, with head tilted slightly forward, to prevent any swallowing of blood.
2. Have the child breath through his/her mouth.
3. Firmly grasp the child's nostrils (lower half) and squeeze together for at least five minutes before releasing the pressure (Figure 10–11).
4. If bleeding continues, pinch the nostrils together for another 10 minutes.
5. Have the child play quietly for the hour or so to prevent bleeding from restarting.
6. Encourage parents to discuss the problem with the child's physician if nosebleeds occur repeatedly.

---

heat stroke – *failure of the body's sweating reflex during exposure to high temperatures; causes body temperature to rise.*

FIGURE 10–11

Firmly grasp and squeeze the child's nostril to stop nosebleeds.

Seizures

Infants and young children experience seizures for a variety of reasons. Simple precautionary measures can be taken during and immediately after a seizure to protect a child from injury, and should include the following:

1. Call for emergency medical assistance if this is the first time a child has experienced a seizure. If the child has a known seizure disorder, call for emergency help if the seizure lasts longer than three to four minutes or the child experiences severe difficulty breathing or stops breathing.
2. Encourage everyone to remain calm.
3. Carefully lower the child to the floor.
4. Move furniture and other objects out of the way.
5. Do not hold the child down.
6. Do not attempt to force any protective device into the child's mouth.
7. Loosen tight clothing around the child's neck and waist to make breathing easier.
8. Watch carefully to make sure the child is breathing.
9. Place the child in the recovery position (on one side) with head slightly elevated when the seizure ends. This prevents choking by allowing oral secretions to drain out of the mouth.

When the seizure has ended, the child can be moved to a quiet area and encouraged to rest or sleep. A teacher should continue to monitor the child closely. Always notify parents whenever their child has experienced a seizure.

Splinters

Most splinters under the skin's surface can be easily removed with a sterilized needle and tweezers. Clean the skin around the splinter with soap and water or alcohol before starting and after it is removed. Cover the area with a bandage. If the splinter is very deep, do not attempt to remove it. Inform the child's parents to seek medical attention. Also, make sure the child's tetanus immunization is current.

Sprains

A sprain is caused by injury to the ligaments and tissue surrounding a joint and often results in pain and considerable swelling. In most cases, only an X-ray can confirm whether an injury is a sprain or fracture. If there is any doubt, it is always best to splint the injury and treat it as if it were broken. Elevate the injured part and apply ice packs intermittently for 15 to 20 minutes at a time for several hours. Notify the child's parents and encourage them to have the child checked by a physician.

Tick Bites

Ticks are small, oval-shaped insects that generally live in wooded areas and on dogs. On humans, ticks frequently attach themselves to the scalp or base of the neck. The child is seldom aware of the tick's presence. Rocky Mountain Spotted Fever and Lyme disease are rare complications of a tick bite. If a child develops chills, fever, or rash following a known tick bite, medical treatment should be sought at once.

Ticks should be removed carefully. Grasp the tick closely to the skin with tweezers, pulling steadily and straight out to remove all body parts; do not squeeze or twist. Wash the area thoroughly with soap and water and apply a disinfectant such as alcohol. Watch the site closely and contact a physician if any signs of infection and/or rash develop.

Tooth Emergencies

The most common injuries to children's teeth involve chipping or loosening of a tooth. A tooth that has been knocked loose by a blow or fall will often retighten itself within several days. Care should be taken to keep the tooth and gum clean and avoid chewing on hard foods.

If a tooth is completely dislodged, the child should be seen by a dentist and monitored for signs of infection. While dentists will seldom attempt to replace a baby tooth, they are more likely to try and reimplant children's permanent teeth. Successful reimplantation depends on prompt emergency treatment, including:

- handling the tooth with care not to touch the root-end
- keeping the tooth wet by immediately wrapping it in a damp cloth or placing it in a small cup of water or milk
- getting the child to a dentist within an hour of the injury (AAP, 1998; Child Health Alert, 1990).

FOCUS ON FAMILIES • Poison Prevention in the Home

Children under the age of six are the most frequent victims of unintentional poisonings. Their curiosity and limited experience often lead them unknowingly into risky situations. In many households, items such as cleaning products, garden chemicals, automobile waxes, charcoal lighter, lamp oil, and medications are commonly left in places accessible to young children. Often, simple precautions can be taken to make children's environments safe.

- Always place potentially dangerous substances in a locked cabinet. Don't rely on your child's ability to "know better."

- Supervise children closely whenever using harmful products. Take them with you if the doorbell rings or if you must leave the room.

- Teach children not to put anything into their mouths unless it is given to them by an adult.

- Test the paint on your house, walls, children's furniture, and toys to be sure it doesn't contain lead. Contact the National Lead Information Center for information (1-800-424-LEAD).

- Check before purchasing plants and flowers (indoor and outdoor) to make certain they are not poisonous.

- Insist that medications, including those purchased over-the-counter, are in child-resistant containers.

- Post the number of the nearest Poison Control Center near the telephone.

- Caution visitors to keep purses and suitcases out of children's reach.

CASE STUDY

The assistant director of the Cactus Kids Child Care Center was surprised one morning when a child care licensing surveyor from the local public health department paid an unannounced visit. She was confident that her center was in tip-top shape and would have no problem passing its annual safety inspection. As the surveyor entered one of the classrooms, she observed teachers attending to a child who appeared to be having a seizure. The director thought the child had a history of seizures, but ran back to the office to check her file.

1. What first aid measures should the teachers be administering?
2. How would their management strategies differ if the child has had no previous seizures?
3. Should the child's parents be called? Why?
4. What conditions in the classroom could potentially cause a seizure?
5. If the child's seizure continues longer than five minutes, what should the teachers do?
6. What information should be recorded during and following the seizure?

SUMMARY

- Emergency care is administered for life-threatening conditions.

- First aid treatment is given for conditions that are not life-threatening.

- Early education programs should have policies and procedures in place for managing childhood emergencies, including:
  - personnel who are trained in first aid and CPR.
  - emergency contact information and telephone numbers.
  - first aid supplies.

- Teachers never offer a diagnosis or medical advice.

- Parents are responsible for obtaining additional medical treatment after teachers have provided initial emergency or first aid care.

SUGGESTED ACTIVITIES

1. Complete basic CPR and first aid courses.

2. Design a poster or bulletin board illustrating emergency first aid for a young child who is choking. Offer your project to a local early education center where it can be displayed for parents to see.

3. Divide the class into small groups of students. Discuss and demonstrate the emergency care or first aid treatment for each of the following situations. A child:
   - burned several fingers on a hot plate
   - ate de-icing pellets
   - splashed turpentine in his/her eyes
   - fell from a climbing gym
   - is choking on popcorn
   - slammed fingers in a door
   - is found chewing on an extension cord

4. As a class project, prepare listings of emergency services and telephone numbers in your community. Distribute them to local early childhood centers or family day care homes.

CHAPTER REVIEW

A. **Complete each of the given statements with a word selected from the following list. Take the first letter of each answer and place it in the appropriate space following question 10 to spell out one of the basic principles of first aid.**

airway	evaluate
breathing	plans
diagnose	pressure
elevating	responsible
emergency	resuscitation

1. Always check to be sure the child is _____.

2. The immediate care given for life-threatening conditions is _____ care.

3. Early childhood programs should develop _____ for handling emergencies.

4. If an infant is found unconscious and not breathing, begin mouth-to-nose/mouth _____ immediately.

5. The first step in providing emergency care is to quickly _____ the child's condition.

6. Bleeding can be stopped by applying direct _____.

7. When evaluating a child for life-threatening injuries, be sure to check for a clear _____, breathing and circulation.

8. Parents are _____ for any additional medical treatment of a child's injuries.

9. Treatment of shock includes _____ the child's legs 8 to 10 inches.

10. Teachers never _____ or give medical advice.

   A basic principle of first aid is __ __   __ __ __ __ __ __ __ __

REFERENCES

Adeboye, K., &. Armstrong, L. (2002). Pattern and severity of injuries in micro-scooter related accidents. *Emergency Medicine Journal, 19*(6), 571–572.

American Academy of Pediatrics (AAP). (1999) *Choking prevention and first aid for infants and children.* Elk Grove, IL: Author.

American Academy of Pediatrics (AAP). (1998). *Caring for your baby and young child.* New York: Bantam Books.

American Academy of Pediatrics (AAP) & American Public Health Association (APHA). (2002). *Caring for Our Children: National Health and Safety Performance Standards: Guidelines for Out-of-Home Child Care Programs.* Washington, DC: Authors.

American Diabetes Association. (1999). Care of children with diabetes in the school and day care setting. *Diabetes Care, 22*(1), 163–166.

American Heart Association. (2001). *New guidelines for use of CPR.* Dallas, TX: Author. Accessed May 29, 2003, from http://www.aha.org.

American Heart Association. (1997). *Basic life support for healthcare providers: 1997–99.* Dallas, TX: Author.

Aronson, S. (2002). *Health young children: A manual for programs.* (4th ed.). Washington, DC: NAEYC.

Centers for Disease Control and Prevention (CDC). (2002). *Fact Book for 2001–2002: Water-Related Injuries.* Washington, DC: National Center for Injury Prevention and Control (NCIPC).

Centers for Disease Control and Prevention (CDCP). (2002). *Childhood drowning.* Washington, DC: National Center for Injury Prevention and Control.

Child Health Alert. (2002, April). First aid. A clever way to remove particles from a child's eye. *Child Health Alert, 20,* 2.

Child Health Alert. (1990, September). Teeth that get knocked out: A dental emergency. *Child Health Alert,* 2–3.

Child Health Alert. (1999). Helmets recommended for skiing, snowboarding. *Child Health Alert, 18,* 2.

Delfino, R. J., Gong, H., Linn, W. S., Pellizzari, E. D., & Hu, Y. (2003). Asthma symptoms in Hispanic children and daily ambient exposures to toxic and criteria air pollutants. *Environmental Health Perspectives, 111*(4), 647–656.

Dixon, J. K. (2002). Kids need clean air: air pollution and children's health. *Family & Community Health, 24*(4), 9–26.

Lalloo, R. & Sheiham, A.. (2003). Risk factors for childhood major and minor head and other injuries in a nationally representative sample. *Injury, 34*(4), 261–266.

Liebelt, E. L., & DeAngelis, C.D. (1999, September 22). Evolving trends and treatment advances in pediatric poisoning. *JAMA, 282*(12), 1113–1115.

Litovitz, T. L., Klein-Schwartz, W., Rogers, G., Cobaugh, D., Youniss, J., Omslaer, J., May, M., Woolf, A., & Benson, B. (2002). 2001 Annual Report of the American Association of Poison Control Centers Toxic Exposures Surveillance System. *American Journal of Emergency Medicine, 20*(5), 391–452.

Marin Child Care Council. (2002). *Childhood emergencies.* San Rafael, CA: Author.

Marotz, L. R. (2000). Childhood and classroom injuries. In J. L. Frost (Ed.), *Children and injuries.* Tucson, AZ: Lawyers & Judges Publishing Co.

MMWR. (2002). Nonfatal choking-related episodes among children—United States, 2001. *Morbidity & Mortality Weekly Report (MMWR), 51*(42), 945–948.

National SafeKids Campaign. (2003). *Injury facts: Airway obstruction.* Accessed on May 29, 2003, from http://www.safekids.org.

Preboth, M. (2002). Preventing unintentional injuries and deaths in schools. *American Family Physician, 65*(10), 2167–2170.

Simon, R. A. (2002). The allergy-asthma connection. *Allergy & Asthma Proceedings, 23*(4), 219–222.

Siwula, C. M. (2003). Managing pediatric emergencies: No small matter. *Nursing, 33*(2), 48–51.

Slack-Smith, L. M., Read, A. W., & Stanley, F. J. (2002). Experience of respiratory and allergic illness in children attending childcare. *Child Care Health & Development, 28*(2), 171–177.

Wong, D. (2003). *Whaley & Wong's nursing care of infants and children.* (7th ed.). St. Louis, MO: Mosby.

Ying, S. Y., & Ho, W. S. (2001). Playing with fire—a significant cause of burn injury in children *Burns, 27*(1), 39–41.

ADDITIONAL READING

American Academy of Pediatrics (AAP). (1997). Toy-related injuries among children and teenagers in the U.S. *Pediatrics, 46*(50), 118.

American Academy of Pediatrics (AAP). (1998, April). In-line skating injuries in children and adolescents. *Pediatrics, 101*(4), 720.

Aronson, S. (2001). Reducing the risk of injury in child care. *Child Care Information Exchange, 101*(3), 64–66.

Bosque, E., & Watson, S. (1997). *Safe and sound: How to prevent the most common childhood emergencies.* New York: St. Martin Press.

Boudreaux, E. D., Emond, S. D., Clark, S., & Camargo, C. A. (2003). Race/ethnicity and asthma among children presenting to the emergency department: differences in disease severity and management. *Pediatrics, 111*(5 Pt 1), 615–621.

Brady, R. E. (2001). Day care and asthma? *Pediatrics, 108*(5):1237.

Child Health Alert. (1999). Children can strangle on window covering cords. *Child Health Alert, 17,* 3.

Child Health Alert. (1998, October). Serious allergy in school and child care: Prevention and management. *Child Health Alert, 16,* 1.

Copeland, M. (1996). Code blue! Establishing a child care emergency plan. *Child Care Information Exchange, 107,* 17–21.

Daisey, J. M., Angell, W. J., & Apte, M. G. (2003). Indoor air quality, ventilation and health symptoms in schools: an analysis of existing information. *Indoor Air, 13*(1), 53–64.

Goldberg, E. (1994). Including children with chronic health conditions: Nebulizers in the classroom. *Young Children, 49*(2), 34–37.

Mahalick, D. M., McDonough, M., & Levitt, J. K. (1999). Head injuries in adults and children. *Trauma, 37,* 4.

Mitka, M. (1999, June 16). Why the rise in asthma? New insights, few answers. *JAMA, 281*(2), 2171–72.

Kostelnik, M. J., Onaga, E., Rohde, B., & Whiren, A. (2002). *Children with Special Needs: Lessons for Early Childhood Professionals. Early Childhood.* Williston, VT: Teachers College Press.

Loubeau P. R. (2000). Exploration of the barriers to bicycle helmet use among 12 and 13 year old children. *Accident Analysis & Prevention, 32*(1), 111–115.

McKinlay, A., Dalrymple-Alford, J. C., Horwood, L. J., & Fergusson, D. M. (2002). Long term psychosocial outcomes after mild head injury in early childhood. *Journal of Neurology, Neurosurgery, & Psychiatry, 73*(3), 281–288.

Qureshi, S., & Mink, R. (2003). Aspiration of fruit gel snacks. *Pediatrics, 111*(3), 687–689.

Satz, P. (2001). Mild Head Injury in Children and Adolescents. *Current Directions in Psychological Science, 10*(3), 106–109.

Shallcross, M. A. (1999). Family child care homes need health and safety training and an emergency rescue system. *Young Children, 54*(5), 70–73.

HELPFUL WEB SITES

Canadian Health Network	http://www.hwc.ca
Children's Safety Network	http://www.edc.org/HHD/csn/
National Safe Kids Campaign	http://www.safekids.org
National Safety Council	http://www.nsc.org/index/
Parent Time	http://www.parenttime.com/health/ poisonprev/
U.S. Consumer Product Safety Commission (bicycle helmet safety standards)	http://www.cpsc.gov/cpscpub/pubs/helmet

For additional health, safety, and nutrition resources, go to
http://www.EarlyChildEd.delmar.com

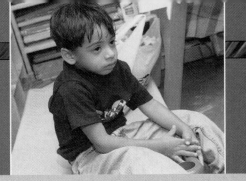

CHAPTER 11

Child Abuse and Neglect

OBJECTIVES

After studying this chapter, you should be able to:

- Distinguish between abuse and neglect.
- Identify three types of abuse and two types of neglect.
- State four ways that teachers can help abused or neglected children.
- Describe characteristics of abusive adults and abused children.
- Identify six sources of support and assistance for abusive and neglectful parents.
- Describe actions the teacher should take in a case of suspected child abuse.

For many reasons, the incidence(s) of **abuse** and **neglect** is difficult to determine with any accuracy. Current estimates suggest that more than three million cases are reported in the United States each year (Administration for Children & Families, 2001). However, many more instances of maltreatment are known to go unreported. An estimated one to two thousand children die each year as a result of abuse and/or neglect, but this number is probably much higher than the data reveal (Johnson, 2002; Sedlak & Broadhurst, 1996). Thousands of additional children suffer serious injury and long-term physical and emotional disabilities as a result of abusive treatment.

---

abuse – *to mistreat, attack, or cause harm to another individual.*
neglect – *failure of a parent or legal guardian to properly care for and meet the basic needs of a child under 18 years of age.*

HISTORICAL DEVELOPMENTS

Accounts of child abuse date from ancient times to the present. Throughout history, young children, especially those with developmental disabilities, have suffered abusive and neglectful treatment. They were also subjected to cultural practices that today would be considered inhumane. In many societies, children had no rights or privileges whatsoever, including the right to live.

One of the first child abuse cases in this country to attract widespread public attention involved a young girl named Mary Ellen. Friends and neighbors were concerned about the regular beatings Mary Ellen received from her adoptive parents. However, in 1874 there were no organizations responsible for dealing with the problems of child abuse and neglect. Consequently, Mary Ellen's friends contacted the New York Society for the Prevention of Cruelty to Animals on the basis that she was a human being and, therefore, also a member of the animal kingdom. Her parents were found guilty of cruelty to animals and eventually Mary Ellen was removed from their home. This incident brought gradual recognition to the fact that some form of care and protection was needed for the many maltreated, abandoned, and developmentally delayed children in this country.

Although child abuse continued to be a major problem, it wasn't until 1961 that the subject once again received national attention. For a period of years, Dr. C. Henry Kempe studied various aspects of child abuse and was concerned about these children whose lives were endangered. He first introduced the phrase "battered child syndrome" in 1961 during a national conference that he organized to address problems related to the harsh treatment of children (Kempe & Helfer, 1982).

The passage of Public Law (PL) 93–247, the Child Abuse Prevention and Treatment Act (CAPTA) on January 31, 1974, signified a turning point in the history of child abuse and neglect. For the first time, national attention was drawn to the maltreatment of young children. The law also created the National Center on Child Abuse and Neglect, and required individual states to establish a central agency with legal authority to investigate and prosecute incidences of maltreatment. PL 93–247 also mandated states to develop policies, procedures, definitions, and laws that addressed the problems of child abuse and neglect. In October 1996, CAPTA was reauthorized and amended to more clearly define circumstances related to the withholding of medical treatment in life-threatening situations (National Clearinghouse on Child Abuse and Neglect Information, 1997).

Although child abuse and neglect have occurred throughout history, it is only in recent years that public attention has been drawn to the magnitude of the problem. And, only now are professionals realizing the full extent and long-term effects of child abuse and neglect as they currently exist in our society.

DISCIPLINE VS. PUNISHMENT

The term **discipline** is derived from the word disciple and refers to the act of teaching or guiding. The appropriate use of discipline can be effective for teaching children socially acceptable ways of behaving. However, when it is used improperly or involves threats, fear, or harsh physical **punishment**, it only teaches children anger and violence.

For decades, the right to punish or discipline children as families saw fit was considered a parental privilege. Consequently, outsiders often overlooked or ignored incidences of cruelty to children so as not to interfere in a family's personal affairs. However, public attitudes regarding

---

discipline – *training or enforced obedience that corrects, shapes, or develops acceptable patterns of behavior.*

punishment – *a negative response to what the observer considers to be wrong or inappropriate behavior; may involve physical or harsh treatment.*

family privacy and the rights of families to discipline children as they wished began to change. Educators, health and law enforcement professionals, neighbors, and concerned friends grew intolerant of the abusive and neglectful treatment of young children. They began speaking out against such behavior and serving as advocates for innocent children who were being victimized by adults.

One of the most difficult aspects of this problem is deciding at what point discipline or punishment becomes abuse or neglect. For example, when does a spanking or verbal **reprimand** constitute abuse? Is sending a child to his room without dinner neglect? In an attempt to establish clear guidelines, federal legislation was passed forcing states to define abuse and neglect and to establish policies and procedures for handling individual cases.

ABUSE AND NEGLECT

The terms *abuse* and *neglect* are generally defined as any situation or environment in which a child is not thought to be safe due to inadequate protection, exposure to hazardous conditions, exploitation, mistreatment, or harm **intentionally** inflicted by adults. For legal purposes, a child is defined as an individual under 18 years of age (Figure 11–1). The most commonly recognized categories of abuse and neglect include:

- physical abuse
- emotional or verbal abuse
- sexual abuse

- physical neglect
- emotional or psychological neglect

Physical abuse is often the form most easily identified due to the visible nature of indicators, such as cuts, burns, welts, fractures, scratches, missing hair, or other nonaccidental injuries. Explanations given for these injuries are often inconsistent or unreasonable based on the child's age and level of development. A combination of new and older or untreated injuries may suggest repeated abuse. In almost every instance, observable changes in the child's behavior, including shyness, fearfulness, passiveness, anger, or apprehension will accompany any physical injury (Table 11–1).

FIGURE 11–1

The legal definition of a child is an individual under 18 years of age.

---

reprimand – *to scold or discipline for unacceptable behavior.*
intentionally – *a plan of action that is carried out in a purposeful manner.*
physical abuse – *injuries, such as welts, burns, bruises, or broken bones, that are caused intentionally.*

TABLE 11-1 Observation List for Recognizing Abused and Neglected Children

Physical Abuse

- repeated or unexplained injuries, e.g., burns, fractures, bruises, bites, eye or head injuries
- frequently complains of pain
- wears clothing to hide injuries; may be inappropriate for weather conditions
- reports harsh treatment
- frequently late or absent; arrives too early or stays after dismissal from school
- unusually fearful of adults, especially parents
- appears malnourished or dehydrated
- avoids logical explanations for injuries
- withdrawn, anxious or uncommunicative or may be outspoken and disruptive
- lacks affection, both giving and seeking
- may be given inappropriate food, beverage, or drugs

Emotional Abuse

- generally unhappy; seldom smiles or laughs
- aggressive and disruptive or unusually shy and withdrawn
- reacts without emotion to unpleasant statements and actions
- displays behaviors that are unusually adultlike or childlike
- delayed growth and/or emotional and intellectual development

Sexual Abuse

- underclothing torn, stained, or bloody
- complains of pain or itching in the genital area
- has venereal disease
- has difficulty getting along with other children, e.g., withdrawn, babylike, anxious
- rapid weight loss or gain
- sudden failure in school performance
- involved in delinquency, including prostitution, running away, alcoholism, or drug abuse
- fascination with body parts, talks about sexual activities

Physical Neglect

- repeatedly arrives unclean; may have a bad odor from dirty clothing or hair
- is in need of medical or dental care; may have untreated injuries or illness
- frequently hungry; begs or steals food while at school
- dresses inappropriately for weather conditions; shoes and clothing often sized too small or too large
- is chronically tired; falls asleep at school, lacks the energy to play with other children
- has difficulty getting along with other children; spends much time alone

Emotional Neglect

- poor academic performance
- appears apathetic, withdrawn and inattentive
- frequently absent or late to school
- uses any means to gain teacher's attention and approval
- seldom participates in extracurricular activities
- engages in delinquent behaviors, e.g., stealing, vandalism, sexual misconduct, abuse of drugs or alcohol

The **Shaken Baby Syndrome**, another form of physical abuse, is typically seen in infants. It is caused by the vigorous shaking or tossing of an infant into the air, often because a baby won't stop crying. The resulting whiplash-like motion can cause serious bleeding and bruising in the infant's brain, death, or long-term complications, including blindness, deafness, fractures, learning disabilities, and seizures (American Academy of Pediatrics, 2000). Understanding the harmful effects of shaking a baby and recognizing that crying is a baby's main form of communication are important for preventing this senseless tragedy.

Physical abuse frequently begins as an **innocent** act of frustration or punishment. In other words, most adults do not set out to intentionally harm a child. However, during the process of disciplining the child, quick tempers and uncontrollable anger may lead to punishment that is severe and sufficiently violent to cause injuries and sometimes even death (Table 11–1). Predicting whether the abusive behavior will be repeated is often difficult, since it is more likely to occur during times when an adult has lost control (Mammen, Kilko, & Pilkonis, 2002). Thus, days, weeks, and even months may pass between attacks.

Emotional or **verbal abuse** occurs when adults repeatedly and unpredictably criticize, verbally assault, ignore, or belittle a child's behavior and/or achievements (Hamarman, Pope, & Czaja, 2002). Their demands and expectations are often unrealistic given the child's age and developmental abilities. Chronic exposure to negative statements, such as "Why can't you ever do things right?" or "I knew you were too stupid" have lifelong effects on children's emotional and intellectual development. In many cases, verbal assaults turn into physical abuse over time. Understandably, toddlers and preschoolers are the most common victims of this form of abuse.

Notable changes in a child's behavior are often an early indicator of verbal abuse. Careful observation and documentation of adult–child interactions can be useful for the early identification of potential emotional abuse. Unlike the immediate harm caused by an act of physical abuse, the effects of verbal abuse often do not appear until years later. This fact makes it difficult to identify and treat before the abuse leaves permanent scars on the child's personality and development. Sadly, many of these children will experience serious psychiatric disorders later in life (Feerick, Haugaard, & Hien, 2002; Johnson, 2002; Brodsky, Oquendo, Ellis, Hass, Malone, & Mann, 2001).

Sexual abuse includes any sexual involvement between an adult and a child, such as fondling, exhibitionism, rape, incest, child pornography, and prostitution. Such acts are considered abuse regardless of whether or not the child agreed to participate (Kolvin & Trowell, 1996). This belief is based on the assumption that children may not be free of adult pressure or are incapable of making a rational decision in these situations. Girls are sexually abused at a rate nearly twice that of boys (Johnson, 2002; Burkhardt & Rotatori, 1995). More often, the perpetrator is male and not a stranger to the child, but rather someone the child knows and trusts, for example, a babysitter, relative, caretaker, stepparent, or teacher (Kolvin & Trowell, 1996). For this reason, the incidence of sexual abuse is probably much greater than reported and often not discovered until years later.

A caretaker's failure to provide for a child's basic needs and care is considered *physical neglect*. More than half of all substantiated cases of maltreatment involve some form of neglect, including inadequate or inappropriate food, shelter, clothing, cleanliness, or medical and dental care. In many states, parents who fail to send their children to school or to encourage regular attendance are also considered guilty of neglect.

Shaken Baby Syndrome – *forceful shaking of a baby that causes head trauma, internal bleeding, and sometimes death.*

innocent – *not guilty; lacking knowledge.*

emotional abuse – *repeated humiliation, ridicule, or threats directed toward another individual.*

verbal abuse – *to attack another individual with words.*

sexual abuse – *any sexual involvement between an adult and child.*

TABLE 11–2 Tips for Determining if Children Are Ready to be Left Home Alone

- Has your child expressed interest in staying home alone?
- Does your child typically understand and abide by family rules?
- Is your child reliable and able to handle responsibility in a mature manner?
- Does your child handle unexpected events in a positive way?
- Is your child able to entertain her/himself for long periods of time or does she/he require constant supervision?
- Have you rehearsed safety and emergency procedures so your child knows how to respond in the event of a fire, an unwanted telephone call, or someone knocking at the front door?
- Does your child know how to reach you if necessary? Is there another adult your child can contact if you are not available?
- Has your child experienced being home alone for short periods?
- Does your child have any fears which would be a problem if left alone?

Leaving young children unsupervised can also result in charges of physical neglect. The term **latch-key** was originally used to describe the large number of school-aged children who were home alone during the hours before and after school. *Self-care* children, a newer term in the literature, may more accurately describe this growing phenomenon. A shortage of programs and lack of trained personnel have made it difficult for many working parents to locate adequate before- and after-school care for school-aged children. Many unanswered questions have been raised about whether these children are at greater risk for accidental injury and/or feelings of loneliness and fear of being left alone (Mayer, 1999; Lovko & Ullman, 1989). In the meantime, parents should have access to guidelines that can help them decide when and if a child can be safely left home alone (Table 11–2).

ISSUES TO CONSIDER • Cultural Practices and Child Abuse

Members of a local Vietnamese community were irate following the arrest of a boy's 23-year-old parents for child abuse. Teachers had noted purple "bruises" on the little boy's back and chest when he arrived at school one day. The couple denied any wrongdoing, insisting they were merely performing "cao gio," a traditional Vietnamese practice used to cure fever. Following the application of medicated oil to the skin, a warm coin or spoon is scraped along the spine and chest until reddened patches appear. The boy's parents believed this would eliminate "bad winds" that had caused the fever.

- Is this abuse?
- How do cultural differences affect parental practices and values?
- Should parents be expected to give up traditional cultural practices related to healing and medicine when they immigrate to this country?
- Why is it important for teachers to acquire an understanding of cultural differences?

latch-key – *a term that refers to school-age children who care for themselves without adult supervision before and after school hours.*

Emotional or psychological neglect is perhaps the most difficult of all types to identify and document (Hamarman, Pope, & Czaja, 2002). For this reason, many states do not include it in their reporting laws. Emotional neglect reflects a basic lack of parental interest or responsiveness to a child's psychological needs and development. Parents fail to see the need, or do not know how, to show affection or converse with their child. The absence of any emotional connection, such as hugging, kissing, touching, conversation, or facial expressions revealing pleasure or displeasure, can lead to developmental delays and stunted physical growth. The term **failure to thrive** is used to describe this condition when it occurs in infants and young children. A lack of measurable gains in weight and/or height is often one of the first indicators of psychological neglect (Diaz, Simantor & Rickert, 2002).

REPORTING LAWS

Reporting laws support the philosophy that parenthood carries with it certain obligations and responsibilities toward children (Figure 11–2). Therefore, punishment of abusive adults is not the primary objective. Rather, the purpose of these laws is to protect children from maltreatment and exploitation. Every attempt is made to maintain family unity by helping families find solutions to problems that may be contributing to the abuse or neglect. Contrary to common belief, removing children from their homes is not always the best solution. Criminal action against parents is usually reserved for those cases where the adults are unwilling or unable to cooperate with prescribed treatment programs.

Each case of child abuse and/or neglect involves a unique and complex set of conditions, including home environments, economic pressures, individual temperaments, cultural differences, along with many other factors. For this reason, most child abuse laws and definitions are purposely written in general terms. This practice allows the legal system and social agencies greater flexibility in determining whether or not an adult has acted irresponsibly.

FIGURE 11–2

Parenthood involves the acceptance of certain obligations and responsibilities toward children.

---

failure to thrive – *a term used to describe an infant whose growth and mental development is severely slowed due to lack of nurturing or mental stimulation.*

REFLECTIVE THOUGHTS

Teachers (including assistants, aides, and students) are required to report suspected incidences of child abuse and/or neglect. How do you determine what to report? Should the family be informed when a report has been filed? What are your feelings about making a report when it is likely the family will know who filed the complaint? What professional responsibilities do you have to the child and family?

Laws in every state identify certain groups and professionals who are required to report suspected incidences of abuse or neglect, including:

- teachers, including assistants and student teachers
- center directors and principals
- health care providers, e.g., doctors, nurses, dentists, pharmacists, psychologists
- law enforcement personnel
- social workers
- clergy

Every center should establish a written plan for handling suspected incidences of abuse and neglect (Nunnelly & Fields, 1999). Policies and procedures should be reviewed frequently with staff to ensure understanding and compliance. In most large centers, teachers often report their observations to the director or health consultant who then contacts appropriate local authorities and files a report. However, if at any time teachers are not satisfied that their concerns have been reported, they must personally carry out this obligation. In home-based programs or smaller centers, an individual staff member may be responsible for initiating the report. Failure to do so may prolong a potentially harmful situation for the child, and can result in criminal prosecution and fines for the teacher.

Initial reports are usually made by telephone, and a written report is completed within several days (Table 11–3). All information is kept strictly confidential, including the identity of the person making the report. Protection against liability and criminal charges is afforded by most reporting laws to anyone who reports abuse or neglect without deliberate intent to harm another individual.

It is not the teacher's role to prove suspicions of abuse and neglect before making a report. If there is any reason to believe that a child is being mistreated or inadequately cared for, child protective services should be contacted immediately. As long as a report is made in good faith, the teacher is merely indicating that a family may be in need of help. The law does not require that the

TABLE 11–3 Items to Include in a Written Child Abuse/Neglect Report

1. The name and address of the child and the parents or caretakers (if known).
2. The child's age.
3. The nature and extent of the child's injuries or description of neglect including any evidence of previous injuries or deprivation.
4. The identity of the offending adult (if known).
5. Other information that the reporting person believes may be helpful in establishing the cause of injuries or neglect.
6. The name, address, telephone number, and professional title of the individual making the report.

family or adult be notified when a report is filed. In some cases, doing so could place the child in additional danger, especially if sexual or harsh physical abuse is involved. Other families may experience relief when their problems are finally recognized. Therefore, the decision of whether or not to inform the family or adult may depend on the particular circumstances.

Reporting a parent, colleague, or acquaintance is often difficult. However, as advocates for children's rights, teachers must always be concerned about children's well-being. If the child is not in immediate danger, trained personnel will usually meet with the family or adult, evaluate circumstances surrounding the incident, and work with them in an attempt to improve conditions.

PROTECTIVE MEASURES FOR PROGRAMS AND TEACHERS

It is essential that early childhood programs take steps to protect themselves from potential accusations of child abuse and neglect. Special attention should be given to careful hiring practices, policy development, and ongoing training of personnel, including:

- conducting background checks on new employees for any prior record of child abuse or felony convictions. (These are mandated in most states and conducted by state law enforcement agencies)
- hiring individuals with formal training in early education and child development
- requesting and contacting an applicant's references (nonrelative)
- reviewing an employee's past employment record, including reasons for leaving previous jobs
- establishing a code of conduct regarding appropriate child–teacher behavior (Table 11–4)

TABLE 11–4 Strategies for Positive Behavior Management

- **Reinforce** desirable behaviors. Give lots of verbal praise, hugs and pats, and adult attention for things the child is doing appropriately; this reinforcement should be given often and immediately following the appropriate behavior. "I really like the way you are sharing your toys" or "That was nice of you to let Mat have a turn on the bike."

- **Redirect** the child to another activity or area when he/she is behaving inappropriately; don't comment on the inappropriate behavior. "Juan, could you come and help me set the table?" or "Let's go to the block area and build a zoo together."

- **Rules** help children understand their limits and how adults expect them to behave. Rules should be simple and state what behavior is appropriate. Limit explanations or reasons for the rule. "Mika, you need to sit on the sofa; feet go on the floor." or "We need to walk in the halls."

- **Consequences** can be used together with other management strategies. Most children understand consequences from an early age on. "When your hands are washed we can eat." or "I will have to take the ball away if you throw it at the window again."

- **Ignoring** undesirable behaviors, such as tantrums or throwing things can be effective for decreasing the attention-getting response children may be looking for. Don't look at the child or discuss the behavior.

- **Practice** desirable behaviors when the child behaves inappropriately. For example, if the child scatters crayons across the floor he/she needs to pick them up and then be praised for doing what was asked. An adult may also model the desired behavior by helping the child pick up the crayons.

- providing continued inservice training, especially on topics related to identification of abuse/neglect, and teaching children self-protection skills
- establishing a policy of nontolerance toward any form of abusive behavior, including harassment and harsh discipline

There are additional measures teachers can take to protect themselves against the possibility of false accusations (Mikkelsen, 1997). By conducting daily health checks and recording the findings, a child's condition can be documented upon arrival, thus eliminating opportunities for teachers to be blamed for a bruise or scratch that may have occurred elsewhere. It is also good practice not to leave a teacher alone with children. A second teacher can serve as an eyewitness to avoid any suspicions of wrongdoing. Teachers should also continually seek out training opportunities to improve their understanding of child abuse and the important role they play in intervention.

UNDERSTANDING THE DYNAMICS OF ABUSE AND NEGLECT

Abusive adults come from all levels of social, economic, educational, racial, religious, and occupational backgrounds (Administration for Children & Families, 2001; Murry, 2000). They live in rural areas, as well as small towns and large cities. It is a common misconception that child abuse and neglect are committed by people who are uneducated, alcoholics, drug abusers, or of low income. While the incidence of abuse and neglect is higher among these groups, such generalizations are often too simplistic where complex social and economic issues are involved.

Perhaps one explanation for why a larger percentage of individuals are identified from disadvantaged families is because of their greater use of, and dependency on, public and social services. Furthermore, daily living is often more stressful for low-income families. Simply finding adequate food, clothing, housing, and transportation can be overwhelming demands (Brown, Cohen, Johnson, & Salzinger, 1998). In contrast, families with greater financial resources can afford private medical care, move from doctor to doctor, and even seek treatment in neighboring cities. This flexibility and inconsistent contact with a single health care provider makes it to easier to avoid immediate suspicion, especially if children's injuries are minor, and allegations of abuse or neglect (Herendeen, 2002).

In an attempt to understand the complex nature of child abuse and neglect, three major risk factors have been identified and studied extensively:

- characteristics of adults with potential for abuse/neglect
- presence of a "special" child
- family and environmental stresses

It is believed that for abuse and neglect to take place, all three risk factors must be present at the same time.

Characteristics of Abusive/Neglectful Adults

Certain adult behaviors and predispositions are commonly associated with abusive tendencies, including:

- a history of repeated fear, anger, and rejection (Pears & Capaldi, 2001)
- low self-esteem
- difficulty in forming long-term relationships, e.g., friendships, marriage, that leads to social isolation and loneliness
- lack of trust
- early marriage and pregnancy

- use of harsh punishment to "discipline" children
- impulsive tendencies
- low tolerance for stress
- drug and alcohol addictions
- poor problem-solving abilities

While not every adult who exhibits these characteristics is abusive or neglectful, likewise not every abusive or neglectful caregiver will necessarily fit this description (Simons, Whitbeck, Conger, & Chyi-in, 1991). In many cases, adults simply lack the knowledge and skills to be a successful parent—to provide proper care and protect children's well-being. A lack of understanding about child development leads to expectations that are often unrealistic and developmentally inappropriate based on the child's age and abilities (Milner, 2003; Baumann & Kolko, 2002). For example, a parent may become upset because a 15-month-old wets the bed, a toddler spills milk, or a seven-year-old loses a mitten. Intolerance, frustration, and uncontrolled anger can, in turn, lead to a subsequent outlash of abusive behavior.

Presence of a "Special" Child

Occasionally an abusive or neglectful caregiver will single out a child whom they consider to be different in some way from their **expectations**. These differences may be real or only imagined, but the adult is convinced that they actually exist. Qualities that are often cited by abusive adults include a child who is:

- developmentally delayed
- disobedient or uncooperative
- physically unattractive
- unintelligent
- hyperactive
- fussy
- clumsy
- frequently ill
- very timid or weak
- resembles someone the adult dislikes

Children under three years and those with developmental disabilities experience the highest incidence of child abuse (Administration for Children & Families, 2001; Goldson, 1998). However, the rate is also high among children born out of wedlock, from unwanted or unplanned pregnancies, and stepchildren. Infants and children over the age of six years are more likely to suffer from neglect. The percentage of boys and girls who become victims of abuse and neglect is nearly equal.

REFLECTIVE THOUGHTS

In many families, economic pressures contribute to the problem of child abuse and neglect. How does poverty increase the probability of child abuse? How might cultural values affect this association? What are some resources available to families in poverty to help with everyday living expenses? What potential effects might poverty and an abusive childhood have on a child's self-concept?

---

expectations – *behaviors or actions that are anticipated.*

Family and Environmental Stresses

All individuals and families face conflict and crises from time to time. However, some are better able to cope with stressful events than others. In many cases of abuse or neglect, stress is the **precipitating** factor. That is, conflict is sufficient to push them to action (abuse) or withdrawal (neglect) as a caretaker (Bugental & Shennum, 2002).

Abusive or neglectful adults often react to stressful events without distinguishing the true magnitude of the conflict. Instead, they find all crises equally overwhelming and difficult to handle. The following examples illustrate the diversity of personal and environmental stresses that might lead to a loss of control, especially when they occur in combination with other events that are perceived as stressful:

- flat tire
- clogged sink
- broken window
- lost keys
- job loss

- illness, injury, or death
- financial pressures
- divorce or other marital problems
- moving
- birth of another child

Some of these events may seem trivial in comparison to others. Yet, any one may become the "straw that breaks the camel's back" and trigger abusive behavior. The adult's response may also be inappropriate or out of proportion to the actual event. It is typically at this point that anger and frustration are taken out on the child.

THE ROLE OF THE TEACHER

Teachers are in an ideal position to identify and help children who are being abused or neglected (Bolen, 2003; Anderson, Weston, Doueck, & Krause, 2002; Wright, 2000). Daily health checks and frequent interactions make it possible for teachers to recognize early changes in children's behavior and appearance. In many cases, a teacher may be the only person whom a child trusts enough to reveal abusive or neglectful treatment.

Child abuse and neglect is often exhibited as a pattern of behavior. Therefore, careful written documentation of each incident is important (Tower, 1993). Written reports should be precise and include the following information:

- the type, location, size, and severity of any injury (Figure 11–3)
- the child's explanation of how the injury occurred
- any explanation provided by the parents or caretakers of how the injury happened
- obvious signs of neglect, e.g., malnutrition, uncleanliness, inappropriate dress, excessive fatigue, lack of medical or dental care
- recent or drastic changes in the child's behavior
- quality of parent/child interactions.

A teacher's written observations can provide valuable evidence for child protective authorities. They may also be useful for determining which services and treatment programs are appropriate to meet the immediate needs of children and their families.

Helping Abused or Neglected Children

Teachers play an important role in helping maltreated children cope with the effects of abuse and neglect (NAEYC, 1997). As a positive role model, the teacher must accept children for who they

---

precipitating – *factors that trigger or initiate a reaction or response.*

FIGURE 11–3

A form for recording the location, size, and nature of a child's injury.

Child's Name: _____

Date: _____

Comments: _____

          Description of Injury: _____

          Location and Size of Injury: _____

          Color of Injury: _____

          Desciption of Child's Behavior: _____

Additional Comments/Concerns: _____

Reported by: _____

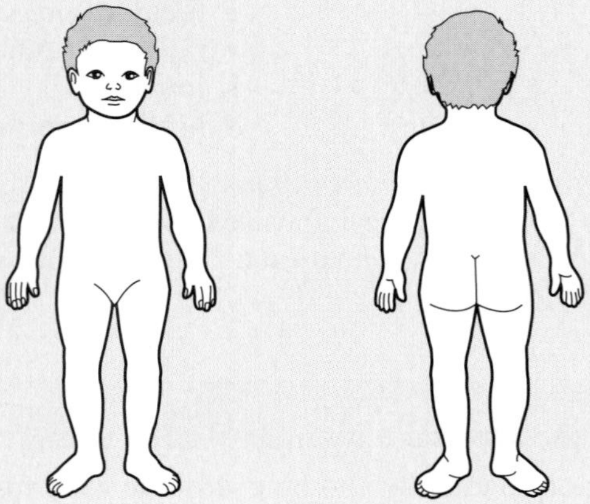

are, listen to their problems, encourage their efforts and praise their successes (Lowenthal, 1999). For many children it may be the first time any adult has shown a sincere interest in them without threatening or causing them harm (Eaton, 1997).

As a trusting relationship is established, children may begin verbalizing their feelings. Play therapy can be especially effective with young children by providing opportunities for acting out anger, fears, and anxieties related to abusive treatment. Housekeeping activities and doll play are ideal activities for this purpose. Talking about how the doll (child) feels when it is mistreated can help to draw out a child's true feelings. At the same time, teachers can model good parenting skills, such as appropriate ways to talk with, treat, and care for the dolls.

Artwork can also be an effective means for helping young children express their feelings and concerns. For example, self-portraits may reveal an exaggeration of certain body parts or emotions that children have experienced. Pictures may also depict unusual practices that children have been subjected to, such as being tied up, locked in a closet, or struck with an object.

Extreme caution must always be exercised when attempting to interpret children's artwork. A child's immature drawing skills and lack of perspective can easily lead an inexperienced observer to misinterpretation and false conclusions. Therefore, it is best to view unusual items in children's drawings as additional clues, rather than absolute indicators of abuse or neglect.

Some children exhibit behaviors that adults find extremely annoying or irritating in order to gain attention. Repetitive use of such behaviors may prove especially frustrating for adults who have a low tolerance point or lack an understanding of how to manage these situations in a positive manner. In some instances, this intense frustration is sufficient to trigger an abusive response

(Brodsky, 2001; Murry, Baker, & Lewin, 2000; Lowenthal, 1999). Teachers can be effective in helping children learn to manage and express their feelings in ways that are both appropriate and socially acceptable. For example, a teacher might say, "Rosa, if you want another cracker, you need to use your words to ask for it. No one can understand when you whine or cry." They can also do much to build and strengthen trusting relationships with these children. Over time, the abused or neglected child's self-esteem and self-concept may gradually improve through the teacher's persistent encouragement and supportive efforts to:

- respond to children in a loving and accepting manner
- set aside a private space that children can call their own
- establish gradual limits for acceptable behavior; set routines and schedules that provide order in children's lives that often have been dominated by turmoil
- let children know they are available whenever they need someone, whether it be for companionship, extra attention, or reassurance (Figure 11–4)
- take time to prepare children for new experiences; knowing what is expected enhances the "safeness" of the child's environment
- encourage children to talk about their feelings, fears, and concerns

A number of educational programs and materials have been developed to help improve children's awareness and ability to respond to maltreatment (Table 11–5). Many of these resources are available through local public libraries. Materials should be selected carefully so that they are instructive and not frightening to young children (Aronson, 2000). Social workers, nurses, doctors, mental health specialists, and public service groups can also be called upon to provide special programs for children and parents.

It is also important for all children to learn good communication and self-protection skills. Even when they do not fully understand the complexity of abuse or neglect, these skills enable children to recognize "uncomfortable" situations, how and when to tell a trusted adult, and how to assert themselves by saying no when someone attempts a behavior that is inappropriate. Informed children can be the first line of defense against abuse and neglect if they are aware that being beaten, forced to engage in sexual activity, or left alone for long periods is not normal or the type of treatment they deserve.

FIGURE 11–4

Caring adults can provide extra companionship, reassurance, and individualized attention.

TABLE 11–5   Books for Children about Child Abuse

A stranger in the park, by Stuart Fitts & Donna Asay. Agreka Books (1999).
A very touching book . . . for little people and for big people, by Jan Hindman. Alexandria
   Associates (1983).
I told my secret: A book for kids who were abused, by Eliana Gil. Launch Press (1986).
He told me not to tell, by Jennifer Fay, J. Stowell & W.M. Dietzel. ACT for Kids (1991).
My body is private, by Linda W. Girard. Albert Whitman & Co. (1992).
My very own book about me: A personal safety book, by Jo Stowell & M. Dietzel. ACT for Kids
   (2000).
Never talk to strangers: A book about personal safety, by Irma Joyce. Golden Books Pubishing Co.
   Inc (2000).
No more secrets for me, by Oralee Wachter. Little Brown & Co. (2002).
Private zone: A book teaching children sexual assault prevention tools, by Francis Dayee. Warner
   Books (1985).
Red flag, green flag people, by Kecia Freed (Illustrator). Rape & Abuse Crisis Center (1985).
Something happened and I'm scared to tell: A book for young victims of abuse, by Patricia Kehoe.
   Parenting Press (1987).
Stranger safety, by Pati Myers Gross. Roo Publishing (1996).
The right touch: A read-aloud story to help prevent child sexual abuse, by Sandy Kleven.
   Illumination Arts (1998).
Trouble with secrets, by Karen Johnsen. Parenting Press (1986).
*The safe child book: A commonsense approach to protecting children and teaching children to pro-
   tect themselves,* by Sherryll Kraizer. Fireside Press (1996).
Who is a stranger and what should I do?, by Linda W. Girard. Concept Books (1993).
Your body belongs to you, by Cornelia Maude Spelman. Albert Whitman & Co. (1997).

Helping Parents

Parenting is a demanding task. Many parents today have not had the same opportunities to learn parenting skills that past generations once had. They have often grown up in smaller families and had fewer opportunities to practice parenting firsthand. Their jobs frequently require relocation to distant cities and the resulting loss of immediate family support. And, more often than not, today's parents are also employed outside of the home, adding yet another challenge to the task of raising children. A lack of adequate knowledge and resources can cause some parents to react to stressful pressures by causing harm to their child. However, their circumstances in no way excuse this type of behavior but rather signal the importance of early recognition and intervention. Without sound knowledge and adequate resources, everyday stresses can lead to abusive and neglectful treatment of children.

There are many ways teachers can help parents. Daily contacts with parents provide opportunities for recognizing families in crises and directing them to appropriate community services and programs, including:

- child protective services
- day care and "crisis" centers
- family counseling
- help or "hot lines"
- temporary foster homes
- homemaker services
- transportation
- financial assistance

- parenting classes
- employment assistance
- home visitors
- self-help or support groups

Teachers can also share valuable information about issues, such as child development, discipline, and health, with parents to strengthen their child-rearing skills. Teachers must, however, be sensitive to cultural differences in parenting practices that could be misinterpreted as abusive. Establishing supportive partnerships and maintaining effective lines of communication with parents are also effective strategies that teachers can use for both prevention and intervention. On a more structured basis, teachers can offer seminars and workshops through local schools, child development centers, or community agencies on topics of interest to most parents, including:

- child growth and development
- identification and management of behavior problems
- principles of good nutrition; feeding problems
- how to meet children's social and emotional needs at different stages
- preventive health care for children at various ages
- locating and utilizing community resources
- stress and tension relievers for parents
- financial planning
- organizing a parent self-help group

Inservice Training

Teachers are morally and legally responsible for identifying the early signs of child abuse and neglect. However, to be effective, they must be well informed. Through inservice training sessions, teachers can gain the basic knowledge and understanding necessary to perform this function. Suggested topics for inservice programs might include:

- an explanation of relevant state laws.
- teachers' rights and responsibilities.
- how to identify child abuse and neglect.
- development of school policies and procedures for handling suspected cases.
- exploration of teachers' and staff reactions to abuse and neglect.
- identifying community resources and services.
- classroom strategies for helping abused and neglected children.
- stress reduction and time management.

FOCUS ON FAMILIES • Anger Management

Being a parent has many positive rewards, but it can also be a challenging and stressful role to fulfill. At times, children are likely to behave in ways that we find upsetting and cause us to react in anger. While this behavior is understandable, it does not teach children how to handle their feelings of frustration or disappointment in a positive manner. Instead, our actions may teach children how to shout, say hurtful words, and respond in an emotional, rather than in a rational, way. When adults practice effective strategies for managing their anger, they become positive role models for children. The next time your child makes you angry, try several of the following techniques:

- Take a deep breath. Thoroughly assess the situation before you react.

- Leave the room. Take a brief "time out" and regain control of your emotions.

- Consider whether the situation or the child's behavior is actually worth your becoming upset. Could the outcome affect the long-term relationship you have with your child?

- Tell children what has upset you, and why.

- Avoid lengthy explanations and arguments with your child. Children are more likely to understand statements when they are brief and to the point.

- Learn to recognize your tolerance limits and what behaviors are most likely to make you upset.

- Always find something good to say about your child soon afterward. This helps children understand that you still love them despite their unacceptable behavior.

CASE STUDY

When it was time for snacks, four-year-old Jimmy said he wasn't hungry and refused to come over and sit down. At the teacher's gentle insistence, Jimmy reluctantly joined the other children at the table. Tears began to roll down his cheeks as he tried to sit in his chair. Jimmy's teacher watched for a few moments and then walked over to talk with him. Initially, he denied that anything was wrong, but later told the teacher that he "had fallen the night before and hurt his leg."

The teacher took Jimmy aside and comforted him. She asked Jimmy if he would show her where he had been hurt. When Jimmy loosened his jeans, the teacher observed what appeared to be a large burn with some blistering approximately two inches in length by one inch in width on his left buttock. Several small bruises were also evident along one side of the burn. Again, the teacher asked Jimmy how he had been hurt and again he replied that "he had fallen."

1. What actions should Jimmy's teacher take? Should she tell anyone else?

2. Would you recommend that Jimmy's teacher report the incident right away or wait until she has gathered more evidence? Why?

3. To whom should the teacher report what she observed?

4. Using the information provided, write up a complete description of Jimmy's injury.

5. If you were Jimmy's teacher, would your feelings and responses be any different if this was a first-time versus a repeated occurrence?

6. Is it necessary for the teacher to notify Jimmy's parents before making a report?

7. In what ways can the teacher be of immediate help to Jimmy?

8. What should the teacher do if this happens again?

SUMMARY

- Public Law 93–247, the Child Abuse Prevention and Treatment Act:
  - raised public awareness to the problems of child abuse.
  - provides legal protection to abused children.

- Laws governing child abuse:
  - are developed and passed by individual states.
  - are intended to preserve the family unit.
  - require certain professionals, including teachers, to report suspected incidences of abuse and/or neglect.
  - are designated to grant a central agency in each state authority to investigate and handle child abuse/neglect cases.

- Most states recognize four categories of abuse/neglect, including physical abuse, sexual abuse, emotional abuse, and emotional/psychological neglect.

- Potential for abuse/neglect is thought to be greatest when three factors exist simultaneously: an adult who has abusive tendencies, a child who is viewed as "special," and environmental stressors.

- Teachers play an important role in the prevention and treatment of child abuse/neglect through early identification and reporting, providing emotional support to children, educating parents, helping children learn socially acceptable behaviors, and advocating on behalf of children.

SUGGESTED ACTIVITIES

1. Gather statistics on the incidence of child abuse and neglect for your city, county, and state. Compare them to the national rates.

2. Write a two-minute public service announcement for radio and television alerting the community to the problems of child abuse and neglect.

3. Locate at least five agencies or services in your community that provide assistance to abusive or neglectful families. Collect materials from these agencies and prepare a written description of their services.

4. Develop a pamphlet that illustrates self-protection skills for young children. Use it with a group of three- to four-year-olds. Evaluate their response.

5. Identify organizations in your community that work with parents of sexually abused children. Do they also offer programs for children?

6. Develop a bibliography of resources on parenting issues.

7. Conduct a search on the Web to learn more about the CASA (Court Appointed Special Advocates) program. What role do they play in helping abused and neglected children? Is there a CASA program in your area? What qualifications are required of volunteer participants?

CHAPTER REVIEW

A. **Briefly define each of the following terms:**

1. child
2. abuse
3. neglect
4. reporting laws
5. environmental stresses

B. **Complete the given statements by selecting a correct answer from the following list.**

teachers
trust
physical
psychological
neglect
confidential

sexual
childhood
definition
expectations
identify
reported

1. A child's excessive fascination with body parts and talk about sexual activities may be an indication of _____ abuse.

2. Public Law 93–247 requires states to write a legal _____ of child abuse and neglect.

3. Injury that is intentionally inflicted on a child is called _____ abuse.

4. Malnutrition, lack of proper clothing, or inadequate adult supervision are examples of physical _____.

5. Verbal abuse sometimes results because of unrealistic parent demands and _____ .

6. Emotional or _____ neglect is one of the most difficult forms of neglect to identify.

7. Reporting laws usually require _____ to report suspected cases of child abuse and neglect.

8. Information contained in reports of child abuse or neglect is kept _____.

9. Many abusive adults were abused during their own _____.

10. Lack of _____ makes it difficult for many abusive and neglectful adults to form friendships.

11. Daily contact with children helps teachers to _____ children who are abused or neglected.

12. Suspected abuse or neglect does not have to be proven before it should be _____.

C. **Briefly answer each of the following questions:**

1. List five clues that would help teachers recognize a child who is being physically abused.

2. What should teachers do if they suspect that a child is being abused or neglected?

3. What information should be included in both an oral and written report?

4. Discuss four ways that teachers can help abused and neglected children in the classroom.

5. List six types of services that are available in most communities to help abusive or neglectful families.

6. Why does the incidence of child abuse and neglect appear to be higher among disadvantaged families?

REFERENCES

Administration for Children & Families, Children's Bureau. (2001). *Child maltreatment 2001.* Department of Health & Human Services. Accessed on June 4, 2003, at http://www.acf.hhs.gov/programs/cb/publications.

American Academy of Pediatrics (AAP). (2000). *Prevent shaken baby syndrome.* Morton Grove, IL: Author.

Anderson, L. E, Weston, E. A., Doueck, H. J., & Krause, D. J. (2002). The child-centered social worker and the sexually abused child: Pathway to healing. *Social Work, 47*(4), 368–378.

Aronson, S. (2002). *Healthy young children: A manual for programs.* (4th ed.). Washington, DC: NAEYC.

Baumann, B. L., & Kolko, D. J. (2002). A comparison of abusive and nonabusive mothers of abused children. *Child Maltreatment, 7*(4), 369–376.

Bolen, R. M. (2003). Child sexual abuse: Prevention or promotion? *Social Work, 48*(2), 174–185.

Brodsky, B. S., Oquendo, M., Ellis, S. P., Haas, G. L., Malone, K. M., & Mann, J. J. (2001). The relationship of childhood abuse to impulsivity and suicidal behavior in adults with major depression. *American Journal of Psychiatry, 158*(11), 1871–1877.

Brown, J., Cohen, P., Johnson, J. G., & Salzinger, S. (1998, November). A longitudinal analysis of risk factors for child maltreatment: Officially recorded and self-reported child abuse and neglect. *Child Abuse & Neglect, 22*(11), 1065–78.

Bugental, D. B., & Shennum, W. (2002). Gender, power, and violence in the family. *Child Maltreatment, 7*(1), 56–64.

Burkhardt, S. A., & Rotatori, A. F. (1995). *Treatment and prevention of childhood sexual abuse.* Washington, DC: Taylor and Francis.

Cohen, P., Brown, J., & Smaile, E. (2002). Child abuse and neglect and the development of mental disorders in the general population. *Developmental Psychopathology, 13*(4), 981–989.

Diaz, A., Simantov, E., & Rickert. (2002). Effect of abuse on health: results of a national survey. *Archives of Pediatric & Adolescent Medicine, 156*(8), 811–817.

Eaton, M. (1997). Positive discipline: Fostering self-esteem of young children. *Young Children, 52*(6), 43–46.

Feerick, M. M., Haugaard, J. J., & Hien, D. A. (2002). Child maltreatment and adulthood violence: the contribution of attachment and drug abuse. *Child Maltreatment, 7*(3), 226–240.

Goldson, E. (1998, July). Children with disabilities and child maltreatment. *Child Abuse & Neglect, 22*(7), 663–65.

Hamarman S., Pope, K. H., & Czaja, S. J. (2002) Emotional abuse in children: variations in legal definitions and rates across the United States. *Child Maltreament, 7*(4), 303–311.

Herendeen, P. M. (2002). Evaluation of physical abuse in children. Solid suspicion should be your guide. *Advanced Nurse Practioner, 10*(8), 32–36.

Johnson, C. F. (2002). Child maltreatment 2002: recognition, reporting and risk. *Pediatrics International, 44*(5), 554–560.

Johnson, J. G. (1999). Childhood abuse ups risk for adult mental illness. *Archives of General Psychiatry, 56,* 600–606.

Kempe, C. H., & Helfer, R. (Eds.). (1982). *The battered child.* Chicago: University of Chicago Press.

Kolvin, I., & Trowell, J. (1996). Child sexual abuse. In I. Rosen (Ed.). *Sexual deviation* (3rd ed.). Oxford, England: Oxford University Press, 337–360.

Lovko, A. M., & Ullman, D. (1989). Research on the adjustment of latchkey children: Role of background/demographic and latchkey situation variables. *Journal of Clinical Child Psychology, 18*(1), 16–24.

Lowenthal, B. (1999). Effects of maltreatment and ways to promote children's resiliency. *Childhood Education, 75*(4), 204–206.

Mammen, O. K., Kolko, D. J., & Pilkonis, P. A. (2002). Negative affect and parental aggression in child physical abuse. *Child Abuse and Neglect, 26*(4), 407–424.

Mayer, D. (1999). *At home alone: Safety tips for latchkey children.* Manitoba, Canada: Manitoba Child Care Association. Child & Family—Canada Web site <http//www.cfc-efc.ca>.

Mikkelsen, E. (1997). Responding to allegations of sexual abuse in child care and early childhood programs. *Young Children, 52*(3), 47–51.

Milner, J. S. (2003). Social information processing in high-risk and physically abusive parents. *Child Abuse & Neglect, 27*(1), 7–20.

Moriarty, A. (1990). Deterring the molester and abuser: Pre-employment testing for child and youth care workers. *Child and Youth Quarterly, 19*(1), 59–66.

Murry, S. K., Baker, A. W., & Lewin, L. (2000). Screening families with young children for child maltreatment potential. *Pediatric Nursing; 26*(1), 47–54.

National Association for the Education of Young Children (NAEYC). (1997). NAEYC position statement on the prevention of child abuse in early childhood programs and the responsibilities of early childhood professionals to prevent child abuse. *Young Children, 52*(3), 42–46.

Nunnelly, J. C., & Fields, T. (1999). Anger, dismay, guilt, anxiety—the realities and roles in reporting child abuse. *Young Children, 54*(5), 74–80.

Pears, K. C., & Capaldi, D. M. (2001). Intergenerational transmission of abuse: A two-generational prospective study of an at-risk sample. *Child Abuse & Neglect, 25*(11), 1439–1461.

Sedlak, A., & Broadhurst, D. (1996). *Executive summary of the third national incidence study of child abuse and neglect.* Washington, DC: U.S. Department of Health and Human Services, Administration for Children and Families, Administration on Children, Youth and Families, National Center on Child Abuse and Neglect.

Simons, R. L., Whitbeck, L. B., Conger, R. D., & Chyi-in, W. (1991). Intergenerational transmission of harsh parenting. *Developmental Psychology, 27*, 159–171.

Tower, C. (1993). *Understanding child abuse and neglect.* Boston: Allyn and Bacon.

Wright, C. M. (2000). Identification and management of failure to thrive: a community perspective. *Archives of Disease in Children, 82*(1), 5–9.

ADDITIONAL READING AND RESOURCES

The Association for Early Childhood Education. (1990). *Child abuse: A handbook for early childhood educators.* Ontario, Canada: Author.

Bowman, B. (1992). Who is at risk for what and why? *Journal of Early Intervention, 16*(2), 101–108.

Caughey, C. (1991). Becoming a child's ally: Observations in a classroom for children who have been abused. *Young Children, 46*(4), 22–28.

Cloud J. (2002, April 29). Pedophilia. *Time, 29;159*(17), 42–46.

Engeland, B, & Erickson, M. F. (1990). Rising above the past: Strategies for helping new mothers break the cycle of abuse and neglect. *Zero to Three, 11*(2), 29–35.

Gargarino, J., & Kostelny, K. (1992). Child maltreatment as a community problem. *Child Abuse and Neglect, 16*(4), 455–464.

Gray, E., & Coolsen, P. (1987). How do kids really feel about being home alone? *Children Today, 16*(4), 30–32.

Gregory, T. (1999). Skin lesions that mimic child abuse. *Patient Care, 33*(9), 169.

Marino, R., Weinman, M. L., & Soudelier, K. (2001). Social work intervention and failure to thrive in infants and children. *Health & Social Work, 26*(2), 90–7.

McNulty, C. (1994). Adult disclosure of sexual abuse: A primary cause of psychological distress? *Child Abuse and Neglect, 18*(7), 549–555.

National Clearinghouse on Child Abuse and Neglect Information. (1999). *What is child maltreatment?* Washington, DC: Author.

Newman, M. G., Clayton, L., Zuellig, A., Cashman, L., Arnow, B., Dea, R., & Taylor, C. B. (2000). The relationship of childhood sexual abuse and depression with somatic symptoms and medical utilization. *Psychology of Medicine, 30*(5), 1063–1077.

Tourigny, M., & Bouchard, C. (1994). Incidence et Characteristiques des Signalements D'enfants Maltraite's Comparaison Interculturelle. *Child Abuse and Neglect, 18*(10), 797–808.

U.S. Advisory Board on Child Abuse and Neglect. (1995, April). *A nation's shame: Fatal child abuse and neglect in the United States.* Washington, DC: Author.

HELPFUL WEB SITES

American Professional Society on Abuse of Children	http://www.apsac.org
Boys and Girls Clubs of America	http://www.bgca.org
Child Abuse Prevention Center	http://www.capcenter.org
Child Welfare League of America (CWLA)	http://www.cwla.org
Children's Bureau/National Center on Child Abuse and Neglect (NCCAN)	http://www.acf.dhhs.gov
National Clearinghouse on Child Abuse and Neglect Information	http://www.calib.com/nccanch
Shaken Baby Alliance	http://www.shakenbaby.com

For additional health, safety, and nutrition resources, go to http://www.EarlyChildEd.delmar.com

CHAPTER 12

Planning for Children's Health and Safety Education

TERMS TO KNOW

attitudes
values
incidental learning

inservice
concepts
objectives

retention
evaluation

OBJECTIVES

After studying this chapter, you should be able to:

- Explain the four principles of instruction.
- Develop a lesson plan for teaching health and safety concepts.
- Explain the importance of including parents in children's learning experiences.
- List five health/safety topics that are appropriate for toddlers, and five that are appropriate for preschool-aged children.

Many of today's health problems result from a combination of environmental and self-imposed factors (Lowry, Wechsler, Galuska, Fulton, & Kann, 2002). Poor eating habits, lack of exercise, pollution, increased stress, poverty, violence, and substance abuse (alcohol, drugs, and tobacco) are challenging the quality of children's health (Belfield, 2003; U.S. Department of Health and Human Services, 2000; Valentine, 1997).

Education is fundamental to assuring a healthy and productive life (Fodor, 2003; Cicchetti, Rappaport, Sandler, & Weissberg, 2000; Allensworth, Lawson, Nicholson, & Wyche, 1997). Many of the health behaviors, **attitudes**, and **values** formed during the early years will be carried over into adulthood (Berg, Buechner, & Parham, 2003). It is also a time when children are more receptive to new ideas, changes, and suggestions. Thus, it is important to help children acquire basic information and establish skills that will promote good health. This includes raising children's awareness of factors that influence health- and safety-related behaviors, encouraging positive decisions, and motivating them to assume an active role in personal health care and safety matters.

---

attitudes – *beliefs or feelings one has toward certain facts or situations.*
values – *the beliefs, traditions, and customs an individual incorporates and utilizes to guide behavior and judgments.*

PARENT INVOLVEMENT IN HEALTH AND SAFETY EDUCATION

Parents are a child's first and most important teachers. Young children acquire many of their attitudes and health/safety practices from parents through combinations of direct instruction, **incidental learning**, and modeling. Daily routines often provide valuable opportunities for spontaneous learning. Early education teachers can continue to build on this foundation of skill and understanding by planning and integrating learning experiences for children across the curriculum (Workman & Gage, 1997). For children to attain the ultimate goal of health/safety education programs, that is, to make choices and decisions that will improve the quality of their lives, they must understand the reasons and purposes for their behavior.

It is important that teachers work closely with parents to ensure consistency in the information children receive (Aronson, 2002; Jaffe, 1997). Health/safety concepts that children receive in school can be shared with parents and ultimately enhance what the child learns at home. Most parents welcome additional information and ideas that can be shared with children.

Successful parent education is built on collaboration and involvement (Lundgren & Morrison, 2003; Pena, 2000; Diffily & Morrison, 1997) (Figure 12–1). There are many resourceful ways parents can be included in children's health/safety instructional programs, including:

- newsletters
- parent meetings
- observations
- participation in class projects, demonstrations, films, lectures
- assisting with field trips, health assessments, or making special arrangements
- preparing and presenting short programs on special topics

Parent involvement and collaboration encourage greater uniformity of health/safety information and practices between the child's home and school. This partnership also helps reduce

FIGURE 12–1

Successful parent education is built on involvement.

---

incidental learning – *learning that occurs in addition to the primary intent or goals of instruction.*

REFLECTIVE THOUGHTS

Historically, it was considered a family's right and responsibility to teach children values and attitudes associated with health and safety. Teachers were expected to focus their efforts on academic instruction. Is this assumption true today? What factors may be contributing to this change? How does a teacher determine what values and attitudes are important to teach young children? What steps can a teacher take to be sure that learning experiences are bias-free?

frustration that occurs when children receive information that conflicts with family practices and values. Other advantages of sharing health/safety instruction with parents include:

- better understanding of children's developmental needs
- improved parental esteem
- increased parental knowledge and competence
- reinforcement of children's learning
- strengthening good parenting skills
- improved communication between home and school

The resources and efforts of parents, children, and teachers can be united to bring about long-term improvements in health and safety behaviors.

THE ROLE OF TEACHER INSERVICE AND HEALTH AND SAFETY EDUCATION

Learning experiences that address health and safety issues are essential to include in children's educational programs. Yet, few teachers are adequately prepared to assume this responsibility. Most teachers have had only limited formal training in health education. However, **inservice** opportunities can provide the teacher with useful information about developmentally appropriate content and instructional techniques for teaching health and safety.

Inservice education should be an ongoing process and focused on expanding and updating teachers' information and skills. Many professionals in the community can be called upon to present informative inservice programs on topics, such as:

- early education programs and the law
- emergency preparedness
- identifying child abuse
- advances in health screening
- review of sanitary procedures
- stress management
- working with parents
- communicable disease updates
- information on specific health problems, e.g., epilepsy, spina bifida, HIV/AIDS, allergies
- review of first aid techniques and CPR training
- health promotion practices
- nutrition education

inservice – *educational training provided by an employer.*

- food and nutrition
- consumer health, e.g., taking medicines, understanding advertisements, reading labels, quackery
- factors affecting growth
- mental health, e.g., personal feelings, making friends, family interactions, getting along with others
- roles of health professionals
- communicable illnesses
- safety and accident prevention, e.g., bicycle, pedestrian, playground and home safety, first aid techniques
- coping with stress
- physical fitness

Objectives

The ultimate goal of health and safety education is the development of positive knowledge, behavior, and attitudes. Learning is demonstrated when children are able to make good decisions and carry out health and safety practices that maintain or improve their present state of health. **Objectives** describe the precise quality of change in knowledge, behavior, attitude, or value that can be expected from the learner upon completion of the learning experiences (Redican, Olsen, & Baffi, 1993).

Objectives serve several purposes:

- as a guide in the selection of content material
- to identify desirable changes in the learner
- as an aid in the selection of appropriate learning experiences
- as an evaluation or measurement tool

To be useful, objectives must be written in terms that are clear and meaningful: for example, "The child will be able to select appropriate clothing to wear when it is raining." The key word in this objective is "select." It is a specific behavioral change that can be evaluated and measured. In contrast, the statement, "The child will know how to dress for the weather," is too vague and cannot be accurately measured. Additional examples of precise and measurable terms include to:

- draw
- list
- discuss
- explain
- select
- write
- recognize
- describe
- identify
- answer
- demonstrate
- match
- compare

Measurable objectives are more difficult to develop for learning experiences that involve values, feelings, and/or attitudes. The behavioral changes associated with this type of learning are often not immediately observable. Rather, it must be assumed that at some later point, children's behaviors will reflect what they have previously learned.

Curriculum Presentation

Teachers serve as facilitators in the educational process, selecting strategies that are appropriate for children and support the stated objectives (Gordon & Browne, 2004). How a teacher presents health

---

objectives – *clear and meaningful descriptions of what an individual is expected to learn as a result of learning activities and experiences.*

REFLECTIVE THOUGHTS

Planning effective learning experiences for young children requires a great deal of time and effort. The Internet now offers easy access to a wealth of information, particularly in the areas of health, safety, and nutrition. Can all of this information be trusted? What criteria can you use to evaluate the accuracy of information found on Web sites? What additional steps can you take to assure that material you use for developing learning experiences is reliable?

and safety information, skills, and values to children will depend on the instructional method that is selected. This can be one of the most challenging, yet creative steps in the instructional process (Ames, Trucaro, Wan, & Harris, 1995). When deciding on a method, teachers should consider:

- presenting only a few, simple concepts or ideas during each session
- limiting presentations to a maximum of 5 to 10 minutes for toddlers and 10 to 15 minutes for preschool and school-aged children
- class size, age group, type of materials being presented, and available resources
- emphasizing the positive aspects of concepts; avoid confusing combinations of do's and don'ts, good and bad
- incorporating learning experiences that involve children in hands-on activities with real-life materials
- ways to include simple explanations so children become familiar with common terms
- opportunities for repetition (to improve learning)
- ways to use encouragement and positive reinforcement to acknowledge children's accomplishments

There are a variety of methods that can be used to present health/safety instruction, including:

- group discussion
- media, e.g., filmstrips, records, models, specimens, videos and audio tapes
- demonstrations and experiments
- teacher-made displays, e.g., posters, bulletin boards, booklets, flannel boards
- art activities
- printed resource material, e.g., pamphlets, posters, charts (See Table 12–1 for ways to evaluate printed resource material.)

TABLE 12–1 How to Evaluate Printed Resource Material

Look for materials that:

- are prepared by authorities or a reliable source
- contain unbiased information; avoid promotion or advertisement of products
- present accurate, up-to-date facts and information
- involve the learner, e.g., suggested projects, additional reading
- are thought provoking, or raise questions and answers
- are attractive
- add to the quality of the learning experience
- are worth the costs involved
- support your program's philosophy

- books and stories
- guest speakers
- personal example

Methods that actively involve young children in learning experiences are the most desirable and effective (Gordon & Browne, 2004; Essa, 2003). When learning activities involve participation, they will hold children's attention longer and improve what is remembered. Such methods are also more appealing to young children and increase learning and **retention** of ideas. Examples of methods that actively engage children in learning include:

- dramatic play, e.g., dressing up, hospital, dentist office, restaurant, traffic safety, supermarket
- field trips, e.g., visits to a hospital, dental office, exercise class, supermarket, farm
- art activities, including posters, bulletin boards, displays, pictures or flannelboards created by children
- hands-on experiences, e.g., handwashing, brushing teeth, grocery shopping, cooking projects, growing seeds, animal care
- puppet shows, e.g., care when you are sick, protection from strangers, health checkups, good grooming practices
- games and songs
- guest speakers, e.g., firefighter, dental hygienist, nurse, aerobics or dance instructor, nutritionist, poison control staff, mental health professional

Combinations of these approaches may also be very useful for maintaining interest among children, especially when several sessions will be presented on a similar topic or theme. Incorporating health and safety concepts into children's play activities reinforces learning and assures an integrated approach (Figure 12–3).

Many governmental and commercial agencies offer excellent educational materials on health, safety, and nutrition topics that are appropriate for young children. Some educational materials and lesson plans are also available through various Web sites, including those listed at the end of

FIGURE 12–3

Health and safety concepts can be incorporated into play activities.

---

retention – *the ability to remember or recall previously learned material.*

this chapter. Educational materials and curriculum plans can also be obtained by writing to the organization (see Appendix C).

Evaluation

Ongoing **evaluation** is an integral part of the educational process. It is also an important step during all stages of health/safety instruction. Evaluation provides feedback concerning the effectiveness of instruction. It reveals whether or not students have learned what a teacher set out to teach. Evaluation procedures also help teachers determine the strengths, weaknesses, and areas of instruction that need improvement (Pealer & Dorman, 1997; Ames, Trucano, Wan, & Harris, 1995).

Evaluation is accomplished by measuring positive changes in children's behavior. The goals and objectives established at the onset of curriculum development are used to determine whether or not the desired behavioral changes have been achieved. Do children remember to wash their hands after using the bathroom without having to be reminded? Do children check for traffic before dashing out into the street after a runaway ball? Do children brush their teeth at least once daily? Are established rules followed by children when they are alone on the playground? In other words, evaluation is based on demonstrations of change in children's behaviors. Many of these changes can simply be observed.

Evaluation must not be looked upon as a final step. Rather, it should add a dimension of quality throughout the entire instructional program. The following criteria may be used for the evaluation process:

- Do the objectives identify areas where learning should take place?
- Are the objectives clearly stated and realistic?
- Were children able to achieve the objectives?
- Was the instructional method effective? Were children involved in the learning experiences?
- How can the lesson be improved?

Evaluation should be a nonthreatening process. Results of an evaluation can be used to make significant improvements in the way future health/safety programs are presented to children. It then becomes a tool that teachers can use to improve the communication of health/safety knowledge, and skills to young children.

ISSUES TO CONSIDER • Fire Safety

The headlines read, "Three young children found dead after fire guts basement apartment." Firefighters had worked frantically, but intense flames forced them out of the burning building before the small children could be found. The children had been playing with matches in their mother's closet when flames spread to nearby clothing. Smoke inhalation claimed the lives of all three children.

- **What developmental characteristics might have contributed to this incident?**
- **What skills do young children need to learn to avoid a similar tragedy?**
- **What do parents need to know?**
- **What classroom learning experiences can teachers introduce to help children behave safely in the event of a house fire?**
- **Describe how these learning experiences can be integrated across the curriculum.**

---

evaluation – *a measurement of effectiveness for determining whether or not educational objectives have been achieved.*

ACTIVITY PLANS

A teacher's day can be filled with many unexpected events. Activity plans encourage advanced planning and organization. They improve the efficiency of classroom experiences because teachers are better organized and can have instructional materials ready.

A written format for activity plans is often as individualized as are teachers. However, activity plans for health/safety instruction should include several basic features:

- subject title or concept to be presented
- specific objectives
- materials list
- step-by-step learning activities
- evaluation and suggestions for improvement

Activity plans should contain enough information so they can be used by anyone, including a substitute teacher, classroom aide, or volunteer. Objectives should clearly indicate what children are expected to learn. Activities can then be modified to meet the needs of a particular age group. A description of materials, how they are to be used, and safety precautions required for an activity are also important to include. Following are examples of several activity plans.

Activity Plan #1: Germs and Prevention of Illness

CONCEPT: Sneezing and coughing release germs that can cause illness.

OBJECTIVES:
- Children will be able to identify the mouth and nose as major sources of germs.
- Children will cover their coughs and sneezes without being reminded.
- Children will be able to discuss why it is important to cover coughs and sneezes.

MATERIALS LIST: Two large balloons and a small amount of confetti, dolls or stuffed animals, doctor kit, stethoscopes, old lab coats or men's shirt to wear as uniforms. (*Note:* Check before conducting this activity to be sure no one has a latex allergy).

LEARNING ACTIVITIES:
A. Fill both balloons with a small amount of confetti. When the activity is ready to be presented to children, carefully inflate one of the balloons by blowing into the balloon.

> *Caution: Remove your mouth from the balloon each time before inhaling.*

When it is inflated, quickly release pressure on the neck of the balloon, but do not let go of the balloon itself. Confetti will escape as air leaves the balloon, imitating germs as they leave the nose and mouth during coughs and sneezes. Repeat the procedure. This time, place your hand over the mouth of the balloon as the air escapes (as if to cover a cough or sneeze). Your hand will prevent most of the confetti from escaping into the air.

B. Discuss the differences between the two demonstrations with the children:

"What happens when someone doesn't cover their mouth when they cough?"

"How does covering your mouth help when you cough or sneeze?"

C. Include a discussion of why it is important to stay home when you are sick or have a cold.

D. Help children set up a pretend hospital where they can care for "sick" dolls or animals. Encourage children to talk about how it feels to be sick or when they must take medicine. Reinforce the importance of covering coughs and hand washing to keep from getting sick.

FIGURE 12–4

Children learn to cover their coughs and sneezes.

E. Have several books available for children to look at and discuss:

Berger, M. (1995). *Germs make me sick.* New York HarperCollins.

Capeci, A. (2001). *The giant germ (Magic School Bus Chapter Book 6).* New York: Scholastic.

Katz, B. (1996). *Germs! Germs! Germs!* New York: Cartwheel Books.

Rice, J. (1997). *Those mean, nasty, dirty, downright disgusting but invisible germs.* St. Paul, MN: Redleaf Press.

Romanek, T. (2003). *Achoo: The most interesting book you'll read about germs.* Toronto, ON: Kids Can Press.

EVALUATION:

- Children can begin to describe the relationship between germs and illness.
- Children can identify coughs and sneezes as a major source of germs.
- Children voluntarily cover their own coughs and sneezes (Figure 12–4).

Activity Plan #2: Handwashing

CONCEPT: Germs on our hands can make us sick and/or spread illness to others.

OBJECTIVES:

- Children can describe when it is important to wash their hands.
- Children can demonstrate the handwashing procedure without assistance (Figure 12–5).

FIGURE 12–5

A good handwashing technique is important for children to learn.

- Children will value the concept of cleanliness as demonstrated by voluntarily washing their hands at appropriate times.

MATERIALS LIST: Liquid or bar soap, paper towel, sink with running water.

LEARNING ACTIVITIES:

A. Present the fingerplay, "Bobby Bear and Leo Lion." Have children gather around a sink to observe a demonstration of the handwashing procedures as the story is read.

"One bright, sunny morning, Bobby Bear and Leo Lion (make a fist with each hand, thumbs up straight), who were very good friends, decided to go for a long walk in the woods (move fists in walking motion). They walked and walked, over hills (imitate walking motion raising fists) and under trees (imitate walking motion lowering fists) until they came to a stream where they decided to cool off.

Bobby Bear sat down on a log (press palm of hand on faucet with adequate pressure to release water) and poured water on Leo Lion and Leo Lion danced and danced under the water (move hand and fingers all around underneath the water) until he was all wet. Then it was Bobby Bear's turn to get wet, so Leo Lion (hold up other fist with thumb up) sat down on a log (press palm of hand on faucet with adequate pressure to release water) and Bobby Bear danced and danced under the water until he was all wet (move other hand under water).

This was so much fun that they decided to take a bath together. They found some soap, picked it up (pick up bar of soap), put a little on their hands (rub a little soap on hands), then laid it back down on the bank (place soap in dish on side of sink). Then they rubbed the soap on their fronts and backs (rub hands together four or more times) until they were all soapy.

After that, Bobby Bear jumped back on his log (press faucet) and poured water on Leo Lion until all his soap was gone (move hand under water). Then Leo Lion jumped back on his log (press other faucet) and poured water on Bobby Bear and rinsed him until all his soap was gone (move other hand under water).

Soon the wind began to blow and Bobby Bear and Leo Lion were getting very cold. They reached up and picked a leaf from the tree above (reach up and take a paper towel from the dispenser) and used it to dry themselves off (use paper towel to dry both hands). When they were all dry, Bobby Bear and Leo Lion carefully dropped their leaves into the trash can (drop paper towel into wastebasket). They joined hands (use fists, thumbs up and joined; walking motion, rapidly) and ran merrily back through the woods."[1]

B. Discuss the proper handwashing procedure with small groups of children. Ask simple questions and encourage all children to contribute to the discussion.

"When is it important to wash our hands?"

"What do we do first? Let's list the steps together."

"Why do we use soap?"

"Why is it important to dry our hands carefully after washing them?"

C. Talk with children about the importance of washing hands after blowing their nose, coughing into their hands, playing outdoors, using the bathroom, and before eating. Model these behaviors and set a good example for children.

D. Set up a messy art activity, e.g., fingerpaint, clay, glue. Practice handwashing. Have children look at their hands before and after washing them. Point out the value of washing hands carefully.

[1]The authors would like to acknowledge Rhonda McMullen, a former student and graduate of the Early Childhood Program, University of Kansas, for sharing her delightful story and creative ways with young children.

E. Have children practice washing their hands for as long as it takes them to sing the complete ABC song.

F. Read and discuss with the children several of the following books:

Adams, P. (1990). *Six in a bath*. New York: Child's Play International.

Cobb, V. (1989). *Keeping clean*. New York: HarperCollins Children's Books.

Cole, B. (1980). *No more baths*. New York: Doubleday.

Edwards, F. B. (2000). *Mortimer Mooner stopped taking a bath*. Kingston, Ontario: Pokeweed Press.

Gantos, J. (1980). *Swampy alligator*. New York: Windmill/Wanderer Books.

Katz, A. (2001). *Take me out of the bathtub, and other silly dilly songs*. New York: Scholastic.

Ross, R. (2000). *Wash your hands!* LaJolla, CA: Kane/Miller Book Publishers.

Showers, P. (1991). *Your skin and mine*. New York: HarperCollins Juvenile Books.

Woodruff, E. (1990). *Tubtime*. New York: Holiday House, Inc.

G. Observe children washing their hands from time to time to make sure they continue to follow good procedures.

H. Observe children at different times throughout the day to determine if they are using correct technique and washing hands at appropriate times.

EVALUATION:
- Was the fingerplay effective for demonstrating the handwashing technique?
- Can children wash their hands correctly and alone?
- Do children wash their hands at the appropriate times, without being prompted?

Activity Plan #3: Dressing Appropriately for the Weather

CONCEPT: Clothing helps to keep us healthy.

OBJECTIVES:
- When given a choice, children will be able to match appropriate items of clothing with different kinds of weather, e.g., rainy, sunny, snowy, hot, cold.
- Children will be able to perform two of the following dressing skills: button a button, snap a snap, or zip up a zipper.
- Children will demonstrate proper care and storage of clothing by hanging up their coats, sweaters, hats, etc., at least two out of three days.

MATERIALS LIST: Items for a clothing store, such as clothing, cash register, play money, mirror; old magazines and catalogues containing pictures of children's clothing, paste, and paper or newspaper; buttons, snaps and zippers sewn on pieces of cloth; dolls and doll clothes; books and pictures.

LEARNING ACTIVITIES:
A. Read and discuss with the children several of the following books:

Andersen, H. C. (2002). *The emperor's new clothes*. New York: North South Winds Press.

Calder, L. (1991). *What will I wear?* Racine, WI: Western Publishing Co.

Jennings, P. (1996). *What should I wear?* New York: Random House.

Neitzel, S. (1994). *The jacket I wear in the snow*. New York: Morrow Books.

Scarry, R. (2002). *Richard Scarry's what will I wear?* New York: Random House.

Watanabe, S. (1992). *How do I put it on?* New York: Collins.

B. Help children set up a clothing store. Provide clothing appropriate for boys and girls. Include items that could be worn for different types of weather conditions. Talk about the purpose of clothing and how it helps to protect our bodies. Help children identify qualities in clothing that differ with weather conditions, e.g., short sleeves vs. long sleeves, light colors vs. dark colors, lightweight fabrics vs. heavyweight fabrics, etc.

C. Have children select two different seasons or weather conditions. Give children old magazines or catalogues from which they can choose pictures of appropriate clothing. Display completed pictures where parents can see them. Younger children can point to and name various items of clothing.

D. Provide children with pieces of cloth on which a button, zipper, and snap have been sewn. Working with a few children at a time, help each child master these items. Have several items of real clothing available for children to practice putting on and taking off.

EVALUATION:

- Children can select at least two appropriate items of clothing for three different types of weather.
- Children can complete two of the following skills—buttoning a button, snapping a snap, zipping a zipper.
- Children hang up their personal clothing, e.g., hats, coats, sweaters, raincoats, at least two out of three days.

Activity Plan #4: Dental Health

CONCEPT: Good dental care helps to keep teeth healthy.

OBJECTIVES:

- Children will be able to identify at least two purposes that teeth serve.
- Children can name at least three foods that are good for healthy teeth.
- Children can describe three ways to promote good dental health.

MATERIALS LIST: Gather men's old shirts (preferably white) to use as dental uniforms, stuffed animals, tongue blades, children's books on dental health, old magazines, plastic fruits and vegetables, and gardening tools.

LEARNING ACTIVITIES:

A. Locate learning and resource materials about children's dental care on the following Web sites:

American Dental Association (www.ada.org); American Academy of Pediatric Dentistry (www.aapd.org); Head Start (www.nhsa.org); Health Resources & Services Administration (www.ask.hrsa.gov).

B. Read one or more of the following books during group time. Talk with the children about the role teeth play (e.g., for chewing, speech, smiling, a place for permanent teeth) and why it is important to take good care of them.

Dowdy, L. (1997). *Barney goes to the dentist.* Allen, TX: Barney Publications.

Frost, H. (1999). *Going to the dentist.* Mankato, MN: Pebble Books.

Mercer, M. (2001). *Just going to the dentist.* New York: Golden Books.

Schoberle, C. (2000). *Open wide! A visit to the dentist.* New York: Simon Spotlight.

Showers, P. (1991). *How many teeth?* New York: Harper Collins Juvenile Books.

Smee, N. (2000). *Freddie visits the dentist.* Hauppauge, NY: Barrons Educational Series.

C. Set up a "dentist" office for dramatic play. Have old white shirts available for children to wear as uniforms. Place stuffed animals in chairs so children can practice their "dentistry" skills using wooden tongue blades and cotton balls.

D. Spread out plastic fruits, vegetables, child-size gardening tools, and baskets on the floor. Have children plant a garden with foods that are healthy for their teeth.

E. Discuss ways children can help to keep their teeth healthy, e.g., daily brushing with a fluoride toothpaste; regular dental checkups; eating nutritious foods/snacks (especially raw fruits, vegetables); avoiding chewing on nonfood items, e.g., pencils, spoons, keys; limiting sweets.

F. Help children construct "good food" mobiles. Use old magazines to cut out pictures of foods that are good for healthy teeth. Paste pictures on paper, attach with string or yarn and tie to a piece of cardboard cut in the shape of a smile.

G. Have children help plan snacks for several days; include foods that are nutritious and promote healthy teeth.

EVALUATION:

- Children can identify at least two functions that teeth serve.
- Children can name at least three foods that are good for healthy teeth.
- Children can describe three good dental health practices that help to keep teeth healthy.

Activity Plan #5: Toothbrushing

CONCEPT: Teeth should be brushed after meals and snacks to stay white and healthy.

OBJECTIVES:

- Children can state appropriate times when teeth should be brushed.
- Children can demonstrate good toothbrushing technique.
- Children can describe one alternate method for cleaning teeth after eating.

MATERIALS LIST: One white egg carton per child, cardboard, pink construction paper; several old toothbrushes, cloth, and grease pencil. Toothpaste and toothbrushes (donated).

LEARNING ACTIVITIES:

A. Invite a dentist or dental hygienist to demonstrate toothbrushing to the children. Ask the speaker to talk about how often to brush, when to brush, how to brush, alternate ways of cleaning teeth after eating, what type of toothpaste to use, and care of toothbrushes. This may also be a good opportunity to invite parents to visit so they can reinforce toothbrushing skills at home.

B. Help children construct a set of model teeth from egg cartons (Figure 12–6). Cut an oval approximately 14 inches in length from lightweight cardboard; crease oval gently along the center. Cut the bottom portion of an egg carton lengthwise into two strips. Staple egg carton "teeth" along the small ends of the oval. Glue pink construction paper along the edges where "teeth" are fastened to form "gums." Also cover the backside of the oval with pink construction paper. Use a grease pencil to mark areas of plaque on the teeth. Cover the head of an old toothbrush with cloth and fasten. With the toothbrush, have children

FIGURE 12–6

A set of "egg carton" teeth.

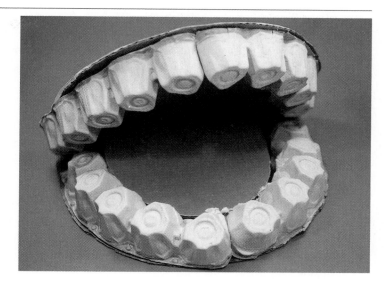

demonstrate correct toothbrushing technique to remove areas of plaque (grease pencil markings).

C. Obtain pamphlets on children's dental health from your local dental health association. Prepare a newsletter article reinforcing the concepts children have been learning.

D. Send a note home to parents and request that children bring a clean toothbrush to school. Practice toothbrushing, step-by-step with small groups of children.

E. Older children will enjoy designing posters or bulletin board displays that reinforce good dental hygiene.

F. Read and discuss with children several of the following books:

McGuire, L. (1993). *Brush your teeth please.* New York: Reader's Digest.

Keller, L. (2000). *Open wide: Tooth school inside.* New York: Henry Holt & Co.

Luttrell, I. (1997). *Milo's toothache.* New York: Puffin Books.

Quinlan, P. (1992). *Brush them bright.* Toronto, Ontario: Somerville House.

West, C. (1990). *The king's toothache.* New York: HarperCollins.

EVALUATION:
- Children can identify times when teeth should be brushed.
- Children can demonstrate good toothbrushing technique.
- Children can correctly identify at least one alternate method for cleaning their teeth after eating.

Activity Plan #6: Understanding Feelings (Mental Health)

CONCEPT: Feelings affect the state of one's mental as well as physical well-being.

OBJECTIVES:
- Children will be able to name at least four feelings or emotions.
- Children can express their feelings in words.

MATERIALS LIST: Old magazines, glue, paper; large, unbreakable mirror; shoe boxes.

LEARNING ACTIVITIES:

A. Read and discuss with the children several of the following books:

Anglund, J. (1993). *A friend is someone who likes you.* San Diego, CA: Harcourt, Brace & Jovanovich.

Bang, M. (1999). *When Sophie gets angry—Really, really, angry.* New York: Scholastic.

Blumenthal, D. (1999). *The chocolate-covered-cookie tantrum.* New York: Clarion Books.

Carle, E. (2000). *The grouchy ladybug.* New York: Scholastic.

Carle, E. (2000). *The very lonely firefly.* New York: Scholastic.

Carlson, N. (1998). *I like me.* New York: Scholastic.

Crary, E. (1996). *I'm scared.* Seattle, WA: Parenting Press.

Crary, E. (1996). *I'm mad.* WA: Parenting Press.

Gainer, C. (1998). *I'm like you, you're like me: A child's book about understanding and celebrating each other.* Minneapolis, MN: Free Spirit Publishing.

Lewis, P. (2002). *I'll always love you.* Wilton, CT: Tiger Tales.

Spelman, C. M. (2000). *When I feel angry.* Morton Grove, IL: Albert Whitman & Co.

Thomas, P. (2000). *Stop picking on me.* Hauppaugne, NY: Barron's Juveniles.

B. During large or small group time, encourage children to talk about different feelings people experience. Stress that many of these feelings are normal and that it is important to learn acceptable and healthy ways of expressing them. Ask children, one at a time, to name a feeling, e.g., happy, sad, tired, bored, special, excitement, surprise, fear, lonely, embarrassed, proud, or angry. Have children act out the feeling. Encourage children to observe the expressions of one another. Help children learn to recognize these feelings. "Have you ever seen someone look like this?" "Have you ever felt like this?" "What made you feel like this?" Role play healthy and acceptable ways of coping with these feelings.

C. Place an unbreakable mirror where children can see themselves. Encourage them to imitate some of the feelings they have identified and observe their own facial expressions.

D. Make a collage of feelings using pictures of people from old magazines. Help children identify the feelings portrayed in each picture.

E. Construct "I Am Special" boxes. Have children decorate old shoe boxes with pictures of things that reflect their individuality, such as favorite foods, activities, toys, etc. Have children fill their boxes with items that tell something special about themselves; for example, a hobby, favorite toy, photograph, souvenirs from a trip, pet, picture of their family. Children can share their boxes and tell something special about themselves during "Show and Tell" or large group time.

F. Older children can be involved in role play. Write out problem situations on small cards; for example, "you and another child want the same toy," "someone knocks down the block structure you just built," "another child pushes you," "a friend says they don't like you anymore." Have pairs of children select a card and act out acceptable ways of handling their feelings in each situation. Discuss their solutions.

EVALUATION:

• Children can name at least four different feelings or emotions.
• Children begin using words rather than physical aggression to handle difficult or emotional situations.

Activity Plan #7: Safety in Cars

CONCEPT: Good safety rules are important to follow in and around vehicles.

OBJECTIVES:
- Children will begin to understand the purpose and importance of wearing seat belts or sitting in an appropriate safety car seat (Figure 12–7).
- Children can name at least one important safety rule to follow in and around cars.

MATERIALS LIST: Order pamphlets about seat belt restraints and car safety from:
National Passenger Safety Association
1050 17th Street, N.W., Suite 770
Washington, DC 20036

    OR

National Highway Traffic Safety Administration
U.S. Department of Transportation
400 Seventh Street, S. W.
Washington, DC 20590

Prepare photographs of children demonstrating the following safety rules:

a. Always hold an adult's hand when going to and from the car; never dash ahead.

b. Always get in and out of a car on the curbside.

c. Open and close car doors properly. Place both hands on the door handle to reduce the possibility of getting fingers caught in the door.

d. Sit in the car seat; never ride standing.

e. Put on seat belt or use safety car seat.

f. Lock all car doors before starting out.

g. Ride with arms, legs, head, and other body parts inside the car.

h. Don't play with controls inside of the car.

i. Ride quietly so as not to disturb the driver.

FIGURE 12–7

Children weighing 20–40 pounds (9.1–18.2 kg) must be buckled securely in a child safety seat.

FIGURE 12–8

Learning safety signs.

LEARNING ACTIVITIES:

A. Discuss with the children information found in the pamphlets. Stress the importance of wearing seat belts or riding in an appropriate car seat restraint. Later, have children take the pamphlets home to share with parents.

B. Mount photographs of safety rules on posterboard or display on a table. Encourage children to identify the safe behavior demonstrated in each picture (Figure 12–8).

C. Use large group time to discuss with the children the importance of each safety rule pictured in the photographs.

D. For dramatic play, use large wooden blocks, cardboard boxes or chairs, and a "steering wheel" to build a pretend car. Have children demonstrate the car safety rules as they play.

E. Prepare a chart with all of the children's names. Each day, have children place a checkmark next to their name if they wore their seat belt on the way to school.

F. Establish a parent committee to plan a "Safe Riding" campaign. On randomly selected days, observe parents and children as they arrive and depart from the center; record whether or not they were wearing seat belt restraints. Enlist children's artistic abilities to design and make awards to be given to families who ride safely. Repeat the campaign again in several months.

EVALUATION:

- Children can be observed wearing seat belts or sitting in a proper safety car seat.
- Children can name one safety rule to observe when riding in a car.

TEACHER RESOURCES:

Seat Belts Activity Book (Teacher's Guide). U.S. Department of Transportation, National Highway Traffic Safety Administration, Washington, DC 20590.

We Love You, Buckle Up (Preschool curriculum kit on use of seat belt restraints). Order from: NAEYC, 1834 Connecticut Avenue, NW, Washington, DC 20009.

Activity Plan #8: Pedestrian Safety

CONCEPT: Young children can begin to learn safe behaviors in and around traffic and a respect for moving vehicles.

OBJECTIVES:
- Children will be able to identify the stop, go, and walk signals.
- Children can describe two rules for safely crossing streets.
- Children will begin to develop respect for moving vehicles.

MATERIALS LIST: Flannelboard and characters; cardboard pieces, poster paint, wooden stakes; masking tape, yarn or string; six-inch paper plates; red, green, and yellow poster paint; black marker.

LEARNING ACTIVITIES:
A. Obtain the booklets (5): *Preschool Children in Traffic* from the American Automobile Association, 1000 AAA Drive, Heathrow, FL 32746. NAEYC also has the following booklets available: *Walk in Traffic Safely; We Cross the Street Safely: A Preschool Book on Safety;* and *When We Cross the Street: A First Book on Traffic Safety.* Also read:

Berenstain, S. & Berenstain, J. (1999). *My trusty car seat: Buckling up for safety.* New York: Random House.

Committee, C. B. (2000). *Buckles buckles everywhere.* Palmetto Bookworks.

Rathmann, P. (1995). *Officer Buckle and Gloria.* New York: Putnam Publishing Group.

B. Discuss rules for safe crossing of streets:

   a. always have an adult cross streets with you (this is a must for preschool children)

   b. only cross streets at intersections

   c. always look both ways before stepping out into the street

   d. use your ears to listen for oncoming cars

   e. don't walk out into the street from between parked cars or in the middle of a block

   f. ask an adult to retrieve balls and toys from streets

   g. always obey traffic signs

C. Introduce basic traffic signs (only those that have meaning to young pedestrians), e.g., stop, go, walk, pedestrian crossing, one-way traffic, bike path, railroad crossing. Help children learn to recognize each sign by identifying certain features, such as color, shape, location.

D. Help children to construct the basic traffic signs using cardboard and poster paint. Attach signs to wooden stakes. Set up a series of "streets" in the outdoor play yard using string, yarn or pieces of cardboard to mark paths; place traffic signs in appropriate places. Select children to ride tricycles along designated "streets" while other children practice pedestrian safety.

E. Prepare a flannelboard story and characters to help children visualize pedestrian safety rules.

F. Help children construct a set of stop-go-walk signs. Have each child paint three paper plates—one red, one green, one yellow. On a plain white plate write the word WALK. Fasten all four plates together with tape or glue to form a traffic signal.

EVALUATION:
- Children respond correctly to the signals stop, go, walk.
- Children can state two rules for safely crossing streets. (Puppets can be used to ask children questions.)
- Children demonstrate increased caution in the play yard while riding tricycles and other wheeled toys and also as pedestrians.

Activity Plan #9: Poisonous Substances— Poison Prevention

CONCEPT: Identification and avoidance of known and potentially poisonous substances.

OBJECTIVES:
- Children will be able to name at least three poisonous substances.
- Children can identify at least one safety rule that will help prevent accidental poisoning.

MATERIALS LIST: Old magazines, large sheet of paper, glue; small squares of paper or self-adhesive labels, marking pens.

LEARNING ACTIVITIES:
   A. Invite a guest speaker from your local hospital emergency room or Public Health Department to talk with the children about poison prevention.

   B. Show children pictures and/or real labels of poisonous substances. Include samples of cleaning items, personal grooming supplies, medicines, perfumes, plants, and berries.

   C. Discuss rules of poison prevention:
   - a. only food should be put into the mouth (Figure 12–9)
   - b. medicine is not candy and should only be given by an adult

FIGURE 12–9

Only food belongs in children's mouths.

    c. an adult should always inform a child that they are taking medicine, not candy

    d. never eat berries, flowers, leaves, or mushrooms before checking with an adult

D. Make a wall mural for the classroom displaying pictures of poisonous substances. Be sure to include a sampling of cleaning products, personal grooming supplies, medicines, plants, products commonly found in garages, such as insecticides, fertilizers, gasoline, and automotive fluids. Glue pictures of these products on a large sheet of paper. Display the mural where parents and children can look at it.

EVALUATION:

- Children can point to or name at least three poisonous substances.
- Children can state and role-play at least one safety rule that can help prevent accidental poisoning.

TEACHER RESOURCES:

Common poisonous plants and mushrooms of North America, by N. J. Turner & A. F. Szczawinski, (1995). Portland, OR: Timber Press.

Poison: Keeping your family safe (booklet). Channing Bete, 200 State Road, South Deerfield, MA 01373 or call 1-800-628-7733.

Protect your child from poisons in your home. (2000). Washington, DC: Department of Health & Human Services. Available online at www.fda.gov.

Teachers guide to poison prevention. (2002). Obtain a free copy from Washington Poison Center at 1-800-222-1222 or write to the Washington Poison Center, 155 NE 100th St., Suite 400, Seattle, WA 98125–8012.

Activity Plan #10: Fire Safety

CONCEPT: Fire safety rules are important to know in the event of a fire.

OBJECTIVES:

- Children can describe what they would do if there was a fire at their house or school.
- Children can demonstrate stop, drop and roll.
- Children can state what a firefighter does and how they put out fires.

MATERIALS LIST: Large cardboard boxes; posterboard; photograph of each child; chalk and paint in fire colors (red, orange and yellow); small spray bottles; paper and plastic wrap; rolling pin; tape.

LEARNING ACTIVITIES:

A. Invite a firefighter to the classroom. Ask the speaker to discuss important safety skills such as stop-drop-and-roll crawling on the floor to stay away from smoke and heat, and having alternative evacuation routes.

B. Construct a fire obstacle course. Build a tunnel out of cardboard boxes. Establish a "designated meeting place" at the end of the tunnel by displaying a poster with children's photographs. Have children begin the obstacle course by demonstrating the correct stop, drop, and roll technique. Next, have children crawl through the tunnel on their hands and knees; this shows children the appropriate way for navigating through a smoke-filled room before arriving at the designated safe area. Be sure to encourage and reinforce children's efforts.

C. Take cardboard boxes outside and have the children decorate them to look like buildings. Have children draw fire on the buildings using red, yellow, and orange chalk. Children can then use small spray bottles filled with water to put out the fire.

D. Add firefighter figures, ladders, fire trucks, and other fire-related materials to the block area.

E. Create a fire painting. Have the children paint a picture with red and yellow paint. While the paint is still wet, cover with plastic wrap and secure to the back of the painting with tape. Have the child use a rolling pin to roll out their painting.

Evaluation:

- Children can describe how they would get out of their house or school safely during a fire and where they would go once outside the building.
- Children can demonstrate stop, drop, and roll.
- Children can state what firefighters do and how they put out fires.[2]

FOCUS ON FAMILIES • Evaluating Health-Safety Information on the Internet

The Internet has substantially increased consumer access to health and safety information. As a result, we are often more aware of current developments and better able to make informed decisions. However, the lack of any regulatory control has also allowed considerable misinformation to be posted on Web sites, particularly in the areas of health and safety. Thus, consumers must approach such information with caution. Consider:

- What individual or group is responsible for this site? Check the URL (Web address): information on sites maintained by the government (www.gov) and educational institutions (www.edu) is generally considered more reliable.

- Are the individuals who prepared and run the site qualified? Often the credentials of advisory board members or the Webmaster will be included.

- Who is the intended audience? Is the purpose to entertain, inform, or educate? Judging this can be helpful in determining whether a site is a source of legitimate information.

- Is the site current? How recently was the information updated? It may be difficult to know if the date posted on a Web page refers to when the information was originally written, last revised, or actually posted.

- Does the information appear to be objective and free of bias? Sites run by private individuals or commercial groups may reflect personal opinion or attempt to sell a product. Facts and figures should include a reference to the original source of information.

- What links are included? Anyone can establish a link to any other Web page, so this may not prove to be a valid strategy for evaluating a site's credibility.

- Does the site include a way to contact the owner if you have questions or wish further information?

---

[2] The authors would like to thank Allison Moore, a former student and graduate of the Early Childhood program, Department of Human Development and Family Life, University of Kansas, for her innovative lesson plan.

CASE STUDY

Eduardo, a new assistant, was asked by his head teacher to develop a lesson on "Healthy eating helps us grow." Although eager to be given this assignment, Eduardo was also apprehensive about planning something that four-year-olds would enjoy. He arrived early that morning and set up a grocery store for dramatic play, books about food for the children to read, and magazine pictures of foods for the children to sort into categories using the Food Pyramid. The children played "grocery shopping" for a while, looked at several of the books, but weren't interested in the sorting activity.

1. Were the activities Eduardo planned appropriate for four-year-olds?
2. How effective was this lesson for teaching children about healthy eating habits?
3. What are some realistic learning objectives that Eduardo might have established in preparation for this lesson?
4. How would Eduardo evaluate what the children may have learned from these activities?
5. What changes would you make in Eduardo's instructional strategies?

SUMMARY

- Poor lifestyle practices and attitudes contribute to many of today's health problems.

- Education is a key element in reducing health problems.
  - It raises individual awareness and ability to make informed decisions.
  - Education enables individuals to begin assuming some responsibility for personal health.
  - It contributes to improved health and safety behaviors and quality of life.

- Effective health and safety education requires long-range planning to ensure that children receive comprehensive instruction.

- Objectives describe the changes in an individual's behavior that can be expected as the result of instruction.
  - They can be used to identify appropriate content material and learning experiences for children.
  - Objectives evaluate the effectiveness of instruction and behavioral outcomes.

- Including parents in children's health and safety education encourages consistency between school and home.
  - Parents can reinforce information, practices, and values that children are learning.
  - Teachers become more aware of family diversity issues and can create learning experiences that are more responsive to children's needs.

- Ongoing inservice opportunities help teachers stay informed, especially in the areas of health and safety where new developments and information appear frequently.

SUGGESTED ACTIVITIES

1. Interview a teacher of toddler or preschool children and a first or second grade teacher. Ask them to describe the health and safety concepts that are stressed with each group. Arrange to observe one of the teachers conducting a health/safety session with children. What were the teacher's objectives? Was the instructional method effective? Did the teacher involve children in learning activities? Were the children attentive? Were the objectives met?

2. Write to several organizations for materials on seat belt restraints and car safety seats. Read and compare the information. Do all statements agree? Do the statements disagree? For whom is the material written, e.g., parents, children, professionals?

3. Develop a lesson plan for a unit to be taught on "What Makes Us Grow?" Include objectives, time length, materials, learning activities, measures for evaluation and any teacher resource information. Exchange lesson plans with another student; critique each other's lesson plan for clarity of ideas, thoroughness and creativity.

4. Select, read, and evaluate three children's books from the reference lists provided in this unit.

CHAPTER REVIEW

A. Matching. Match the definition in column I with the correct term in column II.

Column I	Column II
1. to assess the effectiveness of instruction	a. education
2. favorable changes in attitudes, knowledge and/or practices	b. outcome
3. a sharing of knowledge or skills	c. positive behavior changes
4. ideas and values meaningful to a child	d. attitude
5. subject or theme	e. relevance
6. feeling or strong belief	f. topic
7. occurs in conjunction with daily activities and routines	g. incidental learning
8. the end product of learning	h. evaluation

B. Following is a list of suggested health/safety topics. Place an A (appropriate) or NA (not appropriate) next to each of the statements. Base your decision on whether or not the topic is suitable for preschool-aged children.

_____ dental health

_____ feelings and how to get along with others

_____ primary causes of suicide

_____ consumer health, e.g., understanding advertisements, choosing a doctor, medical quackery

_____ eye safety

_____ the hazards of smoking

_____ how to safely light matches

_____ physical fitness for health

_____ cardiopulmonary resuscitation

_____ the values of rest and sleep

_____ safety at home

_____ animal families

C. **Questions for individual or small group discussion.**

1. Why is health and safety education so important during a child's early years?

2. What purpose does evaluation play in health and safety education? How can this information be used to improve future lessons?

3. Why should parents be included in any health and safety instruction for children?

4. What value does long-range planning play in children's health and safety education?

5. How can teachers determine if health and safety resource materials are reliable?

REFERENCES

Allensworth, D., Lawson, E., Nicholson, L., & Wyche, J. (Eds.). (1997). *Schools and health: Our nation's investment.* Washington, DC: National Academy Press.

Ames, E., Trucano, L., Wan, J., & Harris, M. (1995). *Designing school health curricula.* Dubuque, IA: Brown & Benchmark.

Aronson, S. (2002). *Healthy young children: A manual for programs.* (4th ed.). Washington, DC: NAEYC.

Belfield , J. (2003). Childhood obesity—a public health problem. *School Nurse News, 20*(1), 20, 22, 24.

Berg, F., Buechner, J., Parham E. (2003). Guidelines for childhood obesity prevention programs: promoting healthy weight in children. *Journal of Nutrition Education & Behavior, 35*(1), 1–4.

Cicchetti, D., Rappaport, J., Sandler, I., & Weissberg, R. (Eds.). (2000). *The promotion of wellness in children and adolescents (Issues in children's and families' lives).* Washington, DC: Child Welfare League of America.

Diffily, D., & Morrison, K. (Eds.). (1997). *Family-friendly communication for early childhood programs.* Washington, DC: NAEYC.

Essa, E. (2003). *Early childhood education.* (4th ed.). Clifton Park, NY: Delmar Learning.

Fodor, J. T. (2003). Using the Internet as a phone service: an improved technology that can benefit health promotion and education. *Promoting Education, 9*(4), 151.

Gordon, A. & Browne, K. (2004). *Beginnings and beyond.* (6th ed.). Clifton Park, NY: Delmar Learning.

Jaffe, M. (1997). *Understanding parenting.* Dubuque, IA: William C. Brown Publishers.

Locke, D. (1998). *Increasing multicultural understanding.* Thousand Oaks, CA: Sage.

Lowry, R., Wechsler, H., Galuska, D. A., Fulton, J. E., & Kann, L. (2002). Television viewing and its associations with overweight, sedentary lifestyle, and insufficient consumption of fruits and vegetables among US high school students: differences by race, ethnicity, and gender. *Journal of School Health, 72*(10), 413–421.

Lundgren, D., & Morrison, J. W. (2003). Involving Spanish-speaking families in early education programs. *Young Children, 58*(3), 88–95.

Pealer, L. N., & Dorman, S. M. (1997). Evaluating health related web sites. *Journal of School Health Education, 67*(6), 232–235.

Pena, D. (2000). Parent involvement: Influencing factors and implications. *Journal of Educational Research, 94,* 42–54.

Redican, K., Olsen, L., & Baffi, C. (1993). *Organization of school health programs.* Dubuque, IA: Brown & Benchmark.

Seefeldt, C., & Barbour, N. (1998). *Early childhood education.* Columbus, OH: Merrill.

Summerfield, L. M. (1995). National standards for school health education. *ERIC Digest* (ED 387483).

U.S. Department of Health and Human Services. (2000). *Healthy people 2010.* Washington, DC: National Center for Chronic Disease Prevention and Health Promotion.

Valentine, J. (1997). Schools and communities work together for healthy children. *Wellness Management, 13*(1), 11.

Workman, S. H., & Gage, J. A. (1997). Family-school partnerships: A family strengths approach. *Young Children, 52*(4), 10–14.

ADDITIONAL READING

Association for the Advancement of Health Education. (1994). *Cultural awareness and sensitivity: Guidelines for health educators.* Reston, VA: Author.

Eldridge, D. (2001). Parent involvement: It's worth the effort. *Young Children, 56*(4), 81–83.

Glanz, K., Lewis, F., & Rimer, B. (Eds.). (1990). *Health behavior and health education.* San Francisco: Jossey-Bass Publishers.

Hendricks, C., Peterson, F., Windsor, R., Poehler, D., & Young, M. (1988). Reliability of health knowledge and measurement in very young children. *Journal of School Health, 58*(10), 21–25.

Henry, C. J., Allison, D. J., & Garcia, A. C. (2003). Child nutrition programs in Canada and the United States: comparisons and contrasts. *Journal of School Health, 73*(2), 83–85.

Hodges, E. A. (2003). A primer on early childhood obesity and parental influence. *Pediatric Nursing, 29*(1), 13–16.

Kaufman, H. (2001). Skills for working with all families. *Young Children, 56*(4), 81–83.

Mahoney, B., & Olsen, L. (1993). *Health education: Teacher resource handbook.* Millwood, NY: Kraus International Publications.

Matiella, A. (Ed.). (1994). *The multicultural challenge in health education.* Santa Cruz, CA: ETR Associates.

Mayesky, M. (2002). *Creative activities for young children.* (7th ed.). Clifton Park, NY: Delmar Learning.

McKenzie, J. F. (1987). A checklist for evaluating health information. *Journal of School Health, 57*(1), 31–32.

NAEYC. *Walk in traffic safely (WITS): A traffic safety kit.* Washington, DC: Author.

NAEYC. *We love you—buckle up!* Curriculum packet. Washington, DC: Author.

National Center for Health Education. (1989). *Growing health: Health education curricular progression chart.* New York: Author.

Nelson, G. D., & Hendricks, C. (1988). Health education needs in child care programs. *Journal of School Health, 58*(9), 360–364.

Roths, B., Fees, B. S., Bailey, G., & Fitzgerald, K. (2002). Let's move, learn, and have fun! *Journal of Nutrition Education & Behavior, 34*(6), 343–344.

Werner, P., Timms, S., & Almond, L. (1996). Health stops: Practical ideas for health-related exercise in preschool and primary classrooms. *Young Children, 51*(6), 48–56.

Wisconsin Department of Public Instruction. (1992). *Healthy kids: A team approach to integrating developmental guidance and health education K–6.* Madison, WI: Author.

HELPFUL WEB SITES

American Automobile Association	http://www.aaa.com
American Dental Association	http://www.ada.org
American Heart Association	http://www.amhrt.org
Awesome Library, The	http://www.neat-schoolhouse.org/health.html
Canadian Early Childhood Care & Education	http://www.childcarecanada.org
Center for Disease Control & Protection	http://www/cdc.gov
Children, Stress, & Natural Disasters; University of Illinois	http://www.ag.uiuc.edu/~disaster/teacher.html
Consumer Product Safety Commission	http://www.cpsc.gov
Dole Food Company	http://www.dole5aday.com
Environmental Protection Agency	http://www.epa.gov
Early Childhood Parenting Collaborative	http://ecap.crc.uiuc.edu
KidSource Online	http://www.kidsource.com

National Clearinghouse on Child
   Abuse & Neglect   http://www.calib.com/nccanch

National Dairy Council   http://www.ndc.org

National Fire Protection Association   http://www.nfpa.org

National Highway Traffic Safety
   Administration   http://www.nhtsa.dot.gov

National Institutes of Health   http://www.nih.gov

National Safety Council   http://www.nsc.org

PE (physical education) Central   http://www.pe.central.vt.edu

The Weather Channel on the Web   http://www.weather.com/twc/homepage.twc

For additional health, safety, and nutrition resources, go to
http://www.EarlyChildEd.delmar.com

FOODS AND NUTRIENTS: BASIC CONCEPTS

CHAPTER 13

Nutritional Guidelines

OBJECTIVES

After studying this chapter, you should be able to:

- Outline the steps required to evaluate the nutrient content of a meal or meals.
- Apply the Dietary Guidelines for Americans to your personal nutritional goals.
- Classify foods according to the Food Guide Pyramid.
- Identify nutrient strengths and weaknesses for each major food group in the Food Guide Pyramid.
- Evaluate the nutritional quality of a food from its package label.

TERMS TO KNOW

nutrition	Dietary Reference Intake	protein
nutrients	(DRI)	Percent Daily Values (%DV)
malnutrition	Dietary Guidelines for	nutrition claims
undernutrition	Americans	
essential nutrient	calcium	

Good nutrition affects the health and well-being of individuals of all ages. It is important to note that all persons throughout life need the same nutrients, but in varying amounts. Small children need nutrients for growth and energy; adults need nutrients to maintain or repair body tissue and to provide energy.

To teach good food habits, the teacher or parent must first set a good example. Children frequently model behaviors they see in people they love and admire, such as parents and teachers. To set a good example, the teacher must possess the knowledge to maintain good personal nutrition. A good basic understanding of one's own nutrient needs is essential for good personal dietary practices. The ability to apply nutrition knowledge to the care of children will hopefully follow.

Nutrition is the study of food and how it is used by the body. Nutritionists study foods because foods contain **nutrients**, which are chemical substances with specific uses in the body. The body has three main uses for nutrients:

- sources of energy
- materials for growth and maintenance of body tissue
- regulation of body processes

---

nutrition – *the study of food and how it is used by the body.*
nutrients – *the components or substances that are found in food.*

TABLE 13–1   Nutrients: Their Functions

	Calories per Gram	Energy	Build Body Tissues	Regulators
carbohydrates	4	X		
fats	9	X		
proteins (needed for every function)	4	X	X	X
minerals			X	X
water			X	X
vitamins				X*

*are required in a regulatory role only.

Table 13–1 shows the relationship between nutrients and their functions.

Nutrients are needed in adequate amounts for normal body function to take place. An inadequate supply of nutrients or poor utilization of nutrients may lead to **malnutrition** or **undernutrition** resulting in abnormal body function and general poor health. Malnutrition may also result from excessive intake of one or more nutrients and this, too, may interfere with normal body functions and be health-threatening. Currently there is much concern about excessive consumption of fats and cholesterol in the diet and of minerals and vitamins from self-supplementation.

Approximately 50 nutrients are known to be essential for humans. An **essential nutrient** is one that must be provided by food substances, as the body is unable to manufacture it in adequate amounts. Scientists have been able to determine the approximate amounts of many nutrients needed by the body. Information listing the amounts of many nutrients found in specific foods is also available.

Good nutrition is dependent upon combinations of foods that provide nutritious meals on a daily basis. What to eat? What not to eat? How much to eat? The answers to these important questions have led to the development of a number of meal plans or guidelines. Any of the guidelines discussed will promote healthful eating habits; the choice lies with the individual and may depend on time available, ease of use, and interest.

Regardless of the guideline selected, the common factor necessary for good nutrition is the inclusion of a wide variety of foods. A variety of foods is most likely to supply the greatest number of nutrients. Some foods contain many nutrients, while others contain only a few nutrients. No single food contains enough of all nutrients to support life. The only exception is breast milk, which contains all the nutrients known to be needed by an infant until about six months of age.

malnutrition – *prolonged inadequate or excessive intake of nutrients and/or calories required by the body.*
undernutrition – *an inadequate intake of one or more required or essential nutrients.*
essential nutrient – *nutrient that must be provided in food because it cannot be synthesized by the body at a rate sufficient to meet the body's needs.*

DIETARY REFERENCE INTAKE (DRI)

The "master guideline" for nutrition planing is **Dietary Reference Intake (DRI)**. Known since 1941 as the Recommended Daily Dietary Allowances (RDA), the most recent revision of this plan has brought about major changes in both format and philosophy. The updated guideline is now presented as four components and is being released stepwise over several years. Table 13–2 illustrates the first two portions of the up-dated guideline. The DRI consists of:

- Recommended Daily Allowance (RDA)—goals for nutrient intake by individuals
- Adequate Intake (AI)—goals for nutrient intake when an RDA has not been determined.
- Estimated Average Requirement (EAR)—amount of a nutrient that is estimated to meet the requirements of half the individuals in a life-stage or gender group
- Tolerable Upper Intake Level (UL)—the highest intake level that is likely to pose no health risk

The primary uses for DRIs are in *assessing* intakes of individuals or groups and in *planning* diets for individuals or groups. It is suggested that RDAs, AIs, and ULs be used in planning diets for individuals, while the EAR is more useful in planning for groups. EARs are believed to be important in the assessment of intakes of both individuals and groups (Yates, Schlicloe, & Suitor, 1998).

For the Dietary Reference Intake guidelines to be meaningful, the nutrient content of foods must be known. (Check the references at the end of this chapter.) Evaluation of a diet by means of the Dietary Reference Intake guidelines requires the following steps:

1. List the amounts of all foods and beverages consumed during one 24-hour period.
2. Use nutrient value tables or a computer program to determine the nutrient content of each food and beverage consumed.
3. Total the amount of each nutrient consumed during the day.
4. Determine if nutrients consumed are in sufficient amounts by comparing the total amount of each nutrient consumed with the Dietary Reference Intake for the appropriate age and sex group (Table 13–2).

DIETARY GUIDELINES FOR AMERICANS

The National Nutrition Monitoring and Related Research Act of 1990 requires that the Secretaries of Health and Human Services (HHS) and the U.S. Department of Agriculture (USDA) jointly issue a report, **Dietary Guidelines for Americans**, at least every five years.

At this time, the *Dietary Guidelines* has come to serve as the basis for nearly all nutrition information in the United States. While the Dietary Reference Intakes (DRI) address nutrients only, the *Dietary Guidelines* relates to food and behaviors and their impact on health.

The recommendations contained in the *Dietary Guidelines* are based on current scientific knowledge about the role of nutrition in maintaining health and minimizing disease risks. Periodical updates allow incorporation of new findings about the relationship between food and health.

The *Dietary Guidelines for Americans* are grouped into the ABC's of nutrition:

- **Aim for Fitness . . .**
- **Aim for a healthy weight.** Calories are essential to a child's growth and development. However, it is imperative to balance calorie intake with physical activity to prevent childhood obesity.

Dietary Reference Intake (DRI) – *a plan that presents the recommended goals of nutrient intakes for various age and gender groups.*
Dietary Guidelines for Americans – *report that provides recommendations for daily food choices, to be balanced with physical activity, to promote good health and reduce certain disease risks.*

TABLE 13-2 Food and Nutrition Board, Institute of Medicine—National Academy of Sciences—Dietary Reference Intakes: Recommended Levels for Individual Intake

Life Stage Group	Calcium (mg/d)	Chromium (µg/d)	Copper (µg/d)	Fluoride (mg/d)	Iodine (µg/d)	Iron (mg/d)	Magnesium (mg/d)	Manganese (mg/d)	Molybdenum (µg/d)	Phosphorus (mg/d)	Selenium (µg/d)	Zinc (mg/d)
infants												
0–6 mo	210*	0.2*	200*	0.01*	110*	0.27*	30*	0.003*	2*	100*	15*	2*
7–12 mo	270*	5.5*	220*	0.5*	130*	**11**	75*	0.6*	3*	275*	20*	3
children												
1–3 y	500*	11*	340	0.7*	90	7	80	1.2*	17	464	20	3
4–8 y	800*	15*	440	1*	90	10	130	1.5*	22	500	30	5
males												
9–13 y	1,300*	25*	700	2*	120	8	240	1.9*	34	1,250	40	8
14–18 y	1,300*	35*	890	3*	150	11	410	2.2*	43	1,250	55	11
19–30 y	1,000*	35*	900	4*	150	8	400	2.3*	45	700	55	11
31–50 y	1,000*	35*	900	4*	150	8	420	2.3*	45	700	55	11
51–70 y	1,200*	30*	900	4*	150	8	420	2.3*	45	700	55	11
>70 y	1,200*	30*	900	4*	150	8	420	2.3*	45	700	55	11
females												
9–13 y	1,300*	21*	700	2*	120	8	240	1.6*	34	1,250	40	8
14–18 y	1,300*	24*	890	3*	150	15	350	1.6*	43	1,250	55	9
19–30 y	1,000*	25*	900	3*	150	18	310	1.8*	45	700	55	8
31–50 y	1,000*	25*	900	3*	150	18	320	1.8*	45	700	55	8
51–70 y	1,200*	20*	900	3*	150	8	320	1.8*	45	700	55	8
>70 y	1,200*	20*	900	3*	150	8	320	1.8*	45	700	55	8
pregnancy												
≤18 y	1,300*	29*	1,000	3*	220	27	400	2.0*	50	1,250	60	12
19–30 y	1,000*	30*	1,000	3*	220	27	350	2.0*	50	700	60	11
31–50 y	1,000*	30*	1,000	3*	220	27	360	2.0*	60	700	60	11
lactation												
≤18 y	1,300*	44*	1,300	3*	290	10	360	2.6*	50	1,250	70	13
19–30 y	1,000*	45*	1,300	3*	290	9	310	2.6*	50	700	70	12
31–50 y	1,000*	45*	1,300	3*	290	9	320	2.6*	50	700	70	12

Note: This table presents Recommended Dietary Allowances (RDAs) in **bold type** and Adequate Intakes (AIs) in ordinary type followed by an asterisk (*). RDAs and AIs may both be used as goals for individual intake. RDAs are set to meet the needs of almost all (97 to 98 percent) individuals in a group. For healthy breastfed infants, the AI is the mean intake. The AI for other life stage and gender groups is believed to cover needs of all individuals in the group, but lack of data or uncertainty in the data prevent being able to specify with confidence the percentage of individuals covered by this intake.

Sources: Dietary Reference intakes for Calcium, Phosphorus, Magnesium, Vitamin D, and Fluoride (1997); Dietary Reference Intakes for Thiamin, Riboflavin, Niacin, Vitamin B6, Folate, Vitamin B12, Pantothenic Acid, Biotin, and Choline (1998); Dietary Reference Intakes for Vitamin C, Vitamin E, Selenium and Carotenoids (2000); and Dietary Reference Intakes for Vitamin A, Vitamin K, Arsenic, Boron, Chromium, Copper, Iodine, Iron, Manganese, Molybdenum, Nickel, Silicon, Vanadium, and Zinc (2001). These reports may be accessed via www.nap.edu.

- **Be physically active each day.** Maintain or improve your weight. Many chronic diseases are associated with excess weight and sedentary lifestyles. The teacher has a responsibility not only to plan appropriate physical activities but also to demonstrate participation and enjoyment of those activities.
- **Build a Healthy Base . . .**
- **Let the Pyramid guide your food choices.** The Food Guide Pyramid is a guide for building a healthy diet. With no single food being able to provide all the nutrients individuals need, the pyramid is used to stress the framework for a balanced diet.
- **Choose a variety of grains daily, especially whole grains.** Whole grains are an excellent source of fiber and other nutrients essential to a balanced diet. They are also a low-fat food. Six or more servings are recommended daily.
- **Choose a variety of fruits and vegetables daily.** Fruits and vegetables are rich sources of many vitamins and minerals. These foods are also naturally high in fiber.
- **Keep food safe to eat.** Young children are at a higher risk for food-borne illnesses. Washing hands, cooking food to proper temperatures, storing foods in proper refrigeration, and following food labels are key tips to reducing food-borne illness.
- **Choose Sensibly . . .**
- **Choose a diet that is low in saturated fat and cholesterol and moderate in total fat.** High fat intake is also associated with development of chronic diseases and when coupled with minimal physical activity, promotes development of obesity. This guideline suggests that no more than 30 percent of calories be derived from fats. Please note that grains, vegetables, and fruits eaten in their simplest forms are very low in fat.
- **Choose beverages and foods to moderate your intake of sugars.** Current recommendations suggest that over half of calories be derived from carbohydrates. While it is suggested that most of the carbohydrates be complex—such as whole grains—sugar in small amounts is not thought to be harmful as long as the diet is balanced. Individual foods should not be labeled "good" or "bad" and may be enjoyed as part of a variety of foods.
- **Choose and prepare foods with less salt.** Excess sodium and salt is also associated with a number of chronic diseases. While it is essential for life, most people can get enough sodium from food without adding extra salt. Again, vegetables, fruits, and grains in their simplest forms contain little sodium or salt. Most processed foods and fast foods are quite high in sodium and salt.
- **If you drink alcoholic beverages, do so in moderation.** This guideline includes a list of persons who should not drink (1) children or teens, (2) persons who cannot restrict their drinking to moderate levels, and (3) women who are pregnant, trying to become pregnant or breast-feeding.

Other Nutrition Guidelines

Healthy People 2010 originated with the U.S. Public Health Service. Some pertinent directives include:

- reduce prevalence of growth retardation to less than 5 percent among low-income children age five years or younger
- increase the proportion of persons aged two years and older who consume no more than 30 percent of calories from total fat
- increase the proportion of persons aged two years and older who consume at least six daily servings of grain products, with at least three being whole grain
- increase the proportion of consumers who follow key food safety practices

The American Heart Association has issued guidelines addressing fat, cholesterol, sodium, and alcohol in the diet. The National Cancer Institute's guidelines call for increased vegetable, fruit, and grain consumption, along with decreased fat and alcohol consumption.

ISSUES TO CONSIDER • Food Guide Pyramid Controversy

The Food Guide Pyramid, developed by the U.S. Department of Agriculture, was initially designed to be used as a teaching tool in conjunction with the *Dietary Guidelines for Americans.* While the *Dietary Guidelines* are reviewed and updated every five years, the Pyramid has not been reassessed since its inception in 1992. The Pyramid has become part of a growing controversy questioning the nutritional guidelines it promotes. One criticism is that the tip of the Pyramid identifies all fats as bad when recent research shows that there may be fat beneficial to the American diet (Richards, 2002).

- What are other possible criticisms of the current Food Guide Pyramid?
- With the growing grates of obesity in children and adults, would you consider the Food Guide Pyramid a useful guideline for healthy eating?
- What are some recommendations you would make considering the design or the nutritional information offered through the Pyramid to make it more useful for educating consumers?

THE FOOD GUIDE PYRAMID

The graphic illustration of the *Dietary Guidelines for Americans* is the Food Guide Pyramid (Figure 13–1). If the age-related recommended number and size of servings of foods from the Food Guide Pyramid are consumed, the nutrient needs of children and adults should be met. A pattern of consuming the same foods over time provides the same nutrient strengths but also the same nutrient weaknesses.

The food groups that constitute the Food Guide Pyramid are:

- the Bread, Cereal, Rice, and Pasta Group
- the Vegetable Group
- the Fruit Group
- the Milk, Yogurt, and Cheese Group
- the Meat, Poultry, Fish, Dry Beans, Eggs, and Nuts Group
- the Fats, Oils, and Sweets Group

The Bread, Cereal, Rice, and Pasta Group

Such foods as breads, breakfast cereals, pastas, and flour make up the Bread and Cereal Group. Food choices from this group should be whole grain or enriched products. Whole grain products retain all of the grain. Enriched breads and cereals are products that have been processed and specified amounts of nutrients have been added. The nutrients that are added are iron, thiamin, riboflavin, and niacin. In an effort to reduce the incidence of birth defects, grain products are now also fortified with folacin. The amounts of these added nutrients are equal to those found in the whole grain. Whole grain bread and cereals are better choices for children and adults. In the processing of cereals, some minerals and vitamins are removed that are not put back into enriched cereals. Whole grain products also provide needed fiber.

A serving from this group consists of one slice of bread, one cup of dry, ready-to-eat cereal, or 1/2 cup of cooked cereal or pasta. As with the other groups, the child's serving is one-half the size of the adult serving. The Pyramid plan recommends six or more servings of bread and cereal daily.

FIGURE 13–1

The USDA Food Guide Pyramid was designed to illustrate what Americans should eat each day. (Courtesy of the U.S. Department of Agriculture.)

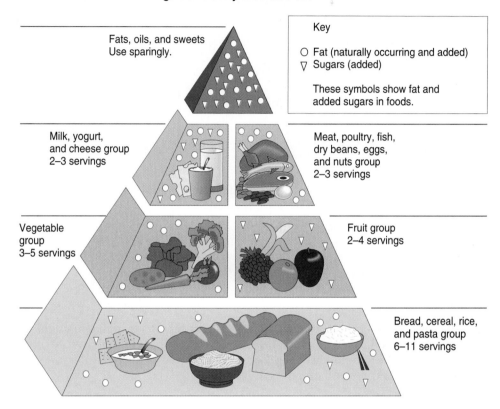

The Food Guide Pyramid
A guide to daily food choices

Fats, oils, and sweets
Use sparingly.

Key

○ Fat (naturally occurring and added)
▽ Sugars (added)

These symbols show fat and added sugars in foods.

Milk, yogurt, and cheese group
2–3 servings

Meat, poultry, fish, dry beans, eggs, and nuts group
2–3 servings

Vegetable group
3–5 servings

Fruit group
2–4 servings

Bread, cereal, rice, and pasta group
6–11 servings

Nutrient Summary: Bread, Cereal, Rice, and Pasta Group

Nutrient Strengths	Nutrient Weaknesses
Iron	Calcium
Thiamin	Vitamin A
Niacin	Vitamin C
Riboflavin	
Folic Acid	
Complex Carbohydrates	

The Vegetable Group and the Fruit Group

The Vegetable Group and the Fruit Group indicate a separation of the "Fruits and Vegetable Group" of the Basic Four Food Groups. Careful study of the Pyramid reveals that more servings of vegetables (3–5) are recommended than of fruit (2–4). Vegetables are emphasized on the Food Guide Pyramid because they contribute notable amounts of minerals and vitamins, whereas fruits contribute mainly vitamins (*Journal of American Dietetic Association*, 1997) (Figure 13–2).

FIGURE 13-2

A variety of foods is most likely to supply the greatest number of nutrients.

One example of the effort to promote increased consumption of vegetables and fruits is the "5 a Day for Better Health" campaign. The key points are:

- eat five servings of vegetables and fruits a day
- eat at least one Vitamin C-rich selection every day (Table 13–3)
- eat at least one Vitamin A-rich selection every day (Table 13–4)
- eat at least one high-fiber selection every day
- eat cabbage-family vegetables several times a week (i.e., cabbage, broccoli, cauliflower, brussels sprouts)

Fiber in the diet has received increasing attention. Very high fiber intake in childhood could have adverse effects. A practical recommendation for fiber intake for children over two years of age is the "Age + 5" rule. For example, Tasha, age three years, would require eight grams of fiber/day. See Table 13–5 for food sources and amounts of fiber.

Milk, Yogurt, and Cheese Group

This group includes milk and dairy products. Children should have a total of three cups of milk or the equivalent from this group daily. The servings may be divided into one-half cup portions in consideration of children's smaller appetites and capacity. Adults need two cups of milk or the

TABLE 13-3 Good to Excellent Sources of Vitamin C

orange*	tomatoes*
orange Juice*	grapefruit*
strawberries*	mustard greens
cauliflower	spinach
broccoli	cabbage
sweet peppers, red or green	tangerine*

*May cause allergic reactions

TABLE 13–4 Good to Excellent Sources of Vitamin A

cantaloupe	winter Squash
carrots	greens
pumpkin	apricots
sweet potatoes	watermelon*
spinach	broccoli

*May cause allergic reactions

equivalent daily. Equivalent foods include cheese, yogurt, ice cream, custards, and puddings. Equivalent amounts of foods may vary due to the addition of other ingredients such as fruit or sugar. Foods that provide **calcium** equal to that in one cup of milk are:

1 1/2 ounces cheddar cheese
1 cup pudding
1 3/4 cups ice cream
1 cup plain yogurt

Nutrient Summary: Milk, Yogurt, and Cheese Group

Nutrient Strengths	**Nutrient Weaknesses**
Calcium	Vitamin C
Protein	Iron
Riboflavin	

TABLE 13–5 Dietary Fiber Content of Some Commonly Eaten Foods

Food	Amount	Fiber (gm)
cornflakes	1/2 cup	0.5
oatmeal	1/4 cup	1.4
wheat flakes	1/2 cup	1.5
macaroni	1/2 cup	1.1
bread, whole wheat	1/2 slice	0.8
bread, white	1/2 slice	0.5
graham crackers	1 square	0.7
apple with skin	1/2	1.5
banana	1/2	0.9
raisins	1 Tbsp.	0.5
potato, baked with skin	1/2	1.1
green beans	1/4 cup	0.5
pinto beans	1/2 cup	3.4

Courtesy of Pennington, J. A. T. (1994). *Bowes and Church's food values of portions commonly used.* (16th ed.). Philadelphia: Lippincott, Williams, & Wilkins.

calcium – *mineral nutrient; a major component of bones and teeth.*

Meat, Poultry, Fish, Dry Beans, Eggs, and Nuts Group

The recommended daily amount from the Meat, Poultry, Fish, Dry Beans, Eggs, and Nuts Group is two or more servings. The amount of food in a serving varies with the age of the individual. Small children need and often will eat only one to one-and-one-half ounces in a serving, while the adult serving consists of two to three ounces of meat or equivalent. Beef, veal, pork, lamb, fish, and poultry are included in the Meat, Poultry, Fish, Dry Beans, Eggs, and Nuts Group. Other foods included in this group are eggs, legumes such as dry peas and beans, nuts, and nut butters such as peanut butter. Cheese may also be substituted for meats; however, it should be remembered that cheeses do not contain iron, which is a nutrient strength of this group. The following foods contain **protein** equal to that in one ounce of meat:

> 1 egg
> 1 ounce of cheese
> 1/4 cup cottage cheese
> 1/2 cup dried peas or beans
> 2 tablespoons peanut butter

> Nutrient Summary: Meat, Poultry, Fish, Dry Beans, Eggs, and Nuts Group

Nutrient Strengths	Nutrient Weaknesses
Protein	Calcium
Thiamin	Vitamin C
Riboflavin	Vitamin A
Niacin	
Iron	

Fats, Oils, and Sweets Group

The tip of the Pyramid is called the Fats, Oils, and Sweets Group. Most items in the tip are condiments or contribute no important nutrients. Examples of items in the tip of the Pyramid are butter or margarine, jelly, and honey. *Note:* Symbols for fat and sugar have been added. Circles on the Pyramid signify added or naturally occurring fat; inverted triangles signify added but not naturally occurring sugar. The purpose of the symbols is to teach that fat and sugar are found in all food groups.

In general, the nutrient content of this group is low and the calorie content is high. The addition to the diet of large amounts of foods from the Fats, Oils, and Sweets Group can dilute the nutrient content of foods from the Pyramid. Table 13–6 illustrates the dilution of the Vitamin C in an apple by the addition of sugar and fat. Calorie content increases with the addition of sugar. Further increases in calories occur with the addition of fat and flour in making apple pie. At the same time the calories are increasing, the amount of Vitamin C decreases.

TABLE 13–6 Comparison of Caloric Increase and Nutrient Decrease When Sugar and Fats Are Added to the Diet

	Calories	Vitamin C
apple, raw 3/#	80	6 mg
applesauce, sweetened, 1 cup	230	3 mg
apple pie, 1/7 pie	342	2 mg
pie a la mode, 1/7 plus 1/2 cup ice cream	480	2 mg

Courtesy of Home and Garden Bulletin No. 72.

protein – *class of nutrients used primarily for structural and regulatory functions.*

REFLECTIVE THOUGHTS

The use of the Pyramid as a guide for making healthy food choices requires recognition that individual foods within one food group vary greatly in nutrient content relative to sugar, fat, and calorie content. Choose different foods within a given pyramid food group and try to assign them to one of the following groups:

    a. Unrestricted—eat any amount every day (high nutrient content but low in fat and sugar)

    b. Moderately restricted—eat only one to three times per day (moderately high in fat and/or sugar)

    c. Very restricted—eat only two to three times per week (high in fat and/or sugar and calories)

NUTRITIONAL LABELING

The Nutritional Labeling and Education Act, passed in 1990, resulted in many changes in the labeling of food products. The food label was revised in 1994 and is regulated by the Food and Drug Administration (FDA) and the U.S. Department of Agriculture (USDA) (Figure 13–3). This resulted in a label that provides:

- Easy-to-read nutrition information on packaged foods.
- Serving sizes in commonly consumed amounts. This prevents using small serving sizes to make food products that are high in fat, cholesterol, sodium, or calories look better than they are.
- A list of all ingredients (in decreasing order relative to amount) on their label.
- **Percent Daily Values (%DV)** that show how a serving of food fits into a total day's diet. (This replaces the previously used USRDA.)
- **Nutrition claims** that mean the same on every product (Figure 13–4).
- Voluntary information for the most commonly eaten fresh fruits and vegetables, raw fish, and cuts of meat. This information may appear on posters or in brochures in the same area as the food.

CALORIES FROM FAT

Labels now provide both the amount of fat and the amount of saturated fat. Also provided are calories from fat. With the amount of fat and calories from fat given on the label, determining the percent of calories from fat is simple.

$$\text{Percent of calories from fat} = \frac{\text{fat calories/serving}}{\text{total calories/serving}} \times 100$$

To calculate the number of calories from fat, use this formula:

calories from fat = grams (g) of fat/serving $\times$ 9 (cal/g)

Percent Daily Values (%DV) – *measures of the nutritional values of food; used in nutrition labeling.*
nutrition claims – *statements of reduced calories, fat, or salt on the food labels.*

FIGURE 13–3

A food label.

Nutrition Facts
Serving Size 3/4 cup (30g)
Servings Per Container about 15

Amount Per Serving	Cereal	Cereal with 1/2 cup Skim Milk
Calories	100	140
Calories from Fat	5	5

	% Daily Value**	
Total Fat 0.5g*	1%	1%
Saturated Fat 0g	0%	0%
Polyunsaturated Fat 0g		
Monounsaturated Fat 0g		
Cholesterol 0mg	0%	0%
Sodium 220mg	9%	12%
Potassium 190mg	5%	11%
Total Carbohydrate 24g	8%	10%
Dietary Fiber 5g	21%	21%
Soluble Fiber 1g		
Insoluble Fiber 4g		
Sugars 6g		
Other Carbohydrate 13g		
Protein 3g		

Vitamin A	15%	20%
Vitamin C	0%	2%
Calcium	0%	15%
Iron	45%	45%
Vitamin D	10%	25%
Thiamin	25%	30%
Riboflavin	25%	35%
Niacin	25%	25%
Vitamin B6	25%	25%
Folate	25%	25%
Vitamin B12	25%	35%
Phosphorus	15%	25%
Magnesium	15%	20%
Zinc	10%	15%
Copper	10%	10%

*Amount in Cereal. One half cup skim milk contributes an additional 40 calories. 65mg sodium, 200mg potassium, 6g total carbohydrate (6g sugars), and 4g protein.

**Percent Daily Values are based on a 2,000 calorie diet. Your daily values may be higher or lower depending on your calorie needs:

	Calories:	2,000	2,500
Total Fat	Less than	65g	80g
Saturated Fat	Less than	20g	25g
Cholesterol	Less than	300mg	300mg
Sodium	Less than	2,400mg	2,400mg
Potassium		3,500mg	3,500mg
Total Carbohydrate		300g	375g
Dietary Fiber		25g	30g

FIGURE 13–4

Definitions of commonly used food labeling terms. (Courtesy of **FDA Consumer,** September 1995.)

WHAT SOME CLAIMS MEAN

high-protein: at least 10 grams (g) high-quality protein per serving

good source of calcium: at least 100 milligrams (mg) calcium per serving

more iron: at least 1.8 mg more iron per serving than reference food. (Label will say 10 percent more of the Daily Value for iron.)

fat-free: less than 0.5 g fat per serving

low-fat: 3 g or less fat per serving. (If the serving size is 30 g or less or 2 tablespoons or less, 3 g or less fat per 50 g of the food.)

reduced or fewer calories: at least 25 percent fewer calories per serving than the reference food

sugar-free: less than 0.5 g sugar per serving

light (two meanings):

- one-third fewer calories or half the fat of the reference food. (If 50 percent or more of the food's calories are from fat, the fat must be reduced by 50 percent.)

- a "low-calorie," "low-fat" food whose sodium content has been reduced by 50 percent of the reference food.

The following calculations of percent of calories from fat in some selected foods will show how fat content reports on labels may be misleading:

Cheddar cheese—1 ounce = 115 calories and 9 g of fat:
  Calories from fat = 9 × 9 = 81
  Percent calories from fat × 81/115 × 100 = 70%

Eggs—one egg = 75 calories and 6 g of fat:
  Calories from fat = 6 × 9 = 54
  Percent calories from fat = 54/75 × 100 = 72%

90% fat-free ground beef—3 ounces = 185 calories and 10 g fat:
  Calories from fat = 10 × 9 = 90
  Percent calories from fat = 90/185 × 100 = 49%

For all of these examples, the grams of fat (9, 6, and 10) are low, yet they all presented more than 30 percent of calories from fat.

The recommendation that only 30 percent of calories should come from fat does not mean that all healthy food choices must derive less than 30 percent of their calories from fat. This would virtually eliminate all red meat and most dairy products. However, it does mean that if you eat a lean hamburger with 49 percent fat-calories, it might be better to skip the french fries at 47 percent fat-calories and substitute an apple, banana, or orange with less than 10 percent of calories from fat.

The calculations for percent of fat-calories seem tedious at first, but after a few calculations you will find that you can skim a label and judge its nutrient density or fat-calorie level. You will not need to take a calculator with you when you go grocery shopping.

FOCUS ON FAMILIES • Dietary Guidelines for Americans

One major recommendation of the *Dietary Guidelines for Americans* encourages a diet that is moderate in sugar consumption. Many foods such as milk/dairy products and fruit have naturally occurring sugar. Foods that have sugar added in processing or preparation add unnecessary calories and are low in many vitamins and minerals. Sugar is thought not to be harmful if it is used in limited amounts in the diet.

- Know your food labels: A *reduced sugar* food item contains at least 25 percent less sugar than the reference food. *No added sugar* or *without added sugar* foods indicate that no sugars were added during processing or packaging. *Sugar free* foods contain less than 0.5 grams sugar per serving.

- The following terms, if listed as the first or second ingredient of a food label, indicate the food is likely high in sugar: Brown sugar, corn sweetener or corn syrup, fructose, fruit juice concentrate, glucose, dextrose, high-fructose corn syrup, honey, lactose, maltose, molasses, raw sugar, table sugar (sucrose), syrup.

- Major food sources of sugar in the United States are sodas, cakes, cookies, pies, fruit ades, fruit punch, and dairy desserts such as ice cream. Healthy foods that contain added sugar should be limited in the diet: chocolate milk, presweetened cereals, and fruits packed in syrup. If these foods are eaten, do so in moderation and choose smaller serving sizes (a serving of soda in the 1950's was 6$\frac{1}{2}$ ounces compared to a 20-ounce serving today!).

CASE STUDIES

1. Betsy, age three-and-one-half years, drinks milk to the exclusion of adequate amounts of food from other food groups. What nutrient is Betsy receiving in excess? What two nutrients are most likely to be deficient?

2. Jason, age four years, refuses to eat vegetables. He will occasionally accept a small serving of applesauce but no other fruits. What two nutrients are probably deficient in Jason's diet?

3. Jeremy, age three years, is allergic to milk and dairy products. What nutrient is deficient in Jeremy's diet?

4. Tommy, two years old, by choice will eat only high carbohydrate foods, preferably those that are sweet. He rejects high-protein, high-fat foods such as meats and cheese. How would you change his diet to provide adequate protein and fat for normal growth and nerve development without increasing his carbohydrate intake with high-fat pastries, cakes, etc?

5. Mary, age four, refuses milk and all milk products; she likes to drink a variety of juices. How would you adjust her diet to assure that she meets her calcium requirement?

SUMMARY

- The study of nutrition is concerned with what nutrients are, why the human body needs them, how much of each is needed, and where they may be obtained from foods.

- Food Guidelines are provided to aid in making food choices that assure meeting the essential nutrients in adequate amounts without consuming excesses of nutrients that might be unhealthful.

- The most practical guide for making healthful food choices is the Pyramid, which groups foods that contain similar kinds and amounts of nutrients.

- Dietary Reference Intake (DRI) gives a more precise evaluation of nutrient needs for persons in various age and sex groups.

- The *Dietary Guidelines for Americans* advises on food selections that meet nutrient needs and avoids known harmful effects of over consumption of some nutrient groups.

- *Healthy People 2010* is a comprehensive set of disease-prevention and health-promotion objectives for the nation to achieve over the first decade of the century.

- Eating a variety of foods from all food groups is the best assurance of consuming a health-promoting diet.

SUGGESTED ACTIVITIES

1. Using the following format, summarize each of the food groups from the Food Guide Pyramid:
   a. Recommended number of servings
      - child
      - adult (where different)

b. Recommended size of serving
  - child
  - adult
c. Nutrient strengths
d. Nutrient weaknesses

2. Plan a day's diet for a four-year-old child. Include the recommended number of servings and the appropriate serving sizes from the Food Guide Pyramid.

3. Assume that a child is allergic to citrus fruit and strawberries (common food allergies). What fruit and/or vegetable choices could be substituted to provide adequate vitamin C?

4. Visit a child care center. Analyze the posted menus according to the Food Guide Pyramid. Identify nutrient strengths of each food served.

5. The next time you eat pizza, note the amount that you ate and use the Pyramid as a guide to evaluate the number of servings that you received from the different food groups. You might have a green salad with your pizza and see what it might add.

CHAPTER REVIEW

A. **Match the foods in column I to the appropriate food group in column II. Some foods may include more than one food group.**

Column I

1. navy beans
2. rice
3. spaghetti
4. hamburger pizza
5. macaroni and cheese
6. peanut butter sandwich
7. french fries
8. ice cream
9. popcorn
10. carbonated beverages

Column II

a. Milk, Cheese, and Yogurt Group
b. Meat, Poultry, Fish, Dry Beans, Eggs, and Nuts Group
c. Bread, Cereal, Rice, and Pasta Group
d. Vegetable Group/Fruit Group
e. Fats, Oils, and Sweets Group

REFERENCES

American Dietetic Association. (1997). Vegetarian diets. *Journal of the American Dietetic Association, 97,* 1317–1321.

Mahan, K. L., & Escott-Stump, S. (1996). *Krause's food, nutrition, and diet therapy* (9th ed.). Philadelphia: W. B. Saunders Company.

Pennington, J. A. T. (1994). *Bowes and Church's food values of portions commonly used* (16th ed.). Philadelphia: J. B. Lippincott Co.

Richards, Linda (2002). Food Pyramid controversies. *Today's Dietitian.* 4, 34–37.

U.S. Department of Agriculture. (1999). Nutritive values of foods. *Home and Garden Bulletin No. 72.* Washington, DC: Author.

U.S. Department of Health and Human Services and U.S. Department of Agriculture (2000). *Dietary Guidelines for Americans.* Washington, DC: Authors.

Yates, A. A., Schlicker, S. A., & Suitor, C. W. (1998). Dietary Reference Intakes: New baseline recommendations for calcium and related nutrients. *Journal of the American Dietetic Association, 98,* 699–706.

ADDITIONAL READING

Bureau of Nutritional Services. (1990). *Recommended nutrient intakes for Canadians.* Ottawa, Canada: Author.

Christian, J. L., & Geigher, J. L. (1988). *Nutrition for living* (2nd ed.). Menlo Park, CA: Benjamin Cummings Publishing Company.

Digital System Research, Inc. (1992). *Health and diet pro for windows.* San Diego, CA: Author.

Duyff, R. L. (2002). *The American Dietetic Association's complete food and nutrition guide* (2nd ed.). New York: John Wiley & Sons.

FDA Consumer Publication. (1994, April). *Food label close-up.* Washington, DC: U.S. Department of Agriculture.

FDA Consumer Publication. (1998, January/February). *Skimming the milk label.* Washington, DC: U.S. Department of Agriculture.

FDA. *The Food Guide Pyramid.* (1992). Washington, DC: U.S. Department of Agriculture.

Franz, M. J. (1997). *Fast food facts* (5th ed.). Minneapolis, MN: International Diabetes Center.

Garrison, R., & Sumer, E. (1995). *The nutrition desk reference.* New Canaan, CT: Keats Publishing, Inc.

Herbert, V., & Subak-Sharpe, G. E. (1994). *Total nutrition—The only guide you'll ever need.* New York: St. Martin's Griffin.

U.S. Department of Agriculture. (1990). *Nutrition and your health: Dietary guidelines for Americans.* Washington, DC: Author.

U.S. Department of Agriculture. (1999). Composition of foods. *Agriculture Handbook No. 8.* Washington, DC: Author.

U.S. Department of Agriculture. (1999). *Home and Garden Bulletin No. 252.* Washington, DC: Author.

Whitney, E. & Sizer, F. S. (2003). *Nutrition concepts and controversies with Infotrac* (9th ed.). Belmont, CA: Wadsworth Publishing.

HELPFUL WEB SITES

Federal Citizen Information Center	http://www. pueblo.gsa.gov/food.htm
Food and Drug Administration (FDA) Labeling	http://vmcfsan.fda.gov.label.htm
Kids Pyramid	http://www.usda.gov/cnpp/KidsPyra
Tufts University Center on Nutrition Communication	http://www.navigator.tufts.edu
United States Department of Agriculture (USDA) News Site	http://www.usda.gov/Newsroom/
United States Department of Agriculture (USDA) Search	htttp://www.usda.gov/search

For additional health, safety, and nutrition resources, go to
http://www.EarlyChildEd.delmar.com

CHAPTER 14

Nutrients That Provide Energy
(Carbohydrates, Fats, and Proteins)

OBJECTIVES

After studying this chapter, you should be able to:

- Identify the three classes of nutrients that supply energy.
- State the amount of energy supplied by each class of nutrients.
- List three factors that determine individual energy requirements.
- Identify foods containing good sources of energy-supplying nutrients.
- Calculate daily caloric requirements of a child based on the child's weight.
- Plan a day's diet eliminating refined sucrose.
- Plan a day's diet that meets the recommended 30 percent of calories from fat, and is low in saturated fatty acids and cholesterol.

TERMS TO KNOW

energy	basal metabolic rate (BMR)	metabolize (metabolism)
calories	thermic energy of food	linoleic acid
enzymes	digest (digestion)	linolenic acid
coenzymes	absorb (absorption)	PUFAs
gram		

Energy is generally defined as the ability to do work. Examples of work done by the body are (1) moving the body, (2) building new tissues, (3) maintaining body temperature, and (4) digesting, absorbing, and metabolizing food. Energy is required for all body functions. In terms of survival, the need for energy is second only to the need for oxygen and water.

The amount of potential energy in a food is expressed in **calories**, for example, a one-cup serving of ice cream supplies 185 calories. The energy cost of a given activity is also measured and expressed in calories, for example, swimming for 30 minutes expends about 150 calories.

Carbohydrates, fats, and proteins found in foods supply energy for the body's activities. Vitamins, minerals, and water do not supply calories but they are essential for the functioning of

---

energy – *power to perform work.*
calories – *units used to measure the energy value of foods.*

346

enzymes, **coenzymes**, and hormones. Enzymes and coenzymes are vitamin-containing substances that initiate and participate in the many metabolic reactions that are necessary for the release of energy from carbohydrates, fats, and proteins. Hormones, such as thyroxin and insulin, while not directly involved in energy-releasing reactions, do regulate many of these reactions. For example, several are required to maintain a blood sugar level that provides an adequate supply of energy for all body needs. The caloric value of any given food is determined by its carbohydrate, fat, and protein content. The relative numbers of calories contained in carbohydrates, fats, and proteins are:

- carbohydrates—four calories per gram
- fat—nine calories per gram
- proteins—four calories per gram

A **gram** is a metric unit of measurement for weight. There are 28 grams in one ounce, and 454 grams in one pound. A metal paper clip weighs about one gram.

Every individual has different energy requirements; these requirements vary slightly on a day-to-day basis. Individual energy requirements are determined by:

- basal metabolic rate (BMR)
- physical activity
- energy spent to release energy from food (thermic energy of food)

Basal metabolic rate (BMR) is a term used to describe the energy needed just to carry on vital involuntary body processes. The BMR, which varies little from day to day, is a measure of the energy required for blood circulation, breathing, cell activity, body temperature maintenance, heartbeat, and other involuntary activities. A child's BMR will be higher than an adult's because of additional energy required for growth. It does not measure voluntary activity; however, physical activity to the aerobic level will increase heart beat and breathing rate. This will temporarily increase the BMR. For most children and adults, the energy required to meet basal metabolic needs is greater than energy expended for voluntary physical activity.

Physical activity is the aspect of energy need that is subject to the greatest conscious control. For instance, participation in tennis or swimming as a recreational activity requires far more energy than reading or watching television (Figure 14–1). Children should be encouraged to participate in physical activity. The benefits of physical activity include motor development, the opportunity for socialization, a sense of accomplishment, and increased fitness. The additional calories required by increased physical activity provide the opportunity to increase food intake and thus make it easier to meet other nutrient requirements.

Thermic energy of food refers to the energy required to **digest**, **absorb**, transport, and **metabolize** nutrients in food. This factor accounts for approximately 10 percent of the total energy requirement.

---

enzymes – *proteins that catalyze body functions.*
coenzymes – *a vitamin-containing substance required by certain enzymes before they can perform their prescribed function.*
gram – *a metric unit of weight; approximately 1/28 of an ounce.*
basal metabolic rate (BMR) – *minimum amount of energy needed to carry on the body processes vital to life.*
thermic energy of food – *energy required to digest, absorb, transport, and metabolize nutrients in food.*
digestion – *the process by which complex nutrients in foods are changed into smaller units that can be absorbed and used by the body.*
absorption – *the process by which the products of digestion are transferred from the intestinal tract into the blood or lymph or by which substances are taken up by the cells.*
metabolism – *all chemical changes that occur from the time nutrients are absorbed until they are built into body tissue or are excreted.*

FIGURE 14–1

Quiet activities require lesser amounts of energy than more strenuous activities.

FIGURE 14–2

The energy needs of active growing children are relatively greater than those of an adult.

Growing children need more energy per unit of body weight than adults (Figure 14–2). Growth requires energy for division and/or enlargement of existing cells (Alford & Bogle, 1982). Rates of growth, physical activity, and body size cause variations in the amount of energy needed by individual children. The number of calories needed daily is calculated on the basis of normal body weight. A four-year-old child needs approximately 40 calories per pound of body weight. (The energy needs of infants are detailed in Chapter 17.) For comparison, a moderately active adult female requires approximately 18 calories per pound; a moderately active adult male needs approximately 21 calories per pound. (Moderately active has been described as equal time "on the feet and on the seat.") Males have a higher BMR because they have a higher muscle/fat ratio than females. Muscles require BMR energy, while fat requires zero energy for storing or retrieving it.

Balancing the number of calories eaten with the number of calories expended results in stable body weight (see *Dietary Guidelines for Americans* in Chapter 13). Eating fewer calories than are needed leads to weight loss. The result of eating too few calories is more serious in growing children than in adults. Too few calories can result in slowed growth as a result of burning body tissue to provide needed energy for body function. Children need sufficient calories from carbohydrates and fat to spare protein that is needed for growth. For children as well as adults, it is better to get one half or more of their calories from carbohydrates; starch is the preferred carbohydrate because its food sources contribute needed vitamins, minerals, and fiber as well as energy.

TABLE 14–1 Tips for Managing an Overweight Child

- Increasing exercise is often the most effective way to help a child control weight.
- Slight changes in snacks can help a child control weight. For example, offer fat-free animal crackers rather than a chocolate cookie or chips.
- Reduce intake of sweetened beverages and encourage water intake between meals.
- No clean plate requirements.
- Do not exclude desserts; this only increases their importance for the child. Substitute fresh fruit or low-fat, low-sugar dairy-based desserts for high calorie desserts.

Too many calories consumed over a period of time may lead to obesity. Obese children are often less active than their slimmer playmates and may require fewer calories due to their lower activity level. The obese child's bulkier body can lead to less coordinated movements and greater danger of accidents. This may result in the obese child shunning play that involves much physical activity, which may lead to more weight gain. It is important that this vicious cycle be stopped early in the child's life because there is strong evidence that child obesity results in adult obesity. Obese children are often teased by their playmates and excluded from play activities. Exclusion from play groups often adds to problems encountered by the obese child, such as poor self-image, decreased fitness level, and fewer opportunities for socialization. The child with a weight problem should be encouraged to exercise and be offered adequate amounts of nutrient-dense foods (Table 14–1). Calories should not be drastically reduced, as reduction of calories may result in reduction of essential nutrients (Twin Cities District Dietetic Association, 1990). One safe plan is to adjust calorie intake to keep body weight stable while the child grows linearly. Over time, this will bring the weight:height ratio (also known as Body Mass Index, or BMI) back into a normal range.

According to the 2000 *Dietary Guidelines for Americans*, children need enough food for proper growth. Physical activity, not food restriction, is recommended to encourage weight loss. Children on weight-reduction programs must be under the supervision of a physician to ensure that their nutritional needs are met.

CARBOHYDRATES AS ENERGY SOURCES

Carbohydrates that yield four calories per gram should be primary sources of energy for children. At least half the energy required by a child should be derived from carbohydrates. A child requiring 1,600 calories should derive at least 800 calories from carbohydrates; 800 calories are supplied by 200 grams of carbohydrates. Many experts recommend a minimum intake for adults of 125 grams (500 calories) of carbohydrates daily. Children need more, but the exact minimum amount needed is not known. The main portion of carbohydrates should be complex with no more than 10 percent of calories coming from refined sugar.

Foods that contain complex and unprocessed carbohydrates are wise choices for children's snacks. Fresh fruits and vegetables, fruit and vegetable juices, and whole grain products such as breads, cereals, and crackers are nutritious and readily accepted snack foods for growing children. Carbohydrates are present in foods in simple and complex forms.

Consumption of refined sugar has increased since 1900; the use of complex carbohydrates, such as starches, has dropped during that same period. Current nutrition recommendations suggest increased amounts of complex carbohydrates and decreased amounts of refined sugars. This simply means less sugar and more starch and fiber from the Bread, Cereal, Rice, and Pasta Group, the Vegetable Group, and the Fruit Group. Three general classes of carbohydrates are found in foods: simple sugars, compound sugars, and complex carbohydrates.

ISSUES TO CONSIDER • Are We Having an Obesity Epidemic?

The media, almost daily, tell us that we are fat and getting fatter. Depending upon the source, the story will be that "30–50 percent of all Americans are obese" i.e., 20 percent above normal body weight. The message will then proceed to tell us that obesity increases our risk for several diseases.

- Why do Americans not take these warnings seriously enough to really try to achieve and maintain body weight and thus reduce risk of disease?
- How much attention is or should be given to helping children balance energy input with energy output so that as adults they may not face an obesity problem?
- Discuss the importance of including physical activity as routine programming in child care and educational institutions.

It is reported that families with young children are more frequently eating away from home and that this is often at a fast food restaurant.

- What are the usual menu choices for children and adults in these restaurants?
- Consider the amount of high fat foods available, the lack of fruit, vegetables, and milk as menu items, and the average total calorie count of fast food offerings.
- Could the accelerated use of fast food offerings be contributing to the increase of obesity in children and adults?

Simple Sugars

Simple sugars consist of one sugar unit that needs no further digestion prior to absorption. Examples of simple sugars are:

- glucose
- fructose
- galactose

Glucose is the form in which sugar is used by body cells. However, most glucose in the blood is a result of digestion of more complex carbohydrates (starches).

Fructose is present in honey and high-fructose corn syrup; it is sweeter than all other sugars. In some cases, smaller amounts of fructose may be used to give a desired degree of sweetness.

Galactose is not found free in foods. It results from the digestion of "milk sugar."

Compound Sugars

Compound sugars are made up of two simple sugars joined together. Compound sugars must be digested to their component simple sugars before they can be absorbed and utilized by the body. Two important examples of compound sugars are:

- sucrose
- lactose

In its refined form, sucrose is commonly known at table sugar. Sucrose is found in sugar beets and sugar cane and in fruits, vegetables, and honey. When sucrose occurs in fruits and vegetables, it is accompanied by other essential nutrients such as vitamins, minerals, and water

FIGURE 14–3

Sugar in fruits is accompanied by other essential nutrients.

(Figure 14–3). Refined sucrose, or table sugar, is the cause of concern in several aspects of health. Refined table sugar contributes no nutrients—only calories. For this reason, calories from table sugar are frequently called "empty calories." Eating too many empty calories can lead to obesity accompanied by a deficiency of some essential nutrients. Children who are allowed to eat too many foods containing refined sugar may not be hungry for more healthful foods containing the nutrients they need.

Refined sucrose has also been linked to tooth decay in children. Other important factors contributing to tooth decay are the stickiness of the food containing the sugar, the frequency of eating, the frequency of toothbrushing, whether the sugar is contained in a meal with other foods or in a snack, and whether the sugar-containing food is accompanied by a beverage.

Lactose is found in milk and is referred to as "milk sugar." It is the only carbohydrate found in an animal-source food. Lactose occurs in milk of mammals, including breast milk. It is the least sweet of all common sugars which explains why one cup of 2 percent milk with the equivalent of one tablespoon of sugar in the form of lactose does not taste sweet. It has advantages over other sugars in that lactose aids in establishing and maintaining beneficial intestinal bacteria. Calcium is more efficiently used by the body if lactose is also present. Fortunately, calcium and lactose occur in the same food—milk.

While usually a beneficial sugar, lactose can present problems to some individuals. Some persons do not produce the enzyme to break lactose down to its component simple sugars that can be absorbed. This lactose intolerance may cause intestinal discomfort, cramping, gas, and diarrhea. Often small amounts of milk (1–2 cups a day in small feedings) are tolerated. Dairy products such as yogurt and buttermilk are tolerated better than milk. Lactose intolerance is seen more frequently and severely in adults than in children.

Complex Carbohydrates

Complex carbohydrates are composed of many units of simple sugar joined together. Complex carbohydrates must be broken down to their component simple sugars before the body can absorb and use them. Digestion of only one complex carbohydrate can result in thousands of simple sugars. Complex carbohydrates that are important to human nutrition are:

- starch
- cellulose
- glycogen

Starches are the only digestible complex carbohydrates found in foods. They are found in large amounts in grains, legumes, root vegetables such as potatoes, breads, and cereals. When contained in these foods, starches are accompanied by vitamins and minerals that the body needs. Starches are desirable components of a healthful diet.

Cellulose is an indigestible complex carbohydrate. Because humans cannot digest cellulose, it cannot be absorbed and used by body cells. Cellulose, because it cannot be absorbed, is a good source of insoluble fiber that increases the rate of transit of food through the intestinal tract and increases the frequency of elimination of intestinal waste material. This action by cellulose results in decreased time for digestion and absorption of food components and cholesterol. Rapid transit of materials through the gastro-intestinal tract may reduce absorption of substances that could cause cancer formation. Cellulose is found in whole grains, nuts, fruits, and vegetables. It is also thought to provide some detergent effect to teeth, thus aiding good dental health.

Another complex carbohydrate of physiological importance is glycogen. Glycogen is often referred to as animal starch. It is the form in which carbohydrate is stored in the body for future conversion into sugar and subsequent use for performing body activity.

The use of artificial sweeteners to replace sugar as a means of reducing calorie intake has become a common practice. The four FDA-approved artificial sweeteners are saccharin, aspartame (Nutrasweet), acesulfame potassium (Sunett), and Sucralose (Splenda, approved in 1998). Used in moderation, these sweeteners are accepted as safe for adult consumption. The herbal sweetener Stevia has not received FDA approval but is currently being sold as a dietary supplement. Adequate evidence has not been received by the FDA to designate Stevia as a safe food additive (U.S. Food and Drug Administration, 1999). The use of the non-calorie artificial sweeteners in a child's diet is questionable because foods containing them are usually poor sources of needed nutrients. Also, most children have from birth a strong preference for a sweet taste that does not need to be enhanced by "fake" sweets. Children with phenylketonuria (PKU), a genetic disease characterized by an inability to properly metabolize the essential amino acid phenylalanine, must not use aspartame. It contains phenylalanine. Accumulation of this toxic substance may cause severe and irreversible brain damage.

FATS AS ENERGY SOURCES

For the past several decades, fats have been given much "bad press" and the food market has been deluged with low-fat and fat-free foods. Fat is a very essential nutrient for the young child. It is required for growth and production of body regulators as well as being the most concentrated dietary source of energy. The very young child has a small stomach capacity and cannot meet energy needs without fat.

Fats are the richest food source of energy, supplying nine calories per gram consumed. Foods in which fats are readily identified are butter, margarine, shortening, oils, and salad dressings. Less obvious sources of fats are meats, whole milk, egg yolks, nuts, and nut butters. Fruits and vegetables

REFLECTIVE THOUGHTS

Fat intake seems to be a prime dietary concern of most Americans, and yet American children have higher blood cholesterol levels than children anywhere else in the world. How can we reduce cholesterol, a fatlike substance found only with animal-source fats, without limiting food fat for children who still need more fat for growth and brain development?

The American Academy of Pediatrics (AAP) recommends that fat intake not be reduced before two years of age because infants and young children need 50 percent of their energy from fat to assure normal growth and brain development. After the child has reached age two, the AAP recommends a gradual decrease in fat to result in 30 percent of energy from fat by age four or five years. This fat reduction is particularly important for children in families with a history of early heart disease.

- Which of the Pyramid food groups would contribute the most animal fat and cholesterol?
- Which three food groups contribute little fat and no cholesterol?
- How could a green vegetable become a source of fat and cholesterol?

contain little fat; with the exception of the avocado, which is quite rich in fat. Bread and cereal products are naturally low in fat. However, the many baked goods such as cakes, pies, doughnuts, and cookies that use grain products are high in added fat. Some dietary fat is required for good health. Recommendations have been made to reduce average fat intake to about 30 percent of total calories. The American Academy of Pediatrics Nutrition Policy (Barnes, 1999) states that there should be no dietary fat restriction for children under two years of age. The 2000 *Dietary Guidelines for Americans* advises that after age two, children "should gradually adopt a diet that, by about five years of age contains no more than 30 percent of calories from fat." For a child requiring 1,600 calories, this means 480 calories or 50–55 grams of fat in the diet. This is equivalent to approximately four tablespoons of butter or oil.

Although they provide more than twice as much energy per gram as carbohydrates, fats are a less desirable energy source for children. Fats are harder to digest than carbohydrates and are accompanied by fewer essential nutrients. Fats should not be reduced below the level of providing 30 percent of calories because fats perform important functions for the child:

- allow normal growth and development of brain and nerve tissues
- provide the essential fatty acids (**linoleic** and **linolenic**)
- are carriers of the required fat-soluble vitamins
- allow infants and children with limited stomach capacity to meet their calorie needs

The practice of lowering a very young child's fat intake through the use of skim milk is not an acceptable safe choice. Most authorities believe that this practice may lead to insufficient calorie intake and essential fatty acid (EFA) deficiency. Infants or children (under two years of age) who consume the same amount or more of skim milk as they previously consumed of breast milk or formula will receive a higher and possibly excessive amount of protein and minerals. These excesses may require excretion of greater amounts of waste and minerals, which the child's kidneys may not be mature enough to handle (Williams & Caliendo, 1984). Children under two years of age should not be given skim milk in an effort to lower fat. Beyond two years

---

linoleic acid – *a polyunsaturated fatty acid, which is essential (must be provided in food) for humans.*
linolenic acid – *one of the two polyunsaturated fatty acids that are recognized as essential for humans.*

of age, low fat (2 percent) milk may be given and might be advised for a child if there is a high incidence of cardiovascular disease (CVD) among adult relatives.

Before fats present in foods can provide energy they must undergo digestion and absorption into the body. Digestion of dietary fats produces:

- fatty acids
- glycerol

The resulting fatty acids and glycerol can be absorbed for use by the body. Fatty acids in foods are either saturated or unsaturated.

Fats found in animal-source foods such as meat, milk, and eggs contain fatty acids that are saturated. Fats containing predominantly saturated fatty acids are solid at room temperature and are often accompanied by cholesterol. Cholesterol and saturated fats have been extensively investigated as undesirable dietary components. However, after years of study, few definite conclusions have been reached regarding the role of dietary cholesterol in cardiovascular disease or the advisability of lowering the saturated fatty acid and cholesterol intake of children. It is important to remember that cholesterol is found only in animal-source food fats. Do not equate high fat with high cholesterol. For example, coconut derives 83 percent of its calories from fat and 89 percent of its fatty acids are saturated, but it has no cholesterol.

Unsaturated fats are usually soft at room temperature or are in oil form. Monounsaturated fatty acids (MUFA), which have only one point of unsaturation, are currently being reported to be most effective in controlling the kind and amount of fat and cholesterol circulating in the blood. Thus olive oil and canola oil, high in MUFA, are recommended for use by CVD-prone persons.

Fats found in plant-source foods such as corn oil or sunflower oil contain mostly unsaturated fatty acids. Many plant oils are polyunsaturated, which means the fatty acids contain numerous unfilled attachment sites. Polyunsaturated fatty acids are often called **PUFAs**. Linoleic and linolenic acids are polyunsaturated fatty acids that are essential for all humans, but are needed in greater amounts for infants and children than for adults. These essential fatty acids cannot be produced by the body and so must be obtained from food sources. Plant-source foods are better sources of these essential fatty acids than animal-source foods and do not give cholesterol. Protein links with fat to produce lipoproteins, which are involved in the transport of fat and cholesterol in the blood. A high blood level of High Density Lipoproteins (HDLs), which have a high ratio of protein to fat, are currently considered to reduce the risk of cardiovascular disease. Physical exercise has been identified as the most effective way to increase HDL (good cholesterol) levels in blood.

PROTEINS AS ENERGY SOURCES

Proteins are the third class of nutrients that the body can use as an energy source. Proteins supply four calories per gram; the same amount of energy as that derived from carbohydrates. "Eating protein to meet energy needs . . . represents a waste like burning furniture for heat when firewood is available" (Longacre, 1976). Proteins must be digested to their component amino acids prior to absorption and utilization by the body.

Each protein is unique in the number, arrangement, and specific amino acids from which it is built. Since proteins (amino acids) function as materials to build body tissues and as regulators of body functions, they will be discussed in detail in subsequent chapters.

PUFAs – *polyunsaturated fatty acids; fatty acids that contain more than one bond that is not fully saturated with hydrogen.*

FOCUS ON FAMILIES • Healthy Families

Calculate and graph your child's Body Mass Index (BMI) using the following method: (Teachers can provide parents with a BMI table from the CDC Web site: www.cdc.gov)

Example: Height: 4 ft. 0 in.   Weight: 75 lbs.

1. Multiply weight (pounds) by 703. $75 \times 703 = 52,725$

2. Multiply height (inches) by 48 (inches) $48 \times 48 = 2,304$

3. Divide the answer in step 1 by the answer in step 2 $52,725/2,304 = 23$

The higher a child's BMI, the greater the risk for certain health related diseases. Regardless of where a child's BMI appears on the graph, all families should consider adopting the following lifestyle changes.

- Sit as a family at mealtime. All distractions such as televisions, video games, and computers should be turned off. Mealtime is the time to begin healthy, nonstressful conversations with your family.

- Use the Food Guide Pyramid to guide your food choices and to incorporate a wide variety of foods into your family's diet. Limit foods from the top of the pyramid, as they contain high amounts of sugar and fat.

- Encourage healthy snacking at planned times. Empty-calorie snacking throughout the day will cause a child to eat poorly at meals.

- Shop sensibly and avoid purchasing "junk" food. If those foods are readily available, it is difficult to engage in healthy snacking.

CASE STUDY

Terry, age five, has several decayed teeth. His dentist has suggested a program of good dental hygiene plus limiting his intake of refined sucrose.

Plan a day's diet for Terry that contains at least 150 grams of carbohydrates without any refined sucrose (table sugar). Use the following average amounts of carbohydrates:

bread, cereals, pastas	15 grams/slice or ounce
fruits and juices	10 grams/1/2 adult serving
starchy vegetables	10 grams/1/2 adult serving
milk	6 grams/1/2 cup

SUMMARY

- Energy is needed to do the work of the body, including internal involuntary activity and voluntary physical activity.
- A person's total energy need is a composite of (a) basal metabolic need, (b) voluntary physical activity, and (c) metabolism to release energy for activities (a) and (b) above.
- During periods of active growth, children need energy for the increase in body size.
- The nutrient classes that yield energy are carbohydrates (four calories/gram), proteins (four calories/gram), and fats (nine calories/gram).
- Carbohydrates come in different forms: simple sugars (glucose and fructose), compound sugars (sucrose and lactose), and complex carbohydrates (starch). Cellulose is a carbohydrate that does not give energy but is important as a source of fiber.
- The fatty acids of different fats may be saturated or unsaturated and all yield nine calories per gram.
- Two unsaturated fatty acids (linoleic and linolenic) are very important for children because they are essential for growth.
- Cholesterol (a fatlike substance) and saturated fats, if consumed in generous amounts, are believed to increase risk of cardiovascular disease.
- Proteins are inefficient sources of energy and are not usually burned for energy unless there are not enough carbohydrates and fats available to meet energy needs.

SUGGESTED ACTIVITIES

1. Using the cereal label in Figure 14–4, determine the following:
   a. the number of calories derived from carbohydrate
   b. the approximate percentage of total calories derived from sucrose and other sugars
2. Which of the nutrient contributions of this cereal are increased by the addition of milk?
3. a. Explain why cereal with milk has a higher carbohydrate value than cereal alone.
   b. Is this cereal predominantly starch or sucrose?
   c. Do starches and complex carbohydrates increase with the addition of milk?
4. Calculate the caloric requirement of a four-year-old child who weighs 42 pounds.
5. Determine the number of calories in a serving of food that contributes the following:

   carbohydrate—12 grams

   protein—8 grams

   fat—10 grams

FIGURE 14–4

Cereal label.

Nutrition Facts

Serving Size 3/4 cup (30g)
Servings Per Container about 15

Amount Per Serving	Cereal	Cereal with 1/2 cup Skim Milk
Calories	100	140
Calories from Fat	5	5

	% Daily Value**	
Total Fat 0.5g*	**1**%	**1**%
Saturated Fat 0g	**0**%	**0**%
Polyunsaturated Fat 0g		
Monounsaturated Fat 0g		
Cholesterol 0mg	**0**%	**0**%
Sodium 220mg	**9**%	**12**%
Potassium 190mg	5%	**11**%
Total Carbohydrate 24g	**8**%	**10**%
Dietary Fiber 5g	**21**%	**21**%
Soluble Fiber 1g		
Insoluble Fiber 4g		
Sugars 6g		
Other Carbohydrate 13g		
Protein 3g		

Vitamin A	15%	20%
Vitamin C	0%	2%
Calcium	0%	15%
Iron	45%	45%
Vitamin D	10%	25%
Thiamin	25%	30%
Riboflavin	25%	35%
Niacin	25%	25%
Vitamin B6	25%	25%
Folate	25%	25%
Vitamin B12	25%	35%
Phosphorus	15%	25%
Magnesium	15%	20%
Zinc	10%	15%
Copper	10%	10%

*Amount in Cereal. One half cup skim milk contributes an additional 40 calories, 65mg sodium, 200mg potassium, 6g total carbohydrate (6g sugars), and 4g protein.

**Percent Daily Values are based on a 2,000 calorie diet. Your daily values may be higher or lower depending on your calorie needs:

	Calories:	2,000	2,500
Total Fat	Less than	65g	80g
Saturated Fat	Less than	20g	25g
Cholesterol	Less than	300mg	300mg
Sodium	Less than	2,400mg	2,400mg
Potassium		3,500mg	3,500mg
Total Carbohydrate		300g	375g
Dietary Fiber		25g	30g

CHAPTER REVIEW

A. Match the terms in column II to the correct phrase in column I.

Column I

1. a simple sugar

2. digestible complex carbohydrate

3. found in meats, dairy products, legumes, and eggs

4. building blocks of proteins

5. found in grains, fruits, vegetables, and milk products

6. richest source of energy

7. indigestible complex carbohydrate

8. table sugar (complex sugar)

Column II

a. amino acids
b. cellulose
c. protein
d. carbohydrate
e. glucose
f. fats
g. starch
h. sucrose

REFERENCES

Alford, B., & Bogle, M. L. (1982). *Nutrition during the life cycle.* Englewood Cliffs, NJ: Prentice Hall, Inc.

Barnes, L. (Ed.). (1999). *Pediatric nutrition handbook.* Elm Grove, IL: American Academy of Pediatrics.

Longacre, D. J. (1976). *More-with-less cookbook.* Scottsdale, PA: Herald Press.

Twin Cities District Dietetic Association. (1990). *Manual of pediatric nutrition.* St. Paul, MN: Author.

U.S. Department of Health and Human Services and U.S. Department of Agriculture. (2000). *Dietary guidelines for Americans.* Washington, DC: Authors.

U.S. Food and Drug Administration (1999). Sugar substitutes: Americans opt for sweetness and lite. *FDA Consumer.* College Park, MD: Author.

Williams, E. R., & Caliendo, M. A. (1984). *Nutrition: Principles, issues and applications.* New York: McGraw Hill Book Company.

ADDITIONAL READING

Christian, J. L., & Geiger, J. L. (1988). *Nutrition for living.* Menlo Park, CA: Benjamin/ Cummings Publishing Co.

Cryon, J., & Johns, R. K. (1997). Should the current recommendations for energy in infants and children be lowered? *Nutrition Today, 32,* 69–74.

Dietz, W., & Stern, L. (1999). *Guide to your child's nutrition.* New York: Random House, Inc.

Dwyer, J., & Johns, R. K. (1998). Predictors of overweight or overfatness in a multiethnic pediatric population. *American Journal of Clinical Nutrition, 67,* 602–610.

Forman, A. K. (1998, September). Environmental nutrition position on sugar substitutes. *Environmental Nutrition Publications, 22,* 1–3.

Garrison, R., & Sumer, E. (1995). *The nutrition desk reference.* New Canaan, CT: Keats Publishing, Inc.

Hamilton, E. M. N., Whitney, E. N., & Sizer, F. S. (2000). *Nutrition: Concepts and controversies* (2nd ed.). St. Paul, MN: West Publishing Co.

Hegarty, V. (1988). *Decisions in nutrition.* St. Louis, MO: C. V. Mosby Co.

Hill, J. O., & Trowbridge, F. L. (1998, March, Supplement). The cause and health consequences of obesity in children. *Pediatrics, 101,* 497–574.

Manhan, L. K., & Arlin, M. (2000). *Krause's food, nutrition, and diet therapy.* Philadelphia: W. B. Saunders Co.

Ronzio, R. A. (1997). *The encyclopedia of nutrition and good health.* New York: Random House, Inc.

Satter, E. (1987). *How to get your kid to eat . . . But not too much.* Palo Alto, CA: Bull Publishing Company.

Tamborlane, W. (1997). *The Yale guide to children's nutrition.* New Haven, CT: Yale University Press.

Wardlaw, G. W., & Insel, P. M. (2000). *Perspectives in nutrition* (6th ed.). New York: McGraw-Hill.

HELPFUL WEB SITES

Center for Science in Public Interest (CSPI)	http://www.cspinet.org
Nutrition Health Reports	http://www.nutritionhealthreports.com
Women, Infants, and Children (WIC)	http://www.fns.usda.gov/wic/
WebMD	http://www.webmd.com

For additional health, safety, and nutrition resources, go to
http://www.EarlyChildEd.delmar.com

CHAPTER 15

Nutrients That Promote Growth of Body Tissues
(Proteins, Minerals, and Water)

OBJECTIVES

After studying this chapter, you should be able to:

- State how growth occurs.
- Name three classes of nutrients that promote growth of body tissue and list food sources for each.
- Describe the role that proteins, minerals, and water play in body growth.
- Differentiate between nonessential and essential amino acids.
- Identify food sources for complete protein and for incomplete protein.
- Identify examples of complementary incomplete protein combinations.

TERMS TO KNOW

amino acids
complete protein
incomplete proteins

complementary proteins
supplementary proteins
minerals

collagen
hemoglobin
iron-deficiency anemia

Growth may be defined as an increase in physical size of either the entire body or of any body part. Growth may occur by (1) an increase in the number of cells, or by (2) an increase in the size of individual cells. At various stages of the child's life, either or both types of growth may be occurring. Young children do not grow at a steady rate. They will grow linearly for a period of time and then stop and just gain weight for a while. Their appetite and their need for nutrients is greatest during their linear growth phase. Failure to meet nutrient needs for growth may result in a small-for-age child, with decreased resistance to disease, poor utilization of food eaten, and delays in expected physical and mental behavior.

Infancy and early childhood are periods of rapid growth (Figure 15–1). During the first six months of life, infants can be expected to approximately double their birth weight. By the end of the first year, their birth length should have increased by 50 percent. Birth weight and length are the baselines for evaluating infant growth. Head circumference is another measure used to evaluate growth and development of a child.

FIGURE 15–1

Infancy is a period of rapid growth.

PROTEINS FOR GROWTH

Proteins play an important role in growth. Protein is the material from which all body cells are built. Approximately 15 percent of body weight is protein. Examples of types of body tissues that consist of large amounts of protein are muscles, glands, organs, bones, blood, and skin.

Proteins are composed of hundreds of individual units called **amino acids**. The human body is able to manufacture some of the amino acids needed to build proteins; these amino acids are termed nonessential amino acids. Amino acids that the body cannot manufacture in needed amounts must be provided by proteins in foods; these amino acids are termed essential amino acids.

When all essential amino acids occur in adequate amounts in food protein, that protein is said to be a **complete protein**. Complete proteins occur in animal-source foods such as meats, milk, eggs, and cheese.

Incomplete proteins are those that lack adequate amounts of one or more essential amino acids. Proteins from plant sources such as grains, legumes, and vegetables are incomplete proteins. One exception is the soybean, which supplies adequate amino acids to support growth in young children. However, soybean consumption in large amounts can decrease iron absorption. Gelatin, an animal-source food, is also an incomplete protein.

---

amino acids – *the organic building blocks from which proteins are made.*

complete protein – *protein that contains all essential amino acids in amounts relative to the amounts needed to support growth.*

incomplete proteins – *proteins that lack required amounts of one or more essential amino acids.*

Complete protein intake may be achieved by combining two or more complementary incomplete proteins. A food that supplies an amino acid that is absent or in low quantities in another food is said to complement that food. For example, wheat, which is deficient in lysine, may be combined with peanuts, which contain adequate amounts of lysine but lack another essential amino acid provided by wheat (Vyhmeister, 1984). The resulting combination of wheat and peanuts contains all the essential amino acids and is equivalent to a complete protein. The wheat-peanut combination could be served as a peanut butter sandwich. Plant proteins tend to be less costly than complete animal proteins.

Rapidly growing children need some complete protein or equivalent combinations daily to support that growth. A greater amount of incomplete protein is needed to achieve the equivalent of a complete protein (Lappe, 1975). For instance, one cup of beans is required to complement 2 2/3 cups of rice (Longacre, 1976).

Small children may not have enough stomach capacity to hold the larger amounts of food they must eat to meet their protein needs solely from incomplete protein. Children on such diets grow and thrive but are often small for their age (Mahan & Arlin, 1992). Free amino acids resulting from digestion of food protein must be used within a short time, as they are not stored for future use. All essential amino acids must be provided several times each day. Therefore, the more efficient complete proteins are better able to support rapid growth.

Many favorite dishes are good examples of combinations of proteins that result in the equivalent of a complete protein. Foods may be combined in either of two ways to obtain adequate protein for less money than by using the more costly complete protein sources:

- **complementary proteins**—incomplete protein combined with another incomplete protein to equal complete protein.
  Examples: peanut butter sandwich, beans and rice, chili, peas and rice, macaroni salad with peas, lentil soup with crackers, navy beans with cornbread, baked beans and brown bread
- **supplementary proteins**—incomplete protein combined with a small amount of complete protein to equal complete protein.
  Examples: macaroni and cheese, rice pudding, cheese sandwich, cheese pizza, cereal and milk

Protein Requirements

The total amount of protein needed daily is based on desirable body weight. An infant's requirements for protein and other nutrients are shown in Table 13–2. Due to the infant's extremely rapid rate of growth, nutrient needs are greater in relation to size during infancy than at any other period of life.

Growing children need more protein per pound than adults. A four- to six-year-old child needs approximately 2/3 of a gram of protein for each pound of body weight. Thus, a child weighing 45 pounds needs 30 grams of protein each day. To be meaningful, these figures must be considered in terms of amounts of food. The following selection of foods provides slightly more than the 30 grams of protein recommended for a four-year-old child.

Food	Protein
2 cups of milk	16 grams
1 1/2 slices bread	3 grams
2 ounces meat or meat alternate	14 grams
	TOTAL 33 grams

complementary proteins – *proteins with offsetting missing amino acids; complementary proteins can be combined to provide complete protein.*

supplementary proteins – *a complete protein mix resulting from combining a small amount of a complete protein with an incomplete protein to provide all essential amino acids.*

TABLE 15–1 Menu Supplying Recommended Daily Allowances of Protein for Four- to Six-Year-Olds

Breakfast	Grams of Protein
1/2 c fruit juice	trace
1/2 c dry oat cereal	1
1/2 c milk*	4
1/2 banana	trace
Midmorning Snack	
1/2 c milk*	4
1/2 slice buttered toast	1
Lunch	
1/2 peanut butter and jelly sandwich (1 slice bread, 1/2 tablespoon peanut butter, 1/2 tablespoon jelly)+	4
carrot sticks	1
1/2 apple	trace
1/2 c milk*	4
Midafternoon Snack	
1/2 c fruit juice	trace
2 rye crackers	1
Dinner	
1 chicken leg (1 oz)*	6
1/4 c rice	1
1/4 c broccoli	trace
1/4 c strawberries	trace
1/2 c milk*	4
TOTAL:	**31 grams of protein**

*Complete protein
+ Complementary proteins

Table 15–1 shows a menu for one day that would provide the daily recommended amount of protein for a four- to six-year-old child.

MINERALS FOR GROWTH

Minerals are inorganic elements that help to regulate body functions and build body tissue. The following discussion deals with minerals that help to build body tissue. The regulatory functions performed by minerals will be covered in Chapter 16. (Check Table 16–4, the mineral summary, for more information on minerals.)

Minerals provide no energy. They are required in far smaller amounts than are energy-producing nutrients. For example, the RDA for protein is 19 grams for a four-year-old child; this amount is slightly more than two and one-half servings of meat. In contrast, the RDA for calcium for that same child is 0.8 gram. Other minerals are required in even smaller amounts.

---

minerals – *inorganic chemical elements that are required in the diet to support growth and repair tissue and to regulate body functions.*

Growth involves creating increased amounts of body tissue, which requires attention to receiving adequate amounts of specific minerals. Two types of body tissues most dependent on minerals for growth are bones and teeth, and blood.

Building Bones and Teeth

Calcium and phosphorus are the major minerals found in bones and teeth (Figure 15–2). Bones are formed by the deposition of phosphorus and calcium crystals on **collagen**, a flexible protein base composed of amino acids. Young children's bones are soft and pliable; as growth occurs, the amount of calcium and phosphorus deposited in their bones increases, resulting in larger, harder bones. While bones appear to be solid and unchanging, calcium and phosphorus are replaced on a regular basis. The calcium content of adult bone is thought to be replaced every five years. Children need calcium not only for bone growth but also for replacement of existing bone. Adults need calcium only for replacement. Other minerals are also needed for normal bone and tooth formation, but they are rarely limiting factors in the development of these tissues.

Sources of Calcium.   Milk and milk products are the major food source of calcium. With the exception of the vegetables broccoli, collard greens, kale, and Chinese cabbage or the soy products tofu and miso, there are no good food sources of calcium other than milk and products made from it. A one-cup serving of the above vegetables and soy products will only provide about one-half the amount of calcium available in one cup of milk. Milk, cheese, and yogurt are excellent sources of calcium. Custards, pudding, and ice cream provide calcium, but they also contain varying amounts of added sugar and fat, which reduce their nutrient density relative to calcium.

The calcium content of many dishes may be increased by the addition of nonfat dry milk. The addition of nonfat dry milk to casseroles, cooked cereals, breads, and ground meat dishes not only

FIGURE 15–2

Calcium and phosphorus are needed for strong teeth and bones.

---

collagen – *a protein that forms the major constituent of connective tissue, cartilage, bone, and skin.*

ISSUES TO CONSIDER • Nutrient-fortified Foods

Tufts University Health and Nutrition Letter poses two interesting questions in the February 2000 issue: "Too many calcium-fortified foods?" "Has the calcium craze gone too far?" Our common current concern with not meeting our calcium needs makes us vulnerable to advertisements of extra calcium sources. As yet, the answer to the two questions above is "no," but this could change if food industry competition in this area increases. Already one bakery is making a claim that its bread is better than another because two slices of its bread have the same amount of calcium as one glass of milk. Several fruit juices have calcium added at a level making them a source of calcium equal to milk.

- Does this mean that these fortified products can be substituted for milk?
- Do these fortified foods give us the protein and vitamins A and D that milk does?

The upper, adult tolerable level for calcium intake is 2,500 milligrams per day. An amount above this limit may increase the risk for kidney stone formation. Children's smaller bodies may reduce their tolerance level.

- Is there a need for regulation of the kinds and amounts of nutrients used to fortify foods?
- What foods might be fortified with the least danger of exceeding tolerance levels?

increases the amount of calcium and protein in those dishes but also improves the quality of the incomplete proteins in pastas, cereals, or flours. Calcium is added to some brands of orange juice. This is a good combination; the vitamin C of the orange juice will increase the absorption of the calcium.

Sources of Phosphorus.
Phosphorus is also found in milk and milk-containing foods as well as other high-protein and whole grain foods. Good sources of phosphorus are milk, meats, fish, eggs, and grain products. Calcium and phosphorus occur in approximately equal amounts in milk. It is easier to obtain phosphorus than calcium, since it occurs in more kinds of foods. The balance between calcium and phosphorus may be upset if a child is permitted to drink large amounts of carbonated beverages that contain phosphorus. If the child drinks more carbonated beverages than milk, phosphorus in the diet outweighs calcium and calcium absorption may be impaired. This could result in reduced deposition of calcium in the bones and, in extreme cases, withdrawal of calcium from the bones. When carbonated beverages are substituted for milk as a child's beverage, the potential calcium available for consumption is further reduced.

The Role of Fluoride.
Fluoride should be considered in connection with bone and tooth formation. Many communities add fluoride to the community water supply in an effort to reduce tooth decay in children. Fluoride-containing toothpastes are also recommended for use by children. Fluoride incorporated into a growing tooth from drinking water makes the tooth harder and more resistant to decay. Fluoride applied to the exterior surface of the tooth is less effective in hardening of the tooth, but it is also thought to reduce the incidence of decay. Excess amount of fluoride may cause mottling and brown-staining of the teeth. Children who are drinking fluoridated water should be taught not to swallow toothpaste after brushing to prevent possible excess consumption that could result in discoloration of teeth.

The most consistent source of fluoride is the local water supply, either as naturally occurring fluorine or as fluoride added to a level of one p.p.m. (one part fluoride per million parts of water). Food sources of fluoride are variable and depend on the fluorine content of the soil where grown.

Building Blood

Iron is a mineral that is essential to the formation of hemoglobin. **Hemoglobin** is the iron-containing protein in red blood cells that carries oxygen to the cells and removes waste (carbon dioxide) from the cells. Normal growth depends on a healthy blood supply to nourish an increasing number of cells. Iron plays an important role in the formation of healthy blood.

Iron-deficiency anemia is often found in children two to three years of age. Iron-deficiency anemia is characterized by low levels of hemoglobin in red blood cells, which results in the cells' reduced ability to carry oxygen to tissues. The end result is reduced growth rate, fatigue, lack of energy, possible reduction in learning ability, and reduced resistance to infections.

Sources of Iron. The Meat, Poultry, Fish, Dry Beans, Eggs, and Nuts Group and the iron fortified Bread, Cereal, Rice, and Pasta Group are the best sources of iron. Liver is an especially rich source of iron. It is not a well-accepted food by adults or children; however this does not mean that liver should never be included in meal plans. Milk, which is usually a major part of the diet of young children, contains very little iron. A child who drinks large amounts of milk to the exclusion of iron-containing foods may not receive enough iron to support a growing blood supply.

Studies of the nutritional status of preschool children have repeatedly indicated that neither calcium nor iron is received in adequate amounts. There may be several reasons for this. One reason may be that neither calcium nor iron are widely distributed in foods. Also, many factors affect the absorption of calcium and iron. Therefore, the presence of either mineral in foods does not always assure that the mineral will be absorbed for use by body cells. Another factor may be that many foods containing calcium or iron are expensive.

Factors That Affect Absorption of Calcium and Iron

Calcium	Factor	Iron
↑	Adequate Vitamin C	↑
↑	Increased Need	↑
↓	Large Dose	↓
↓	Fiber (bulk) in Diet	↓
↓	High Protein Level	↑

Factors that *increase* the absorption of calcium and iron:

- Vitamin C aids in keeping calcium and iron more soluble and, therefore, more readily absorbed by the body.
- Vitamin C maximizes the absorption of iron in foods in the same meal.
- In cases where need is increased, inadequate intake or rapid growth-absorption of calcium and iron is increased.

Factors that *decrease* the absorption of calcium and iron:

- Large single doses of calcium and iron are not as well-absorbed as several smaller doses.
- Large amounts of fiber in the diet speed intestinal movement, decreasing the time calcium and iron are in contact with absorption surfaces.

Proteins aid the overall absorption of iron; the iron in meats (known as heme iron) is more readily absorbed than the iron in grains and other nonmeat foods. In addition to the minerals

---

hemoglobin – *the iron-containing, oxygen-carrying pigment in red blood cells.*
iron-deficiency anemia – *a failure in the oxygen transport system caused by too little iron.*

calcium, phosphorus, and iron there are "trace" minerals that are critical for growth. The required amounts of these minerals are small and are met with the average diet. Zinc and selenium are two of these minerals that are currently getting attention via TV, newspapers, and magazines.

THE ROLE OF WATER

Water is an important constituent of all body tissues. Approximately 60 percent of normal adult body weight is water; an infant's body weight is nearly 75 percent water. A gradual decline in water content occurs throughout the life cycle. Need for water is affected by body surface area, environmental temperature, and activity. Water is essential for survival; humans can survive much longer without food than they can without water. Water is supplied to the body through drinking water and other beverages, solid foods, and water that results from energy metabolism.

Vomiting and diarrhea cause excess loss of water that can very rapidly cause dehydration. This is especially threatening to infants, toddlers, and small children, since the amount of water loss necessary to produce dehydration is small in comparison to that of an adult.

Children experience more rapid loss of water through evaporation and dehydration than do adults. Since children are busily involved in other activities, they may need reminders to drink fluids (Figure 15–3). This is important at any time but especially in hot weather. Both

FIGURE 15–3

Young children absorbed in play may need to be reminded to drink fluids.

children and adults should be encouraged to drink water rather than sugared beverages, since the presence of sugar is known to slow the absorption of water (DeVries, 1980). Many children request fruit juice instead of water to drink. This practice should be discouraged. While nutritious juices can contribute to a healthy diet in children, excess intake of juices can lead to a number of problems:

- stunted growth. Toddlers who fill up on fruit juice may not get the fuel they need to grow. They will have less room for milk and other foods that are richer in calories and other important nutrients, including protein and fat, which should not be restricted in very young children.
- Diarrhea. Too much fluid in itself can cause loose stools. Some juices, notably apple juice, also contain sorbitol, a natural sugar that can be difficult to digest in large quantities, compounding that effect. Most children who drink a lot of juice experience only loose stools; some develop diarrhea.
- Tooth decay. Toddlers sometimes use a bottle more for comfort than nourishment or refreshment. Overreliance on a bottle, especially as a way to fall asleep, can lead to nursing-bottle caries—dental decay resulting from prolonged exposure to sugars, in juice or in milk (Consumers Union, September 1995).

THE ROLE OF VITAMINS

Vitamins are not structural parts of growing tissue; however, some of them play critical roles in the use of minerals and proteins as building material for the body. For example, bones could not be properly formed or maintained without vitamins A, D, and C, and blood components could not be produced without vitamins C, B_6, B_{12}, and folic acid. (See Chapter 16, Table 16–1.) Vitamins, although not structural parts of any of the growth products, are essential for cell division for new cells and for increase in mass of all cells.

REFLECTIVE THOUGHTS

Single nutrients are often discussed as if functioning alone. Actually a single nutrient can rarely complete any function alone. A look at the critical needs of an actively growing child shows many nutrient dependencies. A protein deficiency is often looked upon as the only cause of retarded growth in children in some poor, underdeveloped countries. If that is true, how can their protein deficiency and growth retardation be so easily corrected by feeding the children generous amounts of flour and sugar? When a child is provided with sufficient energy, the small amounts protein in their diet can be used for growth.

- How does vitamin C help maximize the availability of calcium from food sources?
- Why is growth depressed when a diet has adequate protein but lacks folic acid or vitamin B_{12}?
- Lack of a single vitamin can keep carbohydrates from yielding energy. Explain how this can happen.
- How is calcium dependent upon vitamin D?
- Make a list of as many nutrient interdependencies that you can.

FOCUS ON FAMILIES • Nutrients That Promote Growth

Calcium is a major mineral found in bones and teeth and is needed in the diet to support normal bone formation. Children ages one through eight require 500 to 800 mg of calcium daily to meet nutritional needs. Teachers can support calcium intake by regularly including calcium-rich foods into meal patterns and by encouraging parents to provide these foods in the child's diet at home. Some excellent sources of calcium are:

Milk Group:	Serving Size	Calcium (mg)
yogurt	1 cup	452
cheese (cheddar, Swiss)	1 ½ oz.	300–400
milk	8 oz.	300
calcium-fortified orange juice	8 oz.	300
lasagna	1 cup	286
calcium-fortified cereal	1 cup	250
cheese pizza	1 slice	220
string cheese	1 ounce (1 slice)	214
cheeseburger	1	182
macaroni and cheese	½ cup	180

CASE STUDY

The following chart shows a fairly typical daily intake for Timothy, age four and a half. Consider this daily pattern in terms of balance between calcium and phosphorus.

Breakfast:
    1 slice of toast
    1 scrambled egg
    1/2 cup orange juice

Midmorning Snack:
    2 graham crackers (milk offered but refused)

Lunch:
    2 fish sticks
    1/4 cup peas
    1/2 slice bread
    water (milk offered but refused)

Midafternoon Snack:
    1 small soft drink

Dinner:
    hamburger
    french fries
    1 small soft drink

1. What foods provide calcium?
2. What foods provide phosphorus?
3. Change the menu to eliminate the phosphorus/calcium imbalance.

SUMMARY

- Growth is an increase in size of the entire body or any part of the body.

- Growth occurs first by an increase in the number of cells. This type of growth has a definite time schedule for each organ and a lack of nutrient during this time schedule cannot be corrected later.

- Growth by an increase in the size of cells continues during most of the total growth period. Deficiency of nutrients during this period may be reversed later.

- The nutrients most needed during the growth periods are protein, minerals, and water. Proteins are components of all living cells; the amino acids that they provide are critically needed for synthesis of specific cellular proteins.

- The best sources of protein that provide all of the amino acids required for growth are meat, fish, poultry, and dairy products.

- Calcium and phosphorus, major components of bones and teeth, crystallize upon a protein base. As they are deposited, the bones and teeth harden.

- Calcium is found primarily in dairy products while phosphorus is found in milk and in meats, grains, beans, nuts, and cereal products.

- Iron is a part of hemoglobin, a protein found in red blood cells that is necessary for the carrying of oxygen to all body cells.

- Best food sources of iron are red meats and iron-fortified breads and cereals.

- Many factors can interfere with the absorption of both calcium and iron.

- The limited sources of iron and calcium and their absorption problems means that special attention must be given to food choices to assure that adequate amounts of these minerals are provided for the growing child.

- Water is a major constituent of all living body cells; 60 to 75 percent of total body weight is water. Water need is first in line for survival of body cells. During active growth periods, water is a most critical need.

SUGGESTED ACTIVITIES

1. Compare nutrition information labels from prepared cereals. Common iron content levels are 98 percent Daily Value, 45 percent Daily Value, and 25 percent Daily Value. After reviewing the "Factors that Affect Absorption of Calcium and Iron," discuss which cereal(s) would be the wisest choice in terms of iron absorption. What other step(s) could be taken to increase the absorption of the iron available in the cereal?

2. Explain why early childhood is a time of risk for iron-deficiency anemia. Consider factors such as food groups in which iron occurs, typical food preferences, and relative ease of eating various foods.

3. Determine the amount of protein recommended for a child who weighs 42 pounds.

CHAPTER REVIEW

A. **Match the terms in column II with the definition in column I. Use each term in column II only once.**

Column I

1. an essential amino acid

2. a nutrient class that functions both to build tissues and provide energy

3. the mineral component of hemoglobin

4. the mineral that is a major component of bones and teeth

5. the food group that provides the greatest amounts of calcium

6. the food group that provides the greatest amounts of iron

7. a nutrient class that helps to regulate body processes and also helps to build body tissue

8. comprises approximately 60 percent of normal adult body weight

Column II

a. calcium
b. Milk, Yogurt, and Cheese Group
c. iron
d. Meat, Poultry, Fish, Dry Beans, Eggs, and Nuts Group
e. lysine
f. minerals
g. protein
h. water

REFERENCES

Consumers Union. (1995, September). *Consumer reports on health.* Yonkers, NY: Author.

Dennison, B. A., Rockwell, H. L., & Baker, S. L. (1997). Excessive fruit juice consumption by preschool-aged children is associated with short stature and obesity. *Pediatrics, 99,* 15–22.

DeVries, H. A. (1980). *Physiology of exercise for education and athletics.* (3rd ed.). Dubuque, IA: William C. Brown Company.

Lappe, F. M. (1975). *Diet for a small planet.* (Revised ed.). New York: Ballantine.

Longacre, D. J. (1976). *More-with-less cookbook.* Scottsdale, PA: Herold Press.

Mahan, L. K., & Arlin, M. (1992). *Krause's food, nutrition, and diet therapy.* Philadelphia: W. B. Saunders Co.

U.S. Department of Health and Human Services and U.S. Department of Agriculture. (2000). *Dietary Guidelines for Americans.* Washington, DC: Authors.

Vyhmeister, I. B. (1984). Vegetarian diets—issues and concerns. *Nutrition and the MD, May.*

ADDITIONAL READING

American Dietetic Association. (1995). ADA's child nutrition and health campaign. *Journal of the American Dietetic Association, 95,* 1121–1149.

Barnes, L. (Ed.). (1999). *Pediatric nutrition handbook.* Elm Grove, IL: American Academy of Pediatrics.

Gershoff, S., & Whitney, C. (1990). *The Tufts University guide to total nutrition.* New York: Harper Roe Publishers.

Ronzio, R. A. (1997). *The encyclopedia of nutrition and health.* New York: Facts on File.

Schard, T. D. (1998, December). Magnesium special feature. *Nutrition Action Health Letter.* Washington, DC: Centre for Science in the Public Interest.

Tufts University. (2000). *Tufts University Health and Nutrition Letter 2000, 17,* 1.

Williams, S. R., & Worthington-Roberts, B. S. (1988). *Nutrition throughout the life cycle.* St. Louis, MO: Times Mirror/Mosby College Publishing.

HELPFUL WEB SITES

American Academy of Pediatrics   http://www.aap.org

National Association for the Education   http://www.NAEYC.org
of Young Children (NAEYC)

Tufts University Nutrition Navigator   http://navigator.tufts.edu/

For additional health, safety, and nutrition resources, go to
http://www.EarlyChildEd.delmar.com

CHAPTER 16

Nutrients That Regulate Body Functions

(Proteins, Minerals, Water, and Vitamins)

OBJECTIVES

After studying this chapter, you should be able to:

- Name general types of body functions regulated by nutrients.
- Identify nutrients that perform regulatory functions in the body.
- List at least one specific function performed by each of the four nutrient classes identified as regulators.

TERMS TO KNOW

milligram (mg)
microgram (mcg)
neuromuscular
megadose
macrocytic anemia

toxicity
synthesis
DNA
RNA
catalyzes (catalyst)

microcytic anemia
coenzymes
adenosine triphosphate
 (ATP)
hormones

Energy cannot be produced or released from carbohydrates, proteins, and fats without specific nutrients catalyzing sequential steps. New tissues such as bone, blood, or muscles cannot be formed unless specific vitamins, minerals, and proteins are available for their specific functions in each of these processes. Nerve impulses will not travel from one nerve cell to another, nor will muscles contract, unless the required nutrients are available in adequate amounts at the appropriate times. Some body functions may be regulated by one or two nutrients in one or two reactions. Many other functions involve intricate sequences of reactions that require many nutrients. All body functions are subject to regulation by nutrients.

Regulation of body functions is an extremely complex process. While much has been learned about the role of nutrients in regulation, there is still much that is unknown. It is important to remember that nutrients and functions are intricately interrelated. No single nutrient can function alone; thus regulation of body functions depends on many nutrients. This unit briefly discusses four nutrient classes involved in regulating body functions:

- vitamins
- minerals
- proteins
- water

Protein has been discussed earlier in terms of both energy and growth. Minerals and water were introduced as tissue-building nutrients and will now be considered as regulatory nutrients. Vitamins are able to perform only regulatory functions. They do not yield energy directly, nor do they become part of body structure. However, no energy can be released or any tissue built without benefit of the specific regulatory activities performed by vitamins.

Vitamins and minerals are needed in extremely small amounts. In Chapter 13, Tables 13–2, you will find that their RDAs are in **milligrams (mg)**, which are one-thousandth of a gram and in **micrograms (mcg)**, which are one-millionth of a gram. One standard size metal paper clip weighs approximately one gram. Imagine that you smash that paper clip into 1,000 pieces or 1,000,000 pieces and try to envision one milligram or one microgram. Would you expect to see a particle that was one microgram in size?

The regulatory functions discussed in this chapter are crucial to the normal growth and development of young children (Table 16–1 and Table 16–4). Generally these functions are:

- energy metabolism
- cellular reproduction and growth
- bone growth
- **neuromuscular** development and function
- blood composition control

Other functions are also crucial to normal development. However, these functions were chosen because of their critical relationship to normal growth, learning, and general good health of infants, toddlers, and young children.

VITAMINS AS REGULATORS

Vitamins are needed in extremely small amounts, but they are essential for normal body function. Each vitamin plays a specific role in a variety of body activities (Table 16–1). Vitamins frequently depend upon one another to perform their functions. For example, the vitamins thiamin and niacin are both needed as crucial coenzymes for the release of energy, but thiamin cannot function in the place of niacin, nor can niacin function in the absence of thiamin's action in a prior step. Study Table 16–1 and note that most vitamins are involved in several different functions; vitamin E has only one general function, but this function is performed in almost every cell in the body.

Vitamins are needed and used in specific amounts. Large excesses do not serve any useful function and in some instances are known to be harmful. Toxic effects have long been known for excesses of vitamin A and vitamin D. Recent research has described neurological damage resulting from large amounts of vitamin B_6 and kidney stone formation and destruction of vitamin B_{12} stores as a result of **megadose** of vitamin C (ascorbic acid). Megadoses are usually defined as 10 times the recommended daily amount for an adult. There is not enough information to define

milligram (mg) – *a metric unit of measurement; one milligram equals one-thousandth of a gram.*
microgram (mcg) – *a metric unit of measurement; one microgram equals one-millionth of a gram.*
neuromuscular – *pertaining to control of muscular function by the nervous system.*
megadose – *an amount of a vitamin or mineral at least 10 times that of RDA.*

TABLE 16-1 Vitamin Summary

VITAMIN	FUNCTIONS	SOURCES	DEFICIENCY SYMPTOMS	TOXICITY SYMPTOMS
Fat-soluble Vitamins vitamin A	maintenance of: • remodeling of bones • all cell membranes • epithelial cells; skin • mucous membranes, glands regulation of vision in dim light	liver, whole milk, butter, fortified margarine, orange and dark green vegetables, orange fruits (apricots, nectarines, peaches)	depressed bone and tooth formation, lack of visual acuity, dry epithelial tissue, increased frequency of infections related to epithelial cell vulnerability	headaches, nausea, vomiting, fragile bones, loss of hair, dry skin infant: hydrocephalus, hyperirritability
vitamin D	regulates calcium/phosphorus absorption mineralization of bone	vitamin D fortified milk, exposure of skin to sunlight	rickets (soft, easily bent bones), bone deformities	elevated blood calcium; deposition of calcium in soft tissues resulting in cerebral, renal, and cardiovascular damage (Dubick & Rucker, 1983)
vitamin E	antioxidant	vegetable oils, wheat germ, egg yolk, leafy vegetables, legumes, margarine	red blood cell destruction; creatinuria	fatigue, skin rash, abdominal discomfort
vitamin K	normal blood coagulation	leafy vegetables, vegetable oils, liver, pork; synthesis by intestinal bacteria	hemorrhage	none reported for naturally occurring vitamin K
Water-soluble Vitamins vitamin C (ascorbic acid)	formation of collagen for: • bones/teeth • intercellular cement • wound healing aid to calcium/iron absorption conversion of folacin to active form neurotransmitter synthesis	citrus fruits, strawberries, melons, cabbage, peppers, greens, tomatoes	poor wound healing, bleeding gums, pinpoint hemorrhages, sore joints, scurvy	nausea, abdominal cramps, diarrhea precipitation of kidney stones in susceptible person; "conditioned scurvy" (Dubick & Rucker, 1983)

(Continued)

TABLE 16–1 Vitamin Summary (Continued)

VITAMIN	FUNCTIONS	SOURCES	DEFICIENCY SYMPTOMS	TOXICITY SYMPTOMS
thiamin	carbohydrate metabolism energy metabolism neurotransmitter synthesis	whole or enriched grain products, organ meats, pork	loss of appetite, depression, poor neuromuscular control, beriberi	none reported
riboflavin	metabolism of carbo-hydrates, fats, and proteins energy metabolism	dairy foods, meat products, enriched or whole grains, green vegetables	sore tongue, cracks at the corners of the mouth (cheilosis)	none reported
niacin	carbohydrate, protein, and fat metabolism; energy metabolism; conversion of folacin to its active form	meat products, whole or enriched grain products, legumes	dermatitis, diarrhea, depression, and paranoia	flushing, itching, nausea, vomiting, diarrhea, low blood pressure, rapid heart beat, low blood sugar, liver damage (Dubick & Rucker, 1983)
pantothenic acid	energy metabolism; fatty acid metabolism; neuro-transmitter synthesis	nearly all foods	uncommon in humans	none reported
vitamin B$_6$ (Pyridoxine)	protein and fatty acid synthesis; neurotrans-mitter synthesis; hemoglobin synthesis	meats, organ meats, whole grains, legumes, bananas	nervous system: • irritability • tremors } infants • convulsions }	unstable gait, numbness, lack of coordination (Schaumberg et al., 1983) *(Continued)*

TABLE 16–1   Vitamin Summary (Continued)

VITAMIN	FUNCTIONS	SOURCES	DEFICIENCY SYMPTOMS	TOXICITY SYMPTOMS
folacin	synthesis of DNA and RNA: cell replication protein synthesis	liver, other meats, green vegetables	macrocytic anemia characterized by unusually large red blood cells; sore tongue, diarrhea	none reported (large amount may hide a B$_{12}$ deficiency)
vitamin B$_{12}$ (Cobalamin)	synthesis of DNA and RNA: conversion of folacin to active form; synthesis of myelin (fatty covering of nerve cells); metabolism of carbohydrates for energy	animal foods, liver, other meats, dairy products, eggs	macrocytic anemia, nervous system damage, sore mouth and tongue, loss of appetite, nausea, vomiting (pernicious anemia results from faulty absorption of B$_{12}$)	none reported
biotin	carbohydrate and fat metabolism; amino acid metabolism	organ meats, milk, egg yolk, yeast; synthesis by intestinal bacteria	nervous disorders, skin disorders, anorexia, muscle pain	none reported

macrocytic anemia – *a failure in the oxygen transport system characterized by abnormally large immature red blood cells.*

TABLE 16–2 Characteristics of Vitamins

	FAT-SOLUBLE VITAMINS	WATER-SOLUBLE VITAMINS
examples	A, D, E, K	vitamin C (ascorbic acid), thiamin, niacin, riboflavin, pantothenic acid, B_6 (Pyridoxine), biotin, folacin, B_{12} (Cobalamin)
stored in body	yes	no (B_{12} is an exception)
excreted in urine	no	yes
needed daily	no	yes
deficiency	develop slowly (months, years)	develop rapidly (days, weeks)

toxic doses of all vitamins for young children; it is certainly smaller than the amount required to produce **toxicity** symptoms in an adult. Therefore, extreme caution should be used if giving children vitamin supplements without the advice of a physician. The most frequent nutrient toxicity seen in children is of iron. Iron is found in many of the vitamin supplements for children and adults. Iron toxicity causes serious illness and may cause death. "If a little bit is good, a lot is better" is a dangerous practice relative to vitamins.

Vitamins have been the subject of much attention in the press, having been promoted as "cures" for numerous conditions including cancer, common colds, and mental illness (Consumers Union, 1998). Many people take vitamins and give them to their children as an "insurance policy." Vitamins can supplement a "hit-or-miss" diet but should not be given as a replacement for an adequate diet. There are a number of reasons why supplements cannot add up to an adequate diet by themselves. Vitamin and/or mineral supplements do not provide all of the nutrients known to be needed by humans, nor do they provide any calories, a primary need. Poor diets may lack fiber or essential amino acids or essential fatty acids, which will not be corrected by vitamin/mineral supplements. Also, there may be substances as yet unknown, but essential, which are derived from foods that are not included in vitamin/mineral preparations. The 2000 *Dietary Guidelines for Americans* states "because foods contain many substances that promote health, use the Food Guide Pyramid when choosing foods. Don't depend on supplements to meet your usual nutrient needs."

Vitamins are classified as fat-soluble (dissolved in or carried in fats) or water-soluble (dissolved in water). Fat-soluble vitamins differ from water-soluble vitamins both chemically and functionally. Table 16–2 provides a summary of the characteristics of these two classes of vitamins.

Vitamins in Energy Metabolism

A slow steady release of energy is important to body needs. If energy is released in a haphazard fashion, much of it is lost as heat. Since young children require greater amounts of energy per pound, they cannot afford to lose energy in such a fashion. The primary vitamins involved in the regulation of metabolism for the release of energy are:

- thiamin
- niacin
- riboflavin
- pantothenic acid

toxicity – *a state of being poisonous.*

As parts of coenzymes, these four vitamins act as a team to release energy from carbohydrates and fats. These four vitamins are not the only nutrients involved in this process; all the other nutrients required must also be available in adequate amounts at the time needed.

Vitamins in Cellular Reproduction and Growth

Two vitamins that are absolutely essential for cell growth are folacin and cobalamin (B_{12}). Both vitamins participate in the **synthesis** of **DNA** and **RNA**, which are the chemicals that provide the pattern for cell division and growth. So crucial are these vitamins for cell division and growth that deficiencies of them are quickly noticeable in tissues that are frequently replaced, such as red blood cells or the cells lining the intestine.

Young children may be considered at risk for both folacin and B_{12} deficiency; both of these vitamins are critical requirements for the synthesis of protein. Requirements for these nutrients are always increased during periods of rapid growth such as that typical of early childhood. Another factor that must be considered is the fact that B_{12} is found only in food from animal sources. Parents who are vegetarians will find that very careful planning is required in order to meet their child's needs for vitamin B_{12} and other nutrients (Table 16–3).

Vegetarian diets are classified by the extent to which the diet includes animal foods:

- lacto-ovo-vegetarian—diary foods and eggs included.
- lacto-vegetarian—dairy foods included, but no eggs.
- vegan—no animal source foods included.

It was formerly thought that vegan diets could not meet the needs of infants and children. In a 1997 position paper on vegetarianism, the American Dietetic Association stated "vegan diets tend to be high in bulk, care should be taken to ensure that calorie intakes are sufficient to meet every need." Infants and children who consume well-planned vegetarian diets can generally meet

---

TABLE 16–3 Replacing Animal Sources of Nutrients

Vegetarians who eat no animal products need to be more aware of nutrient sources. Nutrients most likely to be lacking and some nonanimal sources are:

- **vitamin B_{12}**—fortified soy beverages and cereals
- **vitamin D**—fortified soy beverages and sunshine
- **calcium**—tofu processed with calcium, broccoli, seeds, nuts, kale, bok choy, legumes (peas and beans), greens, lime-processed tortillas, and soy beverages, grain products, and orange juice enriched with calcium
- **iron**—legumes, tofu, green leafy vegetables, dried fruit, whole grains, and iron-fortified cereals and breads, especially whole-wheat. (Absorption is improved by vitamin C, found in citrus fruits and juices, tomatoes, strawberries, broccoli, peppers, dark-green leafy vegetables, and potatoes with skins.)
- **zinc**—whole grains (especially the germ and bran), whole-wheat bread, legumes, nuts, and tofu
- **protein**—tofu and other soy-based products, legumes, seeds, nuts, grains, and vegetables

Courtesy of *FDA Consumer.* October 1995.

---

synthesis – *the process of making a compound by the union of simpler compounds or elements.*
DNA – *deoxyribonucleic acid; the substance in the cell nucleus that codes for genetically transmitted traits.*
RNA – *ribonucleic acid; the nucleic acid that serves as messenger between the nucleus and the ribosomes where proteins are synthesized.*

all of their nutritional requirements for growth. Table 16–3 lists those nutrients most likely to be deficient in the vegetarian diet and nonanimal sources of those nutrients.

Some general recommendations include:

- Minimize intake of less nutritious foods such as sweets and fatty foods.
- Choose whole or unrefined grain products instead of refined products.
- Choose a variety of nuts, seeds, legumes, fruits, and vegetables, including good sources of vitamin C to improve iron absorption.
- Choose low fat varieties of dairy products, if they are included in the diet.
- Vegans should use properly fortified sources of vitamin B12, such as fortified soy beverages or cereals, or take a supplement (FDA Consumer, October 1995).

In addition to needs for folacin and B_{12}, cellular reproduction and increase in cell size are also dependent on proteins. One vitamin that is essential to the metabolism of proteins is pyridoxine (B_6). Pyridoxine **catalyzes** the chemical changes that permit the building of proteins from amino acids or the breakdown of proteins to provide needed amino acids.

Vitamins That Regulate Bone Growth

The minerals calcium and phosphorus are the major structural components of bones and teeth. However, bone growth also depends on a number of other nutrients as regulators, including vitamins A, C, and D (Figure 16–1).

Vitamin A regulates the destruction of old bone cells and their replacement by new ones. This process is known as "remodeling."

Vitamins C functions in two ways in the formation of bone tissue:

- maintains the solubility of calcium, making it more available for absorption
- aids in the formation of collagen, the flexible protein foundation upon which phosphorus and calcium are deposited

FIGURE 16–1

Body function is regulated by many nutrients.

---

catalyzes – *accelerates a chemical reaction.*

Vitamin D is necessary for the absorption of calcium and phosphorus, the major constituents of bones and teeth. It is also needed to assure blood levels of calcium and phosphorus that allow for deposition of these minerals in bones and teeth.

Vitamins That Regulate Neuromuscular Function

Vitamins play a role in a neuromuscular function either through the synthesis of neurotransmitters (chemical messengers) or through growth or maintenance of nerve cells.

Vitamin B_6 and vitamin C, thiamin, and niacin catalyze the synthesis of neurotransmitters that carry messages to all organs and that regulate nerve-muscle activities. Deficiencies of these vitamins result in neurological abnormalities.

Vitamins B_6 and B_{12} are necessary for the formation and maintenance of the myelin sheath, the insulative layer surrounding nerve cells. Faulty myelin sheath formation and maintenance results in abnormal passage of nerve impulses, which may result in numbness, tremors, or loss of coordination.

Recent research has indicated that maternal deficiency of folacin may result in neural tube defects that developed during the first months of fetal life. Prenatal vitamins contain folacin; however, neural tube defects occur before the mother is aware that she is pregnant. A recent attempt to remedy this situation has been the fortification of most grain products with folacin.

Vitamins That Regulate Blood Formation

Some vitamins play an important role in the formation of blood cells and hemoglobin. Hemoglobin, the red pigment of the red blood cells, carries oxygen to all cells of the body and carries the waste product, carbon dioxide, away from the cells to the lungs. Vitamins needed for the production of red blood cells and hemoglobin are:

- vitamin E
- pantothenic acid
- vitamin B_6 (pyridoxine)
- folacin
- vitamin B_{12} (cobalamin)

MINERALS AS REGULATORS

Many body functions require the presence of specific minerals (Table 16–4). The amounts of minerals required for regulatory purposes are smaller than those required directly to build or repair body tissue. Minerals used by the body for regulatory purposes are usually parts of enzymes or coenzymes or catalyze their action.

Minerals in Energy Metabolism

Minerals also play an important role in the steady, efficient release of energy. This process of energy metabolism (production, storage, and release) depends on adequate amounts of:

- phosphorus
- magnesium
- iodine
- iron

TABLE 16–4 **Mineral Summary**

MINERAL	FUNCTIONS	SOURCES	DEFICIENCY SYMPTOMS	TOXICITY SYMPTOMS
calcium	major component of bones and teeth; collagen formation; muscle contraction; secretion/release of insulin; neurotransmitters; blood	dairy products, turnip or collard greens, canned salmon or sardines, soybeans or soybean curd (tofu)	poor growth, small adult size, fragile and deformed bones, some form of rickets	unlikely: absorption is controlled; symptoms usually result from excess vitamin D or hormonal imbalance
phosphorus	major component of bones and teeth; energy metabolism; component of DNA and RNA	dairy products, meats, legumes, grains; additive in soft drinks	rare with normal diet	large amounts may depress calcium absorption
magnesium	major components of bones and teeth; activator of enzymes for ATP use; required for synthesis of DNA and RNA and for synthesis of proteins by RNA	nuts, seeds, green vegetables, legumes, whole grains	poor neuromuscular coordination, tremors, convulsions	unlikely
sodium	nerve impulse transmission; fluid balance; acid-base balance	meats, fish, poultry, eggs, milk, (naturally occurring sodium); many processed and cured foods (added sodium), salt, MSG	rare (losses from sweat may cause dizziness, nausea, muscle cramps)	linked to high blood pressure in some persons; confusion; coma

(Continued)

TABLE 16–4 Mineral Summary (Continued)

MINERAL	FUNCTIONS	SOURCES	DEFICIENCY SYMPTOMS	TOXICITY SYMPTOMS
potassium	nerve impulse transmission; fluid balance; acid-base balance	fruits (bananas, orange juice), vegetables, whole grains, fresh meats, fish	weakness, irregular heartbeat	unlikely from food sources
iron	component of hemoglobin; enzymes involved in oxygen utilization	liver, oysters, meats, enriched and whole grains, leafy green vegetables	microcytic anemia (characterized by small, pale red blood cells), fatigue, pallor, shortness of breath	unlikely (may be due to genetic defect)
zinc	component of many enzymes involved in: protein metabolism, DNA/RNA synthesis collagen formation wound healing	liver, oysters, meats, eggs, whole grains, legumes	retarded growth, loss of senses of taste and smell, delayed wound healing	excess supplementation may interfere with iron/copper metabolism nausea, vomiting, diarrhea, gastric ulcers
iodine	component of thyroxin, which regulates basal metabolic rate; regulates physical and mental growth	iodized salt, seafoods, many processed foods	goiter, physical dwarfing, cretinism if deficiency occurs during fetal life	iodism; rashes; bronchitis

microcytic anemia – *a failure in the oxygen transport system characterized by abnormally small red blood cells.*

REFLECTIVE THOUGHTS

What are your thoughts about vitamin and/or mineral pills? They are staples in the lives of millions of Americans, but are they necessary? Vitamin/mineral pills are safe for adults if they provide no more than 100 percent daily RDIs.

- Are they a good buy if they only have a placebo affect?
- Would you recommend vitamin/mineral pills for toddlers and preschoolers?

Think about some of the dangers of these for the very young child. Using them as candy because they look and taste like candy makes it easy to ingest some minerals at a toxic level. Having adult vitamin/mineral pills available to children has caused many serious cases of iron toxicity and some fatalities. There are times when these supplements benefit adults and children.

- Think of the benefit risk ratio for both children and adults.

Phosphorus is necessary for the production of enzymes and **coenzymes** required for energy-releasing metabolism and also for the formation of **adenosine triphosphate (ATP)**, the chemical substance in which potential energy is stored in body cells. Another mineral, magnesium, is necessary for both the storage and the release of the energy trapped in ATP. Iron functions as part of one of the key enzyme systems in the final stages of energy metabolism. Iodine is a component of the hormone thyroxin. As such, iodine aids in the control of the rate at which the body uses energy (the basal metabolic rate) for involuntary activities.

Minerals in Cellular Reproduction and Growth

Minerals required for cellular reproduction and growth include:

- phosphorus
- magnesium
- zinc

Phosphorus is a structural component of both DNA and RNA. Magnesium is required both for the synthesis of DNA and for synthesis of proteins from the pattern provided by DNA. Zinc functions as part of an enzyme system that must be active during DNA and RNA synthesis. DNA allows cells to reproduce and to synthesize proteins needed for growth.

The effect of an inadequate zinc supply is reflected by signs and symptoms such as stunted growth, decreased acuity of taste and smell that may further decrease food intake, and delayed sexual maturity. Zinc is chemically related to iron; its absorption is affected by many of the same factors. Zinc availability may be seriously reduced by excessive supplements with calcium and/or iron.

Minerals That Regulate Neuromuscular Function

Passage of nerve impulses from nerve cell to nerve cell or from nerve cell to muscle is dependent on the presence of:

- sodium
- potassium
- calcium
- magnesium

---

coenzymes – *a vitamin-containing substance required by certain enzymes before they can perform their prescribed function.*

adenosine triphosphate (ATP) – *a compound with energy-storing phosphate bonds that is the main energy source for all cells.*

Sodium and potassium act to change the electrical charge on the surface of the nerve cell, allowing the passage of the nerve impulse. Calcium is required for the release of many neurotransmitters from nerve cells. The passage of a nerve impulse to a muscle cell causes the contraction of muscles. Calcium is required for the actual contraction of a muscle, while ATP, which contains phosphorus as a structural component, provides the energy for the contraction to take place. Sodium and potassium promote the relaxation phase of muscle contraction. Magnesium regulates neuromuscular activity and causes muscle relaxation.

Minerals in Blood Formation

Blood is the transport medium of all regulatory minerals. Iron is a structural part of hemoglobin, an important component of blood. Copper aids iron with absorption and in its being incorporated into hemoglobin. Calcium is necessary for production of substances to induce blood coagulation.

PROTEINS AS REGULATORS

Proteins are the only class of nutrients that can perform all three general functions of nutrients. They build and repair body tissue, regulate body functions, and provide energy.

Proteins in Energy Metabolism and Growth Regulation

Proteins (amino acids) are important components of enzymes and some hormones and thus play a major role in regulation of energy metabolism. The body must have an adequate supply of protein in order to produce these important enzymes and hormones.

ISSUES TO CONSIDER • Food Supplement Safety

"Food supplements" are appearing in the food market in increasing numbers and are often in the news. Traditionally, food supplements were made of one or more essential nutrients believed to be needed in the diet in greater amounts or they were promoted as cures for something. Now the term has been broadened to include products ingested to supplement the diet, such as herbs and other plant-derived substances that might improve health. The magic of using the term "food supplement" is that it can be used to advertise a substance as a cure for a condition or disease without showing any proof. Manufacturers do not have to submit their product to the Food and Drug Administration (FDA) for testing and approval before it can be offered for sale. Promoting herbs, often as pills, for the cure of many conditions is a concern of nutritionists, professional health care personnel, and pharmacists. A food supplement must now carry on its label the statement: "This product is not approved by the FDA."

- Will this label serve as a warning that this may not be a safe product to use?
- Does using the term "natural" give assurance that a product is safe?
- Why is it important that a person check with their doctor and pharmacist before using any of these products?
- Why is there so much concern about the increasing use of herbs as food supplements?

All body functions are dependent on the presence and activity of enzymes. Enzymes are defined as protein catalysts. A catalyst is a substance that regulates a chemical reaction without becoming part of that reaction. The sequential metabolism for release of energy requires many steps; each step requires at least one enzyme specific for the particular reaction. Many enzymes require vitamin-containing coenzymes to enable them to catalyze their specific chemical reactions.

Hormones are substances that are secreted by glands for action on tissue elsewhere in the body. As such, they regulate many body functions. While not all hormones are composed of amino acids, two amino-acid dependent hormones are required in energy metabolism. These hormones are thyroxin and insulin.

Thyroxin regulates the rate at which energy is used for involuntary activities. It is secreted by the thyroid gland. Insulin is secreted by the pancreas. Its presence is necessary for glucose to be absorbed by the body cells so that it may be used as an energy source for cellular activity. Insulin and adrenalin (another amino acid-dependent hormone) act together to maintain normal blood glucose levels.

WATER AS A REGULATOR

The initial step of processing food for use by the body is digestion. Digestion is the process by which food is broken down mechanically and chemically into nutrients that can be used by the body. Food composition is changed during chemical digestion through the breaking down of nutrient molecules by the addition of water. Water is added at appropriate places in the molecules of protein, fats, and carbohydrates to break them into units small enough to be absorbed and used by the cells. Water is essential for many processes as the medium in which chemical reactions take place (Figure 16–2).

After food is digested and the nutrients absorbed, the nutrients are carried in solution by the blood and lymph to the cells of the body. Water again is necessary as it is the main transporting agent of the body comprising all body fluids including blood, lymph, and tissue fluid. Water also is the major component of body secretions such as salivary juice, gastric juice, bile, perspiration, and expirations from the lungs. Water plays a major role in ridding the body of waste material. Soluble body waste is carried out in urine, which is 95 percent water. Water regulates body temperature during changes in environmental temperature and activity-related heat production. It is important that children be given plain water rather than juice or other sweetened beverages. Sugar greatly reduces the absorption of water.

SUMMARY FOR UNIT 4

Approximately 40 nutrients are recognized as essential for providing energy, allowing normal growth for the child and maintenance for the adult. Each nutrient has its special function(s). Some nutrients share functions and in many cases the function of any given nutrient is dependent upon one or more other nutrients being present. The purpose of the following summary chart is to help you understand some of these functional interrelationships and reduce some confusion about what nutrients really do in the body. You might make this a personal study by associating each functional unit with the part of your own body. For example, when listing nutrient needs for bones and teeth, envision your own bones and teeth and what these nutrients are doing for them.

---

hormones – *special chemical substances produced by endocrine glands that influence and regulate certain body functions.*

FIGURE 16–2

Water is essential for regulation of body functions.

Summary of Biological Functions of Nutrients

FUNCTIONAL UNIT	NUTRIENTS INVOLVED	SPECIFIC FUNCTION
blood formation and maintenance	calcium vitamin K protein	blood clotting
	iron copper vitamin B_6 folacin	hemoglobin production
	folacin vitamin B_{12}	production of red blood cells
		(Continued)

Summary of Biological Functions of Nutrients (Continued)

FUNCTIONAL UNIT	NUTRIENTS INVOLVED	SPECIFIC FUNCTION
bone and teeth development	calcium phosphorus magnesium	components of bones and teeth
	vitamin C vitamin A vitamin D	building and remodeling of bones
nerve-muscle development and activity	vitamin C thiamin niacin vitamin B_6 pantothenic acid calcium potassium	transmission of nerve impulses
	calcium magnesium potassium sodium thiamin pantothenic acid	regulates muscle contraction and relaxation
growth and maintenance of body parts	protein phosphorus zinc selenium vitamin B_6 folacin	regulates cell division and synthesis of needed cell proteins
	iodine	regulates physical and mental growth
availability of energy for cellular activity	carbohydrates fats proteins	may be "burned" to release energy
	phosphorus magnesium thiamin riboflavin niacin pantothenic acid biotin	roles in enzyme and coenzyme production to release energy
	iodine	regulates basal metabolic energy needs

FOCUS ON FAMILIES • Nutrients That Regulate Body Functions

Water is essential for the regulation of body functions. Although water is abundantly available, it continues to be a challenge getting adequate amounts in the diet. Water has many competitors such as sodas, fruit drinks, fruit beverages and fruit ades that children often find more appealing. These beverages, however, provide little nutritional value while adding large amounts of calories and sugar. With concerns of childhood obesity and dental caries, the lack of water intake by children has become an important issue for parents and teachers to consider. Parents should regularly consume water and set an example for their children.

- Limit or avoid purchasing sweetened beverages. If these items are not readily available in the home, your child is more likely to drink water and other nutritious beverages such as milk and 100 percent fruit juice.

- Keep a pitcher of water available in the refrigerator with small cups within the child's reach. Smaller cups are less intimidating and more manageable.

- When traveling from home or participating in physical activities, encourage your child to carry a water bottle to quench thirst. This is more economical than purchasing beverages from vending machines or convenience stores and will provide more health benefits in comparison to sodas, fruit drinks, fruit beverages, and fruit ades.

CASE STUDY

Tony, age four-and-one-half, is allergic to citrus fruits. Even a few drops of juice cause him to break out in hives.

1. For what nutrient should Tony's diet be closely monitored?
2. a. If Tony's diet is actually deficient in this nutrient, would symptoms appear rapidly or slowly?
   b. Why?
3. Suggest foods other than citrus fruits that could also provide this nutrient.
4. List two symptoms that Tony might display.
5. a. Should Tony be given large doses of this nutrient to offset possible deficiencies?
   b. Why or why not?

SUMMARY

- Proteins, minerals, and vitamins are nutrient classes that regulate body activity.
- Vitamins function only as regulators, but they are essential for reactions involved with energy release, growth by cell division, bone and blood formation, and brain and nerve activities.

- Minerals are required for the same regulatory functions as vitamins in addition to regulating water balance in the body.

- Proteins, in addition to providing energy and supporting growth, function in many regulatory reactions.

- Enzymes are special proteins needed by the body in the many stages of metabolism to provide energy for all cells of the body.

- Proteins, or their amino acids, are parts of hormones that control the rate of many reactions that release energy for body use.

- Water, as the medium in which most nutrient functions take place, regulates a majority of nutrient activity and transports all nutrients after they enter the body. Water is also the prime regulator of body temperature.

SUGGESTED ACTIVITIES

1. Using the vitamin and mineral summaries in Tables 16–1 and 16–4, list two specific foods or types of foods that are rich sources of each of the following nutrients:
magnesium   thiamin
calcium   riboflavin
   a. What foods are good sources of more than one of these nutrients?
   b. Which nutrients occur in the same types of foods?
   c. Which nutrients do not occur in the same types of foods?
   d. Which nutrients are found mostly in animal-source foods?
   e. Which nutrients are found mostly in plant-foods?

CHAPTER REVIEW

A. **Briefly answer the following questions.**

   1. What two minerals are required for energy metabolism?
   2. What two minerals are required for cellular division and growth?
   3. What is the medium in which nutrient-related chemical reactions take place in the body?
   4. Name an important nutrient component of enzymes and some hormones.
   5. Which nutrient is the prime regulator of body temperature?

REFERENCES

American Dietetic Association. (1997). Vegetarian diets. *Journal of the American Dietetic Association, 97,* 1317–1321.

Consumers Union. (1998, April). *Consumer reports on health—1998: Vitamins and minerals and herbs.* Yonkers, NY: Author.

Dubick, M. A., & Rucker, R. B. (1983, February). Dietary supplements and health aids—A critical evaluation. Part I vitamins and minerals. *Journal of Nutrition Education, 15,* 47–51.

FDA Consumer Publication. (1995, October). *More people trying vegetarian diets.* Washington, DC: U.S. Department of Agriculture.

Schaumberg, H. A., et al. (1983, August 25). Sensory neuropathy from pyridoxine abuse. *New England Journal of Medicine, 309,* 445–48.

U.S. Department of Health and Human Services and U.S. Department of Agriculture. (1995). *Dietary guidelines for Americans.* Washington, DC: Authors.

ADDITIONAL READING

Centre for Science in the Public Interest. (1995). *Vitamin smarts.* Washington, DC: Nutrition Action Health Letter.

Christian, J. L., & Gregor, J. L. (1990). *Nutrition for living.* Menlo Park, CA: Benjamin/Cummings Publishing Co.

Garrison, M. A., & Somer, E. (1995). *The nutrition desk reference.* New Canaan, CT: Keats Publishing, Inc.

Hegarty, V. (1988). *Decisions in nutrition.* St. Louis, MO: C. V. Mosby Co.

Kreutler, P. A. (1990). *Nutrition in perspective.* Englewood Cliffs, NJ: Prentice Hall.

Kurtweil, P. (1998, September/October). Guide to dietary supplements. *FDA Consumer.* Pittsburg, PA: Superintendent of Documents.

Mahan, L. K., & Arlin, M. (2000). *Krause's food, nutrition, and diet therapy.* Philadelphia: W. B. Saunders Company.

Pipes, P. (1997). *Nutrition in infancy and childhood.* New York: McGraw-Hill.

Reed, P. B. (1980). *Nutrition: An applied science.* St. Paul, MN: West Publishing Company.

Satter, E. (2000). *Child of mine.* Palo Alto, CA: Bull Publishing Company.

Tamborlane, W. V. (1995). *The Yale guide to children's nutrition.* New Haven, CT: Yale University Press.

Tufts University. (1997, November). 100% juice isn't necessarily better. *Tufts University Health and Nutrition Letter.* 15, 1.

Whitney, E. N., & Rolfes, S. R. (2001). *Understanding nutrition with Infotrac.* (9th ed.). Belmount, CA: Wadsworth Publishing.

Williams, E. R., & Calienda, M. A. (1984). *Nutrition: Principles, issues, and applications.* New York: McGraw-Hill Book Company.

HELPFUL WEB SITES

Federal Consumer	http://www.pueblo.gsa.gov/food.htm
Mayo Clinic Health Letter	http://www.mayoclinic.com
Tufts University Nutrition Center	http://navigator.tufts.edu
United States Department of Agriculture (USDA)	http://www.fns.usda.gov/fncs

*For additional health, safety, and nutrition resources, go to
http://www.EarlyChildEd.delmar.com*

NUTRITION AND THE YOUNG CHILD

CHAPTER 17

Infant Feeding

After studying this chapter, you should be able to:

- Discuss the advantages of breast-feeding.
- Describe the proper way to bottle-feed an infant.
- Describe ways to feed the breast-fed infant in a child care setting.
- Identify the appropriate ages at which to introduce semi-solid foods to infants.
- Name recommended safe foods to use as first semi-solid foods.
- Give criteria for selecting nutritious solid food for the baby and evaluate benefits of commercial versus home-prepared semi-solid food.
- Evaluate nutrient contributions of different types of commercial baby food and make appropriate choices.

TERMS TO KNOW

prenatal	aseptic procedures	developmental readiness or
low-birthweight (LBW)	distention	physiological readiness
infant	regurgitation	Type I diabetes
antibodies	bottle-mouth syndrome	electrolyte(s)

PROFILE OF AN INFANT

During the first year of a child's life, the rate of growth and development is more rapid than at any other period in the life cycle. Infants will double their weight during the first four to five months and will approximately triple their birth weight by the end of the first year. Birth length may be expected to increase by 50 percent by the child's first birthday.

Infants are totally dependent upon parents and/or teachers to protect them from environmental hazards, such as temperature change and pathogenic organisms, and to provide the necessary nutrients in a safe and useable form. The giving of food must be coupled with socializing and much tender loving care (TLC). Without TLC, infants' growth and development can be seriously delayed even when they are receiving all of the nutrients they need. Infants need much stimulation to help them learn and food can serve as an important medium for stimulating the infant—by

TABLE 17–1   Infant Feeding Guidelines

| Food | Age (months) | | | | | |
	0–2	2–4	4–6	6–8	9–10	11–12
human milk/formula (ounces)	18–28	25–32	27–45	24–32	24–32	24–32
iron-fortified cereal (Tbsp.)			4–8	4–6	4–6	4–6
zwieback, dry toast				1	1	1–2
vegetable, plain, strained (Tbsp.)				3–4	6–8	7–8 (soft, chopped)
fruit, plain, strained (Tbsp.)				3–4	6–8	8 (soft, cooked, chopped)
meat, plain, strained (Tbsp.)				1–2	4–6	4–5 (ground or chopped)
egg yolk (Tbsp.)					1	1
fruit juice (ounces)				2–4	4	4
potatoe, rice, noodles (Tbsp.)						8

Reprinted by permission from Morrison Management Specialists, *Manual of clinical nutrition management.* Atlanta, GA, 2003.

providing a variety of tastes, colors, temperatures, textures, etc. Within the first 12 months, infants will progress from a diet solely of breast milk or formula to gradually include semi-solid foods to finally a modified adult diet that includes them in the family group at meal time (Table 17–1).

MEETING NUTRITIONAL NEEDS OF THE INFANT

The rapid rate of growth and development that is characteristic of infancy must be supported by adequate nutrient intake. The nutrient needs during this first year are high, while the volume capacity of the infant's stomach is small. This explains the infant's need for frequent feedings of nutrient-dense food.

The calorie needs during the first four months are particularly high relative to an infant's size because of the high energy requirements for the rapid growth taking place. A newborn needs 45–55 calories per pound daily. One-fourth to one-third of these calories are used for growth. As the infant progresses through the first year, fewer calories are needed for growth and more are needed for physical activity as the infant becomes more mobile (Figure 17–1). By six months of age the infant requires only 40–45 calories per pound. The infant's needs for all nutrients are very high in proportion to their body size. In addition, a child's social and emotional needs must also be met to ensure optimal growth and development.

The nutritional needs of the infant may be conditioned by the nutritional status of the mother during pregnancy. A common consequence of poor **prenatal** (conception to birth) nutrition is a

prenatal – *the period from conception to birth of the baby.*

FIGURE 17–1

Older infants need fewer calories for growth and more calories for physical activity.

low-birthweight (LBW) infant. The incidence of serious illness and death is very high for low-birthweight infants during their first year. LBW infants present with serious problems such as:

- poor regulation of body temperature
- increased susceptibility to infection
- difficulty in metabolizing carbohydrates, fats, and proteins
- delayed development of kidneys and digestive organs
- poorly calcified bones—reduced bone density
- poor iron stores resulting in neonatal anemia
- presentation of vitamin deficiencies during neonatal period (birth to 28 days): vitamin E, folacin, and pyridoxine deficiencies are most common

The infants at high risk for these problems are those born of teen-age mothers who must meet their own high nutrient needs to complete their growth in addition to providing nutrients for the growth and development of the fetus.

Common prenatal nutritional deficiencies that produce low-birthweight babies are:

- protein
- energy
- folacin
- vitamin D
- pyridoxine

Prenatal nutrient deficiencies may be partially corrected, but rarely totally reversed, by the generous provision of the nutrient needs of the baby immediately after birth. The WIC (Women, Infants, and Children) program, which provides food supplements for pregnant and breast-feeding women, infants, and children up to the age of five, has been very effective in reducing the incidence of prenatal, infant, and child malnutrition. WIC serves approximately 45 percent of all infants born in the United States and provides nutrition and child care information in a number of languages (Figure 17–2).

---

low-birthweight (LBW) infant – *an infant who weighs less than 5.5 pounds (2,500 grams) at birth.*

FIGURE 17–2

WIC provides nutrition and child care information in several languages. Developed by South Los Angeles Health Projects, REI WIC Progarm (2003).

Cómo Atender A Un Bebé Molesto

Cargar y abrazar a su bebé es muy importante y le dará la seguridad y el amor que ella necesita para crecer. **Esto NO la va a malcriar.**

Si su bebé esta molesta, o llora mucho, ella posiblemente . . .

. . .tenga hambre.

Dé pecho cada vez que ella tenga hambre. Signos de que el bebé tiene hambre incluyen: chuparse las manos, o mamar y mover la cabeza como si buscara el pecho.

. . .necesite atención.

"Abrace" a su bebé en vez de usar un portador de bebés.

. . . esté muy agitada o muy cansada.
♥ Cálmela meciéndola suavemente de lado a lado, muchísimo contacto de piel con piel, baños tibios, luces bajas y música suave.

. . . esté teniéndo un periodo de crecimiento rápido.
♥ A las 2, 6, y 12 semanas su bebé puede que tenga hambre más seguido porque está creciendo más rápido. Aliméntela cuando ella parezca que tenga hambre.

. . . puede ser sensible a la cafeína.
♥ Trate de no tomar café, refrescos de cola ó té.

. . . está enferma.
♥ llame al doctor, especialmente si tiene fiebre, y siga dando pecho.

El Programa WIC es un empleador y proveedor de igualdad de oportunidad

Developed by South Los Angeles Health Projects, REI WIC Program FB5/03s

The First Six Months

During the first six months, the infant's nutritional needs can be met solely with breast milk or formula. The full-term infant is born with a store of iron and vitamin A to supply these nutrients for six months. A premature infant may require supplements of these nutrients during this period. No semi-solid foods are needed or advisable until the infant is at least five months of age. Younger infants are not developmentally or physiologically ready to ingest solid foods (discussed later in this chapter). Breast milk is the preferred food for an infant; Table 17–2 presents some advantages of breast milk over formula. However, after considering health factors and lifestyle, a mother may select formula feeding as the best approach for her and her infant. Some conditions that might cause a mother to choose formula feeding are:

- illness of the mother
- mother needs to take medications
- mother needs to be away from the child for long periods of time
- mother wishes not to nurse
- mother uses addictive drugs

The Teacher and the Breast-Feeding Mother

The mother who is employed outside the home may choose to continue to breast-feed. She may use a breast pump or hand express her milk to be fed to her baby by the teacher while she is at work. Breast milk may be refrigerated in a sterile container for up to 24 hours or may be frozen in a plastic bag for up to two weeks. The teacher should be flexible and willing to assist the mother who wants to breast-feed her infant.

Safe Handling of Breast Milk. Human milk varies in color, consistency, and odor, depending on the mother's diet and storage container used. Since breast milk is not homogenized,

TABLE 17–2 Advantages of Breast-Feeding

Breast Milk:

- has all of the nutrients needed by the infant for the first six months
- contains proteins that are more digestible than cow's milk protein
- contains lactose, the carbohydrate present, which aids in calcium absorption and in establishing beneficial intestinal flora
- provides **antibodies** (immunoglobulins) that protect the infant from some infectious illnesses
- has a higher content of the essential fatty acids
- provides taurine*
- provides dietary nucleotides**
- is less likely to cause food allergies
- reduces the risk of bacteria entering the infant's body from unsanitary formula preparation
- is inexpensive, convenient, and is always at the correct temperature
- contains less sodium (salt) than formulas
- fosters emotional bonding between mother and infant
- is a biologically active substance, changing in nutrient composition to meet the infant's changing needs

*Taurine is a free amino acid (not found in proteins), that is particularly important for the normal growth and development of the central nervous system. It is now added to some formulas, especially those for premature infants.
**Dietary Nucleotides play a role in the infant's ability to produce antibodies in response to infectious organisms they may be exposed to. The American Academy of Pediatrics currently recommends that these be added to all prepared formulas.

---

antibodies – *special substances produced by the body that help protect against disease.*

cream may rise to the top of the container. Safe handling by the teacher includes following these steps:

- Wash hands well before touching any milk containers. Avoid touching the inside of bottles or caps.
- Request that mothers label containers with the date when milk was collected; use the oldest milk first.
- If breast milk is to be stored for more than 24 hours, it should be frozen. (See Table 17–3 for safe thawing instructions.)
- Frozen breast milk may be safely stored in a refrigerator freezer for six months or in a deep freeze (0 to −10°F) for up to 12 months.

The Teacher and the Formula Fed Infant

Most infants in child care centers are formula fed. The type of formula to be fed will have been determined by the infant's parents and health care provider. Formula for infants is prepared to closely resemble breast milk in composition relative to the amount of protein, carbohydrate, and fat. Infant formula may be made from cow's milk, soy, or meat products. The formula may be purchased in powder or liquid concentrates or as ready-to-feed liquids. Unmodified cow's milk should not be given to infants prior to one year of age because it often causes digestive disorders and may cause intestinal bleeding.

Preparation of Formula

Safe preparation of formula is primarily dependent on two factors:

1. Sanitation—Sanitary formula preparation using **aseptic procedures** prevents serious illness that might result from bacteria introduced into the formula. This requires careful sanitizing of all utensils used in preparing formula and thorough handwashing prior to mixing the formula. When preparing formula from a powdered concentrate, the water to be used for dilution must be sterilized before it is used. Honey should never be added to a formula for an infant less than one year of age.

Caution: Honey contains Clostridium botulinum *spores, which in an infant's intestine, can produce a dangerous toxin that can be life-threatening.*

TABLE 17–3 Thawing Frozen Breast Milk Safely

1. Wash your hands with soap and water before touching the breast milk container.
2. Place the sealed container of breast milk in a bowl of warm water for about 30 minutes, or hold the container of 4 ounces of human milk under warm running water for approximately 4 minutes. **NEVER MICROWAVE BREAST MILK!** Microwaving can alter the nutritional composition of breast milk and may result in burning the baby.
3. Swirl the container to blend any fat that may have separated and risen during thawing.
4. Feed thawed milk immediately or store in the refrigerator for a maximum of 24 hours.
5. **NEVER REFREEZE BREAST MILK.**

---

aseptic procedure – *treatment to produce a product that is free of disease-producing bacteria.*

Infant formulas are packaged in different forms. Parents can choose from ready-to-feed (RTF), concentrated liquid, or powder formulas. Each type of formula requires different preparation techniques, that are specified on product labels.

2. Accuracy—Accurate measuring and mixing of formula (according to directions) assures the provision of needed calories and nutrients to allow for optimal growth and development. Adding too much water results in diluted formula that cannot provide adequate daily nutrients within the volume of formula that an infant will consume. Adding too little water results in an "over-rich" formula that may cause digestive problems. If given over a long period of time, this rich formula results in excessive caloric intake and obesity. Skim milk or low-fat milk should not be used in formula preparation because infants need the fat to meet their calorie needs within the volume of feedings that can be comfortably taken in each day. Adequate fat in the diet is also a critical need relative to normal nerve development; fat is needed for myelin, the insulation on new nerve fibers. It is recommended that 30–50 percent of the infant's calories come from fat. The fat in the formula also must provide the essential fatty acids (linolenic and linoleic) that are required for cell growth. The equivalent of one tablespoon of a polyunsaturated fat, such as corn oil or safflower oil, will meet the infant's need for essential fatty acids. Table 17–4 provides a summary of the formulas available for infants.

TABLE 17-4 Example of Infant Formula

Standard Formulas

Enfamil with Iron	20 cal/oz	modified cow's milk
Enfamil	20 cal/oz	modified cow's milk
Similac with Iron	20 cal/oz	modified cow's milk
Similac	20 cal/oz	modified cow's milk
SMA	20 cal/oz	modified cow's milk
SMA Lo Iron	20 cal/oz	modified cow's milk
Carnation Good Start	20 cal/oz	modified cow's milk

Soy Formulas

Isomil	20 cal/oz	hypoallergenic formula
Nursoy	20 cal/oz	hypoallergenic formula
Prosobee	20 cal/oz	hypoallergenic formula
Soyalac	20 cal/oz	hypoallergenic formula
Carnation Alsoy	20 cal/oz	hypoallergenic formula

Therapeutic Formulas

Nutramigen	20 cal/oz	hypoallergenic formula
Pregestimil	20 cal/oz	hypoallergenic formula
Alimentum	20 cal/oz	hypoallergenic formula
Lofenalac	20 cal/oz	for phenylketonurics (PKU)
Pedialyte	3 cal/oz	electrolyte/fluid replacement
Mead Johnson Lactofree	20 cal/oz	lactose-free milk
Ross Lactose Free	20 cal/oz	lactose-free milk
Enfamil Premature	20 or 24 cal/oz	premature infant formula
Enfamil 22	22 cal/oz	premature infant formula
Similac Special Care	20 or 24 cal/oz	premature infant formula
Similac Neosure Advance	22 cal/oz	premature infant formula

FEEDING TIME FOR THE INFANT

How frequently a baby is fed is determined by the parents, infant, and health care provider. For the first four months it is generally considered best to feed an infant on demand. Infants vary greatly as to how much food they can comfortably handle at one time and in how often they require food. The individual infant is the best source of information on when to feed. There is much variation in the frequency and amount of feeding. Some common guidelines suggest:

0–1 months	6 feedings of 3–4 oz./feeding
1–2 months	6 feedings of 3–5 oz./feeding
2–3 months	5 feedings of 4–6 oz./feeding
4–5 months	5 feedings of 5–7 oz./feeding
6–7 months*	5 feedings of 6–8 oz./feeding
8–12 months*	3 feedings of 8 oz./feeding

*Also taking solid foods

If the infant has at least six wet diapers a day, she probably is receiving enough formula.

How to feed a baby involves much more than getting the nipple into the mouth. Cleanliness is of first importance at feeding time. The teacher's hands must be soap-washed prior to feeding. The formula should not be too warm or too cold. If it feels slightly warm when tested against the inside of the wrist, it is the right temperature.

Caution: Infant formula in the bottle should not be heated in the microwave. The fluid formula may become dangerously hot while the outside of the bottle feels cool. This method of heating has severely burned some infants.

Feeding time should be relaxed with actual feeding preceded by a few minutes of talking and playing with the infant. The infant should be held in a sitting position with the head against the teacher's upper arm. The infant should be cuddled and talked to with eye-to-eye contact while being fed. This makes feeding time a pleasant social time for the infant. It also gives needed close human contact (bonding) (Figure 17–3). The nipple of the bottle should be kept full of formula so that the baby does not swallow air, which can cause gas and **distention** of digestive organs. The

FIGURE 17–3

Feeding time is a time for infant and parent bonding.

distention – *stretched or enlarged.*

FIGURE 17–4

Types of nipples.

Regular nipple
Available in slow,
medium,
and fast flow

Newborn nipple

Orthodontic Nipple

Cleft-palate nipple

infant should not be hurried; infants require at least 20 minutes per feeding. See Figure 17–4 for examples of types of nipples available with which to facilitate bottle feeding.

The teacher should stop two or three times during each feeding and after the feeding to burp the baby (Figure 17–5). This may be done by placing the infant over the shoulder or face-down across the lap and gently patting or rubbing the back. After feeding, the infant should be placed on

FIGURE 17–5

The teacher should stop during and after feeding to burp the baby.

its right side to aid passage of feeding into the stomach. This also prevents distention of the stomach and **regurgitation**. Infants should not be placed on their stomachs for sleeping. This position may put a child at a higher risk for sudden infant death syndrome (Wong, 1993).

> *Caution:* *The bottle should never be propped and the baby left unattended while feeding. Infants do not have the motor control to remove the bottle from their mouth and may aspirate the formula after they fall asleep. This practice also increases the risk of* **bottle-mouth syndrome** *or baby bottle tooth decay (BBTD) and ear infections.*

Until solid foods are added, breast milk or formula should meet the water needs of the baby. However, since the infant has a great need for water, it is not safe to assume that the formula has supplied all that is necessary. A thirsty baby acts much like a hungry baby. So, if the baby appears hungry after only a short interval after feeding, unflavored water can be offered. Water sweetened with sugar or flavored drinks are discouraged. Also, if the temperature of the environment is high, water should be offered to the infant with increased frequency.

Vitamin and/or mineral supplements are sometimes recommended for the infant. Breast milk or formula is adequate to meet the nutritional needs of the infant except perhaps for vitamin D and the mineral fluoride. The breast-fed infant may benefit from a vitamin D supplement but the formula-fed infant is getting adequate amounts of vitamin D and should not be supplemented with this vitamin. Fluoride is not found in effective amounts in breast milk even though the mother may be drinking fluoridated water, and this mineral is not generally added to infant formulas. The infant who has no fluoride in his diet and consumes little water would also benefit from a fluoride supplement. Fluoride supplements started at birth may reduce tooth decay in a child's permanent teeth by 50–60 percent. The recommended level of supplementation is 0.25 mg fluoride per day starting at six months of age.

> *Caution:* *Be sure to monitor an infant's fluoride intake; fluoride in excess is toxic and at 0.5 mg/day levels may cause tooth discoloration. Fluoride supplements combined with vitamin D are not safe to use with the formula-fed infant. That is because formulas are already supplemented with vitamin D and excessive intake of vitamin D may have serious consequences for the infant.*

INTRODUCING SEMI-SOLID (PUREED) FOODS

The teacher, parent, and health care professional must cooperate closely in introducing semi-solid foods to the infant. Finely cut, pureed foods high in fluid content, such as cereals, and pureed fruits and vegetables, are introduced between five and six months of age. Introducing semi-solid foods prior to five months of age is inappropriate because the infant does not demonstrate **developmental or physiological readiness**.

Developmental Readiness

At approximately five months of age, the baby changes from only being able to suck to being able to move food to the back of the mouth and to swallow without an initial sucking action. At this point, the baby is able to chew, to sit with some comfort, and to lean forward toward the spoon.

---

regurgitation – *the return of partially digested food from stomach to mouth.*
bottle-mouth syndrome – *a pattern of tooth decay, predominantly of the upper teeth, that develops as the result of permitting a child to go to sleep with a bottle containing juice, milk, or any other caloric liquid that may pool in the mouth.*
developmental or physiological readiness – *growth (both physical and cognitive) and chemical processes that lead to the ability to perform a function.*

FIGURE 17–6

Infants sometimes find more pleasure in touching their food while tasting it.

At four to five months, the infant shows interest in touching, holding, and tasting objects—food and otherwise (Figure 17–6). It is important to note that at this age the baby can turn his head away from food when satisfied, signalling a desire to stop eating. This signal should be watched for, respected, and the offering of food should be stopped.

Physiological Readiness

By the age of five to six months the infant's digestive system has developed the capability of digesting complex carbohydrates and proteins other than milk protein. At about the same time the iron stores that were present at birth have become exhausted. These happenings signal readiness to begin adding semi-solid foods such as iron-enriched cereals and pureed vegetables and fruits

 REFLECTIVE THOUGHTS

Missy T. is the mother of six-week-old Hayden. Hayden is Missy's first child. Missy's mother lives nearby and is happy to help with Hayden's care. Missy complains of being tired and mentions to her mother that Hayden had awakened several times during the night acting hungry. Her mother advises her to add cereal to his bedtime bottle in order to "fill him up so he will sleep through the night." She also advises cutting larger holes in the nipple so the cereal won't clog it.

- Should Missy follow her mother's advice?
- What, if any, dangers would feeding cereal from the bottle at six weeks of age involve?
- Do child care practices change from generation to generation?
- Consider possible short- and long-term outcomes of feeding semi-solid food from a bottle.
- If you were a teacher and a parent requested that you feed an infant in this way, how would you respond?

TABLE 17–5   Age-Related Infant Behaviors

AGE	COMMON INFANT BEHAVIORS
4–6 months	• assumes more symmetrical sitting position • grasps for objects • puts objects in mouth • may close hands around bottle • turns head away from food when no longer hungry • leans toward food-containing spoon
6–7 months	• teeth erupt • shows up and down chewing motions • grasps finger foods and gets them to mouth • drinks small amounts of liquid from a cup • holds bottle with both hands
7–8 months	• sits alone with little support • can manipulate food in the mouth better • more successful when drinking from a cup • begins self-feeding with help
9–12 months	• can more precisely grasp and release objects • reaches for the spoon • feeds self with some help • drinks successfully from a cup • more aware of environment • mimics motions and activities observed

to the diet. By the age of six to seven months the infant's kidneys are sufficiently developed to handle the nitrogen-containing wastes resulting from the addition of high protein meat products to the diet.

Table 17–5 describes age-related, developmental factors that may influence feeding behavior. It is important to remember that infants vary greatly in rate of development. That is why there is no need for concern if a baby presents some of these behaviors ahead of or behind schedule.

New foods should be introduced slowly with a few baby spoonfuls offered one or two times daily. The food may be thinned with formula, breast milk, or water to make it more acceptable to the infant. Semi-solid foods should be fed by spoon rather than by feeder or bottle. Iron-fortified infant cereal is usually the first addition. Rice or barley cereals are less likely to cause allergic reactions and are therefore wise choices for the first semisolid food offered.

A suggested sequence for introducing solid foods is:

4–6 months	iron-enriched cereals
6–8 months	vegetables and fruits
6–8 months	meat or meat substitutes

Initially, it is better to offer individual foods rather than mixtures. If an allergy or sensitivity develops, the offending food can be identified more readily. Sugar, salt, or butter should not be added to an infant's food. When an infant begins to eat semi-solid food, parents may prepare the pureed food at home or use commercially prepared food. Either is acceptable as long as the types of food are nutritionally adequate. Food may be pureed in a blender using foods from the table before it has been seasoned for the rest of the family. Doing this allows more control over what food shall be offered and usually presents a greater variety of food to the infant. Initially, it may be wise to offer only those family foods that are not too high in fiber. If the family is having baked

ISSUES TO CONSIDER • Does Infant Formula Cause Type I Diabetes?

Recent reports have questioned a possible link between formula feeding and an increased incidence of **Type I diabetes**. The implication is that protein in cow's milk might precipitate Type I diabetes; elevated antibodies to these proteins have been observed in diabetic children. A recent report stated that to date, studies have failed to take into consideration the wide variety of formulas on the market. However, the American Academy of Pediatrics strongly encourages breast-feeding and avoidance of cow's milk and products containing cow's milk proteins during the first year, for infants born into a family with a strong history of Type I diabetes. This applies especially if a sibling has diabetes.

- What implications does this study have for breast-feeding recommendations?
- If an infant in a family is receiving formula, what options are available?
- Why do you think the American Academy of Pediatrics only recommends avoidance of cow's milk protein for the first year?

Source: Marincic, P. Z., McCune, R. W., & Hendricks, D. G. (1999). Cows-milk-based infant formula: Heterogeneity of bovine serum albumin content. *Journal of the American Dietetic Association, 99*, 1575–1578.

chicken, peas, and rice, an appropriate serving for the infant might be 2T chicken, 2T peas, and 1/4 c rice pureed in a blender. Home-prepared pureed food may be frozen in ice cube trays; when frozen the cubes may be removed, stored in the freezer in a tightly sealed container, and removed, thawed, and used as needed. If the decision is to use commercially prepared baby food, it is better to use plain fruits, vegetables, and meats rather than "dinners," or "desserts," which are often extended with starches and other additives. The labels on commercially prepared foods for infants and young children are helpful in making wise selections (Figure 17–7). Ingredients on food

FIGURE 17–7

Special labeling rules apply to foods for infants and young children. Courtesy of Kurtzweil, P. (1995, May). Labeling rules for young children's food. *FDA Consumer.*

Nutrition Facts	
Serving Size 1 jar (140g)	
Amount Per Serving	
Calories 110	
Total Fat	0g
Sodium	10mg
Total Carbohydrate	27g
Dietary Fiber	4g
Sugars	18g
Protein	0g
% Daily Value	
Protein 0% •	Vitamin A 6%
Vitamin C 45% •	Calcium 2%
Iron 2%	

Nutrition Label for Foods for Children Under Four Years Old.

Nutrition Facts	
Serving Size 1 jar (140g)	
Amount Per Serving	
Calories 110 Calories from Fat 0	
Total Fat	0g
Saturated Fat	0g
Cholesterol	0mg
Sodium	10mg
Total Carbohydrate	27g
Dietary Fiber	4g
Sugars	18g
Protein	0g
% Daily Value	
Protein 0% •	Vitamin A 6%
Vitamin C 45% •	Calcium 2%
Iron 2%	

Nutrition Label for Foods for Children Two to Four Years Old.

Type I diabetes – *a disease distinguished by a lack of insulin production; usually diagnosed in childhood or young adulthood.*

FIGURE 17–8

The six- to eight-month-old infant really enjoys finger food.

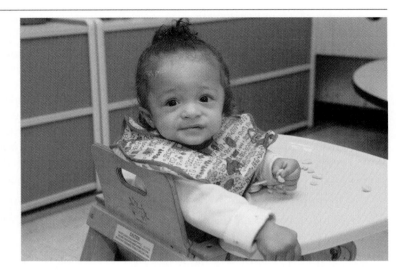

labels are listed in descending order according to amount present. The first ingredient in an acceptable infant food should be fruit, vegetable, or meat, not water or starch. When feeding a child prepared baby food, it is better to remove the small portion that you will use, put it in a small bowl, and put the rest of the jar's contents into the refrigerator. This will reduce the chance of bacterial contamination of the remaining food. Enzymes in the saliva can also cause the food to break down and become "watery." Removing only the amount of food to be eaten from the container will prevent contaminations.

Infants may begin to drink small amounts of liquid from a cup around six to seven months of age. At six to seven months they may grasp finger foods and chew on them (Figure 17–8). At this age, teeth are beginning to erupt and the provision of "chew foods" such as dry toast or baby biscuits helps the teething process. (Refer to Table 17–1.)

Some Common Feeding Concerns

Allergies. The most common chronic condition affecting infants is allergies. Allergic responses to food may result in a variety of symptoms such as runny nose, diarrhea, vomiting, abdominal pain, hives, and eczema. These symptoms are not specific for any given food or for allergies in general. Occurrence of any of these symptoms should be discussed with the infant's physician.

If there is a history of family members with allergies, it is recommended that the introduction of semi-solid foods be delayed as long as possible. Certain foods such as citrus juice(s), egg, cereal products other than rice, chocolate, and nut butters are common allergens. Their addition to the baby's diet should be delayed until late infancy.

If allergic reactions seem to be linked with a specific food, the food should be eliminated from the diet and reintroduced at a later time. If a milk-based formula seems to be the offending food, it may be necessary to replace it with one formulated from soybeans or meat derivatives.

Vomiting and Diarrhea. There are many different causes for vomiting or diarrhea in the infant. Some common causes include:

- food allergies or food sensitivities
- overfeeding
- infections: systemic or food-borne

- feeding food that the baby is not yet ready for
- incorrect formula preparation
- use of fruit juice
- swallowed air
- reflux

When vomiting and diarrhea occur, the primary concern is to replace fluid and **electrolytes** that have been lost. The child with diarrhea should receive a liquid intake of approximately three ounces of fluid per pound of body weight. There are numerous RTF rehydrating formulas available for use (Pedialyte, Infalyte, and Rehydralyte). Baby juices, carbonated beverages, tea, or adult electrolyte formulas are not recommended because of their high sugar and low electrolyte content. The goal is gradual progression to the diet normal for the infant's age.

Acute diarrhea due to an infection, and characterized by accompanying fever, must be attended to immediately. The infant's physician should be contacted and immediate and consistent attention should be given to replacing the fluid and electrolytes lost.

Anemia. Inadequate iron intake can result in low-hemoglobin type anemia that may delay the growth process and cause the infant to be lethargic. The iron stores present at birth are usually exhausted by six months of age unless the infant is on an iron-fortified formula. The addition of iron-enriched cereals at this age will provide iron needed to prevent anemia. Some infants may experience intestinal problems if on iron-fortified formula. These infants are given plain formula and should receive iron supplements by six months of age.

Bottle-Mouth Syndrome. Babies who are allowed to recline or go to sleep with a bottle in their mouth may develop bottle-mouth syndrome. This condition is characterized by a high rate of tooth decay caused by the pooling of sugar-containing formula, breast milk, or juices in the baby's mouth.

Ear Infection. Propping the bottle so the infant may lie down and feed without being held may lead to ear infections. A child should be held in a semi-seated position during feedings to prevent milk from traveling into the eustachian tubes and into the ears.

Obesity. Obesity results when energy intake exceeds an infant's need for energy for growth, maintenance, and activity. Some infant feeding practices that are thought to play a role in obesity are overeating during bottle feeding, too early introduction of semi-solid foods, and feeding cereal in the bottle.

It is important to be alert to signs that a baby is satisfied. Stopping periodically during the feeding gives infants a chance to assess their own hunger and respond appropriately when the bottle is again offered. It is important to respect an infant's judgment of the amount of food needed at a given time.

Since the parent or teacher receives visual indicators of how much the child has drunk from a bottle, the bottle-fed infant is frequently urged to finish the feeding. In so doing, the parent or teacher may ignore the infant's signs of fullness. Such signs include:

- closing the mouth or turning away from the bottle
- falling asleep
- fussing at repeated attempts to continue feeding
- biting or playing with the nipple

---

electrolytes – *substances which, when in solution, become capable of conducting electricity; examples include sodium and potassium.*

Some authorities believe that continuously ignoring these signs may cause the infant to stop such signaling, thus ending a means of regulating food intake. This could have serious consequences later for the toddler, the preschooler, and the adult who does not know when to stop eating. To establish the point at which the infant is satisfied, the teacher might stop after a few minutes of solid-food feeding and play with the child before offering food again. This helps determine whether the infant is eating because of hunger or to get attention.

Introducing semi-solid foods to the infant before they are needed or giving foods that are too high in sugar or fat may lead to babies taking more calories than they need with the consequence of obesity. Continuing to offer solid food after the baby seems satisfied also contributes to obesity and may set the stage for overeating later in life.

Choking. This can be avoided during breast or bottle feeding by holding the child properly with the head elevated as previously described. Allowing the infant to lie down with the bottle propped up greatly increases the danger of choking. The six- to seven-month-old infant wants and should be given finger foods such as dry bread, crackers, or dry cereal. However, these foods may cause choking. This danger can be minimized by having the child sit in an upright position and offering only foods that do not break into large pieces that are difficult for the infant to swallow. Offering semi-solid food that is finely ground and somewhat diluted will also minimize choking. Due to the high incidence of choking among infants, CPR training for parents and teachers is vitally important.

Teething. Teeth begin to erupt around six months of age. This can be a stressful period for some infants. Teething may temporarily disrupt an infant's feeding pattern. As a result, some infants may begin to wean themselves from breast or bottle feedings. They may prefer foods that can be chewed such as dry toast or teething biscuits. Diarrhea accompanying teething is usually due to infectious organisms and is not caused by the teething process. Appropriate toys and food items should be made available for chewing to discourage infants from picking up inappropriate or unsafe objects to chew on. In a child care center, it is important to ensure that toys are frequently sanitized to reduce the risk of spreading infectious organisms.

Constipation. Infants who have difficulty with infrequent, hard bowel movements may be helped by increasing their intake of water and fibrous foods such as whole grain cereals, fruits, and vegetables. If the infant is still primarily on bottle feeding, the health care provider should be consulted about possible formula changes.

FOCUS ON FAMILIES • Infant Feeding

A majority of food preferences carried into adulthood evolve from childhood and childhood eating experiences. Birth (or before) is the ideal time to begin addressing a child's nutritional well-being.

- Breast milk and/or infant formula is recommended as the infant's primary source of nutrition for the first year. Cow's milk cannot meet the nutritional requirements needed for the rapid growth rate of an infant and should not be offered during the first year.

- Always hold and bond with an infant during feedings. This is essential in preventing choking and bottle-mouth syndrome.

- The first food that should be introduced into an infant's diet is a single-grain iron-fortified cereal. Introduce foods one at a time in order to detect possible allergies/intolerances.

- Be wary of food additives, especially in commercially produced baby food. "Desserts" and "Dinners" often contain additives and offer less nutritional value than plain cereal, vegetables, fruits, and meats.

- 100 percent fruit juice can be introduced at approximately six to seven months of age. Avoid fruit beverages, fruit drinks, sodas, and tea.

- Avoid foods that cause choking: grapes, peanuts, hotdogs, and popcorn.

CASE STUDY

Lindsey, five months old, has been brought to child care as her mother has returned to work. Lindsey was started on cereal mixed with pureed fruit prior to entering child care. Lindsey's mother pumps her breast milk and delivers it to child care frozen to be thawed and fed to Lindsey as needed. The infant is now experiencing some diarrhea and apparent abdominal pain.

1. What are some possible causes of Lindsey's discomfort?
2. Do you know how the breast milk is handled at home?
3. What are safe procedures for handling breast milk at child care?
4. Given Lindsey's age, is she ready to have fruit added to her diet?
5. What other food/liquids could be used to mix her cereal; what type of cereal should be fed?

SUMMARY

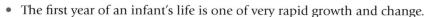

- The first year of an infant's life is one of very rapid growth and change.
  - The baby will have tripled its birth weight.
  - Length will have increased by 50 percent.

- Good nutrition is a major factor contributing to physical growth.
  - Breast milk is the preferred nutrition for the first four to six months.
  - Formula is an acceptable alternate when breast-feeding is not feasible.
  - Unmodified cow's or goat's milk should not be given during the first year.

- At the age of four to six months, the infant is developmentally and physiologically ready for semi-solid foods.
  - Single grain cereals are the first semi-solid foods added.
  - Vegetables, fruits, and meats are added over the next three months.

- Social aspects of infant feeding are important.
  - The infant should be held when feeding.
  - Cuddling, eye-contact, and talking should be part of the infant feeding experience.
  - Feeding is a key aspect of the infant–parent bonding.

SUGGESTED ACTIVITIES

1. Mrs. Jones, mother of two-month-old Kelly, has been on maternity leave from her job. At present, she is breast-feeding Kelly. She is preparing to return to work and place Kelly with a teacher.
   She is concerned that she must switch Kelly to formula, although she has found breast-feeding quite rewarding. What feeding options can her teacher offer her?

2. Visit the baby food section of the local grocery store and read the ingredients that are listed on the labels. Based on the ingredients listed, select several kinds of foods that are good choices to feed to a young infant.

3. Plan an instructional package with which to instruct a new employee in an infant care facility. What social aspects of infant feeding should be included in addition to nutritional and infant-handling factors?

4. If applicable, review state regulations for child teachers relating to infant feeding.

5. Review the common problems associated with low-birthweight infants and report the prenatal nutrient deficiencies that most frequently result in the birth of low-birthweight infants.

CHAPTER REVIEW

Briefly answer each of the following questions.

1. List three reasons for not propping the infant's bottle when the infant is feeding.

2a. In what order should the following foods be introduced?
   pureed peas   pureed meat products   iron-fortified cereal
   crisp toast   pureed peaches

2b. At approximately what ages should each of these foods be introduced?

3. Describe three social factors that make feeding time more enjoyable for an infant.

4. Why should unmodified cow's or goat's milk not be given to an infant before one year of age?

5. Why should reduced fat milk or skim milk not be used for preparing an infant's formula feeding?

6. Describe several feeding practices that are considered to contribute to infant obesity.

7. What should be evaluated if an infant is experiencing vomiting and/or diarrhea?

REFERENCES

Duyff, R. L. (1996). *The American Dietetic Association's complete food and nutrition guide*. Minneapolis, MN: Chromined Publishing.

Georgia Department of Human Resources. (1990). *Infant feeding guide*. Atlanta, GA: Author.

Kurtzweil, P. (1995, May). Labeling rules for young children's food. *FDA Consumer*.

Mahan, L. K., & Escott-Stump, S. (1996). *Krause's food, nutrition, and diet therapy* (9th ed.). Philadelphia: W. B. Saunders Company.

Marincic, P. Z., McCune, R. W., & Hendricks, D. G. (1999). Cows-milk-based infant formula: Heterogeneity of bovine serum albumin content. *Journal of the American Dietetic Association, 99,* 1575–1578.

Research & Education Institute, Harbor-UCLA Medical Center. (1990). *WIC Program.* Los Angeles, CA: Author.

The Chicago Dietetic Association & The South Suburban Dietetic Association. (1996). *Manual of clinical dietetics.* Chicago, IL: Authors.

WIC Program, Research & Education Institute, Inc., Harbor-UCLA Medical Center. (1990). *Nutrition and child care information.* Los Angeles, CA: Author.

Wong, D. L. (1993). *Essentials of pediatric nursing.* St. Louis, MO: Mosby-Year Book.

ADDITIONAL READING

Carver, J. D., Pimenthal, B., Cox, W. J., & Marness, L. A. (1991). Dietary nucleotide effects upon immune function in infants. *Pediatrics, 88*(2), 359–363.

Committee on Nutrition, American Academy of Pediatrics. (1981). Nutritional aspects of obesity: Infancy and childhood. *Pediatrics, 68,* 880.

Gershoff, S. (1991). *Total nutrition.* New York: Harper and Row.

FDA. (1995, March). Labeling rules for young children's food. *FDA Consumer.*

Liebman, B. (1990). Baby formula: Missing key fats. *Nutrition Action Health Letter, 17*(8), 8–9.

Pipes, P. L. (1997). *Nutrition in infancy and childhood.* St. Louis, MO: Times Mirror/Mosby.

Roberts, S. B. (1988). Energy expenditure and intake in infants born to lean or overweight mothers. *New England Journal of Medicine, 318,* 461.

Samour, P. Q., & Helm, K. K. & Lang, C. E. (1999). *Handbook of pediatric nutrition.* Sudbury, MA: Jones and Bartlett Publishing.

Satter, E. (1986). *Child of mine; Feeding with love and good sense.* Palo Alto, CA: Bull Publishing Co.

Satter, E. (1991). *How to get your child to eat . . . But not too much.* Palo Alto, CA: Bull Publishing Co.

Satter, E. (1980). The feeding relationship. *Journal of the American Dietetic Association, 86,* 352–356.

HELPFUL WEB SITES

Child Care Bureau	http://www.acf.dhhs.gov
LaLeche League	http://www.lalecheleague.org
National Network for Childcare	http://www.nncc.org
The National Women's Health Information Center	http://www.4woman.gov/breastfeeding/
Gerber	http://www.gerber.com
Nestlé Carnation Infant Nutrition	http://www.verybestbaby.com

For additional health, safety, and nutrition resources, go to
http://www.EarlyChildEd.delmar.com

CHAPTER 18

Feeding the Toddler and Preschool Child

OBJECTIVES

After studying this chapter, you should be able to:

- Outline three major responsibilities of the teacher in feeding the toddler.
- Estimate appropriate serving sizes of food for toddlers and preschoolers.
- Describe the possible consequences of overreliance on milk as a food for toddlers.
- List two strategies that will enable the teacher to promote good eating habits.
- Name three health problems that are thought to be related to unhealthy eating habits acquired at an early age.

TERMS TO KNOW

neophobic
individuality

reward(s)
dental caries

hypertension
refusal

PROFILE OF TODDLERS AND PRESCHOOLERS

Toddlers (one- to two-and-a-half-year-olds) are a challenge! They want to assert their independence but need and want limits. As they become increasingly mobile and active, they need to be protected from and taught about environmental hazards. Their insatiable curiosity can get them into trouble. Their daily routine, including food experiences, is affected by societal and cultural factors that affect their family. Children of working parents may spend considerable time each day outside of their home with teachers and other children. This will give the child social experiences that differ from those in their home. The child thus learns that different people do things in different ways.

Toddlers begin to be avid television watchers, and what they see will affect their behavior including their reactions to food (Figure 18–1). The hours spent sitting in front of the TV reduce valuable time that should be spent in physical activity (Figure 18–2). This inactivity reduces the child's caloric needs and could contribute to child obesity problems. There is also cause for concern about the foods advertised during children's prime TV time. Recent research shows that even brief exposures to commercials can influence children to choose low-nutrition junk food (Borzekowski & Robinson, 2001). Many of these foods create a desire for foods that are high in sugar and fat and are highly refined.

414

FIGURE 18–1

Some young children spend too many hours sitting and watching television.

The toddler grows less rapidly than the infant but still has a high nutrient need and limited stomach capacity. The infant was best fed on demand, but the toddler needs a consistent schedule for eating. In their struggle for independence, toddlers may resist this schedule and frequently reject the food served. They have learned the power of the word "no" and use it constantly. They quickly learn to shape parents' behavior by refusing to eat or, at other times, by eating to gain adult favor.

The toddler is described as being **neophobic**—having a fear of anything new (Satter, 1988). This may interfere with getting the child to eat an increasing variety of foods. However,

FIGURE 18–2

It is better for toddlers and preschoolers to be physically active than to sit and watch television.

neophobic – *fear of things that are new and unfamiliar.*

recognizing this quality in the toddler may help parents and teachers be a bit more patient and ingenious as they introduce new foods.

Preschool-aged children (two and a half to five years) are easier to manage. They still assert their independence but they want to please and learn to express their **individuality** in ways that are more appropriate. They are very sociable and want to be liked by peers, as well as by parents and teachers. The preschool-aged child wants structure and respects it more than the toddler did. However, they do not suddenly become overly compliant persons and are still somewhat hesitant to accept new things.

Preschoolers are involved with discovering ways to become individuals, while also being extremely social and making new friends. Many of these changes will be reflected in their reactions to food and eating.

THE CHALLENGE OF FEEDING A TODDLER

Toddlers, in asserting their independence, begin to make their preferences known. This includes their firm announcement of what foods they will or will not eat. Fortunately, their "will" and "will not" foods change almost daily. Great care must be taken so that the parent or teacher does not become involved in a battle of wills over what the toddler will eat and when it will be eaten.

Basic to minimizing this friction is a clear understanding of the primary responsibilities of parent/teacher and child in the feeding relationship. The teacher is responsible for:

- serving a variety of nutritious foods
- deciding when food is offered
- setting a good example by eating a variety of foods

The child is responsible for:

- choosing what foods will be eaten from those that have been offered
- deciding how much of the offered food to eat

What Foods Should Be Served and How Much

Parents and teachers have a responsibility to provide a variety of nutritious foods each day. As discussed in Chapter 13, the Food Guide Pyramid guidelines are easy to follow and ensure meeting daily nutritional needs. To review, the Food Guide Pyramid Groups and recommended daily servings for toddlers are (see Figure 18–3):

- Bread, Cereal, Rice, and Pasta Group (6 servings)
- Vegetable Group (3 servings)
- Fruit Group (2 servings)
- Milk, Yogurt, and Cheese Group (2 servings)
- Meat, Poultry, Fish, Dry Beans, and Eggs Group (2 servings)
- Fats, Oils, and Sweets Group (use sparingly)

Foods from all food groups should be offered at each meal. They may be offered individually:

- ground beef patty
- green beans
- whole grain bread
- sliced peaches
- milk

individuality – *qualities that distinguish one person from another.*

FIGURE 18–3

Food Guide Pyramid for young children: a daily guide for (two to six year olds). USDA Center for Nutrition Policy and Promotion.

or be combined in one main dish:

- tuna noodle casserole with peas
- milk
- diced pineapple

Toddlers usually prefer foods presented individually. Toddler serving sizes are approximately one-fourth that of an adult serving for each food group with the exception of the milk group (Figure 18–4):

- milk and milk products—1/2 to 3/4 cup
- meat and meat alternates—1 to 1 1/2 ounces
- fruits and vegetables—2 tbsp
- breads and cereals—2 tbsp rice, cereal, or pasta

When feeding a toddler, it is preferable to serve slightly less than what the teacher thinks the child will eat and let the child ask for more. In this way toddlers are not overwhelmed by the serving size and are allowed to assert their independence by asking for more. The toddler's decreased rate of growth typically causes a decrease in appetite and lack of interest in food. This often causes parents and teachers great concern. However, it is important that this concern does not lead to begging or forcing the child to eat more food than the child wants or needs.

Table 18–1 presents some age-related eating behaviors that may help understand a child's changing responses to food. This table also gives adults who are feeding the toddler some clues as to how to help maximize positive feeding experiences at different ages.

When to Serve Food

Timing of meals and snacks is important when feeding the toddler. Too much time between feedings will result in an overhungry, cranky child who is less likely to accept the food presented.

FIGURE 18–4

Menu suitable for a toddler.

BREAKFAST	**LUNCH**	**DINNER**
Whole milk (1/2 cup)	Whole milk (1/2 cup)	Whole milk (1/2 cup)
Cream of wheat (1/4 cup)	Beef patty (1 1/2 oz)	Finely chopped chicken (1 1/2 oz)
Banana (1/2)	Whole-wheat bread (1 slice)	Dinner roll (1/2)
Margarine (1 tsp)	Broccoli (2 tbsp)	Cooked carrots (2 tbsp)
Whole-wheat toast (1/2 slice)	Margarine (1 tsp)	Margarine (1 tsp)
Jam or jelly (1 tsp)	Canned peaches (1/4 cup)	Mashed potatoes (2 tbsp)
MIDMORNING SNACK	**MIDAFTERNOON SNACK**	**EVENING SNACK**
Vanilla wafers (2)	Fruit yogurt (1/2 cup)	Applesauce (1/4 cup)
Orange juice (1/2 cup)		Graham crackers (2)

TABLE 18–1   Expected Eating Behaviors According to Age

AGE	BEHAVIOR
12–24 months	has a decreased appetite sometimes described as a finicky or fussy eater; may go on food jags uses spoon with some degree of skill helps feed self
2 year old	appetite is fair often has strong likes and dislikes; may go on food jags likes simple food, dislikes mixtures, wants food served in familiar ways learns table manners by imitating adults and older children
3 year old	appetite is fairly good; prefers small servings, likes only a few cooked vegetables feeds self independently, if hungry uses spoon in semi-adult fashion; may even spear with fork dawdles over food when not hungry
4 year old	appetite fluctuates from very good to fair may develop dislikes of certain foods and refuse them to the point of tears if pushed likes to help with meal preparation uses all eating utensils; becomes skilled at spreading jelly or peanut butter or cutting soft foods such as bread
5 year old	eats well, but not at every meal likes familiar foods often adopts food dislikes of family members and teachers makes breakfast (pours cereal, gets out milk and juice) and lunch (spreads peanut butter and jam on bread)

Adapted from Allen, K. E., & Marotz, L. R. (2003).

Meals and snacks spaced too closely will not allow ample time for a child to become hungry, again resulting in a poor eating response. Most young children also eat better at meals if they are not too tired and if they have been given a little warning so that they can "wrap up" their current play activity. Allowing time for reading a quiet story just before a meal may set the stage for a pleasant and more satisfying meal-time experience for both child and teacher.

Because of toddlers' great need for nutrients and small stomach capacity, they must eat more often than the three-meal family pattern. A good eating pattern is:

- breakfast
- midmorning snack
- lunch
- midafternoon snack
- dinner
- bedtime snack, if needed

Snacks should be chosen from the Food Guide Pyramid and be planned carefully as part of the day's total food intake. If a food is appropriate to be in a child's meal, it is a good snack choice. Snacks for the toddler cannot be those commonly promoted on TV as "snacks." Foods such as chips, snack cakes, rich cookies, candy bars, fruit "drinks," and sodas have no place in the toddler's daily food plan. These foods contain empty calories, which provide little if any nutritional value. Some appropriate food choices for snacks are:

- cheese cubes
- lightly sweetened puddings
- crackers with peanut butter
- 100 percent fruit juice—orange or other juices fortified with vitamin C
- raw vegetables—broccoli flowerettes, cauliflower pieces, carrots (cut in small pieces to reduce risk of choking)
- lightly cooked vegetables—green beans, carrots, lima beans
- fruits—apple and orange wedges, bananas, applesauce, diced peaches/pears
- whole grain crackers or bread
- dry, nonsweetened cereal
- yogurt

How to Make Eating Time Comfortable, Pleasant, and Safe

Children are more likely to eat in comfortable surroundings. Furniture should be at an appropriate size; table height should be at a comfortable height for children to eat from and the chairs should allow their feet to rest flat on the floor. If a highchair or youth chair is used, it must allow support for the child's feet and have a comfortable eating tray. Eating utensils should be child-sized and non-breakable. An upturned rim around plates provides a means of "trapping" elusive bits of food. Use of plates that are divided into two or three compartments may help reduce frustration for toddlers as they develop their feeding skills. Small (4–6 ounce) cups with broad bases are easy for children to hold and reduce spilling. Forks chosen for children should have short, blunt tines and broad, short easy-to-grasp handles. Spoons should also have short, blunt handles and shallow bowls for easy use. While most toddlers and preschoolers will have difficulty using knives for cutting, they should be encouraged to use them occasionally for spreading in order to help them develop this skill.

During the toddler and preschool years, children are developing better fine motor skills and hand/eye coordination. This enables them to better handle utensils and feed themselves (Figure 18–5). They should be encouraged to use these skills but should not be given too many

FIGURE 18–5

Toddlers and preschoolers develop fine motor skills enabling them to better use eating utensils.

FIGURE 18–6

Toddlers and preschoolers must learn the importance of washing hands before handling food.

hard-to-manage foods at one time. Serving finger foods along with those foods that require using a fork or spoon reduces mealtime frustration.

Finger foods encourage self-feeding; they are well accepted and easy to handle. Meats and cheeses may be cut into cubes or strips, vegetables into sticks, and fruits into slices. Toddlers enjoy turning some nonfinger foods into finger foods and often accept them better because it was their individual choice. A parent may not think peas, mashed potatoes, and rice are finger foods, but some toddlers do. A little flexibility in the choice of eating methods often pays off in the toddler's increased willingness to try eating by conventional methods.

Sanitation is an important consideration in feeding the toddler. The aseptic environment with which we surround the infant is not necessary or possible with the toddler. However, cleanliness is of prime importance when preparing, serving, and eating food. The teacher and toddler must thoroughly wash their hands before handling or eating food and again after eating or before returning to work or play (Figure 18–6). Handwashing is mandatory since this age group does a lot of eating with their hands.

AS THE TODDLER BECOMES A PRESCHOOLER

As children grow older, they begin to eat more willingly. However, preschoolers will have even firmer ideas of what they will and will not eat. The preschooler grows in "spurts" that are followed by periods of little or no growth, only weight gain. During active growth periods the child's appetite and food acceptance is usually good. However, as growth slows, so does the child's appetite. It is during this latter stage that parents and teachers often are unduly concerned. (This concern can have the consequence of establishing a food–emotion link that can lead to long-lasting feeding problems.) There is no real cause for concern; a growing energetic child will never starve. Remember that during this age, food is offered frequently. If Johnny does not eat a good lunch, it will soon be snack time and he can get the needed nutrients then. The important thing is to be sure that the snack food presented is of the same nutritious quality as the lunch.

During the preschool years, attitudes about food and eating patterns are formed that will be carried throughout adult life. The teacher and parents share responsibilities for forming positive feelings about food and promoting healthful eating practices in the young child. Preschoolers like rules even though they resist them. Rules about acceptable eating behavior should be consistent to establish good mealtime behaviors. However, rules should allow flexibility for parent and child in order to avoid stressful eating situations.

Guidelines for Feeding the Preschooler

As with toddlers, the Food Guide Pyramid provides a simple guideline for feeding preschoolers (Figure 18–7). The main difference is in amount of food served. Suggested serving sizes for the preschooler are:

1/2 to 3/4 cup milk
1/2 to 1 slice of bread
1 tbsp for each year of age for:
    fruits
    vegetables
    meats and meat alternates

Serving the preschooler a little less than you expect them to eat does not overwhelm them but rather gives them an opportunity to ask for more. Three- to five-year-old children are also very aware of the appearance of food. Attention should be given to presenting a variety of colors, shapes, and textures in a meal. Doing so makes the food more attractive and increases its acceptance. At this age the child prefers foods that are lukewarm. Hot or cold foods are often rejected or

FIGURE 18–7

Menu suitable for a preschool child.

BREAKFAST	LUNCH	DINNER
2% milk (1/2 cup)	2% milk (1/2 cup)	2% milk (1 cup)
Cream of wheat (1/2 cup)	Beef patty (2 oz)	Chopped chicken (2 oz)
Banana (1/2)	Whole-wheat bread (1 slice)	Cooked carrots (2 tbsp)
Margarine (1 tsp)	Broccoli (3 tbsp)	Dinner roll (1 medium)
Whole-wheat toast (1 slice)	Ketchup (1 tbsp)	Margarine (1 tsp)
Jam or jelly (2 tsp)	Canned peaches (1/4 cup)	Mashed potatoes (3 tbsp)
MIDMORNING SNACK	**MIDAFTERNOON SNACK**	**EVENING SNACK**
Vanilla wafers (3)	Cheese (3/4 oz)	Applesauce (1/3 cup)
Orange juice (1/2 cup)	Crackers (5)	Graham crackers (2)

FIGURE 18–8

Children enjoy preparing some of the food that they will eat.

played with until they reach an acceptable temperature. Involving the children in the preparation of a food to be served may enhance their interest in eating that food and the entire meal (Figure 18–8).

The same rules for making mealtime comfortable for the toddler also apply for the pre-schooler. The three-to five-year-old child still has trouble managing eating utensils and is more co-operative if some finger foods are provided and if unintentional messes are ignored.

GOOD EATING HABITS

Life-long eating habits are formed between the ages of one to five years. This makes the feeding of toddlers and preschoolers a very important task. Parents and teachers can promote good eating habits in two ways:

- serving and enjoying a variety of nutritious foods
- eating with the children and showing enjoyment of a variety of nutritious foods

One of the most important goals in developing good eating habits is to gain the toddler's and preschooler's acceptance of a variety of foods from each of the various food groups. It is especially important to cultivate an interest for the fruit and vegetable group because there is a great differ-ence in nutrient contribution from individual foods within this group. Children should be en-couraged to accept a variety of new foods and familiar foods should be prepared in different ways. Toddlers and preschoolers may learn to like things that are sweet and not to like most vegetables. This presents a real challenge to teachers to downplay sweets and increase children's interest in vegetables. Teachers should eat a variety of vegetables in front of the children, comment on how delicious they are and usually display pleasure (such as smiling). This should help to promote healthy life-long eating habits.

Children are often avid mimics of the adults in their lives and of peers in a child care setting. Consequently, it is particularly important that adults sit with the children at mealtime and show pleasure in eating all kinds of food, never showing dislike for a food. Children quickly pick up on negative reactions to food and imitate them. Table 18–2 gives some suggestions for introducing new foods that may increase their acceptance by the young child.

TABLE 18-2   Introducing New Food

1. Introduce only one new food at a time.
2. Serve new food with familiar foods.
3. Serve only small amounts of the new food—begin with one teaspoonful.
4. Introduce new food only when the child is hungry.
5. Talk about the new food—taste, color, texture, etc.
6. Let the child help prepare the new food.
7. Encourage the child to taste the new food. If rejected, accept the refusal and try again later. As foods become more familiar, they are more readily accepted.
8. Find out what is not liked about a rejected food. The food may be accepted if it is prepared in a different way.
9. Let the child see you eat the new food and enjoy it!

Adapted from: *Food for the Preschooler. Vol. 2.* Washington State Department of Social and Health Services.

Rewards should not be offered for trying a new food. Also, foods should never be used as a reward for any type of behavior. Studies with preschool children have shown that rewards for trying new foods increased the frequency of tasting a new food but did not increase the long-term acceptance of the new food. Adults are often tempted to use food (especially dessert or popular sweet snacks) as a reward for eating nutritious foods presented in the meal. This practice makes these foods assume undue importance for the child. Appropriate desserts should be nutritious and planned as an important part of the meal. If they are nutritious, they can be served to the child along with the main dish, bread, and vegetables. Also, a child should never be asked to present a "clean plate" before receiving their dessert. This is one sure way to start the child on a road to obesity.

HEALTH PROBLEMS RELATING TO EATING HABITS

Teaching the child healthful eating practices can benefit the child on through adulthood. A number of health problems are now thought to be directly or indirectly related to foods eaten. Examples are:

- **dental caries** (tooth decay)
- obesity (excess body fat)
- **hypertension** (high blood pressure)
- cardiovascular disease (CVD)
- diabetes mellitus
- some cancers

The occurrence of dental caries may be affected by sugar in the diet. However, the kind of sugar (soluble or not), the form it is in (adheres to tooth surface or not), and the time it is eaten

---

rewards – *things given for appropriate behavior.*
dental caries – *tooth decay.*
hypertension – *elevation of blood pressure above the normally accepted values.*

(meals versus snacks) determine the decay potential more than total sugar intake. Providing sugar in the form of fruits and vegetables may give protection from tooth decay. They also provide needed nutrients for the actively growing young child.

Prevention of obesity should start with infant feeding. Look for the infant's signals of satiety and then stop feeding when they occur. The toddler and preschooler will usually stop feeding when they have had enough food, unless eating or not eating is their best way to get attention. A genetic potential for obesity exists in some families; this does not mean that obesity is inevitable for all family members. Children with one or two obese parents should be helped during early childhood years to make wise choices of nutrient-dense foods. Approximately 15 percent of children are overweight. This rate of overweight has tripled in the last 20 years (Kaiser Permanente, 2003). Involving children in physical activity and limiting sedentary activities such as television viewing and computer/video games will also help the child maintain normal body weight (Figure 18–9).

For many years hypertension (high blood pressure) has been correlated with a high intake of salt (sodium). At-risk children are those from families where hypertension is common. They may

FIGURE 18–9

The Physical Activity Pyramid is designed to help children get fit and stay healthy.

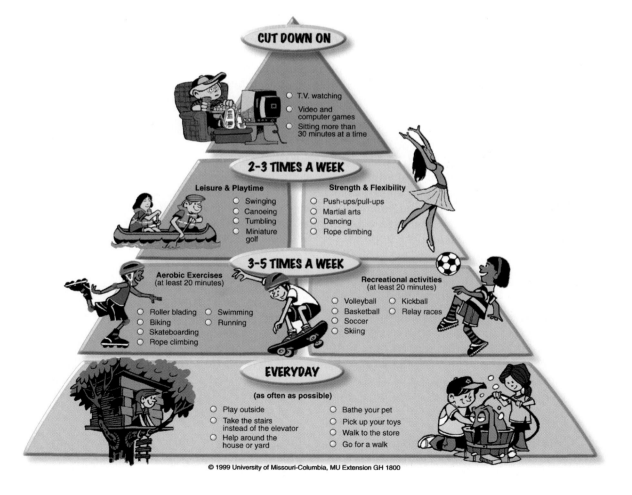

© 1999 University of Missouri-Columbia, MU Extension GH 1800

benefit from reducing the intake of salt. Sodium is an essential nutrient for infants and young children, but this need can be met easily without the use of the salt shaker. The increased use of convenience foods in the home, plus an increased frequency of eating out in fast food restaurants, may increase the intake of salt by both adults and children.

Cardiovascular disease (CVD) is most often associated with high levels of certain fatty substances in the blood. Cholesterol is most often associated with CVD; however, a high intake of saturated fatty acids and/or total fat are primary contributors to CVD. Sixty percent of overweight children ages 5 to 10 will already have one risk factor for heart disease (CDC, 2000).

The possible health benefit of testing and monitoring blood cholesterol levels in young children is a controversial issue. The American Academy of Pediatricians recommends that no cholesterol testing be done before the child is two years old. The two- to eight-year-old child should be tested for cholesterol only if there is a family history of early (<55 years of age) cardiovascular disease.

Fats, including cholesterol, should not be restricted in the diet of the infant or toddler; fats are a source of essential fatty acids and are required for normal nerve development.

The diet for a child with high blood cholesterol levels should be carefully monitored to not have more than 30 percent of calories from fat and 10 percent or less calories from saturated fat. If a child's diet must be adjusted for any reason, the first priority must be that it meets all of the nutrient requirements for normal growth and development. Involving the child in more physical activity may also lower blood cholesterol.

While Type I diabetes is not caused by the child's diet, the disease does have a profound effect on the diabetic child's eating habits and growth. There is no one "diabetic diet." The primary goal in feeding a diabetic child is to provide food to meet her nutritional needs. The purpose is to find a balance between food, medication (insulin), and activity to achieve normal blood sugar levels.

Typical meal plans for diabetic children include limitation of concentrated sugars, meals planned with food exchanges, and matching the amount of medication taken to the amount of carbohydrates in meals and snacks.

It is important that the diabetic child eat as many foods as possible similar to her peers so as not to feel that she is "different."

It had been thought that Type I diabetes occurred only in children and young adults, while Type II diabetes occurred primarily in overweight, middle-aged, and older adults. Recent years have seen a rapid increase in Type II diabetes in younger children due to the epidemic of childhood obesity. According to the American Academy of Pediatrics, research shows that 30 to 50 percent of children newly diagnosed with diabetes have Type II diabetes. This figure was less than 4 percent in 1990 (*Food Insight*, 2000).

Some Common Feeding Concerns During Toddler and Preschool Years

Consuming Excessive Amounts of Milk. The child who drinks milk to the exclusion of other foods may be at risk for iron-deficiency anemia and vitamin C (ascorbic acid) deficiency. Milk is very deficient in iron and in vitamin C. The child who drinks more than 16–24 ounces of milk daily usually does not consume enough foods from the other three food groups to adequately meet nutrient needs. Offering the child water between meals to satisfy thirst may help in solving this problem. Including iron-rich foods in the child's daily meals will also protect against iron-deficiency anemia. Table 19–1 presents some good food sources of iron.

Child's Refusal to Eat. Toddlers and preschoolers may refuse food either because they are not hungry or because they are asserting their newly found independence. Whatever the cause, the best response is to ignore it. Remember that active growing children will not let themselves starve—they will get hungry and eat. If nutritious food is provided for meals and snacks and if parents and teachers do not give in to substituting the less nutritious foods that the child requests, hunger will eventually win over the challenge of **refusal**. However, it is important that the teacher does not "try too hard." This can lead to battles and emotion-packed feeding sessions.

Dawdling and Messiness.   These are the trademarks of the toddler and preschooler and cannot be avoided; however, they can be controlled. Children dawdle for various reasons—they have eaten enough, they'd rather eat something else, or they have learned that it gets attention. Establishing mealtime rules and consistently enforcing them will usually end dawdling. The teacher should decide upon an appropriate length of time for eating (approximately 20–25 minutes), warn the child when there is not much time left, and then remove the child from the table. This may result in some unhappiness for a time, but the young child learns quickly. However, it is always important to avoid hurrying children at mealtime and to allow sufficient time for eating.

Children need to learn to feed themselves and manage proper eating utensils, even though some foods may present a real challenge. This results in understandable and forgivable messiness and should be ignored. Attention-getting messiness should be ignored also; otherwise, the behavior will be reinforced. However, the teacher has some rights too, and continuous, avoidable messiness may be handled by removing the child from the table.

Food Jags.   This problem can best be solved by prevention. Foods served to young children should be chosen so that a specific food does not appear too frequently. This helps to avoid the child getting fixed on a given food. Food jags occur when children consume a limited variety of foods and eventually results in a deficient intake of certain nutrients. Fortunately, children usually tire of these limited foods and will return to their normal eating behaviors.

Inconsistencies in Adult Approaches to Feeding Problems.   This concern relates to several problems already cited. It is very important that parents and teachers communicate and agree on the manner that certain food-related problems are going to be handled. It doesn't matter if the problem is weaning from excessive milk intake, decreasing dawdling and messiness behaviors, refusal to eat, or dealing with food jags, it is essential that a procedure to handle the problem is established and carried out consistently. The child cannot be expected to learn acceptable behavior if the rules constantly change.

REFLECTIVE THOUGHTS

Many parents report that their children are allergic to specific foods. However, actual documented food allergies are reported to affect up to 8 percent of children. Those foods most commonly responsible for allergic reactions are milk, eggs, soy, peanuts, tree nuts (cashews and almonds), wheat, fish, and shellfish. Not all food-related reactions are caused by allergies; some result from food intolerances. Many symptoms of food intolerance are identical to allergic symptoms.

- Can you tell the difference between food allergies and food intolerances?
- Is the difference important in terms of meal planning?
- Review the list of common foods causing allergic reactions. What similarities do you see between those foods and substances used to make infant formula?

---

refusal – *the act of declining or rejecting.*

Food Additives and Hyperactivity. Since 1973, when the Feingold diet was published, there has been considerable interest in the possible link between food additives and behavior problems, particularly hyperactivity and ADHD (see Chapter 5). Several early double-blind studies failed to show a link between additives and/or sugar and hyperactivity; however, more recent studies of specific additives have indicated some responses related to the amount of the additive given (Wolraich, 1996). Research has still not provided clear-cut answers. No doubt some children may be affected by certain additives in an allergic-type reaction. For these children, the offending agent should be eliminated from their diet. Sugar has also been thought to be a cause of hyperactivity, but this, too, has been unproven. Restricting a child's sugar intake has not been shown to improve behavior or learning. Actually, a biochemical case can be made for sugar as a calming and sleep-inducing agent (Sizer & Whitney, 1999, p. 126). Avoidance of additives or dyes is certainly not harmful if the diet still includes sufficient amounts of foods from all food groups. The parent–child interaction involved is thought to benefit hyperactive children.

Fast Food Consumption by Toddlers and Preschoolers. The current cultural pattern of increased numbers of two-working-parent and single-parent families has changed family eating practices. More meals are eaten outside of the home, especially in fast food restaurants. There is growing concern about the repeated and long-term consumption of fast food and its effect on young children. One concern centers around the lack of suitable seating and utensils for the young child. However, the major nutritional concern is that fast foods are very high in calories, fat, and salt. These may later contribute to health problems such as cardiovascular disease, hypertension, diabetes, or obesity. Fast foods are also low in vitamins A and C and calcium, unless milk is the selected beverage. A too frequent scenario is a mother and preschooler at a fast food shop. The mother shares a few bites of her hamburger with the child, whose meal is rounded out with french fries and a small cola. An occasional fast food meal for the preschool child is no problem if care is taken when selecting food and lacking nutrients are made up when selecting food for the other meals served that day.

Effect of Television on Food Preferences and Food Choices. Television advertising affects a child's attitudes toward food more than TV programs do. Preschoolers watch TV for many hours each day. It is estimated that a child is exposed to three hours of commercials per week and to 19,000–22,000 commercials each year. Over one-half of these commercials are for food. Cereals (mostly sweetened), cookies, candy, sweetened beverages, and fast food offerings

---

ISSUES TO CONSIDER • "Surfing the Web" for Information

Many of us "surf the Web" for information. A recent report in the *American Journal of Public Health* noted that 29 percent of Americans access the Internet for medical information.

- Do you think all the information available on the Internet is factual?
- Do you feel you can judge which is factual and which is not?
- Where would you turn for guidance?

Clues to unreliable sources include:

- information based on testimonials.
- information provided by someone who stands to profit.
- unpublished information available only on the Internet.

Source: American Dietetic Association. (1999). *Journal of the American Dietetic Association, 99*(12).

are the most frequently advertised foods. Many of these foods are high in sugar or fat and are too calorie-dense to be healthful choices for the young child. An additional concern is the extent to which a teacher's choice of food in the market is influenced by the child's food preferences that were learned from TV food commercials.

FOCUS ON FAMILIES • Feeding the Toddler and Preschool Child

Mealtimes with children can be filled with many emotions and learning experiences. It can be a joyful time for families to form strong positive bonds, or it can be a time when conflicts erupt and eating no longer becomes a pleasurable experience. Many families are faced with the latter if they have a picky eater in the family. It is challenging, but not impossible, to get picky eaters to explore and accept new foods in their diet. With careful planning, families can work to make their eating experiences positive ones.

- Let children help with menu planning. Take them to the grocery store to help pick out fresh fruits and vegetables.

- Serve foods that a child does not like with a favorite food they are familiar with.

- Use different preparation techniques to prepare food in a fun way.

- Do not give up on a food if your child does not accept it the first time around. It can take 10 to 15 exposures to an unfamiliar food before a child may accept it.

- Serve regular meals and snacks. Children are more likely to eat better if their meals and snacks are adequately spaced apart.

- Avoid sharing and passing your own food dislikes to your child.

- Finally, most children will get what they need nutritionally. Continue offering a wide variety of foods and making mealtime a positive, pleasant experience.

CASE STUDY

Maria, age three years, is enrolled in your care. Maria's parents speak very little English. Maria, having interacted with other English-speaking children, speaks and understands some English. Her food preferences, however, reflect those of her culture and she eats little of what you provide.

1. Can you meet Maria's needs?
2. What plans have you made or could you make in order to communicate with Maria's parents?
3. Do you have access to appropriate printed materials to aid in Maria's care/communication with her family?
4. Is an interpreter available for assistance? How would you find out?

SUMMARY

- After the first birthday:
  - physical growth rate slows.
  - behavioral change is rapid.
- Food can serve as a source of friction. The adult's responsibility is to:
  - serve a *variety* of nutritious foods.
  - decide when to offer food.
  - set a good example by eating a variety of nutritious foods.
- The child will decide:
  - what to eat.
  - how much to eat.
- Long-term food habits are formed during the preschool years.
  - Make self-feeding as successful as possible to foster self-esteem.
  - Make feeding as nutritious as possible to minimize food-related health problems such as obesity, anemia, and hypertension

SUGGESTED ACTIVITIES

1. Eighteen-month-old Jason has recently been enrolled in a child care center. His health assessment reveals that he is anemic. Observation of his eating habits reveals that he dislikes meat and vegetables but eats large quantities of fruits and drinks at least two cups of milk at every meal and snack. What changes in eating habits should the teacher try to foster to improve Jason's iron status?

2. Formulate plans for the dining area of a child care center that will help develop self-feeding skills. Include a discussion of appropriate furniture and eating utensils. Plan a menu for one day (one meal and two snacks) that will further enhance the child's self-feeding skills.

3. Four-year-old Traci arrives at her teacher's home every morning with a bag of doughnuts. Her mother has told her that her daughter does not need to eat the food served to her but may eat her doughnuts instead. The other children have also begun to ask for doughnuts. How should the teacher handle this situation? What factors must be considered?

CHAPTER REVIEW

A. Briefly answer the following questions.

1. Name three ways that mealtimes can be made pleasant for children.

2. Explain the teacher's major responsibilities in toddler feeding situations.

3. Suggest serving sizes for a two-year-old and for a four-year-old for each of the following foods:

bread	peas
applesauce	orange juice
banana	cooked chicken
noodles	baked beans

B. **Suggested Class Projects**

1. Watch one hour of Saturday morning cartoons on television and answer the following:
   a. What foods were presented in the commercials?
   b. What adjectives were used in describing the foods that were advertised?
   c. Imagine you are a four-year-old. On your next trip to the grocery store with your mother, what products would you want her to buy?

2. Go to a fast food restaurant featuring hamburgers and observe the following:
   a. How many toddlers and preschoolers are there?
   b. What are the children eating and drinking?
   c. What foods can be ordered from the restaurant to provide a more nutritious, healthier meal?
   d. Ask the restaurant for nutritional information or visit its Web site.

3. Go to the local supermarket and observe advertising techniques geared toward children's foods.
   a. What cereals are sold at a child's eye level?
   b. What types of foods are displayed at the end of aisles?
   c. What types of free food samples are offered by the store to young children?

REFERENCES

Allen, K. E., & Marotz, L. R. (2003). *Developmental profiles: Pre-birth through twelve* (4th ed.). Clifton Park, NY: Delmar Learning.

American Dietetic Association. (1999). *Journal of the American Dietetic Association, 99*(12).

Borzekowski, D. L., & Robinson, T. N. (2001). The 30-second effect: An experiment revealing the impact of television commercials on food preferences of preschoolers. *Journal of the American Dietetic Association. 101*(1), 42–46.

International Food Information Council Foundation (January/February 2003). The Challenge of Type 2 Diabetes in children. *Food Insight.*

Kaiser Permanente (2003). The epidemic of obesity: Challenges and opportunities for Kaiser Permanente. *The Permanente Journal, 7,* 2.

Mahan, L. K., & Escott-Stump, S. (1996). *Krause's food, nutrition, and diet therapy* (9th ed.). Philadelphia: W. B. Saunders Company.

Satter, E. (1988). *How to get your child to eat . . . But not too much.* Palo Alto, CA: Bull Publishing Co.

Sizer, F., & Whitney, E. (1999). *Nutrition concepts and controversies* (8th ed.). Belmont, CA: Wadsworth/Thomson Learning.

United States Department of Health and Human Services: CDC (Winter, 2000). Preventing obesity among children. *Chronic Disease Notes and Reports, 13,* 1.

Washington State Department of Social and Health Services. (1992). *Food for the preschooler, Vol. 2.* Olympia, WA: Author.

Wolraich, M. L. (1996). Diet and behavior: What the research shows. *Contemporary Pediatrics, 13*(12), 29–39.

ADDITIONAL READING

Brackenridge, B. P., & Rubin, R. R. (1996). *Sweet kids.* Chicago: The American Diabetes Association.

Burt, J. V., & Hertzler, A. A. (1980). Parental influence on the child's food preference. *Journal of Nutritional Education, 12,* 200.

Dietz, W., & Gortmaker, S. L. (1985). Do we fatten our children at the television set? Obesity and television viewing in children and adolescents. *Pediatrics, 75,* 807.

Duyff, R. L. (2002). *The American Dietetic Association's complete food and nutrition guide* (2nd ed). New York: John Wiley & Sons.

Ephron, D. (1978). *How to eat like a child and other lessons in not being grown up.* New York: Viking Press.

Essa, E. (1999). *Practical guide to solving preschool behavior problems* (4th ed.). Albany, NY: Delmar.

Koerner, C. B. (1998). *Food allergies.* Chicago: The American Dietetic Association.

National Cholesterol Education Program Coordinating Committee. (1991). *Highlights of the report of the expert committee on blood cholesterol levels in children and adolescents.* Washington, DC: Author.

Pipes, P. L. (1997). *Nutrition in infancy and childhood.* St. Louis, MO: Times Mirror/Mosby.

Satter, E. (2000). *Child of mine; Feeding with love and good sense.* Palo Alto, CA: Bull Publishing Co.

Shapiro, L. R., Crawford, P. B., Clark, M. J., Pearson, D. J., Raz, J., & Huenemann, R. L. (1984). Obesity prognosis: A longitudinal study of children from the age of 6 months to 9 years. *American Journal of Public Health, 74,* 968–972.

HELPFUL WEB SITES

Diabetes Care	http://care.diabetesjournals.org
Journal of Pediatrics	http://www.us.elsevierhealth.com
Texas Department of Health	http://www.tdh.state.tx.us

For additional health, safety, and nutrition resources, go to http://www.EarlyChildEd.delmar.com

CHAPTER 19

Planning and Serving Nutritious and Economical Meals

OBJECTIVES

After studying this chapter, you should be able to:

* Identify the criteria for adequate menus for young children.
* State where information can be obtained regarding licensing requirements for food and nutrition services.
* Plan meals and snacks that meet nutritional requirements for young children.
* Outline a simple cost control plan.

TERMS TO KNOW

sensory qualities
ethnic
weekly menus
cycle menus
odd-day cycle menus

whole grains
enriched
full-strength juice
fruit drinks

cost control
(First-In-First-Out) FIFO
  inventory method
procurement

One of the basic human needs is nourishing the body. Eating is an activity that most people, including infants and young children, enjoy. Eating is a sensory, emotional, social, and learning experience. It is associated with the young child's feeling of well-being. As many infants and young children spend much of their early years in the care of teachers other than parents, it is important that teachers help the children establish appropriate attitudes toward meals. This can be accomplished by planning nourishing meals that are acceptable to children and serving these meals in a pleasant atmosphere that helps build the child both socially and emotionally.

MEAL PLANNING

A menu is a list of foods that are to be served; it is the basis of any food service. Menu planning requires thought and careful evaluation of the physical, developmental, and social needs of those for whom it is planned. Thought and planning are as necessary for a menu designed to feed a family of three as they are for an institution serving thousands of meals a day. The difference between the two situations is largely one of scale. The same careful planning must be applied to the development of menus suitable for young children. To be adequate, a menu planned for children must:

- meet the nutritional needs of children
- meet any existing funding or licensing requirements
- be appealing (have taste, texture, and eye appeal)
- make children comfortable by serving familiar foods
- encourage healthy food habits by introducing new foods
- provide safe food prepared and served in clean surroundings
- stay within budgetary limits
- provide alternatives for children with food allergies

A Good Menu Meets Nutritional Needs

The primary criterion for a good menu is nutritional adequacy. A menu must meet the nutritional needs of those for whom it is intended. When planning menus for young children in a care center, it is important to first determine what share of the day's total intake must be included in the menu. To determine the nutritional needs of young children, the Food Guide Pyramid and/or the *Dietary Guidelines for Americans* for that age group should be reviewed. Menus should be planned around servings from the Food Guide Pyramid.

Iron, calcium, and vitamin C are nutrients for which young children are most at risk; these nutrients should be provided daily. Tables 19–1 through 19–4 give sources for these nutrients and suggestions for preparation.

Federally funded food programs for children are required to provide one-third of the recommended daily requirements for calcium, iron, vitamin A, and vitamin C. However, it is recommended that nearly one-half the day's nutrients be included in the event that meals at home do not provide the other two-thirds of the needed nutrients. Federal guidelines for child care centers, Child and Adult Care Food Program (CACFP), receiving federal reimbursement require the following menu pattern in order to ensure minimum nutritional adequacy:

1. Minimum Breakfast Requirement
   - whole grain or enriched bread or bread alternate
   - full-strength fruit or vegetable juice, or a fruit or vegetable
   - milk, fluid

REFLECTIVE THOUGHTS

The Pyramid represents an idea that has become very popular. Review the Food Guide Pyramid illustrated in Chapter 13. The Pyramid has now been adapted to include the Children's Pyramid, a Vegetarian Pyramid, and a Mediterranean Pyramid. The idea has been expanded to other areas such as Activity Pyramids and Stress Relief Pyramids.

- Why do you think the Pyramid has become so widely used?
- Is the Food Guide Pyramid pertinent to your daily life/work?
- Do you use it to plan meals?
- What portion of the Pyramid do you have the greatest difficulty achieving?

TABLE 19–1 Sources of Iron and Suggested Preparation

Liver
strips, baked
loaf
braised, with tomato sauce
braised, with apple slices and onion

Beef
ground beef and macaroni casserole
ground beef patty
meat loaf
roast beef
hot beef sandwich with gravy
beef stew
meat balls and spaghetti
meat sauce and spaghetti
roast beef sandwich

Dried Peas, Beans, and Lentils
with rice
with small amounts of meat
with vegetables
in soup

Ham
creamed ham and peas
ham salad
ham and sweet potato casserole
scalloped ham and potatoes
sliced baked ham
ham sandwich

Prunes
stewed
whip
fruit soup

Chicken
chicken and rice
chicken and dumplings
chicken and noodles
creamed chicken
baked chicken
chicken salad

Grain Products (Whole or Enriched)
pasta with tomato or meat sauce
gingerbread
bran or cornmeal muffins
rice pudding

Raisins
in bread or rice pudding
plain
stewed
in cereal

Spinach
raw
salad with onions and bacon
cooked and buttered
with hard cooked eggs
with cheese sauce
with onions and bacon

TABLE 19–2 Sources of Calcium and Suggested Preparation

Milk
plain
in custards
in puddings

Cheese
in sandwiches
in cream sauce
cubes
in salads

Yogurt
plain
with fruit
as dip for fruits or vegetables

Salmon
patties
loaf

Vegetables
broccoli stir-fried with cheese sauce

TABLE 19–3 Sources of Vitamin C and Suggested Preparation

RICH SOURCES

Oranges
  juice
  sections
  slices
  wedges
  juice in gelatin

Strawberries
  plain
  with milk
  in fruit cup

Cantaloupe
  cubed or balled
  in fruit cup

Cauliflower
  raw
    florets
    with yogurt dip
  cooked
    buttered
    with cheese sauce
    with cream sauce

Green Pepper
  strips
  rings
  seasoning in sauces, casseroles

Broccoli
  raw
    strips
    chunks
    florets with yogurt dip
  cooked
    buttered
    with cheese sauce
    with lemon sauce

Tomatoes
  raw
    slices
    wedges
    cherry
    juice
    in tossed salad
  cooked
    baked
    broiled
    sauce
    scalloped
    stewed

GOOD SOURCES

Cabbage
  raw
    coleslaw
    wedges
    in tossed salad
  cooked
    buttered
    in stew

Spinach
  raw
    salad with onions and bacon

Tangerine
  sections
  slices
  in fruit cup

2. Minimum Snack Requirement (choose two different components) Refer to "Supplemental Foods" in Table 19–5.
   - whole grain or enriched bread or bread alternate
   - milk, fluid
   - full-strength fruit or vegetable juice, or a fruit or vegetable
   - meat or alternate
3. Minimum Lunch or Supper Requirement
   - meat or alternate
   - fruits and/or vegetables, two or more different kinds

TABLE 19–4   Sources of Vitamin A and Suggested Preparation

Rich Sources	Good Sources

Liver
  strips, baked
  loaf
  braised, with tomato sauce
	Apricots
	  raw
	  canned
	    plain
	    in fruit cup
	    whip
	    nectar

Carrots
  raw
  sticks, curls, coins
  salad, with raisins
  cooked
    with celery
    with peas
    creamed
	Cantaloupe
	  balls
	  cubes
	  in fruit cup

Pumpkin
  mashed
  bread
  custard
	Broccoli
	  raw
	    strips
	    chunks
	    florets with yogurt dip
	  cooked
	    buttered
	    with cheese sauce
	    with lemon sauce
	    stir-fried with celery, onions

Sweet Potatoes
  baked
  mashed
  bread	

Spinach
  raw
    salad with onions and bacon
  cooked
    buttered
    with hard cooked eggs
    with cheese sauce
    with onions and bacon	

- whole grain or enriched bread or alternate
- milk, fluid

Minimum serving sizes are determined by the child's age in categories of one to three years and three to six years (USDA, 1995).

A Good Menu Meets Funding or Licensing Requirements

Many child care organizations depend on some form of government monies for their funding. Perhaps the best known of these government programs is the Child and Adult Care Food Program (CACFP). This is a program that provides reimbursement for meals served to children in child care centers and home child care programs. Meal service includes cost of food, labor, and administration. Funds are provided by the Food and Nutrition Service of the U.S. Department of Agriculture; the program is administered within most states by the Department of Education. The meal plan cited in Table 19–5 is the minimum that must be served in order to qualify for reimbursement

TABLE 19–5 Meal Plans for Children Ages One Through Five

Breakfast. The minimum amount of food components to be served as breakfast are as follows:

Components	Ages 1 and 2	Ages 3 through 5
Milk, Fluid	1/2 cup[1]	3/4 cup
Vegetables and Fruits or	1/4 cup	1/2 cup
full-strength vegetable or fruit juice or an equivalent quantity of any combination of vegetable(s), fruit(s), and juice	1/4 cup	1/2 cup
Bread and Bread Alternatives[2]		
bread or	1/2 slice	1/2 slice
cornbread, biscuits, rolls, muffins, etc.[3] or	1/2 serving	1/2 serving
cold dry cereal[4] or	1/4 cup or 1/3 ounce	1/3 cup or 1/2 ounce
cooked cereal or	1/4 cup	1/4 cup
cooked pasta or noodle products or	1/4 cup	1/4 cup
cooked cereal grains or an equivalent quantity of any combination of bread/bread alternate	1/4 cup	1/4 cup

[1] For purposes of the requirements outlined in this subsection, a cup means a standard measuring cup.
[2] Bread, pasta, or noodle products, and cereal grains, shall be whole grain or enriched; cornbread, biscuits, rolls, muffins, etc., shall be made with whole grain or enriched meal or flour; cereal shall be whole grain or enriched or fortified.
[3] Serving sizes and equivalents to be published in guidance materials by FNS.
[4] Either volume (cup) or weight (ounces) whichever is less.

Lunch. The minimum amount of food components to be served as lunch are as follows:

Components	Ages 1 and 2	Ages 3 through 5
Milk, Fluid	1/2 cup[1]	3/4 cup
Vegetables and Fruits[2]		
vegetables(s) and/or fruit(s)	1/4 cup total	1/2 cup total
Bread and Bread Alternates[3]		
bread or	1/2 slice	1/2 slice
cornbread, biscuits, rolls, muffins, etc.[4] or	1/2 serving	1/2 serving
cooked pasta or noodle products or	1/4 cup	1/4 cup
cooked cereal grains or an equivalent quantity of any combination of bread/bread alternate	1/4 cup	1/4 cup
Meat and Meat Alternates		
lean meat or poultry or fish[5] or	1 ounce	1 1/2 ounces
alternate protein products[6] or	1 ounce	1 1/2 ounces
cheese or	1 ounce	1 1/2 ounces
egg (large) or	1/2	3/4
cooked dry beans or peas or	1/4 cup	3/8 cup
peanut butter or soynut butter or other nut or seed butters or	2 tablespoons	3 tablespoons
peanuts or soynuts or tree nuts or seeds[7] or	1/2 ounce[8] = 50%	3/4 ounce[8] = 50%
yogurt, plain or flavored, unsweetened or sweetened or an equivalent quantity of any combination of the above meat/meat alternates	4 ounces or 1/2 cup	6 ounces or 3/4 cup

[1] For purposes of the requirements outlined in this subsection, a cup means a standard measuring cup.
[2] Serve 2 or more kinds of vegetables(s) and/or fruit(s). Full-strength vegetable or fruit juice may be counted to meet not more than one half of this requirement.
[3] Bread, pasta, or noodle products, and cereal grains, shall be whole grain or enriched; cornbread, biscuits, rolls, muffins, etc., shall be made with whole grain or enriched meal or flour.
[4] Serving sizes and equivalents to be published in guidance materials by FNS.
[5] Edible portion as served.
[6] Must meet the requirements of Appendix A of this table (Alternate Foods for Meals).
[7] Tree nuts and seeds that may be used as meat alternates are listed in program guidance.
[8] No more than 50% of the requirement shall be met with nuts or seeds. Nuts or seeds shall be combined with another meat/meat alternate to fulfill the requirement. For purpose of determining combinations, 1 ounce of nuts or seeds is equal to 1 ounce of cooked lean meat, poultry, or fish.

(Continued)

TABLE 19–5 Meal Plans for Children Ages One Through Five (Continued)

Supper. The minimum amount of food components to be served as supper are as follows:

Components	Ages 1 and 2	Ages 3 through 5
Milk, Fluid	1/2 cup[1]	3/4 cup
Vegetables and Fruits[2]		
vegetables(s) and/or fruit(s)	1/4 cup total	1/2 cup total
Bread and Bread Alternates[3]		
bread or	1/2 slice	1/2 slice
cornbread, biscuits, rolls, muffins, etc.[4] or	1/2 serving	1/2 serving
cooked cereal grains or an equivalent quantity of any combination of bread/bread alternate	1/4 cup	1/4 cup
Meat and Meat Alternates		
lean meat or poultry or fish[5] or	1 ounce	1 1/2 ounces
alternate protein products[6] or	1 ounce	1 1/2 ounces
cheese or	1 ounce	1 1/2 ounces
egg (large) or	1/2	3/4
cooked dry beans or peas or	1/4 cup	3/8 cup
peanut butter or soynut butter or other nut or seed butters or	2 tablespoons	3 tablespoons
peanuts or soynuts or tree nuts or seeds[7] or	1/2 ounce[8] = 50%	3/4 ounce[8] = 50%
yogurt, plain or flavored, unsweetened or sweetened or an equivalent quantity of any combination of the above meat/meat alternates	4 ounces or 1/2 cup	6 ounces or 3/4 cup

[1] For purposes of the requirements outlined in this subsection, a cup means a standard measuring cup.
[2] Serve 2 or more kinds of vegetables(s) and/or fruit(s). Full-strength vegetable or fruit juice may be counted to meet not more than one half of this requirement.
[3] Bread, pasta, or noodle products, and cereal grains, shall be whole grain or enriched; cornbread, biscuits, rolls, muffins, etc., shall be made with whole grain or enriched meal or flour.
[4] Serving sizes and equivalents to be published in guidance materials by FNS.
[5] Edible portion as served.
[6] Must meet the requirements of Appendix A of this table (Alternate Foods for Meals).
[7] Tree nuts and seeds that may be used as meat alternates are listed in program guidance.
[8] No more than 50% of the requirement shall be met with nuts or seeds. Nuts or seeds shall be combined with another meat/meat alternate to fulfill the requirement. For purpose of determining combinations, 1 ounce of nuts or seeds is equal to 1 ounce of cooked lean meat, poultry, or fish.

Supplemental (Snack) Food. The minimum amount of food components to be served as supplemental foods are as follows. Select two of the following four components. (For children, juice may not be served when milk is served as the only other component.)

Components	Ages 1 and 2	Ages 3 through 5
Milk, Fluid	1/2 cup[1]	1/2 cup
Vegetables and Fruits		
vegetable(s) and/or fruit(s) or	1/2 cup	1/2 cup
full-strength vegetable or fruit juice or an equivalent quantity of any combination of vegetable(s), fruit(s), and juice	1/2 cup	1/2 cup
Bread and Bread Alternates[2]		
bread or	1/2 slice	1/2 slice
cornbread, biscuits, rolls, muffins, etc.[3] or	1/2 serving	1/2 serving
cold dry cereal or	1/4 cup or 1/3 ounce	1/3 cup or 1/2 ounce
cooked cereal[4] or	1/4 cup	1/4 cup
cooked pasta or noodle products or	1/4 cup	1/4 cup
cooked cereal grains or an equivalent quantity of any combination of bread/bread alternate	1/4 cup	1/4 cup

(Continued)

TABLE 19–5 Meal Plans for Children Ages One Through Five (Continued)

Supplemental (Snack) Food (Continued)

Components	Ages 1 and 2	Ages 3 through 5
Meat and Meat Alternates		
lean meat or poultry or fish[5] or	1/2 ounce	1 1/2 ounces
alternate protein products[6] or	1/2 ounce	1 1/2 ounces
cheese or	1/2 ounce	1 1/2 ounces
egg (large) or	1/2	1/2
cooked dry beans or peas or	1/4 cup	3/8 cup
peanut butter or soynut butter or other nut or seed butters or	1 tablespoon	1 tablespoon
peanuts or soynuts or tree nuts or seeds[7] or	1/2 ounce	1/2 ounce
yogurt, plain or flavored, unsweetened or sweetened or an equivalent quantity of any combination of the above meat/meat alternates	2 ounces or 1/4 cup	2 ounces or 1/4 cup

[1] For purposes of the requirements outlined in this subsection, a cup means a standard measuring cup.
[2] Bread, pasta, or noodle products, and cereal grains, shall be whole grain or enriched; cornbread, biscuits, rolls, muffins, etc., shall be made with whole grain or enriched meal or flour; cereal shall be whole grain or enriched or fortified.
[3] Serving sizes and equivalents to be published in guidance materials by FNS.
[4] Either volume (cup) or weight (ounces) whichever is less.
[5] Edible portion as served.
[6] Must meet the requirements of Appendix A of this table (Alternate Foods for Meals).
[7] Tree nuts and seeds that may be used as meat alternates are listed in program guidance.

Appendix A—Alternate Foods for Meals

Alternate Protein Products

A. What are the criteria for alternate protein products used in the Child and Adult Care Food Program?
    1. An alternate protein product used in meals planned under the provisions in ;st226.20 must meet all of the criteria in this section.
    2. An alternate protein product whether used alone or in combination with meat or meat alternate must meet the following criteria:
        a. The alternate protein product must be processed so that some portion of the nonprotein constituents of the food is removed. These alternate protein products must be safe and suitable edible products produced from plant or animal sources.
        b. The biological quality of the protein the alternate protein product must be at least 80 percent that of casein, determined by performing a Protein Digestibility Corrected Amino Acid Score (PDCAAS).
        c. The alternate protein product must contain at least 18 percent protein by weight when fully hydrated or formulated. ("When hydrated or formulated" refers to a dry alternate protein product and the amount of water, fat, oil, colors, flavors, or any other substances which have been added.)
        d. Manufacturers supplying an alternate protein product to participating schools or institutions must provide documentation that the product meets the criteria in paragraphs A2.a through c of this appendix.
        e. Manufacturers should provide information on the percent protein contained in the dry alternate protein product and on an as prepared basis.
        f. For an alternate protein product mix, manufacturers should provide information on:
        (1) The amount by weight of dry alternate protein product in the package; (2) Hydration instructions; and (3) Instructions on how to combine the mix with meat or other meat alternates.

B. How are alternate protein products used in the Child and Adult Care Food Program?
    1. Schools, institutions, and service institutions may use alternate protein products to fulfill all or part of the meat/meat alternate component.
    2. The following terms and conditions apply:
        a. The alternate protein product may be used alone or in combination with other food ingredients. Examples of combination items are beef patties, beef crumbles, pizza topping, meat loaf, meat sauce, taco filling, burritos, and tuna salad.
        b. Alternate protein products may be used in the dry form (nonhydrated), partially hydrated, or fully hydrated form. The moisture content of the fully hydrated alternate protein product (if prepared from a dry concentrated form) must be such that the mixture will have a minimum of 18 percent protein by weight or equivalent amount for the dry or partially hydrated form (based on the level that would be provided if the product were fully hydrated).

C. How are commercially prepared products used in the Child and Adult Care Food Programs?
Schools, institutions, and service institutions may use a commercially prepared meat or meat alternate product combined with alternate protein products or use a commercially prepared product that contains only alternate protein products.

Source: Food and Nutrition Service, United States Department of Agriculture 2000.

> ## ISSUES TO CONSIDER • Benefits of CACFP
>
> A recent study indicated that meals provided by the CACFP have the potential to improve the diets of young children. The children in the center participating in the CACFP had fewer sick days. The study further found that almost one-fourth of the children in the study were overweight. The number of overweight children was almost equally distributed between the center not receiving CACFP funding and the center which did.
>
> - Consider the practical implications of this study for families of children in child care.
> - Of what importance are the results of this study to menu planners?
> - What is the "take home lesson" from this study for parents and/or teachers?

under this program. At this time, meals are planned using food-based menu planning, using Nutrient Standard or Assisted Nutrient Standard Menu Planning, or adopting an alternate menu planning approach developed by a state agency or by the school food authority with state agency approval. The guidelines are quite specific as to the minimum amounts of food required to fulfill a serving. Guidelines are also available listing specific foods that are permitted as alternatives within each food group (Table 19–6). The menu planner working within these guidelines must take great care to keep up with the current information as this program undergoes frequent and sometimes sweeping changes. The National School Lunch Act requires that school meals comply with *Dietary Guidelines for Americans*. The ABC's of the *2000 Dietary Guidelines for Americans* include: (1) Aim for fitness; (2) Build a Healthy Base; and (3) Choose Sensibly.

Licensing of child care facilities is administered by state agencies, usually the Department of Health. Each state has its own licensing requirements with regard to nutrition and food service. Teachers who provide food for children should check the licensing requirements for their particular state. Aspects pertaining to nutrition often covered by licensing regulations include:

1. Administration and record keeping
   - sample menus and appropriate menu substitutions
   - production records
   - number of meals served daily
2. Food service
   - specifications for kitchens and equipment
   - sanitation of dishes, utensils, and equipment
   - requirements for transport of food when kitchen facilities are not available
   - feeding equipment required for specific age groups
3. Staffing
   - requirements of person in charge of food service
4. Nutrition policies
   - number of meals and snacks to be served within the current week
   - posting of menus and their availability to parents
   - seating of adults at the table with children
   - posting of food allergies in kitchen and eating area

A Good Menu Is Appealing

The French say, "We eat with our eyes." Menu planners who take into consideration how the food will look on the plate are likely to develop meals that are appealing and accepted by the children

TABLE 19–6 Acceptable Bread and Bread Alternates

Important Notes:

- All products must be made of whole grain or enriched flour or meal.
- Serving sizes listed below are specified for children under six years of age
- A "full" serving (defined below) is required for children six years of age and older.
- USDA recommends that cookies, granola bars, and similar foods be served in a snack no more than twice a week. They may be used for a snack only when:
  - whole grain or enriched meal or flour is the predominant ingredient as specified on the label or according to the recipe; and
  - the total weight of a serving for children under six years of age is a minimum of 18 grams (0.6 0z.) and for children over six years, a minimum of 35 grams (1.2 0z.)
- To determine serving sizes for products in Group A that are made at child care centers, refer to "Cereal products" in FNS-86, "Quantity Recipes for Child Care Centers."
- Doughnuts and sweet rolls are allowed as a bread item in breakfasts and snacks only.
- French, Vienna, Italian, and Syrian breads are commercially prepared products that often are made with unenriched flour. Check the label or manufacturer to be sure the product is made with *enriched* flour.
- The amount of bread in a serving of stuffing should weigh at least 13 grams (0.5 ounces).
- Whole grain, enriched, or fortified breakfast cereals (cold, dry, or cooked) may be served for breakfast or snack only.

Group A

When you obtain these items commercially, a *full* serving should have a minimum weight of 25 grams (0.9 ounces). The serving sizes specified below should have a minimum weight of 13 grams (0.5 ounces).

Item	Serving Size
bagels	1/2 bagel
biscuits	1 biscuit
boston brown bread	1/2 serving
breads, sliced	1/2 slice
all types (white, rye, whole-wheat, raisin, quick breads, etc.)	
buns and sweet buns	1/2 bun
cornbread	1 piece
croissants	1/2 croissant
doughnuts (all types)	1/2 doughnut
egg roll/wonton wrappers	1 serving
english muffins	1/2 muffin
french, Italian, or Vienna bread	1/2 slice
"fry" bread	1/2 piece
muffins	1/2 muffin
pizza crust	1 serving
pretzels, Dutch (soft)	1 pretzel
rolls and sweet rolls	1/2 roll
stuffing (bread)	1/2 serving
syrian bread (pita)	1/2 round

(Continued)

TABLE 19-6 Acceptable Bread and Bread Alternates (Continued)

Group B
When you obtain these items commercially, a *full* serving should have a minimum weight of 20 grams (0.7 ounces). The serving sizes specified below should have a minimum weight of 10 grams (0.4 ounces).

Item	Serving Size
batter and/or breading	
bread sticks (dry)	2 sticks
chow mein noodles	1/4 cup
graham crackers	2 squares
melba toast	3 pieces
"pilot" bread	1 piece
rye wafers (whole grain)	2 wafers
saltine crackers	4 squares
soda crackers	2 crackers
taco shells (whole, pieces)	1 shell
zwieback	2 pieces

Group C
When you obtain these items commercially, a *full* serving should have a minimum weight of 30 grams (1.1 ounces). The serving sizes specified below should have a minimum weight of 15 grams (0.5 ounces).

Item	Serving Size
dumplings	1/2 dumpling
hush puppies	1/2 serving
meat or meat alternate pie crust	1/2 serving
meat or meat alternate turnover crust	1/2 serving
pancakes	1/2 pancake
popovers	1/2 popover
sopaipillas	1/2 serving
spoonbread	1/2 serving
tortillas	1/2 tortilla
waffles	1/2 serving

Group D
When you serve these items, a *full* serving should have a minimum of 1/2 cup cooked product. The serving sizes specified below are the minimum *half* servings of cooked product.

Item	Serving Size
barley	1/4 cup
bulgur	1/4 cup
corn grits	1/4 cup
lasagna noodles	1/4 cup
macaroni or spaghetti	1/4 cup
noodles (egg)	1/4 cup
ravioli (pasta only)	1/4 cup
rice (white or brown)	1/4 cup

Courtesy of USDA, 1995.

FIGURE 19–1

Orange "smiles" are a novel way to serve a familiar food in order to make it more appealing to children. Courtesy of *The Sunshine Cookbook,* © State of Florida, Department of Citrus, 1976.

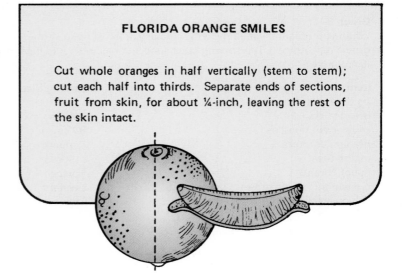

FLORIDA ORANGE SMILES

Cut whole oranges in half vertically (stem to stem); cut each half into thirds. Separate ends of sections, fruit from skin, for about ¼-inch, leaving the rest of the skin intact.

to whom they are served. Figure 19–1 shows an interesting way to serve orange slices that will make them more appealing to children. Appeal can be increased by contrasting the following **sensory qualities**:

- color
- flavor (strong or mild; sweet or sour)
- texture (crisp or soft)
- shape (round, cubed, strings)
- temperature (cold or hot)

These sensory qualities of foods play an important part in a young child's choice of foods. Toddlers and young children think of foods in terms of color, flavor, texture, and shape rather than the nutrient content. Color plays a major role in children's knowledge of food (Rush, 1984; Contento, 1981). Using sensory qualities of food to appeal to young children takes advantage of their developmental level of interpreting their environment through the physical senses.

A comparison of the following two menus illustrates how menus can be made more appealing:

Menu #1
Grilled Cheese Sandwiches
Celery Sticks
Banana Chunks
Milk

Menu #2
Grilled Cheese Sandwiches
Buttered Broccoli
Red Apple Wedges
Milk

sensory qualities – *aspects that appeal to sight, sound, taste, feel, and smell.*

Menu #1 is essentially tones of yellow and light brown. Substituting broccoli for celery sticks adds color and increases the amount of vitamins A and C. Substituting red apples for bananas improves color contrast and adds a crunchier texture.

The sensory contrasts that contribute to the attractiveness of a meal also provide many opportunities for the teacher or parent to expand the young child's language development. The child can be encouraged to identify foods and describe their qualities such as round, rectangular, red, yellow, hot, or cold.

While color is an important factor in food appeal, other aspects also contribute to acceptability. Young children often prefer mildly flavored, simple foods. Softer textured foods such as chicken or ground meats are often preferred because they are easy to chew. Many young children prefer plain foods that do not touch each other as opposed to mixed dishes. Sweet foods are frequently preferred. Since the basis for this preference may be biological, fruits and nutritious whole grain baked products could be offered if such a preference is shown.

A Good Menu Includes Familiar Foods and New Foods

While it is important to introduce nutritious new foods to children, it is also important to use many foods with which the children in the group are familiar. Familiarity plays a large part in young children's food choices. Familiarity of a food is a result of family food practices. Sharing of information, menu plans, recipes and the like with parents may be important in expanding family food choices that could give the child a better base of familiar foods.

Acceptance of a meal may depend on the number of familiar foods included. When introducing new foods, it is a good idea to include them along with familiar ones. It is a good idea to back up one unfamiliar new food with familiar foods; if the new food is not well-accepted, the children will not leave the table hungry. (See Table 18–2 for suggestions for introducing new foods to young children.) The menu planner might also consider introducing unfamiliar foods at snack time. Introducing unfamiliar foods at snack time prevents the new food from being labeled "breakfast food" or "lunch food."

When feeding young children, it is wise to include numerous finger foods (Table 19–7). Some children may not be skilled in the use of tableware and find finger foods to be reassuring. New foods should be introduced with little fanfare. Child involvement in preparation of an unfamiliar food may enhance its acceptance.

TABLE 19–7 Suggested Finger Foods

apple wedges	grapefruit sections (seeded)
banana slices	green pepper sticks
berries	meat cubes
cabbage wedges	melon cubes
cauliflowerets	orange sections
celery sticks*	pitted plums
cheese cubes	pitted prunes
dried peaches	tangerine sections
dried pears	tomato wedges
fresh peach wedges	turnip sticks
fresh pear wedges	zucchini sticks
fresh pineapple sticks	

*May be stuffed with cheese or peanut butter
Courtesy of *A Planning Guide for Food Service in Child Care Centers.* USDA, FNS-64, 1981.

Most centers care for children from a variety of cultural and ethnic backgrounds. A good menu planner draws on this wealth of backgrounds and includes foods that are familiar to a number of cultures. The inclusion of **ethnic** foods serves several purposes:

- The children from the culture being featured are familiar with these foods. Since they accept them at meals or snacks, other children in the group are more willing to try them too.
- Foods of different cultural groups add variety to the meals and may serve as a basis for educational activities concerning various cultures.
- Serving ethnic food helps the teacher establish rapport with the children and their families. This may foster increased parental participation in the center's activities.
- Educating children about various cultures fosters greater respect for children who are from a culture different from theirs.
- The sharing of food is often an effective way of helping the ethnic child feel comfortable and accepted.

STEPS IN MENU PLANNING

Menu planning should be organized so that it may be done efficiently and effectively. Some of the materials that are helpful in menu planning are:

- menu forms
- a list of foods on hand that need to be used
- list of allergies
- recipe file
- old menus with notes and suggestions
- calendar with special events and holidays noted
- grocery ads for short-term planning
- USDA list of commodity foods available

The menu form shown in Figure 19–2 could be used for a child care center or home. The form may be adapted to provide only the meals that are served in the individual center. Components of each meal or snack are included in the form to serve as reminders of kinds of foods that should be included to provide a nutritious menu.

Step 1. List the main dishes to be served for lunch during the week. These should include a meat or meat alternate. Include alternatives for children with food allergies. Appropriate combinations (see Chapter 13) of whole grain products, dried peas, beans, lentils, cheese, nuts, or nut butters may be acceptable protein-source substitutes for meat, eggs, or fish. However, many of these combinations do not contribute as much iron as meat would. To ensure that the iron needs are met attention should be given to including other iron-rich foods in the menu planned with a meat substitute.

Tuna noodle casserole with cheese	BBQ beef	Scrambled eggs	Chili	Macaroni and cheese	Protein

Step 2. List vegetables and fruits, including salads, for the main meal. Be sure to use fruits and vegetables in season. Fresh produce in season is less expensive and more nutritious than canned

---

ethnic – *pertaining to races or groups of people who share common traits or customs.*

FIGURE 19–2

A sample menu form.

		Monday	Tuesday	Wednesday	Thursday	Friday
Breakfast	Fruit/Vegetable Bread Milk					
Snack (supplement)	Bread Fruit/Vegetable or Milk					
Lunch	Protein Fruit/Vegetable Fruit/Vegetable Bread Milk					
Snack (supplement)	Bread Fruit/Vegetable or Milk					
Notes	# Served					

and some frozen foods. Fresh fruits and vegetables also offer excellent materials for learning activities. If planning seasonal menus months in advance, local County Extension Offices can provide information concerning produce in season and predicted supplies.

Peas Orange wedges	Broccoli Peach slices	Tomatoe juice 1/2 banana	Carrots and celery Canned pear slices	Green beans Apple wedges	Fuits and Vegetables

Step 3. Add enriched or whole grain breads and cereal products.

Enriched noodles (in casserole)	Enriched bun	Whole wheat toast	Corn muffin	Enriched macaroni (in casserole)	Bread

Step 4. Add beverage. Be sure to include the required amount of milk.

Milk	Milk	Milk	Milk	Milk	Milk

Step 5. Plan snacks to balance the main meal. Especially check for vitamin C, vitamin A, iron, and calcium.

A.M. Snack	Prepared oat cereal Milk	Bran muffin Apple juice	Pumpkin bread Milk	Raisin toast Orange juice	Rye crackers Milk
P.M. Snack	Carrot curls Wheat crackers Water	Cheese crackers Peanut butter Milk	Pizza biscuits Pineapple juice	Oatmeal cookies Milk	Brown-white sandwich Apricot-orange juice

Step 6. Review your menu. Be sure it includes the required amounts from the Food Guide Pyramid.

- Does it meet funding or licensing requirements?
- Does it include a variety of contrasting foods?
- Does it contain familiar foods?
- Does it contain new foods?

Step 7. Post the menu where it can be seen by staff and parents (Figure 19–3). Be sure to note any changes made and the likes and dislikes of the children. Communication between care center staff and parents is very important to ensure that each child's nutrient needs are met for the day and the week.

Step 8. Evaluate the menu. Did the children appear to like the foods that were served? Was there much plate waste? Keep a copy of the notes with menu planning materials. However, do not eliminate a food from the menu because it resulted in too much plate waste. A child's likes and dislikes are constantly changing and the rejected food of this week may become a favorite in a week or two.

FIGURE 19–3

Menus should be available to the parents.

			WEEKLY MENUS Week of _____		
			Lunch and Snacks		
	Monday	**Tuesday**	**Wednesday**	**Thursday**	**Friday**
Snack	Bagel with Cream Cheese Orange Juice	Blueberry Muffin Milk	Sausage Biscuit Milk	Waffles Applesauce Milk	Apple Butter Graham Crackers Orange Juice
Lunch	Turkey with Gravy Mashed Potatoes Peas Peaches Bread & Butter Milk	Macaroni & Cheese Bread & Butter Celery, Carrots Green Peppers Orange Slices Milk	Tomato Soup with Rice Bologna Sandwich Apple Slices Milk	Beef Barbecue Green Beans Bread Pears Milk	Spaghetti with Meatballs Tossed Salad Bread Sticks Fruit Cup Milk
Snack	Peanut Butter Celery Stick Milk	Yogurt Pineapple Tidbits Water	Granola Bar Pineapple/Orange Juice	Oatmeal Cookies Milk	Jello with Fruit Milk

WRITING MENUS

There are several methods of writing menus that the planner may wish to consider: weekly menus, cycle menus, and odd-day cycle menus. Among the factors that influence the method chosen are the child care center's schedule and hours, and the personnel who will be preparing the foods on the menu. The means of buying food and sources of food supply also influence the chosen method of menu planning.

Weekly menus list the foods that are to be prepared and eaten for one week at a time. This is a very time-consuming method and should be extended to include a minimum of two or three weeks at a time. Planning more than one week allows utilization of larger, more economical amounts of food. It also permits an outline of all the foods to be served over a period of time, so that too frequent repetitions of foods may be avoided.

Cycle menus incorporate a series of weekly menus that are reused or cycled over a period of two or three months. Frequently, cycle menus are written to parallel the seasons and reflect the fruit and vegetable offerings that are most available and affordable in a given season. A well-planned cycle menu is quite efficient since, after the initial expenditure of time in planning the cycle, little additional time is required for menu planning. Food ordering also becomes less time-consuming and the use of food is more efficient. However, the planner should not hesitate to change parts of the cycle that prove difficult to produce or that are not well accepted by the children. Seasonal cycle menus may be used for a period of years with timely revisions.

weekly menus – *menus that are written to be served on a weekly basis.*
cycle menus – *menus that are written to repeat after a set interval, such as every three to four weeks.*

Odd-day cycle menus involve planning menus for periods of days other than a week. Cycles of any number of days may be used. This type of cycling avoids the association of specific foods with certain days of the week. This type of menu requires very careful planning to avoid dishes or foods that require advance preparation in Monday-to-Friday child care centers.

NUTRITIOUS SNACKS

A snack is suitable if it is a nutrient-dense food and makes a serious contribution to meeting the nutrient needs of the child for that day. Calorie-dense snacks, high in sugar and fat, are not appropriate for the young child.

Snacks should contribute to the child's daily food needs and educational experiences. Snacks should contribute vitamins, minerals, and other nutrients important in health, growth, and development (Figure 19–4). Snack foods should include nutrients that were not adequately provided by lunch and/or breakfast.

New or unusual foods can often be better introduced at snack time. This may often be accomplished in a party atmosphere such as a taste-testing party.

Snacks are a means of providing nutrients and energy between meals, since children have small stomach capacities and may not be able to eat enough at one meal to sustain them until the next meal. One and one-half or two hours between meals seems to be the best spacing for most children in order to prevent them from becoming too hungry or spoiling their appetite for the next meal.

Suitable Snack Foods

A variety of raw fruits and vegetables are ideal for snack foods. Raw fruits and vegetables are excellent sources of vitamin C, vitamin A, and fiber and should be included often. The teacher must be sure the fruits and vegetables are sectioned or sliced so the children can chew them. The crispness of fruits and vegetables helps to remove food clinging to the teeth. The crispness and texture also

FIGURE 19–4

Snacks should provide nutrients to balance the meals.

---

odd-day cycle menus – *menus planned for a period of days other than a week that repeat after the planned period; cycles of any number of days may be used. These menus are a means of avoiding repetition of the same foods on the same day of the week.*

stimulate the gums so they stay healthy. Fresh fruits and vegetables provide cellulose, which aids elimination. Another important factor not to be forgotten is exposure to the subtle flavors of fruits and vegetables.

Whole grains and cereal products or enriched breads and grain products are also good high-fiber snack foods. The flavor of **whole grains** adds variety to the diet. **Enriched** breads and cereals are refined products to which iron, thiamin, niacin, riboflavin, and folic acid are added in amounts equal to the original whole grain product.

Unsweetened beverages such as **full-strength** fruit and vegetable juices are good choices for snacks. Juices made from oranges, grapefruits, tangerines, and tomatoes are rich in vitamin C. Vitamin C may also be added to apple, grape, and pineapple juices. Check the labels of these juices to determine if they are fortified with vitamin C. Carbonated beverages, **fruit drinks**, and fruit ades are unacceptable for snacks. These beverages contain large amounts of sugar and no other nutrients, except perhaps some added vitamin C.

Careful attention to beverage labels enables one to avoid these expensive sugar-water offerings. Some guidelines are:

- fruit juice must be 100 percent juice
- juice drink may have as little as 39 percent fruit juice
- fruit drink has from 0–10 percent real juice

Water is also essential for good health; children should drink 6 to 8 small glasses of water a day (Figure 19–5).

Water should be available to children at all times and may be served with their meals and snacks. Allowing children to pour the water from a pitcher, as they want it, may encourage them to

FIGURE 19–5

Children should drink six to eight glasses of water daily.

---

whole grains – *grain products that have not been refined; they contain all parts of the kernel of grain.*
enriched – *adding nutrients to grain products to replace those lost during refinement; thiamin, niacin, riboflavin, and iron are nutrients most commonly added.*
full-strength juice – *undiluted fruit or vegetable juice.*
fruit drinks – *products that contains 10 percent fruit juice, added water, and sugar.*

drink more water. Special attention should be given to water intake after a period of physical activity and when the environmental temperature is high. A good plan might be to stop at the drinking fountain on the way in after a period of active outdoor play.

SERVING MEALS

A nutritious meal is of no value to a child if it is not eaten and enjoyed. The atmosphere in which meals are served can either forestall or further contribute to eating problems. All meals should be served in a relaxed, social atmosphere. The classroom should be tidied prior to mealtimes. This eliminates the distraction of scattered toys or unfinished games. The resulting uncluttered environment provides a more restful atmosphere in which to eat.

The table should be made as attractive as possible. Placemats made by the children add interest to the meal and give children the opportunity to contribute to the meal setting. Centerpieces may be constructed during art or assembled from objects gathered on field trips or nature hikes. Plates, cups, utensils, and napkins should be laid out neatly and appropriately. Table setting can be a learning experience for children and can provide positive experiences that enhance self-esteem. In addition, the food served should be made as attractive as possible to increase its appeal. Food can be more appealing by preparing it appropriately to retain its color and shape and neatly arranging it in serving dishes or on plates. (White or warm-hued plates enhance natural food colors; cool-hued plates tend to detract from most food colors.) Fresh, edible garnishes may be used if time and budget permit. Contrived or "cute" foods are time-consuming to prepare and may actually result in the children wanting to save them as "souvenirs" rather than eating them.

Food may be served in a variety of styles:

- plate service
- family-style service
- combination of the above

Plate service is when the food is placed on the plates in the kitchen. This style of service permits the greatest degree of portion control and leftover food. Thus, it permits the greatest degree of **cost control**.

In family-style service, the food is placed on the table in serving dishes. The children are then asked to help themselves and to pass the dish to the next child. Beverages are placed in small, easily managed pitchers, and each child pours the amount desired before passing it to the next child. While this method does not permit the degree of portion control of plate service, it promotes decision making by the children. The child chooses how much food to serve and eat and thus enhances and acknowledges the very important aspect of self-regulation of food intake. The motor skills used to dip, serve, pass, and pour are practiced, as well as the social skills of cooperating and sharing. Many teachers feel that the positive aspects of family-style service outweigh the benefits of lesser portions and cost control of plate service.

Positive aspects of both styles of service may lead the teacher to choose a combination of the two. For example, the teacher may place servings of the entree on the plates (the amount is determined by each child's request) while the children pass the bread, fruit, and vegetables. This style of service allows portion control, a very positive aspect since the entree is the most expensive item on the menu, and safety, since the entree is usually a hot food. If the vegetables are hot, they may also be served by the teacher.

---

cost control – *reduction of expenses through portion control inventory and reduction of waste.*

TABLE 19–8 Make Mealtime a Happy Time

Feeding young children can be fun if you know:

- What foods children should have.
- How to bring children and foods together happily. Pleasant eating experiences are as important as nutritious foods. They provide pleasant associations with food and eating. Food habits and attitudes that form during the preschool years remain with most people throughout life.
- Try to understand each child's personality and reaction to foods.
- Children need to do as much for themselves as they are able to do. First efforts may be awkward, but encourage them. These efforts are a step toward growth.
- Children may be in no hurry to eat once the first edge is taken off their hunger. They do not have adults' sense of time. Urging them to hurry may spoil their pleasure in eating.
- Most one-year-old children can handle bite-sized pieces of food with their fingers. Later they can handle a spoon by themselves. Since they are growing slower than infants, they may be less hungry. They may be choosy and refuse certain foods. Don't worry or force them to eat. Keep on offering different foods.
- Sometimes children three to six years old go on food "jags." They may want two or three servings of one food at one meal. Given time they will settle down and eat a normal meal. The overall pattern from week to week and month to month is more important.

Courtesy of *A Planning Guide for Food Service in Child Care Centers.* USDA, FNS-64, 1981.

It is important that teachers eat meals with the children as this offers the children role models for appropriate behavior and attitudes. Mealtime should be a time when teachers sit and engage in pleasant conversions with the children about things that interest the children. Children should also be encouraged to talk with one another. Dwelling on table manners and behavior during meals should be avoided as much as possible. Only positive reinforcement of good behavior should be mentioned. Problem eaters need special positive reinforcement of good eating behavior; if possible, negative behavior should be ignored during mealtime. Table 19–8 gives some additional ideas on making mealtimes happy times.

THE MENU MUST STAY WITHIN THE BUDGET

While the menu lists what foods are to be served, the budget defines the resources allotted for preparation of the menu. Items that must be included in the budget are food, personnel, and equipment. The food budget can be controlled through careful attention to:

- menu planning
- food purchasing
- food preparation
- food service
- recordkeeping

Cost control is essential if a food service is to stay within the budget. The goal is to feed the children appetizing, nutritious meals at a reasonably low cost. Cost control should never be attempted at the expense of good nutrition.

Menu Planning

Cost control begins at the menu-planning stage. To plan menus that stay within a budget, it is important to begin by including inexpensive foods. To do so, the planner must be aware of current prices and seasonal supplies.

To lower food costs, the menu planner should make careful use of leftovers and supplies on hand. To ensure that quality foods are selected from supplies on hand, the **First-In-First-Out (FIFO) inventory method** should be used. This food storage system places newly purchased foods at the back of storage and older foods at the front so they can be used first. This method of rotating stocks of food can be facilitated by dating all supplies as they come into the storage area.

Food Purchasing

Food purchasing, or **procurement**, is a crucial step in cost control. Lowering food costs during the purchasing phase can be accomplished by utilizing food from local suppliers, using USDA donated foods, and keeping abreast of price trends and the market availability of various foods. Purchasing of too much food or inappropriate foods can transform a menu that is planned around inexpensive foods to an expensive menu at service. The key step is to determine as accurately as possible the amount of food that is needed to feed everyone an adequate amount. The use of standardized recipes can be a great help in determining how much and what kinds of food are needed. One such set of recipes is that developed by the U.S. Department of Agriculture for use in school lunches or Child Care Food Programs. These recipes provide the ingredients needed as well as the amounts required to produce the recipe for groups of various sizes.

Before purchasing food, a written food order should be prepared. Written product specifications are used to clarify the following information:

- name of product
- federal grade
- packaging procedures and type of package
- test or inspection procedures
- market units—ounces, pounds, can size, cases, etc.
- quantity (number) of units needed
- style of food desired—pieces, slices, halves, chunks, etc.

For those who purchase food at local retail stores, a simple form that follows the floor plan of the store(s) where food is purchased may be helpful. When completing the market order, list the foods needed for the entire period of time for which food must be purchased in the following order:

- main dishes
- fruits and vegetables
- breads, cereals, pastas
- dairy products

Frozen foods should be selected last to minimize thawing between store freezer and food service freezer.

Food Preparation

Careful preparation methods that are appropriate for the specific food contribute both to the nutritional quality of the food and to cost control. Fruits and vegetables should be peeled only if necessary, as more nutrients are retained if the skin is left intact. If peeling is necessary, as it may be for very young children, only a thin layer of skin should be removed.

Correct heat and cooking time are important factors in cost control as well as nutrient retention. Foods cooked too long or at excessively high heat may undergo shrinkage or be burned. In either case, food costs increase because burned food is not usable and shrinkage results in fewer

---

First-In-First-Out (FIFO) inventory method – *a method of storage in which the items stored for the longest time will be retrieved first.*

procurement – *the process of obtaining services, supplies, and equipment in conformance with applicable laws and regulations.*

FIGURE 19-6

A sample attendance and meal count form. (Courtesy of Douglas County Child Development Association.)

CRR ATTENDANCE AND MEAL COUNT

MONTH OF _____ 19____   PROVIDER: _____

Number of Children Licensed For: _____

CHILD'S FULL NAME		1	2	3	4	5	6	7	8	9	10	11	12	13	14	15	16	17	18	19	20	21	22	23	24	25	26	27	28	29	30	31	TOTALS
	B.																																
	S.																																
	L.																																
	S.																																
	D.																																
	B.																																
	S.																																
	L.																																
	S.																																
	D.																																
	B.																																
	S.																																
	L.																																
	S.																																
	D.																																
	B.																																
	S.																																
	L.																																
	S.																																
	D.																																

FOR OFFICE USE ONLY

1. Total Breakfasts served _____ X _____ = $ _____
2. Total Lunches served _____ X _____ = $ _____
3. Total Suppers served _____ X _____ = $ _____
4. Total Supplements served _____ X _____ = $ _____

Date Paid _____   Check # _____   TOT _____

portions than originally planned. Nutrients, such as thiamin and vitamin C, are readily destroyed when exposed to heat.

Standardized recipes, such as those available from the U.S. Department of Agriculture, help to ensure correct amounts of ingredients and to reduce leftovers. Leftover foods that have not been placed on the table may be promptly frozen and used when serving the same dish again. Leftovers should be reheated in a separate pan and not mixed with freshly prepared portions. Leftovers should be reheated only once.

Food Service

If the recipe specifies a serving size, that amount should be served, for example, "one-half cup or 1 1/2" × 1 1/2" square." In child care centers using family-style service, the staff may serve standard portions to the children as a means of portion control. In centers where children are encouraged to serve themselves, each child should be asked to take only as much as can be eaten.

Serving utensils that are made to serve specific portions are an aid to portion and cost control. Examples of such utensils are soup ladles and ice cream scoops, which are available in a number of standardized sizes. These tools are available at restaurant supply companies.

Recordkeeping

Complete, accurate records should be kept of the amount of money spent for food, and the number of children and staff served daily. These records provide an idea of how much money is being spent for food and whether this amount is within the projected budget. Figure 19–6 shows an example of a form used to report the number of meals served.

A record of expenses for each month should be kept. For further accuracy, an inventory of foods on hand should be done and the cost of the inventory determined and deducted from the raw food cost for that month. (If inventories tend not to differ much from month to month, this last step may be omitted.) At the end of each month:

- calculate the total number of individuals served
- calculate the total food bills
- divide the total dollars spent by the total number served to determine monthly food costs per person

---

FOCUS ON FAMILIES • Meal Planning

Parents should use the Food Guide Pyramid as the basis for planning healthy, nutritious meals. Meal planning may require additional time, but proves to be worthwhile for the following reasons:

1. You can ensure that all food groups from the Pyramid are included.

2. It helps you to balance meals (serving meat that is high in salt, such as ham, with foods that do not contain large amounts of salt, such as steamed vegetables.

3. By using a grocery list, you will make fewer unnecessary trips to the store and be less likely to buy foods on impulse.

Preparing a grocery list for the first time may feel overwhelming, but following these principles can help get you started:

- Build the main part of your meal around complex carbohydrates (rice, pastas, other grains).

- Add variety and try different ethnic cuisines.

- Use planned leftovers to save time and money (serve half of a beef pot roast for one meal and use the other half in a stew). If time allows, cook a double batch of your family's favorite dish and freeze for later use.

- Avoid purchasing these high-fat snacks: doughnuts, croissants, pastries, high-fat cookies, high-fat crackers, and chocolate candy.

- Try purchasing these foods for healthy, nutritious snacks: animal crackers, fig bars, Cheerios, graham crackers, saltines, pretzels, fruit, vanilla wafers.

CASE STUDY

Ms. R. is responsible for planning menus for a child care center that cares for 50 children. She wants to plan a menu according to the Food Guide Pyramid featuring a variety of foods from each section of the Pyramid. Her purpose is to introduce new or unusual foods to the children. She starts with the Grain Group and features bagels, tortillas, fried rice, hush puppies, and pita bread. The next group to be highlighted will be vegetables.

1. Suggest some unusual vegetables to prepare.
2. How can these vegetables be presented to increase acceptance?
3. How will refusals be handled?
4. What food group would you highlight next? Why?

SUMMARY

- The menu is the basic tool of food service.
  - The menu should meet the nutritional needs of those served.
  - The menu should introduce new foods.
  - Familiar, well-liked foods should be served frequently.
  - Foods should be cooked and served in sanitary surroundings.
  - Menus should be planned within budgetary limits.

- Careful menu planning is essential to cost control.
  - Including seasonal foods in the menu lowers costs.
  - Using good quality food products appropriate to menu items saves money.
  - Prompt storage of food at the correct temperature limits waste.
  - Use of standardized recipes and appropriate serving sizes controls costs.
  - Accurate record keeping enables the menu planner to be aware of food costs.

SUGGESTED ACTIVITIES

1. Plan a five-day menu appropriate for four-year-old children that includes morning snack, lunch, and afternoon snack. The menu should provide one-half of the foods needed according to the Food Guide Pyramid. Provide one good source each of vitamin C, calcium, and iron daily. Provide at least three good sources of vitamin A during the five-day period.

2. Four-year-old Jamie often comes to the child care center without having had breakfast at home. (Both his parents work and must leave early every day.) His mother often buys him a doughnut on the way to the center, explaining that she felt "he should have something to eat." During circle times, he's often inattentive and seems to be "in his own world" and somewhat lethargic. He rarely engages in large-motor activities voluntarily. At snack times and mealtimes, he tends to select only milk or juices and is resistant to eating vegetables and meats.
   a. What may be the cause of Jamie's behavior during circle times?
   b. How would you characterize Jamie's nutritional status?
   c. What eating patterns need to be corrected?
   d. What steps should be taken to improve Jamie's participation in activities, as well as his nutritional patterns and status?

3. Review the criteria given for menus. Rank the criteria as you perceive their degree of importance. Are there other factors that you feel should also be considered in planning adequate menus? Consider the needs of individual child care centers, child care homes, or family homes. Are the important factors the same or different for each situation?

4. Three-year-old Eiswari is allergic to eggs. Explain how this affects menu planning.

5. Using the listing of food sources of nutrients for which a vegan vegetarian child would be at risk, plan a menu that would enable the child to meet her needs for one day. Modify the menu for a lacto-ovo-vegetarian child. Include appropriate sizes of servings (refer to Chapter 16).

6. The following menu is planned for a child care center for one week in January:

Meat loaf	Bread with margarine
Creamed new peas and potatoes	Fresh strawberry-banana fruit cup
Peach half in cherry gelatin	Milk

   a. Evaluate this menu and suggest changes that could make it less expensive but equally or more nutritious.
   b. How would the cost of this menu served in January compare to the cost of the same menu served in June?

CHAPTER REVIEW

Briefly answer the following questions.

1. State the serving size for a child three to six years old for each of the following foods:
   a. milk
   b. dry cereal
   c. fruit
   d. vegetable
   e. bread

2. Where can information relative to licensing requirements for nutrition and food services for young children be obtained?

3. Name four sensory qualities that can be contrasted to make food appealing.

4. What are two reasons for using fresh fruits and vegetables in season?

5. List two ways the menu planner can control food costs.

6. Outline three ways to control food costs when preparing food.

7. Name three ways that mealtimes can be made pleasant for children.

REFERENCES

Child and Adult Care Food Program (CACEP). (1992). *Nutrition guidance for child care.* Washington, DC: United States Department of Agriculture.

Child nutrition programs: School meal initiatives for healthy children; final rule. (1995, June 13). *Federal Register.*

Contento, I. (1981). Children's thinking about food and eating—A Piagetian-based study. *Proceedings of the Workshop on Nutrition Education Research.* Chicago: The American Dietetic Association.

Douglas County Child Development Association. (1996). *Child and adult care food programs.* Lawrence, KS: Author.

Rush, J. (1984). *Identification and description of some dimensions of young children's food knowledge and attributes.* Master's Thesis, University of Kansas.

State of Florida Department of Citrus. (1976). *The sunshine cookbook.* Lakeland, FL: Author.

U.S. Department of Agriculture. (1981). *A planning guide for food service in child care centers.* FNS-64. Washington, DC: Author.

U.S. Department of Agriculture, Food and Consumer Service. (1995, September) *Child and adult care food program. Nutrition guidance for child care centers.* Washington, DC: Author.

U.S. Department of Health and Human Services and U.S. Department of Agriculture. (1995). *Dietary guidelines for Americans.* Washington, DC: Authors.

ADDITIONAL READING

Edelstein, S. (1992). *Nutrition and meal planning in childcare programs.* Chicago: The American Dietetic Association.

Egan, M. C. (1981). Federal nutrition support programs for children. In H. S. Wright & L. S. Sims, (Eds.), *Community nutrition: People, policies, and programs.* Belmont, CA: Wadsworth/ Thomson Learning

Endres, J. B., & Rockwell, R. E. (1994). *Food, nutrition and the young child* (4th ed.). New York: Merrill Publishing Co.

Essa, E. (2002). *Introduction to early childhood education* (4th ed.). Albany, NY: Delmar Learning.

Essa, E. (2002). *A practical guide to solving preschool behavior problems* (5th ed.). Albany, NY: Delmar Learning.

Food and Nutrition Service, United States Department of Agriculture. (1992, April). *Building for the future: Nutrition guidance for the child nutrition programs.* FNS-279.

Gordon, A., & Browne, K. (2004). *Beginnings and beyond: Foundations in early childhood education* (6th ed.). Clifton Park, NY: Delmar Learning.

Rolfes, S. R., & DeBrugne, L. K. (1990). *Life span nutrition: Conception through life.* St. Paul, MN: West Publishing Co.

Pamphlets

Conserving the Nutritive Value in Foods, USDA Home and Garden Bulletin No. 90. Superintendent of Documents, U.S. Government Printing Office, Washington, DC 20402.

Food is More than Just Something to Eat, Nutrition, Pueblo, CO 81009.

Growing Up with Breakfast, Kellogg Company, Department of Home Economics Services, 235 Porter Street, Battle Creek, MI 49016.

Buying Food, Superintendent of Documents, U.S. Government Printing Office, Washington, DC 20402.
Fun with Good Foods, USDA, PA-1204. Superintendent of Documents, U.S. Government Printing Office, Washington, DC 20402.

Video

The Child and Adult Care Food Program. *Nutrition guidance for child care.* (1992). Washington, DC: United States Department of Agriculture. Running Time: 30 minutes.

HELPFUL WEB SITES

American Dietetic Association	http://www.eatright.org
FDA—Center for Food Safety and Applied Nutrition	http://vm.cfsan.fda.gov/list.html
Florida State Farmers Markets	http://www.fl-ag.com
Multicultural Food Guide Pyramids	http://multiculturalhealth.org
The Pumpkin Patch Produce Availability Guide	http://www.thepumpkinpatch.com/availability.html
Tri-County Farm-Fresh Produce Growers Co-op	http://www.tricountyfarm.org
USDA—Center for Nutrition and Public Policy	http://www.usda.gov/cnpp
USDA—Food and Nutrition Service	http://www.fns.usda.gov/fns

For additional health, safety, and nutrition resources, go to
http://www.EarlyChildEd.delmar.com

CHAPTER 20

Food Safety

After studying this chapter, you should be able to:

- State aspects of personal hygiene that relate to food safety.
- Describe proper ways to store food.
- Describe methods of sanitizing food preparation areas and equipment.
- Identify proper dishwashing practices.
- Explain how to prevent contamination of food.
- Cite examples of food-borne illnesses.

TERMS TO KNOW

food-borne illness
food-borne illness outbreak
HACCP—Hazard Analysis
   Critical Control Point
critical control point

pasteurized
sanitized
disinfected
bacteria
viruses

parasites
irradiation
food infections
food intoxications

This unit introduces factors other than the menu that contribute to effective food service in the child care setting. The success of a carefully planned menu depends upon the food being safe to eat.

FOOD SAFETY DEPENDS ON SANITATION

The safety of meals prepared for young children is of equal importance to the nutritional value. Food-borne illness is a major public health issue; food-illnesses are dangerous and may be fatal to young children. A **food-borne illness** is a disease or illness that is carried or transmitted by food.

---

food-borne illness – *a food infection due to ingestion of food contaminated with bacteria, viruses, some molds, or parasites.*

A **food-borne illness outbreak** occurs when two or more people become ill after ingesting the same food and a laboratory analysis confirms that food was the source of the illness. The United States Centers for Disease Control estimates 76 million people become ill each year as a result of food-borne illnesses. This accounts for 325,000 hospitalizations and 5,000 deaths yearly. Those groups at greatest risk are:

- infants and children
- pregnant women
- elderly individuals
- persons with chronic diseases
- persons with weakened immune systems

While food-borne illness outbreaks associated with fast food chains and manufactured foods receive media coverage, most cases are caused by home-cooked meals. (Remember the Thanksgiving when the whole family had "the flu" after the holiday dinner?)

Causes of Food-Borne Illness

Food can become unsafe in several ways. Hazards to food are present in the air, in water, in other foods, on work surfaces, and on hands and bodies of food service workers. Such hazards can be divided into three categories (Figure 20–1):

- biological
- chemical
- physical

FIGURE 20–1

Food hazards.

Hazard	Examples
Biological	Bacteria
	Parasites
	Viruses
	Molds, yeasts
Chemical	Pesticides
	Metals
	Cleaning chemicals
Physical	Dirt
	Hair
	Broken glass
	Metal shavings
	Plastic
	Bones
	Rodent droppings

food-borne illness outbreak – *two or more persons become ill after ingesting the same food. Laboratory analysis must confirm that food is the source of the illness.*

The greatest threat to food safety is bacteria. Bacteria occur in the environment; some are even beneficial (blue cheese, yogurt, etc.); others can cause serious and dangerous illnesses. Primary techniques to lessen the danger of environmental contamination of food are:

- following good personal health and cleanliness habits
- maintaining a sanitary food service operation

Hazard Analysis and Critical Control Point (HACCP)

HACCP, or **Hazard Analysis and Critical Control Point**, is a food safety and self-inspection system that highlights potentially hazardous foods and how they are handled in the food service environment. The U.S. Food and Drug Administration (FDA) recommend implementation of HACCP because it is the most effective and efficient way to ensure products are safe. There are seven principles of a HACCP plan:

1. **Conduct a hazard analysis.** In this phase, a HACCP team is assembled. The team should list all food items used in the establishment with the product code, preparation techniques, and storage requirements for each one. A flow chart should be developed that follows the food from receiving to serving in order to identify potential hazards during this process (Figure 20–2).
2. **Determine the critical control point (CCP).** These are points during food preparation where hazards are identified and can be prevented or controlled (i.e., cooking foods to appropriate temperatures, proper thawing techniques).
3. **Establish critical limits.** Develop procedures and operating guidelines to help prevent or reduce hazards in the food service area. Establish requirements and ensure that these are being met.
4. **Establish monitoring procedures.** This principle needs to be accomplished through consistent documentation in temperature logs, observation and measurement of requirements, and frequent feedback and monitoring by the food service manager.
5. **Establish corrective actions.** Specific actions need to be developed and implemented if a critical control point procedure is not met. These episodes should be accurately documented so that future occurrences can be prevented.
6. **Establish record-keeping and documentation procedures.** Records of importance include recipes, time/temperature logs, employee training documentation, cleaning schedules, and job descriptions.
7. **Establish verification procedures.** Continued training is essential and management must be diligent in observing staff's routine behaviors.

For the HACCP plan to be successful in any food service establishment, continuous monitoring and improvement are essential (Food Code, 2001).

Personal Health and Food Safety

Those who are involved in food preparation and service must take great care to maintain a high level of personal health. The food handler must meet health standards. Those working in licensed

---

Hazard Analysis Critical Control Point (HACCP) – *a food safety and self-inspection system that highlights potentially hazardous foods and how they are handled in the food service department.*

critical control point (CCP) – *a point or procedure in a specific food system where loss of control may result in an unacceptable health risk.*

FIGURE 20–2

Recipe flow charts identify potential hazards in a food service establishment.

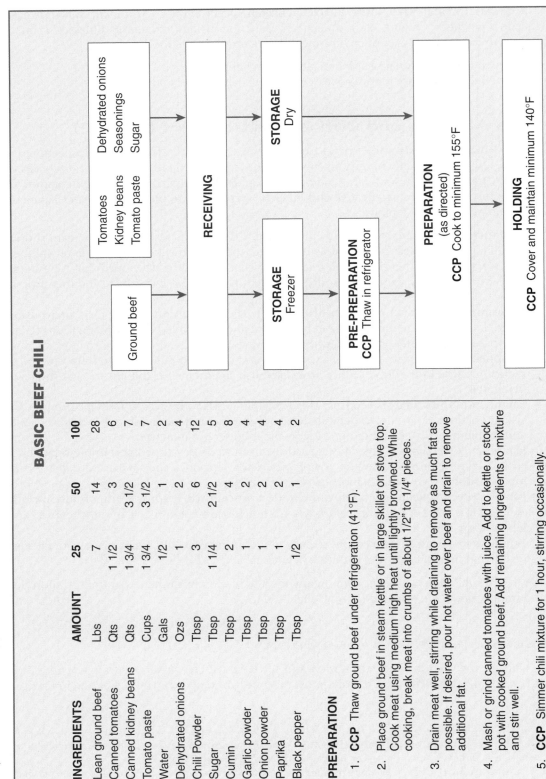

BASIC BEEF CHILI

INGREDIENTS	AMOUNT	25	50	100
Lean ground beef	Lbs	7	14	28
Canned tomatoes	Qts	1 1/2	3	6
Canned kidney beans	Qts	1 3/4	3 1/2	7
Tomato paste	Cups	1 3/4	3 1/2	7
Water	Gals	1/2	1	2
Dehydrated onions	Ozs	1	2	4
Chili Powder	Tbsp	3	6	12
Sugar	Tbsp	1 1/4	2 1/2	5
Cumin	Tbsp	2	4	8
Garlic powder	Tbsp	1	2	4
Onion powder	Tbsp	1	2	4
Paprika	Tbsp	1	2	4
Black pepper	Tbsp	1/2	1	2

PREPARATION

1. **CCP** Thaw ground beef under refrigeration (41°F).

2. Place ground beef in steam kettle or in large skillet on stove top. Cook meat using medium high heat until lightly browned. While cooking, break meat into crumbs of about 1/2" to 1/4" pieces.

3. Drain meat well, stirring while draining to remove as much fat as possible. If desired, pour hot water over beef and drain to remove additional fat.

4. Mash or grind canned tomatoes with juice. Add to kettle or stock pot with cooked ground beef. Add remaining ingredients to mixture and stir well.

5. **CCP** Simmer chili mixture for 1 hour, stirring occasionally. Temperature of cooked mixture must register 155°F or higher.

Reprinted by permission from La Vella Food Specialists, *HACCP for Food Service, Recipe Manual and Guide*, 1998.

Continued

FIGURE 20-2

Recipe flow charts identify potential hazards in a food service establishment (Continued).

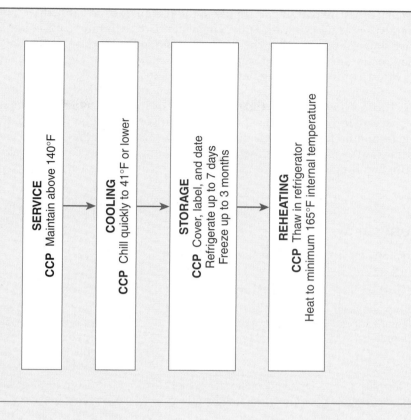

BASIC BEEF CHILI (cont'd)

PREPARATION (cont'd)

6. **CCP** Remove from heat and portion into service pans. Cover and hold for service (140°F).

7. Portion: 1 cup (8 ounces) per serving

SERVICE

1. **CCP** Maintain temperature of finished product above 140°F during entire service period. Keep covered whenever possible. Take and record temperature of unserved product every 30 minutes. Maximum holding time, 4 hours.

STORAGE

1. **CCP** Transfer unserved product into clean, 2-inch deep pans. Quick-chill. Cooling temperature of product must be as follows: from 140°F to 70°F within 2 hours and then from 70°F to 41°F or below, within an additional 4 hour period. Take and record temperature every hour during chill-down.

2. **CCP** Cover, label, and date. Refrigerate at 41°F or lower for up to 7 days (based on quality maintained) or freeze at 0°F for up to 3 months.

REHEATING:

1. **CCP** Thaw product under refrigeration, if frozen (41°F).

2. **CCP** Remove from refrigeration, transfer into shallow, 2-inch deep pans and immediately place in preheated 350°F oven, covered. Heat for 30 minutes or until internal temperature reaches 165°F or above.

Discard unused product.

SERVICE
CCP Maintain above 140°F

COOLING
CCP Chill quickly to 41°F or lower

STORAGE
CCP Cover, label, and date
Refrigerate up to 7 days
Freeze up to 3 months

REHEATING
CCP Thaw in refrigerator
Heat to minimum 165°F internal temperature

Reprinted by permission from La Vella Food Specialists, *HACCP for Food Service, Recipe Manual and Guide,* 1998.

child care facilities are required to supply to the school or child care center written proof that they are currently free of tuberculosis. Sufficient evidence of their tuberculosis-free status is afforded by a negative skin test or a negative chest X ray. Food handlers should also undergo periodic physical examinations to document their state of general good health. Health standards for food service workers vary according to the regulations of individual states.

Everyone who is involved in food preparation and service should be free of communicable diseases. Those suffering from colds, respiratory or intestinal types of influenza, gastrointestinal upsets, or severe throat infections should not be involved in food handling. Even though persons suffering from mild forms of these diseases frequently feel that they are well enough to work, to do so may transmit their illness to others. Those suffering from any communicable disease should refrain from handling food (Figure 20–3). An emergency store of simply prepared foods can solve

FIGURE 20–3

Restrictions for preventing disease transmission.

Illness	Restrictions	Comments
Abscess, skin lesions, boils (infected)	No direct customer contact or food preparation; use impermeable cover	May return to work when drainage ceases and lesion has healed or employee has a negative culture; can work if affected area is covered by impermeable cover.
Diarrhea (acute stage)	No direct customer contact or food preparation	May return to work when symptoms resolve and infection with Salmonella*, Shigella* or Campylobacter** is ruled out
Hepatitis A	No direct customer contact or food preparation	Until 7 days after onset of jaundice (local health department should be contacted)
HIV/AIDS	No restrictions	Counsel employee to ensure he/she observes safe work and hygiene practices
Lacerations, abrasions and burns (non-infected)	May have customer contact and prepare food with proper precautions	Proper precautions include keeping affected area covered by clean bandage and wearing disposable gloves if on hands or lower arms
Respiratory infection (no fever)	May have customer contact and prepare food with proper precautions	If no fever, wash hands frequently and observe safe work practices. If excessive coughing or fever, restrict from foodservice operation.
Strep throat	No direct customer contact or food preparation	Until 24 hours after effective treatment is started

*Restrict until 2 consecutive negative cultures, at least 24 hrs apart.
**Restrict until symptoms resolve or appropriate antibiotic treatment has been in effect for 48 hrs.

(From *Managing Food Protection* by James W. Kinner. Copyright 1998 by Dietary Managers Association. Used with permission of Kendall/Hunt Publishing Company.)

the problem of what to feed the children when the cook is ill. Foods that could be available for emergency use include:

- canned soups
- peanut butter
- canned or frozen fruits and vegetables
- tuna or chicken, canned

An adequate supply of these foods can provide meals that require a minimum of time or cooking skill to prepare.

Food handlers should wear clean, washable clothing and should change aprons frequently if they become soiled. Hair should be covered by a net, cap, or scarf while the worker is handling food. Head coverings should be put on and shoulders checked carefully for loose hair prior to entering the kitchen. Fingernails should be properly maintained and no polish or artificial nails should be allowed. Jewelry should not be worn with the exception of a plain ring, such as a wedding band.

Food handlers should refrain from chewing gum or smoking while working with food. Both practices can introduce saliva to the food handling area.

The Importance of Handwashing

Handwashing is of utmost importance to personal cleanliness (Figure 20–4). Hands should be washed thoroughly:

- before work
- before putting on gloves to work with food
- before touching food
- after handling nonfood items, such as cleaning or laundry supplies
- between handling different food items

FIGURE 20–4

Hands should be thoroughly washed before handling food.

- after using the bathroom
- after coughing, sneezing, or blowing the nose
- after using tobacco, eating, or drinking
- after touching bare body parts (face, ears) or hair

Hands should be washed with a cleaning compound after handling raw foods, such as fish, shellfish, meat and poultry, and before handling other foods. Current recommendations suggest that soap and water remains the accepted method of cleaning hands in non-health-care settings. Health care settings are increasing their use of waterless, alcohol-based gels. This is an acceptable method for hand hygiene but is not a sensible choice for child care settings. The harm posed by children coming into contact with or ingesting these potentially toxic substances may not be worth the protection they provide. If these alcohol-based gels are used, they should be made inaccessible to children. To encourage young children to thoroughly wash their hands, have them count to 20 and then say their full name while washing their hands. If the food handler has cuts or abrasions on hands or arms, they should be bandaged and gloves should be worn. Gloved hands should be washed as often as bare hands because the gloves can also pick up bacteria. See Figure 20–5 for an example of good handwashing technique.

Safe Food Handling

Food.   All raw produce should be inspected for spoilage upon delivery and should be thoroughly washed before use. Fresh fruits and vegetables can carry bacteria and pesticide residues. Produce that won't be peeled, such as strawberries, potatoes, and green onions, can be washed with plain water. If necessary, use a small brush to remove surface dirt. Lettuce leaves should be washed individually. Produce that will be peeled should be washed with soapy water and rinsed well to prevent spreading bacteria from the peel or rind to the hands and edible parts of the fruit or vegetable. All dairy products must be **pasteurized**. Tops of cans should be washed before opening; contaminants on cans can be passed to other cans or work surfaces by a dirty can opener. The can opener should also be washed daily. Food in cans which "spew" when opened should be discarded immediately. All other food packages should be in good condition with the integrity of the product protected.

After washing raw meat, fish, or poultry, rinse the sink with hot, soapy water. The kitchen sink, drain, and faucet handles should also be sanitized periodically by pouring down the sink a solution of one teaspoon of chlorine bleach per one quart of water. Food particles trapped in the drain and disposal along with moisture in the drain provide an excellent environment for bacterial growth.

Food Storage.   Careful storage and handling of food at appropriate temperatures are essential factors of food safety. Refrigerators should be maintained at 38°F to 40°F. A thermometer hung from a shelf in the warmest area of the refrigerator can be used to check whether appropriate temperatures are being maintained. Freezers should be maintained at 0°F or below. Frozen foods should be thawed:

- in the refrigerator
- in cold water (place food in watertight, plastic bag; change water every 30 minutes)
- in a microwave oven
- while cooking

Caution: Frozen food should never be thawed at room temperature!

---

pasteurized – *heating a food to a prescribed temperature for a specific time period to destroy disease-producing bacteria.*

FIGURE 20–5

Good handwashing techniques.

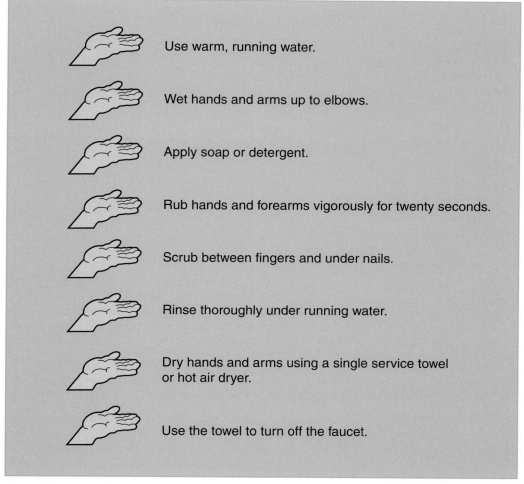

Use warm, running water.

Wet hands and arms up to elbows.

Apply soap or detergent.

Rub hands and forearms vigorously for twenty seconds.

Scrub between fingers and under nails.

Rinse thoroughly under running water.

Dry hands and arms using a single service towel or hot air dryer.

Use the towel to turn off the faucet.

(From *Managing Food Protection* by James W. Kinner. Copyright 1998 by Dietary Managers Association. Used with permission of Kendall/Hunt Publishing Company.)

Transport. Food should be covered or wrapped during transport. Covering provides additional temperature control and avoids the possibility of contamination during transport. When serving foods, each serving bowl, dish, or pan should have a spoon; spoons should not be used to serve more than one food.

Food Service. Food that has been on the tables should not be saved. Exception to this rule are fresh fruits and vegetables that may be washed after removal from the table and served later. Food that has been held in the kitchen at safe temperatures (160°F for hot food or 40°F or below for cold foods) may be saved. Food should not be held longer than two hours. Foods that are to be saved should be placed in shallow (three inches or less) pans and refrigerated or frozen immediately. Spreading food in a thin layer in shallow pans allows it to cool more rapidly.

FIGURE 20–6

Kitchen sanitation depends on frequent, systematic cleaning.

CLEANING SCHEDULE

Daily
- ▼ Cutting boards sanitized after each use
- ▼ Counter tops washed and sanitized between preparation of different foods
- ▼ Tables washed with sanitizing solution
- ▼ Can openers washed and sanitized
- ▼ Range tops cleaned
- ▼ Floors damp mopped

Weekly
- ▼ Ovens cleaned
- ▼ Refrigerator cleaned and rinsed with vinegar water

As Needed
- ▼ Refrigerator/freezer defrosted
- ▼ Walls washed
- ▼ Floors scrubbed

Foods such as creamed dishes, meat, poultry, or egg salads that are especially prone to spoilage should be prepared from chilled ingredients as quickly as possible and served or refrigerated in shallow containers immediately. All such foods should be maintained at temperatures below 40°F until cooked or served.

Sanitation of Food Preparation Areas and Equipment

The cleanliness of the kitchen and kitchen equipment is a vital factor of safe food service. These areas should be cleaned on a regular schedule. Minimizing traffic through the kitchen reduces the amount of dirt brought in. Schedules, such as that shown in Figure 20–6, should be maintained for the cleaning of floors, walls, ranges, ovens, and refrigerators. The equipment used in the direct handling of food must receive extra care. Surfaces on which food is prepared should be **sanitized** or **disinfected** with chlorine bleach solution each time a different food is prepared on it. Cutting boards should be non-porous and should be washed with hot, soapy water and sanitized with bleach solution after each use. Designated cutting boards should be used for specific foods (e.g., raw poultry). Labeling or color coding may be used to distinguish the boards. Disinfecting may be done with a liquid chlorine bleach solution (1/4 cup bleach to each gallon of water). This solution should be made daily.

*Caution: **Never mix bleach with anything other than water—A poisonous gas can result!***

Dishwashing. Dishes may be washed by hand or with a mechanical dishwasher. If washing by hand:

- wash dishes with hot water and detergent
- rinse dishes in hot, clear water
- sanitize dishes with chlorine bleach solution or scald with boiling water

---

sanitized – *cleaned or sterilized.*
disinfected – *killed pathogenic organisms.*

REFLECTIVE THOUGHTS

How safe is your kitchen? While regulations are written for organizational kitchens, what about the kitchens in our homes?
Do you:

- sanitize counter surfaces and cutting boards? Do you use an antibacterial product or dilute chlorine bleach?
- sanitize utensils? Do you immerse in hot (170°) water for a least 30 seconds? Do you wash them in the dishwasher?
- wash your hands frequently? Wash briskly with soap? Dry them with a clean towel or paper towels?
- sanitize spills from raw meats, fish, seafood, and poultry?
- wash fruits and vegetables thoroughly?
- cook foods to proper temperatures?
- ensure refrigerators/freezers are maintained at appropriate temperatures?

All dishes, utensils, and surfaces must be air dried (not dried with a towel).

If dishes are washed by a mechanical dishwasher, the machine must meet local health department standards. Some state licensing regulations provide guidelines as to the method of dishwashing to be used based on the number of persons served.

Sanitation of Food Service Areas

The eating area requires special attention. Cleanliness of the tables can be a problem, especially if they are also used as classroom tables. In order to maintain adequate sanitation, the tables should be washed with chlorine bleach solution:

- before each meal
- after each meal
- before each snack
- after each snack (Figure 20–7)

FIGURE 20–7

Tables should be washed properly before and after meals.

The children should be taught to wash their hands carefully before eating. They should also be taught that serving spoons should be used to serve food and then replaced in the serving dishes. Children should never be allowed to eat from serving utensils.

The guidelines for sanitation evaluation shown in Figure 20–8 are a useful tool in assessing food service sanitation on a regular basis.

FIGURE 20–8

Guidelines for sanitation evaluation.

SANITATION EVALUATION

	EX	GOOD	FAIR	POOR
FOOD				
1. Supplies of food and beverages must meet local, state, and federal codes.				
2. Meats and poultry must be inspected and passed for wholesomeness by federal or state inspectors.				
3. Milk and milk products must be pasteurized.				
4. Home canned foods must not be used.				
FOOD STORAGE				

1. Perishable foods are stored at temperatures that will prevent spoilage:
  a. Refrigerator temperature: 40°F (4°C) or below
  b. Freezer temperature: 0°F (-18°C) or below				

2. Thermometers are located in the warmest part of each refrigerator and freezer and are checked daily.				
3. Refrigerator has enough shelves to allow space between foods for air circulation to maintain proper temperatures.				
4. Frozen foods are thawed in refrigerator or quick-thawed under cold water for immediate preparation, or thawed as part of the cooking process. (Never thawed at room temperature.)				
5. Food is examined when brought to center to make sure it is not spoiled, dirty, or infested with insects.				
6. Foods are stored in rodent-proof and insect-proof covered metal, glass, or hard plastic containers.				
7. Containers of food are stored above the floor (6 inches) on racks that permit moving for easy cleaning.				

Continued

FIGURE 20–8

Guidelines for sanitation evaluation (Continued).

SANITATION EVALUATION

	EX	GOOD	FAIR	POOR
8. Storerooms are dry and free from leaky plumbing or drainage problems. All holes and cracks in storeroom are repaired.				
9. Storerooms are kept cool: 50°F to 70°F (10°C to 21°C)				
10. All food items are stored separately from nonfood items.				
11. Inventory system is used to be sure that stored food is rotated.				
FOOD PREPARATION AND HANDLING				
1. All raw fruits and vegetables are washed before use. Tops of cans are washed before opening.				
2. Thermometers are used to check internal temperatures of: a. Poultry—minimum 170°F (74°C)				
b. Pork and pork products— minimum 160°F (66°C).				
3. Meat salads, poultry salads, potato salads, egg salad, cream-filled pastries and other potentially hazardous prepared foods are prepared from chilled products as quickly as possible and refrigerated in shallow containers or served immediately.				
4. All potentially hazardous foods are maintained below 40°F (4°C) or above 140°F (60°C) during transportation and holding until service.				
5. Foods are covered or completely wrapped during transportation.				
6. Two spoons are used for tasting foods.				
7. Each serving bowl has a serving spoon.				
8. Leftover food from serving bowls on the tables is not saved. An exception would be raw fruits and vegetables that could be washed. Food held in kitchen at safe temperatures is used for refilling bowls as needed.				

Continued

FIGURE 20–8

Guidelines for sanitation evaluation (Continued).

SANITATION EVALUATION

	EX	GOOD	FAIR	POOR
9. Food held in the kitchen at safe temperatures is reused.				
10. Foods stored for reuse are placed in shallow pans and refrigerated or frozen immediately.				
11. Leftovers or prepared casseroles are held in refrigerator or frozen immediately.				

STORAGE OF NONFOOD SUPPLIES

	EX	GOOD	FAIR	POOR
1. All cleaning supplies (including dish sanitizers) and other poisonous materials are stored in locked compartments or in compartments well above the reach of children and separate from food, dishes, and utensils.				
2. Poisonous and toxic materials other than those needed for kitchen sanitation are stored in locked compartments outside the kitchen area.				
3. Insect and rodent poisons are stored in locked compartments in an area apart from other cleaning compounds to avoid contamination or mistaken usage.				

CLEANING AND CARE OF EQUIPMENT

	EX	GOOD	FAIR	POOR
1. A cleaning schedule is followed: a. Floors are wet mopped daily, scrubbed as needed.				
b. Food preparation surfaces are washed and sanitized between preparation of different food items (as between meat and salad preparation).				
c. Cutting boards are made of hard nontoxic material, and are smooth and free from cracks, crevices, and open seams.				

Continued

FIGURE 20–8

Guidelines for sanitation evaluation (Continued).

SANITATION EVALUATION

	EX	GOOD	FAIR	POOR
d. After cutting any single meat, fish, or poultry item, the cutting board is thoroughly washed and sanitized.				
e. Can openers are washed and sanitized daily.				
f. Utensils are cleaned and sanitized between uses on different food items.				
2. Dishwashing is done by an approved method:				
a. *Hand washed*—3-step operation including sanitizing rinse.				
b. *Mechanical*—by machine that meets local health department standards.				
3. Range tops are washed daily and as needed to keep them clean during preparation.				
4. Ovens are cleaned weekly or as needed.				
5. Refrigerator is washed once a week with vinegar.				
6. Refrigerator is defrosted when there is about 1/4" thickness of frost.				
7. Tables and other eating surfaces are washed with a mild disinfectant solution before and after each meal.				
8. All food contact surfaces are air-dried after cleaning and sanitizing.				
9. Cracked or chipped utensils or dishes are not used; they are disposed of.				
10. Garbage cans are leakproof and have tight-fitting lids.				
11. Garbage cans are lined with plastic liners and emptied and cleaned frequently.				
12. There is a sufficient number of garbage containers available.				

Continued

FIGURE 20–8

Guidelines for sanitation evaluation (Continued).

SANITATION EVALUATION

	EX	GOOD	FAIR	POOR
INSECT AND RODENT CONTROL				
1. Only an approved pyrithren base insecticide or fly swatter is used in the food preparation area.				
2. The insecticides do not come in contact with raw or cooked food, utensils, or equipment used in food preparation and serving, or with any other food contact surface.				
3. Doors and windows have screens in proper repair and are closed at all times. All openings to the outside are closed or properly screened to prevent entrance of rodents or insects.				
PERSONAL SANITATION				
1. Health of food service personnel meets standards: a. TB test is current.				
b. Physical examination is up to date.				
2. Everyone who works with or near food is free from communicable disease.				
3. Clean washable clothing is worn.				
4. Hairnets or hair caps are worn in the kitchen.				
5. There is no use of tobacco or chewing gum in the kitchen.				
6. Hands are washed thoroughly before touching food, before work, after handling nonfood items, between handling of different food items, after using bathroom, after coughing, sneezing, blowing nose.				

FOOD-BORNE ILLNESSES

Food poisoning refers to a variety of food-borne illnesses that may be caused by the presence of **bacteria**, **viruses**, **parasites**, or some kinds of molds growing on foods (Table 20–1). Foods that are visibly molded, soured, or beginning to liquefy should not be used; nor should food from bulging cans or cans in which the liquid is foamy or smells strange. Foods containing most food poisoning organisms carry few signs of spoilage. The food usually appears and smells safe, but still can cause severe illness. Proper sanitation procedures, preparation, and food handling should prevent most food-borne illnesses (Cody & Keith, 1991).

The introduction of **irradiation** as a new food preservation technique may in time reduce the incidence of food-borne disease. Irradiation has recently been approved by the Food and Drug Administration as an "additive" for food to kill microorganisms that might cause illness. This procedure involves exposing food to low levels of gamma radiation with the amount of exposure and the kinds of food to be irradiated being controlled by the FDA. Irradiated foods must carry the symbol and message shown in Figure 20–9 on page 482. Irradiation is allowed in nearly 40 countries and is endorsed by the World Health Organization, the American Medical Association, and the CDC, among others.

The use of irradiation as a preservative for food is still controversial, and some people feel uncomfortable consuming food preserved in this manner. Irradiated foods are not radioactive. They have been changed chemically, so there may be considerable loss of some nutrients. Vitamins A, E, and C, beta carotene, and thiamin are particularly vulnerable to destruction by irradiation. Recently, the USDA released specifications for the purchase of irradiated ground beef

ISSUES TO CONSIDER • An *E. coli* Outbreak

E. coli 0157:H7 is a deadly bacteria that is frequently in the news. Most people associate outbreaks with contaminated and undercooked meats—especially ground beef. Those are not always the source of poisoning. One such outbreak occurred at a popular water park when an infected child was brought with a group of children. It is thought that the child accidentally defecated in the wading pool while the water chlorine levels were lower than safe. This incident resulted in 26 infections reported in several surrounding states. One child ultimately died from the effects of *E. coli* 0157:H7 poisoning.

- Are your sanitation procedures adequate to prevent spreading illness through water play?
- Are your food preparation and service methods safe?
- What sanitation precautions should you observe when taking children on an outing?

---

bacteria – *one-celled microorganisms; some are beneficial for the body but pathogenic bacteria cause diseases.*
viruses – *any of a group of submicroscopic infective agents, many of which cause a number of diseases in animals and plants.*
parasites – *organisms that live on or within other living organisms.*
irradiation – *food preservation by short-term exposure of the food to gamma ray radiation.*

TABLE 20–1   Food-Borne Illnesses

DISEASE AND ORGANISM THAT CAUSES IT	SOURCE OF ILLNESS	SYMPTOMS	PREVENTION METHODS
salmonellosis *Salmonella* (bacteria; more than 1,700 kinds)	May be found in raw meats, poultry, eggs, fish, milk, and products made with them. Multiplies rapidly at room temperature.	Onset: 12–48 hours after eating. Nausea, fever, headache, abdominal cramps, diarrhea, and sometimes vomiting. Can be fatal in infants, the elderly, and the infirm.	• Handling food in a sanitary manner • Thorough cooking of foods • Prompt and proper refrigeration of foods
E. coli *E. coli 0157:H7*	May occur in beef (primarily ground beef) unpasteurized apple cider, raw milk, raw potatoes, mayonnaise. Organism is naturally present in food animals.	Onset: 12–72 hours. Watery, profuse diarrhea, fever. Diarrhea may be bloody.	• Cooking ground meats to 165°F. This temperature is high enough to inactivate *E. coli.* • Pasteurization
staphylococcal food poisoning staphylococcal enterotoxin (produced by *Staphylococcus aureus* bacteria)	The toxin is produced when food contaminated with the bacteria is left too long at room temperature. Meats, poultry, egg products; tuna, potato and macaroni salads; and cream-filled pastries are good environments for these bacteria to produce toxin.	Onset: 1–8 hours after eating. Diarrhea, vomiting, nausea, abdominal cramps, and prostration. Mimics flu. Lasts 24–48 hours. Rarely fatal.	• Sanitary food handling practices • Prompt and proper refrigeration of foods
botulism botulinum toxin (produced by *Clostridium botulinum* bacteria)	Bacteria are widespread in the environment. However, bacteria produce toxin only in an anaerobic (oxygen-less) environment of little acidity. Types A, B, and F may result from inadequate processing of low-acid canned foods, such as green beans, mushrooms, spinach, olives, and beef. Type E normally occurs in fish.	Onset: 8–36 hours after eating. Neuro-toxic symptoms, including double vision, inability to swallow, speech difficulty, and progressive paralysis of the respiratory system. OBTAIN MEDICAL HELP IMMEDIATELY. BOTULISM CAN BE FATAL.	• Using proper methods for canning low-acid foods • Avoidance of commercially canned low-acid foods with leaky seals or with bent, bulging, or broken cans • Toxin can be destroyed after a can is opened by boiling contents hard for 10 minutes—NOT RECOMMENDED

(Continued)

TABLE 20-1 Food-Borne Illnesses (Continued)

DISEASE AND ORGANISM THAT CAUSES IT	SOURCE OF ILLNESS	SYMPTOMS	PREVENTION METHODS
Listeriosis *Listeria monocytogenes*	Raw animal products and dairy foods, contaminated water.	Mild fever and diarrhea, severe sore throat, meningitis, encephalitis, still birth, or abortion.	• Pasteurization • Sanitation • Hygiene
parahaemolyticus food poisoning *Vibrio parahaemolyticus* (bacteria)	Organism lives in salt water and can contaminate fish and shellfish. Thrives in warm water.	Onset: 15–24 hours after eating. Abdominal pain, nausea, vomiting, and diarrhea. Sometimes fever, headache, chills, and mucus and blood in the stools. Last 1–2 days. Rarely fatal.	• Sanitary handling of foods • Thorough cooking of seafood
gastrointestinal disease enteroviruses, rotaviruses, parvoviruses	Viruses exist in the intestinal tract of humans and are expelled in feces. Contamination of foods can occur in three ways: (1) when sewage is used to enrich garden/farm soil, (2) by direct hand-to-food contact during the preparation of meals, and (3) when shellfish-growing waters are contaminated by sewage.	Onset: After 24 hours. Severe diarrhea, nausea, and vomiting. Respiratory symptoms Usually lasts 4–5 days but may last for weeks.	• Sanitary handling of foods • Use of pure drinking water • Adequate sewage disposal • Adequate cooking of foods
hepatitis hepatitis A virus	Chief food sources: shellfish harvested from contaminated areas, and foods that are handled a lot during preparation and then eaten raw (such as vegetables).	Jaundice, fatigue. May cause liver damage and death.	• Sanitary handling of foods • Use of pure drinking water • Adequate sewage disposal • Adequate cooking of foods
mycotoxicosis mycotoxins (from molds)	Produced in foods that are relatively high in moisture. Chief food sources: beans and grains that have been stored in a moist place.	May cause liver and/or kidney disease	• Checking foods for visible mold and discarding those that are contaminated • Proper storage of susceptible foods *(Continued)*

TABLE 20-1 Food-Borne Illnesses (Continued)

DISEASE AND ORGANISM THAT CAUSES IT	SOURCE OF ILLNESS	SYMPTOMS	PREVENTION METHODS
giardiasis *Giardia lamblia* (flagellated protozoa)	Protozoa exist in the intestinal tract of humans and are expelled in feces. Contamination of foods can occur in two ways: (1) when sewage is used to enrich garden/farm soil, and (2) by direct hand-to-food contact during the preparation of meals. Chief food sources: foods that are handled a lot during preparation.	Diarrhea, abdominal pain, flatulence, abdominal distention, nutritional disturbances, "nervous" symptoms, anorexia, nausea, and vomiting.	• Sanitary handling of foods • Avoidance of raw fruits and vegetables in areas where the protozoa is endemic • Proper sewage disposal
amebiasis *Entamoeba histolytica* (amoebic protozoa)		Tenderness over the colon or liver, loose morning stools, recurrent diarrhea, change in bowel habits, "nervous" symptoms, loss of weight, and fatigue. Anemia may be present.	• Sanitary handling of foods • Avoidance of raw fruits and vegetables in areas where the protozoa is endemic • Proper sewage disposal
perfringens food poisoning *Clostridium perfringens* (rod-shaped bacteria)	Bacteria are widespread in environment. Generally found in meat and poultry and dishes made with them. Multiply rapidly when foods are left at room temperature too long. Destroyed by cooking.	Onset: 8–22 hours after eating (usually 12). Abdominal pain and diarrhea. Sometimes nausea and vomiting.	• Sanitary handling of foods especially meat and meat dishes and gravies • Thorough cooking of foods • Prompt and proper refrigeration
shigellosis (bacillary dysentery) *Shigella* (bacteria)	Food becomes contaminated when a human carrier with poor sanitary habits handles liquid or moist food that is then not cooked thoroughly. Organisms multiply in food stored above room temperature. Found in milk and dairy products, poultry, and potato salad.	Symptoms last a day or less and are usually mild. Can be more serious in older or debilitated people. Onset: 1–7 days after eating. Abdominal pain, cramps, diarrhea, fever, sometimes vomiting, and blood, pus, or mucus in stools. Can be serious in infants, the elderly, or debilitated people.	• Handling food in a sanitary manner • Proper sewage disposal • Proper refrigeration of foods
campylobacterosis *Campylobacter jejuni* (rod-shaped bacteria)	Bacteria found on poultry, cattle, and sheep and can contaminate the meat and milk of these animals. Chief food sources: raw poultry and meat and unpasteurized milk.	Onset: 2–5 days after eating. Diarrhea, abdominal cramping, fever, and sometimes bloody stools. Lasts 2–7 days.	• Thorough cooking of foods • Handling of food in a sanitary manner • Avoid unpasteurized milk *(Continued)*

TABLE 20-1 Food-Borne Illnesses (Continued)

DISEASE AND ORGANISM THAT CAUSES IT	SOURCE OF ILLNESS	SYMPTOMS	PREVENTION METHODS
gastroenteritis *Yersinia enterocolitica* (non-spore-forming bacteria)	Ubiquitous in nature; carried in food and water. Bacteria multiply rapidly at room temperature, as well as at refrigerator temperatures of 39.2°F (4° to 9°C). Generally found in raw vegetables, meats, water, and unpasteurized milk.	Onset 2–5 days after eating. Fever, headache, nausea, diarrhea, and general malaise. Mimics flu. An important cause of gastroenteritis in children. Can also infect other age groups, and, if not treated, can lead to other more serious diseases (such as lymphadenitis, arthritis, and Reiter's syndrome).	• Thorough cooking of foods • Sanitizing cutting instruments and cutting boards before preparing foods that are eaten raw • Avoidance of unpasteurized milk and unchlorinated water
cerus food poisoning *Bacillus cereus* (bacteria and possibly their toxin)	Illness may be caused by the bacteria, which are widespread in the environment, or by an enterotoxin created by the bacteria. Found in raw foods. Bacteria multiply rapidly in foods stored at room temperature.	Onset: 1–18 hours after eating. Two types of illness: (1) abdominal pain and diarrhea, and (2) nausea and vomiting. Lasts less than a day.	• Sanitary handling of foods • Thorough cooking of foods • Prompt and adequate refrigeration
cholera *Vibrio cholera* (bacteria)	Found in fish and shellfish harvested from waters contaminated by human sewage. (Bacteria may also occur naturally in Gulf Coast waters.) Chief food sources: seafood, especially types eaten raw (such as oysters).	Onset: 1–3 days. Can range from "subclinical" (a mild uncomplicated bout with diarrhea) to fatal (intense diarrhea with dehydration). Severe cases require hospitalization.	• Sanitary handling of foods • Thorough cooking of seafood

Courtesy of "Who, Why, When, and Where of Food Poisons (And What to Do About Them)." *FDA Consumer,* July–August 1982.

FIGURE 20–9

Irradiated food must bear this radura symbol plus the message that it has been irradiated.

through the National School Lunch Program. It became available for schools to purchase in January 2004.

Irradiation is not as dangerous as its critics claim, but neither is it the solution to all food-borne illness problems as its promoters claim. Probably the most serious concerns should be that irradiation could be used to cover up unsanitary food processing procedures or that consumers will rely too much upon radiation protection and become careless in the handling of food. Until more is known about the safety of irradiation and the degree of protection that it affords, it is important that the prescribed procedures for sanitary handling of food be consistently and carefully practiced.

Steam pasteurization is a technique developed to produce safer meat products. In this process the carcass is immersed in pressurized steam for six to eight seconds. This technique covers the entire carcass, killing all bacteria uniformly.

Researchers are also looking at spraying baby chicks with antibiotic mist to reduce *Salmonella* infections in poultry. Other research is looking at changing cattle feeding practices immediately before slaughter to control *E. coli* in beef.

CONDITIONS FOR BACTERIAL GROWTH

Since our environment contains numerous bacteria, why do food-borne illnesses not occur even more frequently than they do? For illness to occur the following conditions must be present:

- *Potentially hazardous food*—bacteria generally prefer foods that are high in protein; such as meat, poultry, eggs, and dairy products.
- *Oxygen*—some bacteria require oxygen. Others cannot tolerate oxygen. Other bacteria grow with or without oxygen.
- *Temperature*—temperature is probably the most critical factor in bacterial growth. The hazard zone of 41°F–140°F is the range in which bacteria grow most rapidly.
- *Time*—a single bacterial cell can multiply into one million cells in five hours under ideal conditions.
- *Water*—bacteria grow in foods with a higher water content.
- *Acidity*—bacteria prefer conditions that are near neutral (pH 7.0).

FIGURE 20–10

Safe-handling instructions are given with packaged meats and poultry.

SAFE-HANDLING INSTRUCTIONS

THIS PRODUCT WAS PREPARED FROM INSPECTED AND PASSED MEAT AND/OR POULTRY. SOME FOOD PRODUCTS MAY CONTAIN BACTERIA THAT COULD CAUSE ILLNESS IF THE PRODUCT IS MISHANDLED OR COOKED IMPROPERLY. FOR YOUR PROTECTION, FOLLOW THESE SAFE-HANDLING INSTRUCTIONS.

KEEP REFRIGERATED OR FROZEN. THAW IN REFRIGERATOR OR MICROWAVE.

KEEP RAW MEAT AND POULTRY SEPARATE FROM OTHER FOODS. WASH WORKING SURFACES (IN-CLUDING CUTTING BOARDS), UTENSILS, AND HANDS AFTER TOUCHING RAW MEAT OR POULTRY.

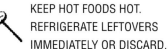

COOK THOROUGHLY.

KEEP HOT FOODS HOT. REFRIGERATE LEFTOVERS IMMEDIATELY OR DISCARD.

Food infections result from ingestion of large amounts of viable bacteria in foods that cause infectious disease. Symptoms usually develop relatively slowly (12–24 hours) since incubation of the bacteria takes time.

Food intoxications result from eating food containing toxins that are produced in the food by bacterial growth. Symptoms usually develop more rapidly (within 1–6 hours) than those associated with infections (Williams, 1997), except for botulinum toxins, which produce symptoms later (8–36 hours). The incidence of food-borne illnesses appears to be on the rise and is a frequent cause of illness in infants and toddlers in day care centers. The most common food carriers of infectious agents and/or toxins are milk, eggs, meat, fish, and poultry. Poultry products are one of the most frequent causes of food poisoning, which explains the recommendation that a separate cutting board be provided for poultry and raw meat products. An additional reason for concern is that the U.S. Department of Agriculture has relaxed its inspection rules, has no standards for bacterial contamination, and allows federal inspectors of poultry products only two seconds to examine each bird. The consumer must assume full responsibility for choosing, storing, and preparing these products so that they do not cause illness. Safe-handling instructions attached to packaging aid the consumer in safely preparing these foods (Figure 20–10). Very thorough cooking of poultry, eggs, and other meat products will kill bacteria and destroy most toxins. It is NEVER safe to allow young children to eat raw or poorly cooked eggs, meat products, fish, or seafood. Their less than fully developed immune systems leave them more vulnerable to, and less able to cope with, a food-borne illness. It is important to remember that cold temperature **STOPS** bacterial growth. Heat **KILLS** bacteria. Figure 20–11 outlines safe cooking temperatures.

---

food infections – *illnesses resulting from ingestion of live bacteria in food.*
food intoxications – *illnesses resulting from ingestion of food containing residual bacterial toxins in the absence of viable bacteria.*

FIGURE 20–11

Safe cooking temperatures.

Download this form online at http:// www.Early ChildEd.del mar.com

Product	Fahrenheit	Product	Fahrenheit
Eggs and Egg Dishes		**Poultry**	
Eggs	Cook until yolk and white are firm	Chicken, whole	180
Egg dishes	160	Turkey, whole	180
Ground Meat and Meat Mixtures		Poultry breasts, roast	170
Turkey, chicken	165	Poultry thighs, wings	Cook until juices run clear
Veal, beef, lamb, pork	160		
Fresh Beef		Stuffing (cooked alone or in bird)	165
Medium rare	145	Duck and goose	180
Medium	160	**Ham**	
Well done	170	Fresh (raw)	160
Fresh Veal		Pre-cooked (to reheat)	140
Medium rare	145	**Seafood**	
Medium	160	Fin fish	145
Well done	170	Minced fish such as fish sticks, fish or seafood patties	155
Fresh Lamb		Stuffed fish or seafood stuffing	165
Medium rare	145	Oysters, clams, mussels	165
Medium	160	Shrimp, lobster, crab or other seafoods	145
Well done	170		
Fresh Pork			
Medium	160		
Well done	170		

Source: USDA. (1996, November).

FOCUS ON FAMILIES • Handwashing

Food safety is everyone's responsibility, and it is never too early to introduce children to safe hygiene behaviors. Handwashing is the single most effective tool for reducing illness by germs transferred from people and surroundings. In teaching children the importance of sound eating behaviors and practices, teaching the art of handwashing is essential. As the primary role model for children, parents and teachers should consistently practice good handwashing techniques and be active in getting children to adopt this behavior.

- Children should wash their hands with warm, soapy water before eating, after using the toilet, after playing with a pet, and after nose blowing.

- Keep a step stool nearby to make it easier for the child to reach the sink.

- Post a chart near the sink and make a mark for every time hands are washed. Praise your child for a job well done.

- Make handwashing fun. Hand and soap dispensers are available in different shaped bars/bottles.

- Be creative . . . create your own song using the melodies from favorite childhood songs or nursery rhymes such as "Row, row, row your boat" or "Old McDonald had a farm. " Have your child wash hands for the length of the song. This will be fun and ensure the appropriate amount of time is spent properly cleaning hands.

CASE STUDY

The health department is investigating an outbreak of food poisoning at a local child care center. The children were served a menu that included tacos, tossed salad, fresh fruit cubes, and milk. Annie, the cook, had forgotten to put ground beef to thaw under refrigeration a few days earlier, so she allowed it to thaw on the counter overnight. After dividing the partially thawed raw ground beef with her bare hands, she continued preparations for lunch and chopped the ingredients for the tossed salad. Using the same knife that she used to open the packages of ground beef, she cut the fruit sections for the fruit salad.

1. What are the possible causes of the food-borne illness outbreak at the child care center?

2. How could the outbreak have been prevented?

SUMMARY

- Basic food safety is an integral factor in the quality of a food service.
  - Wash hands before and after preparation of food.
  - Keep raw meats and poultry separate from other foods.
  - Clean and disinfect cutting boards and kitchen surfaces after preparing food.
  - Keep hot foods hot and cold foods cold.
  - Do not leave food out at room temperature for longer than two hours.
  - Refrigerate leftovers promptly in shallow containers or tightly wrapped bags.
  - Meat and poultry should be cooked all the way through until the juices run clear.
  - Hamburgers should be cooked to a temperature of 165°F and should be brown inside, not pink.
  - Do not taste or eat raw, rare, or even pink ground meat or poultry in any form. When eating out, order ground meats thoroughly cooked.
  - Cook seafood until it is opaque and flaky. Do not eat raw shellfish, such as oysters or clams, even if marinated.
  - Cook eggs thoroughly; they should be firm and not runny.
  - Avoid eating other foods that contain raw or undercooked eggs, such as Caesar salad dressing or cookie dough.

- HACCP (Hazard Analysis and Critical Control Point) is a food safety and self-inspection system that highlights potentially hazardous foods and how they are handled in the food service environment.

- Food safety depends on personal cleanliness and careful food handling.

- Personal health and cleanliness includes:
  - negative tuberculosis test.
  - periodic physical examinations.
  - clean work clothing.
  - head coverings.
  - frequent, thorough hand washing.

- Sanitation of the food service area requires systematic attention including:
  - cleaning schedules.
  - spot cleaning spills as they happen.
  - thorough daily cleaning.

- Safe food handling requires temperature control.
  - Temperature above 140°F to kill bacteria.
  - Temperature below 40°F to prevent bacterial growth.

SUGGESTED ACTIVITIES

1. The cook at your child care center has strep throat. Using the emergency stock discussed in this chapter, plan a menu for lunch that will meet menu-planning guidelines outlined in Chapter 19.

2. Invite a laboratory technician to class to make culture plates of a
   a. hand before washing
   b. hand after washing with water only
   c. hand after washing with soap and water
   d. strand of hair

   The technician should then return to the class with the cultures after the cultures have incubated for two to three days.
   e. Is there bacterial growth on any of the culture plates?
   f. Which cultures have the most bacterial growth?
   g. Discuss how these results could be best utilized in terms of
      (1) food preparation and service
      (2) child care center meal and snack times

CHAPTER REVIEW

Briefly answer the following questions.

1. List three means of keeping the food preparation area clean and germ free.

2. Describe the care, uses, and handling of cutting boards necessary for safe food service.

3. How could ground meat be safely thawed if there is too little time to thaw it in the refrigerator?

4. Terry, the cook, has a cut on her hand. What precautions should she take?

REFERENCES

Cody, M. M., & Keith, M. (1991). *Food safety for professionals,* Chicago: The American Dietetic Association.
Cooke, R. (1998, August). Antibacterial soaps can aid resistance in bacteria, doctors say. *Ladies Home Journal.*

FDA. (1982, July–August). Who, why, when, and where of food poisons (and what to do about them). *FDA Consumer.*

Kinner, J. W. (1998). *Managing food protection.* Dubuque, IA: Kendall/Hunt Publishing Company.

United States Department of Agriculture. (1996, November). *Keeping kids safe: A guide for safe food handling and sanitation.* Washington, DC: Author.

United States Department of Health and Human Services, Public Health Service and Food and Drug Administration (2001). *2001 Food Code.*

Williams, S. R. (1997). *Nutrition and diet therapy* (8th ed.). St. Louis, MO: C. V. Mosby Company.

ADDITIONAL READING

Cody, M. M. (1996). *Safe food for you and your family.* Minneapolis, MN: Chromined Publishing.

Farber, J. M., & Hughes, A. General guidelines for the safe handling of foods. *Dairy, Food and Environmental Sanitation, 18*(2), 70–78.

FDA. (1995, October). Can your kitchen pass the food safety test? *FDA Consumer.*

Jacobson, M., Lefferts, L. Y., & Garland, A. W. (1990). *Safe food: Eating wisely in a risky world.* Washington, DC: Center for Science in the Public Interest.

Kroger, M. (1991). Food safety: What are the real issues? *Annual Editions: Nutrition 91/92.* Guilford, CT: Dushkin Publishing Group Inc.

Lefferts, L. Y., & Schmidt, S. (1991, July/August). Name your (food) poison. *Nutrition Action Health Letter, 18*(6), 3–11 Washington, DC: USDA.

Wardlow, G. M., & Insel, P. M. (1990). *Perspectives in nutrition.* St. Louis, MO: Times Mirror/Mosby College Pub.

Williamson, C. C. (1992). The storm seasons: Handling food after tornados, hurricanes, floods, and fires. *Food News for Consumers, 9,* 1.

HELPFUL WEB SITES

1999 Food Safety Project, Iowa State University Extension — http://www.extension.iastate.edu/foodsafety/

Centers for Disease Control and Prevention — http://www.cdc.gov/health/disease

Center for Food Safety and Applied Nutrition — http://www.FoodSafety.gov

Fight Back — http://www.fightbac.org

Food and Drug Administration — http://www.fda.gov

The National Food Safety Database — http://foodsafety.gov

Recall Information:

FDA — http://www.fda.gov/opacom/Enforce.html

USDA — http://www.fsis.usda.gov/OA/news/xrecalls.htm

University of Nebraska (Food Safety and Self-Inspection for Child Care Facilities) — http://www.ianr.unl.edu/pubs/foods/g1232.htm

For additional health, safety, and nutrition resources, go to http://www.EarlyChildEd.delmar.com

CHAPTER 21

Nutrition Education Concepts and Activities

OBJECTIVES

After studying this chapter, you should be able to:

- Identify the primary goal of nutrition education for preschool children.
- List four basic concepts important to nutrition education.
- Explain the various roles child care personnel play in nutrition education.
- Describe four ways that nutrition education activities contribute to child development.
- Describe the general principles of safety that must be observed in planning nutrition education activities for children.

TERMS TO KNOW

nutrition education	hands-on	objectives
concepts	serrated	attitudes
sensorimotor	preplan	peer
harvest	evaluation	

In the simplest of terms, **nutrition education** is any activity that tells a person something about food. These activities may be structured, planned activities or very brief, informal happenings. The primary goal of nutrition education at the preschool level is to introduce children to some simple, basic principles of nutrition and to encourage them to eat and enjoy a variety of nutritious foods.

BASIC CONCEPTS OF NUTRITION EDUCATION

Some basic **concepts** for teaching young children that nutrition is important for good health are:

1. Children must have food to grow and to have healthy bodies.
   - All animals and plants need food.
   - Eating food helps children grow, play, learn, and be happy.

---

nutrition education – *activities that impart information about food and its use in the body.*
concepts – *combinations of basic and related factual information that represent a more generalized statement or idea.*

488

- Many foods are good for us.
- Eating food makes us feel good.
2. Nutrients come from foods. It is these nutrients that allow children to grow and be healthy.
    - After food is eaten these nutrients are set free to work in our bodies.
    - Nutrients do different things in our bodies.
    - Many different nutrients are needed each day.
    - Foods are the sources of all of the nutrients that we know are needed.
3. A variety of foods need to be eaten each day. No one food gives all of the needed nutrients.
    - Different foods provide different nutrients so we need to eat many kinds of food.
    - Nutrients need to work together in our bodies; we need many different nutrients each day.
    - Children should be exposed to and encouraged to accept a variety of foods from each of the Food Guide Pyramid Groups.
    - Children should explore how foods differ relative to color, shape, taste, and texture. They can learn to group and to identify certain kinds of foods such as fruits, breads, and meats.
4. Foods must be carefully handled before they are eaten to ensure that they are healthful and safe.
    - Cleanliness of all materials and persons involved with food handling is most important.
    - Some foods need to be cooked and eaten hot.
    - Some foods must be kept refrigerated and may be served cold.
    - Involving children with food handling helps them learn about the preparation that must be done to foods before they may be eaten.
    - Eating food that has not been handled properly can make children very ill.

These conceptual points require that the persons responsible for nutrition education have a basic knowledge of nutrition, in relation to both foods and nutrients.

Parents often ask the child care staff questions about nutrition topics or about something they have read about nutrition. It is important that they get the correct information. If the staff person does not know the answer, they might provide a list of local allied health personnel (dietitians, health department officers, USDA extension service, etc.) that could answer their questions.

To evaluate resource material for parents or for use in planning a food activity for children certain questions should be asked:

1. Is the resource known for its reliability in reporting?
2. What are the professional credentials of the author(s)?
3. Is the resource accurate and does it deal with known nutritional facts rather than theories?
4. Are unsubstantiated health claims presented?
5. Is the resource trying to sell something?
6. Is the material presented at the appropriate level or adaptable?
7. Are the suggested nutrition education projects healthful?
8. Are the projects safe?

Nutrition knowledge should be combined with a knowledge of educational techniques appropriate for the age group. Food activities should be planned with consideration for the developmental level of the age group and individual children in the group who will be participating in the lesson. Food experiences should be fun and enhance a child's positive feelings about healthful food.

RESPONSIBILITY FOR NUTRITION EDUCATION

All personnel involved in the nutrition program are responsible for nutrition education. Effectiveness of the nutrition education program depends on cooperation between the director, teacher,

FIGURE 21–1

The effectiveness of the nutrition education program depends on cooperation between the director, teachers, and food service personnel.

and cook or food service personnel (Figure 21–1). While programs vary in their organizational structure, these people generally have the responsibility for nutrition education.

The director's role is mainly supportive. The director should stress to the staff the importance of nutritious meals and snacks. The director should see that financial support is available for nutrition education in the curriculum.

The teacher is usually responsible for planning and executing the nutrition education program and for creating a pleasant atmosphere for meals and snacks. For this reason, the preschool teacher should be familiar with the conceptual framework behind nutrition education. The teacher should be aware of the nutritional value of foods and of educational methods. The teacher should be able to clearly state objectives and realistically evaluate the results of nutrition activities.

The food service personnel are responsible for planning, preparing, and serving nutritious, attractive meals. Food service personnel can be a great asset to a nutrition education program by including foods in the menu that reinforce what the children have learned from nutrition activities. The cook is a valuable resource person for food preparation methods. Since the cook is also responsible for the kitchen equipment, the cook may determine what is available for food preparation experiences.

Underlying the effectiveness of the above child care personnel as nutrition educators is one very simple, basic concept: *Set a good example.* Children who observe a teacher eating and enjoying a variety of nutritious foods will learn to eat more nutritiously than children who observe adults drinking soft drinks and eating other calorie-dense junk foods.

Parental Involvement in Nutrition Education

Parent involvement is vital to nutrition education in child care centers. Part of the nutrition program should involve helping parents understand their role in the provision of adequate nutrition for the child and the development of healthful eating habits. Communication between staff and parents is important so that parents may provide additional reinforcement for what has been learned at school.

To be effective, this communication should involve a real commitment of time and effort from both parents and teachers. Some ways that child care centers could encourage parental involvement with nutrition education are:

- Weekly posting of menus plus suggestions for foods that provide nutritional complements to each menu.
- Provide parents with a report of, and recipes for, new foods that their children have recently been introduced to.

- Provide a report on nutrition education units (food experiences) to the parents and ask for parental feedback on the child's reaction to these experiences.
- Present some evening meetings or workshops for parents. These could include talks or questions/answer sessions with local health agency personnel, demonstrations of food preparation by a local chef, or presentations by a parent who may have some food or nutrition experience to share.

Other ways for parents to participate in nutrition education are:

- accompany children to food-related field trips
- occasionally eat lunch with their child at the day care center
- help plan menus
- share special recipes that are nutritious and family favorites
- share ethnic or traditional foods with care-center children and/or other parents
- assist and observe one food experience activity with their child
- help in developing guidelines for acceptable foods that parents could bring to the day care center to celebrate a birthday or other holidays

Regardless of the degree of involvement chosen by the individual teachers and parents, the overriding common goal is the optimal growth and development of the child. Such a goal can best be met when open, understanding, two-way communication exists between teacher and parents.

RATIONALE FOR NUTRITION EDUCATION IN THE EARLY YEARS

There are several reasons for presenting information on nutrition to young children. Simple basic principles of good nutrition and how they relate to health can be effectively taught through nutrition education. Another advantage is that nutrition education activities foster child development in the following areas that relate directly to the preschool curriculum:

- *Promotion of language development*
  Children learn and use food names, food preparation terms, and names of utensils. Children also use language to communicate with their peers and teachers throughout the nutrition activity. A variety of children's literature and music can also be introduced to reinforce both language skills and nutrition concepts.
- *Promotion of cognitive development*
  Children learn to follow step-by-step directions in recipes. Math concepts are learned through activities that involve measurement of food (cups, ounces, teaspoons), counting, and time periods. Science concepts, such as changes in form, are reinforced through activities that involve heating, mixing, cooking, or chilling foods.
- *Promotion of **sensorimotor** development*
  Hand and finger dexterity are developed through measuring, cutting, mixing, spreading, and serving food. Shapes, textures, and colors are learned through a variety of foods.
- *Promotion of social/emotional development*
  Through nutrition activities, children learn to work as part of a team in either large or small groups. Their knowledge and acceptance of cultural differences may also be enhanced through food activities that feature ethnic foods. In addition, children gain a more positive self-concept when they master such skills as pouring juice into a glass for themselves.

---

sensorimotor – *Piaget's first stage of cognitive development, during which children learn and relate to their world primarily through motor and sensory activities.*

FIGURE 21–2

Resources for children's activities involving food.

Alley, H. (1992). *Nutrition for children ages two through twelve.* For the health of it. Athens, GA: Cooperative Extension Service, The University of Georgia College of Agricultural and Environmental Sciences.

American Institutes for Cancer Research. *Good-news-letter. The good news about good food.* Bimonthly Newsletter, Children Ages 7–10. Washington, DC: Author.

Arapahoe County Extension Service (1999). *ACE child care food program correspondence course.* Littleton, CO: Author.

Berman, C., & Froman, J. (1997). *Meals without squeals.* Palo Alto, CA: Bull Publishing Co.

Dole Food Company (1994). *Fun with fruits and vegetables: Kid's cookbook.* San Mateo, CA: Author.

Galloway, J., Ivey, J., & Volster, G. (1990). *Daily plans for active preschoolers.* West Nyack, NY: The Center for Applied Research in Education.

Harms, Thelma and Veitch, Beverly (1981). *Cook and learn: Nutritious food from various cultures.* Red Leaf Press.

Mayer, Marianna (1998). *The Mother Goose cookbook: Rhymes and recipes for the very young.* William Morrow and Company.

Nasco nutrition teaching aids (Catalog). 901 Janesville Ave., Fort Atkinson, WI 53538, or 4825 Stoddard Rd., Modesto, CA 95356. Email: info@eNASCO.com

National Cattlemen's Beef Association. *Munchster recipes.* Denver, CO: Author.

National Dairy Council (1990). *Airplane, choo-choo and other games parents play: A feeding guide for the first two years.* Rosemont, IL: Author.

National Dairy Council. The Family Food Zone. www.familyfoodzone.com

National Dairy Council: *Food models and food models guide for teachers and other leaders.* Rosemont, IL: Author.

National Dairy Council: *Nutrition Explorations.* www.nutritionexplorations.com/index.asp

National Network for Child Care. *Cooking with children: Kid's in the Kitchen.* www.nncc.org/Curriculum/fc46_cook.kids.html

Nutrition counseling education services (Catalog). 1904 East 123rd St., Olathe, KS 66061.

Pipes, P. (1997). *Nutrition in infancy and childhood* (6th edition). St. Louis, MO: C.V. Mosby Co.

Pugliese, M. *Nutrition and all that jazz: A nutrition handbook for preschool teachers.* Boston: Simmons College.

Sherman, G. (1994). *Hot food facts for cool kids.* Olathe, KS: Nutrition Counseling Education Services.

The Food and Drug Administration. FDA Kid's Home Page. www.fda.gov/oc/opacom/kids/

Warner, Penny (1999). *Healthy snacks for kids.* Bristol Publishing Enterprise.

Westcott, Nadine Bernard (1998). *Never take a pig out to lunch and other poems.* New New York: Orchard Books.

PLANNING A NUTRITION EDUCATION PROGRAM

The nutrition education program should consist of well-planned activities that lead to specific outcomes. (A list of resources for children's activities involving nutrition education is given in Figure 21–2.) The desired outcome behaviors are the objectives of the program.

The overall program should be planned around some or all of the four basic nutrition education concepts. Concepts should be chosen that are appropriate for the children in the group according to their age and developmental level. Young children have the ability to comprehend that food is good. They can benefit from an introduction to a variety of nutritious foods. Older children can begin to understand the concept of food groups based on similar nutrient contributions.

The preschool nutrition program is the ideal place to increase familiarity with a variety of new foods. It is also an effective tool for showing children that common foods may be prepared in a

FIGURE 21–3

Sample outline for incorporating nutrition education concept #1 into learning experiences for the young child.

CONCEPT: CHILDREN NEED FOOD TO GROW AND HAVE HEALTHY BODIES

OBJECTIVES: The children should learn that
- ▼ all living things need food
- ▼ food is important for growth and for good health

SUGGESTED ACTIVITIES
- ▼ caring for animals in the classroom with special attention to their diets
- ▼ taking field trips to the zoo or farm to learn what animals eat
- ▼ caring for plants in the classroom
- ▼ planting a vegetable garden in containers or a small plot of ground
- ▼ weighing and measuring the children periodically
- ▼ tracing outlines of each child on large sheets of paper

QUESTIONS FOR EXTENDING LEARNING EXPERIENCES
- ▼ What do animals eat?
- ▼ Do all animals eat the same foods?
- ▼ Do animals eat the same foods as people?
- ▼ Do animals grow faster or slower than people?
- ▼ What do plants eat?
- ▼ Can people see plants eating?
- ▼ Do plants eat the same foods as people?
- ▼ What does it mean to be healthy?
- ▼ Do people need food to be healthy?
- ▼ Do children need food to grow?

EVALUATION
- ▼ Children can name what animals and plants eat.
- ▼ Children can describe some effects of not feeding plants and animals.

number of ways. The three-year-old, for instance, may not yet realize that a head of lettuce, a leaf of lettuce on a sandwich, and torn lettuce in a salad are all the same food. Tasting parties are easy ways to introduce new foods, or different forms of the same food.

Nutrition education activities should be part of a coordinated program designed to explore each of the concepts chosen. They should be planned to meet specified goals rather than simply serving as a means of filling time or keeping the children busy.

The results of the program should be measurable in order to determine its effectiveness. Results may be evaluated by determining whether any of the desired behaviors outlined in the objectives are observed. Figures 21–3 and 21–4 give examples of how a nutrition concept can be outlined and incorporated into learning experiences for young children.

It should be remembered that setting goals does not imply that the activity should be rigidly imposed. As in any other curricular activity, the interests of the children and their optimal development should be the governing factors for planning and extending learning activities.

FIGURE 21–4

Sample outline for incorporating nutrition education concept #4 into learning experiences for the young child.

CONCEPT: FOODS MUST BE CAREFULLY HANDLED BEFORE THEY ARE EATEN

OBJECTIVES: Children should understand
- ▼ where foods come from
- ▼ how foods are handled

SUGGESTED ACTIVITIES
- ▼ Grow, *harvest*, and prepare foods from a garden.
- ▼ Sprout alfalfa, radishes, or bean seeds.
- ▼ Discuss and illustrate the different parts of plants used as food (leaves, roots, fruit, seeds).
- ▼ Conduct simple experiments that show change in color or form of food.
- ▼ Play "store" or "farm".
- ▼ Take children on a field trip to a farm, dairy, bakery, or grocery store.

QUESTIONS FOR EXTENDING LEARNING EXPERIENCES
- ▼ From where does food come?
- ▼ Where do grocery stores get food?
- ▼ Is food always eaten the way it is grown?
- ▼ Who prepared different foods?
- ▼ Does all food come from the store?

EVALUATION
- ▼ Children can name sources of specific foods.
- ▼ Children can name who handles such foods as bread, milk, etc.

harvest – *to pick or gather fruit or grains.*

GUIDELINES FOR NUTRITION EDUCATION ACTIVITIES

1. Nutrition activities should be suitable for the developmental level of the participating children.

   Caution: Special consideration should be given to the chewing ability of the children involved, especially when raw fruits, nuts, popcorn, peanut butter, or vegetables are to be used in the activity.

2. With consideration to food safety, funds, equipment available, and any known food allergies, actual foods should be used in nutrition projects as often as possible. These may be accompanied by pictures, games, and stories to reinforce what is learned in real food activities.

   Caution: The teacher should always check for allergies to any foods (or similar foods) introduced in the nutrition activity.

3. The foods used should be nutritious. A variety of healthy foods should be chosen from the Food Guide Pyramid. Foods from the Fats, Oils, and Sweets Group are usually not as nutritious as the other groups and should be limited. Cakes, pies, and cookies, although made from grain products, are high in added sugars, fats, and calories. Foods in this group should be included only if all nutrient needs are met and there is still need for more calories; this rarely happens with the young child.

4. The end products of a nutrition activity should be edible and should be eaten by the children. Pasta collages and chocolate pudding finger paintings are not suitable nutrition projects since it is not possible to eat the end product. These activities say to the child that it is OK to play with food; this is not a desirable behavior to develop in a young child.

5. The children should be involved in the actual food preparation. **Hands-on** experiences such as cleaning vegetables, rolling dough, spreading butter, and cutting biscuits increase learning and help to develop a child's positive feelings about food (Figure 21–5). These

FIGURE 21–5

Hands-on experiences foster the development of positive feelings about food.

---

hands-on – *active involvement in a project; actually doing something.*

FIGURE 21–6

Foods prepared during nutrition activities should be eaten within a short period of time after the activity is completed.

activities not only enhance food experiences, but aid in the development of other skills such as manual dexterity, counting, or learning to follow directions. Children will often accept new, unfamiliar foods more readily if they have helped in its preparation.

6. Once the nutrition activity is completed, the food should be eaten within a short period of time (Figure 21–6). Delays between the completion of the activity and use of the food lessen the impact of the activity.

SAFETY CONSIDERATIONS

Attention to the following points can contribute to the increased success and safety of all food experiences.

Basic Guidelines

- Be aware of all food allergies identified in children. Post a list of the names of these children, along with the foods they cannot eat. Some of the more common foods to which children may be allergic are: wheat; milk and milk products; juices such as orange or grapefruit juice that have a high acid content; chocolate; eggs; and nuts.
- Avoid serving foods such as nuts, raw vegetables, peanut butter, and popcorn that could cause young children to choke.
- Children should always sit down to eat.
- Use low work tables and chairs.
- Use unbreakable equipment whenever possible.
- Supply enough tools and utensils for all of the children in the group.
- Use blunt knives or **serrated** plastic knives for cutting cooked eggs, potatoes, bananas, etc. Vegetable peelers should be used only under supervision and only after demonstrating their proper use to the children.

---

serrated – *saw-toothed or notched.*

REFLECTIVE THOUGHTS

Americans are heavy and getting heavier. Our supermarket shelves provide the widest selection of foods in the world. Low-fat, fat-free, and sugar-free foods are available in increasing numbers. Books, magazines, and newspapers feature the "Diet of the Week/Month/Year."

- What kinds of nutrition education experiences and activities could you provide to promote healthy eating habits?
- What kinds of foods or eating patterns should be stressed?
- What lifestyle factors contribute to obesity?
- Review Issues to Consider from Chapter 19; what implications does that study have for planning nutrition education experiences?

- Have only the necessary tools, utensils, and ingredients at the work table. All other materials should be removed as soon as they are no longer needed. Plan equipment needs carefully to avoid having to leave the work area during the activity. The teacher should never leave the activity area when utensils or foods are present that have the potential for causing injury.
- **Preplan** the steps of the cooking project; discuss these steps with the children before beginning. Children should understand what they are expected to do and what the adults will do before the cooking materials are made available to them.
- Long hair should be pulled back and fastened; floppy or cumbersome clothing should not be worn. Aprons are not essential, but may be helpful.
- Wash hands before beginning the activity.
- Begin with simple recipes that require little cooking. Once the children feel comfortable with those cooking projects, move on to slightly more complex ones.
- Allow plenty of time for touching, tasting, looking, and comparing, as well as for discussion. Use every step in the cooking project as an opportunity to expand the learning experience for the children.

Food Safety

- Wash hands before and after cooking project; this applies to teachers as well as children.
- Children and adults with colds should not help with food preparation.
- Children and adults with cuts or open sores on their hands should have them properly covered during food preparation.
- Keep all cooking utensils clean. Have extra utensils available in case one is dropped or is put into a child's mouth.
- Teach children how to taste foods that are being prepared. Give each child a small plate and spoon to use. Never let the children taste foods directly from the bowl or pan in which the foods are being prepared.
- Avoid using foods that spoil rapidly. Keep sauces, meats, and dairy products refrigerated.

preplan – *outline a method of action prior to carrying it out.*

Cooking Safety

- Match the task to the children's developmental levels and attention spans.
- Instruct children carefully regarding the safe use of utensils.
- Emphasize that all cooking must be supervised by an adult.
- Adults should do the cooking over stove burners. Pot handles should always be turned away from the edge of the stove.
- Use wooden utensils or utensils with wooden handles for cooking. (Metal utensils conduct heat and can cause painful burns.)

DEVELOPING ACTIVITY PLANS FOR NUTRITION ACTIVITIES

The success of each classroom activity as it contributes to the total nutrition education program depends upon the careful development of a plan for each activity. The principles of instruction for general health education programs including topic selection, development of objectives, instructional procedures, and **evaluation** are covered in depth in Chapter 8. Reviewing this material will be helpful in planning nutrition education activities.

Some special considerations when developing plans for an effective nutrition program are:

- The title (subject) and **objectives** chosen for each activity should contribute to the understanding of one or more of the four nutrition concepts considered appropriate for the young child.
- Classroom activities that involve hands-on experience with real food are most effective in teaching children about nutrition.
- Careful preplanning is essential for making each activity safe as well as a good learning experience. Most plans need a cautions list.
- Preplanning allows a sequencing of activities so that each new activity reinforces things that have been learned from prior lessons.
- Evaluation, in addition to giving feedback on the current activity, should be used in planning future activities.

Figure 21–7 presents a nutrition activity planning form to help in developing individual classroom activities.

Activity Plan #1 Weighing and Measuring Children

FOOD ACTIVITY (TITLE): ___Weighing and Measuring Children___

DATE: _____ LENGTH OF TIME REQUIRED: ___10–15 minutes___

TYPE OF GROUP: Individual _____ Small ___x___ Large _____

---

evaluation – *a measurement of effectiveness for determining whether or not educational objectives have been achieved.*

objectives – *clear and meaningful descriptions of what an individual is expected to learn as a result of learning activities and experiences.*

FIGURE 21–7

Nutrition activity planning form.

FOOD ACTIVITY (TITLE): _____

DATE: _____ LENGTH OF TIME REQUIRED: _____

TYPE OF GROUP: Individual _____ Small _____ Large _____

NUTRITIONAL CONCEPTS TO BE REINFORCED:

    Children must have food to grow and have healthy bodies _____

    Nutrients come from foods _____

    A variety of foods must be eaten each day _____

    Foods must be handled carefully before they are eaten _____

OBJECTIVES OF ACTIVITY (Reasons for choosing activity):

    1.   3.

    2.   4.

Motor Skills Involved:	mixing	dipping	pouring
	beating	peeling	spreading
	grinding	measuring	cutting
	grating	rolling	other _____
Sensory Experiences	smelling	feeling	tasting
	seeing	hearing	

Related Concepts/Developmental Areas

MATERIALS/EQUIPMENT:

    1.   5.

    2.   6.

    3.   7.

    4.   8.

PRE-LESSON PREPARATION NEEDED: _____ yes _____ no

    Describe.

PROCEDURE (step-by-step)/Discussion Questions:

    1.   6.

    2.   7.

    3.   8.

    4.   9.

    5.   10.

CAUTIONS:

EVALUATION AND COMMENTS:

SUGGESTIONS FOR FOLLOW-UP ACTIVITIES:

NUTRITIONAL CONCEPTS TO BE REINFORCED:

Children must have food to grow and have healthy bodies ____x____

Nutrients come from foods _____

A variety of foods must be eaten each day _____

Foods must be handled carefully before they are eaten _____

OBJECTIVES OF ACTIVITY (Reasons for choosing activity):

1. Children learn that their growth is maximized by eating good food.
2. Children learn that growth may be measured by (1) height and (2) weight.

Motor Skills Involved:	mixing	dipping	pouring
	beating	peeling	spreading
	grinding	(measuring)	cutting
	grating	rolling	other _____
Sensory Experiences:	smelling	feeling	tasting
	(seeing)	hearing	

Related Concepts/Developmental Areas: Math: numbers on scale, units of measure (pounds, inches). Language: comparisons of size. Social skills: acceptance of individual differences.

MATERIALS/EQUIPMENT:

1. Balance-beam scale or bathroom scale
2. Yardstick
3. Sheets of paper

SETTING FOR ACTIVITY: Classroom or child care center

PRE-LESSON PREPARATION NEEDED: _____ yes ____x____ no

Describe.

PROCEDURE (step-by-step)/Discussion Questions

1. Help each child onto scale.
2. Help child read his/her weight.
3. Measure height.
4. Help child read his/her height.
5. Record height.
6. Record weight.

1. Does everybody weigh the same?
2. Is everyone the same height?
3. Do children stay the same size? Do adults?
4. What makes children grow?
5. Name some foods that help children grow.

CAUTIONS:

EVALUATION AND COMMENTS:

Each child can tell the teacher his/her height and weight.

Children can name foods that contribute to health and growth.

SUGGESTIONS FOR FOLLOW-UP ACTIVITIES:

Trace outline of each child on large sheets of paper.

Repeat this activity periodically to monitor each child's rate of growth.

Discuss individual differences between children, such as concepts of tall and short.

(The discussion should be positive—these differences are what make each child special.)

Activity Plan #2 Making Indian Fried Bread

FOOD ACTIVITY (TITLE):   _Indian Fried Bread_

TYPE OF GROUP: Individual _____ Small ____x____ Large _____

NUTRITIONAL CONCEPTS TO BE REINFORCED:

Children must have food to grow and have healthy bodies _____

Nutrients come from foods _____

A variety of foods must be eaten each day ____x____

Foods must be handled carefully before they are eaten _____

OBJECTIVES OF ACTIVITY (Reasons for choosing activity):

1. To introduce foods from another culture.

2. To provide tactile sensations from kneading dough.

Motor Skills Involved:	(mixing)	dipping	(pouring)
	beating	peeling	spreading
	grinding	(measuring)	cutting
	grating	(rolling)	other kneading
Sensory Experiences:	(smelling)	(feeling)	(tasting)
	(seeing)	(hearing)	

Related Concepts/Developmental Areas: Science: melting butter, browning bread, addition of water to dough. Language: discussion of American Indian heritage. Social skills: learning safe cooking procedures.

MATERIALS/EQUIPMENT:

1. Electric skillet
2. Bowl
3. Spoon
4. Measuring cups
5. Measuring spoons

6. Recipe:

2 c. whole-wheat flour
2 c. unbleached white flour
1 tsp. salt
3 Tbsp. corn oil
Water to make soft dough
(See Figure 21–8.)

FIGURE 21–8

Picture recipe for Indian fried bread.

SETTING FOR ACTIVITY:

Kitchen (or use electric skillet in the classroom)

PRE-LESSON PREPARATION NEEDED: _____x_____ yes _____ no

Describe. Gather equipment as listed.

PROCEDURE (step-by-step)/Discussion Questions

1. Wash hands.
2. Mix together and knead dough 5–10 minutes.
3. Put dough in bowl, cover with cloth.
4. Let dough stand for 1 hour.
5. Shape dough into balls the size of a marble and roll and pat them flat.
6. Melt butter in pan.
7. Fry 3–4 pieces of dough at one time.
8. Serve bread warm with butter, jelly, or honey.

1. Is this bread like the bread you have at home?
2. Can you describe the bread you usually eat?
3. How did Indians make their bread?

> *Cautions:*
> *Adults must cook the bread.*
> *Table with electric skillet should be against the wall.*
> *Check for food allergies; provide an alternative, if necessary.*

EVALUATION AND COMMENTS:

Children's social skills were further developed by working together to make the bread.

The children experienced the feel of dough by kneading it.

Kneading helped to develop motor skills.

Children learned about American Indian food customs.

Children tasted a new food from another culture.

SUGGESTIONS FOR FOLLOW-UP ACTIVITIES:

Have children make another type of bread, e.g., corn pone.

Activity Plan #3 Tasting Party

FOOD ACTIVITY (TITLE): __Tasting Party for Dairy Foods__

DATE: _____ LENGTH OF TIME REQUIRED: __10–15 minutes__

TYPE OF GROUP: Individual _____ Small _____ Large ____x____

NUTRITIONAL CONCEPTS TO BE REINFORCED:

Children must have food to grow and have healthy bodies ____x____

Nutrients come from foods ____x____

A variety of foods must be eaten each day ____x____

Foods must be handled carefully before they are eaten ____x____

OBJECTIVES OF ACTIVITY (Reasons for choosing activity):

1. Children learn that common foods may be served in a variety of ways.
2. Children learn to recognize foods that belong to the dairy group.

Motor Skills Involved:

(mixing)	(dipping)	(pouring)
beating	peeling	spreading
grinding	(measuring)	(cutting)
grating	rolling	other _____

Sensory Experiences:

| (smelling) | feeling | (tasting) |
| (seeing) | hearing | |

Related Concepts/Developmental Areas: Social skills: task delegation, cooperation. Cognitive skills: classify foods as part of dairy group even though they look different than milk. Science: changes that took place to make cheese, yogurt, etc.

MATERIALS/EQUIPMENT:

1. Pitcher of milk
2. Yogurt, plain
3. Cottage cheese
4. Cheddar cheese
5. Bowl of apple chunks
6. Small bowl of granola
7. Orange juice concentrate
8. Cutting board
9. Bowls
10. Spoons
11. Cups
12. Blender

SETTING FOR ACTIVITY: Classroom or child care center

PRE-LESSON PREPARATION NEEDED: ____x____ yes _____ no
Describe. Assemble necessary equipment and materials.

PROCEDURE (step-by-step)/Discussion Questions

1. Wash hands.
2. Blend part of cottage cheese with orange juice, using blender. Leave remainder as is.
3. Spoon yogurt into bowl.
4. Cut cheddar cheese into cubes.
5. Wash tables.
6. Wash hands.
7. Place all foods on table.
8. Taste small servings of each food.

1. Are all these foods made from milk?
2. Do they look alike?
3. Do they taste alike?
4. Is cottage cheese like cheddar cheese? How is it different?
5. Why were these foods chilled before preparation and why should they be eaten immediately?

Cautions:

Instruct and demonstrate safe use of knife and blender.

Check for milk or dairy product allergies of any children in group; provide alternative, if necessary.

Stress that refrigeration and sanitation are very important when working with protein foods, such as milk and milk products.

EVALUATION AND COMMENTS:
Children can identify foods made from milk.
Children will taste each food served.
Children help with cleaning the tables.

SUGGESTIONS FOR FOLLOW-UP ACTIVITIES:
Make yogurt or cheese from milk.
Mix fruit with yogurt and discuss fruit and milk as "healthful" foods.

Activity Plan #4 Trip to the Grocery Store

FOOD ACTIVITY (TITLE): _____Trip to the Grocery Store_____

DATE: _____ LENGTH OF TIME REQUIRED: __varies__

TYPE OF GROUP: Individual _____x_____ Small _____x_____ Large _____

NUTRITIONAL CONCEPTS TO BE REINFORCED:

Children must have food to grow and have healthy bodies _____x_____

Nutrients come from foods _____x_____

A variety of foods must be eaten each day _____x_____

Foods must be handled carefully before they are eaten _____x_____

OBJECTIVES OF ACTIVITY (Reasons for choosing activity):

1. Children are encouraged to make decisions about foods and to taste a variety of foods.

2. Children buy a food with which they are not familiar.

Motor Skills Involved:	mixing	dipping	pouring
	beating	peeling	spreading
	grinding	measuring	cutting
	grating	rolling	other _____

Sensory Experiences: (smelling) (feeling) (tasting)
(seeing) hearing

Related Concepts/Developmental Areas: Language: names of foods on list, color/shape/size concepts. Cognitive skills: classification (food sections in the store). Math: paying for food, number concepts (pick two red fruits). Social skills: working as a team to complete a task, interacting with grocers/clerks.

MATERIALS/EQUIPMENT:

1. Shopping list

SETTING FOR ACTIVITY: Grocery store, child care center

PRE-LESSON PREPARATION NEEDED: _____x_____ yes _____ no

Describe. Secure parental permission for field trip; make up grocery list.

PROCEDURE (step-by-step)/Discussion Questions

1. Select one to three children.
2. Travel to store.
3. Find produce section.
4. Find fruits.
5. Find red fruits.
6. Select two varieties of red fruit.

7. Count the number of each fruit needed.

8. Purchase fruit.

9. Return to child care center.

10. Ask cook to prepare fruit for snack or meal.

1. What will this fruit taste like?

2. What is the name of this food?

3. How does this fruit grow?

4. Is the skin peeled or eaten?

5. Will this fruit have seeds?

6. What ways can this fruit be prepared?

> *Cautions:*
> *Permission must be obtained from parents for field trip.*
> *Fasten restraints if driving to store.*
> *If walking to store, review safety rules for walking, crossing streets, etc.*
> *Check for allergies; provide alternatives, if necessary.*

EVALUATION AND COMMENTS:

Children are able to identify two varieties of red fruit.

Children eat and enjoy the prepared fruit.

SUGGESTIONS FOR FOLLOW-UP ACTIVITIES:

Children play "store" with some children acting as grocers, some acting as clerks, and some acting as shoppers. Have children select two types of green vegetables.

Activity Plan #5 Safe Lunches

FOOD ACTIVITY (TITLE):   __Packing a Safe and Healthy Lunch__

DATE: _____   LENGTH OF TIME REQUIRED: __varies__

TYPE OF GROUP: Individual _____   Small ___x___   Large _____

NUTRITIONAL CONCEPTS TO BE REINFORCED:

Children must have food to grow and have healthy bodies ____x____

Nutrients come from foods ____x____

A variety of foods must be eaten each day ____x____

Foods must be handled carefully before they are eaten ____x____

OBJECTIVES OF ACTIVITY (Reasons for choosing activity):

1. Children learn how to select and eat food safely.

2. Children buy a food with which they are not familiar.

Motor Skills Involved:	mixing	dipping	pouring
	beating	(peeling)	spreading
	grinding	measuring	cutting
	grating	rolling	other
Sensory Experiences:	(smelling)	(feeling)	(tasting)
	(seeing)	hearing	

Related Concepts/Developmental Areas: Language: Discussion among the group regarding the differences in foods. Cognitive skills: Relating a variety of foods to groups within the Food Guide Pyramid. Science: Learning how to safely prepare and store foods in order to prevent illness.

MATERIALS/EQUIPMENT:

1. Obtain certain foods that may be available in school cafeteria/kitchen as examples of items for children to pack in a lunchbox (e.g., sandwich, milk, juice, soup, carrot sticks, cheese cubes, ice cream, apple, banana, potato chips, pretzels, yogurt, salad, etc.)
2. Empty lunchbox with thermos

SETTING FOR ACTIVITY: Classroom or child care center

PRE-LESSON PREPARATION NEEDED: ____x____ yes _____ no

1. Obtain foods needed for lesson just prior to activity to avoid spoilage.
2. Preparation of certain foods may be necessary.

PROCEDURE (step-by-step)/Discussion Questions

1. Have children volunteer to participate in activity allowing every child an opportunity. (May allow children to participate in groups of two).
2. Have children wash hands prior to food selection.
3. Child will approach table where foods are displayed.
4. Have child select foods from those provided that he/she would pack in a lunchbox to bring to school.
5. Encourage child to choose a variety of foods based on the Food Guide Pyramid.
6. Have discussion regarding chosen foods.
7. After every child has had an opportunity to participate, children may be allowed to sample food.

1. Which foods need to be kept cold?
2. Which foods need to be kept hot?
3. Which foods need to be wrapped or stored in special containers to be kept safe?
4. Which foods need to be washed before eating them?
5. Are there any other foods you would choose for your lunch box that are not shown here?

> *Cautions:*
>
> *Check for food allergies in children prior to activity.*
>
> *Recommend sampling only those foods that do not require storage at extreme temperatures to avoid illness (i.e., avoid milk, yogurt, ice cream, soup).*

EVALUATION AND COMMENTS:

Children are able to participate in choosing their own food at mealtime.

Children are learning to choose a variety of foods in their diet.

Children are learning how to eat foods safely.

SUGGESTIONS FOR FOLLOW-UP ACTIVITIES:

Take children on an actual picnic lunch. Allow children to assist in the preparation and safe storage of the foods for the event.

Activity Plan #6 Eating Five Fruits and Vegetables Daily

FOOD ACTIVITY (TITLE): ____Eating 5-A-Day____

DATE: _____ LENGTH OF TIME REQUIRED: ____15–20 minutes____

TYPE OF GROUP: Individual _____ Small ____x____ Large _____

NUTRITIONAL CONCEPTS TO BE REINFORCED:

Children must have food to grow and have healthy bodies ____x____

Nutrients come from foods ____x____

A variety of foods must be eaten each day ____x____

Foods must be handled carefully before they are eaten ____x____

OBJECTIVES OF ACTIVITY (Reasons for choosing activity):

1. Children learn that there are a wide variety of fruits and vegetables.
2. Children learn that a particular fruit or vegetable may be prepared and eaten in a variety of different ways.
3. Fruits and vegetables taste good and keep us healthy.

Motor Skills Involved:	mixing	dipping	pouring
	beating	(peeling)	spreading
	grinding	measuring	cutting
	grating	rolling	other _____
Sensory Experiences:	(smelling)	(feeling)	(tasting)
	(seeing)	hearing	

Related Concepts/Developmental Areas: Language: Discussion comparing various sizes, colors, and tastes of foods. Social skills: Acceptance of new foods and new food preparation techniques. Cognitive skills: Recognizing differences/similarities of the same food. Math: Counting amounts of chosen food items.

MATERIALS/EQUIPMENT:

1. Disposable plates and napkins
2. Examples of a variety of fruits, emphasizing different sizes, colors, and shapes (apples, bananas, oranges, kiwi, etc.)
3. Examples of a variety of vegetables, emphasizing different preparation techniques (i.e. Baked potato, mashed potato, french fries)

SETTING FOR ACTIVITY: Classroom or child care center

PRE-LESSON PREPARATION NEEDED: ____x____ yes _____ no

1. Food should be prepared prior to lesson.
2. Maintain proper temperatures of food. If food is prepared in advance of class, store necessary foods in the refrigerator. Prior to the activity, reheat food and maintain at the proper temperature.

PROCEDURE (step-by-step)/Discussion Questions

1. Wash hands prior to food handling
2. Allow children to select a total of five fruits and vegetables for their plate.
3. Encourage children to pick a variety of foods, particularly those they have never eaten before.
4. Allow children to sample the foods they have selected.
5. Have a discussion regarding the differences of the foods they have selected.

1. What are some of the different colors of fruits and vegetables?
2. What are the different ways of preparing the same food? Do you know of any more?
3. Is there a food you tried today that you have never eaten before? Will you try it again?
4. Did you know that if you eat a total of five fruits and vegetables every day, it can keep you from getting sick? Discuss.

> *Cautions:*
>
> *Check for food allergies in children prior to activity.*
>
> *Maintain foods at appropriate temperatures to avoid illness.*

EVALUATION AND COMMENTS:

Children learn that there is a variety of fruits and vegetables to include in their daily diet.

Children learn that food can be prepared in many ways in order for them to be accepted and liked.

Children learn that a diet providing five fruits and vegetables daily can prevent disease.

SUGGESTIONS FOR FOLLOW-UP ACTIVITIES:

Take the children for a visit to the local supermarket. Call the store manager prior to the visit. He/she may be able to arrange for a special tour which may include food sampling in the produce department.

OTHER SOURCES OF INFORMATION ABOUT FOOD

Children learn about food from informal sources as well as from planned programs of instruction. The family, teachers, other children, and television are additional sources of information about food and all have an effect on children's eating habits (Figure 21–9).

The Family

Food preferences and **attitudes** of the family unit are of primary importance in the formation of the young child's attitudes about and preferences for food. Family food choices are subject to cultural influences, money available for food, educational level, and specific preferences of family members. Since familiarity with a food is often a factor in choices, the child who comes from a family that eats a wide variety of foods is more willing to try new foods, because that is acceptable behavior in the home.

Teachers

Teachers exert considerable influence over children's attitudes about food. For this reason the teacher should display positive attitudes about food and demonstrate both with actions and words enjoyment of food and enthusiasm for trying new foods.

FIGURE 21–9

Additional sources of information about food have an effect on children's eating habits.

**ADDITIONAL FACTORS THAT EFFECT
CHILDREN'S EATING HABITS:**

▼ Parents of children with strong preferences for high-fat foods have higher BMI scores than parents who do not have a strong preference for high-fat foods.

▼ Young children who observe adults eating a certain food are more likely to eat it themselves.

▼ There is a strong relationship between the food preferences of toddlers and their mothers, fathers, and older siblings.

▼ Involving parents in a nutrition education program for students increases the diversity of quality of the students' diets.

▼ In general, the more hours women work outside the home, the fewer hours they spend preparing meals, and the more meals their children eat away from home.

▼ The nutrition knowledge and practices of food service personnel in child care centers has a major influence on the menus served there. (Escobar, 1999)

attitudes – *beliefs or feelings one has toward certain facts or situations.*

ISSUES TO CONSIDER • Food Trend Predictions

Health-conscious consumers are looking for "Better-for-You Twists." Projected hot products include herbals, organic foods, more full-flavor fat-frees, and nutrition products on the run, such as sports bars, smoothies, and shakes.

- Do you perceive these trends to be positive or negative?
- Will these trends impact young children?
- How will these trends affect children in your care?

Source: Kansas Beef Council. (2000, Winter) *Nutrition news—A nutrition & health publication.* Topeka, KS: Author

Other Children

Young children's choices of food are frequently made on the basis of approval or disapproval of others within their group. A child with a strong personality who eats a variety of foods can be a positive influence on other children. On the other hand, children who are "picky eaters" can also spread their negative influence. A simple statement from the teacher, such as, "You don't have to eat the broccoli, Jamie, but I can't allow you to spoil it for Tara and Pablo," should be effective in curbing this negative influence. Younger children may base their choices on familiarity of food and its taste. Older children (five–six) are more subject to **peer** influence when deciding whether or not to eat a food.

Television

Television is a major source of information about food for many children and their families. Unfortunately, nutrient-dense foods are rarely featured on television. Preferred foods for television advertising are those that taste good, are chocolaty, are really fun, or come with a prize. The role of television in determining food choices by the young child is discussed in Chapter 18. Both parents and teachers can help counteract the influence of television by monitoring the programs that children view and by pointing out differences between programs and commercials. The child needs to learn that the purpose of a commercial is to sell a product.

FOCUS ON FAMILIES • 5 A Day for Better Health

Parents can take an active part in ensuring that their child consumes a total of five fruits and vegetables daily. Consuming five to nine servings of fruits and vegetables daily can improve health and reduce the risk of cancer, heart disease, hypertension, diabetes, and obesity. Parents can create activities to include this health message.

- Make homemade vegetable soup or a fresh fruit salad. Have your child name each vegetable or fruit contained in the recipe. This increases your child's awareness of how fruits and vegetables can be included into daily meal plans while providing a nutritious meal or snack.

peer – *one of the same rank; equal.*

- Take a visit to the nearest farmer's market. Not only will your child develop an appreciation for fresh produce, but it will also stimulate questions for learning.

- Teach your child the importance of eating seasonal fruits and vegetables not only for the taste but also the cost savings it can provide for your family. Below is a sampling of some fruits and vegetables you will find plentiful every season.

  Spring: apples, grapefruits, pears, strawberries, broccoli, cabbage, carrots, celery
  Summer: berries, cantaloupes, grapes, melons, corn, green beans, cucumbers, okra
  Fall: oranges, peaches, prunes, plums, brussel sprouts, tomatoes, peppers, lima beans
  Winter: apples, grapefruits, lemons, beets, cauliflower, potatoes, spinach, squash

- Try planting one of the foods listed above. Your child will learn about the growing process and realize that foods do not always originate in the supermarket.

CASE STUDY

Marcus, age four years, has been ill several times recently. His mother mentions that she is now giving him an herbal supplement to "boost his immune system" so he won't be ill so often. She asks you if you think the supplement will help Marcus and if you feel it is safe for Marcus to take.

1. What information do you need to answer her questions?
2. What resources are available to find the necessary information?
3. How will you evaluate the information available to you?
4. Are you qualified to advise Marcus's mother on this issue?

SUMMARY

- Nutrition education is any activity that tells a person something about food.
  - Children must have food for growth and healthy bodies.
  - Nutrients come from food.
  - A variety of foods must be eaten to provide needed nutrients.
  - Foods must be handled carefully to be safe to eat.

- Nutrition education must be appropriate for the persons being taught.
  - Nutrition activities should promote skills in all developmental areas.
  - Activities should illustrate basic nutrition concepts.

- The primary goal of nutrition education is to teach children to choose a healthful diet.
  - Food used in activities should be nutritious.
  - The end product should be edible.
  - All activities should be planned with an emphasis on safety.

SUGGESTED ACTIVITIES

1. Prepare lesson plans for a two-day nutrition education activity. Plans may be for two consecutive days or for any two days within one week. The lesson plan for each day should be in the format presented in this unit.

2. From the following list, choose three foods as the subjects of food experiences. Upon what criteria were the choices based? What was the primary basis for the decision to work with each food? What other considerations affected the choice of some foods and not others?
   a. raisin-oatmeal cookies
   b. granola
   c. brownies
   d. honey
   e. greens (lettuce, spinach) for salad
   f. pancakes

3. Outline an equipment list and safety plan for a food experience in which four- and five-year-olds make pancakes in the classroom. Cooking will be done in an electric skillet on a table. What precautions should be taken? How should the room be safely arranged? What instructions should be given to the children?

4. Select 15–20 library books appropriate for young children. Note those instances where food is portrayed either in the story or pictures. What types of foods are shown? Chart these foods according to the Food Guide Pyramid. What percentage of foods were noted within each group? What was the general message about food presented in these books?

5. Watch one hour of children's television programs on Saturday morning.
   a. Determine the percent of observed advertisements that were for "sweets" (gum, candy, soft drinks, snack cakes, and pre-sweetened cereals).
   b. Which food groups were least represented in these commercials?

6. Review an article about nutrition from a popular magazine. Apply the suggested criteria for a good nutrition resource. Is this a good article? Why or why not?

CHAPTER REVIEW

A. **Briefly answer the following questions.**

1. What is the teacher's role in providing nutrition education activities for the young child?

2. List four ways that nutrition education activities aid child development.

3. What are the criteria used for choosing appropriate nutrition education concepts for young children?

4. Report four ways that parents may share in the nutrition education of their child.

REFERENCES

Goodwin, M. T., & Pollen, G. (1981). *Creative food experiences for children.* Washington, DC: Center for Science in the Public Interest.

Kansas Beef Council. (1994). *Nutrition news for the 90s.* Topeka, KS: Author.

Kansas Beef Council. (2000, Winter). *Nutrition news—A nutrition & health publication.* Topeka, KS: Author.

ADDITIONAL READING

American Dietetic Association. (1987). Position paper on standards in daycare for children. *Journal of the American Dietetic Association, 87,* 502.

Escobar, A. (1999). Factors influencing children's dietary practices: A review. *Family Economics and Nutrition Review, 12,* 45–55.

Gahagan, G. (Not Dated). *CCFP nutrition education and training project.* Ottawa, KS: East Central Kansas Community Action Program Head Start Comprehensive Nutrition Education Program.

Jacobson, M., & Hill, L. (1991). *Kitchen fun for kids.* Washington, DC: Center for Science in the Public Interest.

Mahan, K. L., & Escot-Stump, S. (2000). *Krause's food, nutrition and diet therapy.* Philadelphia: W. B. Saunders Co.

National Center for Nutrition and Dietetics of the American Dietetic Association. (1998). *Good nutrition reading list.* Chicago: Author.

Richard, K. A., et al. (1995). The play approach to learning in the context of families and schools: An alternative paradigm for nutrition and fitness education in the 21st Century. *Journal of the American Dietetic Association, 95,* 1121–1126.

Singleton, J. C., Achterberg, C. L., & Shannon, B. M. (1992). Role of food and nutrition in the health perceptions of young children. *Journal of the American Dietetic Association, 92,* 67–70.

Williams, S. R. (2000). *Basic nutrition and diet therapy* (11th ed.). St. Louis, MO: Mosby.

Williams, S. R., & Worthington-Roberts, B. S. (1999). *Nutrition throughout the life cycle.* (4th ed.). St. Louis, MO: Times Mirror/Mosby.

HELPFUL WEB SITES

5 a Day for Better Health	http://www.5aday.com
American Dietetic Association	http://www.eatright.org
U.S. Food and Drug Administration	http://www.fda.gov
Healthy People 2010	http://www.healthypeople.gov/
Journal of Nutrition Education & Behavior	http://www.jneb.org
Teaching Strategies, Inc.	http://www.TeachingStrategies.com
Tufts University Nutrition Navigator	http://www.navigator.tufts.edu
U.S. Department of Agriculture	http://www.usda.gov

For additional health, safety, and nutrition resources, go to http://ww.EarlyChildEd.delmar.com

APPENDICES

APPENDIX A
Nutrient Information: Fast Food Vendor Websites

Arby's	http://www.arbys.com
Back Yard Burgers	http://www.backyardburgers.com
Blimpie	http://www.blimpie.com
Burger King	http://www.burgerking.com
Carl's Jr.	http://www.carlsjr.com
Chick-fil-A	http://www.chick-fil-a.com
Church's Fried Chicken	http://www.churchs.com
Dairy Queen	http://www.dairyqueen.com
Domino's Pizza	http://www.dominos.com
Hardee's	http://www.hardees.com
KFC	http://www.kfc.com
Krystal	http://www.krystal.com
Little Caesars	http://www.littlecaesars.com
Long John Silvers	http://www.ljsilvers.com
McDonald's	http://www.mcdonalds.com
Pizza Hut	http://www.pizzahut.com
Subway	http://www.subway.com
Taco Bell	http://www.tacobell.com
Wendy's	http://www.wendys.com
White Castle	http://www.whitecastle.com

For more information on food and nutrition, visit the Food and Nutrition Information Center at http://www.nal.usda.gov/fnic.

APPENDIX B
Growth and BMI Charts for Boys and Girls

Instructions for Using Charts:

1. Locate the child's age along the bottom of the chart.

2. Locate the child's height/weight along the right-hand side of the chart.

3. Place an *X* at the point where the two lines cross. This point represents a percentile (child's height/weight ranked in comparison to other children of the same age).

   For example: A five-year-old male who is 43.3 inches tall would be ranked at the fiftieth percentile. This means that approximately 50 percent of five-year-old males are taller; 50 percent are shorter.

4. Body Mass Index is a relatively accurate measure of body fat and risk of obesity. To calculate BMI use the following formula:

   weight (pounds) ÷ height (inches) ÷ height (inches) × 703.

   Plot the result on the graphs provided (pp. 520 and 523).

Source: Developed by the National Center for Health Statistics in collaboration with the National Center for Chronic Disease Prevention and Health Promotion (2000).

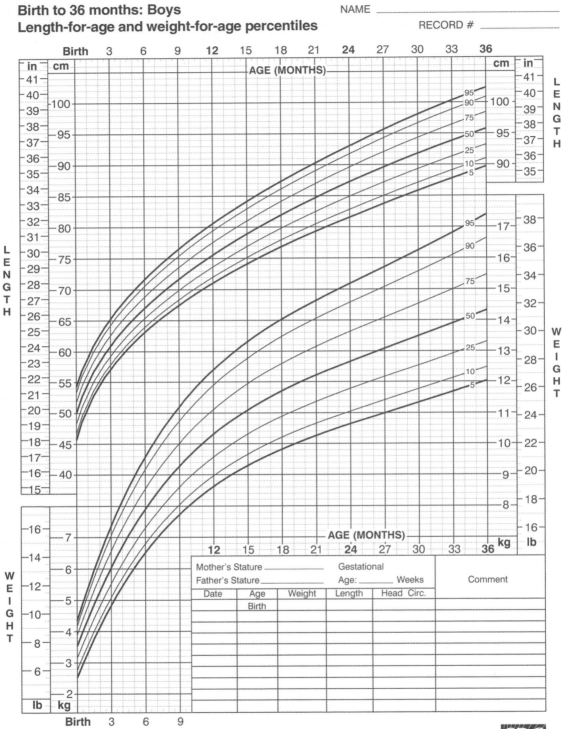

Birth to 36 months: Boys
Length-for-age and weight-for-age percentiles

NAME _____

RECORD # _____

Published May 30, 2000 (modified 4/20/01).
SOURCE: Developed by the National Center for Health Statistics in collaboration with
the National Center for Chronic Disease Prevention and Health Promotion (2000).
http://www.cdc.gov/growthcharts

SAFER · HEALTHIER · PEOPLE™

2 to 20 years: Boys
Stature-for-age and weight-for-age percentiles

NAME _____

RECORD # _____

Mother's Stature _____ Father's Stature _____

Date	Age	Weight	Stature	BMI*

*To Calculate BMI: Weight (kg) ÷ Stature (cm) ÷ Stature (cm) x 10,000
or Weight (lb) ÷ Stature (in) ÷ Stature (in) x 703

AGE (YEARS)

STATURE

WEIGHT

Published May 30, 2000 (modified 11/21/00).
SOURCE: Developed by the National Center for Health Statistics in collaboration with
the National Center for Chronic Disease Prevention and Health Promotion (2000).
http://www.cdc.gov/growthcharts

SAFER·HEALTHIER·PEOPLE™

2 to 20 years: Boys
Body mass index-for-age percentiles

NAME _____

RECORD # _____

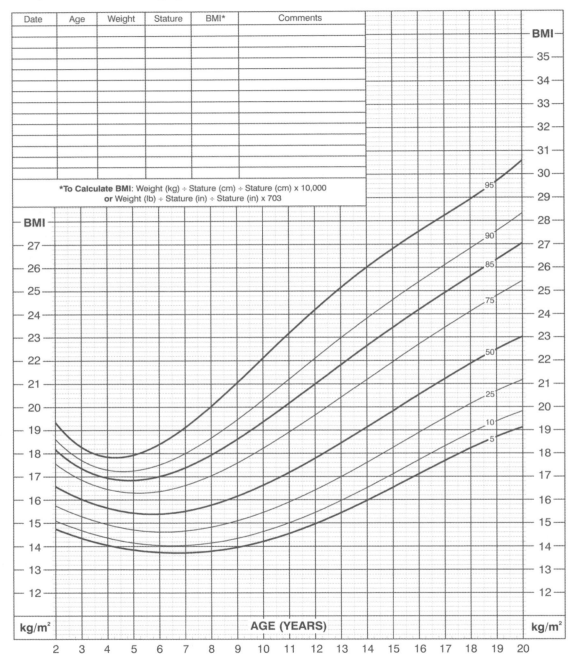

*To Calculate BMI: Weight (kg) ÷ Stature (cm) ÷ Stature (cm) x 10,000
or Weight (lb) ÷ Stature (in) ÷ Stature (in) x 703

AGE (YEARS)

Published May 30, 2000 (modified 10/16/00).

SOURCE: Developed by the National Center for Health Statistics in collaboration with
the National Center for Chronic Disease Prevention and Health Promotion (2000).
http://www.cdc.gov/growthcharts

SAFER · HEALTHIER · PEOPLE™

Birth to 36 months: Girls
Length-for-age and weight-for-age percentiles

NAME _____

RECORD # _____

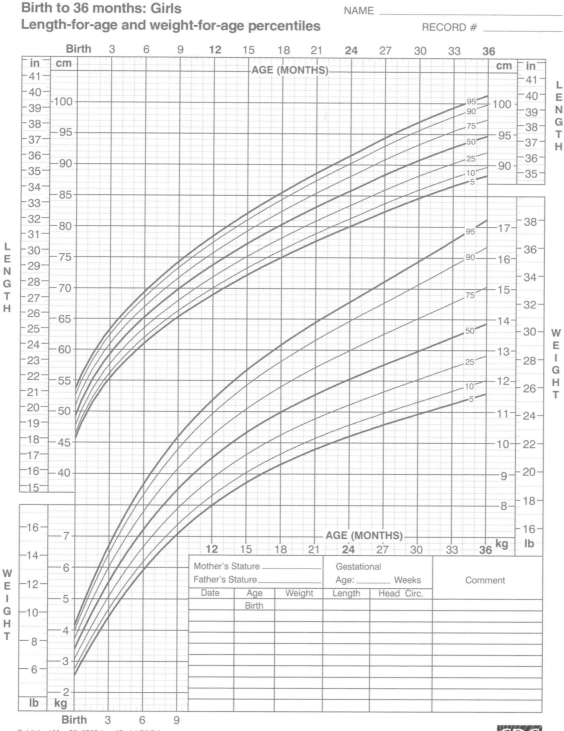

Published May 30, 2000 (modified 4/20/01).

SOURCE: Developed by the National Center for Health Statistics in collaboration with
the National Center for Chronic Disease Prevention and Health Promotion (2000).
http://www.cdc.gov/growthcharts

SAFER·HEALTHIER·PEOPLE™

2 to 20 years: Girls
Stature-for-age and weight-for-age percentiles

NAME _____

RECORD # _____

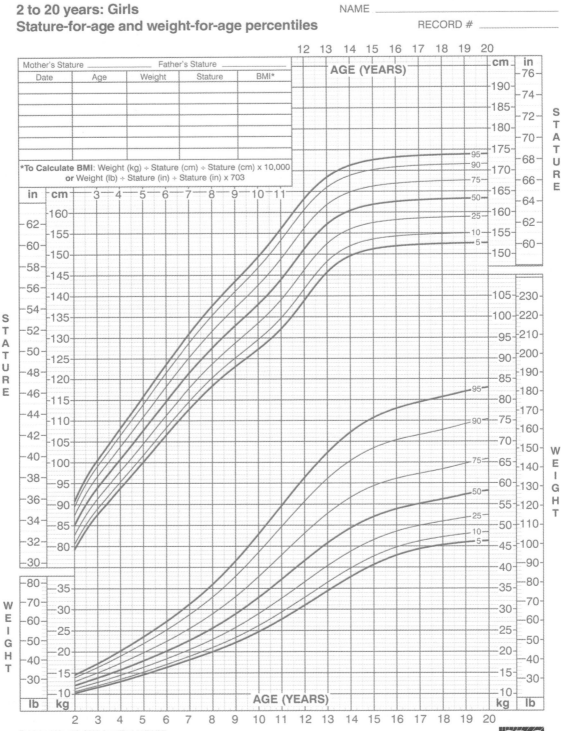

*To Calculate BMI: Weight (kg) ÷ Stature (cm) ÷ Stature (cm) x 10,000
or Weight (lb) ÷ Stature (in) ÷ Stature (in) x 703

Published May 30, 2000 (modified 11/21/00).
SOURCE: Developed by the National Center for Health Statistics in collaboration with
the National Center for Chronic Disease Prevention and Health Promotion (2000).
http://www.cdc.gov/growthcharts

SAFER · HEALTHIER · PEOPLE™

2 to 20 years: Girls
Body mass index-for-age percentiles

NAME _____

RECORD # _____

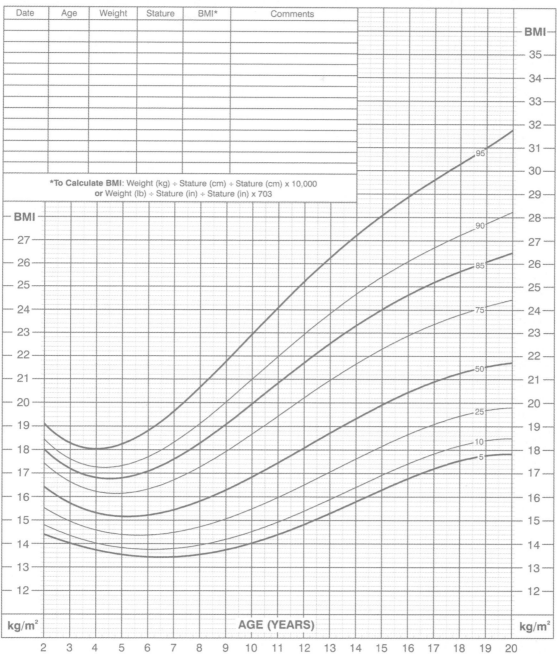

Date	Age	Weight	Stature	BMI*	Comments

*To Calculate BMI: Weight (kg) ÷ Stature (cm) ÷ Stature (cm) x 10,000
or Weight (lb) ÷ Stature (in) ÷ Stature (in) x 703

Published May 30, 2000 (modified 10/16/00).
SOURCE: Developed by the National Center for Health Statistics in collaboration with
the National Center for Chronic Disease Prevention and Health Promotion (2000).
http://www.cdc.gov/growthcharts

SAFER·HEALTHIER·PEOPLE™

APPENDIX C
Educational Resources: Health, Safety, and Nutrition

Abbott Laboratories
100 Abbott Park Road
Abbott Park, IL 60064-3500
http://www.abbott.com

Administration for Children and Families
370 L'Enfant Promenade, SW
Washington, DC 20447
http://www.acf.hhs.gov/

Aetna Life, Casualty, and Health Companies
151 Farmington Avenue
Hartford, CT 06156
http://www.aetna.com

Agricultural Research Service, USDA
National Agricultural Library, Room 105
10301 Baltimore Avenue
Beltsville, MD 20705-2351
http://www.nal.usda.gov/fnic

Alexander Graham Bell Association
   for the Deaf, Inc.
3417 Volta Place, NW
Washington, DC 20007
http://www.agbell.org

Alliance to End Lead Poisoning
227 Massachusetts Avenue
Suite 200
Washington, DC 20002
http://www.afhh.org

American Academy of Pediatrics
141 Northwest Point Boulevard
Elk Grove, IL 60007-1098
http://www.aap.org

American Academy of Pediatric Dentistry
211 E. Chicago Avenue, Suite 700
Chicago, IL 60611-2663
http://www.aapd.org

American Academy of Allergy, Asthma,
   & Immunology
611 East Wells Street
Milwaukee, WI 53202
http://www.aaaai.org

American Automobile Association
1000 AAA Drive
Heathrow, FL 32746
http://www.aaa.com

American Cancer Society
1599 Clifton Road
Atlanta, GA 30329
http://www.cancer.org

American Dairy Association
10255 W. Higgins Rd., Suite 900
Rosemont, IL 60018-5616
http://www.3aday.org

American Dairy Products Institute
116 N. York Street, Suite 200
Elmhurst, IL 60126
http://www.ilovecheese.com

American Dental Association
211 E. Chicago Avenue
Chicago, IL 60611
http://www.ada.org

American Diabetes Association
1701 N. Beauregard Street
Alexandria, VA 22311
http://www.diabetes.org

American Dietetic Association
120 South Riverside Plaza, Suite 2000
Chicago, IL 60606-6995
http://www.eatright.org

American Foundation for the Blind
11 Penn Plaza, Suite 300
New York, NY 10001
http://www.afb.org

American Heart Association
7272 Greenville Avenue
Dallas, TX 75231
http://www.americanheart.org

American Hospital Association
One N. Franklin
Chicago, IL 60606-3421
http://www.aha.org

American Institute of Baking
1213 Bakers Way
P.O. Box 3999
Manhattan, KS 66505-3999
http://www.aibonline.org

American Insurance Association
1130 Connecticut Avenue, NW
Suite 1000
Washington, DC 20036
http://www.aiadc.org

American Lung Association
61 Broadway, 6th Floor
New York, NY 10006
http://www.lungusa.org

American Medical Association
515 N. State Street
Chicago, IL 60610
http://www.ama-assn.org

American Red Cross National Headquarters
431 18th Street, NW
Washington, DC 20006
http://www.redcross.org

American Optometric Association
243 North Lindbergh Boulevard
St. Louis, MO 63141
http://www.aoanet.org

American Printing House for the Blind
1839 Frankfort Avenue
P. O. Box 6085
Louisville, KY 40206-0085
http://www.aph.org

American Public Health Association
800 I Street, NW
Washington, DC 20001-3710
http://www.apha.org

American School Health Association
7263 State, Rt. 43
P.O. Box 13827
Kent, OH 44240
http://www.ashaweb.org

American Social Health Association
P. O. Box 13827
Research Triangle Park, NC 27709
http://www.ashastd.org

American Speech, Language, and
   Hearing Association
10801 Rockville Pike
Rockville, MD 20852-3226
http://www.asha.org

America's Promise: The Alliance for Youth
909 N. Washington St., Suite 400
Alexandria, VA 22314-1556
http://www.americaspromise.org

The Arthritis Foundation
P. O. Box 7669
Atlanta, GA 30357-0669
http://www.arthritis.org

The Arc of the United States
1010 Wayne Avenue, Suite 650
Silver Spring, MD 20910
http://www.thearc.org

Association for the Care of Children's Health
19 Mantua Road
Mount Royal, NJ 08061
http://www.acch.org

Asthma and Allergy Foundation of America
   (AAFA)
1233 20th Street, NW, Suite 402
Washington, DC 20036
http://www.aafa.org

Autism Society of America
7910 Woodmont Avenue, Suite 300
Bethesda, MD 20814-3067
http://www.autism-society.org

Better Vision Institute, Inc.
1700 Diagonal Road, Suite 500
Alexandria, VA 22314
http://www.visionsite.org

Centers for Disease Control
National Prevention Information Network
P. O. Box 6003
Rockville, MD 20849-6003
http://www.cdcnpin.org

Children's Defense Fund.
25 E Street, NW
Washington, DC 20001
http://www.childrensdefense.org

Committee for Children
568 First Avenue South, Suite 600
Seattle, WA 98104-2804
http://www.cfchildren.org

Comprehensive Health Education
   Foundation
22419 Pacific Hwy S
Seattle, WA 98198-5106
http://www.chef.org

Consumer Information Center
Pueblo, CO 81009
http://www.pueblo.gsa.gov

Council for Exceptional Children
1110 North Glebe Road, Suite 300
Arlington, VA 22201
http://www.cec.sped.org

Cystic Fibrosis Foundation
6931 Arlington Road
Bethesda, MD 20814
http://www.cff.org

Department of Community Health
   & Epidemiology
Royal University Hospital
University of Saskatchewan
Saskatoon, Saskatchewan, Canada
http://www.usask.ca/healthsci/che

Department of Health and Wellness
P.O. Box 510
Fredericton, N.B. Canada E3B 5G8
http://www.gnb.ca/0051/index-e.asp

Environmental Protection Agency
Ariel Rios Building
1200 Pennsylvania Avenue, NW
Washington, DC 20460
http://www.epa.gov

Epilepsy Foundation of America
4351 Garden City Drive
Landover, MD 20785-7223
http://www.epilepsyfoundation.org

Federal Citizen Information Center
Office of Citizen Services and
   Communications
U.S. General Services Administration
1800 F Street, NW
Washington, DC 20405
http://firstgov.gov
(parenting, safety, health)

Federal Emergency Management Agency
500 C Street, NW
Washington, DC 20472
http://www.fema.gov

Feingold Association of the United States
P.O. Box 6550
Alexandria, VA 22306
http://www.feingold.org

Florida Department of Citrus Fruit
P.O. Box 148
Lakeland, FL 33802-0148
http://www.fred.ifas.ufl.edu/citrus/index

Food and Nutrition Service
U.S. Department of Agriculture
Washington, DC 20250
http://www.fns.usda.gov/fns

Ford Motor Company
Customer Relationship Center
P.O. Box 6248
Dearborn, MI 48126
http://www.ford.com/en/innovation/safety/
    familySafety.htm
(traffic safety, seat belts)

General Mills
Educational Services
Box Tops for Education
P.O. Box 8998
Young America, MN 55551
http://www.boxtops4education.com

Health Education Associates, Inc.
327 Quaker Meeting House Road
East Sandwich, MA 02537-1300
http://www.healthed.cc

Health Insurance Association of America
1201 F Street, NW, Suite 500
Washington, DC 20004-1204
http://www.hiaa.org/consumer

Health Resources and Services
    Administration
U. S. Department of Health and Human
    Services
Parklawn Building
5600 Fishers Lane
Rockville, MD 20857
http://www.ask.hrsa.gov
(formerly the National Maternal and Child
    Health Clearinghouse)

Healthy Child Care America
American Academy of Pediatrics
Department of Community Pediatrics
141 Northwest Point Blvd.
Elk Grove Village, IL 60007
http://www.healthychildcare.org/

Huntington's Disease Society of America
158 West 29th Street, 7th Floor
New York, NY 10001-5300
http://www.hdsa.org/

International Lefthanders Society
P. O. Box 10198
5521 West Center Street
Milwaukee, WI 53210

International Life Sciences Institute
One Thomas Circle, 9th Floor
Washington, DC 20005
http://www.ilsi.org

Johnson and Johnson Health Care Division
New Brunswick, NJ 08903
(first aid, dental health)
http://www.jnj.com/home.htm

The Joseph P. Kennedy, Jr. Foundation
1325 G Street, NW, Suite 500
Washington, DC 20005
http://www.jpkf.org

Kellogg Company
One Kellogg Square
Department of Consumer Education
Battle Creek , MI 49016
http://www.kelloggs.com

Learning Disabilities Association of America
4156 Library Road
Pittsburgh, PA 15234-1349
http://www.ldanatl.org

Learning Disabilities Resource Community
Adaptive Technology Resource Centre
University of Toronto
130 St. George St., First Floor
Toronto, Ontario Canada, M5S 3H1
http://www.ldrc.ca

Lefties
http://www.umkc.edu/imc/lefties.htm

Lever Brothers Company (USA)
45 River Road
Edgewood, NJ 07020
http://www.leverbrothers.com

March of Dimes Birth Defects Foundation
1275 Mamaroneck Ave.
White Plains, NY 10605
http://www.modimes.org

Metropolitan Life Insurance Company
Health and Safety Division
1 Madison Ave.
New York, NY 10010
http://www.metlife.com
(health, safety, first aid)

Muscular Dystrophy Association
3300 E. Sunrise Drive
Tucson, AZ 85718
http://www.mdause.org

National Academy of Sciences
Institute of Medicine
500 Fifth Street NW
Washington DC 20001
http://www.iom.edu

National Association for Down Syndrome
P.O. Box 4542
Oak Brook, IL 60522
http://www.nads.org

National Association for the Education
of Young Children
1509 16th Street, NW
Washington, DC 20036
http://www.naeyc.org

National Association for the Visually
Handicapped (NAVH)
22 West 21st Street, 6th Floor
New York, NY 10010
http://www.navh.org

National Attention Deficit Disorder
Association (ADDA)
P.O. Box 1303
Northbrook, IL 60065-1303
http://www.add.org

National Clearinghouse on Child Abuse and
Neglect Information
330 C Street, SW
Washington, DC 20447
http://www.calib.com/nccanch

National Dairy Council
10255 W. Higgins Rd., Suite 900
Rosemont, IL 60018
http://www.nationaldairycouncil.org

National Down Syndrome Society
666 Broadway
New York, NY 10012
http://www.ndss.org

National Easter Seals
230 West Monroe Street, Suite 1800
Chicago, IL 60606
http://www.easter-seals.org

National Eczema Association
4460 Redwood Hwy.
Suite 16, Box D
San Rafael, CA 94903-1953
http://www.nationaleczema.org

National Eye Institute
2020 Vision Place
Bethesda, MD 20892-3655
http://www.nei.nih.gov

National Fire Protection Association (NFPA)
1 Batterymarch Park
Quincy, MA 02169-7471
http://www.nfpa.org

National Health Council
1730 M Street, NW, Suite 500
Washington, DC 20036
http://www.nhcouncil.org

National Health Information Center
U. S. Department of Health and Human
Services
Office of Disease Prevention and Health
Promotion
P.O. Box 1133
Washington, DC 20013-1133
http://www.health.gov/nhic

National Hemophilia Foundation
116 West 32nd Street, 11th Floor
New York, NY 10001
http://www.hemophilia.org

National Information Center for Children
    and Youth with Disabilities (NICHCY)
U. S. Department of Education
P.O. Box 1492
Washington, DC 20013-1492
http://www.nichcy.org

National Institutes of Health (NIH)
U. S. Department of Health and Human
    Services
9000 Rockville Pike
Bethesda, MD 20892
http://www.nih.gov

National Kidney Foundation
30 East 33rd St., Suite 1100
New York, NY 10016
http://www.kidney.org

National Organization on Fetal Alcohol
    Syndrome
216 G Street, NE
Washington, DC 20002
http://www.nofas.org

National Pediculosis Association
50 Kearney Road
Needham, MA 02494
http://www.headlice.org

National Reye's Syndrome Foundation
P. O. Box 829
Bryan, OH 43506-0829
http://www.reyessyndrome.org

National SAFE KIDS Campaign
1301 Pennsylvania Ave., NW
Suite 1000
Washington, DC 20004
http://www.safekids.org

National Safety Council
1121 Spring Lake Drive
Itasca, IL 60143-3201
http://www.nsc.org

National Security Agency
9800 Savage Road
Ft. Meade, MD 20755-6248
http://www.nsa.gov

National Sudden Infant Death Syndrome
    Resource Center
2070 Chain Bridge Road, Suite 450
Vienna, VA 22182
http://www.sidscenter.org

National Wildlife Refuge Association
1010 Wisconsin Ave., NW
Suite 200
Washington, DC 20007
http://www.refugenet.org

Parents Anonymous, Inc.,
675 West Foothill Boulevard, Suite 220,
Claremont, CA 91711
http://www.parentsanonymous-natl.org

Poison Prevention
P.O. Box 1543
Washington, DC 20013
http://www.poisonprevention.org

Prevent Blindness America
500 E. Remington Road.
Schaumburg, IL 60173
http://www.preventblindness.org

Public Health Services
The U.S. Department of Health and Human
    Services
200 Independence Avenue, SW
Washington, DC 20201
http://www.os.dhhs.gov/

Sex Information and Education Council
    of the United States (SIECUS)
130 West 42nd Street, Suite 350
New York, NY 10036-7802
http://www.siecus.org

State Farm Insurance Companies
One State Farm Plaza
Bloomington, IL 61710
http://www.statefarm.com/educate
(Educational materials and kits)

Sudden Infant Death Syndrome Alliance
1314 Bedford Avenue, Suite 210
Baltimore, MD 21208
http://www.sidsalliance.org

Tufts University—Child & Family WebGuide
105 College Ave.
Medford, MA 02155
http://www.cfw.tufts.edu

United Cerebral Palsy Association
1660 L Street, NW
Washington, DC 20036-5602.
http://www.ucpa.org.

USDA/ARS Children's Nutrition Research
  Center
1100 Bates Street
Houston, TX 77030
http://www.bcm.tmc.edu/cnrc/resources/
  hottopics

U. S. Department of Education
400 Maryland Avenue, SW
Washington, DC 20202
http://www.ed.gov

U.S. Government Printing Office
Superintendent of Documents
710 N. Capitol Street, NW
Washington, DC 20402
http://www.access.gpo.gov

U. S. Department of Health & Human
  Services
Drug and Food Information
200 Independence Avenue, SW
Washington, DC 20201
http://www.hhs.gov/drugs

U. S. Department of Health and Human
  Services
Office of Disease Prevention and Health
  Promotion
Office of Public Health and Science
200 Independence Avenue SW., Room 738G
Washington, DC 20201
http://odphp.osophs.dhhs.gov

U.S. Department of Homeland Security
Washington, DC 20528
http://www.ready.gov
(Emergency preparation)

Veterans of Safety
Dr. Robert Baldwin, Executive Director,
Central Missouri State University
Humphreys Suite 201
Warrensburg, MO 64093
http://www.veteransofsafety.org

World Health Organization
Office of Public Information
525, 23rd Street, N.W.
Washington, DC 20037
http://www.who.int

APPENDIX D
Federal Food Programs

Federal food programs are funded and regulated by the U. S. Department of Agriculture and administered at the state level by the Department of Education or the Public Health Department. Information about food programs available in a given locality may be obtained from City or County Health Departments, State Public Health Departments, or the State Department of Education.

CHILD NUTRITION PROGRAMS

Child nutrition programs provide cash and/or food assistance for children in public schools, nonprofit private schools, early education centers, home-based child care programs, and summer day camps.

National School Lunch Program (NSLP)

The National School Lunch Program (NSLP) is the oldest and largest federal child feeding program in existence, both in terms of number of children reached and dollars spent. The NSLP is administered at the national level by the United States Department of Agriculture and at the state level by the Department of Education. The U.S. Department of Agriculture reimburses the states for nutritionally adequate lunches served according to federal regulations. The amount of money received per meal depends upon whether the student must receive free meals or is able to pay either full or reduced price. The families of those students receiving free or *reduced price meals* must submit statements of income and meet family size and income guidelines to be eligible. These guidelines are adjusted periodically according to national *poverty guidelines.* Statements of family income must be submitted to the local school district at the beginning of each school year.

Meals funded by NSLP include five food components: meat or meat alternatives, such as peanut butter, eggs or beans, two or more servings of fruits and/or vegetables, bread, and milk. The meals must provide at least one-third of the Recommended Daily Dietary Allowances for the age group served.

School Breakfast Program (SBP)

The School Breakfast Program was authorized by the Child Nutrition Act of 1966. This program also makes provision for free or reduced price meals along with full price meals. The same income eligible guidelines are used for the School Breakfast Program as for the School Lunch Program. The School Breakfast Program is available to schools and public or licensed nonprofit residential child care facilities.

Child and Adult Care Food Program (CACFP)

The Child and Adult Care Food Program provides money for food and commodities for meals served to children in licensed early childhood centers, home-based child care programs (*Federal Register,* August 20, 1982), and adults in adult care programs. The program benefits children 12 years old and under, disabled persons in an institution serving a majority of persons 18 years old and under, migrant children 15 years old and younger, and adults with disabilities. Infant meal patterns are different, and include infant formula, milk, and other foods. The CACFP program is administered by the U.S. Department of Agriculture's Food and Nutrition Service (FNS). In most states it is administered by the Department of Education.

Reimbursement is for two meals and one snack or one meal and two snacks. Reimbursements are determined by income eligibility. The meal pattern is the same as that required in the National School Lunch Program, adjusted by age in categories of infants 1–2 years, children 3–5 years and 6–12 years of age, and adults.

Family Nutrition Programs

Two governmental programs that help to provide the family with adequate food are the Special Supplemental Program for Women, Infants and Children, better known as WIC, and the Food Stamp Program.

Special Supplemental Program for Women, Infants, and Children (WIC)

The WIC program may be operated by either public or nonprofit health agencies. It provides nutrition counseling and supplemental foods rich in protein, iron, and vitamin C to pregnant or lactating women, infants, and children up to five years of age who are determined to be at risk by professional health assessment. Participants receive specified amounts of the following foods:

- iron-fortified infant formula
- iron-fortified cereal
- fruit/vegetable juices high in vitamin C
- fortified milk
- cheese
- eggs
- peanut butter
- dried beans and legumes

The Food Stamp Program

The Food Stamp Program may be administered by either state or local welfare agencies. It is the major form of food assistance in the United States. Its purpose is to increase the food purchasing power of low income persons. Those who meet eligibility standards may buy stamps that are worth more than the purchase price. The very poor receive stamps free. Stamps may be used to buy *allowed foods* or seeds from which to grow foods. Items not allowed include soap, cigarettes, paper goods, alcoholic beverages, pet foods, or deli foods that may be eaten on the premises.

APPENDIX E
One-Week Sample Menu

	Breakfast	Lunch	Snack (Supplement)
Monday	muffin 100% fruit juice milk	spaghetti with meat sauce green beans diced peaches milk	applesauce graham crackers water
Tuesday	dry cereal banana milk	baked chicken mashed potatoes green peas whole grain bread milk	saltines cheese slices water
Wednesday	waffle sticks syrup 100% fruit juice milk	hamburger patty baked sweet potato broccoli whole grain bread milk	mixed raw vegetables & dip pita bread wedges water
Thursday	cinnamon toast 100% fruit juice milk	turkey tetrazzini carrots diced pears milk	yogurt blueberries water
Friday	pancakes strawberries milk	vegetable soup PB/J sandwich sliced plums milk	cheese cubes whole wheat tortilla water

APPENDIX F
Children's Book List

Dental Health

Civardi, A. (1992). *Going to the Dentist.* Usborne, London: E. D. C. Publications.
Dowdy, L. (1997). *Barney Goes to the Dentist.* New York: Lyric.
Frost, H. (1999). *Going to the Dentist.* Mankato, MN: Pebble Books.
Keller, L. (2000). *Open Wide: Tooth School Inside.* New York: Henry Holt & Company.
Lewison, W. (2002). *Clifford's Loose Tooth.* New York: Scholastic.
Mayer, M. (2001). *Just Going to the Dentist.* New York: Golden Books.
McGuire, L. (1993). *Brush Your Teeth Please.* New York: Reader's Digest.
Minarik, E. (2002). *Little Bear's Loose Tooth.* New York: HarperFestival.
Munsch, R. (2002). *Andrew's Loose Tooth.* New York: Scholastic.
Murkoff, H. (2002). *What to Expect When You Go to the Dentist.* New York: HarperFestival.
Rogers, R. (1989). *Going to the Dentist.* New York: G. P. Putman & Sons.
Schoberle, C. (2000). *Open Wide! A Visit to the Dentist.* New York: Simon Spotlight.
Showers, P. (1991). *How Many Teeth?* New York: HarperCollins.
Smee, N. (2000). *Freddie Visits the Dentist.* Hauppauge, New York: Barrons Educational Series.

Illness/Germs

Berger, M. (1995). *Germs Make Me Sick!* New York: HarperCollins.
Berger, M. (2002). *Why I Sneeze, Shiver, Hiccup, & Yawn.* New York: HarperCollins.
Capeci, A. (2001). *The Giant Germ.* New York: Scholastic Paperbacks.
Cole, J. (1995). *The Magic School Bus Inside Ralphie: A Book About Germs.* New York: Scholastic.
Cote, P. (2002). *How Do I Feel?* New York: Houghton Mifflin. (Spanish & English).
Dealey, E. (2002). *Goldie Locks Has Chicken Pox.* New York: Scholastic.
Demuth, P. (1997). *Achoo!: All About Colds.* New York: Grosset & Dunlap.
Katz, B. (1996). *Germs! Germs! Germs!* New York: Cartwheel Books.
O'Brien-Palmer, M. (1999). *Healthy Me: Fun Ways to Develop Good Health and Safety Habits: Activities for Children 5–8.* Chicago, IL: Chicago Review Press.
Rice, J. (1997). *Those Mean, Nasty, Dirty, Downright Disgusting but Invisible Germs.* St. Paul, MN: Redleaf Press.
Romanek, T. (2003). *Achoo: The Most Interesting Book You'll Ever Read About Germs.* Kids Toronto, CA: Can Press.
Ross, T. (2000). *Wash Your Hands!* New York: Kane/Miller.
Showers, P. (1991). *Your Skin and Mine.* New York: HarperCollins.
Wenkman, L. (1999). *Body Buddies Say . . . "Wash Your Hands!"* Bloomington, IN: Sunrise Publications.

Mental Health (feelings)

Agassi, M. (2000). *Hands Are Not for Hitting.* Minneapolis, MN: Free Spirit Publishing.
Anglund, J. (1993). *A Friend Is Someone Who Likes You.* New York: Harcourt Brace Jovanovich.
Anholt, C. (1998). *What I Like.* Cambridge, MA: Candlewick Press.
Anholt, C. (1998). *What Makes Me Happy?* Cambridge, MA: Candlewick Press.
Baker, L. (2001). *I Love You Because You're You.* New York: Cartwheel Books.
Bang, M. (1999). *When Sophie Gets Angry–Really, Really Angry.* New York: Scholastic.
Blumenthal, D. (1999). *The Chocolate-Covered-Cookie Tantrum.* New York: Clarion Books.
Cain, J. (2000). *The Way I Feel.* Seattle, WA: Parenting Press.
Carle, E. (2000). *The Grouchy Ladybug.* New York: Scholastic.
Carle, E. (1999). *The Very Lonely Firefly.* New York: Philomel Books.

Carlson, N. (1997). *How to Lose All Your Friends.* New York: Puffin Books.

Carlson, N. (1990). *I Like Me!* Parsippany, NJ: Pearson Learning.

Cole, J. (1997). *I'm a Big Brother.* New York: William Morrow & Co.

Cole, J. (1997). *I'm a Big Sister.* New York: William Morrow & Co.

Crary, E. (1992). *I'm Mad.* Seattle, WA: Parenting Press.

Crary, E. (1996). *I'm Scared.* Seattle, WA: Parenting Press.

Cruz, R. (1992). *Alexander and the Terrible, Horrible, No Good, Very Bad Day.* New York: Aladdin.

Cutis, J. L. (2002). *I'm Gonna Like Me: Letting Off a Little Self-Esteem.* New York: Joanna Cotler.

Cutis, J. L. (1998). *Today I Feel Silly: And Other Moods That Make My Day.* New York: HarperCollins.

Demi. (1996). *The Empty Pot.* New York: Henry Holt & Co. (honesty)

Eisnberg, P. (1992). *You're My Nikki.* New York: Dial Books for Children.

Gainer, C. (1998). *I'm Like You, You're Like Me: A Child's Book About Understanding and Celebrating Each Other.* Minneapolis, MN: Free Spirit Publishing.

Hammerseng, K. (1996). *Telling Isn't Tattling.* Seattle, WA: Parenting Press.

Henkes, K. (1996). *Chrysanthemum.* New York: HarperTrophy.

Hudson, C., & Ford, B. (1990). *Bright Eyes, Brown Skin.* Just Us Books.

Krasny, L., & Brown, M. (2001). *How to Be a Friend: A Guide to Making Friends and Keeping Them.* Boston, MA: Little Brown & Co.

Kubler, A., & Formby, C. (1995). *Come Play with Us.* Ashworth Road, Bridgemead, Swindon, Wiltshire, SN5 7YD: Child's Play International, Ltd.

Lachner, D. (1995). *Andrew's Angry Words.* New York: North South Books.

Lalli, J. (1997). *I Like Being Me: Poems for Children, About Feeling Special, Appreciating Others, and Getting Along.* Minneapolis, MN: Free Spirit Publishing.

Lewis, J. (1993). *Claire and Friends.* Brookline, MA: Creative License Press.

Lewis, P. (2002). *I'll Always Love You.* Wilton, CT: Tiger Tales.

Lovell, P. (2001). *Stand Tall, Molly Lou Melon.* New York: Scholastic.

Naylor, P. (1994). *King of the Playground.* New York: Aladdin.

O'Neill, A. (2002). *The Recess Queen.* New York: Scholastic.

Parr, T. (2001). *It's Okay to be Different.* Boston, MA: Little, Brown.

Payne, L. (1994). *Just Because I Am: A Child's Book of Affirmation.* Minneapolis, MN: Free Spirit Publishing.

Payne, L. (1997). *We Can Get Along: A Child's Book of Choices.* Minneapolis, MN: Free Spirit Publishing.

Pinkney, A., & Pinkney, B. (1997). *Pretty Brown Face.* Lake Worth, FL: Red Wagon Books.

Spelman, C. (2000). *When I Feel Angry.* New York: Albert Whitman & Co.

Thomas, P. (2000). *Stop Picking on Me.* Hauppauge, New York: Barrons.

Vail, R. (2002). *Sometimes I'm Bombaloo.* New York: Scholastic.

Viorst, J. (1992). *The Good-bye Book.* New York: Aladdin.

Weninger, B., & Marks, A. (1995). *Good-bye Daddy.* New York: North-South Books.

Personal Health & Self-Care

Aliki. (1992). *I'm Growing.* New York: HarperCollins.

Aliki. (1991). *My Five Senses.* New York: HarperCollins.

Brown, M. (1991). *Good Night Moon.* New York: HarperFestival.

Cazet, D. (1992). *I'm Not Sleepy.* New York: Orchard Books.

Edwards, F. (1990). *Mortimer Mooner Stopped Taking a Bath.* Kingston, Ontario: Pokeweed Press.

Fox, M. (1997). *Time for Bed.* Lake Worth, FL: Red Wagon Books.

Gordon, J. R. (1991). *Six Sleepy Sheep.* New York: St. Martin's Press.

Himmelman, J. (1995). *Lights Out!* Mahwah, NJ: Troll.

Katz, A. (2001). *Take Me Out of the Bathtub.* New York: Scholastic.

Keats, E. J. (1992). *Dreams.* New York: Aladdin Books.

Leonard, M. (1998). *Getting Dressed.* New York: Bantam Books.

Murkoff, H. (2000). *What to Expect at Bedtime.* New York: HarperFestival.
Murkoff, H. (2000). *What to Expect When You Go to the Doctor.* New York: HarperFestival.
Pfeffer, W. (1999). *Sounds All Around.* New York: HarperCollins.
Reidy, H. (1999). *What Do You Like to Wear?* New York: Larousse Kingfisher Chambers.
Rowland, P. (1996). *What Should I Wear?* New York: Random House.
Showers , P. (1997). *Sleep Is for Everyone.* New York: HarperCollins.
Showers, P. (1993). *The Listening Walk.* New York: HarperTrophy.
Showers, P. (1990). *Ears Are for Hearing.* New York: Ty Crowell Co.
Sykes, J. (1996). *I Don't Want to Go to Bed.* Wilton, CT: Tiger Tales.
Time-Life. (1993). *What Is a Bellybutton?* Alexandria, VA: Time-Life Books.
Watanabe, S. (1992). *How Do I Put It On?* New York: Philomel
Wood, A. (1996). *The Napping House.* San Diego, CA: Harcourt Brace & Co.

Safety

Berenstain, S., & Berenstain, J. (1999). *My Trusty Car Seat: Buckling Up for Safety.* New York: Random House.
Best, C. (1995). *Red Light, Green Light, Mama and Me.* New York: Orchard Books.
Boxall, E. (2002). *Francis the Scaredy Cat.* Cambridge, MA: Candlewick Press.
Committee, C. B. (2000). *Buckles Buckles Everywhere.* Columbia, SC: Palmetto Bookworks.
Cuyler, M. (2001). *Stop, Drop, Roll.* New York: Simon & Schuster.
Dubowski, C. (1990). *Fire Engine to the Rescue.* New York: McClanahan Book Company.
Girard, L. (1987). *My Body Is Private.* Morton Grove, IL: Albert Whitman & Co.
Hayward, L. (2001). *A Day in the Life of a Firefighter.* New York: Dorling Kindersley Publisher.
Hindman, J. (1986). *A Very Touching Book . . . for Little People and Big People.* Alexandria, VA: Alexandria Press.
Johnsen, K. (1986). *Trouble with Secrets.* Seattle, WA: Parenting Press.
MacLean, C. K. (2002). *Even Firefighters Hug Their Moms.* New York: Dutton.
Mitton, T. (2001). *Down by the Cool of the Pool.* New York: Orchard Books.
Palatini, M. (2002). *Earthquack!* New York: Simon & Schuster.
Prigger, M. (2002). *Aunt Minnie and the Twister.* New York: Clarion.
Rathmann, P. (1995). *Officer Buckle and Gloria.* New York: Putnam.
Reasoner, C. (2003). *Bee Safe (The Bee Attitudes).* Los Angeles, CA: Price Stern Sloan Publishers.
Rylan, C. (1991). *Night in the Country.* New York: Aladdin.
Schwartz, L. (1995). *The Safety Book for Active Kids: Teaching Your Child How to Avoid Everyday Dangers.* Santa Barbara, CA: Learning Works.
Tekavec, H. (2002). *Storm Is Coming!* New York: Dial.
Weeks, S. (2002). *My Somebody Special.* San Diego, CA: Harcourt, Inc.
Weidner, T. (1997). *Your Body Belongs to You.* Morton Grove, IL: Albert Whitman & Co.

Special Needs

Aseltine, L., Mueller, E., & Tait, N. (1987). *I'm Deaf and It's Okay.* Morton Grove, IL: Albert Whitman & Co.
Bunnett, R. (1996). *Friends at School.* Long Island City, New York: Star Bright Books. (Special needs)
Fassler, J. (1987). *Howie Helps Himself.* Morton Grove, IL: Albert Whitman & Co. (Special needs)
Gosselin, K. (1998). *Taking Diabetes to School.* Valley Park, MO: JayJo Books.
Gosselin, K. (1996). *Zooallergy: A Fun Story About Allergy and Asthma Triggers.* Valley Park, MO: JayJo Books
Harrison,T. (1998). *Aaron's Awful Allergies.* Buffalo, New York: Kids Can Press.
Lakin, P. (1994). *Dad and Me in the Morning.* Morton Grove, IL: Albert Whitman & Co. (Special needs)

London , J. (1997). *The Lion Who Had Asthma.* Morton Grove, IL: Albert Whitman & Co.

Maguire, A. (2000). *Special People, Special Ways.* Arlington, TX : Future Horizons. (Special needs)

Mayer, G., & Mayer, M. (1993). *A Very Special Critter.* New York: Golden Books. (Special needs)

Millman, I. (2000). *Moses Goes to School.* New York: Frances Foster Books/Farrar, Straus & Giroux. (Special needs)

Nausau, E. (2001). *The Peanut Butter Jam.* Albuquerque, NM: Health Press. (Allergies)

Powers, M. (1987). *Our Teacher's in a Wheelchair.* Morton Grove, IL: Albert Whitman & Co.

Shriver, M. (2001). *What's Wrong with Timmy?* New York: Little Brown & Co. (Special needs)

Smith, N. (1999). *Allie the Allergic Elephant: A Children's Story of Peanut Allergies.* Jungle Communications, Inc.

Stuve-Bodeen, S. (1998). *We'll Paint the Octopus Red..* Woodbine House. (Down syndrome)

Weiner, E. (1999). *Taking Food Allergies to School.* Valley Park, MO: JayJo Books.

White Pirner, C. (1994). *Even Little Kids Get Diabetes.* Morton Grove, IL: Albert Whitman & Co.

Nutrition

Appleton, J. (2001). *Do Carrots Make You See Better?* St. Paul, Minnesota: Red Leaf Press.

Barkan, J. & Wheeler, J. (1989). *My Measuring Cup.* New York: Warner Juvenile Books.

Berenstain, S., & Berenstain, J. (1995). *The Berenstain Bears and Too Much Junk Food.* New York: Random House.

Carle, E. (1998). *Pancakes, Pancakes!* New York: Aladdin Books.

Carle, E. (1986). *The Very Hungry Caterpillar.* New York: Putnam.

Cole, J. (1990). *The Magic School Bus: Inside the Human Body.* New York: Scholastic.

Compestine, Y. (2001). *The Runaway Rice Cake.* New York: Simon & Schuster.

French, V. (1998). *Oliver's Fruit Salad.* New York: Orchard Books.

Geeslin, C. (1999). *How Nanita Learned to Make Flan.* New York: Atheneum

Gershator, D. (1998). *Bread Is for Eating.* New York: Henry Holt.

Hall, Z. (1996). *The Apple Pie Tree.* New York: Scholastic.

Harms, T. (1981). *Cook and Learn: Nutritious Foods from Various Cultures.* St. Paul, MN: Red Leaf Press.

Katzen, M. (1994). *Pretend Soup and Other Real Recipes:A Cookbook for Preschoolers and Up.* Berkeley, CA: Tricycle Press.

Krauss, R. (1989). *The Carrot Seed.* New York: HarperTrophy.

Lin, G. (2001). *Dim Sum for Everyone.* New York: Knopf.

Lin, G. (1999). *The Ugly Vegetables.* Watertown, MA: Charlesbridge Publishing.

Loreen, L. (1996). *The Edible Pyramid: Good Eating Every Day.* New York: Holiday House.

Mayer, M. (1998). *The Mother Goose Cookbook: Rhymes and Recipes for the Very Young.* New York: William Morrow & Co.

McGinley, N. (1999). *Pigs in the Pantry: Fun with Math and Cooking.* New York: Simon & Schuster.

Paulsen, G. (1998). *The Tortilla Factory.* San Diego, CA: Harcourt Brace.

Peterson, C. (1996). *Harvest Year.* Homedale, PA: Boyd Mill Press.

Priceman, M. (1996). *How to Make an Apple Pie and See the World.* New York: Knopf.

Reiser, L. (1998). *Tortillas and Lullabies.* New York: Greenwillow Books.

Rockwell, L. (1999). *Good Enough to Eat: A Kid's Guide to Food and Nutrition.* New York: Harper-Collins.

Sanger, A. (2001). *First Book of Sushi.* Berkeley, CA : Tricycle Press.

Sharmat, M. (1989). *Gregory, the Terrible Eater.* New York: Scholastic.

Swain, G. (1999). *Eating.* St. Paul, MN: Red Leaf Press.

Wells, P. (2003). *Busy Bears: Breakfast with the Bears.* London, England: Sterling Publications.

Westcott, N. (1998). *Never Take a Pig Out to Lunch and Other Poems.* New York: Orchard Books.

Woods, D., & Woods, A. (2000). *The Big Hungry Bear.* Swindon, England: Child's Play Publishers.

abdomen – the portion of the body located between the diaphragm (located at the base of the lungs) and the pelvic or hip bones.

absorption – the process by which the products of digestion are transferred from the intestinal tract into the blood or lymph or by which substances are taken up by the cells.

abuse – to mistreat, attack, or cause harm to another individual.

accident – an unexpected or unplanned event that may result in physical harm or injury.

accreditation – the process of certifying an individual or program as having met certain specified requirements.

acuity – sharpness or clearness, as in vision.

acute – the stage of an illness or disease during which an individual is definitely sick and exhibits symptoms characteristic of the particular illness or disease involved.

adenosine triphosphate (ATP) – a compound with energy-storing phosphate bonds that is the main energy source for all cells.

AIDS (Acquired Immunodeficiency Syndrome or Acquired Immune Deficiency Syndrome) – A disease caused by the human immunodeficiency virus (HIV).

airborne transmission – when germs are expelled into the air through coughs/sneezes, and transmitted to another individual via tiny moisture drops.

alignment – the process of assuming correct posture or of placing various body parts in proper line with each other.

alkalis – groups of bases or caustic substances that are capable of neutralizing acids to form salts.

allowed foods – foods that are eligible for reimbursement under School Lunch or Child Care Food Program Guidelines.

amblyopia – a condition of the eye commonly referred to as "lazy eye"; vision gradually becomes blurred or distorted due to unequal balance of the eye muscles. The eyes do not present any physical clues when a child has amblyopia.

amino acids – the organic building blocks from which proteins are made.

anaphylaxis – a severe allergic reaction that may cause difficulty breathing, itching, unconsciousness, and possible death.

anecdotal – a brief note or description that contains useful and important information.

anemia – a disorder of the blood commonly caused by a lack of iron in the diet, resulting in the formation of fewer red blood cells and lessened ability of the cells to carry oxygen. Symptoms include fatigue, shortness of breath, and pallor.

anthropometric – pertains to measurement of the body or its parts.

antibodies – special substances produced by the body that help protect against disease.

apnea – momentary absence of breathing.

appraisal – the process of judging or evaluating; to determine the quality of one's state of health.

*Definitions are based on usage within the text.

aseptic procedure – treatment to produce a product that is free of disease-producing bacteria.

aspiration – accidental inhalation of food, fluid, or an object into the respiratory tract.

assessment – appraisal or evaluation.

asymptomatic – having no symptoms.

attitudes – beliefs or feelings one has toward certain facts or situations.

atypical – unusual; different from what might commonly be expected.

autonomy – a state of personal or self-identity.

bacteria – one-celled microorganisms; some are beneficial for the body, but pathogenic bacteria cause diseases.

basal metabolic rate – minimum amount of energy needed to carry on the body processes vital to life.

biochemical – pertains to chemical evaluation of body substances such as blood, urine, etc.

bonding – the process of establishing a positive and strong emotional relationship between an infant and his or her parent; sometimes referred to as attachment.

bottle-mouth syndrome – a pattern of tooth decay, predominantly of the upper teeth, that develops as the result of permitting a child to go to sleep with a bottle containing juice, milk, or any other caloric liquid that may pool in the mouth.

calories – units used to measure the energy value of foods.

calcium – mineral nutrient; a major component of bones and teeth.

catalyst – a substance that speeds up the rate of a chemical reaction but is not itself used up in the reaction.

catalyzes – accelerates a chemical reaction.

characteristics – qualities or traits that distinguish one person from another.

cholesterol – a fat-like substance found in animal-source foods, that is synthesized by humans and performs a variety of functions within the body.

chronic – frequent or repeated incidences of illness; can also be a lengthy or permanent status, as in chronic disease or dysfunction.

clinical – pertains to evaluation of health by means of observation.

coenzymes – a vitamin-containing substance required by certain enzymes before they can perform their prescribed function.

cognitive – the aspect of learning that refers to the development of skills and abilities based on knowledge and thought processes.

collagen – a protein that forms the major constituent of connective tissue, cartilage, bone, and skin.

communicable – a condition that can be spread or transmitted from one individual to another.

complementary proteins – proteins with offsetting missing amino acids; complementary proteins can be combined to provide complete protein.

complete proteins – proteins that contain all essential amino acids in amounts relative to the amounts needed to support growth.

compliance – the act of obeying or cooperating with specific requests or requirements.

concepts – combinations of basic and related factual information that represent more generalized statements or ideas.

conductive hearing loss – affects the volume of word tones heard, so that loud sounds are more likely to be heard than soft sounds.

contagious – capable of being transmitted or passed from one person to another.

contrasting sensory qualities – differing qualities pertaining to taste, color, texture, temperature, and shape.

convalescent – the stage of recovery from an illness or disease.

cost control – reduction of expenses through portion control, inventory, and reduction of waste.

criteria – predetermined standards used to evaluate the worth or effectiveness of a learning experience.

critical control point (CCP) – a point or procedure in a specific food system where loss of control may result in an unacceptable health risk.

cycle menus – menus that are written to repeat after a set interval, such as every 3–4 weeks.

Daily Value (DV) – a term the FDA has proposed to replace the USDA RDA values in the new nutrition food labels.

deciduous teeth – a child's initial set of teeth; this set is temporary and gradually begins to fall out around 5 years of age.

dehydration – a state in which there is an excessive loss of body fluids or extremely limited fluid intake. Symptoms may include loss of skin tone, sunken eyes, and mental confusion.

dental caries – tooth decay.

dermatitis – inflammation or irritation of the skin, such as in rashes and eczema.

development – commonly refers to the process of intellectual growth and change.

developmental norms – the mean or average age at which children demonstrate certain behaviors and abilities.

developmental or physiological readiness – growth (both physical and cognitive) and chemical processes that lead to the ability to perform a function.

developmentally appropriate practice (DAP) – learning experiences and environments that take into account each child's abilities, diverse needs, and individual interests. DAP also reflects differences among families and values them as essential partners in children's education.

diagnosis – the process of identifying a disease, illness, or injury from its symptoms.

Dietary Guidelines for Americans – report that gives recommendations for daily food choices, to be balanced with physical activity, to assure good health and reduce certain disease risks.

dietary nucleotides – amino acid combinations found to increase an infant's ability to produce antibodies in response to exposure to disease.

Dietary Reference Intake (DRI) – a plan that presents the recommended goals of nutrient intakes for various age and gender groups.

digestion – the process by which complex nutrients in foods are changed into smaller units that can be absorbed and used by the body.

digestive tract – pertains to, and includes, the mouth, throat, esophagus, stomach, and intestines.

direct contact – the passage of infectious organisms from an infected individual directly to a susceptible host through methods such as coughing, sneezing, or touching.

discipline – training or enforced obedience that corrects, shapes, or develops acceptable patterns of behavior.

disinfected – killed pathogenic organisms.

disorientation – lack of awareness or ability to recognize familiar persons or objects.

distention – stretched or enlarged.

DNA (deoxyribonucleic acid) – the substance in the cell nucleus that codes for genetically transmitted traits.

elevate – to raise to a higher position.

electrolytes – substances which, when in solution, become capable of conducting electricity; examples include sodium and potassium.

emotional abuse – repeated humiliation, ridicule, or threats directed toward another individual.

endocrine – refers to glands within the body that produce and secrete substances called hormones directly into the blood stream.

energy – power to perform work.

enriched – adding nutrients to grain products to replace those lost during refinement; thiamin, niacin, riboflavin, and iron are nutrients most commonly added.

environment – the sum total of physical, cultural, and behavioral features that surround and affect an individual.

enzymes – proteins that catalyze body functions.

epithelial tissue – specialized cells that form the skin and mucus linings of all body cavities, such as the lungs, nose, and throat.

essential nutrient – nutrient that must be provided in food because it cannot be synthesized by the body at a rate sufficient to meet the body's needs.

ethnic – pertaining to races or groups of people who share common traits or customs.

evaluation – a measurement of effectiveness for determining whether or not educational objectives have been achieved.

expectations – behaviors or actions that are anticipated.

failure to thrive – a term used to describe an infant whose growth and mental development is severely slowed due to lack of nurturing or mental stimulation.

family nutrition programs – nutrition programs that focus on the family unit. Examples are Food Stamps, WIC, and the Food Distribution Program.

fecal-oral transmission – when germs are transferred to the mouth via hands contaminated with fecal material.

fever – an elevation of body temperature above normal; a temperature over 99.4°F or 37.4°C orally is usually considered a fever.

First-In-First-Out (FIFO) – a method of storage in which the items stored for the longest time will be retrieved first.

food-borne illness – a food infection due to ingestion of food contaminated with bacteria, viruses, some molds, or parasites.

food-borne illness outbreak – two or more persons become ill after ingesting the same food. Laboratory analysis must confirm that food is the source of the illness.

food infections – illnesses resulting from ingestion of live bacteria in food.

food intoxications – illnesses resulting from ingestion of food containing residual bacterial toxins in the absence of viable bacteria.

food pyramid – a guide to daily food choices developed by the USDA.

fortified food – food with vitamins and/or minerals added that were not found in the food originally, or that are added in amounts greater than occur naturally in the food.

fruit drink – a product that contains 10 percent fruit juice, added water, and sugar.

full-strength juice – undiluted fruit or vegetable juice.

giardiasis – a parasitic infection of the intestinal tract that causes diarrhea, loss of appetite, abdominal bloating and gas, weight loss, and fatigue.

gram – a metric unit of weight; approximately 1/28 of an ounce.

growth – increase in size of any body part or of the entire body.

habits – unconscious repetitions of particular behaviors.

hands-on – active involvement in a project; actually doing something.

harvesting – picking or gathering fruit or grains.

Hazard Analysis Critical Control Point (HACCP) – a food safety and self-inspection system that highlights potentially hazardous foods and how they are handled in the food service department.

head circumference – the distance around the head obtained by measuring over the forehead and bony protuberance on the back of the head; it is an indication of normal or abnormal growth and development of the brain and central nervous system.

health – a state of wellness. Complete physical, mental, social, and emotional well-being; the quality of one element affects the state of the others.

health promotion – engaging in behaviors that help maintain and enhance one's health status; includes concern for certain social issues affecting the diet and environment.

heat exhaustion – above normal body temperature caused by exposure to too much sun.

heat stroke – failure of the body's sweating reflex during exposure to high temperatures; causes body temperature to rise.

hemoglobin – the iron-containing, oxygen-carrying pigment in red blood cells.

hepatitis – an inflammation of the liver.

heredity – the transmission of certain genetic material and characteristics from parents to child at the time of conception.

high-density lipoproteins (HDL) – a protein-fat combination with a high protein to fat ratio, which is formed in the blood to aid in fat transport; a high HDL blood value may decrease risk of cardiovascular disease.

high-fructose corn syrup – a frequently used sweetener produced by exposing corn starch to acid and enzyme action to increase the fructose content; it is much sweeter than sucrose.

HIV (human immunodeficiency virus) – the virus that causes AIDS.

hormone – a special chemical substance produced by endocrine glands that influences and regulates certain body functions.

hyperactivity – a condition characterized by attention and behavior disturbances, including restlessness, impulsive, and disruptive behaviors. True cases of hyperactivity respond to the administration of stimulant-type medication.

hyperglycemia – a condition characterized by an abnormally high level of sugar in the blood.

hyperopia – farsightedness; a condition of the eyes in which an individual can see objects clearly in the distance but has poor close vision.

hypertension – elevation of blood pressure above the normally accepted values.

hyperventilation – rapid breathing often with forced inhalation; can lead to sensations of dizziness, lightheadedness, and weakness.

hypothermia – below normal body temperature caused by overexposure to cold conditions.

immunized – a state of becoming resistant to a specific disease through the introduction of living or dead microorganisms into the body, which then stimulate the production of antibodies.

impairment – a condition or malfunction of a body part that interferes with optimal functioning.

incidental learning – learning that occurs in addition to the primary intent or goals of instruction.

incomplete proteins – proteins that lack required amounts of one or more essential amino acids.

incubation – the interval of time between exposure to infection and the appearance of the first signs or symptoms of illness.

indirect contact – transfer of infectious organisms from an infected individual to a susceptible host via an intermediate source such as contaminated water, milk, toys, utensils, or soiled towels.

individuality – qualities that distinguish one person from another.

infection – a condition that results when a pathogen invades and establishes itself within a susceptible host.

ingested – the process of taking food or other substances into the body through the mouth.

innocent – not guilty; lacking knowledge.

inservice – educational training provided by an employer.

intentional – a plan of action that is carried out in a purposeful manner.

intentionally – to do on purpose.

intervention – practices or procedures implemented to modify or change a specific behavior or condition.

intestinal – pertaining to the intestinal tract or bowel.

iron-deficiency anemia – a failure in the oxygen transport system caused by too little iron.

irradiation – food preservation by short-term exposure of the food to gamma ray radiation.

judicious – wise; directed by sound judgment.

lactating – producing and secreting milk.

language – form of communication that allows individuals to share feelings, ideas, and experiences with one another.

latch-key – a term that refers to school-age children who care for themselves without adult supervision before and after school hours.

lethargy – a state of inaction or indifference.

liability – legal responsibility or obligation for one's actions owed to another individual.

licensing – the act of granting formal permission to conduct a business or profession.

linoleic acid – a polyunsaturated fatty acid, which is essential (must be provided in food) for humans.

linolenic acid – one of the two polyunsaturated fatty acids that are recognized as essential for humans.

lipoprotein – protein linked with fat to aid in the transport of various types of fat in the blood.

listlessness – a state characterized by a lack of energy and/or interest in one's affairs.

low-birthweight (LBW) infant – an infant who weighs less than 5.5 pounds (2500 grams) at birth.

low-density lipoproteins (LDL) – a lipoprotein with a low protein to fat ratio that contains a high level of cholesterol; high blood levels of LDL may signal increased risk for heart disease.

Lyme disease – bacterial illness caused by the bite of infected deer ticks found in grassy or wooded areas.

lymph glands – specialized groupings of tissue that produce and store white blood cells for protection against infection and illness.

macrocytic anemia – a failure in the oxygen transport system characterized by abnormally large immature red blood cells.

malnutrition – prolonged inadequate or excessive intake of nutrients and/or calories required by the body.

mandatory – something that is required; no choices or alternatives available.

megadose – an amount of a vitamin or mineral at least ten times that of RDA.

meningitis – a disease, often caused by bacteria, that leads to inflammation of the brain and spinal cord.

metabolism – all chemical changes that occur from the time nutrients are absorbed until they are built into body tissue or are excreted.

microcytic anemia – a failure in the oxygen transport system characterized by abnormally small red blood cells.

microgram – a metric unit of measurement; one-millionth of a gram.

milligram – a metric unit of measurement; one-thousandth of a gram.

minerals – inorganic chemical elements that are required in the diet to support growth and repair tissue and to regulate body functions.

misarticulation – improper pronunciation of words and word sounds.

mold – a fuzzy growth produced by fungi.

monounsaturated fatty acid (MUFA) – a fatty acid that has only one bond in its structure, and that is not fully saturated with hydrogen.

mottling – marked with spots of dense white or brown coloring.

myopia – nearsightedness; an individual has good near vision but poor distant vision.

neglect – failure of a parent or legal guardian to properly care for and meet the basic needs of a child under eighteen years of age.

negligent – failing to practice or perform one's duties according to certain standards; careless.

neophobic – fear of things that are new and unfamiliar.

neural tube deficit – a birth defect involving damage to the brain and spinal cord.

neurological – pertaining to the nervous system, which consists of the nerves, brain, and spinal column.

neuromuscular – pertaining to control of muscular function by the nervous system.

normal – average; a characteristic or quality that is common to most individuals in a defined group.

norms – an expression (e.g., weeks, months, years) of when a child is likely to demonstrate certain developmental skills.

notarized – official acknowledgment of the authenticity of a signature or document by a notary public.

nutrient – the components or substances that are found in food.

nutrient intake – consumption of foods containing chemical substances (nutrients) essential to the human body.

nutrient strengths – nutrients that occur in relatively large amounts in a food or food group.

nutrient weaknesses – nutrients that are absent or occur in very small amounts in a food or food group.

nutrition – the study of food and how it is used by the body.

nutrition claims – statements of reduced calories, fat, or salt on the food labels.

nutrition education – activities that impart information about food and its use in the body.

obesity – a condition characterized by an excessive accumulation of fat.

objectives – clear and meaningful descriptions of what an individual is expected to learn as a result of learning activities and experiences.

observations – to inspect and take note of the appearance and behavior of other individuals.

odd-day cycle menus – menus planned for a period of days other than a week that repeat after the planned period; cycles of any number of days may be used. These menus are a means of avoiding repetition of the same foods on the same day of the week.

ophthalmologist – a physician who specializes in diseases and abnormalities of the eye.

optometrist – a specialist (non-physician) trained to examine eyes and prescribe glasses and eye exercises.

overweight – weight that exceeds (by 20 percent or less) the recommendations for "desirable" body weight.

pallor – paleness.

parallel play – a common form of play among young children in which two or more children, sitting side by side, are engaged in an activity but do not interact or work together to accomplish a task.

paralysis – temporary or permanent loss of sensation, function, or voluntary movement of a body part.

parasites – organisms that live on or within other living organisms.

pasteurized – heating a food to a prescribed temperature for a specific time period to destroy disease-producing bacteria.

pathogen – a microorganism capable of producing illness or infection.

peers – one of the same rank; equals.

Percent Daily Value (%DV) – a measure of the nutritional value of food; used in nutrition labeling.

personal sanitation – personal habits, such as handwashing, care of illness, cleanliness of clothing.

physical abuse – injuries, such as welts, burns, bruises, or broken bones, that are caused intentionally.

poverty guidelines – family-size and income standards for determining eligibility for free or reduced-price meals under the National School Lunch Program.

precipitating – factors that trigger or initiate a reaction or response.

predisposition – having an increased chance or susceptibility.

prenatal – the period from conception to birth of the baby.

preplan – outline a method of action prior to carrying it out.

prevention – measures taken to avoid an event such as an accident or illness from occurring; implies the ability to anticipate circumstances and behaviors.

preventive – the act of taking certain steps and measures so as to avoid or delay unfavorable outcomes, as in preventive health care.

primary goal – the aim that assumes first importance.

procurement – the process of obtaining services, supplies, and equipment in conformance with applicable laws and regulations.

prodromal – the appearance of the first nonspecific signs of infection; this stage ends when the symptoms characteristic of a particular communicable illness begin to appear.

protein – class of nutrients used primarily for structural and regulatory functions.

PUFA (polyunsaturated fatty acids) – fatty acids that contain more than one bond that is not fully saturated with hydrogen.

punishment – a negative response to what the observer considers to be wrong or inappropriate behavior; may involve physical or harsh treatment.

radura symbol – a required symbol placed on all food that has been treated with irradiation.

RDA (Recommended Daily Dietary Allowances) – suggested amounts of nutrients for use in planning diets. RDAs are designed to maintain good nutrition in healthy persons. Allowances are higher than requirements in order to afford a margin of safety.

receptive loss – hearing loss that affects the range of tones heard, so that high tones are more likely to be heard than low tones.

recovery position – placing an individual in a side-lying position.

reduced-price meals – a meal served under the Child Care Food Program to a child from a family which meets income standards for reduced-price school meals.

referrals – directing an individual to other sources, usually for additional evaluation or treatment.

refusal – the act of declining or rejecting.

registration – the act of placing the name of a child care program on a list of active providers; usually does not require on-site inspection.

regulations – standards or requirement that are set to ensure uniform and safe practices.

regurgitation – the return of partially digested food from stomach to mouth.

reimplanted – replaced a part from where it was removed, such as a tooth.

reprimand – to scold or discipline for unacceptable behavior.

resilient – the ability to withstand or resist difficulty.

resistance – the ability to avoid infection or illness.

respiratory diseases – disease of the respiratory tract, such as colds, sore throats, flu.

respiratory tract – pertains to, and includes, the nose, throat, trachea, and lungs.

resuscitation – to revive from unconsciousness or death; to restore breathing and heartbeat.

retention – the ability to remember or recall previously learned material.

rewards – things given for appropriate behavior.

Reye's syndrome – an acute illness of young children that severely affects the central nervous system; symptoms include vomiting, coma, and seizures.

RNA (ribonucleic acid) – the nucleic acid that serves as messenger between the nucleus and the ribosomes where proteins are synthesized.

Salmonella – a bacteria that can cause serious food-borne illness.

salmonellosis – a bacterial infection that is spread through contaminated drinking water, food or milk or contact with other infected persons. Symptoms include diarrhea, fever, nausea, and vomiting.

sanitized – cleaned or sterilized.

sanitizing solution – a solution of diluted chlorine bleach (1/4 cup chlorine to 1 gallon of water), used to sanitize utensils and work surfaces.

saturated fatty acid (SFA) – a fatty acid that has all carbon bonds satisfied by hydrogen.

scald – to rinse with boiling water.

sedentary – unusually slow or sluggish; a lifestyle that implies a general lack of physical activity.

seizures – a temporary interruption of consciousness sometimes accompanied by convulsive movements.

self-care children – children left to care for themselves.

sensorimotor – Piaget's first stage of cognitive development, during which children learn and relate to their world primarily through motor and sensory activities.

sensorineural loss – a type of hearing loss that occurs when sound impulses cannot reach the brain due to damage of the auditory nerve, or cannot be interpreted because of prior brain damage.

sensory qualities – aspects that appeal to sight, sound, taste, feel, and smell.

serrated – saw-toothed or notched.

sexual abuse – any sexual involvement between an adult and child.

Shaken Baby Syndrome – forceful shaking of a baby that causes head trauma, internal bleeding, and sometimes death.

skeletal – pertaining to the bony framework that supports the body.

skinfold – a measurement of the amount of fat under the skin; also referred to as fat-fold measurements.

speech – the process of using words to express one's thoughts and ideas.

spina bifida – a birth defect in which incomplete formation of the body vertebrae allows a portion of the spinal cord to be exposed to the outside. Varying degrees of paralysis and lack of function are common in the portion of the body below the defect.

standardized recipe – a recipe that has been tested to produce consistent results.

Staphylococcus – a bacteria that can cause serious food-borne illnesses.

sterile – free from living microorganisms.

strabismus – a condition of the eyes in which one or both eyes appear to be turned inward (crossed) or outward (walleye).

submerge – to place in water.

supervision – watching carefully over the behaviors and actions of children and others.

supplementary proteins – a complete protein mix resulting from combining a small amount of a complete protein with an incomplete protein to provide all essential amino acids.

susceptible host – an individual who is capable of being infected by a pathogen.

symptoms – changes in the body or its functions that are experienced by the affected individual.

syndrome – a grouping of symptoms and signs that commonly occur together and are characteristic of a specific disease or illness.

synthesis – the process of making a compound by the union of simpler compounds or elements.

taurine – a free amino acid needed by infants for normal growth and development of the central nervous system.

tax exempt – excused from taxation, often on the basis of nonprofit status.

temperature – a measurement of body heat; varies with the time of day, activity, and method of measurement.

thermic energy of foods – energy required to digest, absorb, transport, and metabolize nutrients in food.

toxicity – a state of being poisonous.

tuberculosis – an infectious disease caused by the tubercle bacillus, characterized by the production of lesions.

tympanic – referring to the ear canal.

Type I diabetes – a disease distinguished by a lack of insulin production; usually diagnosed in childhood or young adulthood.

universal infection control precautions – special measures taken when handling bodily fluids, including careful hand-washing, wearing latex gloves, disinfecting surfaces, and proper disposal of contaminated objects.

urination – the act of emptying the bladder of urine.

values – the beliefs, traditions, and customs an individual incorporates and utilizes to guide behavior and judgments.

verbal assault – to attack another individual with words.

viruses – any of a group of submicroscopic infective agents, many of which cause a number of diseases in animals and plants.

vitamins – organic substances needed in very small amounts to regulate many metabolic functions in the body.

weekly menus – menus that are written to be served on a weekly basis.

whole grains – grain products that have not been refined; they contain all parts of the kernel of grain.

WIC (Women, Infants, and Children) – a federal program that provides food supplements for pregnant women, infants, and children to age five.